Cambridge studies in medieval life and thought

HAGIOGRAPHY AND THE
CULT OF SAINTS

Cambridge studies in medieval life and thought
Fourth series

General Editor:

J. C. HOLT

Professor of Medieval History and
Master of Fitzwilliam College, University of Cambridge

Advisory Editors:

C. N. L. BROOKE

Dixie Professor of Ecclesiastical History and
Fellow of Gonville and Caius College,
University of Cambridge

D. E. LUSCOMBE

Professor of Medieval History, University of Sheffield

The series Cambridge Studies in Medieval Life and Thought was inaugurated by G. G. Coulton in 1920. Professor J. C. Holt now acts as General Editor of a Fourth Series, with Professor C. N. L. Brooke and Professor D. E. Luscombe as Advisory Editors. The series aims to bring together outstanding work by medieval scholars over a wide range of human endeavour extending from political economy to the history of ideas.

Titles in the series

HAGIOGRAPHY AND THE CULT OF SAINTS

The Diocese of Orléans, 800–1200

THOMAS HEAD

Yale University

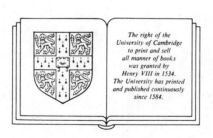

The right of the
University of Cambridge
to print and sell
all manner of books
was granted by
Henry VIII in 1534.
The University has printed
and published continuously
since 1584.

CAMBRIDGE UNIVERSITY PRESS

CAMBRIDGE

NEW YORK   PORT CHESTER

MELBOURNE   SYDNEY

Published by the Press Syndicate of the University of Cambridge
The Pitt Building, Trumpington Street, Cambridge CB2 IRP
40 West 20th Street, New York, NY 10011, USA
10 Stamford Road, Oakleigh, Melbourne 3166, Australia

First published 1990

Printed in Great Britain at the University Press, Cambridge

British Library cataloguing in publication data
Head, Thomas
Hagiography and the cult of saints.
1. France, Loire Valley. Saints. Cults, history
I. Title
274.4'5

Library of Congress cataloguing in publication data
Head, Thomas (Thomas F.)
Hagiography and the cult of saints: the diocese of Orléans,
800–1200 / Thomas Head.
p.   cm. – (Cambridge studies in medieval life and thought;
4th ser., 14)
Includes bibliographical references.
1. Christian saints – Cult – France – Orléans Region – History of
doctrines. 2. Hagiography. 3. Orléans Region (France) – Church
history. I. Title. II. Series.
BX4659.F8H43   1990
235'.2'0944509021 – dc20   89–36839 CIP
ISBN 0 521 36500 7

SE

Dedicated in loving gratitude
to my mother,
Dorothy Lucy Miner Head,
and to the memory of my father,
Dr Thomas Francis Head

CONTENTS

Contents

FIGURES

MAPS

ACKNOWLEDGEMENTS

During the time it has taken for me to develop a research project from a vaguely worded prospectus, first into a dissertation, and later into the present book, I have benefited from the help – or *patrocinium* – of dozens of friends and colleagues. First and foremost stands Giles Constable, now of the Institute for Advanced Study, who served as my adviser on the dissertation. His love for monastic studies has been a constant inspiration, while his perceptive criticism has helped me avoid many blunders. My correspondence with Christopher Brooke, as editor for Cambridge Studies in Medieval Life and Thought, has been a joy. The breadth of his learning and his fine ear for language have eliminated many infelicities along the way. Geoffrey Koziol, Richard Landes, and Frederick Paxton have all shared their knowledge of and enthusiasm for eleventh-century Francia. They will all recognize in this book conversations we have had, perhaps particularly in those cases where we continue to disagree. Even more important to me has been their friendship, which has been a vital personal support.

John Murdoch provided essential guidance during the early stages of my dissertation, Paul Meyvaert added timely advice as it neared completion, and William Graham served as a kindly overseer through the graduate process. Since that time Patrick Geary, Barbara Rosenwein, and Brian Stock have cheerfully served as sounding-boards. Sharon Farmer and Amy Remensnyder have discussed and debated parallel aspects of their own research projects. Bernard Bacharach and Jan Ziolkowski have shared some of my fascination with Letaldus of Micy. Dom Jacques Dubois of the Abbaye de Sainte-Marie and Dom Jean-Marie Berland of the Abbaye de Saint-Benoît-sur-Loire have been most gracious in their welcome and willingness to put the facilities of those abbeys at the disposal of a foreign layman. Barbara Abou-el-Haj, Clarissa Atkinson, Robert-Henri Bautier, Robert Benson, Daniel Callahan, Magdalena Carrasco, François Dolbeau, Richard

Fraher, Cynthia Hahn, Martin Heinzelmann, David Herlihy, Dom David Hurst, Felice Lifshitz, Guy Lobrichon, Thomas Noble, Steven Ozment, Joseph-Claude Poulin, Virginia Reinburg, Geneviève Renaud, Susan Ridyard, Lionel Rothkrug, Richard Rouse, Steven Sargent, Jean-Claude Schmitt, and Marilyn Schmitt have all generously shared their time and their expertise on varied occasions. The encouraging words of a number of colleagues around Claremont – particularly Vincent Wimbush and Harry Liebersohn – have made the process of finishing this book far more bearable. William Davies, Linda Randall, and their colleagues at the Cambridge University Press have shown almost infinite patience at seeing the book through to its conclusion.

I would like to add a particular note of gratitude to two teachers from earlier stages of my education. In secondary school Bishop Ansgar Nelson, OSB, helped to introduce me to the notion of scholarship at once humanistic and Christian. The pellucid scholarship and infectious enthusiasm of Caroline Bynum helped to prompt my original interest in medieval studies as a freshman in college. Their encouragement and example have remained important throughout the intervening years.

Without the help and advice of all these generous people this book would be much the poorer. Any errors which remain are of my own devising.

As the monks and canons of the medieval Orléanais well understood, patronage takes many forms, not least of which is financial. The Danforth Foundation helped to support my graduate education. Grants from the Georges Lurcy Foundation and the Mrs Giles Whiting Foundation helped respectively to fund the research and writing of my dissertation.

An historian is always dependent upon the resources and goodwill of libraries. The staffs of the Bibliothèque Nationale in Paris, the Bibliothèque Municipale of Orléans, the Bibliotheca Apostolica Vaticana, the Bibliothèque Royale in Brussels, the British Library, the Institut de Recherches et d'Histoire des Textes in Paris, the Harry Elkins Widener Library of Harvard University, the University Research Library of the University of California at Los Angeles, and of the Library of the School of Theology at Claremont have all rendered gracious and helpful service. Various research assistants and secretaries, most particularly Kenneth Stenstrup, Helen Young, and Leslie Brown, have valiantly

Acknowledgements

attempted to understand illegible notes, locate books, and satiate my appetite for photocopies.

Finally, I cannot begin to acknowledge the importance of the nurturing love and wisdom shown me by my parents, one living and one now deceased, to whom this book is dedicated in loving gratitude.

ABBREVIATIONS

AASS	*Acta Sanctorum quotquot toto orbe coluntur*, ed. Jean Bolland *et al.* 1st edition. Antwerp and Brussels, 1643–present.
AASSOSB	*Acta Sanctorum ordinis Sancti Benedicti*, ed. Luc d'Achéry and Jean Mabillon. 1st edition. 9 vols. Paris, 1668–1701.
BB	*Abbayes et prieurés de l'ancienne France*, ed. Jean-Martial Besse *et al.* Paris, 1905ff. New edition of Charles Beaunier, ed., *Recueil historique, chronologique, et topographique des archevechez, evêchez, abbayes, et prieurez de France.*
BHL	*Bibliotheca hagiographica latina antiquae et mediae aetatis.* 3 vols. Subsidia hagiographica, 6 and 12. Brussels, 1898–1911.
BM	Bibliothèque municipale.
BS	*Bibliotheca Sanctorum.* 12 vols. Rome, 1961–9.
Catal. Brux.	*Catalogus codicum hagiographicorum bibliothecae regiae Bruxellensis. Pars I. Codices latini membranei.* 2 vols. Subsidia hagiographica, 1. Brussels, 1886–9.
Catal. Paris.	*Catalogus codicum hagiographicorum latinorum antiquiorum saeculo XVI qui asservantur in bibliotheca nationali Parisiensis.* 3 vols. Subsidia hagiographica, 2. Brussels, 1889–93.
Catal. Vat.	*Catalogus codicum hagiographicorum latinorum bibliothecae Vaticanae*, ed. Albert Poncelet. Subsidia hagiographica, 11. Brussels, 1910.
CGMBPF	*Catalogue général des manuscrits des bibliothè-*

	ques publiques de France. Départements. 61 vols. Paris, 1885–present.
DACL	*Dictionnaire d'archéologie chrétienne et de liturgie*, ed. Fernand Cabrol and Henri Leclercq. 15 vols. Paris, 1907–53.
DHGE	*Dictionnaire d'histoire et de géographie ecclésiastiques*, ed. Alfred Baudrillart *et al.* 17 vols. Paris, 1912–present.
DMA	*Dictionary of the Middle Ages*, ed. Joseph Strayer. 9 vols. New York, 1982 present.
DTC	*Dictionnaire de théologie catholique*, ed. A. Vacant *et al.* 15 vols. Paris, 1903–67.
GC	*Gallia Christiana.* 2nd edition. 16 vols. Paris, 1715–1865.
Hist. SS	*Historiae seu Vitae sanctorum . . .*, ed. Laurentius Surius (Laurence Suhr). 5th edition. 13 vols. Marieta, 1875–80.
HLF	*Histoire littéraire de la France.* 41 vols. Paris, 1733–1875.
Jaffé–Wattenbach	*Regesta pontificum romanorum ab condita ecclesia ad annum post Christum natum MCXCVIII*, ed. Phillip Jaffé. 2nd edition, ed. Wilhelm Wattenbach. 2 vols. Leipzig, 1885–8.
MGH	*Monumenta Germaniae historica.*
AA	*Auctores antiquissimi.*
SRM	*Scriptores rerum merovingicarum.*
SS	*Scriptores*, in folio.
Miracula s. Benedicti	*Les Miracles de Saint Benoît écrits par Adrevald, Aimoin, André, Raoul Tortaire et Hugues de Sainte Marie, moines de Fleury*, ed. Eugène de Certain. Paris, 1858.
Nova bibliotheca mss.	*Novae bibliothecae manuscriptorum librorum . . . tomi I et II*, ed. Philippe Labbe. Paris, 1683.
Paris, BN lat.	Paris, Bibliothèque nationale, codex latinus
PL	*Patrologia latina*, ed. J.-P. Migne. 221 vols. Paris, 1844–64.
Regesten des Kaiserreichs	*Regesten des Kaiserreichs unter den Karolingern*, ed. J. F. Böhmer and E. Mühlbacher. 2nd edition. Innsbruck, 1899–1908.

RHF	*Recueil des historiens des Gaules et de la France*, ed. Martin Bouquet. 2nd edition, ed. Léopold Delisle. 24 vols. Paris, 1864–1904.
Vatican, Reg. lat.	Vatican, Bibliotheca Apostolica, codex Reginensis latinus.
VSBP	*Vies des saints et des bienheureux par les révérends pères bénédictins de Paris*, ed. Jules Baudot, Paul Antin, and Jacques Dubois. 13 vols. Paris, 1935–59.

INTRODUCTION

On 25 May 871 Bishop Walter of Orléans issued a set of twenty-five statutes intended to instruct his priests with regard both to the conduct of their own lives and to their guidance of the social and religious lives of the faithful. He covered a variety of topics ranging from the habit which some of his clergy had of drinking in public taverns to the sacred books which they should possess in their churches. He even specified a favoured handbook of virtues and vices to serve as a basis for preaching. Such statutes provide a precious glimpse into the attempts by members of the Carolingian episcopate to mould the practice of Christianity on the parish level.[1]

Set among them was a list of the feastdays which ought to be celebrated in the diocese of Orléans:

[The priests] ought to observe the usual feasts of the saints with solemn cult and come to know those which ought to have been previously observed by their people, that is, the birth of the Lord, [the feast] of Blessed Stephen, of St John the evangelist, of the Innocents, the octaves of the Lord, the epiphany, the nativity of holy Mary, the purification of holy Mary, the Assumption of holy Mary, Holy Saturday, the eight paschal days, the rogation days, the Ascension of the Lord, Pentecost, that of St John the Baptist, of St Peter, of St Paul, of St Martin, and of St Andrew, as well as [the feasts] of our fathers, by whose pious local patronage we are aided before the Lord, [that is] of the death of blessed Evurtius, of the death of blessed Anianus, of blessed Benedict, of blessed Maximinus, similarly of the death of blessed Lifardus, of the invention of the salvation-bringing cross, and of the exaltation of the same life-giving cross.[2]

Walter distinguished between 'usual' (*celebres*) feasts, which might be identified as those of the universal Christian church, and the feasts of the 'fathers' (*patres*) of his diocese whose 'pious local

---

[1] Walter of Orléans, *Capitularia Walterii*, c. 16, p. 191, and c. 7, p. 189. See also Clercq 1936–58, II, 359–61; McKitterick 1977, pp. 66–7; Wallace-Hadrill 1983, pp. 284–5.
[2] Walter of Orléans, *Capitularia Walterii*, c. 18, pp. 191–2.

patronage' (*pium patrocinium vicinum*) interceded on behalf of the people of the diocese with their God. The reforming bishops of the earlier ninth century well understood the need for the celebration of local patrons. A canon of the Council of Mainz (813), for example, required the celebration of a lengthy list of feasts of the universal church, analogous to those described as *celebres* in Walter's text. The bishops added that the feasts of those 'martyrs and confessors whose sacred bodies rest in a given parish and similarly of the dedication of the church' ought also to be observed, thus approving the spirit of Walter's list of local 'fathers'.[3]

While Bishop Walter was not utterly exhaustive in his catalogue of the saints of his diocese, he accurately reflected an important characteristic of the cult of saints in the diocese of Orléans – and, *mutatis mutandis*, other west Frankish dioceses – during the Carolingian periods. In hagiographic writings and liturgical commemorations the clerics of the Orléanais particularly focused on those saints from the Gallo-Roman and Merovingian periods whose relics were currently enshrined in their own or neighbouring churches.[4] Thus clerics celebrated those saints who were most able to provide their religious communities with powerful protective patronage. This focus on the celebration of local saints whose *virtus* was of ancient standing was to continue well into the twelfth century. The cult of the saints in the west Frankish realm was above all else an evocation of the power of the ancient heroes of the local clergy by contemporary members of that same clergy. The patronage thus evoked served the religious hierarchy in its dealings with laity of both noble and servile status.

William Christian, studying the cult of saints in sixteenth-century Nuevo Castile, has made a distinction between the practices of the universal and local churches: 'There were two

---

[3] Council of Mainz, canon 36 in *MGH, Concilia*, II.1, pp. 269–70.

[4] Local 'fathers' were, of course, not the only saintly patrons available to the Frankish world. Many, indeed most, churches bore the appellations of such saints of the universal church as Stephen, Peter, and the Virgin Mary. Cathedrals in particular were bastions of the patronage of these saints and only rarely housed the cult of relics. On the cult of Peter and the apostles, see Ewig 1960a. On the patronage of cathedrals, see Ewig 1960b. Both studies deal only with the background to the period of the present study. Much work remains to be done on the continuity of the cult of such saints in the western Frankish domains. These saints of the universal church, however, were not important to the cult of relics. Their significance has sometimes been slighted because the evidence for it rests on church dedications rather than the presence of shrines and the associated records of the miraculous.

levels of Catholicism – that of the Church Universal, based on the sacraments, the Roman liturgy, and the Roman calendar; and a local one based on particularly sacred places, images, and relics, locally chosen patron saints, idiosyncratic ceremonies, and a unique calendar built up from the settlement's own sacred history.'[5] Like 'local religion' in sixteenth-century Spain, the 'pious local patronage' which the 'fathers' provided for the diocese of Orléans was organized and controlled by the clergy, but also embraced the laity of both high and low standing in a complex system of symbiotic relationships. Monks and canons composed the texts which described the saintly identities of the 'fathers'; they lived under the patronage of those saints; they, along with bishops and the parish clergy, encouraged and directed the faithful in their veneration of those saints. Laypeople, for their part, went to the shrines of the 'fathers' as pilgrims, donated property to their monasteries, and worked the monastic lands as their servants. The cult of the local 'fathers' thus served as one of the most important points of contact between the clergy and laity in the period between the Carolingian reforms and the Fourth Lateran Council.

One of the underlying assumptions of this study is that there was a profound, if gradual, shift in the piety of the cult of saints between the time of Clovis and Gregory of Tours and that of Charlemagne and Theodulf of Orléans. Peter Brown has provided an evocative portrait of what the joining of heaven and earth at the

---

[5] Christian 1981, pp. 1–3. Christian introduced his distinction between 'local' and 'universal' to replace a more common historiographical distinction between 'elite' and 'popular' religion. One traditional view of the cult of relics, which has deep roots both in the historiographical attitudes of the Enlightenment and in the religious attitudes of ultramontane Catholicism, has seen it as a phenomenon of 'popular' religion, implying that it was somehow corrupt, 'magical', and belonging solely to the under classes. In this vein, see K. Thomas' description (1971, pp. 28–31) of popular belief in the miraculous as 'hagiolatry', as well as his implicit categorization of such beliefs as magical, and Finucane's application (1977, p. 27) of the admittedly 'old-fashioned anthropological terms' *mana* and *tabu* to the shrines of the saints. This sense of 'popular religion' has since come under intense criticism; see, for example, Patlagean 1968, pp. 106–8; Manselli 1974; Brown 1981, pp. 17–22; Clark 1983. In the wake of such disquiet, historians have been searching for an acceptable way to describe those forms of medieval Christian practice which were not the sole province of an intellectually or spiritually elite cadre inhabiting monasteries, universities, and episcopal palaces. One pair of writers (Brooke and Brooke 1984, p. 12) notes, 'that there were many overlaps and many different strata among the clergy as well as among the laity, and [much evidence] lies on the frontiers between the two'. The subject matter of this study, located as it is on the interface between the clergy and the laity of the Orléanais, certainly is contained within this more nuanced sense of the phrase 'popular religion'.

3

tombs of the 'very special dead' meant to the people of the western Mediterranean and their Germanic conquerors between the third and sixth centuries.[6] It was the saints of that early period who by and large continued to serve as the 'fathers' of the Orléanais during the period under study here. By the Carolingian period, however, these saints were no longer near-contemporary figures. Their identity and patronage had changed. The fusion of the Mediterranean Christian sense of the 'holy man' and Germanic ideas of charismatic rulership and gift exchange – the very process explored by Brown – produced a new sense of patronage which governed the later cult of the saints.

Beginning in the late eleventh century a second, equally profound, change began to occur in the perception of sanctity in Francia and in western Christendom more generally. Previously the saints who were most commonly venerated were men, and less frequently women, from the distant past. Significant numbers of living Christians now began to be recognized as holy men and women. Eremitic preachers such as Bernard of Tiron and Robert of Arbrissel, to pick only two active in the middle Loire valley, were considered to be saints even before their deaths. Their tombs quickly became important shrines, attracting laity who may have even heard the sermons of the living saints. The cults of such contemporary saints grew in number and importance over the following centuries. The body of the saint continued to be the focus of his or her posthumous cult, but the uses of those bodies changed. The living body of Francis of Assisi, for example, became a virtual relic by bearing the marks of sanctity in the stigmata and the representatives of various towns fought for control of that miraculous body even before the saint's death. At the same time the cults of Jesus and of the Virgin Mary also came once again to the forefront of both clerical and lay piety. Along with the growth of contemporary sanctity came the development of new procedures for the canonization, that is formal recognition, of saints, as well as of a new hagiographic genre, the *processus canonizationis*. In the first decade of the thirteenth century Innocent III made a bold move to place these processes under papal control, a move which was confirmed by the Fourth Lateran Council. The decrees of that council reflected the profundity of the pietistic changes of the previous century and a half. Its effects have been brilliantly charted

---

[6] Brown 1981 and 1982, pp. 222–50.

by André Vauchez, using the evidence of the new hagiographic genre.[7]

The period between these two momentous changes constituted, as Patrick Geary has stressed, a coherent epoch in the piety of relics within western Christendom.[8] In that period the cults of long-dead local 'fathers' such as those of the Orléanais formed the focal point of the cult of saints.

If these assumptions are correct – that the cult of saints as practised in the lands of the old Carolingian empire from the eighth through the twelfth centuries did indeed primarily revolve around the 'pious local patronage' provided by 'fathers' such as those enumerated in Bishop Walter's list – then, in order to understand the cult of saints for this period, it is necessary to study it in terms of a given locale. In this book I will study the identity of the saintly 'fathers' of the diocese of Orléans and analyse how those 'fathers' exerted their 'pious local patronage' on behalf of the clergy and laity of the Orléanais in the period between the ninth and twelfth centuries.[9] The study will focus on the saints of Bishop Walter's list, but will also include others who received similar, if more limited, veneration. In general it will not consider the liturgical and hagiographic commemorations of the saints of the universal church within the diocese, the commemoration of these 'fathers' outside the diocese, or the relics of local saints for whom there was neither liturgical nor hagiographic commemoration, although such topics all fall under the rubric of the 'cult of saints'. Within the boundaries of this period the composition of hagiography in the diocese of Orléans was concentrated in two century-long flowerings: the first stretching from around the year 800 to the promulgation of Bishop Walter's *capitula*, and the second between the 980s and the late eleventh century. There was a continuity in relic piety and the patronage of the diocese's 'fathers' between these two periods.

The Orléanais provides a case study of particular relevance to the

[7] Vauchez 1981. For an excellent case study of the new methods, see Foreville and Keir 1987.   [8] Geary 1978, pp. 25–30.

[9] The geographic scope of this study roughly corresponds to that of the *Histoire d'Orléans et de son terroir* (Debal, 1983). On the history of the social and physical geography of the region, see Babonaux 1983. The authors of the *Histoire religieuse d'Orléanais* (Oury 1983a), on the other hand, have chosen to include the dioceses of both Orléans and Chartres in their definition of the 'pays Orléanais' since the two were inhabited by the same tribe, the *Carnutes*, in the time of the Gauls. On the historical connections of the two, see Villette 1983.

problem at hand. It was a region of central importance within the domains of the western Franks for it served as one of the principal gateways from Francia to the more Romanized south. A series of important episcopal councils were held there in the sixth century. Charlemagne and Louis the Pious placed, in the persons of Bishops Theodulf and Jonas, favoured clerical advisers in its see. In 848 Charles the Bald chose the city as the site for his anointing and coronation as king of the Aquitaine; he frequently thereafter housed his itinerant court in nearby monasteries. At the time of Bishop Walter, Count Robert the Strong was consolidating his considerable military power in this region and his descendants used the Orléanais as an important base throughout the following century. When in 987 that family claimed the royal throne, the coronation of Robert the Pious as an associate of his father Hugh Capet took place in Orléans. Hugh and Robert later issued as many of their proclamations from Orléans as they did from Paris. Rodulfus Glaber, writing in the time of Henry I, still described Orléans in terms of a capital city: 'For this city was of old, as it is at present, the principal royal seat of the kings of Francia particularly for its beauty and its large population, not to mention the fertility of its soil, and the watering of the clear river.'[10] Beyond its importance as a royal seat, the diocese was also the site of the tomb of one of the great saints of western Christendom, that of St Benedict of Nursia at the abbey of Fleury. This tradition makes the Orléanais an inviting region in which to study the continuities between the Carolingian and Capetian periods.

The diocese of Orléans is also particularly rich in hagiographic sources. The abbey of Fleury, for instance, was one of the leading literary centres of the western Frankish lands. One of the most innovative and productive hagiographers of the early eleventh century, Letaldus, came from the abbey of Micy. Many of the textual problems posed by these sources have been considered by previous scholars. Alexandre Vidier, in a *thèse* originally written for the Ecole des Chartes and later both edited and updated by Dom Denis Grémont, surveyed the historiographical and hagiographical traditions of the abbey of Fleury. The Bollandist Albert Poncelet carefully established the relationships of hagiographic texts dealing with the saints of Micy. Geneviève Renaud has edited important texts from the monastery of Saint-Aignan and com-

---

[10] Rodulfus Glaber, *Historiarum libri quinque*, II.5.8, pp. 68–9.

Introduction

mented on the interrelated hagiographic dossiers of Bishops Anianus and Evurtius.[11] These textual studies, while not exhaustive, have provided an invaluable basis for the study of local sanctity and saintly patronage within the region.

Neither the identification of particular 'fathers' of the diocese nor the claim that they exerted a special patronage for its people was an invention of Bishop Walter. The 'fathers' of his list were all saints – or, in the case of the cross, a virtually personified object – whose relics were enshrined in the churches of the region's important monastic and canonical houses. They were also all figures about whom hagiographic texts had been composed by members of those same communities over the course of the century preceding the issue of Walter's *capitula*. These hagiographic works provided the liturgical readings, or *lectiones*, necessary for the feasts required by the bishop's legislation. Thus his canon of 'fathers' already existed in practice. Moreover, in the Carolingian church, bishops bore primary responsibility for decisions on sanctity, particularly within the boundaries of their own diocese.

These saints were striking both for their local origin and for their antiquity. Anianus and Evurtius were Gallo-Roman bishops of Orléans whose relics were venerated in churches located within the city walls, respectively Saint-Aignan, an abbey of Merovingian foundation, and Saint-Euverte, a chapter of canons of Carolingian origin. The recently refounded abbey of Micy, located across the Loire river from the city, housed the relics of its first abbot, a sixth-century monk named Maximinus. Similarly, the abbey of Meung-sur-Loire, located downriver from the city, housed the relics of its first abbot, a sixth-century monk named Lifardus. The geographical origins of the other 'saints' of the list were less immediate, but they were of no less antiquity. Orléans' cathedral housed relics of Christ's cross, allegedly provided by Bishop Evurtius in the fourth century, but probably first venerated there in late Merovingian times. The monks of Fleury claimed to have taken the relics of Benedict of Nursia from their original tomb at Monte Cassino in the seventh century. Thus each 'father' of Walter's list was firmly associated with a particular religious community in his diocese.[12]

[11] Vidier 1965; Poncelet 1904 and 1905; Renaud 1976, 1978a, and 1978b.
[12] These statements raise two problems of nomenclature facing a study which extends from the eighth through the twelfth centuries. The first problem is what to call the larger unit of governance within which the diocese of Orléans was located. 'Neustria' would be more appropriate to the earlier and 'Francia' to the latter halves of the period in question.

7

Moreover, hagiographic texts in local circulation vouched for both their antiquity and their holiness.

These saints were not the only 'fathers' known to the diocese of Orléans. Gregory of Tours had visited the shrine of St Avitus, a sixth-century monk, within the city walls and several versions of that saint's life were composed around the year 800.[13] The relics of other ancient saints, such as Paul Aurelian and Maurus the martyr, were translated into the diocese during the tumults of the tenth century. Suitable hagiographic works and liturgical commemorations came to celebrate the memory of these imported patrons.[14] In the early eleventh century members of newly founded religious communities invented hagiographic traditions for their saintly patrons, making such saints as Laetus remarkably similar in character and achievements to the Merovingian monks of Walter's canon. The term 'fathers' was consistently an accurate description, in terms of gender, of the saints who provided patronage to the Orléanais during our period. The only relics of a female saint venerated in the diocese were those of Montana at Ferrières, but

---

'France' would not seem appropriate until the reigns of Louis VI and Louis VII in the twelfth century. The admittedly cumbersome phrase 'western Frankish lands' has the elasticity and neutrality necessary to refer to the almost constantly shifting patterns of allegiance and governance within the lands north of the Loire. Sometimes the more specific geographic phrase 'middle Loire valley' – meaning the Anjou, the Touraine, the 'pays Chartrain', the Blésois, and the Orléanais – will serve appropriately. The second problem is what to call the houses or foundations of men who who were dedicated to the service of the saints whom I will discuss. In some cases, such as the abbey of Fleury, these houses were communities of monks throughout this period. Such communities originally followed some version of a *regula mixta*, that is customs which combined usages from several monastic rules, and later, after the reforms of Benedict of Aniane, they adopted the sole usage of the Benedictine rule. In other cases, such as the chapter of the cathedral of Sainte-Croix, they were groups of secular canons throughout the period. In still other cases, however, the identity of the communities changed or is difficult to determine with any precision. In the Carolingian period, for instance, the *monasterium* of Saint-Aignan was a community of monks (*Recueil des chartes de Saint-Benoît*, no. 1, 1, 5), but by the later tenth century it was a community of canons (see the charter edited in Vidier 1907, p. 317). In the mid-twelfth century the secular canons of Saint-Euverte were replaced by a community of regular canons. During the period of our study the word *monasterium* tended to be used indifferently with reference to communities of both monks and canons, secular and regular alike. The phrase 'religious community' will be used in the present study to refer to communities of monks, secular canons, and regular canons. Likewise the word 'monastery' will be used in a manner similar to the medieval use of *monasterium* in reference to foundations of both monks and canons. Technical objections could be raised concerning each of these usages, but they seem to be the least problematic terms.

[13] Gregory of Tours, *In gloria confessorum*, c. 97, pp. 810–11. Poncelet 1905, pp. 14–25.

[14] Vidier (1965, pp. 97–102) briefly considers this process for St Maurus and St Paul Aurelian at Fleury.

that cult was of minor importance and she was not regarded as a patron of that house. None of the relics considered here were enshrined in a convent of nuns. Moreover, all the authors considered in this study were male clerics.[15]

The relationship of the 'fathers' of the Orléanais to both the saints of the universal church and to other regional saints can be graphically demonstrated by the arrangement of the church of Saint-Aignan at its rededication in 1029.[16] The main altar of the church was dedicated to St Peter, who shared the patronal title of the foundation with St Anianus. The altar of the rear of the choir was dedicated to Anianus himself, whose relics rested in a crypt directly below the choir. Twelve minor altars lined the sides of the nave. Two of these were dedicated to saintly bishops with whom Anianus had been acquainted: Evurtius of Orléans and Mamertius of Vienne. The remainder were dedicated to saints, such as Stephen and Nicholas, important to the universal church.[17] In addition, the community possessed the bodies of six saints of local importance, but none of them was honoured at this time by an altar, by any form of liturgical celebration, or by any hagiographic text.[18] None of these saints could be considered 'fathers' of the diocese; even the resting place of their relics was left unspecified. A short time later, however, a portion of the relics of one of these saints, Euspicius, was returned to his original resting place at Micy. At that monastery, where Euspicius had allegedly overseen the work of his nephew Maximinus as its first abbot, the monks provided a special altar for the veneration of his relics, began to celebrate his feastday, and composed hagiographic works in his honour.[19] At that point Euspicius could be considered as having been added, at least by the monks of Micy, to the roll of local 'fathers'.

[15] Head (1987b) describes the relationship of a tenth-century female author, Hrotsvit of Gandersheim, to the traditions of monastic and hagiographic literature of concern here.

[16] Helgaud of Fleury, *Epitoma vitae regis Rotberti pii*, c. 22, pp. 106–11.

[17] The dedications of the altars were: Evurtius, Mamertius, Lawrence, George, All the Saints, Martin of Tours, Maurice, Stephen, Anthony, Vincent, Mary, John, the Holy Saviour, Nicholas, and Michael.

[18] These saints were: Euspicius, the uncle of Maximinus of Micy; Monitor and Flosculus, two early bishops of the diocese; Baudelius and Scubilius, two early martyrs (the former identified with a character in the *Vitae s. Aniani*); and Agia, the mother of St Lupus of Sens.

[19] The *Vita et translatio s. Euspicii* was composed at this time and described the saint's life, the return of his relics, and the dedication of the altar. See the sole manuscript exemplar of these texts, Vatican, Reg. lat. 621, fos. 47–54. The 21 July feast of Euspicius is listed in a twelfth-century calendar from Micy: Paris, Bibliothèque d'Arsenal 371, fo. 90. The *lectio*-markings in the text of Reg. lat. 621 suggest that it was read on this feastday.

In addition to its intensely local focus, the most striking characteristic of the cult of the 'fathers' of the Orléanais was the patronage which they afforded to the religious communities which possessed their relics. This special patronage, which Walter described as *pium patrocinium vicinum*, had – like the canon of saints itself – been widely recognized before his time. The clerics and laity of the Orléanais sought the patronage of these 'fathers' through the celebration of their feasts, pilgrimage, and the donation of ex-voto offerings at shrines. The living thus became servants or clients of the holy dead. The saints were people who had entered heaven – for that is the simplest definition of sanctity – through the exercise of spiritual power in their lives. They continued to exhibit that *virtus* posthumously, most particularly at their tombs. As Bertholdus of Micy wrote early in the ninth century, 'The exercise of spiritual virtues speaks forth . . . which even today does not cease to be shown forth at their tombs.'[20] This exercise of *virtus*, whether during the lifetimes of the saints or at their tombs, resulted in miracles. Lives of the saints described their original holiness, while collections of posthumous miracle stories described the *virtutes* which they performed in contemporary times. Around the year 1000 Letaldus of Micy echoed Bertholdus' distinction, 'We thought it right to put down separately whatever we discovered in their narration . . . beginning with those things which Martin [of Vertou] did while living in the body and extending to those things which he accomplished, with Christ working through him, after his death.'[21] Through the devotions of the living to the holy dead and the miracles which these patrons performed for their servants, 'fathers' such as Benedict continued to have an active posthumous existence in the society of the Orléanais.

The focus of the *virtus* of the 'fathers' of the Orléanais – who, after all, had been dead for many centuries – was their relics. To the people of the Orléanais these relics were highly prized objects. According to a Carolingian author, citizens from Orléans and Châteaudun almost fought a pitched battle over the body of St Avitus. The former claimed the relics because the saint had once been a monk of Micy, the latter because he had founded a monastery in their region. The parties eventually reached a Solomonic division in which Orléans received the body, but

---

[20] Bertholdus of Micy, *Vita s. Maximini I*, c. 1, p. 592.
[21] Letaldus of Micy, *Miracula s. Martini Vertavensis*, prologue in *MGH, SRM*, III, 567.

Introduction

Châteaudun retained *reliquia magna*, a phrase which probably indicated the saint's heart. In a celebration to welcome the relics in the streets of Orléans, the populace shouted a variation on a well-known liturgical phrase, clearly demonstrating the sense of Avitus' patronage: 'Gloria in excelsis Deo et in terra pax Aurelianorum in perpetuum sub Avito.'[22]

While this story tells nothing about the historical disposition of Avitus' relics in the sixth century, it clearly indicates clerical attitudes about relics around the year 800. That respect continued unabated throughout the period of our study. After the refoundation of the abbey of Monte Cassino in central Italy, its monks enlisted Pope Zachary and King Pippin III in an attempt to regain the body of its first abbot, Benedict of Nursia, which had been taken by the monks of Fleury. Adrevald of Fleury, a contemporary of Bishop Walter, described their failure as the will of the saint himself.[23] Over two centuries later, a cleric who participated in the liturgy in which the relics of St Lifardus were reburied at Meung-sur-Loire admitted that he had been tempted to steal a piece of the saint's body as it was removed from its tomb. He reminisced,

I am the most miserable of the miserable, the most unhappy of the unhappy, I who thought for a while about a pious theft, although I was not in any way capable of such a theft. I was more sad because I was unable to carry it out than on account of having piously thought of an impious theft.[24]

Later in the twelfth century the relics of Benedict were described as 'a treasure dearer to God than gold or silver and all gems'.[25]

Relics were the manifestation of the saints in the physical world. They provided, in Brown's evocative phrase, a 'joining of Heaven and Earth' at which miracles were more likely to happen than at other points in the world.[26] In the words of our medieval subjects they were variously described as the 'pledges' (*pignora*) or as the 'inheritance' (*reliquia*) of the saint. The saint stood in heaven near Christ, but the living had relics as concrete tokens of the *virtus* possessed by that holy person. As the would-be relic-thief said, 'Behold we believe that blessed Lifardus lives with Christ; in our

[22] *Vita s. Aviti I*, cc. 11–12, pp. 61–2; *Vita s. Aviti III* in Paris, BN lat. 3789, fo. 113.
[23] *Miracula s. Benedicti*, I. 15–17, pp. 37–42.
[24] *Translatio s. Lifardi*, c. 5, p. 158. *Furtum pium* (or *sacrum*) was a common term. Geary (1978) has explored this theme in hagiographic literature of the ninth and tenth centuries, but does not discuss any theft quite so individual in nature.
[25] *Chronique de Saint-Pierre-le-Vif*, p. 152.   [26] Brown 1981, p. 1.

times we happily honour the relics of his mortality.'[27] Miracles
occurred as a result of this felicitous joining of the sacred and the
mundane. Relics served, as Stanley Tambiah has remarked in the
case of Theravada Buddhism, as an objectification of the saint's
charisma, which is simply a sociological phrase for medieval
virtus.[28] The relics themselves, however, were not responsible for
the miraculous; they did not serve as a direct conduit of some
mysterious thaumaturgic radiation. Rather, personal relationships
formed between the living and the dead, relationships which were
balanced on the delicate fulcrum of the saint's pledges or relics,
allowed the saint to exercise his *virtus* on behalf of his living
servants.

The relationships between saints and their living servants were
chronicled in the hagiography composed in the Orléanais.
Adrevald of Fleury, a contemporary of Bishop Walter, collected a
record of the posthumous miracles of Benedict of Nursia, the
earliest such collection from the region. Among his stories
Adrevald told how Count Odo of Orléans mounted a military
expedition and intended to pillage the property of Fleury on the
route of his march as a means of supporting his soldiers. After the
abbot departed with troops raised from the dependants of the
abbey to protect its lands, a monk of Fleury named Hercambaldus
dreamed of St Benedict. The abbot first chastised the monks for
their lack of trust and then offered to make a pact with them:

If you will take care to obey the precepts of the Almighty and will
without hesitation take an oath to follow the commands of the rule which
has been handed down by God through me to you, then all your
adversities will turn to prosperity, your enemies will become friends, and
your patron in his grace will deny you nothing good.[29]

After hearing of the vision, the community prayerfully accepted
the saint's offer, vowing themselves to Benedict's service and
obedience to his rule. A messenger soon arrived, telling them of
Count Odo's death.

The miracles described in the collections from the Orléanais also
included cures performed either at the tomb or through the
invocation of the nearby saint. A particularly detailed text from the

[27] *Translatio s. Lifardi*, c. 7, p. 158.
[28] Tambiah 1984, Part III, 'The cult of amulets: the objectification and transmission of charisma', pp. 195–289. He also calls them (see particularly pp. 4–5) 'indexical symbols', a concept derived from the semiotics of Samuel Pierce.
[29] *Miracula s. Benedicti*, I.20, p. 49.

late eleventh century describes how a German named Henry, who was lame as a result of his sins, was told in a dream that God had decreed that he would be cured through the merits of Maximinus of Micy.[30] After Henry mistakenly journeyed first to the shrine of Maximinus of Trier and then to the shrine of Maximus of Chinon, an angelic vision chastised him for not following the instructions sent by God and told him that the proper shrine was near Orléans. Coming to the abbey of Micy, Henry received a warm welcome from the monks who predicted he would be cured on the coming feastday of the saint. After praying without effect at the saint's tomb during matins on that day, Henry began to leave the church. Then the saint appeared to him and struck him on the legs with an abbatial staff. When he recovered from the blow he found that he was no longer lame. Henry, the monks, and the townspeople who had gathered to celebrate the feast gave thanks to God, and Henry vowed himself a servant of the saint.

For Hercambaldus and his brothers, Benedict was not merely a bag of bones entombed in their church, but a living protector who defended them from their enemies. Similarly, for Henry, Maximinus was a present and powerful person who had cured him. Collections of stories from both Trier and Chinon show that the other saints visited by Henry also had reputations for curing the sick, but his fate was bound in a very special way to Maximinus of Micy, whose servant he eventually became.[31] Similarly the vows taken by Hercambaldus and his fellows renewed the special relationship which they enjoyed with the saint whose relics were enshrined in their monastery. Through such vows of service, as well as through prayers and ex-voto offerings, clerics like Hercambaldus and laypeople like Henry formed firm bonds with the holy dead, seeking the exercise of sacred *virtus* on their behalf. These relationships were both personal and unique. They brought the living into close proximity with the divine. The saints were the 'friends' and 'servants' of God (*amici* or *servi Dei*); they were the inhabitants of heaven, the celestial court of the divine king. Christians sought the aid of these saints – *patroni* or *advocati* who could intercede for them with their God – by becoming their servants. Thus the saints were personally and physically active in society. There was no barrier between heaven and earth. Rather, the members of the societies of both the sinful living and the holy

---

[30] *Miraculum s. Maximini*, pp. 238–51.   [31] Head 1984, p. 238 n. 2, and p. 240 n. 3.

dead mingled their affairs. Jacques LeGoff remarks, 'Hagiography
tells us much about the mental infrastructure [of the middle ages]:
the interpenetration between the tangible world and the supernatural world, the common nature of the corporeal and psychic, are
the conditions which make miracles and related phenomena
possible.'[32] The appearances of Benedict to Hercambaldus and of
Maximinus to Henry betray this 'interpenetration'. The divisions
which the modern mind places between the sacred and the secular,
between the living and the dead, and between heaven and earth
were envisioned very differently by the people whose world and
thoughts we are about to explore.

Hagiography – that is the broad range of literature produced for
the cult of saints – has provided the source material for important
studies concerning both monastic and lay religious practice in the
middle ages. These studies have tended to focus either on the
concept of sanctity or on the laypeople who made up the bulk of
the pilgrim public who attended the shrines of the saints.[33] In the
present study I will focus instead on the religious communities who
possessed the relics of the saints, who produced and used the
hagiographic traditions concerning those saints, and who thus
mediated between the holy dead and their living audiences. In
particular I wish to examine how sanctity, in the period prior to
and contemporary with the development of official canonization
procedures, was constructed and manipulated by religious communities for their own benefit within the context of local
patronage networks. The telling of stories, such as those found in
the hagiographic works which form the basic source material of
this study, is an act of interpretation. A posthumous miracle story,
for example, encapsulates a movement in which the *virtus* of the
saint is mediated through a saint's relics to a social world where the
effects of that *virtus* are interpreted as a miracle. The clerical author
thus related his saintly subject to those people who believed in that
saint's power and who sought that saint's intercession. By

[32] LeGoff 1985, p. 173.
[33] For this definition of hagiography see Graus 1965, p. 25. Sigal (1980) discusses the
relationship of hagiography (repeating this definition) and historiography in medieval
literature. The bibliography on hagiography and the cult of the saints is vast, and it is
impossible to cite here more than a few works of particular relevance to the present
study. The bibliographical essay in Boesch Gajano 1976, pp. 261–300, and the annotated
bibliography in S. Wilson 1983, pp. 309–417, are valuable resources. Review articles by
Gaiffier (1968), Heinzelmann (1977), Pohlkamp (1977), Van Uytfanghe (1977), Schmitt
(1984), and Howe (1986) all survey recent developments in scholarship.

controlling the physical relics themselves and the discourse about the saint whom they represented, clerics controlled both this interpretive process and the patronage relationships between the 'fathers' and the people of the Orléanais. The primary goal of this study, then, is not so much to describe the cult of saints in the diocese of Orléans as it is to analyse both how the people of the Orléanais, the clergy and the laity, related to their saintly 'fathers' and how clerical institutions controlled those relationships.[34]

The crucial relationship of hagiography to the cult of the saints was recognized by medieval clerics themselves. In the early ninth century Bertholdus of Micy opened the *Vita s. Maximini I* with some thoughts on the relationship of hagiographic texts to the veneration of the saints:

The churches of the faithful scattered through the world celebrate together with highest praise the fame of holy men. Their tombs wreathed in the metals of gold and silver as well as in layers of precious stones and in a shell of marble, now bear witness to their pious memory. The exercise of their spiritual virtues speaks forth, both in [the virtues] which they once bodily and spiritually practised and still do today in performances which never cease being exhibited at their tombs. Truly no less for the devotion of the faithful than these works [of the saints] which shine forth the hoped-for proof, the monuments of letters, which are set down on pages, fully inundate the senses of readers and listeners.[35]

For Bertholdus hagiography provided a record of and monument to great heroes of the past. As such it was directly linked to the relics of the holy dead enshrined in monuments of precious metal and stone. These stories, however, had a contemporary utility which

---

[34] As a study of sanctity and hagiography in a particular locale during the period between the Merovingian age and the rise of canonization procedures, this study is by no means novel. The Bollandist Baudouin de Gaiffier wrote his *thèse*, later published (1967), on the hagiography composed in Flanders during the eleventh century. While Gaiffier's primary concern was with the literary production of hagiography, he was also attentive to the institutional contexts within which his subjects composed their texts. Joseph-Claude Poulin (1975) has used the body of hagiography composed in the Aquitaine during the Carolingian period as a source for the exploration of the ideal of sanctity and its function in Carolingian religion and society. Paolo Golinelli (1980) has explored hagiography and the cult of the saints in Reggio Emilia as an example of civic life and religion in an emergent Italian city-state over a period similar to that covered here. Ridyard (1988) has discussed the development of hagiographic traditions concerning Anglo-Saxon royal saints in terms of both spiritual and political concerns. These works have all provided a degree of methodological inspiration for the present study, as well as presenting the rich possibility of comparative studies.
[35] Bertholdus of Micy, *Vita s. Maximini I*, c. 1, p. 592.

made them far more than passive ornament. Like the 'exercise of virtue', that is miracles, which the saints had performed in their lives and continued to perform posthumously, hagiography edified a contemporary audience of clergy and laity. Selections from such hagiographic works served as the *lectiones* which were read out in church on the feastdays of the saints, a practice which was regularized in the diocese of Orléans by Bishop Walter's decree. Bertholdus' fellow authors agreed that the act of writing down stories about the saints served to keep alive the memory of those saints. As a canon of Saint-Aignan wrote of his patron over two centuries later:

I will not allow silence to eclipse the miraculous deeds of such a father . . . therefore we will pluck a few examples from many so that from our devotion he may have some veneration and so that some aid may come to us from his most holy intercession. Just as this saint who has passed over to the joy of the angels is worthily held up in human memory, so too his memory is worthily celebrated.[36]

Without the memory of the saints contained in stories – both those stories which the authors 'set down on pages' and the oral traditions on which they depended – the relics would have been simply bones and ashes buried in the earth rather than holy persons alive in the community. Their audience used the stories told about the saints to interpret the relics of those saints. Miracles were crucial to this hermeneutic interaction of relics, text, and audience. As evidence of a close relationship with God, they served as an authentication of sanctity. The writing of a saint's life by a cleric such as Bertholdus became the exposition of the *virtutes* performed in that saint's life. Hearing such stories of the miraculous, the clergy and laity of the Orléanais had faith in the power of the holy people enshrined in the monuments of metal and stone in their churches. This faith and expectation grounded their experience of the 'hoped-for proof' of posthumous miracles at those shrines. These miracles were in turn collected by later writers, such as the canon of Saint-Aignan, who sought to stimulate not only the pious veneration of his patron, but also the intercessory action – including yet more miracles – of that saint.

In theory, of course, a person did not owe his or her sanctity to

---

[36] *Miracula s. Aniani*, prologue, p. 256. See also, for example, Adrevald of Fleury, *Vita s. Aigulphi*, c. 1, p. 656; *Miracula s. Benedicti*, II.prologue, p. 90; *Miracula s. Euspicii*, c. 1, p. 314.

the public celebration of a feast, the veneration of relics, or the composition of hagiography. A saint was simply a saint: one who had entered the heavenly kingdom. In practice some memory of saints' identity and virtues and some expectation of their miraculous power was central to the veneration of their relics and the celebration of their feasts. This memory and expectation were embedded in texts, whether written or oral. Even in cults which did not win the backing of the institutional church, oral traditions about the saintly virtues of the person represented by relics were central to the public veneration of those relics. Examples can be found in the cult of the inauthentic relics of St Just which was supported with chagrin by William of Volpiano and Rodulfus Glaber in the mid-eleventh century, or that of a noble boy who fell into a well and died on Good Friday which became known to Guibert of Nogent in the early twelfth century, or that of the relics of a dog which was decried by Stephen of Bourbon in the mid-thirteenth century.[37] The putting down of traditions in 'monuments of letters' was crucial to the institutionalization of the veneration of a saint. Rodulfus, Guibert, and Stephen all saw the lack of written texts as symptomatic of deeper problems with these particular cults. In the Orléanais the lack of a written text went hand in hand with the slide into oblivion of various saints of the Merovingian period. The composition of hagiographic texts was also a crucial step in the growth of new relic shrines in the eleventh century, such as that of St Laetus at Pithiviers. The composition and recitation of texts about the saints was thus part of the continuing cycle of the veneration of those saints.

Hagiography was not only an expression of the public piety of the communities which commissioned their composition and listened to their contents, but a private work of piety for the authors themselves. Beyond the usual introductory formulae concerning the humility which an author brought to his task, these authors claimed that their work brought them into closer contact with the saint about whom they wrote, and thus closer to salvation. A canon of Meung-sur-Loire stated that, as 'the one who consigns to memory the marvellous actions of the saints in letters', he hoped that his work would help him win eternal reward.[38] Aimo of Fleury claimed to have written his collection of miracle stories

---

[37] Rodulfus Glaber, *Historiarum libri quinque*, IV.3.7–8, pp. 182–5; Guibert of Nogent, *De pignoribus sanctorum*, 1.5, col. 621, and Stock 1983, p. 246; Schmitt 1979.
[38] *Miracula s. Lifardi*, c. 1, p. 159.

through the intercession of Benedict and the Virgin Mary.[39] By means of an extended simile Hugh of Fleury noted that his miracle stories were designed to help people turn from their own sins and seek salvation. Since the apostle Paul had promised forgiveness to anyone who so helped his fellows, Hugh saw the stories as being an aid in his own salvation.[40] A monk named Hugh was depicted as a suppliant before both Christ and the Virgin in three capitals in the church at Fleury. It has been argued that this monk should be identified as our author and as the sculptor of the capitals. Two of the scenes depict Hugh offering Christ a book, very possibly symbolic of his hagiographic endeavours.[41] In the ninth century the monk Lucifer confronted his audience by concluding his narrative with a direct request: 'hence I beg you, anyone who reads these acts, pray for me to God that I may come to obtain [eternal reward], lest anything bad should come upon me'.[42]

Clerics from the Orléanais composed over sixty extant 'monuments of letters' during the Carolingian and early Capetian periods. Many of these works concerned the saints of Bishop Walter's list, but others detailed the life and miracles of saints who came to be venerated after the ninth century, of saints whose relics were translated into the diocese, of contemporary figures who were considered holy, and even of the patrons of religious foundations of other regions, both near and distant. Still other works are known to have been lost or were written about the saints of the Orléanais by writers from other regions.[43] The exchange of hagiographic works was a mark of friendship among monastic communities. Peter of Poitiers, for example, urged Peter the Venerable, abbot of Cluny, to send two hymns which he had recently composed about St Benedict 'to the monks who keep his body', that is the community of Fleury.[44] The vast majority of all hagiographic works about the saints of the diocese of Orléans were written by authors from the region. A study of the techniques of

---

[39] *Miracula s. Benedicti*, II.prologue, p. 91.

[40] *Miracula s. Benedicti*, IX.prologue, pp. 357–8.

[41] Berland 1979b, pp. 31–2 and 47; Vergnolle 1985, pp. 254–7 and figures 250, 263, and 264.

[42] Lucifer of Orléans, *Vita s. Evurtii II*, c. 20, p. 58.

[43] Andrew of Fleury discussed two lost works on St Benedict by Odo and Arnold, both monks of Fleury: *Vita Gauzlini*, c. 2, p. 34. According to the author of the *De diversis casibus Dervensis coenobii et miraculis s. Bercharii* (p. 849), Abbot Adso of Montierender composed a verse life of Benedict at the request of Abbo of Fleury, but the text has been lost.

[44] Peter the Venerable, *The Letters of Peter the Venerable*, letter 128, I, 325. For the text of the hymns, see I, 320. It is uncertain whether they were ever sent.

composition which they used – a study, if you will, of how they constructed their 'monuments of letters' – will help to reveal both how these clerics attempted to link the past to the present in writing the lives of the saints and how they gathered more contemporary material such as collections of posthumous miracle stories in composing their works.

At the same time it is necessary to remember the 'monuments of stone', as well as the monks and canons who tended them. Works of local hagiography were intimately linked to the shrines and relics of a saint. The geography and chronology of the cults of the 'fathers' of the Orléanais must be charted with some precision in order to understand the ideals of sanctity and patronage contained in those texts. It is also crucial to remember that authors like Bertholdus belonged to religious communities and, as members of those communities, had institutional concerns very much at heart. As Baudouin de Gaiffier has noted for eleventh-century Flanders, 'In that troubled period, it was rare for a hagiographer to write without being preoccupied with the authentication of a relic or the protection of the prerogatives of a saintly patron, the true owner of the goods of a monastery.'[45] The composition of hagiography was controlled by the clergy and the cult of the saints fostered by that hagiography served clerical ends by inspiring devotion, harnessing pious beliefs, promoting certain forms of religious practice, and protecting the saints' property.

Local 'fathers' were some of the most important, although by no means the only elements of the cult of saints in western Christendom from the Carolingian period through the twelfth century. The overall goal of this study is to present a detailed picture of the evolution of the cults of such saints in one locale, showing the institutional and intellectual contexts within which hagiography was composed and relics were venerated. Such an analysis also provides, I think, important evidence about the relationship of clerical and lay religious attitudes in western Frankish society. This study of a single, but important, region will, I hope, help to illuminate the day-to-day practice of the cult of saints, which was itself so crucial to the Christianity of the middle ages.

---

[45] Gaiffier 1967, pp. 420–1.

Chapter 1

THE CAROLINGIAN PERIOD

The Carolingian religious culture of the diocese of Orléans had deep roots in the Gallo-Roman and Merovingian past. When the Romans defeated the local tribe of the Carnutes in 52 BC they latinized the native name of the town to *Cenabum*. By the fourth century the official name of the city had become *civitas Aurelianorum*. The earliest recorded Christian bishop was one 'Diclopetus Aurilianorum' who took part in the Council of Cologne (346). In addition to a bishop, the city had acquired a defensive wall, a theatre, and many other features of a Gallo-Roman *civitas*. According to a text of relatively early date, Bishop Anianus was forced in the mid-fifth century to rebuild the city's virtually ruined cathedral, an act which indicates that the history of the early Christian community was not an unbroken record of success. At that time the cathedral was probably dedicated to St Stephen, whose relics had been discovered and distributed widely through the western empire in the early fourth century.[1]

Bishop Anianus was famed for miraculously saving the city from an attack by the Huns in 451. As early as 478 Sidonius Apollinaris wrote to Anianus' successor apologizing for not having completed an account of the *virtutes* of this man whose prophetic powers were praised by the people (*illa vulgata sacerdotis vaticinatio*).[2] Such an account of the bishop's life was contained in the *Vita s. Aniani I* (*BHL* 473), probably written in the sixth century and thus the earliest extant hagiographic work from the Orléanais.[3] Its

---

[1] Martinière 1939; Debal 1974; Berland 1978b, pp. 19–27. On the disrepair of the cathedral of Orléans, see *Vita s. Aniani I*, c. 2, pp. 108–9. For comparative purposes, see Stancliffe's (1979) account of the Christianization of the neighbouring Touraine.

[2] Sidonius Apollinaris, *Epistolae*, VIII.15, p. 147.

[3] Loyen 1969, pp. 70–2; Renaud 1978a, pp. 86–7. Cf. the arguments of earlier scholars, who attempted to prove that the work either decisively predated or was dependent upon that of Gregory of Tours. Cuissard (1886, pp. 201–2) suggests that it was the completion of Sidonius Apollinaris' work. Krusch (*MGH*, *SRM*, III, 105) dates it to the eighth century, while Theiner (1832, p. 9) dates it to the ninth.

author briefly summarized Anianus' early career in which he spiritually and materially renewed the city's church. Shortly thereafter the Huns under Attila entered Gaul. Anianus set off for Arles to seek the aid of Aetius, the general charged with defending the province. When he arrived at Arles he found many other bishops soliciting aid for their cities, but gained Aetius' attention by providing the exact date on which Attila would attack Orléans. After the Huns laid siege to the city, Anianus went out to warn Attila that God would protect it. Bad weather forestalled the attack for several days. On 14 June, the predicted day, the Huns entered Orléans, but Aetius – informed by the bishop's visionary appearance – led his troops to the barbarian camp, where he massacred his enemies. The story of the siege of Orléans was also known to Gregory of Tours and his continuators.[4]

Elsewhere Gregory mentioned that Bishop Namatius was buried in the *basilica s. Aniani*, the earliest reference to the saint's shrine.[5] By the early seventh century the monastery of Saint-Aignan had been founded in association with this church.[6] Later in the century Queen Balthild supported a reform there which instituted a combination of the monastic rules of St Benedict and St Columbanus.[7] The importance of the shrine was reflected by Fredegar who mentioned it as comparable to that of St Martin of Tours.[8] Gregory knew of one other shrine in the diocese of Orléans, that of an abbot named St Avitus, which he had personally visited.[9] He related the story of a man chastised for not keeping the saint's feast which was celebrated with 'great honour'

[4] Gregory of Tours, *Historia Francorum*, II.7, pp. 48–50; Fredegar, *Chronicon*, II.53, p. 73; *Liber historiae Francorum*, c. 5, p. 246. Gregory, however, placed Aetius' arrival before, rather than after, the breach of the city walls. Compare his account to the *Vita s. Aniani I*, c. 10, pp. 115–16. There are several other differences between the two: (1) the author of *BHL* 473 consistently spelled Aetius as Agetius; (2) the author of *BHL* 473 stated that Maiorianus was emperor at the time, whereas in fact Valentinian III reigned from 425 to 455 (see *MGH, SRM*, III, 110 n. 2); (3) the author of *BHL* 473 identified Thursomodus, not Theodoridus, as the king of the Goths who was allied to Aetius (see *MGH, SRM*, III, 115 n. 3). The two accounts are almost certainly independent and it is impossible to determine which is the earlier.
[5] Gregory of Tours *Historia Francorum*, IX.18, p. 432.
[6] *Recueil des chartes de Saint-Benoît*, no. 1, 1, 5, where Leodebodus of Saint-Aignan referred to himself as *abbas* and his fellows in the community as *monachi*. For a bibliographical summary, see Cottineau 1939–70, cols. 2138–9. The history of Saint-Aignan has been greatly confused by the writings of Robert Hubert (1661), who was himself a canon of the church and forged numerous documents concerning its history.
[7] *Vita s. Balthildis*, c. 9, p. 493.   [8] Fredegar, *Chronicon*, IV. 54, p. 45.
[9] Gregory of Tours, *In gloria confessorum*, c. 97, pp. 810–11; Gregory of Tours, *Historia Francorum*, VIII.2, pp. 371–2.

in the Orléanais. Elsewhere he told how Avitus, a 'powerful churchman of his day', had advised Chlodomir (*c.* 525) not to kill his prisoners.[10]

In Gregory's time the cult of such saints of the old order was an important spiritual defence for the urban Gallo-Roman population against their Frankish conquerors. The cults of these saints developed according to a similar pattern throughout Neustria. First, small churches were erected as shrines over the tombs of the holy dead in the Christian cemeteries located outside the walls of the *civitas*. Later, in many cases after the arrival of the Franks, these churches were enlarged to accommodate communities of monks or canons. Still later these monasteries were encircled by the expanding towns.

In the next century, however, the Franks adopted the veneration of relics wholesale and established it in the countryside as well.[11] In 651 Abbot Leodebodus of Saint-Aignan founded a new abbey on a tract of fertile Loire bottomland located 40 kilometres to the east of the city, land which had been given him by Clovis II.[12] The area was known as *Floriacus* for its fertility, from which the more familiar French epithet 'Fleury' has been derived. Two centuries later the town which huddled next to the monastery's walls was still known as *Vetus Floriacus*.[13] Leodebodus intended the monastery, which he dedicated to St Peter, to serve as a new home for the relics of St Anianus, but the planned translation was never carried out. In the foundation charter he distinguished the new foundation from an extant basilica and monastery dedicated to the Virgin 'which John had built at Fleury', but later implied that the two monasteries had been merged.[14] The monks followed a combi-

[10] Gregory of Tours, *Historia Francorum*, III.6, pp. 101–3. Mabillon (*AASSOSB*, I, 613–14 nn. 2–4) suggests that this is a different Avitus than the monk venerated in later periods, but Poncelet (1905, pp. 15–16) rejects this suggestion.

[11] For a subtle reexamination of the traditional account of the relationship of urban and rural Christianity in the Merovingian period, see Fouracre 1979. For the role of saints' relics in that relationship, see Wood 1979.

[12] *Recueil des chartes de Saint-Benoît*, no. 1, I, 1–19. The only extant text of the foundation charter dates from the eleventh century. Its existence, however, is attested by earlier sources and the general consensus of scholars is that the charter is, if not genuine, at least a reliable reflection of the original document: Bautier and Labory 1965, pp. 32–3; Bautier 1969, p. 76; Laporte, 1979, pp. 109–16. For a bibliographical summary, see BB, I, 345–52; Cottineau 1939–70, cols. 2610–13; *DACL*, V, 1709–60; *DHGE*, XVII, 441–76; Vergnolle 1985, pp. 321–2. [13] *Miracula s. Benedicti*, I.35, p. 77.

[14] On the relationship between Leodebodus and Fleury, see Lesne 1910–45, I, 110 n. 3; I, 119 n. 3; I, 165 n. 3; I, 201 n. 6. On comparable foundation charters, see I, 119, n. 3.

nation of the rules of Benedict and Columbanus similar to that prescribed for Saint-Aignan. In the ninth century there continued to be separate churches dedicated respectively to Peter and to the Virgin at Fleury. By that time they had adopted the sole usage of Benedict's rule.

Within a generation or two of its foundation, Fleury gained enormously in prestige through the acquisition of the relics of St Benedict himself from their original resting place at the then-deserted monastery of Monte Cassino in central Italy.[15] From the late seventh century on Benedict was considered to be a patron of the abbey and began to eclipse the position of St Peter and the Virgin in donation charters.[16] The authenticity of this translation, however, has occasioned considerable debate. Monte Cassino has claimed to possess at least some of Benedict's relics since shortly after its refoundation in the mid-eighth century. In 1066 Abbot Desiderius, in the course of rebuilding the church there, found a tomb which came to be identified as that of the saint, to the exclusion of the Fleury claim.[17]

There is no doubt, however, concerning the antiquity of Fleury's claim to possess relics of St Benedict. The site of Monte Cassino was deserted from 581 until 717 when Petronax of Brescia refounded the monastery. In 750–1 Pope Zachary wrote to the bishops of France on behalf on the monks of Monte Cassino requesting the return of Benedict's relics from an unspecified location.[18] An early manuscript of the Hieronymian martyrology, which may even predate this letter, noted 11 July as the feast of the

---

[15] Two ninth-century documents from Fleury, a set of annals and an abbatial list, dated the translation to the abbacy of Mummolus (*c.* 660). These sources, however, have certain internal inconsistencies, see Vidier 1965, pp. 51 and 271; Hourlier 1979b, pp. 216–17. A date of 703 is given in the *Annales Laureshamenses* (p. 22). Paul the Deacon (*Historia Langobardorum*, VI.2, pp. 164–5) implied that the translation occurred during the reign of Cuncipert (688–700). Hourlier (1979b, pp. 216–18) rejects the evidence of the *Annales Laureshamenses* as being part of a confused German tradition. Goffart (1967, pp. 109–10), on the other hand, argues for the later dates, saying that Paul the Deacon is in 'close agreement' with the *Annales*. In any case, a date in the second half of the seventh century seems reasonable.   [16] Hourlier 1979b, pp. 218–19.

[17] The controversy has continued to the present day among scholars and members of the contemporary monastic communities descended from the medieval foundations. On the Fleury traditions, see Galli 1954; Hourlier 1979b. On the Cassinese tradition, see Meyvaert 1955; Davril 1979a. For a judicious overview, see Goffart 1967, pp. 107–11.

[18] *MGH, Epistolae Carolini aevi*, III, 467–8, edited from Paris, BN lat. 2777. Jaffé-Wattenbach, no. 2290; Kehr 1907–57, VIII, 125, no. 25. This letter itself has occasioned considerable debate, but is now generally accepted to be genuine, see Meyvaert 1955, pp. 9–10; Goffart 1967, pp. 108 and 117; Hourlier 1979a.

translatio to Francia.[19] Late in the eighth century Paul the Deacon, himself a monk of Monte Cassino, noted that 'some Franks, coming from the regions of Le Mans and Orléans and pretending to keep vigil at the venerable body, took away the bones of [Benedict] and likewise of his reverend sister Scholastica'. He also indicated that some minor relics of the saint were left behind at Monte Cassino.[20] The earliest reference to Fleury as the new resting place of the relics was in the *Translatio s. Benedicti* (*BHL* 1116), a brief narrative written about this same time in Germany.[21] In addition, the *Annals of Lorsch* and two early manuscripts of the martyrology of Florus of Lyon (806–37) also specified Fleury.[22] In sum, the evidence indicates that, at some point during the second half of the seventh century, the monks of Fleury acquired relics which they claimed to be – and, more importantly, others accepted as being – those of Benedict of Nursia. The final version of their public claim was not enunciated, however, until the work of Adrevald of Fleury in the second half of the ninth century.

The early history of the other relic shrines of the Orléanais is less clear. Although no pre-Carolingian documents survive from the abbey of Micy, it certainly predated the ninth century.[23] Whether or not the relics of St Maximinus were ever kept at the abbey during its early history is unclear. According to tradition those relics were first enshrined in a cave on the banks of the Loire and later in a church within the town walls of Orléans constructed for that purpose by Bishop Sigobert (*c.* 670–81). In any event the abbey

[19] *AASS*, Nov. II, part 2, p. 368. Quentin 1903, particularly pp. 369–72 on the date of the earliest manuscript to mention the translation.

[20] Paul the Deacon, *Historia Langobardorum*, VI.2, pp. 164–5. Meyvaert 1955, pp. 4–16; Goffart 1967, pp. 108–9; Hourlier 1979e.

[21] Munding 1930; Weber 1952 (a critical edition is provided on pp. 141–2); Hourlier 1979b, pp. 220–3; Goffart 1967, pp. 109 and 115–31. The date of the text is provided by the manuscripts. Bauerreiss (1950) suggests that this account was written by a monk of Benediktbeuren on the occasion of the translation of some of Benedict's relics to that monastery, but that argument has been rejected by Goffart 1967, pp. 121–2.

[22] *Annales Laureshamenses*, p. 22. Quentin discusses the two versions of the martyrology, one called 'Florus-A' (1903, pp. 385–408) and the other 'Florus-M' (p. 313). Goffart (1967, p. 118, n. 1) compares the two texts. See also Hourlier 1979b, pp. 214–18; Goffart 1967, pp. 108–9.

[23] Poncelet 1905, pp. 6–10; 'Chartes de Micy', pp. vi–vii. Cf. the hypercritical remarks of Berland (in Debal 1983, pp. 219–20) who ignores the fact that Theodulf of Orléans accepted the antiquity of Micy's foundation. Berland is correct, however, in pointing out that Micy does not date back as far as the sixth century, as the Carolingian hagiographic traditions suggest. For a bibliographical summary, see BB, I, 353–6; Cottineau 1939–70, cols. 1845–6; *DACL*, XI, 912–27.

itself was sacked in 749.[24] In the early ninth century Bishop Theodulf of Orléans refounded a community in Micy's empty buildings, and his successor Jonas returned the relics of Maximinus.[25] Historians have generally assumed that the abbey of Meung-sur-Loire, allegedly founded by Lifardus in the sixth century, has authentically ancient roots, although, as with Micy, no pre-Carolingian documents survive from it.[26] The chapter of Saint-Euverte was most likely founded in the late eighth century.[27] A cathedral dedicated to the holy cross was probably first constructed in the seventh century and replaced by a cruciform structure in the late eighth. It is uncertain at what point it acquired relics of its 'father'. The earlier cathedral of St Stephen appears to have been included in its *claustrum*.[28]

Through this period the city of Orléans experienced changing fortunes as a centre of ecclesiastical and secular power. In the first half of the sixth century the Merovingian kings five times summoned their bishops to attend a council in Orléans, the two most important being in 541 and 549.[29] While the city declined in significance thereafter, it again became a place of central importance among the west Franks during the early Carolingian period. Theodulf (*c.* 798–818) and Jonas (818–43) – key advisers respectively to Charlemagne and Louis the Pious – occupied the see.[30] By that time the relics of each of the 'fathers' of Bishop Walter's list, as well as those of St Avitus, had been enshrined in the churches of religious communities dedicated to their memory, communities over which they would exercise a form of patronage. One of the most important functions of these communities was to preserve the

---

[24] Bertholdus of Micy, *Vita s. Maximini I*, c. 24, p. 597; Letaldus of Micy, *Miracula s. Maximini*, c. 2, p. 601.

[25] *MGH, Poetae aevi Carolini*, I, 520–2; Bertholdus of Micy, *Vita s. Maximini I*, c. 25, p. 597.

[26] *GC*, VIII, 1513–14. Also see Cottineau 1939–70, col. 1838.

[27] On the rejection of the Merovingian origins of Saint-Euverte, see Martinière 1939, p. 13; Gaillard and Debal 1987, pp. 26–7. Also see the discussion of the *Acta translationis s. Evurtii* below. For a bibliographical summary, see Cottineau 1939–70, col. 2139.

[28] Martinière 1939, pp. 23–32; Berland 1978b, pp. 32–43; Berland, in Debal 1983, pp. 237–40; Gaillard and Debal 1987, p. 22. The earliest indication of any church in Orléans bearing this dedication is a Merovingian coin which bears the notation 'SCA CRUS AURILIANIS' (Blanchet and Dieudonné 1912–36, I, 316). Cf. the attempt by Chenesseau (Chenesseau 1931b and 1938; Chenesseau and Martinière 1939) to defend the historicity of the Carolingian accounts of the foundation of Sainte-Croix during the fourth century. A bull of 1151 (*Cartulaire de Sainte-Croix*, no. 22, p. 47; Jaffé–Wattenbach, no. 9446) stated that a church dedicated to St Stephen was included in the cathedral group.

[29] Wallace-Hadrill 1983, pp. 94–100.

[30] *DTC*, VIII, 1504–8, and XV, 330–4; Debal, in Debal 1983, pp. 226–36.

relics and celebrate the memory of their own 'fathers'. These religious communities and their saintly 'fathers' were central to the religious life and identity of Orléans during the Carolingian period. The identity of those 'fathers' and their powers of *patrocinium* were evidently known to Louis the Pious well before the legislation of Bishop Walter. Ermoldus Nigellus described his visit to the city in 814, 'The triumphant emperor shortly [thereafter] visited the city of Orléans where the remains of the holy cross and of Anianus rest, and where the blessed Evurtius, who first built the cathedral, and holy Maximinus and holy Avitus shine.'[31] Louis returned to the city four years later to 'seek the aid' of two of these 'fathers' – the holy cross and St Anianus – in a campaign against the Bretons.[32]

By the time of Charles the Bald there were four chief relic shrines in the city of Orléans, each with its own community of monks or canons: the cathedral dedicated to the holy cross, Saint-Aignan, Saint-Avit, and Saint-Euverte.[33] In addition, there were three major shrines at abbeys in the surrounding countryside: that of St Benedict at Fleury, to the east of the city; that of St Maximinus at Micy, almost directly across the Loire; and that of St Lifardus at Meung-sur-Loire, situated at the junction of the Loire and the small river Mauve, about 29 kilometres west of Orléans. The shrines of the diocese thus formed an axis running along the Loire river which was centred on the city itself. These communities were not only important for their relics. Bishop Theodulf listed four chief schools in the diocese: Sainte-Croix, Saint-Aignan, Meung-sur-Loire, and Fleury.[34] It should be noted that not all the major abbeys of the diocese possessed important relics. The abbey of Ferrières, for example, which had been founded around 630 by Duke Vandelbert of Etampes, came to be renowned as a centre of learning in the ninth century, and several of its monks were prolific hagiographers, but it did not possess the body of a patron saint.[35]

---

[31] Ermoldus Nigellus, *Poème sur Louis le Pieux*, bk II, lines 790–3, p. 62. Ermold wrote the poem between 826 and 828; the story refers to the journey of Louis to Aix-la-Chapelle for the funeral of Charlemagne. Theodulf of Orléans composed a poem (*MGH, Poetae latini aevi Carolini*, I, 577–8) in honour of the occasion.

[32] Ermoldus Nigellus, *Poème sur Louis le Pieux*, bk III, lines 1532–9, p. 122.

[33] On the city's geography, see Debal, in Debal 1983, pp. 238–43.

[34] *MGH, Capitula episcoporum*, I, 115. These were the schools to which clerics were supposed to send their relatives.

[35] It should be noted that Ferrières is located well away from the communications route provided by the Loire river. The story of its foundation is contained in a bull of Pascal II, dated 11 November 1103 (*GC*, XII, *instrumenta*, pp. 15–16; Jaffé–Wattenbach, no. 5954).

To function in society these communities had this-worldly patrons in addition to saintly ones. Monastic communities, in a situation generally recognized and regretted by reformers, were caught between the competing interests of secular and ecclesiastical authority. Since monasteries constituted an important spiritual presence of Christianity while also owning significant amounts of property, the rights to oversee the election of their abbots and to control the distribution of their temporal possessions were highly prized. Adrevald of Fleury described a typical conflict over church property in the time of Louis the Pious:

> The church of Orléans with the nearby places of the saints, which were considered to be subject to the rule of clerics and monks of the Lord, was afflicted by not a little hardship . . . [Count Odo], who was puffed up above his nature by unwholesome insolence, subjected all the churches of Orléans, with the exception of the mother church [the cathedral], to his law and tried to confiscate the abbatial dignity of Saint-Aignan and even of [Fleury].[36]

He was thwarted in the case of Fleury by a combination of the shrewd leadership of Abbot Boso and the powerful patronage of St Benedict himself, who appeared to one of the monks and promised them his protection. The saints' shrines with their monastic communities had central importance among the properties of the diocese.

Monasteries were, in theory at least, subject in ecclesiastical matters to their bishops, but retained a certain amount of independence in terms of internal government. Likewise, they had a certain amount of economic autonomy, but general oversight – and taxation – of their temporal estates fell under either the direct

---

It confirmed an earlier story, told in the seventh century by Ouenus of Rouen, *Vita s. Eligii*, c. 10, col. 488. The *Exercitiunculae de gestis s. Saviniani*, written in the eleventh century in Sens, was responsible for a later tradition attributing its foundation to St Savinianus, see *VSBP*, XII, 807–11. On the foundation legend of Ferrières, see *DHGE*, XVI, 1278. For further bibliography see BB, VI, 27–9; Cottineau 1939–70, cols. 1130–2; *DHGE*, XVI, 1278–84. Although the abbey was within the medieval boundaries of the diocese of Orléans, it was for all practical purposes contained within the orbit of Sens. Three of its monks became bishops of that diocese: Aldric (828), Walter I (887), and Hildeman (954). The town of Ferrières is located in the modern diocese of Sens. On the hagiography of Abbot Alcuin, see Deug-Su 1983. On that of Ado, see *VSBP*, XII, 482–94; *DHGE*, I, 585. On that of Abbot Lupus, see the discussion below. In the eleventh century Aimo of Ferrières stole the relics of a minor saint, Montana, from a monastery in the Berry. A life of the saint was composed at Ferrières, but her cult never attained great prominence and she was never considered as a patron of the abbey.

36 *Miracula s. Benedicti*, I.20, pp. 47–50.

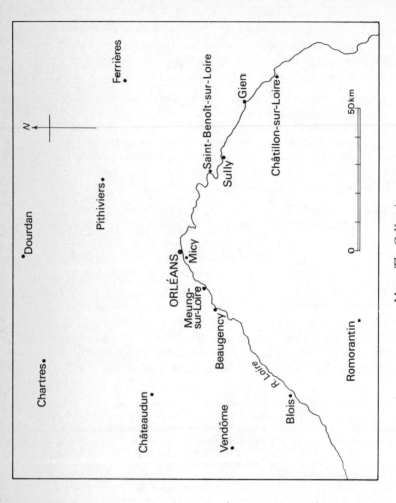

Map 1 The Orléanais

Source: based on Jacques Debal, *el al.*, eds., *Histoire d'Orléans et de son terroir.*
Tome I: Des origines à la fin du XVIe siècle (Roanne: Editions Horvath, 1983), p. 31.

control of the king or the royally deputized control of either the
bishop or a secular lord, such as a count. Such dependence on
outsiders continued, with minor changes, through the Cluniac and
Gregorian reform movements and beyond. To be sure, monastic
communities often exercised a greater degree of independent
control over their spiritual affairs, but the quality of a community's
life was often dependent on the personal power and spiritual gifts
of its abbot. The community which in truth elected its own abbot
was the exception rather than the rule and many communities
suffered under the control of lay abbots. The abbatial office was
often, as in the case of Micy, subject to simony and could even
become, as in the case of Saint-Aignan, the virtually hereditary
possession of a noble family. Even the reform of monastic
communities was usually undertaken at the behest of outside
authority.[37]

The scope and effects of such control can be seen clearly in the
acts of Charles the Bald. Early in his reign the king confirmed
Bishop Jonas' rights over the possessions granted to the bishopric
by Charlemagne and Louis the Pious in order to rescue it from
'miserable collapse, no even destitution'. Thus the bishop was
given rights not only over the cathedral – where 'the hand of God
had appeared' over Bishop Evurtius – and its chapter of canons, but
also over the house of Micy, Saint-Avit, Saint-Euverte, and
Meung-sur-Loire. In addition, the bishop controlled numerous
cellae which did not possess major relics, including one dedicated to
St Lawrence, which later writers would suggest had served as the
original home of St Anianus' body, and another which appears to
be a double monastery dedicated to St Peter. The monasteries
dedicated to the 'fathers' of the diocese, however, held pride of
place in the diploma.[38] Over the next years Charles sometimes
used these episcopal possessions as a residence.[39] They continued to
appear in royal and papal confirmations of the episcopal possessions

---

[37] Lesne's (1910–45, I) analysis of the Carolingian system of control of monastic property is
still the basic work on the subject. See also II.2, 132–43 and 212–16, on the injuries done to
monasteries by lay abbots. For a more summary treatment, see Lot and Fawtier 1962, pp.
26–42, and, on the mutations of this system in the early eleventh century, pp. 49–77.

[38] *Cartulaire de Sainte-Croix*, no. 33, pp. 63–6; new edition in *Recueil des actes de Charles le
Chauve*, no. 25, I, 62–5. Tessier dates the act to between June 840 and August 843.

[39] Muller 1987, pp. 15–18. On Charles' residences more generally, see Brühl 1968, pp. 39–
52. See also the perceptive comments by Nelson (1979, pp. 111–15) on Charles' use of the
wealth of urban and suburban monasteries.

throughout the middle ages.[40] Letaldus' account of the history of Micy in the ninth and tenth centuries demonstrates how complete and detrimental such episcopal control of a monastery could be.[41] The bishop could use his possessions for more spiritual ends, however, as when Jonas sent monks of Micy to reform the house of Curbion, located near Blois.[42] Nor were such houses completely bereft of royal support. Charles extended to Micy an important exemption from certain forms of royal taxation which had originally been granted by Louis the Pious and was similar in form to that given royal monasteries.[43]

In contrast to these monasteries Fleury held a royal grant of immunity and the right to elect its abbots from at least the time of Louis the Pious.[44] The king and the monks of Fleury took this authority seriously. In 855 the monks complained to Charles that 'the prelates of their monastery gave property to laymen in a manner quite out of proportion to what was fitting'. In response the king sent several agents to examine the situation and then issued a diploma which prohibited the abbots from alienating property and required them to look after the welfare of the monks.[45] Bishop Jonas had earlier served as a royal emissary to a *placitum* held to decide a dispute between Fleury and Saint-Denis. The description

---

[40] *Cartulaire de Sainte-Croix*, no. 376, p. 520 (Lothar, 954–72; new edition in *Recueil des actes de Lothaire et de Louis V*, no. 33, p. 81); no. 63, p. 126 (Hugh Capet, 975); no. 39, p. 79 (Hugh Capet, 990); no. 23, p. 51 (Eugenius III, 1151). (Meung-sur-Loire is omitted in no. 376 and in no. 40.) A similar list is included in an act of Robert the Pious for Bishop Arnulf (no. 40, p. 86) which has been judged to be a forgery by Newman (1937a, pp. 136–44). There were, to be sure, interruptions in this episcopal control. In 822 Louis the Pious gave the abbey of Meung-sur-Loire to Count Matfrid of Orléans, but it was returned to the hands of Bishop Jonas in 828 (Muller 1987, pp. 10–13). In 826 Bishop Jonas secured an imperial grant of the right of free abbatial elections for Micy (*Cartulaire de Sainte-Croix*, no. 33, pp. 76–8). In 1112 a charter of Louis VI (*Cartulaire de Saint-Avit*, no. 63, pp. 85–6) described the abbacy of Saint-Avit as 'in manu nostra', while in 1142 a charter of Louis VII (*Cartulaire de Saint-Avit*, no. 40, pp. 66–8) described its abbot as a royal chaplain.

[41] Letaldus of Micy, *Miracula s. Maximini* cc. 14–28, pp. 601–6.

[42] *Recueil des actes de Charles le Chauve*, no. 27, I, 67–71.

[43] *Recueil des actes de Charles le Chauve*, no. 1, I, 1–3; *Recueil des chartes de Saint-Benoît*, no. 15, I, 33–6.

[44] *Recueil des chartes de Saint-Benoît*, no. 15, I, 33–6. In this charter of 818, Louis the Pious confirmed earlier grants of immunity given by Pippin and Charlemagne. Bishop Theodulf was listed in a ninth-century abbatial list from Fleury, see Laporte 1979, pp. 119–24. It is quite possible that Theodulf held the abbacy of Fleury not as a result of his being bishop of Orléans, but as a direct grant from the emperor.

[45] *Recueil des chartes de Saint-Benoît*, no. 22, I, 51–4. New edition in *Recueil des actes de Charles le Chauve*, no. 177, I, 465–9. Tessier dismisses Prou and Vidier's suspicion of this charter. See also Nelson 1979, p. 108.

of the affair makes it clear that Jonas had no authority over Fleury, but was simply an agent of royal interest.[46] Control of Saint-Aignan appears to have rested with the counts of Orléans, from at least the time of Odo. It passed first to the bishops, who seem to have exercised comital powers, and then, in the late ninth century, to the powerful Robertian clan.[47]

As the monks and canons of these communities had a large degree of dependence on their secular patrons, so too the saintly 'fathers' themselves depended to a large degree on their religious servants. The existence of a community under a saint's patronage – a community which guarded the saint's relics and would later produce hagiographic works – was crucial to the survival of a saint's memory and cult. The Hieronymian martyrology (composed *c.* 628) contained the feasts of ten saints connected to the Orléanais. Five of them were saints whose relics were venerated in one of these various shrines: Anianus, Evurtius, Maximinus, Avitus, and Lifardus. In addition several eighth-century manuscripts contained the 11 July feast of the translation of Benedict's relics to Fleury (*translatio*) and the 4 December feast of his burial there (*illatio*). This Merovingian martyrology also, however, contained the feasts of five saints from the diocese whose relics were not venerated at a shrine: Monitor, Prosper, Pastor, Flosculus, and Sichairia.[48] (The feasts of the invention (3 May) and exaltation (14 September) of the cross were introduced in Frankish dioceses somewhat after this time.) By the ninth century the list of feasts of saints associated with the diocese had contracted sharply. The martyrology of Usuard (composed *c.* 858) included only the feasts

[46] *Miracula s. Benedicti*, I.25, pp. 56–7. The story dates to the reign of Louis the Pious. On *placita*, see Nelson 1986, pp. 49–50.

[47] *Miracula s. Benedicti*, I.20, pp. 47–50; Muller 1987, pp. 19 and 21. It is not surprising that, for the Carolingian period, we know far more about a rural monastery, such as Fleury, than about an urban monastery, such as Saint-Aignan. On this question, see McKitterick 1979.

[48] The Hieronymian martyrology is edited in *AASS*, Nov. II, part 2: Anianus (*transitus* 17 November and *translatio* 14 June), pp. 603–5 and 318; Evurtius (7 September) p. 493; Maximinus (15 December), p. 649; Avitus (17 June), p. 323; Lifardus (3 June), p. 301; Monitor (10 November), p. 593; Prosper (29 July), p. 402; Pastor (30 March), p. 167; Flosculus and Sichairia (2 February), pp. 74–5. On its composition, see Dubois 1978, pp. 29–37. According to Adrevald of Fleury the 11 July feast celebrated the arrival of the relics at Fleury and the 4 December feast their actual burial in the church of the Virgin: *Translatio s. Benedicti*, cc. 12 and 15, pp. 10 and 14. The former feast is also referred to as the *adventus* in some liturgical books and calendars, while the latter is sometimes called the *tumulatio* or (confusingly) the *translatio*. On the development of these feasts and their relationship to the Hieronymian martyrology see Chapman 1903; Quentin 1903; Hourlier and Deshusses 1979.

of Anianus, Evurtius, Maximinus, Avitus, Lifardus, Benedict (the *transitus* and the *translatio*), Flosculus, and Laetus.[49] This text provides the earliest evidence for the cult of St Laetus, which later developed in the town of Pithiviers in the early eleventh century.[50]

Those saints whose relics were not possessed by a community under their patronage fell into virtual oblivion.[51] The relics of Monitor and Flosculus, both described as bishops in the Hieronymian martyrology, were located at an unspecified location within the church of Saint-Aignan in the eleventh century.[52] There is no extant record of the relics of Prosper, although he was vaguely remembered as an early bishop of the diocese.[53] The very identity of Pastor remains a mystery, as the notation in the Hieronymian martyrology is the only record of that saint. The tradition which made Sichairia – a virgin and the only known female saint from the Orléanais prior to the thirteenth century – the foundress of the female convent of St Hilary dated, like the convent, to the fourteenth century.[54] None of these saints were included in the canon of Bishop Walter.

As these saints were being forgotten over the course of the eighth and ninth centuries, the second step in the formation of the identity of the 'fathers' of Bishop Walter's list was occurring through the composition of hagiographic works. No less than eleven such works on the lives of Anianus, Evurtius, Maximinus, Lifardus – as well as of Avitus – were composed in this period; most, if not all, of them had been written prior to the promulgation of Walter's *capitula*. The lives of Evurtius also recorded how relics of the holy cross came to be enshrined in the city's cathedral. In addition, Adrevald of Fleury composed a trilogy of works about the cult of Benedict of Nursia and the translation of his relics to Fleury. When Bishop Walter promulgated his diocesan capitulary in 871 there were recently composed texts available to provide the necessary liturgical readings for each local feast whose observance he

---

49 *Le Martyrologe d'Usuard*, pp. 173, 198 (the entry on the feast of Benedict's *transitus* mentions only Monte Cassino), 265 (the entry for the feast of Benedict's *translatio* makes no mention of Fleury), 240, 248, 298, 336, 343, and 360. For a comparison to the entries in the martyrologies of Jerome, Wandelbert, and Adon, see pp. 82–3.

50 See *Le Martyrologe d'Usuard*, p. 73.

51 Other than the notice given of the feast of Flosculus in a thirteenth-century breviary (Paris, BN lat. 1020, fo. 212v) there is no mention of any of these saints in the liturgical books of the Orléanais from the period after 750.

52 Helgaud of Fleury, *Epitoma vitae regis Rotberti pii*, c. 22, p. 110. On Monitor, see *VSBP*, XI, 306. On Flosculus, see *VSBP*, II, 32.   53 *VSBP*, VII, 696.

54 C. de la Saussaye 1615, p. 107; Rocher 1867; Jarossay 1902, pp. 39–40.

required. Bishop Walter's decree was the culmination rather than the inception of the process of the canonization – to use the word in a non-technical sense – of these saints as the 'fathers' of the Orléanais. That process had taken place through the foundation and development of religious communities dedicated to these saints and the composition of hagiographic works about those saints, presumably by members of those same communities. The omission of Avitus from Walter's canon is puzzling, for – as was the case for the other members of that list – a community was dedicated to him and hagiographic works were composed about him during this period. Moreover, calendars from Fleury and Micy show that Avitus' feast was celebrated there in the eleventh and twelfth centuries.[55] In the discussion that follows Avitus will be treated as a *de facto* 'father' of the diocese in the Carolingian period. Walter also did not take notice of the developing cult of St Laetus, who can similarly be numbered among the 'fathers' of the diocese for the Capetian period.

The Carolingian hagiographers were primarily interested in providing foundation narratives, that is texts which described the circumstances surrounding the birth of their communities and the acquisition of their patrons' relics. Such hagiographic works connected the past to the present both by guaranteeing the sanctity of the patron whose relics a community possessed and by safeguarding certain rights and properties of that community by describing the circumstances of its foundation. Given the general lack of extant local literary texts dating from the late antique and Merovingian periods, however, these writers were faced with problems as to how to look into that past. While it seems clear that the scriptoria of such institutions as Micy and Sainte-Croix produced charters in the ninth century, those institutions possessed few if any surviving legal records. Micy, for instance, had been refounded after a long period of abandonment. When its scriptorium produced a foundation charter for the abbey in the eleventh century, it was forged on the basis of Carolingian hagiographic texts. Bertholdus and his later adapter had no access to authentic sixth-century records.[56] Fleury, on the other hand,

---

[55] Paris, BN lat. 7299, fo. 6; Orléans, BM 322, p. 4; Orléans, BM 123, fo. cv; Trier, Seminarbibliothek 187, fo. 6; Orléans, BM 129, fo. 240v; Paris, BN lat. 7521, fo. 19; Paris, Bibliothèque d'Arsenal 371, fo. 92v (which curiously lists the feast on 19 December rather than 17 June); Vatican, Reg. lat. 1263, fo. 69v.

[56] 'Chartes de Micy', pp. lxxxiv–lxxxix.

33

possessed an archive as early as the ninth century.[57] The composition of foundation narratives within hagiography was in part an attempt to organize traditions about a community's past at a time when other forms of written testimony were unreliable.

With the notable exception of Adrevald of Fleury, the Carolingian authors of the diocese rarely discussed the sources for the stories recounted in their lives. The parallel *Vitae s. Aviti* reveal that even these references were formulaic rather than accurate citations. The author of the *Vita s. Aviti I (BHL* 789) claimed that the story of the saint's miraculous birth had been verified and that Leobinus, bishop of Chartres, had provided the story of Avitus' resurrection of his former disciple.[58] The author of the *Vita s. Aviti II (BHL* 881) said more conservatively that 'we hear of' the miraculous birth and named the disciple himself as the source of the resurrection miracle.[59] The author of the *Vita s. Aviti III (BHL* 880) dropped all reference to sources.[60] With only one exception these authors failed to mention sources which they quoted at times verbatim. Several of these Carolingian authors simply redrafted extant texts. Of them Lucifer alone admitted that he was adapting a work already in circulation. He claimed to have rewritten the *Vita s. Evurtii I* in order to put it into a more acceptable style.[61]

Although texts which are no longer extant may have provided some of the stories, it is far more likely that the author of the *Vita s. Aniani III* provided a clue to the origins of most of these Carolingian hagiographic traditions when he remarked, 'We ought not in time keep silent about what we have heard from truthful elders concerning our patron St Anianus and about his life and virtues'.[62] Oral traditions concerning the early saints of the diocese flourished. The confusion of the *Vitae s. Aviti* might have covered just such story-telling. Authors were defensive about such

---

[57] Adrevald of Fleury, *Historia translationis s. Benedicti*, c. 2, p. 3.
[58] 'Natum illum fore beatum nocturno tempore cum magno splendore veridica relatione compertum est.' *Vita s. Aviti I*, c. 1, p. 57. 'Quem rem a sancto beatoque Leobino, Carnotinae civitatis episcopo, divulgatam fuisse comperimus.' *Vita s. Aviti I*, c. 9, p. 61.
[59] Vatican, Reg. lat. 585, fos. 28 and 31v–2; Paris, BN lat. 12606, fos. 54 and 55.
[60] Paris, BN lat. 3789, fos. 105v–6 and 111v–12v.
[61] 'Idcirco justo libramine mercedis unius retributionem diu multumque pensantes ut et nos participes simus eorum, qui praedictorum auctores sunt, maluimus sancti ac beatissimi Evurtii episcopi, qualiter in rebus humanis conversatus est, honorabili stylo vitam pandere, et ad notitiam ignorantium pro imitatione edicere.' Lucifer of Orléans *Vita s. Evurtii II*, prologue, p. 52. In a similar situation the author of the *Vita s. Maximini II* did not mention the earlier work of Bertholdus which he followed very closely: Poncelet 1905, pp. 44–53.   [62] *Vita s. Aniani III*, c. 1, p. 34.

techniques. Lucifer added a colophon to his *Vita s. Evurtii II* in which he ingenuously claimed, 'I Lucifer, a subdeacon, have described in truth these *gesta* of the habits and deeds of holy and most blessed Evurtius the bishop, adding nothing nor speaking superfluously.'[63] Lucifer's claim was in one very obvious, if limited, sense true. In composing his work he had simply adapted a text composed earlier in the century, making only minimal changes.

Lucifer's work was part of a chain or cycle of texts concerning Bishops Anianus and Evurtius which were composed over the course of the ninth century: the *Vita s. Evurtii I* (*BHL* 2800), the *Vita s. Evurtii II* (*BHL* 2799), the *Vita s. Aniani II* (*BHL* 474), and the *Vita s. Aniani III* (*BHL* 476).[64] These texts concerned not only the lives of the bishops, but the alleged foundations of Saint-Aignan, Saint-Euverte, and the cathedral of Sainte-Croix. They provide an excellent case study in the use and development of sources by Carolingian hagiographers. The *Vita s. Aniani I*, the oldest available hagiographic source for the diocese, contained the stories of how Anianus had been miraculously chosen bishop of Orléans, had rebuilt the ruined cathedral originally constructed by his predecessor Evurtius, and had later miraculously saved the city from the invading Huns. The author of that text clearly stated that several men had served as bishop between Evurtius and Anianus.[65]

Despite this assertion, the first Carolingian author in our cycle claimed that Evurtius had consecrated Anianus and had acted as his mentor. In order to provide the relics of his patron with a history, the author associated him directly with the well-known story of Bishop Anianus, in direct contradiction of the extant life of that saint.[66] According to this author Evurtius had passed through

[63] Lucifer of Orléans, *Vita s. Evurtii II*, c. 20, p. 58.
[64] The texts were composed in the order stated, but can be assigned only approximate dates. The *Vita s. Evurtii I* was certainly linked to the growth of Saint-Euverte and the public veneration of the saint's relics there; it may well predate the visit of Louis the Pious to Orléans. The *Vita s. Evurtii II* was composed before 850, the date of the martyrology of Hrabanus Maurus who used it as a source. The two works on St Anianus were probably composed before the end of the century. For fuller consideration, see Renaud 1978a, pp. 87–90.   [65] *Vita s. Aniani I*, c. 2, p. 108.
[66] This tradition was also marred by internal inconsistency. Evurtius allegedly lived during the reign of Constantine (306–37), but Anianus saved the city from destruction by the Huns in 451. Despite these contradictions the succession became generally accepted in the middle ages and was incorporated into an eleventh-century episcopal list; see Duchesne 1894–1915, II, 459–60. Most historians prior to the twentieth century likewise accepted the tradition as genuine. See, for example, C. de la Saussaye 1615, pp. 51–73; Guyon 1647–50, I, 60; Bimbenet 1861, pp. 7–26; Cuissard 1886, pp. 110–24.

Orléans at the time of a contested episcopal election and been chosen for the office by means of a miracle. Later Evurtius saved the city from a large fire through the spiritual force of his prayers and then constructed a new cathedral. During the construction a great treasure was found in the excavations. Rather than keeping the treasure, the bishop sent it to Constantine, who, in amazed gratitude, not only returned the money for the construction of the cathedral, but also sent relics of several martyrs and of the holy cross to be enshrined there. He required that the church be constructed in the shape of the cross, and that the relics of the cross be housed in the main altar in the transept crossing. This work also provided a foundation narrative for the cathedral of Sainte-Croix and its relics.[67] On his death Evurtius was buried by a nobleman on the eastern side of the city (the location of the monastery of Saint-Euverte) 'among the saints and elect bishops'.

A generation or two later the subdeacon Lucifer rewrote this work with the express intent of putting it into 'an honourable style'.[68] He added some details and provided a more elaborate description of the efficacy of the bishop's relics in curing the sick, but did not alter the basic lines of his source. Lucifer did specify that the relics of the holy cross had been brought directly from Jerusalem and that the cathedral had been dedicated on 3 May, the feast of the invention of the Cross.[69] These two narratives successfully clothed both the cathedral of Sainte-Croix and the church of Saint-Euverte with an aura of antiquity: by the late ninth

[67] *Vita s. Evurtii I*, c. 10, p. 316, c. 14, p. 319.

[68] Lucifer of Orléans, *Vita s. Evurtii II*, prologue, p. 52. Lucifer's work received far wider circulation than did its source. Renaud (1978a, p. 88 and nn. 36 and 42) found six medieval manuscripts of the *BHL* 2800 and forty-three of the *BHL* 2799. A number of later authors apparently used Lucifer's work as their source for the tradition of Bishop Evurtius: Adrevald of Fleury, *Miracula s. Benedicti*, I.33, p. 72; Helgaud of Fleury, *Epitoma vitae regis Rotberti pii*, c. 15, p. 84; Rodulfus Glaber, *Historiarum libri quinque*, II.5.9 pp. 66–9; *Le Guide du pèlerin de Saint-Jacques de Compostelle*, c. 8, p. 59. Ademar of Chabannes copied the story of the miraculous election of Evurtius as part of a collection of sources for the Council of Limoges in 1031; Dubois and Renaud 1981, pp. 497–501 (see Paris, BN lat. 2400, fo. 153).

[69] Lucifer of Orléans, *Vita s. Evurtii II*, cc. 12–13, p. 56. An alternative story of the origin of the relics, which described their donation to the cathedral of Orléans by Charlemagne, developed in the twelfth century as part of a dispute between the abbeys of Compiègne and Saint-Denis. The earliest extant version of this story occurred in the *Karlamagnussaga*, a Norwegian saga of the thirteenth century which was based on a lost old French original, itself composed at the abbey of Compiègne some time after 1099. On these texts, see Frolow 1961, pp. 198–202. This tradition was never repeated in the Orléanais, although Hugh of Fleury (*Vita s. Sacerdotis*, c. 21, col. 992) was apparently familiar with the text in question.

century Evurtius was generally accepted as the founder of the cathedral and the immediate predecessor of Anianus.

In the light of these newly composed traditions, one author wrote a new version of the life of St Anianus by adding this new material to the traditions known from the Merovingian life of that saint. His most important innovation was a description of the saint's burial in a church dedicated to St Lawrence on the western side of Orléans and subsequent translation to a church on the eastern side of the city, a foundation which was clearly that of Saint-Aignan.[70] Still later another author wrote the *Vita s. Aniani III* (also known as the *Sermo de adventu s. Aniani*) in order to describe the early life of Anianus with a plausible story, which was little more than a fanciful expansion on earlier traditions. In the complete absence of written sources for these events the author referred instead to the authority of oral tradition.[71] While it seems reasonable to assign the authorship of the two texts about St Anianus to canons of Saint-Aignan, the *Vitae s. Evurtii* may have been composed by canons of either Saint-Euverte or the cathedral chapter.

The hagiographic traditions of the abbeys of Saint-Avit and Micy developed in a similar manner. In the period around the year 800 three lives of St Avitus were composed: *Vita s. Aviti I*, *Vita s. Aviti II*, *Vita s. Aviti III*.[72] The authors described how the sixth-century hermit Avitus became a monk of Micy and studied the monastic life under its first abbot Maximinus. Later Avitus went off into the forest with an anonymous companion, earned a widespread reputation as a holy man, and founded his own monastery near Châteaudun. The authors described how some of his relics had been returned to a church in Orléans, a church whose existence Gregory of Tours had attested in the sixth century. This cycle of texts was most probably developed as a foundation narrative for the monastery of Saint-Avit and its shrine, although it is possible that at least one of the versions was composed by monks from Châteaudun. Shortly thereafter the abbey of Micy was refounded by Bishop Theodulf and the body of its patron returned. Then Bertholdus, a monk of the abbey, wrote his life of Maximinus (*Vita s. Maximini I (BHL 5817)*) based in part on *BHL*

---

[70] *Vita s. Aniani II*, c. 9, p. 33. A church dedicated to St Lawrence appears among the possessions of the bishop in the diploma of Charles the Bald (*Cartulaire de Sainte-Croix*, no. 33, p. 64; *Recueil des actes de Charles le Chauve*, no. 25, I, 64).

[71] *Vita s. Aniani III*, c. 1, p. 34.   [72] Poncelet 1905, pp. 14–25.

880. Bertholdus was careful, however, to alter the story of the
foundation of Micy contained in that work, which ascribed it to
the bishop of Orléans, to one in which Clovis provided the abbey's
lands. Several decades later an anonymous author rewrote
Bertholdus' work (*BHL* 5814–16). [73]

In such cycles of texts each succeeding author canvassed the
available hagiographic sources to produce his narrative. Each
author associated some new material and omitted other older
material, altering the body of tradition. Each author also employed
topoi to flesh out the portrait of his hero. [74] There are even hints that
the author of the *Vita s. Lifardi* (*BHL* 4931) also blended together
traditions from other monastic houses. [75] This association of
traditions about different saints should not be surprising. This was
an era, after all, in which such learned men as Abbots Hilduin and
Hincmar sincerely believed that Bishop Dionysius the evangelist of
Paris, Dionysius the author of the *Celestial Hierarchies*, and
Dionysius the disciple of St Paul were one and the same person.
The sources of any original material, whether it be Maximinus'
miracles at Micy or the miraculous ordination of Evurtius, are open
to speculation. Most probably they represent the oral traditions of
the 'truthful elders'.

These oral traditions were generally, however, ahistorical. Such
invention of new, and even contradictory, traditions and the liberal
reuse of stories from the life of one saint in a work about another
raise the question of plagiarism or forgery. Some historians, such as
Hubert Silvestre, have condemned much of medieval hagiography
as having been forged by clerics for the purposes of misleading an
audience of lay pilgrims. [76] Giles Constable has provided a strong
argument against this historiographical tradition, pointing out that
medieval society held different notions of truth and of personal
specificity of texts from the modern, western standard: 'People in
the Middle Ages also saw what they wanted and needed to see, and
believed to be true what had to be true.' He has described much of
hagiography as an attempt at myth-making, that is of describing
what must have occurred beyond the bounds of collective
memory. As such most medieval hagiography was not properly a

[73] Poncelet 1905, pp. 44–53.
[74] See Poulin (1975, pp. 23–4) on the use of *topoi* in Aquitainian sources of the same period.
[75] On the date of this text, see Poncelet 1905, pp. 90–1. The text certainly antedates some
versions of the martyrology of Florus of Lyon. The author was probably a member of
the community of Meung-sur-Loire.   [76] Silvestre 1960.

forgery or plagiarism, but an accurate rendering of received tradition.[77]

The relics of Benedict of Nursia, unlike those of Anianus and other local saints, had been posthumously translated to the Orléanais from a distant region. Thus Adrevald of Fleury of necessity differed from his contemporaries and concentrated on the relationship between his community and its patron, rather than on the life of the saint which was well known from the work of Gregory the Great. In the *Historia translationis s. Benedicti* (*BHL* 1117), Adrevald described the coming of Benedict's relics to Fleury – a place which he depicted as the saint's consciously chosen home – in terms of a second foundation of the abbey.[78] As Geary had pointed out, Adrevald also imitated Einhard's description of the translation of the relics of Marcellinus and Peter from Rome.[79] According to Adrevald a monk of Fleury named Aigulphus had learned in a dream about the ruined state of the tombs of Benedict and his sister Scholastica. With the blessing of Abbot Mummolus, Aigulphus joined some monks from Le Mans passing by Fleury on their way to Italy to acquire the relics of Scholastica. When the party reached Monte Cassino they found, through miraculous aid, the tomb of the saints as described by Gregory the Great.[80] They smuggled the bodies, again with the aid of miracles, out of Italy, returning them to Fleury. A new monastery was founded in Le Mans to receive the relics of Scholastica.[81] Abbot Mummolus tried to bury the body of Benedict in the larger church of St Peter at Fleury, but a miraculous shaft of light from the church of the Virgin Mary advised the monks to place the relics there instead.

Adrevald's collection of posthumous miracle stories (*BHL* 1123) – the only such collection composed in the Orléanais during the Carolingian period – was the story of this community, the servants of the saint.[82] It began with the life of the saint (adapted directly and with attribution from the *Dialogues* of Gregory the Great) and

---

[77] Constable 1983. The quotation is on p. 24. See, also, the bibliography on forgery cited on pp. 6–9.

[78] The work predates Adrevald's section of the *Miracula s. Benedicti*, but, like that work, may well have been written after the sack of Fleury in 865.

[79] Geary 1978, pp. 145–9.   [80] Gregory the Great, *Dialogues*, II.34, II, 234.

[81] Goffart (1967) has shown that the traditions concerning the acquisition of Scholastica's relics by monks from Le Mans were developed in that city during the early ninth century and were not part of the original traditions concerning the translation.

[82] *BHL* 1123 was composed after 865 and probably before the death of Charles the Bald (877).

the story of the translation of Benedict's relics (quoted directly and again with attribution from Paul the Deacon's *History of the Lombards*). Adrevald also connected these past events to the near-contemporary story of how Benedict had acted as the patron of the monastery through continuing miraculous action. In the *Vita s. Aigulphi* (*BHL* 194) he took up the life story of the monk responsible for the translation. Aigulphus went on to become the reformer of the abbey of Lérins and was murdered by rebellious monks there *c.* 675.[83] Adrevald's trilogy demonstrated how, in the mind of at least one member of the community of Fleury, the histories of that community and of the cult of its patron were inextricably bound together.[84]

Adrevald wrote largely about events no more than two centuries old, but, unlike his contemporaries who treated the late antique and Merovingian past, he considered the implications of the distance which separated him from his subjects. He felt it necessary to defend, for instance, the importance of the relatively recent deeds of Aigulphus, 'For these things are unlike wine, which the older it is, the more pleasing it generally becomes.'[85] In the

---

[83] Modern scholars have questioned this identification of Aigulphus of Fleury with the abbot of Lérins. The only other extant *Vita s. Aigulphi* (*BHL* 193) identifies the abbot as a monk of Fleury, although it makes no mention of the translation of Benedict's relics. The Bollandists have suggested (*AASS*, Sept. 1, p. 729) that Adrevald used *BHL* 193 as a source which is plausible. The only manuscripts of that work, however, are early modern copies and it is impossible to date the text with precision. Since no earlier account of the translation of Benedict's relics identifies by name the monk responsible, it is possible that Adrevald simply chose to identify a holy man whose identity was known from Fleury's early history as the monk responsible for the acquistion of Benedict's relics.

[84] While the same author composed all three works, he did not name himself. The *Historia translationis s. Benedicti* ended with a reference to a forthcoming book of miracles (c. 15, p. 14). In the *Miracula s. Benedicti* the author referred back to the account of the translation when discussing the translation of the relics (1.11, p. 32). In the eleventh century both Aimo (*Miracula s. Benedicti*, ii.prologue and ii.1, pp. 92 and 95) and Andrew (*Miracula s. Benedicti*, iv.prologue, p. 173) referred to Adrevald as the author of these earlier works. Later, however, Rodulfus Tortarius (*Rodulfi Tortarii Carmina*, p. 419) ascribed both works to a monk named Adalbert. This apparent contradiction may be explained by the *explicit* to the miracle collection found in an eleventh-century manuscript (Dijon, BM 1118, fo. 39) which reads, 'Huc usque uenerabilis Adreualdus, qui et Adalbertus estimatur nominatus, historiam miraculorum sancti patris Benedicti texuit: duas uero que secuntur sententias domnus Adelerius adiecit.' Sigebert of Gembloux (*De scriptoribus ecclesiasticis*, c. 100, col. 570) also identified the author of the *Historia translationis s. Benedicti* by both names. As Vidier (1965, pp. 153–7) points out, Rodulfus Tortarius may simply have been choosing the metrically more suitable of two names which he knew for the same person.

[85] Adrevald of Fleury, *Vita s. Aigulphi*, c. 2, p. 657.

Carolingian period it was generally assumed that a saint was by definition a holy man from the distant past. To get in touch with the past Adrevald used both the archives of his monastery and such well-known works on these subjects as those by Gregory the Great and Paul the Deacon.[86] He also used less well-known texts, like the *Relatio s. Scholasticae*, virtually verbatim, but without acknowledgement.[87] Adrevald cited a document – the foundation charter of Fleury known as the 'Testament of Leodebodus' – which could be 'found today in the public archives of our monastery'. [88] In addition to the monastic archives, he had access to a fine and growing library which included such rare items as a fifth-century copy of Sallust, a sixth-century copy of Origen's homilies, and a ninth-century copy of Julius Caesar's *Gallic Wars*.[89] Such record-keeping and library resources distinguished Fleury from its smaller neighbours.

Adrevald was less clear about the sources for the contemporary miracle stories in his collection. He noted that the first miracle story which he related (from the reign of Louis the Pious) could be corroborated by a participant.[90] This episode marked a division in his text between those events of the past which were known only through texts and those events which had occurred in the living memory of the community of Fleury. Adrevald later concluded a group of four curing miracles within his collection:

In that time the Lord saw fit to work, through his servant who had been freed of his burden of flesh, these and many other marvellous things which have been neglected by the laziness of those whose efforts ought to have trumpeted them forth to the public. We, by contrast, try to transmit to the notice of posterity those things which we came to know by our own sight or which we discovered by faithful narration.[91]

Most of the miracle stories recounted by Adrevald had monastic participants or observers. Some stories, however, from *Vetus Floriacus* made their way into the monastic enclosure and to the eager ears of Adrevald.[92]

Men like Lucifer, Bertholdus, and even Adrevald were primar-

---

[86] Adrevald of Fleury, *Historia translationis s. Benedicti*, c. 2, p. 3; *Miracula s. Benedicti*, I.I, p. 17; I.4, p. 21; I.11, p. 32; I.15, pp. 38–9; Hourlier 1979a and 1979c.
[87] Goffart 1967.   [88] Adrevald of Fleury, *Historia translationis s. Benedicti*, c. 2, p. 3.
[89] Lowe 1934–66, VI, xviii–xxi; *DHGE*, XVII, 473–4.
[90] *Miracula s. Benedicti*, I.20, p. 48.   [91] *Miracula s. Benedicti*, I.32, p. 70.
[92] *Miracula s. Benedicti*, I.35, pp. 77–8.

ily involved and interested in the heritage of their own locale. Unfortunately no indication of their origins survive. During the early ninth century there were two authors active in the Orléanais who were also prominent figures in wider court and literary circles: Bishop Jonas and Abbot Servatus Lupus of Ferrières. Both composed works of hagiography at various points in their careers, although none which touched on the saints of the diocese of Orléans.[93] Nevertheless these works by 'court' writers are interesting for our survey because they offer a striking contrast both in terms of literary and pietistic interests to the Carolingian hagiography 'local' to the Orléanais.

In the *Vita et translatio s. Huberti* (*BHL* 3994–5) Jonas told the story of a bishop of Tongres-Liège who had died in 727. In 825 Walcaudus, the contemporary bishop of that diocese, requested Jonas' work on the occasion of the translation of some of the saint's relics to the nearby monastery of Andaine. Jonas rewrote an earlier life of the saint (*BHL* 3993) to which he added an account of the translation based on the reports of eyewitnesses. He accepted the factual accuracy of the earlier account and sought simply to correct that source 'according to the rules of speaking' and thus to add a 'literary surface' to the text. In an aside to Walcaudus he recalled their studies together of the 'science of letters' at the palatine school.[94] A comparison of Jonas' work with his source reveals that in terms of substance he indeed added nothing and subtracted little. His text, however, was significantly longer. The ideas of the earlier writer were – to use Jonas' own term – 'decorated'. New classical and scriptural allusions dotted Jonas' work and such references in the source were elaborated. Jonas likened the hagiographer's task to passing between the Scylla of falsifying the past through un-warranted loquacity and the Charybdis of hiding past virtues by keeping silent. A formulaic excuse of the eighth-century author's rusticity was extended through the use of a metaphor based on the arts of the *trivium*. The citation of two standard scriptural passages for hagiography became a full statement of how God spoke

---

93 On Jonas, see *DTC*, VIII, 1504–8; Manitius 1911–31, I, 374–80; Reviron 1930; Delaruelle 1951. On Lupus, see *DTC*, IX, 963–7; Manitius 1911–31, I, 483–90; *HLF*, V, 255–72; Gariépy 1968; Wallace-Hadrill 1983, pp. 304–14. In addition, Alcuin held the abbacy of Ferrières as a benefice at one time, but was never resident or active in the Orléanais. On his hagiographic method, see Deug-Su 1983, as well as Bullough 1983 on related issues.
94 Jonas of Orléans, *Vita et translatio s. Huberti*, dedicatory letter, p. 806.

through the deeds of the saints.[95] Such changes in the preface set a
tone followed through the remainder of the work.[96]

The explicitly classical references betrayed the fact that Jonas had
learned his 'science of letters' in a different milieu from the local
monastic schools of both his eighth-century predecessor and most
contemporary writers of his own diocese. The elaborations and
changes which Jonas introduced into his source on the grounds of
stylistic improvement were both more numerous and more
accomplished than, for example, those made by Lucifer in the *Vita
s. Evurtii II.* Where Lucifer simply tinkered with his source, Jonas
transformed his. Some other differences between Jonas and his
contemporaries in the Orléanais were due to self-interest as well as
education. Jonas' laudatory description, found in the translation
account, of the benign interest taken in the monastery of Andaine
by Bishop Walcaudus clashed strongly with the growing attempts
of the hagiographers of the abbey of Micy to dissociate their
bishop, that is Jonas himself, from the relic cult of their patron
Maximinus.

Servatus Lupus was born in the Orléanais and first educated at
Ferrières, but left for further study at the abbey of Fulda. He
returned regularly to the abbey, and in 841 became abbot, serving
until his death in 862. While studying under Rabanus Maurus at
Fulda, he composed works on Maximinus of Trier (*Vita s.
Maximini Treverensis* (BHL 5824)) and Wigbert of Hessia (the *Vita
s. Wigberti* (BHL 8879)) at the request of the Austrasian communities which possessed their relics. Like the popular saints of the
Orléanais, Maximinus was an early Merovingian figure. Wigbert,
however, was an abbot of the previous century. Lupus appended a
number of contemporary miracle stories to both lives, making

[95] Jonas of Orléans, *Vita et translatio s. Huberti*, preface, p. 807. In this last case Jonas'
elaboration reads: 'Nam Deus, fons et origo operum justorum, linguas etiam infantium
disertas facit, et ad audendum quodammodo nostram excitans infirmitatem, manu verbi
sui torpentem communefacit dicens: "Aperi os tuum, et ego implebo illud." Redundat
enim in laudem Domini, quicquid generositatis atque nobilitatis pariet in factis
devotissimi servi: maxime cum et Dominus in mirabilibus factis famulorum se
tributorem ac liberalissimum commendaverit datorem, dicendo: "Sine me nihil potestis
facere."' The eighth-century text read more simply: 'Adgrediar tamen facultate qua
valeo, quia ad illum spem erigo qui dixit: "Aperi os tuum, et ego implebo illud." Et
revera illius satis digno praeconio praedicatur quicquid in sanctis ejus mirabile evenitur,
Salvatore testante, qui ait: "Sine me nihil potestis facere."' *Vita s. Huberti I*, preface, p.
798. The differences between the two texts are exemplary of the sort of changes
introduced by Jonas.   [96] See Genicot 1965 for somewhat fuller analysis.

these works chronicles of the cults as well. He acknowledged at length the texts which he used as sources, and for him the word *monimentum* referred not only to the text which he wrote, as it did for Bertholdus of Micy, but also to these sources.[97] He apologized for the mere ninety years which separated him from his subject Wigbert and for the scarcity of source material about Maximi-nus.[98] Both works were brief and contained only such sketchy details of the lives of these saints as Lupus considered verifiable. Since he saw himself as the author of *historia*, he disavowed the use of 'poetic licence' and even bragged that he had not tampered with ugly-sounding Germanic names.[99] He used oral sources for the more recent stories about the translations and miracles of these saints and the availability of such oral sources may explain why his works are weighted so heavily toward them. He used texts as formal models, as well as historical sources. According to Lupus those models included the works of Sallust and Livy, in addition to those of Ambrose and Jerome.[100] The imitation of such models was more important than the collection and collation of historical traditions which were difficult to verify.

In these hagiographic works both Lupus and Jonas were, in their own ways, enterprising textual editors. It is not surprising that Lupus introduced more substantive, as opposed to stylistic, change into his source material than did Jonas, for Lupus was one of the best editors of classical texts of his generation.[101] Both writers,

[97] 'Tam speciosa suae praesentiae meritique monimenta praeclarus ille angelus dereliquit.' Lupus of Ferrières, *Vita s. Maximini Treverensis*, c. 24, p. 82. Also see Lupus' preface (p. 74): 'vix parva gestorum illius monimenta exstant'. Cf. Bertholdus of Micy, *Vita s. Maximini I*, c. 1, p. 592.

[98] Lupus of Ferrières, *Vita s. Wigberti*, preface, p. 673. 'Verum in hoc opere illud me admodum coartat, quod, multis quae, dum adviveret, egit, ut palam est, silentio suppressis, vix parva gestorum illius monimenta exstant, et in his ipsis quaedam fabulosis inveniuntur similia.' Lupus of Ferrières, *Vita s. Maximini Treverensis*, preface, p. 74. 'Iam vero ... summi auctoris Hieronymi testimonio, qui aut contemporalis ei, tametsi puer, fuit aut proxime illius aetatem accessit, licet cognoscere.' *Vita s. Maximini Treverensis*, c. 3, p. 75. 'Ex his quae praemisimus beati Hieronymi verbis, etsi pauca sunt, tamen satis Maximini sanctitas poterit aestimari.' *Vita s. Maximini Treverensis*, c. 4, p. 76.

[99] Lupus of Ferrières, *Vita s. Wigberti*, preface, p. 673.

[100] 'Cum profecto si vel leviter est eruditus, non ignoret Salustium Crispum, Titumque Livium non pauca quae illorum aetatem longe praecesserant, partim auditu, partim lectione comperta narrasse, et ut ad nostros veniam, Hieronymum Pauli sui vitam, quae certe remotissima fuerat, litteris illustrasse, et antistitem Ambrosium virginis Agnes passionem, cui profecto contemporalis non fuerat, editam reliquisse.' Lupus of Ferrières, *Vita s. Wigberti*, preface, p. 673. Cf. Bertholdus of Micy, *Vita s. Maximini I*, c. 1, p. 592.

[101] Beeson (1930) has described Lupus' method in editing the *De oratore* of Cicero.

however, were willing to tamper with received tradition in accordance with explicitly stated principles of textual criticism. They did not simply gather together all available traditions with a primary concern for their social and legal utility, as in essence did the local writers of the Orléanais. A wide gulf separated the intellectual world of Lupus, for instance, from that of his contemporary and near-neighbour Adrevald of Fleury. The world of exemplary literary texts, both Christian and non-Christian, formed the past to which Lupus and Jonas related most easily. As moving forces in Carolingian intellectual circles they were at least as interested in recovering that classical past as they were in recovering the miraculous and legal circumstances surrounding the birth and early growth of any given religious community. Their hagiographic texts were identifiably the works of an individual authorial sensibility, not outgrowths of communal tradition. This difference between 'court' and 'local' hagiography is one which might be fruitfully studied elsewhere in the Carolingian world. Adrevald, at least implicitly, recognized this gulf. In describing the *placitum* held to resolve a legal dispute between Fleury and Saint-Denis, he noted Lupus' presence on the side of Fleury's opponents as 'a doctor of laws from the Gâtinais who was called by a bestial rather than a human name'. The monk of Fleury noted with satisfaction how Benedict struck this adversary dumb, for at least a while.[102]

Such 'court writers' also prominently promoted the ideals of Carolingian royal ideology and the associated 'renaissance' which valued the centralization of political, cultural, and religious discourse. Bishop Jonas, for instance, edited the acts of the Council of Paris in 829 which debated the nature of secular power. Reflecting on that discussion Jonas later produced two linked treatises – the *De institutione regia* and the *De institutione laicali* – which laid out a map of Christian and Frankish society with a strong king supported by a strong episcopacy squarely at its centre.[103] One way in which the Carolingians encouraged uniformity and centralization was in Louis the Pious' patronage of the cult of the cross.[104] Geary has suggested that another way the Carolingians and their advisers pursued this goal was by the promotion of the cults of Roman saints, particularly martyrs. By

---

[102] *Miracula s. Benedicti*, I.25, pp. 56–7. Nelson (1986, p. 63) has also identified this 'bestial' legal expert as Lupus.
[103] Reviron 1930; Delaruelle 1951.   [104] Le Maître 1982.

45

translating the relics of such saints from Rome to various regions in an effort to supplant the local saints of those regions, Carolingian rulers and bishops hoped 'to direct men's loyalties to Rome, and thus to Rome's anointed defender', that is the Carolingian emperors themselves.[105]

One of the translations discussed by Geary is the acquisition of relics of St Sebastian by Abbot Hilduin of Saint-Denis and the subsequent gift of some of those relics to Fleury.[106] While Geary may well be correct in his assessment of Hilduin's motivation in implanting the cult of Sebastian at Saint-Denis, Adrevald's description of the coming of the relics of Sebastian to Fleury – the sole source for that event – suggests that he did not share the same motivation.[107] According to Adrevald, Abbot Boso of Fleury journeyed to the court of Louis the Pious on business of an undisclosed nature. During his return trip to Fleury he stopped at the abbey of Saint-Denis. There Abbot Hilduin gave him minor relics of the abbey's patron, Dionysius; of Dionysius' two companions, Rusticus and Eleutherius; and newly acquired relics of St Sebastian.[108] Boso brought the relics back to Fleury, where they stirred up a great deal of enthusiasm. Since so many laymen, and more importantly laywomen, wished to view the treasure, the monks were forced to build a special wooden structure outside the church of the Virgin to display the relics so that the monastic cloister and routine would not be disturbed. The result of Hilduin's magnanimity was thus profound, but his motivation was probably not the promotion of imperial authority. The abbeys of Fleury and Saint-Denis had recently been involved in a major dispute over land rights, the solution of which had required the intervention of imperial *missi* and, according to Adrevald, the miraculous power of St Benedict himself.[109] Therefore it is reasonable to assume that Boso had been called to the palace in order to make the solution final. Hilduin then most probably gave the relics to Boso – which included not only those of the Roman martyr Sebastian, but also the eminently 'local' relics of Denis and his companions – as a gesture of peace and goodwill between the two houses.

[105] Geary 1979c, the quotation is on p. 19. See also Mikoletzky 1949 on the translation of relics from Rome to the Frankish domains.
[106] Geary 1979c, pp. 15–16.   [107] *Miracula s. Benedicti*, I.28, pp. 63–5.
[108] According to Vidier (1965, p. 157) Adrevald adapted his description of Hilduin's acquisition of the relics from the *Annales Laureshamenses*.
[109] *Miracula s. Benedicti*, I.25, p. 56–7.

Bishops Theodulf and Jonas, as well as Louis the Pious and later Charles the Bald, involved themselves enthusiastically in the cult of the 'fathers' of the Orléanais. At the same time, certain literary ideals of the Carolingian court writers were widely disseminated, as can be seen in the imitation of Einhard by Adrevald.[110] Although Bishop Walter made a distinction between the 'fathers' of his diocese and the saints of the universal church, there does not seem to have been any of the tension between cults of local origin and those promoted by imperial power which Geary has found in other regions during the Carolingian period. Rather the Carolingian period was a time in which the cults of these 'fathers' and their associated hagiography was consciously nurtured and developed with virtually no recorded opposition – and indeed with much support – from the bishop, the count, or the king. What disputes there were occurred over monastic resources, which were in part produced through those cults.

While the ninth century was a period of great activity and achievement for the hagiographers of the diocese of Orléans, as it was for intellectuals throughout the Frankish kingdom, the second half of that century was also a period of great strife, marked by the devastating raids of the Normans in Neustria.[111] The city of Orléans was damaged repeatedly by raiding parties coming up the Loire. The earliest recorded attack was in 841, shortly after the accession of Charles the Bald who focused much of the activity of the early years of his reign in the Orléanais.[112] The bishops played a key role in Charles' administration of the region.[113] Agius, along with Bishop Bouchard of Chartres, organized the defence of the upper Loire which successfully turned back the Normans in 854. The ensuing fifteen years, however, brought three more attacks on the city: on 18 April 856 it was pillaged; in 865 the entire city was burned with the exception of the cathedral; and in 868 the city was again pillaged.[114] Similar disasters plagued the entire middle Loire valley. To protect this region from both the Normans and the newly belligerent Bretons, Charles was forced to create a strong lordship centred on Angers which he conferred on Robert the

---

[110] Geary 1978, pp. 145–9.
[111] See D'Haenens 1969 for a broad treatment of the effects of those raids on the Frankish empire. [112] *Chronique de l'Abbaye de Saint-Bénigne de Dijon*, p. 94.
[113] Muller 1987, pp. 19–20.
[114] *Annales de Saint-Bertin*, pp. 69, 72, 117 and 143. These entries fall into the sections composed by both Prudentius and Hincmar of Reims.

Strong in 862.[115] After Robert's death Hugh the Abbot took over control of this region with the title *dux Francorum*.

In 867 Walter succeeded Agius as bishop, probably with Hugh's support, and extended the episcopal defence of the city by rebuilding its walls.[116] He continued to have close ties to the Robertian family throughout his episcopacy.[117] The persistent threat of the Normans can be sensed in two letters of recommendation which Walter composed in the late 880s on behalf of monks who had fled the 'cruel persecution' of the invaders: the first for a group who had left the community of Saint-Ouen and now sought to make their way back to the relative safety of the county of Bayeux, and the second for an anonymous monk who was undertaking a pilgrimage to Rome.[118] Walter composed the statutes which spoke of the *pium patrocinium vicinum* of the 'fathers' of the diocese in the context of these military struggles.

In promulgating these statutes Walter stood in a tradition of ninth-century bishops who attempted to interpret the general ideals of the Carolingian programme of religious reform into specific practices for their dioceses.[119] The ideals were enunciated as early as the imperial capitulary known as the *Admonitio Generalis* (789).[120] Charlemagne and his ecclesiastical advisers had presented the clergy with a clear statement of their responsibilities to the faithful. Theodulf of Orléans was one of the first, and most influential, bishops to translate this programme into a blueprint for diocesan organization in two sets of statutes, the first dated 802 and the second probably composed after 813.[121] His works were enlivened by a shrewd pastoral sense and a commitment to the precept that his clergy should be exemplars for their flocks. Theodulf lectured his priests, 'You are to be always mindful of your dignity, mindful of your ordination, mindful of the holy unction which you carry in your hands so that . . . conserving cleanliness of heart and of body, you might present an example of

---

[115] On Robert's career, see Lot 1915.
[116] On the rebuilding of the city walls, see *Miracula s. Benedicti*, I.36, p. 79; Letaldus of Micy, *Miracula s. Maximini*, c. 19, p. 603. In a letter of 887 Walter referred to Hugh the Abbot among a list of the bishop's deceased *seniores*, see the edition in Bischoff 1984, p. 129.
[117] In a letter of 888 Walter referred to King Odo and Robert of Neustria as his *seniores*, see the edition in Bischoff 1984, p. 135.
[118] Edited in Bischoff 1984, pp. 126–7 and 128–9.
[119] On episcopal statutes, see Devailly 1966 and 1973a; McKitterick 1977, pp. 45–79; Wallace-Hadrill 1983, pp. 278–92.
[120] *MGH, Capitularia Regum Francorum*, I, 53–62.
[121] *MGH, Capitula episcoporum*, I, 73–142 and 142–84; McKitterick 1977, pp. 53–9.

correct living to the people.'[122] According to Rosamond McKitterick, 'His aim was to strengthen and to propagate the Christian faith, rather than to augment the power and enhance the prestige of the episcopal hierarchy.'[123] His statutes were striking both for their comprehensiveness – each parish was to have a school – and for their specificity – the priests were told exactly how to distribute the Eucharist.[124] The cult of the saints, however, was absent from this programme of inculcating Christianity in the *villae et vici*.

In a much shorter document Walter followed his illustrious predecessor in many matters. He showed more flexibility than had Theodulf, making the earlier requirement of parish schools, for example, into a simple suggestion.[125] His major addition was the requirement of the celebration of the feasts of the saints which has been cited so frequently in the present study. The list of the feasts of the universal church which he employed was taken almost verbatim from an early ninth-century collection of imperial capitularies made by Ansegisus.[126] The list of the 'fathers' of the Orléanais, however, and even his use of the term 'our fathers' to distinguish the local saints from those of the universal church were novel. He was, of course, not the first Carolingian bishop to attempt to increase the prestige of his office by encouraging the veneration of the relics of his Merovingian predecessors. In 825 Jonas of Orléans, for example, had composed the *Vita et translatio s. Huberti* as part of the efforts of Bishop Walcaudus of Liège, which were also supported by Jonas' patron Louis the Pious, to renew the cult of that early bishop by translating his relics to a new monastery.[127] In 835 Bishop Aldric of Le Mans claimed to gather the relics of three of his predecessors (Julian, Turibius, and Pavacius) within his cathedral in an attempt to begin the liturgical commemoration of these saints.[128] In a set of statutes issued only a few years before those of Walter, Archbishop Rodulfus of Bourges had required the commemoration of the feasts of Ursinus, Austregisilus, and Sulpicius, three early bishops of his diocese.[129]

[122] *MGH, Capitula episcoporum*, I, 104–5.   [123] McKitterick 1977, p. 53.

[124] *MGH, Capitula episcoporum*, I, 116 and 129–30.

[125] Walter of Orléans, *Capitularia Walterii*, c. 6, p. 189.

[126] *MGH, Capitula episcoporum*, I, 191 n. 57. For the source text, see *MGH, Capitularia Regum Francorum*, I, 413.

[127] Jonas of Orléans, *Vita et translatio s. Huberti*, pp. 806 and 817–18.

[128] Oury 1978a, pp. 43–6.

[129] *MGH, Capitula episcoporum*, I, 254–5. The exact date of the collection is uncertain. Rodulfus died in 866.

Rodulfus' text might well have provided a formal inspiration to Walter, particularly as Rodulfus had once been an abbot of Fleury, but, unlike the bishops of Le Mans and Bourges, Walter encouraged cults located in rural abbeys as well as those of religious communities located within the episcopal *civitas* itself.[130]

The list which Walter promulgated was the result of over a century of development within his diocese. His enunciation of this list or canon, however, reflects the fact that bishops were responsible for decisions concerning sanctity in the Carolingian world.[131] This text indicates that a serious attempt was made to move the cult of the diocese's 'fathers' outside the walls of the monastic enclosures in which the relics rested and into the parish churches. The celebration of the feasts of the 'fathers' was part of a more general liturgical renewal which was supported by the requirement that each parish possess a set of liturgical manuscripts necessary for the mass, preaching, and the commemoration of saints' feasts.[132] Quite possibly Walter's insistence on the celebration of these feasts and on the *patrocinium* which these 'fathers' provided was in part a response to the havoc which had been wreaked in the fabric of social life by the Norman raids.

Pierre Riché has shown that the cultural life of the west Frankish kingdom was remarkably resilient to the immediate effects of these raids.[133] The fertility of this period in terms of hagiographic composition may well reflect the fact that religious communities of the diocese were, like Bishop Walter, particularly attuned to their need for strong saintly patronage at such a difficult time. The cumulative effect of the attacks, however, severely disrupted the record-keeping and educational institutions of the Orléanais. A diploma of Carloman (dated 883) confirmed certain privileges of Charles the Bald lost in a fire at the cathedral archives which had

---

[130] The relics of Ursinus, Austregisilus, and Sulpicius – the three saints mentioned by Rodulfus – were enshrined at Saint-Ursin (a college of canons), Saint-Aoustrille (a college of canons), and Saint-Sulpice (a community of monks), all of which were located in the city of Bourges. These houses had a similar location and function to the communities of Saint-Aignan and Saint-Euverte in Orléans.

[131] Hermann-Mascard 1975, pp. 84–7.

[132] The list of required manuscripts consisted of a book of gospel readings, a lectionary, a psalter, an antiphonary, a martyrology (probably one of the historical martyrologies produced commonly in Carolingian monastic culture for wider use), and a homiliary. See Walter of Orléans, *Capitularia Walterii*, c. 7, p. 189. On the production of historical martyrologies and *homilaria* in this period, see McCulloh 1983 and Barré 1962.

[133] Riché 1969.

been caused by the 'lamentable persecution of the Normans' and had consumed many 'books of the church and copies of testaments'.[134]

At some later time the author of the *Acta translationis s. Evurtii* (*BHL* 2801), almost certainly a canon of Saint-Euverte, used this confusion to disguise a misleading description of the origins of his community.[135] He related how, at the time of the Muslim (*Vandalicae*) raids in the eighth century, the relics of St Evurtius were translated from a church dedicated to the Virgin Mary outside the walls of the city to the safety of the church of St Stephen within. When the danger had passed, the emperor Charles oversaw the return of the relics to the original church, now referred to as *ecclesia beati confessoris Evurtii*. The author appended a copy of a royal diploma, allegedly executed 'in our palace in Orléans', donating goods and land to the chapter of Saint-Euverte. This charter is an obvious forgery.[136] The earliest genuine reference to the chapter does not occur until 840–3.[137] It seems reasonable to conclude that the relics of the saint were in fact translated from the church of St Stephen (the original cathedral of Orléans) to a church outside the walls in the late eighth or early ninth centuries. That translation would have marked the original foundation, not the refoundation, of the chapter of Saint-Euverte. The author of this text wished to clothe the chapter in a false antiquity, knowing that many monasteries (such as Micy) had actually been devastated at the time of the wars of the eighth century and that many acts of Carolingian rulers (such as those in the cathedral archives) had actually been lost in the late ninth century. Thus the author of the

---

[134] *Cartulaire de Sainte-Croix*, no. 36, pp. 70–2.

[135] The only medieval copy (Vatican, Reg. lat. 623, fos. 93–9), published in the *Acta Sanctorum*, dates from the fifteenth century, see *Catal. Vat.*, p. 391.

[136] The forger intended to ascribe the donation to Charlemagne, who reigned after the Saracen threat had subsided, since he referred to the emperor as a *patricius Romanorum*. He erred, however, by linking his emperor to Bishop Agius (843–67) who served in the time of Charles the Bald. The forger used charters of both Charlemagne and Charles the Bald in composing his document. The forgery was copied by various early modern scholars as an authentic act of Charlemagne; see, for example, *GC*, VIII, *instrumenta*, p. 420. Mühlbacher (*MGH, Diplomata Karolinorum*, I, 331–3) rejected its authenticity on a variety of grounds, including the fact that Agius was not a contemporary of Charlemagne. Historians of the Orléanais began, as early as C. de la Saussaye (1615, pp. 321–2), to ascribe the act to Charles the Bald. Tessier (*Recueil des actes de Charles le Chauve*) however, does not even consider the text in his edition of Charles' acts. The forger sought to lay a claim to properties and rights for which the community of Saint-Euverte did not have a traditional claim.

[137] *Recueil des actes de Charles le Chauve*, no. 25, I, 64.

text sought to alter the memory of the events of the early ninth century.[138] Despite the rather crude nature of his deception, Pope Eugenius confirmed the charter in 1146 as an authentic act of Charlemagne and proof of the antiquity of Saint-Euverte.[139]

The effect of the Norman raids can be seen most vividly at the abbey of Fleury, upriver from Orléans. Adrevald recorded how the monks were twice forced to flee their monastery with the precious relics of their patron. The first time, probably in 854, they were soon able to return and placed the relics of Benedict in their accustomed place in the church of the Virgin.[140] In 865, however, the monks had to take refuge in the city of Orléans, quite possibly in the church built there in the eighth century by Abbot Medo.[141] The monks returned after an extended period of time to find their monastery almost completely devastated. They divided the dormitory, the only building still standing, into two parts. In one they placed the reliquary of Benedict as a makeshift altar. It was in such straitened circumstances that Adrevald must have composed his collection of miracle stories, and quite possibly the rest of his trilogy. He remarked at one point that 'by divine grace God's servants quite miserably wandered, evicted from their threatened home, yet they were solaced by the miracles performed by their most beloved [Benedict]'.[142]

The recovery of the community was rapid. In 876 Count Heccard stood in a rebuilt church of the Virgin, between the main altar and the relics of Benedict, to make a major donation to

---

[138] To describe this composition, which included the production of a false royal diploma for economic self-interest, as a forgery certainly falls under the traditional historiographical use of that term and would seem to meet the criteria set by Constable (1983). I would distinguish the sort of foundation legend set forth in this text, which apparently sought to alter the memory of a monastic community's recent past in part through the falsification of diplomatic material, from the foundation legends contained in hagiographic works such as the *Vitae s. Aviti* or the *Vitae s. Maximini*, which sought to confirm a community's memory of a past too distant to recover in another manner.

[139] *GC*, VIII, 508; Jaffé–Wattenbach, no. 8865. It is impossible to date *BHL* 2801 and its accompanying charter more precisely than pre-1146. The fact that the forger betrays such confusion over the identity of the emperor Charles in question suggests that the work was composed well after the time of Charles the Bald. It may have been written as late as the second quarter of the twelfth century by the Victorine canons who obtained the papal confirmation.

[140] *Miracula s. Benedicti*, I.34, pp. 75–6. Bautier (1969, p. 79) suggests this date.

[141] *Miracula s. Benedicti*, I.34, p. 76. The raid is dated by the *Annales de Saint-Bertin*, p. 117. On the church, see *Miracula s. Benedicti*, I.36, p. 78.

[142] *Miracula s. Benedicti*, I.34, p. 76.

Fleury.[143] Two years later Pope John VIII confirmed all of the royal privileges of Fleury, including the right of free election of its abbots, with no reference to any difficulties experienced by the community.[144] The next year, however, the Normans struck again.[145] Adelarius described this raid in the two chapters which he appended to the work of Adrevald.[146] When the monks of Fleury learned that a raiding party of Normans was approaching, they once again abandoned their monastery, taking the relics of their patron with them. On the road they met up with a small military party under Hugh the Abbot, the *dux Francorum*, returning from an expedition in Burgundy. Although the troops were tired, the count of Auxerre rallied them with the promise that they would be fighting under the protection of St Benedict. They fell on the Norman raiding party not far from the abbey and put them to flight in a bloody rout. After the fight Hugh the Abbot told the monks, 'Certainly St Benedict protected me through the whole battle, for he held the reins of my horse in his left hand and, holding a staff (*baculus*) in his right, he sent many of the enemy falling to their death.'[147] Thus defended by both secular and saintly patronage the abbey survived the last known Norman assault.

In the last decades of the ninth and first decades of the tenth centuries, the power of the Carolingian kings in the Orléanais was slowly usurped by the descendants of Robert the Strong. Both Robert's sons, Odo (888–98) and Robert (922–3), reigned as king of the west Franks.[148] They included the county and diocese of Orléans in the lands which they controlled, and in part based their opposition to the Carolingian succession on that power.[149] The religious communities of the diocese experienced their overlord-

---

[143] *Recueil des chartes de Saint-Benoît*, no. 28, 1, 78–9. On the donation of Perrecy, see Berland 1985.

[144] *Recueil des chartes de Saint-Benoît*, no. 29, 1, 80–5; Jaffé–Wattenbach, no. 3182.

[145] *Miracula s. Benedicti*, 1.41, pp. 86–9. The attack is dated to the time of Louis the Stammerer, who died in 879. Certain is incorrect both in his identification (p. 87 n. 1) of the Hugh discussed in this chapter as the brother of Robert the Strong and in his identification (p. 88 n. 2) of this raid as the one discussed in the 871 entry of the *Annales de Saint-Bertin*.

[146] The addition is contained in three manuscripts of Adrevald's work, see Vidier 1965, pp. 162–4. Aimo of Fleury (*Miracula s. Benedicti*, II.prologue, p. 92) knew of Adelarius' addition.   [147] *Miracula s. Benedicti*, 1.41, pp. 86–9 (the quotation is on p. 89).

[148] On the relationship of the Robertian family to the Carolingian royal house under the last Carolingian kings, see Lemarignier 1955.

[149] Muller (1987, pp. 22–6) provides a detailed listing of their acts in the Orléanais.

ship directly. Odo issued a number of charters in June 889 from the Orléanais, four of which were enacted at Micy, suggesting that the king used that abbey as a residence.[150] Similarly Odo resided at Meung-sur-Loire in July 891 and called an assembly of his major vassals there to maintain the system of royal government.[151] Trohannus, who served as the head of the royal chancery during these years, later received appointment to the see of Orléans as reward.[152] According to Letaldus of Micy, the bishop sold the abbacy of Micy in a drunken stupor to a cleric who proceeded to maltreat the community. The monks responded by calling upon the patronage of St Maximinus, who killed both the bishop and the simoniacal abbot.[153] Robert the Strong served as the lay abbot of Saint-Aignan, a title which was handed on to his son, Robert of Neustria, and which formed part of the family inheritance to at least the time of Robert the Pious.[154] During this period Charles the Simple did, however, retain at least nominal control over Fleury, to the extent of confirming its royal privileges in 900; that monastery never received the Robertian kings.[155]

Mere survival and immunity, however, were not always sufficient for a monastic community. The standard of ascetic practice at Fleury had become extremely lax in the years following the upheavals caused by the Normans. In the 930s Abbot Odo of Cluny was asked to reform the community. According to Odo's biographer, John of Salerno, the monks of Fleury initially opposed the abbot of Cluny: 'When the brethren heard of [Odo's] approach, some arming themselves with swords went up on to the roof of the building, as though to hurl stones and missiles on their enemies from the sky.'[156] The monks eventually relented, persuaded by Odo's humility and by a miraculous vision of St

---

[150] *Recueil des actes d'Eudes*, nos. 1–4, pp. 1–19.

[151] *Recueil des actes d'Eudes,* nos. 27–8, pp. 120–6.

[152] *Recueil des actes d'Eudes*, pp. xxxvi–xxxvii.

[153] Letaldus of Micy, *Miracula s. Maximini*, cc. 19–20, p. 603.

[154] Lot 1891, p. 184; Lauer 1900, p. 6; Lesne 1910–45, I, 201; II.2, 142; II.2, 149 n. 3; II.2, 182; II.3, 15 n. 4; and II.3, 104. For example, Robert of Neustria bore the title 'marchio atque abbas monasterii sancti Aniani' in two charters of 19 June 914 (*Recueil des actes de Charles le Simple*, nos. 77–8, pp. 172–6). The family held similar interests in the monasteries of Marmoutier, Saint-Denis, Saint-Riquier, Saint-Maur-des-Fossés, and Saint-Martin at Tours. In the late 880s Archbishop Walter of Sens (Bischoff 1984, p. 131), referred to Robert's brother, Odo, as the abbot of Saint-Symphorien in Orléans, one of the most important communities in the diocese not to possess a saint's shrine.

[155] *Recueil des chartes de Saint-Benoît*, no. 34, I, 92–5. Also see *Recueil des actes de Charles le Simple*, no. 34, pp. 71–4.   [156] John of Salerno, *Vita s. Odonis*, III.8, 81A.

Benedict. They were sure, however, to present the royal charters which guaranteed them the right of free election. John of Salerno attributed the reform to a count named Elisiardus, who received the abbacy as a royal grant from Ralph of Burgundy (923–36).[157] In a 938 confirmation of the abbey's royal privileges, however, Pope Leo VII attributed the reform to Hugh the Great.[158] In the person of Hugh – who was grandson of Robert the Strong, successor of Hugh the Abbot as *dux Francorum*, brother-in-law of Ralph of Burgundy, and father of the future king, Hugh Capet – the growing influence of the Robertian family, which was strongly tied to the abbey of Cluny, can be sensed at Fleury.

Odo of Cluny was personally devoted to the cult of Benedict's relics, travelling a great distance to be at Fleury on one of the saint's feasts.[159] He also served the cult of Benedict by composing a sermon for the 11 July feast of the translation of St Benedict's relics, as well as a lost account of the translation itself.[160] Odo recognized the powerful attraction exercised by the cult of the saint and began his sermon – in language which brings the *capitulum* of Walter to mind – by describing the large crowds of clerics and laity who came to Fleury to seek the *patrocinium* of the 'holy father'. Admitting the importance of the miracles worked at the saint's tomb, which he even suggested could be signs of the coming of Antichrist, Odo cautioned his monastic audience not to inquire into them too closely. Rather, the monks should be primarily concerned with the content of the rule provided for their lives by that same divinely inspired legislator. The remainder of Odo's sermon became in essence a call for monastic reform. For him, Benedict's role of *legislator* was more important than that of *patronus*, the saint's rule a more impressive legacy than his miracles. Thus it is not too surprising to find Aimo of Fleury later complaining that 'those miracles which the Lord allowed his holy confessor Benedict to perform at his tomb or in other places during the time [of Abbot Odo] remain unknown to us now, partially because of their

---

[157] John of Salerno, *Vita s. Odonis*, III.8, col. 81A. Rosenwein (1982, p. 48) has identified Elisiardus as a man who became a monk of Fleury in the next decade (as recorded in *Receuil des chartes de Saint-Benoît*, no. 47, I, 120–2).

[158] *Receuil des chartes de Saint-Benoît*, no. 44, I, 110–14; Jaffé–Wattenbach, no. 3606.

[159] John of Salerno, *Vita s. Odonis*, III.11, col. 82C.

[160] Odo of Cluny, *Sermo de s. Benedicto*. A thirteenth-century breviary from Orléans used this sermon to provide the readings for the 4 December feast of Benedict's *illatio*: Orléans, BM 125, fo. 265v. On the lost account of the translation of Benedict's relics, see John of Salerno, *Vita s. Odonis*, III.11, col. 83C.

antiquity, partially because the negligence of scribes allowed them to fall into oblivion'.[161]

A few years later the abbey of Fleury substantially enriched its store of relics. During the abbacy of Wulfadus, Bishop Mabbo of Pol-de-Léon in Brittany came to Fleury bearing the relics of St Paul Aurelian, an early bishop who had become the patron of his diocese.[162] He arrived bearing not only the relics, but some ornate gospel books and even liturgical vestments. The relics were immediately interred in the main church at Fleury and the cult flourished for several generations before the monks of Fleury revised the original Breton text of the saint's life according to their own tastes.[163]

Other than the sermon of Odo of Cluny, and possibly the forgery from Saint-Euverte, no hagiographic works were composed in the diocese of Orléans over the first three-quarters of the tenth century.[164] It may be that the cessation of the Norman raids in the late ninth century removed one of the basic motivations for hagiographic composition. By and large the religious communities of the diocese marked time during these years, apparently content to accept the traditional powers of patronage offered by their saints. The relative dearth of hagiographic composition in the Orléanais, while paralleled elsewhere in the middle Loire valley, was largely local. Other regions of Europe produced a relatively

---

[161] *Miracula s. Benedicti*, II.4, p. 101.

[162] *Miracula s. Benedicti*, III.11, pp. 154–5, and VII.16, p. 275. Aimo referred to a now-lost text concerning this translation.

[163] Aimo's text does not substantiate Cousin's claim (1954, p. 46, repeated by Van der Straeten 1982, p. 20) that Mabbo brought a manuscript of the *Vita s. Pauli Aureliani* of Wormonoc of Landévennec (*BHL* 6585) with him to Fleury. Aimo did know the work, however, and a tenth-century copy (identified by Cousin as that of Mabbo) from Fleury's library does survive as Orléans, BM 261, fos. 42–73.

[164] The hagiographic traditions of Micy proved to be a fruitful source for an author from another region, Bertarius of Verdun. In his *Gesta pontificum s. Virdunensis ecclesiae* (c. 4, cols. 509–10) he used the *Vitae s. Maximini* as a source for a discussion of the revolt of that city against Clovis. (On the date (951) and composition of this work see *VSBP*, XI, 296–7.) Bertarius identified the bishop of Verdun as one Firminus and told how Clovis offered the office to Euspicius on the bishop's death. Euspicius refused it for himself, but accepted the post for his nephew, Vitonus, and arranged the abbacy of a new monastery (evidently Micy) for his other nephew, Maximinus. Bertarius claimed (*Gesta pontificum s. Virdunensis ecclesiae*, c. 12, col. 514) to have found a *Vita s. Vitoni* 'on the far side of the Loire'. Dubois (*VSBP*, XI, 297) suggests that this is an allusion to Micy, even though the abbey was in fact on the southern bank of the river. Bertarius evidently composed his account by comparing a local episcopal list to one of the versions of the life of Maximinus. His rewriting of the traditions of Micy were not picked up at that monastery until the 1020s, when the author of the *Vita s. Euspicii* (Vatican, Reg. lat. 621, fos. 47v and 48v) quoted Bertarius almost verbatim.

substantial number of hagiographic texts during this period.[165] In the middle years of the tenth century, for example, Adso of Montierender produced a number of well-researched hagiographic texts, including an elegant foundation narrative for his own house replete with forged diplomas.[166]

It is even more likely that the religious communities of the Orléanais were responding to the ebb and flow of secular patronage and royal authority. Since the time in which Bishop Walter had decreed the canonical list of the 'fathers' of the diocese, the Carolingian dynasty had been losing much of its influence in the Orléanais to the Robertian family.[167] The Robertians directly controlled the monastery of Saint-Aignan throughout the tenth century; through their influence on the bishops of Orléans they virtually controlled the other sanctuaries in or near the city as well. Even at Fleury, which is usually asserted to be a holdout of Carolingian influence, Hugh the Great helped to arrange the reforming mission of Odo of Cluny. The year 987 brought what was effectively a change of royal dynasty to the lands of the western Franks. Over the following decades the monastic communities of the Orléanais responded to the changed circumstances of Capetian rule by renewing the cults of their saintly patrons and composing a new set of hagiographic works in celebration of those 'fathers'.

[165] Zoepf 1908, particularly pp. 31–108. Aimo of Fleury was the only author from the Orléanais considered by Zoepf (p. 185).
[166] Head 1987b, pp. 147 and 152, particularly nn. 27 and 71.
[167] Lot 1891, pp. 171–4.

Chapter 2

THE CAPETIAN PERIOD

In the 980s, after a century of near silence, the monks and clerics of the Orléanais began to compose hagiographic works once again. Sometime after 982 Letaldus of Micy wrote the *Miracula s. Maximini* (*BHL* 5820), a history of Micy, its founder, and that saint's patronage.[1] This work inaugurated the reuse of Carolingian traditions concerning the 'fathers' of the diocese. About the same time (985–7) Abbo of Fleury went to the abbey of Ramsey in England as schoolmaster and representative of monastic reform; while there he was asked to write an account of the life and martyrdom of King Edmund (*BHL* 2392).[2] This work began a new tradition among writers at Fleury of composing works about contemporary and near-contemporary figures – some explicitly regarded as saints, others more simply as models of Christian living. These works in essence presented ideals of abbatial and royal authority.

The next century and a quarter became the second great age of hagiographic composition in the region. Between the 980s and the middle of the eleventh century, local authors composed over thirty

---

[1] The work is usually dated to 986–7 (see, for example, *HLF*, VI, 528–9 and Manitius 1911–31, II, 427). The traditional *terminus post quem* is provided by the fact that Letaldus wrote at least twelve years after the death of Abbot Anno (*Miracula s. Maximini*, c. 39, p. 609). Anno died, however, not in 973 as previously thought (*GC*, VIII, 1428, and Jarossay 1902, p. 534), but in 970. (The abbot died in the same year that Bishop Ermentheus relinquished the episcopal office to his nephew Arnulf. In 973 Arnulf subscribed a charter ('Chartes de Micy', no. 11, p. 67) which was dated to the third year of his episcopate.) The traditional *terminus ante quem* of 987 is provided by Letaldus' reference to Hugh Capet (*Miracula s. Maximini*, c. 16, p. 602) as 'dux' rather than 'rex'. Many authors, however, continued to refer to Hugh as 'dux' after his coronation, particularly in reference to events before 987. See, for example, *Miracula s. Benedicti*, III.7–8, pp. 147–8. Therefore the work is best dated to the decade after 982.

[2] Vidier 1965, pp. 102–3; Mostert 1986. Mostert (1987, p. 45) suggests that Abbo actually composed the work after his return to Fleury in the autumn of 987 and before the death of Archbishop Dunstan (19 May 988).

works related to the cult of the saints.[3] A new vitality can be sensed
as well in schools, libraries, and chanceries during these decades,
most noticeably at Fleury.[4] The following seventy years witnessed
a decrease in the composition of hagiography. Between 1050 and
1120 fewer than ten hagiographic works were composed.[5] The
decline of hagiographic composition continued even more dramatically over the course of the twelfth century. Only three
hagiographic texts were written in the diocese between 1120 and
the end of the century, although it was a fertile period for
hagiographic composition elsewhere in the Capetian kingdom.[6]

[3] This period closely corresponds to what Lemarignier (1959, p. 23), in his discussion on
the relationship of the Capetian monarchy to the foundation and maintenance of
religious communities, has called 'le pullulement de sanctuaires (987–1077)'. Some of
these hagiographic texts were lives of saints whose relics rested in the diocese: the *Vita s.
Euspicii*, the *Vita s. Theodemiri*, the *Vita s. Viatoris*, Vitalis of Fleury's *Vita s. Pauli
Aureliani*, the *Vita s. Laeti*, the *Vita s. Aviti IV*, the *Vita s. Montanae*, and the *Passio s.
Mauri*. Others were texts which concerned the relics of the diocese or the miracles
associated with them: the *Sermo de inventione s. Maximini*, the *Miracula s. Maximini*, the
Translatio s. Euspicii, the *Translatio s. Laeti* (*Vita s. Laeti*, c. 10), Theodoric of Fleury's
Illatio s. Benedicti, the *Miracula s. Benedicti* and the *Miracula s. Abbonis* both of Aimo of
Fleury, the *Miracula s. Benedicti* of Andrew of Fleury, the verse versions of the *Historia
translationis s. Benedicti* by Giraldus and Aimo, and the *Miracula ss. Georgii et Laeti*. Still
others were texts concerned with saints from outside the diocese: Letaldus of Micy's *Vita
s. Juliani*, *Delatio corporis s. Juniani*, *Vita et miracula s. Martini Vertavensis*, and *Vita et
miracula s. Eusicii*; Abbo of Fleury's *Vita s. Edmundi*; Theodoric of Fleury's *Vita s. Martini
papae*, *Passio ss. Tryphoni et Respicii*, and *Vita s. Firmani*; Isembard of Fleury's *Vita,
translatio et miracula s. Judoci*. Finally there were lives of contemporary figures: the
anonymous *Vita s. Gregorii Nicopolitani* and Aimo's *Vita s. Abbonis*, both clearly
hagiographic works, and Helgaud of Fleury's *Epitoma vitae regis Rotberti pii* and Andrew
of Fleury's *Vita Gauzlini*, both works based on hagiographic models. In addition various
hagiographic sermons, liturgical material, contemporary biographies, and related pieces
of historiography were also composed during this time, in some cases (such as Letaldus'
poetry for Saint-Florent, Andrew's *Vita Gauzlini*, and Aimo's *Historiae francorum libri
quatuor*) by writers of hagiography.

[4] On the school of Fleury, see Cuissard 1875; Lesne 1910–45, v, 191–6; Van der Vyver
1929, pp. 443–6, and 1935; Guerreau-Jalabert 1982, pp. 17–23 and 147–75. On other
schools, see Lesne 1910–45, v, pp. 175–91. On the manuscripts produced at Fleury during
this period see the list provided by Guerreau-Jalabert 1982, pp. 177–93, *passim*.

[5] This period corresponds roughly to what Lemarignier (1959, p. 34) has termed 'le
regroupement et l'essor spirituel (1077–1108)' in the royal sponsorship of religious
communities. Two works from Saint-Aignan are difficult to date, but probably were
composed between 1050 and 1070: the *Miracula s. Aniani* and the *Passio et translatio s.
Baudelii*. Two writers from Fleury produced significant bodies of hagiographic and
historiographic works in the first two decades of the twelfth century. Rodulfus Tortarius
wrote the *Passio s. Mauri*, a *Miracula s. Benedicti*, and verse versions of the earlier miracle
collections from Fleury; while Hugh of Fleury wrote a *Miracula s. Benedicti* and the *Vita et
miracula s. Sacerdotis*. In addition the *Miraculum s. Maximini* was composed at Micy *c.*
1074, and the *Translatio s. Lifardi* at Meung-sur-Loire *c.* 1105.

[6] Roger of Saint-Euverte, *Inventio s. Evurtii*, the *Miracula s. Euspicii*, and the *Miracula s.
Lifardi*.

Thereafter virtually no new texts were composed about the traditional 'fathers' of the diocese.

This renewal of the veneration of the diocese's 'fathers' and the rewriting of the stories of their patronage was accomplished within the context of a reconstruction of the church buildings of the diocese, a renewal paralleled elsewhere in Christendom. Rodulfus Glaber later remarked of the first decade of the eleventh century, 'It was as if the very world, by shaking herself and casting off her old age, was clothing herself everywhere in a shining garment of churches. Then finally the faithful changed for the better almost all the churches of episcopal sees, as well as the monasteries of diverse saints, and even smaller parish churches.'[7] The rebuilding of 'monuments of letters' and monuments of stone went hand in hand. According to the witness of Glaber and others, the early decades of the eleventh century were an emotionally charged period in the religious life of the Orléanais. Natural disasters and the passions of nascent persecution mingled to create the atmosphere within which the religious communities of the diocese reconstructed their sanctuaries and began to rewrite their hagiographic records.

The reconstruction of church buildings in this region was not simply a matter of voluntary piety, but a necessity brought about by a series of devastating fires. During the episcopacy of Arnulf (970–1003) the cathedral and virtually the entire city were razed.[8] According to Rodulfus Glaber, writing a half-century later, various omens preceded the fire, including the appearance of tears

---

[7] Rodulfus Glaber, *Historiarum libri quinque*, III.4.13, pp. 116–17. For archaeological confirmation, see Lesne 1910–45, III, 93–6.

[8] Rodulfus Glaber, *Historiarum libri quinque*, II.5.8–9, pp. 64–9. The date of the fire is uncertain, although Bishop Arnulf was in part responsible for the work of reconstruction. The date *octingentesimo octogesimo octavo* (888) is clearly written in a manuscript (Paris, BN lat. 10912) which is in large measure Glaber's autograph. This date implicitly places the fire in 889. (On the relationship of the manuscript to Glaber, see Garand 1983.) The dates are usually corrected to 988–9, based both upon the story's placement in the work and because of the reference to Bishop Arnulf. Nichols (1983, p. 17), on the other hand, has offered a corrected reading of 998–9 without explanation. The apparent reasoning is that the number 888 stood as a symbolic reference to a year of possible apocalyptic expectation. Another reference to the fire is found in a letter which Fulbert of Chartres sent to Robert the Pious in 1024 (*Letters*, no. 94, pp. 170–3) advising the king not to hold a council in Orléans, 'a city ravaged by fire'. The immediacy of Fulbert's reference would suggest a date later than 988. Ademar of Chabannes (*Chronicon*, III.58, p. 184) linked the destruction of Sainte-Croix to a fire at Fleury. There were fires at Fleury in 1002 and 1005 (not 1014 as suggested by Chavanon in a marginal reference). Thus Ademar's imprecise reference also suggests a date late in Arnulf's episcopate. It remains impossible, however, to date the event with any precision.

on a crucifix in the church of Saint-Pierre-le-Puellier and the ringing of the bell of the cathedral by a wolf. After the destruction Arnulf undertook rebuilding the cathedral. During the excavations a treasure was found which was used to finance the construction,

For it was said that the gold had been hidden there by the ingenuity of St Evurtius, an ancient prelate of the same see, for the sake of this reconstruction in the same place. Therefore it was especially granted to him, seeing that the same holy man made the same church better than it had been before, to discover by divine inspiration a gift similar to this one placed there for him.

The other relic shrines (*ceterae basilicae sanctorum*) of the city were also rebuilt at this time. For Glaber this story followed the paradigm of sin followed by purifying destruction and the renewal of forgiveness: 'The people, softened by these punishments and supported by divine affection, recovered all the more quickly, since they wisely accepted the calamity as their own in the form of vengeance for their corruption.' The tale also suggests, however, that the people of the Orléanais interpreted contemporary events in the light of the patronage provided by their 'fathers'.[9]

In 1009 a far more distant church, that of the Holy Sepulchre in Jerusalem, was destroyed by a Muslim caliph, al-Hakim. The Jewish community of Orléans was blamed for having incited this act of desecration. This accusation led to the eviction, and possibly the massacre, of Jews in Orléans and elsewhere.[10] In nearby Sens the entourage of Count Rainard, who was labelled a 'Judaizer', was likewise expelled and some people burnt.[11] The consecration of the reconstructed cathedral of Sainte-Croix occurred around 1016.[12] That event, however, did not end the woes of its chapter of canons. In 1022 several members were found guilty of heresy; King Robert the Pious presided over their trial and execution at the stake.[13] Thus the conjunction of anti-Jewish and anti-heretical

[9] Cf. the interpretation and translation of this passage offered by Nichols 1983, pp. 17–30.
[10] Rodulfus Glaber, *Historiarum libri quinque*, III.7.24–5, pp. 132–7. According to contemporary Byzantine sources, al-Hakim's motivation for the destruction was to abolish the annual 'miracle of the holy fire' which he saw as a hoax perpetrated to incite Christian religious fervour, see Canard 1965.
[11] Rodulfus Glaber, *Historiarum libri quinque*, III.6.23, pp. 132–3.
[12] *Vita s. Theodorici II*, c. 2, p. 197. On the date see *DACL*, XII, 2689.
[13] See particularly Bautier 1975a; Moore 1977, pp. 23–30; Stock 1983, pp. 106–20. Earlier analyses are generally weakened by the misidentification of an account composed in the early twelfth century by Paul of Saint-Père de Chartres as the actual minutes of the council at which the heretics were condemned.

fervour, which R. I. Moore has described as a hallmark of the eleventh century, can be first sensed in Orléans.[14] One of the accusations most commonly levelled at both Jews and heretics was their rejection of the sacraments and the cult of the saints. The Jews of Orléans had allegedly struck at one of the most important Christian pilgrimage sites. In one account of the events of 1022 the canons of Sainte-Croix were accused of denying the efficacy of the spiritual intervention of the saints.[15] The cults of the 'fathers' of the Orléanais did not develop completely without opposition or dissent.

The cycle of destruction and renewal occurred elsewhere in the region. King Robert the Pious sponsored the reconstruction of the church of Saint-Aignan and attended its consecration in 1029.[16] Architectural evidence confirms Rodulfus Glaber's suggestion that the churches of Saint-Euverte and Saint-Avit were rebuilt at about the same time.[17] At Fleury the church of St Peter was destroyed in 974, several minor buildings burned in both 1002 and 1005 when fires erupted on the eve of the 11 July feast of Benedict's *translatio*, and the main church of the Virgin was badly damaged in 1026. In the wake of this last fire, Abbot Gauzlin undertook a major construction programme which would not be completed until well after his death.[18] While the abbey of Micy was not affected by fire, Abbot Albert rebuilt the main church there in the early 1020s. The building programme included the ritual invention of three caskets containing the relics of Maximinus and of men identified as his disciples and successors. Robert the Pious also returned some relics of Maximinus' uncle, Euspicius, to Micy in 1029.[19] There is virtually no evidence concerning Meung-sur-Loire for this period, except for the fact that the bishop of Orléans replaced its monks

---

[14] Rodulfus Glaber implicitly connected the two events by reciting them seriatim (*Historiarum libri quinque*, III.7.24–5 and III.7.26–31, pp. 132–51). Moore (1987, particularly pp. 11–45) has noted these developments as key elements in the development of Christendom as 'persecuting society'.   [15] *Cartulaire de Saint-Père de Chartres*, I, 111.

[16] Helgaud of Fleury, *Epitoma vitae regis Rotberti pii*, c. 22, pp. 106–8. The eleventh-century crypt of this structure survives, see Banchereau 1931a; Rousseau 1975a; Gaillard and Debal 1987, pp. 17–18.

[17] The early eleventh-century crypts of both churches are still extant, see Banchereau 1931b; Chenesseau 1931c; Jouvellier 1975; Gaillard and Debal 1987, pp. 19 and 26–7.

[18] *Miracula s. Benedicti*, II.9, pp. 110–12; III.2, pp. 128–30; and III.19, pp. 166–9. See also Bautier 1969, pp. 88–90 and 100–1.

[19] *Sermo de inventione s. Maximini*, p. 252–3; *Translatio s. Euspicii*, pp. 313–14; Jarossay 1902, pp. 151–2; J. Hubert 1951; Head 1984, pp. 219–20.

with regular canons some time in the mid-eleventh century.[20] In 1103 Leo of Meung led a revolt against Bishop Rainerius. Leo died along with his fellow rebels in a fortified tower 'near the church', probably the bell tower which contains fabric from the Romanesque period.[21] The church was rededicated in 1105 in a ceremony attended by the bishop, King Philip I, the bishops of Tours and Paris, and the abbot of Micy.[22]

Two new sanctuaries were also founded, or at least came into prominence, in the decades around the year 1000. In Tremblevif (now Saint-Viâtre), 42 kilometres south of Orléans, the relics of a saint named Viator were enshrined in a church dedicated to his memory, although there is no evidence of a religious community there.[23] The lords of Pithiviers, 42 kilometres north-east of the city, persuaded Bishop Ermentheus (pre-956–70) to provide the relics of a saint named Laetus which were then enshrined in a newly founded collegiate church.[24] Contemporary authors described both saints as sixth-century hermits who had been disciples of Maximinus and companions of Avitus. Thus they were clothed in an aura of antiquity which made them similar in identity to the traditional 'fathers' of the diocese. The emergence of these towns as important centres indicates that north–south land routes were challenging the Loire as a means of travel and trade.

This renewal of hagiography and the cult of the saints occurred in a period of momentous change for the kingdom of the western Franks. In May 987 Louis V died in a hunting accident. That July Hugh Capet, son of Hugh the Great and *dux Francorum*, was elected to rulership in the place of Louis' uncle, Charles of Lotharingia, by an assembly of magnates.[25] In December Hugh

---

[20] The date usually given is 1068, see *GC*, VIII, 1513; Cottineau 1939–70, col. 1838; *VSBP*, VI, 55. A charter of the cathedral of Chartres from *c.* 1055 (*Cartulaire de Notre-Dame de Chartres*, I, 93), however, described the donation of a church in the Beauce to the *canonices* of St Lifardus in exchange for rights in a church ceded to the bishop of Chartres.

[21] Suger of Saint-Denis, *Vie de Louis VI le Gros*, c. 6, p. 28. Vallery-Radot 1931a, p. 279.

[22] *Translatio s. Lifardi*, c. 1, p. 157. Cf. Molinier (1901–6, no. 1096, II, 36) who provides a date of 1104.

[23] The first appearance of the sanctuary in a charter is as an *ecclesia* in a list of the possessions of the bishop of Orléans confirmed by Eugenius III in 1151 (*Cartulaire de Sainte-Croix*, no. 22, p. 48). The *Vita s. Viatoris*, however, dates to the late tenth or early eleventh centuries, see Poncelet 1905, pp. 64–5. The church, which still houses relics of the saint, has elements which date to the eleventh century. See also *AASSOSB*, I, 613–14; *AASS*, Aug. II, p. 82; Dupré 1854, pp. 190–2; *VSBP*, VIII, 87; and *BS*, XII, 1071–2.

[24] *Vita s. Laeti*, c. 10, p. 76.   [25] Lewis 1981, pp. 16–18.

had his son, Robert the Pious, crowned as his co-ruler in Orléans and later he incarcerated Charles in that city.[26] Helgaud remarked that Robert 'always specially loved' the city where he had been born and crowned.[27] While the accession of the Capetian family was much disputed elsewhere in the kingdom of the west Franks, there was little dissent in the Orléanais. That region had been for over a century under the domination of the Robertian family and now served as one of the foundations of their royal domain.[28] The city of Orléans itself would serve, along with Paris, as one of the two main foci of Capetian royal families' activities until the time of Philip I, who was buried at the abbey of Fleury. The region was thus very much at the centre of religious, social, and political developments among the western Franks over the course of the early eleventh century.

Jean-François Lemarignier has provided a subtle picture of the changing lines of social and ecclesiastical authority in these decades. In particular he has described the efforts of the early Capetian kings to gain control over traditional Carolingian – or, perhaps better, neo-Carolingian – rights, territories, and domains.[29] At the same time the old Carolingian governmental order based on the high nobility was fast disintegrating in a process which he has called 'the dislocation of the *pagus*'. The lesser nobility of the castellans and knights slowly, but consistently, gained more power and rights over the course of the eleventh century.[30] The place of religious communities in society was greatly affected by these changes. Some monastic reformers, such as Abbo of Fleury, sought to shore up relationships with the royal house as a means of protecting monastic rights.[31] Many abbeys and colleges of canons sought to gain grants of immunity and even developed virtually independent lordships in their domains.[32] Still other newly founded houses were directly dependent on either the royal house or various families of both the high and lesser nobility.[33]

An analysis of the relationship of the eleventh-century hagiography from the Orléanais and its social context does much to confirm Lemarignier's theses. In renewing the cults of the diocese's

---

[26] Lot 1903, p. 7 n. 4 and p. 173.
[27] Helgaud of Fleury, *Epitoma vitae regis Rotberti pii*, c. 15, p. 86.
[28] The family exercised a well-documented control over the religious institutions of the diocese, including the episcopal see. For a summary, see Lot 1903, p. 430; Newman 1937b, pp. 88–101 (particularly 91) and 202; Lemarignier 1965, pp. 177–9.
[29] Lemarignier 1965.   [30] Lemarignier 1951.   [31] Lemarignier 1957 and 1977.
[32] Lemarignier 1937 and 1965.   [33] Lemarignier 1959.

'fathers', the religious communities of the region made varied use of the composition of hagiography about their patrons, and the patronage which that hagiography described, according to their varied circumstances. The monasteries under royal protection – Fleury and Saint-Aignan – celebrated the power of their patrons as a means of protecting their traditional rights and properties. The monks of Micy, an abbey under episcopal control, used hagiography as part of a vigorous campaign to win exemptions for their community. The canons of the other communities under episcopal domination – Saint-Avit, Saint-Euverte, and Meung-sur-Loire – remained silent concerning their patron saints over the course of the century.[34] The canons of the newly founded chapter of Pithiviers used hagiography as a means of making their patron similar in both identity and powers of patronage to the traditional 'fathers' of the diocese. While the hagiographers of the Capetian period turned frequently to the works of their Carolingian predecessors, they did not rewrite any of the ninth-century works produced within the Orléanais. Rather they mined earlier works to provide source material for the lives of saints who had not been so honoured in the past.

The best example of such reuse can be found in the related lives of Viator and Laetus. The author of the *Vita s. Viatoris* (*BHL* 8551) told the story of the hermit's life, burial, and cult by freely adapting the Carolingian *Vitae s. Aviti*.[35] In this new work Viator became Avitus' companion during his self-imposed eremitic exile from Micy. After the death of St Maximinus, the monks of Micy made Avitus their abbot, but Viator fled further into the forest and constructed a new hut at *Viatoria*. The site of Viator's tomb – where a church was later built by a nobleman who was cured there – came to be known after the name of that tree under which the saint had died (*Tremulus-vicus*).[36] Thus the story provided a foundation and naming legend not only for the church in which the saint's relics were enshrined, but for the surrounding *villa* as

---

[34] The *Translatio s. Lifardi*, written in 1105, was not composed by a member of the community of Meung-sur-Loire. Moreover its author obscured the purpose of the ritual he described, the reconsecration of the church after people had been killed in it during the revolt of Leo of Meung.

[35] Poncelet 1905, pp. 61–5. The author used his source material in a manner similar to that employed by the authors of the *Vitae s. Carileffi* (*BHL* 1568 and 1569). These ninth-century hagiographers from the diocese of Le Mans had made their local 'father' into a disciple and companion of St Avitus. The author of the *Vita s. Viatoris* used the *Vita s. Aviti III* and the *Vita s. Carileffi II* as his direct sources.

[36] On the later development of that town's name, see *Cartulaire de Sainte-Croix*, p. cvi.

well. The author of the *Vita s. Laeti* (*BHL* 4672), composed during the episcopacy of Odolric (*c.* 1021–36), simply reworked the *Vita s. Viatoris* by substituting his hero, Laetus, for the hero of the original text. This author also appended a lengthy account of the translation of Laetus' relics to Pithiviers.[37]

Just as the development of these two new cults provided a need for composing the lives of hitherto uncelebrated saints, so too Abbot Albert's programme of reconstruction at Micy in the 1020s resulted in the renewal of relic veneration and thus generated a need for new hagiography. An anonymous monk responded by composing three linked texts. In the *Sermo de inventione s. Maximini et eius discipulorum Theodemiri et alterius Maximini* (*BHL* 5821) he described the discovery of the relics of the abbey's patron and his successors, as well as the reconsecration of the new church. He preceded the relatively brief description of contemporary events with a long discussion of the monastic life, borrowed from Jerome, and a précis of the history of Micy, borrowed from Letaldus and the Carolingian lives of Maximinus.[38] Following a similar pattern he composed a life of one of the newly discovered disciples, Theodemir, by prefacing the passages from the lives of Maximinus which mentioned this figure with a long discussion of the Trinity.[39] This author also described the return to Micy of relics of Euspicius, Maximinus' uncle, in the *Vita et translatio s.*

---

[37] Poncelet 1905, pp. 65–71. The only details which are changed are the name of the saint, the place to which Laetus and Avitus go to lead the eremitic life (*Laogium*, that is Saint-Lyé, for *Tremuli vicus*, that is Tremblevif), and the date of the death of the saint (5 November for 5 August). The author even retained *Viatoria*, the name of Viator's hermitage, as the original name of *Laogium*.

[38] Vatican, Reg. lat. 621, fos. 34–46. The concluding portion of the text was printed by Mabillon in *AASSOSB*, VI.1, 252–3. The text can be divided into five sections: the story of Euspicius, Maximinus and the foundation of Micy (fos. 34–7); a discussion of the monastic life followed by them, which included a description of the coenobitical life taken directly and with attribution from a letter of Jerome on the monks of Egypt (fos. 37–9v, cf. Jerome, *Epistola* 22, cc. 34–6, pp. 196–200); a list of the disciples who learned the monastic life from Maximinus (fos. 39–41v); stories of miracles through which Maximinus, and by extension Theodemir, showed their power during their lives (fos. 41v–2); and a narration of the discovery of the tombs and the invention of the relics of the three abbots (fos. 43–6). The description of Maximinus is drawn, at times verbatim, from Letaldus' *Miracula s. Maximini*, augmented with material from the *vitae* (Bertholdus of Micy, *Vita s. Maximini I*, c. 11, p. 594, or *Vita s. Maximini II*, c. 19, pp. 585–6).

[39] The *Vita* has remained unedited and has not been given a *BHL* number. It survives in two late copies: Paris, BN lat. 11773, fos. 71–4v, a manuscript of Saint-Germain-des-Prés copied from an original from Meung-sur-Loire; and Bruxelles, Bibliothèque royale 8949, copied by the Bollandists from an exemplar of the Feuillants, which was itself allegedly copied from an original from Meung. I have only consulted the former. On this text and manuscripts, see Poncelet 1905, pp. 11–12 n. 2, and 82.

Euspicii (*BHL* 2757–8). In this work he introduced a short account of the translation with material about the saint's life once again borrowed directly from the lives of Maximinus.[40] The same author probably also composed the *Vita s. Aviti IV* (*BHL* 882), which was not so much a rewriting of the Carolingian lives of that saint as it was an attempt to reconcile those works with the Carolingian lives of Maximinus (from Micy) and Carileffus (from Le Mans).[41] This work was a pastiche of verbatim quotations and rephrased borrowings from these hagiographic sources, as well as an introduction taken from a work of Letaldus of Micy.[42] This monk combined known hagiographic sources with standard patristic works in order to produce the liturgical readings necessary for new feastdays.

The church of Saint-Aignan, at the time of its reconsecration in 1029, contained relics of a saint named Baudelius who was identified as the subdeacon of Orléans mentioned in the ninth-century lives of Bishop Evurtius. Late in the eleventh century an anonymous canon adapted the traditions of a soldier and martyr from Nîmes who was also named Baudelius into a *Passio et translatio s. Baudelii* (*BHL* 1045 b and c).[43] He told how the subdeacon of Orléans had left that city after the death of Evurtius and had achieved his glorious martyrdom in Nîmes whence some relics had been returned at an indefinite point in the past. The

---

[40] Vatican, Reg. lat. 621, fos. 47v–54. The *translatio* section is printed in *AASSOSB*, VI.1, 314. The author used the *Vita s. Maximini II* as his basic source for the life of Euspicius. He also used several other traditions, including the work of Bertarius of Verdun, in his account of the siege of Verdun. In this account (fo. 49) Euspicius had three nephews in addition to Maximinus: Vitonus, who became bishop of Verdun after Euspicius rejected the honour; Germanus, who became bishop of Auxerre; and Lupus, who ascended to the episcopacy of Troyes.

[41] *AASS*, June III, pp. 351–9. There are two known manuscripts, both dating from the late eleventh or early twelfth centuries: Vatican, Reg. lat. 621, fos. 1–12 (*Catal. Vat.*, p. 390), and Le Mans, BM 217, fos. 13v–17v (*CGMBPF*, xx, 145, and Dolbeau 1976, p. 153). The former manuscript comes from Micy itself, as two folios (fos. 27 and 28) are palimpsests written over charters of Micy.

[42] The sources were the *Vita s. Aviti III*, the *Vita s. Carileffi II*, the *Vita s. Maximini II*, the *Vita s. Leobini*, and the *Vita et miracula s. Martini Vertavensis*. Henschen (*AASS*, June III, pp. 350–1) believed this to be the earliest of the lives of Avitus. Krusch (*MGH, SRM*, III, 380–1) proved that it was derived from the other three lives discussed above. Poncelet (1905, pp. 16–17 and 53–6) identified the bulk of the sources used by the author. He did not realize, however, that the prologue was drawn almost verbatim from that of Letaldus' *Vita s. Martini Vertavensis*: compare *Vita s. Aviti IV* (prologue, p. 351) to *Vita s. Martini Vertavensis* (prologue in *AASS*, Oct. x, p. 805).

[43] Ménard 1750–8, I, 54–6, and *preuves* 4–8; *VSBP*, IX, 145; Renaud 1978b. The original *Passio s. Baudelii* from Nîmes is *BHL* 1043.

author did not substantively alter his source and the clerics of Nîmes paid no regard to the new traditions in the Orléanais. The only major additions made by the author from Saint-Aignan concerned how the saint had gotten from Orléans to Nîmes and, posthumously, back again.

The translation of relics into the diocese posed similar problems concerning the identity of those new saints. After the monks of Fleury received – probably towards the end of the tenth century – the relics of a saint named Maurus from Brittany, an anonymous monk adapted a text concerning a martyr of that name whose relics were venerated in the Istrian city of Porec (Parenzo). The Fleury author changed little in his source except to explain how the relics had travelled from Istria to Brittany, and thence to Fleury.[44] No one in Istria ever seems to have taken notice of the Fleury traditions. In the early decades of the eleventh century Vitalis of Fleury reworked the ninth-century *Vita s. Pauli Aureliani*.[45] Vitalis excused the composition of a new work both because the old one was so tediously lengthy and because the Latin of its author (a Breton named Wormonoc of Landévennec) was so wretched that reading it became 'an onerous burden'.[46] True to his word, Vitalis excised much material from the earlier *vita*. Andrew of Fleury remarked, 'Another man, Vitalis, both in name and deed, corrected with the judgement of his provident incisiveness the life of the excellent Paul, the celebrated eremitcal bishop of the Bretons.'[47]

The monks of Ferrières also acquired relics around the year 1000. The fortunes of the abbey had declined considerably since the ninth century: Abbo of Fleury cited Ferrières as an example of an abbey in need of reform.[48] While residing at Fleury a monk of Ferrières named Aimo was afflicted be severe fevers. In a dream he was

---

[44] Poncelet 1899a; Vidier 1965, pp. 97–100. The Istrian *Passio s. Mauri* is *BHL* 5787, the Fleury text is *BHL* 5789. About a century later Rodulfus Tortarius adapted that prose *passio* into verse (*BHL* 5790).

[45] Vidier 1965, pp. 101–2. Vitalis' text is *BHL* 6586, his source is *BHL* 6585. See also A. Thomas 1889, pp. 219–22. On the Breton author's reworking of his own source, see Smith 1985, pp. 57–9.

[46] Vitalis of Fleury, *Vita s. Pauli Aureliani*, c. 1, p. 112.

[47] Andrew of Fleury, *Vita Gauzlini*, c. 2, pp. 34–6. See also pp. 36–7 n. 1 on Vitalis' text.

[48] 'Quod quam frivolum sit et omnino vacuum, vicinum nobis Sancti Petri monasterium, quod dicitur Ferrarias, indicat, priscis temporibus regia munificentia magnificentissimum Romanae Ecclesiae membrum nunc vero suorum vassalorum beneficio ita corrosum, ut vix aliquid remanserit ad stipendia paucorum fratrum. Haec et alia rogant violentorum lacrymae.' Abbo of Fleury, *Epistolae*, no.1, col. 421A.

informed that he would be cured by the relics of St Montana. He went on pilgrimage to the Berry where he found her relics and was cured. He later stole the relics and transported them back to his own abbey.[49] The *Vita s. Montanae* (*BHL* 6008) was composed sometime thereafter. The author simply adapted the story of another female monastic saint, Gertrude of Nivelles (*BHL* 3490), to provide a past for the relics newly resident at his abbey. The author did little more than substitute the name of Montana and other local details for those found in Gertrude's story.[50] The veneration of saints' relics in general, and that of Montana in particular, never played an important role in the life of the community of Ferrières.[51]

It is striking how freely these authors adapted stories from earlier hagiographic works. Only Vitalis of Fleury and the anonymous monk of Micy limited themselves to texts which specifically concerned their subject. In other cases the saint treated by the author from the Orléanais shared only a name (Baudelius and Maurus), a regional origin (Viator and Laetus), or simply gender (Montana) with the subject of the source text. They frequently did little more than change the names of the saint involved, or add brief descriptions of how the saint's relics had come to the Orléanais. These authors dealt with saints whose veneration was less deeply rooted than that of the long-standing 'fathers' of the diocese. They wrote primarily out of a pressing need to cloak relics with an ancient identity and to provide *lectiones* for their feastdays. Their works bear many of the marks of repetitive story-telling found in oral culture, but it would be wrong to dismiss them as uncreative for that reason. As one anthropologist has remarked about literary endeavours in such cultures, '[A person's] achievement, be it ballad or shrine, tends to get incorporated (or rejected) in an anonymous fashion. It is not that the creative element is absent, though its character is different.'[52] These authors sought to make their

---

[49] The story is printed in *AASS*, Oct. X, p. 860. Mabillon first published it from an unspecified manuscript source. Since the author referred to Ferrières as 'suum monasterium' in reference to Aimo, the author of this brief anecdote was probably from Fleury.

[50] For a comparison of the two texts see Le Cointe 1665–83, III, 470–7.

[51] In the sixteenth century Louis de Blanchfort placed the head of the virgin in a rich reliquary on one of the altars of the church, see *AASS*, Oct. X, p. 861. The relics held by the abbey in the late modern period are listed in a memorial of a revolutionary assembly dated 15 August 1791, published by Giradot 1880.   [52] Goody 1977, p. 27.

subjects similar to the traditional 'fathers' of the diocese, either by directly linking them to those saints as disciples and companions or by giving them similar antiquity and status. Fançois Dolbeau has pointed out that, in texts which are simply a collection of commonplaces adapted from older sources, the use of *topoi* masks a more complex reality.[53] Although none of these saints – with the notable exceptions of Viator and Laetus – became the patrons of their foundations, these works demonstrate that hagiographers of the Capetian period were conscious both of the status of the region's 'fathers' and of the works of their Carolingian predecessors.

The traditional 'fathers' of the diocese appeared in eleventh-century hagiography primarily as the subjects of collections of posthumous miracle stories. Such works celebrated the power of the *patrocinium* exercised by the saints over these religious communities and more generally over the people of the Orléanais. Significantly the first piece of hagiography composed in the diocese during this period – Letaldus of Micy's *Miracula s. Maximini* – was such a work. The author went on to compose similar works for a number of far-flung communities, as well as liturgical and mock-epic verse. Given the importance of the shrine of St Benedict it is not surprising to find the largest miracle collections composed at Fleury.[54] In 1005 Aimo began a collection in two books (*BHL* 1125) intended to bridge the gap from the time of Adrevald to his own.[55] Then in the 1040s Andrew composed another collection in three books which focused on the miracles performed by Benedict at Fleury's many dependencies. A few years later he added a book which returned to Fleury itself (*BHL* 1126).[56] Both monks wrote other works of biography and history.

[53] Dolbeau 1981b, p. 173.

[54] For an overview of the writing of history and hagiography at Fleury during the course of this century, see Bautier 1975b.

[55] *Miracula s. Benedicti*, II.prologue and III.1, pp. 90–2 and 126–8. Vidier 1965, pp. 180–4 and 192–5. The books comprise Books II and III of the Certain edition of the *Miracula s. Benedicti*. Aimo also wrote a brief set of four miracle stories attributed to St Benedict (*BHL* 1136–9), see Vidier 1965, pp. 184–91. On Aimo, also see *DHGE*, I, 1185–7; Manitius 1911–31, II, 239–46; Berland 1983–4.

[56] Vidier 1965, pp. 199–207. These comprise Books IV to VII of the Certain edition of the *Miracula s. Benedicti*. Andrew claimed (IV.prologue, pp. 173–4) to have begun the work eleven years after the death of Abbot Gauzlin (that is in 1041) and he dedicated the work to King Henry I in the twelfth year of his reign (that is in 1043). Most historians agree that Andrew wrote the first three books between those two years, see, for example, Bautier and Labory 1969, pp. 11–13. Vidier (1965, pp. 202–3), on the other hand, claims less convincingly that Andrew began the research for the work in 1041 and then began to

They conceived of their miracle collections as direct continuations of that of Adrevald.[57] In the first decades of the twelfth century Rodulfus Tortarius – a prolific poet – and Hugh of Fleury – a noted historian and author of *A Book on Royal Power and Priestly Dignity* which was of significance to the papal reform movement – each added another collection of miracle stories (*BHL* 1129 and 1135).[58] Rodulfus also wrote versions of the earlier miracle collections (*BHL* 1130–4).

These men were prolific authors who included hagiography within a wide range of literary and other activites. Letaldus was probably the relative of a former abbot of Micy, served as *cancellarius* for the community, and later tried to take the office of abbot through judicial expulsion of the serving abbot.[59] Aimo was the student, friend, and finally biographer of the murdered Abbot Abbo. On the ill-fated trip to La Réole in 1004, Abbo stayed at the *villa* named *Ad Francos* which belonged to Aimo's family and there met his mother.[60] Andrew was the scion of a knightly family, an intimate of Abbot Gauzlin, and seems to have been among the *sapientiores* of Fleury who accompanied that abbot to the trial of heretics at Orléans in 1022.[61] Hugh of Fleury also came from a knightly family and may have helped to execute the decorative columns in the nave of the church of the Virgin.[62] Similarly Helgaud – who composed not a miracle collection but a life of Robert the Pious – held the offices of *chimiliarchus* (guardian of the abbey's relics and treasury) and *precentor* (leader of the monastic

write in 1043. The fourth book was added sometime before 1056. An anonymous continuator added several chapters to that book after that date (*Miracula s. Benedicti*, VII.14–17; *BHL* 1127–8). On Andrew, also see *HLF*, VII, 349–50; Manitius 1911–31, II, 239–46; Head 1987a, pp. 514–15.

[57] *Miracula s. Benedicti*, II.prologue, p. 92, and IV.prologue, p. 173.

[58] Vidier 1965, pp. 209–14. These comprise Books VIII and IX of the Certain edition of the *Miracula s. Benedicti*. Hugh later stated (*Miracula s. Benedicti*, IX.prologue, p. 357) that Rodulfus had left his work incomplete on his death, which occurred *c.* 1114 (see Bar 1975, pp. 1–2). The only extant manuscript of Hugh's work is incomplete. On Rodulfus, also see Manitius 1911–31, II, 872–7; Bar 1937, pp. 3–8, and 1975; *Rodulfi Tortarii Carmina*, pp. ix–lx. On Hugh, also see *DTC*, VII, 239–40; Manitius 1911–31, III, 518–21; *HLF*, X, 285–306; Lettinck 1981, pp. 386–8.

[59] Letaldus of Micy, *Miracula s. Maximini*, cc. 21–2, pp. 603–4; 'Chartes de Micy', no. 11, p. 67; Abbo of Fleury, *Epistolae*, no. 11, cols. 436–8. The fact that the two monks shared a relatively uncommon name and that the author entered the community of Micy as an *infantulus* not long after the abbacy of the earlier Letaldus strongly suggest that they were related.

[60] Aimo of Fleury, *Vita s. Abbonis*, c. 18, p. 53; Berland 1983–4, pp. 7–8.

[61] *Miracula s. Benedicti*, VII.10, pp. 266–7, and VI.20, p. 247; Head 1987a, p. 514 and the bibliography cited there. [62] Vergnolle 1985, pp. 254–7.

choir), used his considerable artisanal talents to improve the abbey's main church and construct a new church to house relics of St Dionysius, and carried out at least one mission on behalf of King Robert.[63] While his family background was never specified, he must also have been of relatively high birth for he was able to purchase in his own right a *villa* for the sum of £9 and donate it to his abbey.[64] Thus at both Micy and Fleury, the community's hagiographers seem to have come from a cadre of important monks who, being men both of good birth and of general artistic and intellectual ability, served their abbeys in a number of different ways.

The authors of miracle collections from other sanctuaries have remained anonymous. The *Miracula s. Aniani* (*BHL* 476 b)[65] was composed, probably by a canon of Saint-Aignan, during the second half of the eleventh century. The *Miracula ss. Georgii et Laeti* (*BHL* 3398d) was composed by a canon of Pithiviers during the episcopacy of Isembard (1033–63).[66] In addition, a monk of Micy added short descriptions of two cures, one of which occurred around Easter of 1041, to Letaldus' *Miracula s. Maximini*,[67] while another wrote, sometime after 1074, a detailed description of the trials and cure of a pilgrim named Henry (*BHL* 5821 b).[68]

This interest in collecting contemporary miracle stories associated with the relics of the 'fathers' was part of the resurgence of the cult of the saints in the years after 1000. Considering newly discovered relics and the churches which housed them, Rodulfus Glaber noted,

When . . . the locations of the relics of many saints, which had long been hidden, were revealed by the signs of various evidences (*diversorum argumentorum indiciis*). As if awaiting some decoration of a resurrection by

---

[63] *Miracula s. Benedicti*, VII.11, p. 267; Andrew of Fleury, *Vita Gauzlini*, c. 2, p. 38, and c. 47, pp. 86–8; *Miracula s. Benedicti*, VI.7, p. 228; Helgaud of Fleury, *Epitoma vitae regis Rotberti pii*, c. 26, pp. 122–4. See also Bautier and Labory 1965, pp. 16–20.

[64] Andrew of Fleury, *Vita Gauzlini*, c. 47, p. 88.

[65] Renaud 1976, particularly p. 253. The work was written after 1053, the date of one source used by the author, and probably around 1070.

[66] *AASS*, Nov. III, p. 68, *commentarius praevius*, n. 3. This work survives only in an incomplete version. C. de la Saussaye (1615, p. 393) lists a group of seven miracle stories from the church at Pithiviers which he read 'in actis ecclesiae Pitverensis manuscriptum'. From his notices it is clear that four of them are those contained in the present version of the work.

[67] *Miracula s. Maximini*, cc. 56–7. This appendix does not have a separate *BHL* number and is included in both known manuscripts of Letaldus' work.

[68] Head 1984, pp. 221–2 and 235–6.

the will of God, they became visible to the consideration of the faithful to whose minds they also brought many a consolation.[69]

For Rodulfus these *indicia* were primarily miracles.[70] Such *indicia* were collected either, in the case of long-venerated relics, to demonstrate the posthumous power of the saints or, in the case of newly venerated relics, to prove their holiness. There was a subtle difference in these enterprises. In addition to the collection of Benedict's posthumous miracles, Aimo of Fleury compiled a second, shorter collection of miracles performed at Abbo's tomb at La Réole immediately after his martyrdom there (*BHL* 4). Such collections which 'manifested' the miracles of a newly deceased saint became very popular in the twelfth century and were eventually adapted into the process of canonization instituted by the Fourth Lateran Council.[71] Aimo's work was the only example of this genre in the Orléanais.

While the authors of the miracle collections apparently gathered stories from oral sources, they rarely discussed that process and in general flatly asserted the truth of the material which they wove together. As Hugh of Fleury wrote introducing his work, 'I will therefore follow a true story, weaving in nothing false, since I know it is written: "The false witness will not go unpunished."'[72] Some contemporary authors from other regions were more specific about their method. Bernard of Angers, who collected the miracles of St Faith at Conques, neatly reversed a common *topos* when he said that he used an oral source 'not only sense for sense, but even word for word'.[73] The recording of the posthumous miracles of the saints developed in the Orléanais during a time in which modes of record-keeping more generally were developing from ones grounded in memory and oral traditions to ones preserved in writing.[74] The general method by which these authors approached their oral sources may be discovered by studying the structure of their works.[75] In the ninth century Adrevald divided his work roughly in half: the first part covering

[69] Rodulfus Glaber, *Historiarum libri quinque*, III.6.19, pp. 126–7.
[70] Cf. Stock (1983, p. 64) who interprets these *indicia* to be written texts.
[71] Finucane 1977, pp. 100–12; Vauchez 1981, pp. 39–68.
[72] *Miracula s. Benedicti*, IX.prologue, p. 357.
[73] Bernard of Angers, *Liber miraculorum s. Fidis*, 'Letter to Fulbert of Chartres', p. 3. See Stock 1983, pp. 65–71.
[74] Clanchy (1979) has provided a model study of this change for England. Unfortunately no such comprehensive study exists for France.
[75] For comparisons see Sigal 1980, pp. 249–56.

events down to the reign of Charlemagne, that is well before Adrevald's lifetime, and the second concerning miracles performed during the reign of Louis the Pious, events which had happened within the memory of people still living in the monastery. Hercambaldus, for example, who had seen Benedict in a vision, could testify *viva voce* to the truth of Adrevald's written account.[76]

This division between the events of a distant past and a past within the living memory of a community was continued in later miracle collections. It was also a common division within medieval historiography as a whole.[77] Aimo chose the election of Hugh Capet as king of the western Franks (987) and the almost contemporaneous election of Abbo as abbot of Fleury (988) as the dividing point for his two books of the *Miracula s. Benedicti*. Since Aimo entered Fleury as a child during the abbacy of Amalbert (*c.* 978–85), this division corresponds roughly to the point at which his own memory would have served as a guide. In the first book, Aimo attributed the lack of records about miracles from the abbacy of Odo of Cluny in part to 'the negligence of writers that has turned them over to oblivion.'[78] In the second book he admitted that he had been absent from Fleury when one miracle occurred, but told it 'from the relation of elders'.[79] Letaldus made a similar division in the *Miracula s. Maximini*, remarking, 'In the time of the same pious Abbot Anno, when I was a small child (for I am now telling not what I hear, but what I have seen) that which I call a miracle occurred.'[80] When Letaldus circulated what amounted to a first draft of his work among the older monks (*venerandi*) of his community, they reminded him of various stories he had neglected to include.[81] Andrew pointed out that, while the witnesses of a miracle at Châtillon-sur-Loire were no longer alive, the provost of that priory had himself heard the story from them and relayed it to him.[82] Hugh included thirteen miracles which occurred at the monastery of Fleury during a period (1114–18) when he was

[76] *Miracula s. Benedicti*, 1.20, p. 48.
[77] Lacroix 1971, p. 45 n. 74; Guenée 1975–6.   [78] *Miracula s. Benedicti*, II.4, p. 101.
[79] *Miracula s. Benedicti*, III.9, p. 150–1.   [80] *Miracula s. Maximini*, c. 34, p. 607.
[81] 'Scribentibus nobis secundum possibilitatem ingenioli nostri de virtutibus praecellentissimi Patris nostri Maximini quosdam contigit venerandos assuisse, quibus petentibus cum ea quae dicta erant revolueremus, multa omisisse, nos quibus ipsi interfuerant confessi sunt, revocabantque nostrae memoriae inter multa hoc quod dicturi sumus miraculum.' *Miracula s. Maximini*, c. 45, p. 610.
[82] *Miracula s. Benedicti*, v.5, p. 199.

resident there and heard the reports of the witnesses.[83] These authors all recognized the reliable boundaries of communal memory and showed a concern for precision in the recording of oral sources.

These authors rarely discussed the exact sources of their tales. Rodulfus Tortarius, for example, attempted to identify the people and properties which figured in his stories as precisely as possible. In one story the two participants were described as 'Hugh, surnamed Bidulfus, one of the knights who inhabited Perrecy' and 'a certain peasant, Guarinus by name, surnamed by the place Cumbis'.[84] In another 'Archembald, surnamed Albus, a strong man' sought to take control of 'a certain possession, called Sulmeriacus, which belonged to Perrecy and which every year provided not inconsiderable supplies of food'.[85] Yet Rodulfus did not detail what sort of sources he used, although some oral or, more likely, written material from Perrecy must have been available for him to tell such detailed stories. The only exception was his relation of a court case of which he learned through the memory of Abbot Hugh (1060–7).[86] Nor were other authors much more forthcoming. Several witnessed miracles themselves.[87] A few people who either received a cure from or had been punished by a saint at a distance from the tomb came to the shrine to report the miracle.[88] A similar report was provided by the Breton hermit Felix, who was saved from drowning by invoking Benedict's name. He not only told the monks of Fleury about the miracle, but joined the community.[89] When Abbot Gervinus of Saint-Riquier was at a gathering of many important abbots from the Capetian realm, including Ragnerius of Fleury (1044–60), he related a story which he had heard at Monte Cassino of a miraculous vision of Benedict in that place.[90] In still other cases witnesses of a miracle later provided testimony about it.[91]

---

[83] *Miracula s. Benedicti*, ix.prologue, p. 357.   [84] *Miracula s. Benedicti*, viii.46, pp. 352–3.
[85] *Miracula s. Benedicti*, viii.48, p. 355.   [86] *Miracula s. Benedicti*, viii.11, p. 287.
[87] *Translatio s. Lifardi* cc. 2–3, pp. 157–8; *Miracula s. Lifardi*, c. 13, p. 162; *Miracula s. Benedicti*, vii.9, pp. 265–6.
[88] For example, *Miracula s. Benedicti*, vi.10, p. 233; viii.12, p. 292; ix.5, p. 363.
[89] *Miracula s. Benedicti*, iii.12, pp. 155–8. On the later career of Felix, see Andrew of Fleury, *Vita Gauzlini*, c. 24, pp. 64–5.   [90] *Miracula s. Benedicti*, vii.15, pp. 272–4.
[91] 'Fit ad hoc miraculum tam clericorum quam ceterorum omnium concursus.' *Miracula s. Aniani*, c. 16, p. 271. 'Complures etiam custodes testati sunt se eum vidisse et ad lumen succendendum virga tactos evigilasse.' *Miracula s. Aniani*, c. 14, p. 270. 'In crastinum vero per semetipsam veniens ad monasterium, totum nostrum exhilaravit conventum.' *Miracula s. Benedicti*, ix.5, p. 363. 'Quaedam mulier Giomensis castri, fama signorum

Hagiography and the cult of saints

Some authors also used written sources. Aimo claimed that his knowledge of the Norman invasions came from both witnesses and the work of Adrevald.[92] Andrew included the text of a peace oath taken in the diocese of Bourges and referred to a charter contained in Fleury's archives.[93] Such archival records, however, were frequently lacking. The author of the *Miracula s. Lifardi* searched the 'library of the diocese of Orléans' for royal, ducal, or pontifical documents bearing the seal of his community. He ascribed the lack of such documents to the fact that his community had not possessed a scriptorium and that its history had frequently been troubled by wars.[94]

When authors described the process of reporting a miracle, it was usually to show either that people had originally doubted its veracity or that onlookers had joined in its celebration. While the monks of Fleury did investigate the authenticity of one cure at their own house in the ninth century and of several cures of women which occurred at their priory of Perrecy in the eleventh century, such critical investigation was not the norm.[95] Adrevald admitted that the former investigation occurred because the monks did not trust the crippled man, who had come to Fleury as a beggar, and Aimo suggested that in the latter case the monks were dubious because Perrecy did not possess sufficient relics of the saint to warrant miraculous cures. The clerics were certainly aware that lay culture differed vastly from their own and that collecting their stories involved an act of translation. Andrew reported Latin versions of the vulgar, that is French, words for the disease of ergotism (*ignis sacer* for *feu sacré*) and the activity of hunting fowl (*panterae* for *panthères*).[96] He also said that one man's description of

adscita patris Benedicti, ad hoc venit coenobium, quae loquendi perdiderat usum, et jam toto triennio linguae caruerat officio . . . At illa surrexit et abiit et mox facultatem loquendi recepit; nos quoque e vestigio signa pulsantes, *Te Deum laudamus* pronunciavimus et fine tenus decantavimus.' *Miracula s. Benedicti*, IX.7, pp. 364–5. 'Tunc quoque domnus abbas et quidam de fratribus procedentes de more ad altare cum turibulis, dum uiderent quod iaceret super pauimentum inmobilis, didicerunt tumultuanti populorum murmure qualiter pedes eius nudati essent calciamentis. Ipse enim nichil omnino loquebatur.' *Miraculum s. Maximini*, p. 248.   [92] *Miracula s. Benedicti*, II.1, p. 95.
[93] *Miracula s. Benedicti*, v.2, pp. 193–4, and VI.9, p. 231.
[94] *Miracula s. Lifardi*, c. 2, p. 160. See the similar sentiments of Paul of Saint-Père de Chartres, who, around 1088, attempted to collect the charters of his community: 'Utrum autem vetustate abolitae sunt, aut hostium igne crematae, aut nunquam scriptae, scribarum penuria, minime scio.' *Cartulaire de Saint-Père de Chartres*, I, 48. See also Stock 1983, pp. 73–7.   [95] *Miracula s. Benedicti*, I.23, p. 54, and III.18, p. 166.
[96] *Miracula s. Benedicti*, IV.1, p. 175 and VI.8, p. 230. Letaldus of Micy (*Miracula s. Martini Vertavensis*, c. 5 in MGH, SRM, III, 571) similarly reported the Latin *ivus* of the vulgar *if*.

76

a vision was affected by the fact that he had a 'peasant's mind'.[97] In any case, reports of miracles by laypeople and investigations of those miracles by clerics occurred on an irregular basis. In one case the monks of Fleury only learned that a man had been released from demonic possession because his shouts attracted them into the church from the nearby chapter-room where they had been gathered.[98] There is no indication that any clerics were specifically charged with recording miracles at the shrines of the 'fathers' of the diocese, offices such as would later develop at Canterbury and elsewhere, although Hugh of Fleury may have informally and briefly served in such a capacity.[99]

The limited but insistent references in the miracle collections to oral sources suggest that a good deal of story-telling about the saints and their miracles occurred among both the members of the religious communities and the laity. According to Rodulfus Tortarius, when a plough which was being used to work a field on a feastday of Benedict broke, the peasants using it reflected on the circumstances of the event and decided that Benedict had punished them.[100] Hugh attributed the visits of many pilgrims to their having heard tales of the prodigies of St Benedict in their villages.[101] In the early Capetian period there was a concerted effort to capture those stories into texts so that they might be preserved. These 'oral circles' were the underpinning of much of the hagiography written in the region.[102] It remains difficult, however, to locate and document the move from 'oral circles' to texts. Aimo provided one tantalizing clue. In introducing the story of a knight of Reims who was chastised by Benedict, he commented, 'We are now entreated to relate one noteworthy work of his, I mean father Benedict, which we happen to know by the relation or writing of a certain brother, who testified that it had been told him by faithful men of the church of Reims.'[103] This passage implies not only that there were sometimes written intermediaries between oral tradition and text, but that stories of far reaching interest were passed from one community to another. Moreover it seems that this story was well known at Fleury and that Aimo's brothers pressed for its inclusion in the collection.

[97] *Miracula s. Benedicti*, v.6, p. 203.   [98] *Miracula s. Benedicti*, VIII.29, p. 326.
[99] Finucane 1977, pp. 100–3 and 125–6; Ward 1982, pp. 89–93.
[100] *Miracula s. Benedicti*, VIII.12, pp. 291–2.
[101] For example, *Miracula s. Benedicti*, IX.4, 5, and 6, pp. 362–3.
[102] I have borrowed this phrase from Stock 1983.   [103] *Miracula s. Benedicti*, II.6, p. 105.

The manuscript of the *Miraculum s. Maximini* provides some insight into how such traditions were preserved and circulated.[104] The work was an extended narrative of how a German nobleman named Henry had come to Micy and been cured of his lameness there through the intercession of St Maximinus. Since Henry remained for seven years as a servant in the abbey, the narrative was almost certainly recorded by a monk who knew him. It was written down in a somewhat careless hand in a crudely fashioned *libellus*. This little booklet was made from several scraps of poor-quality parchment, several of which had been scraped down after previous use as charters. The author recorded a story popular in his community on what was essentially scrap paper saved from the abbey's chancery, possibly with an eye to preserving the story for inclusion in a more formal collection of miracle stories. The booklet was fortuitously preserved, in incomplete form, as part of a collection of various hagiographic works from Micy bound together in the early modern period. It is impossible to determine how many similar booklets were kept in the archives of religious houses, which probably consisted of little more than a wooden cupboard or chest, waiting to serve as source material for later authors. Such works would have provided one bridge to connect the process of story-telling to the process of hagiographic composition.

Reliance on the miraculous powers of their patrons, however, did not completely suffice the needs of these religious communities. In addition to their collections of miracle stories, Aimo composed a life of Abbot Abbo (*BHL* 3) and Andrew one of Abbot Gauzlin of Fleury; their contemporary Helgaud of Fleury composed a life of Robert the Pious which stressed the relationship of the king to the community of Saint-Aignan and their patron saint. In these lives of contemporaries, all steeped in the tradition of hagiography, the monks of Fleury advanced the principles of the monastic reform envisioned by their martyred abbot, some of which had earlier found expression in Abbo's own account of the life of King Edmund. A canon of Pithiviers also wrote an account of the life of Gregory of Nicopolis (*BHL* 3669), a wandering holy man who had come to Pithiviers early in the eleventh century and lived as a hermit there. These were striking new developments. By claiming that these two contemporaries were saints, the clerics of the diocese

---

[104] Vatican, Reg. lat. 621, fos. 29–33; Head 1984, particularly pp. 235–6 on the manuscript.

began to redefine their concept of sanctity by recognizing the possibility of its presence in their own midst. The frank claim that Abbo made for the sanctity of King Edmund of England and the hagiographic overtones in the accounts of the lives of Robert the Pious and Gauzlin significantly expanded the horizons within which sanctity might be found.

Like collections of posthumous miracle stories these lives were largely based on current oral traditions. Some of the stories told in them were remembered by the authors themselves: Aimo was a monk under Abbo and Helgaud was an intimate of the court circles of King Robert. The canon of Pithiviers described his sources: 'In part we saw [these things] with our own eyes; in part we accept them from others who, enjoying [Gregory's] most saintly conversation and friendship, saw them with their own eyes; in part we learned them from parents and friends.'[105] In the case of Abbo's *Vita s. Edmundi* the story was third-generation. There was no written record of the king's life. When the monks of Ramsey discovered that Abbo had, while visiting Canterbury, heard Archbishop Dunstan tell Edmund's story, they asked him to put this *monimentum* into writing. Dunstan's story came *ex antiquitatis memoria*. As Abbo described it, addressing the archbishop in the dedicatory epistle,

You said, your eyes full of tears, that in your youth you had learned [the story] from an old man, who related it simply and in good faith to the most glorious king of the Angles, Athelstan, declaring by oath that he had been armour-bearer to the blessed man, on the very day on which the martyr laid down his life for Christ's sake.[106]

The move from observation, memory, and oral sources to written composition can be most fully observed in Helgaud's *Epitoma vitae regis Rotberti pii*.[107] The sole surviving copy is found in Reginensis latinus 566.[108] The main text is copied in two similar scribal hands. The second copyist corrected some of the work of the first scribe. A third hand – not a professional hand and

---

105 *Vita s. Gregorii Nicopolitani*, c. 11, p. 464.
106 Abbo of Fleury, *Vita s. Edmundi*, prologue, p. 67.
107 Bautier and Labory 1965, pp. 28–47.
108 Vatican, Reg. lat. 566, fos. 7–22. The codex is a collection of hagiographic fragments bound together in the sixteenth century. For a description of the codex, see *Catal. Vat.*, pp. 374–5. Poncelet did not describe the fragment containing Helgaud's work, apparently because he did not consider it to be hagiography. On the relevant fragment, see Bautier and Labory 1965, pp. 28–32.

apparently that of Helgaud himself – made further additions in the margins and corrections in the main body of the text. Thus Helgaud apparently dictated a first version of the work to a scribe of the Fleury scriptorium. Later he massively expanded and revised the work using the services of a different scribe. Still later he corrected the text himself. Moreover Helgaud made a rough copy of his description of one of the most important events in his story. That was the consecration of the rebuilt church of Saint-Aignan under the supervision of Robert the Pious in 1029, of which he quite possibly was an eyewitness. His own copy of the draft, in a hand identical to that of the third hand of Reginensis latinus 566, has fortuitously survived in Reginensis latinus 585.[109] He left blank spaces for certain technical details, such as the dimensions of the church and the number of windows in it, which were filled in by another hand. He seems to have jotted down his own memory of the event and then submitted his work to someone else to fill in forgotten or unknown details. Later he incorporated this description in largely the same manner, and often the same words, into his final, that is dictated, version.[110]

Written sources also played a role in the composition of these lives. Aimo's *Vita s. Abbonis* was in part a florilegium of passages culled from Abbo's own writings, pieced together with factual biographical detail and a few stories which Aimo recalled about his abbot and friend. This method of composition was similar to that employed earlier by Aimo in his *Historiae francorum*.[111] Other writers from Fleury, most particularly Andrew, used the monastery's archives for such materials as charters and letters pertaining to the monastery's property.[112] Helgaud had the *Testamentum Leodebodi*, that is the foundation charter of Fleury, copied at the beginning of his *Epitoma vitae regis Rotberti pii* since he wished to

---

[109] Vatican, Reg. lat. 585, fo. 58. The text is edited and discussed by Auvray 1887. See the further comments of Bautier and Labory 1965, pp. 37–42.

[110] Helgaud of Fleury, *Epitoma vitae regis Rotberti pii*, c. 22, pp. 106–14.

[111] Aimo defended that approach, to Abbo himself, in the dedicatory epistle. 'Calumniabuntur enim tempora, convertent ordinem, res arguent, syllabas eventilabunt, et (quod accidere plerumque solet) negligentiam librariorum ad auctorem referent. Dicent etiam: "En noster historiographus novusque auctor qui aliorum verbis, pro suis utitur." Hoc quidem me fecisse non nego neque me id piget; ac deinde facturum autumo. Habeo bonorum exemplum, quo mihi id licere facere quod illi fecerunt puto. Nec sententiis detrahentium satis moveor: tua laude vel vituperatione doctus esse sufficiens.' *Historiae francorum libri quatuor*, 'Letter to Abbo', col. 628c.

[112] See, for example, the papal and episcopal correspondence reproduced in Andrew of Fleury, *Vita Gauzlini*, c. 18, pp. 52–8.

compare Robert's relation to the monasteries of Fleury and Saint-Aignan to that of Abbot Leodebodus.[113]

Archbishop Dunstan's dinnertable conversation about King Edmund, Aimo's personal memories of his murdered abbot and friend, his aside concerning the origin of the story of Benedict's miracle in Reims, the reminiscences of the friends and relatives of the canon of Pithiviers, the *libellus* containing the story of Henry's cure, and the spaces left blank in the first draft of Helgaud's work all stand as evidence that, no matter how shadowy the oral culture of the middle ages seems now, it was a vibrant and important part of life in religious communities of the eleventh century. Speaking of medieval historiography, Benoît Lacroix has commented that 'oral traditions reigned as a master to such an extent that one might ask if an interpretation of the middle ages is of any value without knowledge of the mechanisms of oral transmission'.[114] As both story-tellers and religious, the hagiographers of the Orléanais themselves were immersed in that culture and served as part of those mechanisms. It was not always an easy task. Aimo complained bitterly about the jealousy which his writings inspired among his fellow monks.[115]

Although many of the texts already discussed would seem to belie the fact, there were signs during this period that a critical attitude toward written sources was becoming more fully developed among some hagiographers.[116] As in the ninth century, the authors of the Orléanais who critically examined their sources usually did so in works requested by clerical communities located outside the region, rather than in the composition of local hagiography. These writers, however, were no longer members of court circles, but monks whose literary corpus was almost exclusively hagiographic and whose audience came from more narrowly defined regions. The best examples of this mentality were Letaldus of Micy and Hugh of Fleury, who worked a century apart.

Letaldus' first work, the *Miracula s. Maximini*, was composed for his own community. It included both a history of that abbey and contemporary miracle stories from the shrine of the saint. In the prologue Letaldus asserted that he accepted only those stories for which he had eyewitnesses or which had been surely handed down

[113] Vatican, Reg. lat. 566, fos. 3–7. For the comparison of king and abbot, see Helgaud of Fleury, *Epitoma vitae regis Rotberti pii*, c. 1, pp. 56–8.   [114] Lacroix 1971, p. 50.
[115] *Miracula s. Benedicti*, III.22, p. 171.   [116] Schreiner 1966a, particularly pp. 14–20.

either by written texts (*litterae*) or by oral tradition (*traditio vivae vocis*). 'And where there is neither of these things, and there is some question as to whether it happened or not, all men will be silent with me.'[117] At various points in the narrative he emphasized the reliability of his sources. He noted, for instance, that a story about the ninth-century abbot Hericus was the 'true relation of elders'.[118] Later he said that he would relate only those things which he himself had seen or which had been told to him by eyewitnesses and reliable informants.[119] While Letaldus thus employed his professed principles in the treatment of Micy's recent history, he composed the more ancient history of his abbey in a fashion reminiscent of Bertholdus and other Carolingian authors. He implied, for instance, that since St Lifardus had been alive at the time of Maximinus, he must have studied the monastic life under the abbot of Micy. That claim ran directly counter to the *Vita s. Lifardi*, which was known to Letaldus, and thus contrary to the critical principles which he claimed to follow.[120]

Over the course of the next two decades Letaldus composed hagiographic works for various ecclesiastical institutions allied to his abbey. Those which he wrote for the monasteries of Saint-Jouin-de-Marnes (*Vita et miracula s. Martini Vertavensis* (BHL 5667–8)) and Selles-sur-Cher (*Vita et miracula s. Eusicii* (BHL 2754 and 2756)) were strikingly similar in form to the *Miracula s. Maximini*. The preface of the *Miracula s. Martini Vertavensis*, for example, contained a touching portrait of a scholarly monk wandering the French countryside in search of sources:

We are going to say scarcely anything about the man of God, Martin, since the book of his life once in the city of Thouars had been burned, and with it the almost incomparable ornaments of his life also perished. Another small volume, however, survived in which various poems were contained, among which is found an abbreviated life of the holy man himself, told in sweet and pleasing rhymes. And so after I had come unworthy and a monk in habit only to the monastery where the remains of the same holy man now rest, I was compelled by the brothers of the place, and most of all by the venerable man Rainald, who holds the office of prefect in the same place, to compose an account in prose from the same

[117] Letaldus of Micy, *Miracula s. Maximini*, prologue, p. 598.
[118] Letaldus of Micy, *Miracula s. Maximini*, c. 16, p. 602.
[119] Letaldus of Micy, *Miracula s. Maximini*, c. 28, p. 605.
[120] Letaldus of Micy, *Miracula s. Maximini*, c. 4, p. 599. Letaldus made a similarly indefensible claim about St Launomaurus both in this passage and in the prologue, p. 598.

poem. Since I was not able to refuse, I composed, in as much as God permitted it, in prose all those things which the book (*libellus*) revealed, with the exception of those things which were said in poetic language; and I expressed [them] in the way of a translator, not word for word, but according to sense; and I expanded it a bit upon the request of the brothers. But, since a group of older men had lived up to our time, who had committed to memory many things from the book of the life of the blessed man, and one of them, that is Rainald, is passing his venerable years right up to today, we thought it right to put down separately whatever we discovered in their account which had not been included in the above mentioned book, making, as it were, another *corpus* of the volume, beginning with those things which Martin did while living in the body and extending on to those things which he accomplished, with Christ working through him, after his death.[121]

Letaldus worked from two separate sources. The first was the relatively abbreviated verse life which was available in the *libellus* at the monastery of Saint-Jouin. It served as the basis for Letaldus' *vita*, as the hagiographer rendered the verse work into prose. Letaldus said that he retold the stories of his written sources 'not word for word, but sense for sense'. The *topos* was a common one to describe the act of translation.[122] The hagiographer regarded the reworking of his source as being in some sense equivalent to translating a text from one language to another.

The writer's second source was a more substantial text which detailed the life of the saint, his posthumous miracles at Vertou, the translation of his relics to Saint-Jouin after the Norman raid of 843, and even miracles performed at the saint's new home. Although the only copy of this work had been destroyed in the fire at Thouars, it served through oral intermediaries as the source for Letaldus' *miracula* (*BHL* 5668). The final story which Letaldus included in his text concerned the chastisement of Duke Rainald of Maine. The duke had taken property from Saint-Jouin, but repented after being confronted by a vision of Martin, John the Baptist, and Peter.[123] Since Rainald died in 885, the lost text probably dated to the late ninth century. Letaldus knew its contents as they were recited to him from memory by the older members of the community, notably the *praepositus*, Rainald. The lost written text was reconstructed by interviewing those members of the

---

[121] Letaldus of Micy, *Miracula s. Martini Vertavensis*, prologue in *MGH, SRM*, III, 567.
[122] Classen 1974, pp. 50–61.
[123] Letaldus of Micy, *Miracula s. Martini Vertavensis*, c. 18 in *MGH, SRM*, III, 575.

community who had earlier heard or read that work. They had probably heard sections of the work as *lectiones* during the liturgy on the saint's feastday. Their familiarity, however, with the broad scope of the work – including the posthumous miracle stories which only rarely served as liturgical *lectiones* – suggests that at least some members of the community had read the text and that its contents had been discussed widely within the community.

The location of the manuscript of the lost hagiographic work is uncertain. The familiarity of the monks with the text suggests that the manuscript had been used at the monastery itself. It was destroyed, however, in a fire at the seat of the local viscounts, approximately 30 kilometres away. The presence of an important hagiographic manuscript with a noble family rather than at the monastery which possessed the saint's relic is puzzling. Usually scholars assume that monastic libraries were the primary repositories of hagiographic works. In this case, however, the local viscount had at the very least borrowed, and may actually have been the primary possessor of, the unique copy of the major hagiographic traditions concerning the monastery's patron. The stress on the age of those who remembered the text indicates that the fire had occurred several decades before Letaldus' commission to produce a replacement. Presumably the alternate verse version of the saint's life had proven insufficient for the liturgical and other needs of the community.

The ability of the older monks of Saint-Jouin to remember the destroyed text of their patron's life and miracles constitutes a remarkable example of what Brian Stock has termed a 'textual community'. These were groups of people who shared the interpretation of a given text in common. Stock chose his examples from groups of intellectuals, reformers, and heretics, not monks using hagiographic traditions. At the beginning of the eleventh century, however, the community at Saint-Jouin seems to have exhibited a similar concern with interpreting and discussing a text even after the written version of that text was no longer available, for, as Stock points out, 'what was essential to a textual community was not a written version of a text'. The monks thus developed, to quote Stock again, 'new uses for orality'.[124] Their concern both with remembering the lost text and with replacing the inadequate verse *libellus* further indicates the important role played by

---

[124] Stock 1983, particularly pp. 90–2.

hagiographic traditions within a community which possessed a saint's relics.

The content of Letaldus' work came from the two original written sources. There is no reason to believe that he added material to the verse *libellus* in the first section of the work, which solely concerned the life of the saint. The latest datable posthumous miracle story in the second section was that which concerned Duke Rainald in the late ninth century. No stories of more recent miracles of Saint-Jouin were added by the monks in their oral transmission of the lost Carolingian text. The manner and language in which the stories were told, however, were formed by the monks' collective memory and, perhaps more importantly, by Letaldus himself. The first story included in the miracle collection demonstrates how this process worked.[125] The story concerned Martin's pilgrimage to Rome. Approaching the city he was joined by St Maximinus of Trier. While Martin was off gathering supplies for the last leg of their journey, Maximinus watched as the ass which they were to use for transport was attacked and consumed by a bear. When Martin returned, he miraculously forced the bear into compliance to take the place of the deceased beast of burden. This incident led to the use of a distinctive type of pectoral chain for bears in the city of Rome.[126] At the end of the story Letaldus observed that 'in our days' such a pectoral chain was still used in Rome. As evidence he cited the eyewitness testimony of a contemporary, Rainald the Thuringian, 'who tells of this and of many other stupendous miracles done by Martin'.[127] It is uncertain whether this reference would have been added by the monks of Saint-Jouin themselves or by Letaldus, but it nevertheless indicates the unabated power of the miracle story for audiences around the year 1000.

At Selles-sur-Cher Letaldus used an *antiquus schedulus* as a source for the life of St Eusicius and interviews with the monks of the community, including the abbot who commissioned the work, to write the collection of posthumous miracles.[128] In both the works for Saint-Jouin and for Saint-Eusice he maintained a strict

---

[125] Letaldus of Micy, *Miracula s. Martini Vertavensis*, c. 1 in *MGH, SRM*, III, 568–9.

[126] Apparently the author of the lost Carolingian text had borrowed this story from Lupus of Ferrières' *Vita s. Maximini Treverensis*, c. 7, p. 77. While attributing the miracle to the *virtus* of his hero, Martin, he was unable to omit Maximinus from the story entirely.

[127] Letaldus refers to Rainald as 'viscount of Angers', the only known occurrence of this title for Rainald. See also Guillot 1972, I, 202–9, and Boussard 1970, pp. 165–6, 170–1, and 192.   [128] Letaldus of Micy, *Miracula s. Eusicii*, prologue, p. 463.

distinction between written (*litterae*) and oral (*traditio vivae vocis*) sources. In both works Letaldus also said that he retold the stories of his written sources 'not word for word, but sense for sense'. The *topos* was a common one to describe the act of translation.[129] Letaldus regarded the reworking of sources from the past for present use to be in some sense equivalent to translating a text from one language to another. That attitude belies an authorial stance of real distance from the events described in those sources.

Since neither the verse *libellus* nor the prose *antiquus schedulus* survives, it is difficult to judge how Letaldus developed his written sources. In the case of the later *Vita s. Juliani* (*BHL* 4544) – a life of the first bishop of Le Mans which Letaldus composed at the request of Bishop Avesgaud of that diocese – it is possible to examine Letaldus' use of such sources in detail.[130] Walter Goffart has shown that Letaldus' source, the *Vita s. Juliani* (*BHL* 4546), was the work of the so-called 'Le Mans forger' in the early ninth century, an author (or authors) who composed a past history of the diocese to support the property claims of the Le Mans cathedral chapter. The 'Le Mans forger' created the life of St Julian by using quotations from earlier hagiographic sources.[131]

Letaldus recognized that his source was corrupt. In the

---

[129] On the *topos*, see Classen 1974, pp. 50–61.

[130] Cf. the treatment of Schreiner 1966a, pp. 28–9.

[131] Goffart 1966, pp. 50–5. *BHL* 4546 has never been published. There are two extant manuscripts, both from Fleury: Vatican, Reg. lat. 318, fos. 235–49v (ninth to tenth centuries: see *Catal. Vat.*, pp. 313–15; Wilmart 1937–45, II, 208–15; Pellegrin 1963, pp. 13–14); and Paris, BN lat. 12606, fos. 13–15 (thirteenth century: see *Catal. Paris.*, III, 142). The work bears close similarities to parts of two other works by the same 'Le Mans forger': the *Vita s. Juliani* (*BHL* 4545) and the first chapter (pp. 28–39) of the *Actus pontificum Cenomannis* (*BHL* 4543). Both works were published by Busson and Ledru in their edition of the *Actus*, although their editions have been made partially obsolete by the work of Goffart (1966, *passim*). The text of the unpublished *BHL* 4546 (Letaldus' source) can in large part be read from the published texts of *BHL* 4543 and *BHL* 4545 (neither of which, in all probability, were used by Letaldus). What follows is a guide. (On this reconstruction of the text of *BHL* 4546, cf. Goffart 1966, p. 54 n. 78.) The text of *BHL* 4546 begins with a unique *incipit* and then follows the text of *BHL* 4543 (p. 28, line 1, to p. 32, line 13). At that point *BHL* 4546 omits a long list of properties given by Count Defensor to the church of St Mary and St Peter. Then *BHL* 4546 continues with the text of *BHL* 4543 (p. 33, line 13, to p. 35, line 13). A unique sentence of connecting material follows. Then *BHL* 4546 continues with the text of *BHL* 4545 (p. 14, line 10, to p. 27 *explicit*). It omits, however, the list of blasphemies (p. 15, lines 17–23) and the cross-references to other works (p. 21, line 26, to p. 22, line 9). The *explicit* of *BHL* 4546 is the same as that of *BHL* 4545. In general the text of *BHL* 4546 follows the texts of *BHL* 4543 and *BHL* 4545 found in a Chartres manuscript (BM 115), whose variants are found in the notes to Busson and Ledru's editions. *BHL* 4546 does, however, include certain minor differences from any published version of the other texts.

dedicatory epistle he explained in detail his task in rewriting that earlier work. He sought to retain what was verifiable and to reject what was not:

I would say that this work [of revision] ought to be one of reverence rather than one of pleasure, for these things should be spoken and written down with the gravity of great reverence. They ought to be recited in the presence of truth . . . For nothing is pleasing to God, except that which is true. Moreover, there are some who, when they seek to exalt the deeds of the saints, offend against the light of truth, as if a lie ought to be raised up for the glory of the saints, who would never have been able to attain the pinacle of sanctity if prevaricators had been in their retinues.[132]

Letaldus concluded that certain stories which could be found 'in the same sense and even in the same words' in the acts of other saints had been falsely added to the original life of Julian. He identified the actual hagiographic sources from which the 'Le Mans forger' had made his pastiche: the *Passio s. Dionysii* (*BHL* 2171), the *Virtutes s. Fursaei* (*BHL* 3213), and the *Passio s. Clementis* (*BHL* 1848).[133] These identifications have since been corroborated in greater detail by modern scholarship.[134] The author of the earlier life stated that Pope Clement had sent Julian, as well as such other early bishops as Dionysius, to France. Letaldus, however, knew from Jerome's translation of Eusebius that Clement had lived under the emperor Trajan. Gregory of Tours also stated that Dionysius and other early bishops came to France in the time of Decius. Moreover Gregory did not mention Julian by name. Thus Letaldus noted that 'neither the reckoning of time nor the authority of the elders agrees with [the earlier life]'.[135]

These conclusions constituted an ingenious piece of historical detection. Both Jerome's translation of Eusebius and Gregory's *History of the Franks* were available in the library at Micy.[136] The

---

[132] Letaldus of Micy, *Vita s. Juliani*, c. 2, cols. 781B–2B.

[133] Letaldus of Micy, *Vita s. Juliani*, c. 3, col. 783B.

[134] Goffart 1966, pp. 50–1 and 54–5.

[135] Letaldus of Micy, *Vita s. Juliani*, c. 3, cols. 783B–4A. See Gregory of Tours, *Historia Francorum*, 1.27, p. 21, and 1.30–1, pp. 23–4. The historical error of placing Dionysius (and hence Julian) in the reign of Trajan comes from the *Passio s. Dionysii*.

[136] Jerome's version of the *Historia Ecclesiastica* is contained in Leiden, University Library, Codex Vossiani Latini Quarto 110 (ninth century: Meyier 1975, pp. 244–6). The *Historia Francorum* is contained in Leiden, Public Library, 21. Both bear an *ex-libris* from Micy. The inscription in the former indicates that it was one of three manuscripts which Abbot Peter placed on the high altar of the Church at Micy during the celebration of Holy Thursday. Letaldus noted elsewhere (*Miracula s. Maximini*, prologue, p. 598) that he was familiar with these manuscripts. For a fuller description of Micy's library, see below pp. 209–11.

identification of the hagiographic works from which the false stories were borrowed demonstrates that Letaldus had a thorough knowledge of hagiographic works. While none of the works can be identified in manuscripts from Micy dating before the twelfth century, they were the sort of texts frequently included in lectionaries, as the feasts of the saints which they commemorated were commonly celebrated.

Having identified his source as corrupt, Letaldus went on to express his desire of seeing through that corruption to an authentic antique tradition: 'We therefore have confirmed, as much as we could from the authority of preceding fathers, what we have written about St Julian, and we have related some things simply according to ancient tradition, but others, which seemed to us less probable, we have omitted.'[137] He likened these traditions to the pleasing rhythms of old songs; to add anything new would be jarring and discordant.[138] Letaldus wished to find the kernel of truth hidden among the falsehoods in his source. The stories which had been added to the life of Julian from the acts of other saints were false and ought to be rejected. What remained would be the actual story of the saint.

Letaldus thus laid down a clear set of criteria for verifying source material and implied that to act contrary to those criteria was to act mendaciously. In these strong condemnations of borrowed stories, he demonstrated a recognition of what would now be called plagiarism or forgery. A comparison of Letaldus' work with his source shows that he did indeed omit much borrowed material. Otherwise he followed – just as he said he would – the order, and sometimes the words, of his source.[139] The earlier author, for example, began with the blessing of Julian by Pope Clement, who then sent Julian on an evangelizing mission to Le Mans, a story adapted from a passage in the *Passio s. Dionysii*.[140] The 'Le Mans forger' thus claimed that Julian's mission was apostolic (although he did not use the word) in that the saint had received his blessing from Clement, who was the successor of Peter. In retelling the story, Letaldus dropped all mention of Clement and stated that

---

[137] Letaldus of Micy, *Vita s. Juliani*, c. 4, col. 784A.

[138] Letaldus of Micy, *Vita s. Juliani*, c. 4, col. 784B.

[139] A full comparison of the two must await a critical edition of the three related texts about St Julian from Le Mans (*BHL* 4543, 4545, and 4546).

[140] *Vita s. Juliani* (*BHL* 4546), p. 28, *incipit* to p. 29, line 7. The source, as identified by Goffart (1966, p. 54 n. 78), is the *Passio s. Dionysii*, cc. 2–3, pp. 102–3. This story tells how Denis was blessed by Clement and then sent to Paris.

Julian's mission was *apostolatus* only in that he was the first apostle of Le Mans.[141] He thus rejected as false a claim concerning the first bishop of Le Mans with the tacit approval of the contemporary bishop of that see.

Letaldus did, however, retain two stories which the 'Le Mans forger' had borrowed from the *Virtutes s. Fursaei*.[142] These concerned Julian's conversion of the Gallo-Roman nobility of Le Mans and the subsequent decision of Count Defensor to donate property to Julian's church, thus renouncing authority over the Christian episcopacy. These stories provided a crucial precedent in the struggle of Bishop Avesgaud, who had commissioned Letaldus' work, against the Count of Le Mans.[143] Although he had enunciated clear canons of verification, and had claimed that to ignore such canons was to lie, Letaldus was willing to retain that part of the earlier text which remained relevant to his client's needs. According to his own criteria Letaldus would seem, in these particular chapters, to be himself guilty of a form of forgery.

The works of Letaldus' contemporary, Theodoric of Fleury, provide an instructive comparison. Theodoric was German in origin, but was drawn to Fleury by its reputation. He later left that monastery in 1002 on an extensive journey, never to return. Over the course of the next decade he composed seven hagiographic works for monastic communities in Italy. While the local circumstances of these texts were far removed from the Orléanais, they still illustrate the mind of an author educated there. Theodoric's three extant works from this period (the *Vita s. Martini papae* (BHL 5596), the *Passio ss. Tryphoni et Respicii* (BHL 8340), and the *Vita s. Firmani* (BHL 3001)) were all reworkings of earlier sources.[144] Like Letaldus he worked with a tradition which he

---

[141] Letaldus of Micy, *Vita s. Juliani*, cc. 8–9, col. 785B. For a discussion of disputes over the claims of 'apostolicity' for other saints venerated in the eleventh century, most particularly St Martial of Limoges, see Schreiner 1966a, pp. 29–31; Landes 1987, pp. 495–7 and the bibliography cited there.

[142] Letaldus of Micy, *Vita s. Juliani*, cc. 15–20, cols. 787A–90A. The first of two source passages in *BHL* 4546 (found in *Actus pontificum Cenomannis*, p. 29, line 8 to line 24) is taken directly from the *Virtutes s. Fursaei*, c. 11, p. 444. The second (p. 30, line 15, to p. 33, line 25) is generally adapted from the story of Haimo, cc. 6–15, pp. 441–5. Cf. Goffart 1966, p. 51 n. 66. This second passage of *BHL* 4546 differs from the printed version of *BHL* 4543 in that it generalizes the specific list of properties donated by Defensor and others to the church of Le Mans (p. 32, line 19, to p. 33, line 8).

[143] For further discussion of the allegiances between Bishop Avesgaud and Micy which constituted the context for this composition, see below chapter 5, pp. 224–9.

[144] For Theodoric's biography, his works, and their sources, see Poncelet 1908.

thought had been corrupted, but what he deemed corruption was not historical inaccuracy, but errors of style. In the prologue to the *Vita s. Martini papae* he wrote:

For [the canons of St Peter] claimed, and the truth bore them out, to have certain *gesta* of the saint, but the *gesta* lied about and falsified [in the saint's life] in such a rustic style that they frightened rather than soothed educated ears. They ascribed the fault for this lying to the scribe (*scriptor*) rather than to the author (*auctor*). For what illiterate man untutored in the grammatical arts would have presumed to undertake the great task of declaring the merits of such a great man? I knew that I would be incapable of fulfilling the request made of me without the help of Him who is incapable of nothing and without whom nothing can be.[145]

Theodoric attempted to subject the source work to 'literary discipline'.

The people who commissioned his other works voiced similar complaints about the extant texts which they asked Theodoric to correct. One, impressed by the success of Theodoric's earlier works, wrote that he wished Theodoric, whom he called a 'doctor' (*medicus*), to improve once again the style of an extant work 'so that just as unlearned writers have made bad from good, so too we strive to make good from bad'.[146] Likewise a monk of Monte Cassino attacked 'a certain very well-known *grammaticus* of that province who, having been led by supercilious arrogance, was thought to have distorted rather than embellished the story of the life of Firmanus in his prolix and shameless telling'.[147]

In the *Vita s. Martini papae*, Theodoric stitched together material from three sources: the *Liber Pontificalis* (*BHL* 5595); a collection of letters concerning Martin made by Theodore Spudaeus (*BHL* 5593); and a *Commemoratio* (*BHL* 5594) also by Theodore. All this material was in essence borrowed from Anastasius the Librarian, who had compiled the first text and translated the latter two. Theodoric, however, referred to Theodore as the author (*auctor*) and to Anastasius merely as the scribe (*scriptor*) of his sources. An analysis of these sources shows that Theodoric introduced virtually no substantive changes in them, although he did much editorial work in the way of original introductory, connecting, and

---

[145] Theodoric of Fleury, *Vita s. Martini papae*, prologue, p. 294.
[146] Theodoric of Fleury, *Passio ss. Tryphoni et Respicii*, prologue, p. 293.
[147] Theodoric of Fleury, *Vita s. Firmani*, prologue, p. 25.

concluding passages.[148] Poncelet's analysis of Theodoric's use of sources in the other extant works shows that he followed a similar course in them.[149] Theodoric did, however, make numerous grammatical changes in his source material, correcting or altering the mood, tense, or form of many words. For Theodoric a story's truth was intimately linked to its style.

Letaldus and Theodoric both felt that the traditions about the saints had been corrupted and tried to remedy that corruption by rewriting the texts in question. Letaldus altered whole stories; Theodoric, simply their language. Letaldus said that it was impious to falsify the deeds of the saints; Theodoric thought it impious to compose those deeds in a bad style. Both authors, however, were concerned with the purity of a tradition; they did not distinguish whether that corruption was stylistic or factual. While both Letaldus and Theodoric were in some sense following in the stylistic footsteps of those ninth-century writers Servatus Lupus and Jonas of Orléans, the eleventh-century writers simply did not have the stature and recognition in international circles which their Carolingian predecessors had enjoyed. They were 'local', not 'courtly', figures. By the eleventh century the principles of critical textual scholarship had moved to the level of local monastic savantes.

Hugh of Fleury's *Vita et miracula s. Sacerdotis* (BHL 7456–9), written *c.* 1107 at the request of the monks of Sarlat, shows how this critical mentality developed in the course of a century.[150] Hugh reworked a no-longer extant source, 'In which there are many

---

[148] The *Vita s. Martini papae* contained five sections. The first is an original passage on the saint's birth and virtues (cc. 1–5, pp. 421–4). This is followed by material borrowed from the *Liber Pontificalis* (cc. 6–9, pp. 424–5, compare *Liber Pontificalis*, c. 76, pp. 181–3). To this material Theodoric added a brief section in chapter 8 which begins 'O praeclara Dei pietas' and runs to the end of the chapter. Next Theodoric changed Anastasius' translations of two letters of Martin into a third person narrative (cc. 9–12, pp. 427–30, compare *PL*, cxxix, cols. 587b–587c). The passage does not include the entire text of the two letters. Fourthly Theodoric transcribed virtually all of Anastasius' translation of Theodore Spudaeus' *Commemoratio* (cc. 15–23, pp. 431–8, compare *PL*, cxxix, cols. 591–9). The concluding section is largely original (cc. 24–6, pp. 438–40). One passage of the final chapter is adapted from the *Commemoratio* (compare *PL*, cxxix, cols. 599d–600a).

[149] Poncelet 1899b, pp. 24–6 n. 1; 1908, particularly pp. 10–14. The sources of both the *Passio ss. Tryphoni et Respicii* and the *Vita s. Firmani* exist only in incomplete manuscripts. A consultation of those manuscripts indicates that Theodoric's use of those sources is similar throughout to those passages quoted by Poncelet.

[150] On the date, see Lettinck 1981, p. 386.

superfluous things. Moreover, noticing certain details distorted by
the fault of the scribes, I have decided to correct it in the modern
time; and to describe more decorously and clearly the text of the
same story, transformed and improved in succinct brevity.'[151]
Abbot Arnaldus of Sarlat had himself realized the factual
corruption of the older work and 'forced' Hugh to undertake the
task of rewriting it, so that the 'light of truth' which had been
obscured by the earlier text would be revealed once more.[152]
Hugh later contrasted the 'hidden speech' of the older work to the
'most open speech' of his own.[153]

In his researches, presumably those which resulted later in the
writing of the *Ecclesiastical History*, Hugh had come across a
number of other stories relating to Sacerdos personally and to his
times. He added these to his *vita*: 'For the sake of polishing and
finishing with care, I have composed many stories myself, as if
polishing, so that [the work] may have nothing except that which
is either splendid or decorous.'[154] Not only did Hugh add episodes
to his narrative, but he arranged his source texts in the margins of
his new work so that he sent the monks of Sarlat not simply a
narrative work, but a glossed manuscript arranged in the manner
of a Bible or copy of Gratian's *Decretum*.[155] Unfortunately that
manuscript has been lost, but Hugh expected his reader to become
involved in a comparative process.[156] Like Letaldus, Hugh
described his task in terms typical of translation,

I desire not to transcribe [the older work] word for word, nor to hammer
out something entirely new in place of the old, but to draw sense out of
sense by improving it according to the poverty of my literary talent, such
as it is. Thus the skill of the reader will easily be able, by investigating each
text carefully, to accept [mine] as true.[157]

---

[151] Hugh of Fleury, *Vita et miracula s. Sacerdotis*, prologue, col. 979D.
[152] Hugh of Fleury, *Vita et miracula s. Sacerdotis*, prologue, cols. 980D–3A.
[153] 'Cuius preciosissimi confessoris vitae seriem, partim in occulto sermone compositam, partim vero scriptorum judicio depravatam conspiciens, nuper corrigere statui; et tempus quo floruit post multorum annorum curricula, moderno tempore designavi; et de ipsius quidem sancti virtutibus, in eadem serie, apertissimo sermone veritatem expressi.' Hugh of Fleury, *Historia ecclesiastica*, as quoted in Couderc 1893, p. 470 n. 1. The phrase *occultus sermo* does not mean that the *series* was composed in French or Provençal as suggested by Chabaneau 1882, pp. 215–17.
[154] Hugh of Fleury, *Vita et miracula s. Sacerdotis*, prologue, cols. 979D–80D.
[155] Hugh of Fleury, *Vita et miracula s. Sacerdotis*, prologue, col. 980D.
[156] There are a few notes in the margins of the prologue in a twelfth-century manuscript of the text (Paris, BN lat. 5575, fos. 79–80v) but these simple glosses are evidently not the original notes discussed by Hugh.
[157] Hugh of Fleury, *Vita et miracula s. Sacerdotis*, prologue, cols. 980D–1A.

For Hugh, as for Letaldus, the truth of that narrative was crucial:

My poor love for Sacerdos was enriched by God's help, to the praise of the confessor, but to add anything in the manner of the [older work] is not worthy praise, but a nefarious deed. For true sanctity and pure religion are not dependent on human lies; they are, on the contrary, obscured when wrapped up in a scheme of falsity.[158]

For Hugh, however, the truth of a saint's life was determined not simply by reaching back to the presumed pure antique tradition through a corrupt intermediary, as Letaldus had done, but by doing research in other sources, and thus discovering as much as possible about the person and his time: 'It is right for the wise man, as I think, to construct the truthful story about an ancient thing, and to replace uncultivated words with more decorous ones.'[159] A little after 1115 Hugh sent the monks of Sarlat a specially abridged version of his *Ecclesiastical History* which highlighted the deeds of Sacerdos and events in their region's history.[160]

The differences between the methodologies of Letaldus of Micy and Hugh of Fleury reflect the slow developments of a literate culture less dependent upon, and integrated with, oral culture than that of the early middle ages.[161] Letaldus used both *litterae* and *traditio vivae vocis* to augment his faulty written source, while Hugh added to his source through research done in written sources. Moreover, he sent his new work to the monks of Sarlat in a manuscript containing some of those new sources as marginalia. Unlike Bertholdus' 'monuments of letters' Hugh's work could not be read and heard in the same way. It was particularly designed for readers who would exercise critical acumen in comparing the text and its marginalia. Letaldus' own criticism and rewriting of the earlier *Vita s. Juliani* had required just this sort of comparison, but his final product was intended for an audience of both listeners and readers who could apprehend his work in a similar manner. Both authors saw the past as something which continued to exist only in so far as it was concretized, truly or falsely, in written texts. Their task as writers was to translate the past for a contemporary audience. Those texts could be corrected, emended, and even augmented by reference to other texts. According to their critical

---

[158] Hugh of Fleury, *Vita et miracula s. Sacerdotis*, prologue, col. 983A.
[159] Hugh of Fleury, *Vita et miracula s. Sacerdotis*, prologue, col. 983C.
[160] A copy of this *Chronicon* (BHL 7460) is found in Bordeaux, BM 11, fos. 180ff. Couderc (1893, pp. 471–4) has edited portions of this work. On the date, see Lettinck 1981, p. 387.
[161] For two overviews of this change, see Clanchy 1979 and Stock 1983.

principles, however, texts should no longer be established out of reference to a body of the *topoi* of sanctity. On the other hand saints continued, through their relics, to work in the contemporary world and those miraculous actions could be recorded by reference to *traditio vivae vocis*. Letaldus and Hugh thus implicitly attacked the approach to the composition of saints' lives employed by their Carolingian predecessors and even by some of their eleventh-century contemporaries in the diocese of Orléans.

A concern over the trustworthiness of just such contemporary oral traditions about the miraculous worried a number of Hugh's contemporaries, most notably Guibert of Nogent who completed his *On the Relics of the Saints* in 1125.[162] The point of departure for the work was the alleged tooth of Christ possessed by the monks of Saint-Medard in Soissons. Guibert attacked this and other relics of Christ as fraudulent and devoted most of the treatise to a discussion of the Eucharist as the truest relic of the Saviour. The focus of the work is the relationship between physical symbols and the spiritual meaning they represent, as in the relationship between the host and Christ. Guibert began by explaining that the cult of the saints belongs, unlike the Eucharist, to the realm of popular, and hence inessential, practice. The veneration of relics could serve pious purposes, but had no doctrinal standing; it could lead to faith, but was not essential to salvation.[163]

Guibert explicitly discussed the relationship of saints' relics, which serve as symbols, to the saints themselves and the role played by documentary evidence in that relationship:

[Relics] are things of reverence and honour for their example and protection. In these matters only that method should be considered authentic, by which a man is called a saint, whom not opinion but the sure tradition of antiquity or of truthful writers confirms. For how can you say that someone, so to speak, is a saint, of whose authority no memory is known, not to mention the fact that it is not supported by texts or by accessible experience of miraculous signs? I say by texts which are efficacious for strengthening, for there are so many stories about some saints, the reputation of which would be better able to cause impiety among the unfaithful than in any way to be illustrious. And even when they are true, they can be brought forth with such ragged, pedestrian, or – if I might use a poetic expression – ground-hugging eloquence and

---

[162] Lefranc 1896; Schreiner 1966a, pp. 31–3; Guth 1970; Morris 1972; Mireux 1977; Stock 1983, pp. 244–52. The critical edition discussed by Mireux has not yet appeared.
[163] Guibert of Nogent, *De pignoribus sanctorum*, I.I, col. 613C.

delivered in the deepest confusion, that, since they are most insignificant, they ought to be believed most false.[164]

Unlike writers such as Letaldus, Guibert considered no documentation to be absolutely free of 'shadow'. While the holiness of a saint could be supported by texts and could result in miracles at the saint's tomb, more frequently than not the veneration of the saint's relics was dubious. For Guibert even the veneration of dubiously authenticated relics could be sinful, although he admitted that the mistaken veneration of inauthentic relics, when done in good faith, was meritorious.[165]

As the words of both Hugh and Guibert attest, attitudes toward the past and toward the writing of history were changing in twelfth-century Europe. The schools of the diocese of Orléans – which boasted such well-known masters as Hilary of Orléans, Bernard of Meung, and Stephen of Tournai – flourished at this time. The city became known as a centre for the study of classical literature and the phrase 'Let Paris be proud of her logic and Orléans of her authors' was repeated by many writers around the year 1200.[166] In the period between the death of Hugh of Fleury and the Fourth Lateran Council, however, the composition of hagiographic texts virtually ceased. Only three texts were written in that period.

In 1145 Victorine canons replaced the secular canons at Saint-Euverte in a reform of a community which had virtually ceased to function.[167] The Victorines were unable to determine the exact location of the relics of their patron. Abbot Roger alleged that the secular canons had not reconstructed their church for fear that they would relocate the tomb and that the discovery of such a 'treasure' would cause the reform of their community.[168] Four years later Roger asked the aid of a visiting dignitary, Abbot Suger of Saint-Denis. Suger suggested that the canons excavate behind the main altar in an area cut off from public access. There they found two coffins.[169] They opened the first on Christmas Eve, only to find it empty. Waiting until the feast of the Holy Innocents, the abbot opened the second and found the relics of the saint within. Soon thereafter Roger wrote a letter, the *Inventio s. Evurtii* (*BHL* 2802),

---

[164] Guibert of Nogent, *De pignoribus sanctorum*, I.1, cols. 613D–14A.
[165] Guibert of Nogent, *De pignoribus sanctorum*, I.1, col. 615A.
[166] Lesne 1910–45, V, 179–91; Häring 1973; Rouse 1979 (quotation on p. 132).
[167] Bernois 1918, pp. 32–3 and 43–56; *DACL*, XII, 2710.
[168] *Inventio s. Evurtii*, cc. 1–2, p. 61.   [169] *Inventio s. Evurtii*, c. 3, p. 61.

to the monks of Saint-Ouen in Rouen, and presumably to other communities as well, announcing the rediscovery of these relics.[170] The canons later reburied the coffins and they apparently remained undisturbed, for they were excavated in the nineteenth century and found arranged in the manner described by Roger.[171] The success of the Victorines in rehabilitating the cult of Evurtius is reflected by the fact that the author of a guide for pilgrims on their way to Compostela advised them to visit the relics of the holy cross and the tomb of Evurtius while passing through Orléans.[172]

Similar neglect of a saintly patron and past traditions had occurred at Meung-sur-Loire, where a canon writing about the same time as Roger frankly regretted the hard times which had long afflicted his community. The property which charters proved had once belonged to it had been alienated. There were few extant written records about their patron saint, Lifardus, and the canon compared the loss of such hagiographic texts to the dispersion of the foundation's property. This canon was textually oriented. He tried and failed to locate references to his community in a search of royal and papal documents contained in the episcopal archives and regretted how cut off his community had become from its own past. He attributed the lack of antique records to the fact that his predecessors had been prevented from preserving them by either the lack of a scriptorium or the unrest of war. He counselled his fellows, 'Since we are unable to restore completely these lost properties . . . let us try to restore that which we can, the praises of God in his saint, lest we seem ungrateful.'[173] To this end he collected seven miracle stories into the *Miracula s. Lifardi* (BHL 4933). Like Abbot Roger this canon sought to restore the ancient authority of his community's patron which had been neglected over the course of the previous century.

Although the canon failed to promote the independence of his own community, Meung became important over the following years as the primary residence of the bishops of Orléans. Manasses of Garland (1146–85) constructed a fortified tower next to the church there, both to protect his possessions and to serve as a

[170] *Inventio s. Evurtii*, c. 1, p. 61.   [171] Lenormant 1862.

[172] *Le Guide du pèlerin de Sainte-Jacques de Compostelle*, p. 59. The author also (p. 60) noted the church of St Samson of Dol in the city of Orléans as the resting place of the paten used at the wedding feast of Cana, but, contrary to tradition, the relics of St Samson were probably never translated to the Orléanais.

[173] *Miracula s. Lifardi* c. 2, p. 160.

sometime residence.[174] Later Manasses of Seignelay (1207–21) constructed a far more elaborate castle which was extensively remodelled in the seventeenth century.[175] Meanwhile a canon of Meung named Bernard added a single miracle story to the *Miracula s. Lifardi*.[176]

At about the same time the miraculous cure of Abbot Andrew of Micy (1171–82) through the intervention of St Euspicius prompted the collection of four miracle stories associated with that saint's relics.[177] The collection was unusual in that Euspicius was not the patron of Micy and his relics were venerated at a side altar in the monastic church. The grateful abbot probably wished to provide his benefactor with some greater prominence. At an earlier time Rodulfus Tortarius had honoured St Maurus the martyr, to whom he had become personally devoted, by including a number of miracles attributed to that saint at Fleury in a larger collection of the patron saint's miracles.[178] Together these constitute the only substantial descriptions made in the region of miracles attributed to saints who were not the patron of their community.

The twelfth-century authors were all trying to revive the veneration of the saints about whom they wrote and their works exhibit little of the vitality present in earlier hagiography. Their works were virtually the last attempts to compose hagiography about the 'fathers' of the Orléanais, whether those promoted by Bishop Walter or those – such as Laetus – who gained prominence later.[179] They represent the final stage of the revival and reorganization of the cult of the saints in the diocese which began with the work of Letaldus in the 980s. Abbot Roger of Saint-Euverte and the anonymous canon of Meung both wrote in episcopally controlled communities where the cult of the patron 'father' had been moribund during the eleventh century. There is no indication that the cult of Avitus was ever to regain importance at Saint-Avit after the fire of 989, although the saint's feastday was remembered in the diocese. These twelfth-century authors wrote in a time of equipoise. The deeds of the 'fathers' of the diocese had

[174] *GC*, VIII, 1450–4; Vallery-Radot 1931a, pp. 295–6.
[175] *GC*, VIII, 1458–62; Vallery-Radot 1931a, pp. 297–301.
[176] *Miracula s. Lifardi*, cc. 18–21, p. 164. It is tempting to identify this Bernard of Meung with the famous author of grammatical texts, but such an identification seems unlikely.
[177] *Miracula s. Euspicii* cc. 1–2, pp. 314–15.
[178] Rodulfus Tortarius, *Miracula s. Benedicti*, VIII.20–3, pp. 304–14.
[179] A minor *Vita s. Dulchardi* was composed in the later middle ages or early modern period; Poncelet 1905, pp. 71–6.

been recovered in as much as was possible. Their works had provided the relics of the diocese with textual guarantees. What was lost, as the canon of Meung suggested, was lost forever. No new relic cults began in the diocese in the twelfth or thirteenth centuries, and certain cults, if these texts are any indication, declined in popularity.[180] The paucity of new hagiography during this period, however, does not necessarily indicate a lapse in the veneration of the saints. New texts were not composed simply because new texts were not needed; the hagiographic material composed in earlier generations retained its force and popularity. The 'fathers' had all been provided with texts adequate for the celebration of their feasts.

The continuing importance of Bishop Walter's canon of local 'fathers' in the twelfth and thirteenth centuries can be seen in the extant liturgical calendars from the diocese, most of which come from either Fleury or Micy. These contain the feasts of all the saints of Walter's list as well as the feast of St Avitus.[181] At Fleury the

---

[180] Two statues of the Virgin gained reputations for working miracles in the later middle ages. Vincent of Beauvais (*Bibliotheca mundi*, VII.83, IV, 251) first mentioned miracles associated with one housed in a church dedicated to St Paul in a suburb of Orléans called *Avenum*. Later called 'Notre Dame des Miracles' this statue played an important role in the career of Jeanne d'Arc. The second statue was located in the nearby town of Cléry. Beginning in 1280 it acquired a reputation for miracles which attracted the active interest of the French royal family.

[181] These include not only the feasts of the deaths of each saint, but of the *translatio* (11 July) and *illatio* (4 December) of Benedict's relics, feasts which were specific to the shrine at Fleury. For the dates of all these feasts see above chapter 1, note 48. There are five extant calendars from Fleury: Paris, BN lat. 7299, fos. 3v–9 (an early eleventh-century calendar from Fleury contained in a collection of *computus* texts); Orléans, BM 322, pp. 1–8 (an incomplete calendar of the late eleventh century from Fleury preceding a text of the Usuard martyrology); Orléans, BM 123, fos. A–F (a calendar of the early twelfth century from a Fleury psalter); Trier, Seminarbibliothek 187, fos. 5–7 (an incomplete calendar of the late twelfth century from a Fleury breviary); Orléans, BM 129, fos. 238–43 (a calendar of the early thirteenth century from the Fleury customary). For a fuller discussion, see Grémont 1975, pp. 204–6. There are three extant calendars from Micy: Paris, BN lat. 7521, fos. 13–29 (a late eleventh-century copy of the Wandelbertian martyrology with additions to the text made at Micy); Paris, Bibliothèque d'Arsenal 371, fos. 87–92 (a twelfth-century calendar of Micy from a collection of *computus* and liturgical texts, see Martin 1885–94, I, 234–35); Vatican, Reg. lat. 1263, fos. 65–74 (a twelfth-century calendar of Micy from a collection of *computus* texts, see Delisle 1876, pp. 489–90). A final calendar is contained in Paris, BN lat. 1020, fos. 1–6 (an early thirteenth-century breviary of the diocese of Orléans, see Leroquais 1934, II, 462–4). None of the calendars from Micy or Fleury mentioned Bishop Flosculus, but the diocesan breviary included his feast. Certain exceptions to the list are caused by the incomplete state of several manuscripts. In addition Paris, BN lat. 7521, omitted the feasts of Evurtius and the *illatio* of Benedict, while Paris, BN lat. 7299, contained neither these diocesan feasts nor other distinctive feasts of Fleury.

The Capetian period

monks also celebrated a group of feasts peculiar to their community. These included the feasts of saints whose relics they had received (Denis and his companions; Paul Aurelian; and Maurus the martyr) as well as of several monks of Fleury (Mummolus, the first abbot; Aigulphus, who became abbot of Lérins; and Abbo).[182] Similarly the reconstruction of Micy in the 1020s inaugurated the celebration of several new feasts which were celebrated in later centuries.[183] The localization of these feasts shows that none of these saints challenged the position of Walter's 'fathers' as far as the whole region was concerned. Of the many saints from outside the diocese whose lives were composed by hagiographers of the Orléanais, only the feasts of Martin of Vertou and Julian of Le Mans were celebrated.[184] Communities sometimes undertook the observance of a feast important to another community as part of an exchange, as when the monks of Fleury agreed to observe the feast of Robert of Chaise-Dieu in return for the observance of the feast of the *illatio* of Benedict at Chaise-Dieu.[185]

Unfortunately little has survived to the present of these buildings except for the magnificent Romanesque church at Fleury and parts of the Romanesque structure at Meung.[186]

[182] The feasts of Dionysius, Rusticus and Eleutherius (9 October) and of both the *transitus* (12 March) and the *translatio* (10 October) of Paul Aurelian were listed in all seven Fleury calendars with the sole exception of Orléans BM 322, which lacked the month of October. Several listed the feast of the translation of Paul in a later hand. The feast of Abbo (13 November) is contained in Paris, nouvelle acquisition latine 7299, fo. 8v; Orléans, BM 322, fo. 8; Orléans, BM, 123, fo. F; Trier, Seminarbibliothek 187, fo. 7; and Orléans, BM 125, fo. 243. The feast of Maurus the martyr (21 November) and that of Aigulphus (3 September) were listed only in Orléans, BM 123, fos. E and F; Trier, Seminarbibliothek 187, fos. 6 and 7; and Orléans, BM 125, fos. 242 and 243. The feast of Mummolus was listed only in Orléans, BM 129, fo. 241v.

According to an eleventh-century text, the *De translatione reliquiarum s. Aigulfi in castrum Pruviense*, Aigulphus' relics were enshrined at Fleury until they were moved to a priory in Provins by four monks of Fleury at the time of the Norman raids, see Godefroy 1937 and 1938. The relics of Abbo were enshrined at La Réole, where he had died, see Davril 1979b. A reliquary of the Merovingian period with Mummolus' name etched in the top does survive, see Berland 1980b, pp. 61 and 69–70.

[183] These included the feasts of the *inventio* of Maximinus' relics, of St Theodemir, of St Euspicius, and of the *translatio* of that saint's relics: Paris, BN lat. 7521, fos. 18v, 21, and 27; Paris, Bibliothèque d'Arsenal 371, fos. 81, 90, 91, and 91v; Vatican, Reg. lat. 1263, fos. 69, 70, 73, and 74.

[184] Martin of Vertou (19 October at Micy): Paris, Bibliothèque d'Arsenal 371, fo. 91. Julian of Le Mans (27 January at both Fleury and Micy): Trier, Seminarbibliothek 187, fo. 1; Orléans, BM 129, fo. 238; Vatican, Reg. Lat. 1263, fo. 55v.

[185] *Recueil des chartes de Saint-Benoît*, II, 135–7.

[186] Chenesseau 1931a; Bautier 1969; Vergnolle 1985.

99

Orléans was burned twice after the twelfth century, first by the English in the famous siege of 1428, and then by the Huguenots on 12 March 1568. The Romanesque cathedral was heavily damaged during the former attack, while the Gothic structure which replaced it was almost completely destroyed by the Huguenots. The church was rebuilt by the Bourbons, and the present structure dates almost entirely from that period.[187] The other churches in the city were also badly damaged both times, although all were rebuilt. The chapter of secular canons at Saint-Aignan and that of Victorine canons at Saint-Euverte, reformed by the Génovefains in the seventeenth century, survived until the Revolution. Both churches stand today, but the only pre-fifteenth-century parts of the buildings which survive are the crypts. Although the church of Saint-Avit survived to the Revolution, the body of the saint disappeared during the wars of religion. The chapter was dissolved when the buildings, which largely still stand, were made into a seminary in 1667. The eleventh-century crypt was rediscovered during excavations made for a new building in 1852.[188] With the exception of Benedict, whose relics attract tourists and pilgrims today, there are few remaining traces of the 'fathers'. A modern visitor would be as hard put to locate the tomb of the patron at Saint-Euverte as was Abbot Roger. At Meung-sur-Loire a statue of Lifardus stands forlornly in the corner of a side chapel facing the reliquary of the saint, while statues of Jeanne d'Arc and Francis of Assisi are surrounded by flowers. When I asked a contemporary priest whether the reliquary was indeed that of the church's patron, he qualified his vaguely positive answer with the words 'if such a person as St Lifardus ever existed'.

The writing down of 'monuments of letters' in the diocese of Orléans was an attempt to link the present patronage of the 'fathers' to their past identity. In the ninth century the religious communities of the region established the holiness of those 'fathers' by composing their lives. In the eleventh and twelfth centuries those same communities – successful foundations under royal patronage, abbeys struggling to win privileges of immunity, unreformed communities of secular canons, and new institutions sponsored by castellans – all used, or failed to use, the patronage provided by the authority of those 'fathers'. In this revival of hagiography the inventive reuse of Carolingian traditions by

187 Chenesseau (1921) discusses the architectural history of the cathedral.
188 Jouvellier 1975.

monastic hagiographers played a crucial role. The clergy of the Orléanais consistently turned to the past, to the Gallo-Roman and Merovingian ages for their saints and to the Carolingian age for literary models, building upon the authority of that past a reality of saintly patronage.

Chapter 3

THE IDEAL OF SANCTITY: FORMATION, IMITATION, AND DISSEMINATION

In the statute of 871, Bishop Walter suggested that the 'fathers' of the diocese of Orléans were to be active in the affairs of the people of his diocese. One of the chief means by which such ancient saints could become present again was through the *vitae* of those saints. Portions of those texts were read out during the liturgy on the feastday of the saint. By reading or hearing these works – for, as Bertholdus of Micy had made clear, the 'audience' of hagiography included both readers and auditors – living Christians came to know the personality and power of these patrons. The *vitae* of the saints described their *virtus*, a word which could equally mean spiritual virtue and miraculous powers. The ways in which the saints had exhibited this *virtus* was also significant. The 'fathers' of Bishop Walter's list were either bishops or monks; they had gained their reputation for sanctity through the traditional paths of the ecclesiastical hierarchy or of asceticism. In their *vitae* hagiographers described and disseminated an ideal of holiness while they implicitly grounded the religious communities of the diocese firmly in the patronage provided by the 'fathers'.

The *virtus* of the saints had gained them entrance into heaven and thus provided those saints with their authority. That authority could help the living in their quest for salvation. Bertholdus described their relationship:

Divine providence provided [us] a shepherd, namely the most blessed Maximinus, who was given to us just as will be explained. He strove, as in the very meaning of his name, to adorn his own life with an abundance of the highest (*maximae*) spiritual virtues. We will attempt to render his great holiness and life worthy of notice . . . and we will attempt this not without a blush in our cheeks . . . since our mind is weak and our hand is slow in the imitation [of his virtues] . . . We commend ourselves to the authority of such great men, who have attained that most safe shore by the most favourable passage, and by whose commands, advice, and repeated entreaty we are allowed to negate our debt, not to mention our servitude.[1]

Bertholdus also made it clear that he wrote for monks (*religiosi*), most particularly for those of his own community who celebrated the feast of their patron saint. One of the purposes of Bishop Walter's legislation, as will be considered below, was to expand the audience of such texts to include the laity as well by causing the feasts of the local 'fathers' to be celebrated in parish churches.

When people heard or read the stories contained in the lives of the saints, they learned not only of the power of the local patron saints, but also of an ideal of behaviour, albeit one almost impossible to attain. Adrevald of Fleury underscored the heroic nature of the lives of saintly people of earlier generations who had earned the appellation 'athletes of Christ': 'We do not value them because of their outward appearances, but because we know them [to be] beautiful on account of their merits. These are placed in our hearts through the recitation of their story, so that they are restored to presence in our mind's eyes as if through some mirror.'[2] For Adrevald 'the signs of their merits' were the miracles which the saints had performed during their lifetimes. He explicitly understood his task to be one of representation, for the recitation of stories about the saints allowed them to become present again as an ideal for the author's contemporaries. Miracles made the saints' interior, or spiritual, characters outwardly apparent. God exercised power through such servants in order to glorify them, but also to help later Christians imitate their interior, that is spiritual, attainments. The saints also continued to be present in the affairs of the living through the performance of posthumous miracles.

Carolingian hagiographers provided portraits of the region's 'fathers' in their lives of those saints, works which constituted by far the most common genre of hagiography during the ninth century. Even Adrevald of Fleury, in his writings about the cult of Benedict's relics, made explicit reference to the well-known life of that saint contained in the *Dialogues* of Gregory the Great. The deeds of such ancient saints as Anianus and Maximinus continued to be of interest to the monks and canons of the communities under their patronage. In the eleventh century hagiographers to a large

[1] Bertholdus of Micy, *Vita s. Maximini I*, c. 2, p. 592.
[2] Adrevald of Fleury, *Vita s. Aigulphi*, c. 1, p. 657.

Hagiography and the cult of saints

degree emulated the work of their predecessors when they wrote about local saints, going so far as to make such saints as Viator and Laetus new 'fathers' of the diocese by directly modelling their lives on Carolingian works.

These 'fathers' – the patrons of Bishop Walter's list and similarly described local saints – belonged to two primary groups: bishops (Anianus and Evurtius), and monks (Avitus, Maximinus, Lifardus, Theodemir, Euspicius, Viator, and Laetus). Certainly there were many other types of sanctity available to medieval hagiographers.[3] It is not that other models were unknown in the Orléanais. Local hagiographers described such minor saints as Baudelius as martyrs and the *Vitae s. Evurtii* recorded how one of the 'fathers' of the diocese had inculcated the cults of other martyrs.[4] Moreover, the works written by authors from the diocese at the request of communities from other regions included many other forms of sanctity.

Those commissioned works included the *vitae* not only of three bishops (Hubertus, Maximinus of Trier, and Julian of Le Mans) and five abbots (Wigbert, Eusicius, Martin of Vertou, Firmanus, and Sacerdos), but also of a pair of martyrs (Tryphonus and Respicius), two royal saints (Edmund and Judocus, who also qualified as a martyr and a hermit respectively), and a pope (Martin). They were all based directly on traditions of a sort apparently unavailable in the Orléanais. Letaldus' picture of Martin of Vertou, for instance, had far more personal depth and detail about the saint's life than any of the traditions about monks from Micy which Letaldus himself used in writing the *Miracula s. Maximini*. So, too, Vitalis of Fleury's *Vita s. Pauli Aureliani*, which was based on a

---

[3] One trend within hagiographic scholarship has been the study of attributes common to a number of related texts in order to analyse the 'ideal' or 'model' of holiness which functioned within a given cultural setting, whether that setting be as large as western Europe or as small as the single diocese analysed here. For comparative material to the present discusion, see Delooz 1969; Poulin 1975; Vauchez 1981, particularly pp. 163–489; Goodich 1982; Weinstein and Bell 1982. The use of the various available models of sanctity differed widely according to region and to period. In the ninth century, for example, Archbishop Rodulfus of Bourges (*MGH, Capitula episcoporum*, I, 254) promoted only the cults of early bishops of his diocese. Poulin (1975, pp. 55–8) identified martyrs, clerics, and evangelists among the 'traditional paths' to sanctity in the contemporary hagiography from the Aquitaine. Gaiffier (1967, pp. 452–6) found the heroes of the hagiography composed in eleventh-century Flanders to be either bishops or monks.

[4] *Vita s. Evurtii I*, c. 13, p. 318; Lucifer of Orléans, *Vita s. Evurtii II*, c. 15, p. 56.

104

Breton original, presented a far more nuanced depiction of episcopal action than any of the lives native to the diocese of Orléans. No matter what the inherent interest of these texts, however, they were not circulated within the Orléanais to any significant degree. Of the saints listed above only the feasts of Paul Aurelian, Julian of Le Mans, and Martin of Vertou were celebrated within the diocese. Therefore it is not, in general, appropriate to include them in a discussion of the ideal of sanctity which was formed and disseminated within the Orléanais.

The hagiographers of the Orléanais did not attempt a full-scale biographical treatment of the saint, rather they composed short works which could be easily abridged into *lectiones* on that saint's feastday. Their purpose was in a very real sense more liturgical than literary. The hagiographers sought to provide in a short compass a convincing argument concerning the saint's *virtus* and his connection to the religious community which each served as patron. Since there was a large degree of interdependence among the *vitae*, there was also a great deal of repetition among them. A review of the identity of the 'fathers' of the diocese and the salient points of their careers is therefore in order.

The foci of the episcopal *vitae* were the election of the bishops and their greatest deeds in the execution of their office. As in the Carolingian Aquitaine, no clear portrait of contemporary bishops emerged from these texts. In contrast to hagiography in the eastern Frankish lands, there was no discussion of the relationships of bishops with the papacy.[5] The *Vitae s. Evurtii* began with the saint's arrival in Orléans at the time of an episcopal election.[6] He was a Roman seeking refuge from the barbarian invasions of the Italian peninsula. While he was sitting amidst the congregation in church a dove descended on him, indicating that he was God's choice for the office.[7] A year later a fire destroyed the city. Saved by Evurtius' prayers, the populace supported his plans to build a new cathedral. His efforts were facilitated by the discovery of a treasure in the excavation pit. The bishop sent the money to Constantine, but the emperor returned it, stunned by the honesty and generosity of a subject he had never met. Constantine also provided relics of the

---

[5] Poulin 1975, pp. 64–7; Zoepf 1908, p. 163; Corbet 1986, pp. 51–8.
[6] Since Lucifer faithfully used the *Vita s. Evurtii I* as a source, there is little factual variation between the two texts.
[7] *Vita s. Evurtii I*, c. 4, p. 313; Lucifer of Orléans, *Vita s. Evurtii II*, c. 4, p. 53.

true cross for the new cathedral.[8] During the mass of consecration God's hands, visible to certain members of the congregation, miraculously appeared over Evurtius' head and blessed him as he was blessing the Eucharistic elements.[9] Evurtius desired that a local abbot, Anianus, be his successor, but did not see fit to impose his will on the faithful. His wish, however, was confirmed by a miraculous pronouncement. When a child, at his request, performed a version of the biblical *sortes* as a means of determining the new bishop, the boy instead spoke the fateful words of commissioning, 'Anianus, Anianus, Anianus, a bishop'.[10]

The ninth-century author of the *Vita s. Aniani II* began with this story of his subject's election.[11] This new story served as an introduction to a retelling of the Merovingian traditions about how Bishop Anianus saved his city from the attack of the Huns.[12] Anianus left Orléans to beseech the protection of the Roman general Aetius for his flock. Through a vision he was able to provide Aetius with the exact time of the barbarian attack on Orléans. When the general arrived a miraculous appearance by the bishop directed him how to defeat the barbarian army. In this retelling, particular emphasis was placed on the miraculous. Anianus' *virtus* was clearly the major rampart which protected the city. In the *vitae* of both early bishops, the civil authorities of the city were noticeably absent. The bishops emerged as the prime governors, both spiritual and temporal, of their region. All three Carolingian authors concluded their works with precise descriptions of the date, location, and means of the saint's burial in suburban cemeteries. These stories functioned as foundation narratives for the communities of Saint-Euverte and Saint-Aignan.[13]

These works included miraculous elements which showed how God worked through the agency of these men. The dove which descended on Evurtius, the divine hands which blessed him, and the child who spoke Anianus' name all vividly demonstrated the close contact between God and these divine *famuli*. The hagiographers first described how each saint had come to be a *patronus* for

[8] *Vita s. Evurtii I*, c. 10, pp. 316–17; Lucifer of Orléans, *Vita s. Evurtii II*, c. 10, pp. 55–6.
[9] *Vita s. Evurtii I*, c. 12, pp. 317–18; Lucifer of Orléans, *Vita s. Evurtii II*, cc. 14–15, p. 56.
[10] *Vita s. Evurtii I*, c. 15, p. 319; Lucifer of Orléans, *Vita s. Evurtii II*, c. 19, p. 58. On biblical *sortes* as practice and hagiographic topos, see Courcelle 1953.
[11] *Vita s. Aniani II*, c. 2, pp. 27–8.   [12] *Vita s. Aniani II*, cc. 3–8, pp. 28–32.
[13] *Vita s. Evurtii I*, c. 16, p. 319; *Vita s. Evurtii II*, c. 20, p. 58; *Vita s. Aniani II*, c. 9, pp. 32–3.

the diocese and then how that saint's patronage benefited its people, Evurtius by building a new cathedral and Anianus by saving the town from destruction. The story of Evurtius' construction of the cathedral also told how the relics of the holy cross came to Orléans, and thus provided the 'election narrative' of another 'father' of Walter's list. Just as Evurtius was consecrated by God, so he consecrated both the cathedral and his successor, Anianus. A web of personal relationships bound the bishops and the relics of the true cross to each other and to God. The authors used the languages of kinship and of service: Anianus was described both as the *frater* and the *famulus* of the older Evurtius.[14] The most important message of these works was that the diocese's patrons formed a close-knit association and that God's providence worked directly through their agency.[15]

The authors of monastic *vitae* portrayed their subjects as teachers of the monastic life and founders of religious communities. They moved from the saint's call to and consecration into the monastic life to the foundation of a community which would continue to exist under their patronage after their deaths.[16] This paradigm was inaugurated in the earliest Carolingian lives from the diocese, the three versions of the *Vitae s. Aviti*. The earliest version provided the basic narrative.[17] Born in the city of Orléans, Avitus entered the religious life at Micy under the tutelage of Maximinus.[18] He became a favourite of the abbot, who raised him to the rank of cellarer, but his success earned him the dislike of many of the other

14 *Vita s. Aniani II*, c. 2, p. 27; *Vita s. Aniani III*, c. 5, p. 35.
15 The stories of the miraculous elections of Evurtius and Anianus were included in a dossier of material prepared, probably by Ademar of Chabannes, for use either at the council held at Limoges in 1031 or in fabricating Ademar's account of that council. They were evidently used as *exempla* to show God's direct interest and involvement in episcopal elections. Dubois and Renaud 1981, pp. 497–501.
16 On the similar descriptions of this ideal in the Carolingian Aquitaine, see Poulin 1975, pp. 67–79.
17 While the later versions differed somewhat in scope from the *Vita s. Aviti I*, Poncelet (1905, pp. 14–25) has shown that there was little substantive difference among the three texts. The *Vita s. Aviti II* ended with the death of the saint, omitting the story of the dispute between Orléans and Châteaudun. The author of the *Vita s. Aviti III*, on the other hand, added the posthumous miracle story told by Gregory of Tours to the narrative of the *Vita s. Aviti I*. Otherwise he imitated the language of the *Vita s. Aviti II*, at times verbatim. The later authors also added little embellishments (such as the fact that Avitus was named for his great-grandfather), omitted or changed certain other minor details (such as the quotation of the words spoken by Christ to Lazarus), and told the saint's story in more elaborate and verbose language.
18 *Vita s. Aviti I*, cc. 1–2, p. 57.

monks. Seeking greater opportunity for contemplation he left one night and stealthily went to the forest of the Sologne, where he established a tiny *cellula* about 17 kilometres from his original abbey.[19] Sought by his former brothers to become their abbot after the death of Maximinus, he fled northward with an anonymous companion, also a former monk of Micy, to establish a new hermitage in the forest of the Perche, near Châteaudun. There he founded an abbey of his own named Poissey.[20] It seems that that community did not receive any of the saint's relics after his death. Some were enshrined at Châteaudun, while the major portions were returned to Orléans.[21] King Childebert, returning from a campaign in Spain on which he had been helped through the intercession of Avitus, built the church over the tomb of the saint which was to become the community of Saint-Avit.[22]

In the Maine an author from the monastery of Saint-Calais (Anisola) elaborated on the *Vita s. Aviti I* to provide a life for the patron of his community, the *Vita s. Carileffi I* (*BHL* 1568) which was probably composed in celebration of the reconstruction of the monastery church *c.* 820. Like the lives of Avitus it was essentially a foundation narrative for the community.[23] Those lives had left anonymous the monk of Micy who accompanied Avitus to the Perche. The author from the Maine identified that companion as Carileffus, who later founded the abbey dedicated to his memory near Le Mans.[24] According to this new tradition Carileffus was a life-long companion of Avitus who came with him from the Aquitaine to enter the monastic life at Micy and later accompanied him to the Perche. When Avitus founded his monastery of Poissey, Carileffus went off further into the wilderness where Clovis later provided him with property for a monastery. In the Capetian

---

[19] *Vita s. Aviti I*, c. 3, pp. 57–8. Larnage (1895) states that the location of this *cellula* was traditionally thought to be the town of Mézières.   [20] *Vita s. Aviti I*, c. 4, p. 58.

[21] *Vita s. Aviti I*, cc. 10–12, pp. 61–2.   [22] *Vita s. Aviti I*, c. 13, pp. 62–3.

[23] Goffart 1966, p. 77. On the relics, see Belton 1893.

[24] There is no complete edition of the *BHL* 1568. The fullest printed text is *Hist. SS*, VII, 71–82. For additions, corrections, and partial reeditions, see *AASS*, July I, p. 102; *Catal. Brux.*, I, 28–9; *Analecta Bollandiana*, 24 (1905), pp. 37–8, 47, and 48; *MGH, SRM*, III, 389–94; and *MGH, SRM*, IV, 769. Poncelet (1905, pp. 31–44) and Goffart (1966, pp. 61–2, 73–7, 220–4, and 361–2) provide a fuller analysis of the text. The work served as an introduction for the *Miracula s. Carileffi* (*BHL* 1572), a collection of miracle stories associated with the saint's relics enshrined at Saint-Calais. The history of that abbey is confused by numerous forged charters, see Poncelet 1905, pp. 31–4; Goffart 1966, pp. 79–80, 92–3, and 141–7.

period both the author of the *Vita s. Viatoris* and his imitator, the author of the *Vita s. Laeti*, described their subjects in similar terms by simply substituting that saint for Carileffus. The one major difference was that neither Viator nor Laetus was made into the founder of a monastic community.

The personality of Maximinus was central to all these traditions, despite the fact that the lives of that saint were actually composed after those of some of his disciples. Maximinus was the first abbot of Micy. He came to the Orléanais as a result of a revolt against Clovis by the citizens of his native city of Verdun. When the Frankish king was about to defeat the rebels, they asked Maximinus' uncle, a priest named Euspicius who was famed for his piety, to act as their envoy. Euspicius not only persuaded Clovis to show mercy, but impressed the king, who offered to build a new monastery for him. The priest accepted this offer, but insisted that his nephew become abbot.[25] Maximinus soon developed a reputation for excellence in the monastic life and drew followers from both the secular and the monastic worlds to study in his 'gymnasium of spiritual philosophy'.[26] It was in this context that the authors from Micy briefly recounted extant traditions about Avitus and Carileffus.[27] A series of miracle stories completed the portrait. In one which used a common hagiographic *topos* Maximinus slew a dragon who inhabited a cave above the Loire.[28] The saint was later buried in that grotto.[29]

The lives of Euspicius and Theodemir, respectively the uncle and successor of Maximinus, presented truncated versions of this model of sanctity, focusing on the saints' entry into the monastic life. As neither saint was the official patron of Micy, and since their lives were taken almost directly out of the *Vitae s. Maximini* by an eleventh-century author, there was simply no need to provide a foundation narrative for the community. In both works Maximinus functioned as the master and teacher; the sanctity of Euspicius and of Theodemir simply mirrored that of the great saint. The

[25] Bertholdus of Micy, *Vita s. Maximini I*, cc. 3–6, pp. 592–3; *Vita s. Maximini II*, cc. 4–13, pp. 582–4.
[26] Bertholdus of Micy, *Vita s. Maximini I*, cc. 13, p. 594; *Vita s. Maximini II*, c. 22, p. 586.
[27] Bertholdus of Micy, *Vita s. Maximini I*, cc. 14–16, pp. 594–5; *Vita s. Maximini II*, cc. 23–5, pp. 586–7.
[28] Bertholdus of Micy, *Vita s. Maximini I*, c. 21, p. 596; *Vita s. Maximini II*, cc. 30–2, p. 589.
[29] Bertholdus of Micy, *Vita s. Maximini I*, c. 22, p. 596–7; *Vita s. Maximini II*, c. 34, p. 589.

author of the *Vita s. Theodemiri* added a long discussion of the Trinity to his account of the saint's life just to demonstrate the knowledge which Theodemir received from Maximinus.[30]

The *Vita s. Lifardi* was not part of this cycle of interrelated texts, but it sounded many of the same themes. The author began with Lifardus' decision, made at age forty, to lead the life of a hermit. He withdrew, with a companion named Urbicius, to a set of buildings at Meung which had been ruined in barbarian raids.[31] As in the Micy texts, the relationship between Lifardus and his disciple, who became the second abbot of Meung-sur-Loire, was highlighted throughout.[32] Some years after they had gone to Meung, a fire-breathing dragon began to scourge the region. Lifardus went to meet the dragon armed only with his staff and he conquered it using the sign of the cross.[33] As his fame spread he was sought out to perform cures and exorcisms, and those miracles in turn attracted disciples. When the bishop heard of his reputation, he consecrated him a priest and had a church constructed which 'still stands today'. After the saint's death this unnamed bishop built more substantial monastic buildings in Lifardus' memory.[34]

Like the episcopal *vitae*, these monastic works developed a network of relationships among their saintly subjects through the rewriting and reassociation of traditions. Discipleship was the keynote of the traditions of Micy. Maximinus served as the mentor for his *discipuli* Theodemir, Avitus, Viator, Laetus, and even – according to Letaldus – Lifardus. Those other monks were his *familia*, that is, people bound to his service.[35] As one author wrote, 'In that time the blessed father Maximinus ruled over the monastery of Micy, and a great multitude of religious monks streamed to his most holy teaching.'[36] The monks of the Orléanais were curious about how their ancestors had practised the monastic life. Eremitic monasticism played a large role in the authors' picture of the Merovingian past.[37] Avitus, Lifardus, Viator, and Laetus were all hermits, although the former two eventually founded coenobitic communities. They presented a Merovingian

---

[30] *Vita s. Theodemiri*, lectio 3, in Paris, BN lat. 11773, fos. 71v–2.
[31] *Vita s. Lifardi*, cc. 2–3, p. 154.   [32] *Vita s. Lifardi*, c. 3, p. 154, and c. 12, p. 156.
[33] *Vita s. Lifardi*, c. 5, p. 155.   [34] *Vita s. Lifardi*, cc. 12–13, pp. 156–7.
[35] *Vita s. Aviti* I, c. 2, p. 57. *Vita s. Viatoris*, c. 7, p. 101.
[36] *Vita s. Laeti*, c. 5, p. 74.
[37] On the revival of eremiticism in the Orléanais during the twelfth century, see Vidier 1906. On the neighbouring Touraine, see Oury 1970–5. More generally on hermits, see Leyser 1984.

world in which the influence of the Egyptian desert had been deeply felt. The rule of Paul and Anthony was ascribed to Avitus' community at Châteaudun and an author from Micy borrowed a long passage from Jerome on those same fathers to describe the life of Maximinus' *familia*.[38] The authors tended to use such stock phrases as 'fasts and vigils' to indicate the asceticism of the saints and paid scant attention to the specifics of their practice. None of the miracle stories in these lives concerned ascetic practices. This stands in stark contrast to Sulpicius Severus' *Vita s. Martini* and the many Frankish monastic lives written on that model.[39] Despite the rhetorical exhortations of Bertholdus and Adrevald, however, there seems to have been very little in these works which their monastic audiences could have imitated in their lives.

These two types of episcopal and monastic sanctity did not significantly change over the course of the Carolingian and Capetian periods. Certain images were commonly used in both episcopal and monastic lives. The saints inhabited a world of competing divine and diabolic powers, sharply etched in a dualistic imagery of light and dark. The author of the *Vita s. Evurtii I* portrayed both the confusion over the episcopal election and the fire in the city of Orléans as having occurred *diabolo instigante*. Thus the stage was set for the two central miracles of the work, the election of Evurtius and the building of the cathedral. In those stories divine power reintroduced order into the world through the actions of St Evurtius.[40] As the author summed up the miraculous election of his hero, 'Then suddenly the whole people, who had been divided through diabolic instigation, were united by divine inspiration.'[41] In the later version of this work, Lucifer suppressed such explicit dichotomies between God and the devil, but he retained much light and dark imagery.

Such dualist imagery was most skilfully used by the author of the *Vita s. Aviti I*. When Avitus arrived at Micy, Maximinus saw a 'celestial light' in him.[42] During Avitus' stay in the forest of the Perche, a mute swineherd, whose cooking fire had been extinguished, was attracted to the saint's cell by the light of his fire

---

[38] *Vita s. Aviti I*, c. 7, p. 60. *Sermo de inventione s. Maximini*, in Vatican, Reg. lat. 621, fos. 37–9.
[39] See, for example, the uses of Sulpicius Severus cited by Poulin 1975, pp. 66–8 and 102–4.
[40] *Vita s. Evurtii I*, c. 1, p. 312; c. 8, p. 319; c. 7, p. 315; c. 3, p. 314.
[41] *Vita s. Evurtii I*, c. 7, p. 315.
[42] *Vita s. Aviti I*, c. 2, as contained in the reedition by Krusch, *MGH, SRM*, III, 384.

shining forth in that wilderness. After being cured by the saint, he
returned along with his brother in the 'light of day' bearing gifts.
The saint requested that the brothers keep his identity hidden, but
they were unable to hide what divine power had caused. Avitus
was forced to leave his hermitage in the dark of night.[43] Later –
when he converted a freed prisoner and cured a blind boy – Avitus
was described as bringing light in those miracles: 'he who was
damned by birth was illuminated by the saint' and 'suddenly the
boy to whom light had been denied since birth deserved to see the
world before him'.[44] In one later version of this work, the author
cited the famous parable that a lamp should not be hidden under a
bushel and called Avitus a *candelabrum Christi*.[45]

Miracles – specifically curing miracles – were one of the most
important expressions of the power for both monastic and
episcopal saints.[46] They were, however, curiously absent from the
lives of both Evurtius and Theodemir. Most cures were performed
through the imposition of the sign of the cross on the invalid.[47] At
other times simple prayer sufficed.[48] In these miraculous cures
there was a hint of an opposition between divine power and the
power of physicians which was to reappear in the posthumous
miracle collections.[49] Lifardus was made to refer to Christ as the
'true doctor'.[50] Bertholdus reminded his audience that divine
grace did not so much serve the holy man himself, as it did 'the faith
of the sick and of those who ask on their behalf'.[51] The saints
literally stood as mediators between heaven and earth. When they
cured the infirm, they acted out that role in their gestures: first they
stretched out their arms to heaven, then implored divine aid, and
finally imparted that power through the sign of the cross. This
position of mediation was graphically illustrated in the eleventh-
century capital from Fleury in which a massively exaggerated right

[43] *Vita s. Aviti I*, cc. 5–7, pp. 58–9.   [44] *Vita s. Aviti I*, c. 8, p. 60.
[45] *Vita s. Aviti II*, in Vatican, Reg. lat. 585, fos. 30v–1, and Paris, BN lat. 12606, fos. 54v–5.
   See Matthew 5:15, Mark 4:24, Luke 8:16.
[46] Poulin (1975, pp. 109–16) discusses the miraculous as one of the constants of Carolingian
   hagiography in the Aquitaine.
[47] *Vita s. Aniani II*, c. 3, p. 28, and c. 4, p. 29; *Vita s. Aviti I*, c. 6, p. 59, and c. 9, pp. 60–1;
   Bertholdus of Micy, *Vita s. Maximini I*, c. 20, p. 596; *Vita s. Viatoris*, c. 4, p. 99; *Vita s.
   Laeti*, c. 4, pp. 73–4; *Vita s. Lifardi*, c. 10, p. 156.
[48] *Vita s. Viatoris*, c. 8, pp. 101–2; *Vita s. Laeti*, c. 8, pp. 75–6.
[49] See particularly *Vita s. Aviti I*, c. 6, p. 59, where the brother of a man cured by Avitus
   'asked after the doctor (*medicus*) and recognized the works of virtue'.
[50] *Vita s. Lifardi*, c. 10, p. 156.
[51] Bertholdus of Micy, *Vita s. Maximini I*, c. 20, p. 596.

hand engaged in a blessing seems to incorporate the right hands of both Christ and St Benedict.[52]

In some miracle stories the saint directly imitated Christ and the apostles by repeating patterns or examples from New Testament stories.[53] Avitus' prayers brought a former disciple back to life, although the authors of all three versions left the parallel to Christ's resuscitation of Lazarus implicit.[54] According to the author of the *Vita s. Aniani I*, the bishop cured the blindness of an abbot by mixing his spittle with dirt and rubbing it on his eyes. That Merovingian author did not mention the precedent of Christ, but emphasized the saint's apostolic stature.[55] His Carolingian successor, however, shortened the story and made the parallel to Christ's action explicit by noting that 'the saint [followed] the example of the saviour'.[56] When Viator met a group of cripples asking him for alms, he quoted the words of Peter in Acts (3:6) 'Silver and gold I have none, but what I have I give you.' He then prostrated himself and prayed that they be cured. The cripples got up and walked. The author commented 'In this affair it happened that blessed Viator imitated the act of Peter the most blessed leader of the apostles ... as Luke the evangelist testified in the Acts of the Apostles.'[57] Through the direct imitation and repetition of the actions of Christ, a saint became more fully identified with divine *virtus*.[58]

The hagiographers occasionally used such traditional phrases as *miles* and *athleta Christi* drawn from the late antique hagiographic tradition to describe their subjects.[59] The images of struggle, however, which such title evoked and which had held preeminence in the age when martyrs were the dominant model of sanctity, had given way throughout western Christendom to an

[52] Christ and the saint are on the front of the capital, while the two side scenes depict miraculous incidents from Gregory the Great's life of the saint. See Vergnolle 1985, pp. 230–1 (including figures 229 and 230).
[53] Gaiffier (1966) analyses the use of biblical *topoi* for miracle stories, primarily in Gregory the Great. For Merovingian hagiography, see Van Uytfanghe 1976 and Fontaine 1979. More generally, see Van Uytfanghe 1984.
[54] *Vita s. Aviti I*, c. 9, pp. 60–1; *Vita s. Aviti II*, in Vatican, Reg. lat. 585, fos. 31v–2, and Paris, BN lat. 12606, fo. 55; *Vita s. Aviti III, lectio* 8, in Paris, BN lat. 3789, fos. 111v–12v. See John 11. [55] *Vita s. Aniani I*, c. 6, pp. 111–12. See John 9:6.
[56] *Vita s. Aniani II*, c. 5, pp. 29–30. [57] *Vita s. Viatoris*, c. 4, pp. 99–100.
[58] For some examples from outside the Orléanais, see Penco 1968.
[59] *Miles* (i.e. *Christi*): Rodulfus Tortarius, *Passio s. Mauri*, part 1, in *Rodulfi Tortarii Carmina*, p. 257. *Athleta Christi*: *Vita s. Lifardi*, c. 5, p. 155; Adrevald of Fleury, *Vita s. Aigulphi*, prologue, p. 656. The hagiographers of the Carolingian Aquitaine continued to employ the late antique titles and models to a far greater degree than did those of the Orléanais: Poulin 1975, pp. 101–3.

image of direct and full dependence on Christ. The saints frequently emphasized this relationship through their gestures, lying prone to beseech the help of their master before attempting a cure.[60] Christ was both the primary model for miraculous action and its ultimate fountainhead. Christ worked directly in the world through the mediation of such *famuli* who themselves did what Christ had once done in the world – although, to be sure, they did so by mediating Christ's power. The use of the sign of the cross in performing miracles provided a concrete expression of this transfer of power from the divine to the mundane realm. This relationship between God and the saints was slowly expanded to include, first, other holy people and, then, people in the world at large. The benediction of Anianus by Evurtius, of Maximinus by Euspicius, and of Avitus, Viator, Laetus, and Theodemir, all by Maximinus, served to transmit the divine *virtus* to a new generation of holy people. When ordinary people requested the aid of the saints, they employed gestures of supplication which symbolically made them servants of the saints, just as the saints themselves supplicated their divine master in gestures of servitude.[61] Thus a network of relationships stretched out from God into the world. Divine power touched people through personal contact and ritual gesture.

Power or *virtus* – be it sacred or secular – was an intensely personal quality in the world of the west Franks. Its possession was defined in terms of corporate groups, such as families, rather than in terms of institutions, such as the monarchy. Thus the 'election' of Hugh Capet as king of the west Franks involved not the accession of a single individual to an office, but the replacement of one familial lineage by another. Michel Sot has argued that the Carolingian authors of *Gesta episcoporum* – works of collective episcopal hagiography and historiography which were begun in the ninth century in dioceses such as Le Mans and Auxerre – consciously used a familial model for describing the early

---

[60] 'Ex more prostratus homo incubuit, et profusis fletibus sanctorum pavimenta metuenda lavabat, atque Omnipotentis throno indesinenter precum suffragia destinavit.' *Vita s. Aviti I*, c. 9, p. 60. 'At vero Lifardus orationi attentius incumbens Dei suffragium . . . flagitabat.' *Vita s. Lifardi*, c. 6, p. 155. 'Tunc orationi ardentius incubuit'. Bertholdus of Micy, *Vita s. Maximini I*, c. 20, p. 596. 'Tunc beatus Viator solo prostratus oravit dicens.' *Vita s. Viatoris*, c. 4, p. 99.

[61] 'Sancti pedibus provolutus immensas gratias pro collata sibi medicina rependit.' *Vita s. Aviti I*, c. 5, p. 59. 'Quod audiens uxor illius, quae matronarum nobilior illis erat in partibus quod S. adveniret ibidem Anianus ejus prostrata pedibus salutem viri sui orabat attentius,' *Vita s. Aniani II*, c. 4, p. 29.

ecclesiastical history of their dioceses.[62] They anticipated a more secular genealogical literature which became important in the eleventh and twelfth centuries in their construction of elaborate lineages for the ecclesiastical offices of a given region.[63] In the *Gesta episcoporum* the bishops of a diocese became members of a sacred family divinely charged with certain powers and responsibilities, rather than holders of an institutionally defined office.

While the hagiographers of the Orléanais did not undertake as explicitly genealogical an enterprise as did the authors of the *Gesta episcoporum*, they achieved a similar result. The hagiographers were profoundly interested in their heroes as the fountainheads of lineages of saints and as the founders of the religious communities of which they were patrons. A monk of Micy acknowledged this when he compared Maximinus to a root which spread out into many branches, 'For as many branches of a tree come forth from one root, thus these and many others, whose names are known to God alone, by springing forth from his [Maximinus'] holy discipline, they and their followers ascended to the heights of virtues.'[64] One underlying assumption of such hagiography was that its audience belonged in some sense to the lineages inaugurated by these saints. The Carolingian authors provided traditions about an early saintly *familia* for the episcopacy of the diocese (in the interconnected stories of Evurtius, Anianus, and the relics of the holy cross), for the abbey of Micy (in the stories of Maximinus and Avitus), and for the abbey of Fleury (in the trilogy of Adrevald). Eleventh-century authors continued this effort of lineage-building for their patrons by connecting the ecclesiastical foundations at Tremblevif and Pithiviers to Micy. Thus the association of the traditions of various saints was not simply a compositional device aimed at providing more material on a given saint, but a conscious attempt to connect the saints into familial lineages.

While bishop and monk were the two models of sanctity found among the 'fathers' of the diocese, there was a third model extant among other local saints. As early as Adrevald, and more

---

[62] Sot 1978 and 1981. In the latter article, Sot explicitly compares the *Gesta episcoporum* to hagiography. On the construction of lineages for saints in later periods see Vauchez 1974 and 1981, pp. 209–14.

[63] On the importance of family lineages respectively in ecclesiastical and political power struggles within the region of the the Loire valley see Devailly 1984. On the importance of lineage ties in a neighbouring region see Hajdu 1977.

[64] *Sermo de inventione s. Maximini, lectio* 4, in Vatican, Reg. lat. 621, fo. 41. This image is strikingly similar to Virgil, *Aeneid*, II, 458.

commonly in the eleventh century, the hagiographers of the Orléanais composed works about saints who did not rank among the 'fathers' of the diocese. The lives of three such saints (Aigulphus, Baudelius, and Maurus) described a third type of sanctity, that of martyr. All three of these lives were revisions of works originally composed outside the Orléanais. This is not surprising, for Aigulphus' relics were not enshrined in the diocese and the relics of both Baudelius and Maurus had been translated there at a relatively recent date.

Adrevald identified Aigulphus as the discoverer of the relics of St Benedict. Similarly, the eleventh-century author of the *Passio et translatio s. Baudelii* identified a subdeacon named Baudelius as one of the witnesses of the divine blessing of Bishop Evurtius during the first mass in the newly built cathedral of the Holy Cross. Like the monastic saints associated with the abbey of Micy, Aigulphus and Baudelius were thus seen as belonging to an extended network of personal relationships stretching out from the 'fathers' of the diocese. Adrevald also altered his source to say that Aigulphus' teacher was Abbot Mummolus – who was venerated as a saint at Fleury – rather than Abbot Leodebodus.[65] Each man went on to martyrdom, Aigulphus at the hands of rebellious monks during his reforming mission to Lérins, Baudelius at the hands of pagans. These stories present a very different image of sanctity from that of the episcopal and monastic *vitae*. Their primary theme is that of struggle, against the paganism of the Goths and the worse sins of apostate monks. Adrevald in particular showed himself adept at using the early Christian heritage of hagiography about martyrs, a heritage which he had recalled explicitly in his prologue.[66]

Still later Rodulfus Tortarius composed a *Passio s. Mauri*, a particular gem of verse hagiography which masterfully expanded the slender received tradition about the saint into a full-scale tale of heroism in the face of fierce persecution. Maurus was an African monk who went on pilgrimage to the tomb of St Peter in Rome in the third century, only to be arrested and martyred there. The long dialogue between the martyr and a Roman prefect debating the merits of their respective religions – an episode which occupied only a few lines in Rodulfus' prose source – fully demonstrated

65 Compare Adrevald of Fleury, *Vita s. Aigulphi*, c. 3, pp. 657–8 with the anonymous *Vita s. Aigulphi*, cc. 4–5, p. 744. This episode recalls how Maximinus attracted Avitus, Viator and Laetus in the Micy traditions.
66 Adrevald of Fleury, *Vita s. Aigulphi*, c. 2, p. 657.

Rodulfus' ability to draw material from a number of sources, Christian and classical, in order to compose a dramatic scene.[67] Rodulfus' verse writing style, which his editors characterize as an artificial combination of classical and Christian traditions, reflected the eclectic content of the tale itself.[68] The primary proof of Maurus' holiness, as in the earlier passions, was his martyrdom and the *constantia* with which he approached it. Rodulfus was personally devoted to this staunch defender of the faith and included several stories of miracles which he attributed to Maurus in his prose miracle collection.

These were the models of sanctity current in the diocese of Orléans. Hagiography served to represent the 'fathers' of the diocese to its contemporary inhabitants and thereby describe the authority and origin of the important relic cults of the region. These particular ideals of sanctity appear to have continued in their dominant position with remarkable stability over the course of the ensuing centuries. Little new hagiography was written about traditional saints and no new holy people from the region were posthumously lauded for their sanctity. The Orléanais was not a major centre for any of those movements, such as the Cistercian or mendicant orders, which consistently produced candidates for canonization during the later middle ages. The traditional saints presented in these lives were in many ways no more than bundles of *topoi*, simple icons of sanctity and *virtus* in distinction to more fully developed holy men such as Sulpicius Severus' Martin or Odo of Cluny's Gerald of Aurillac. Even the life of the contemporary Gregory of Nicopolis lacked the depth of personal detail found in such comparable works as the twelfth-century life of St Gerard, a monk of Saint-Aubin in nearby Angers (*BHL* 3548).

Concerns over the ritualized form of hagiography has led historians such as Pierre Delooz to distinguish the 'real' (*réel*) saint from the saint 'constructed' (*construit*) by society in the perceptions found in hagiographic literature.[69] Such a distinction does violence to the sense and strength with which the hagiographers and their audiences believed in their 'fathers'. The only 'real' St Anianus present in the diocese of Orléans during the Carolingian and Capetian periods was the saint 'constructed' by the hagiographers

[67] Rodulfus Tortarius, *Passio s. Mauri*, c. 2, in *Rodulfi Tortarii Carmina*, pp. 375–9.
[68] Rodulfus Tortarius, *Rodulfi Tortarii Carmina*, pp. xxv–xxvi.
[69] Delooz, 1969, pp. 5–22, particularly pp. 5, 10–11, and 22. Similarly (1962) he distinguishes 'real' and 'constructed' miracles.

in the texts which were read out and heard by an appreciative audience of clerics – and later presumably laity – on the saint's feast. The activity of this saint was focused on, but not limited to, his relics enshrined in the church of Saint-Aignan. The hagiographers, their texts, their audiences, and the saint's relics were involved in a symbiotic process of belief which caused the saint to exist as a very 'real' presence in the Orléanais of the Carolingian and Capetian periods. It was not unusual in medieval culture that texts which claimed to articulate past realities came to stand for those past realities. The truth value of statements, ideas, and events, such as miracles, based on belief is – as philosophers and anthropologists such as Rodney Needham have discussed – notoriously hard to assess.[70] When Robert the Pious was present at the reconsecration of the church of Saint-Aignan in 1029, Helgaud of Fleury described Anianus as Robert's 'particular advocate'.[71] It is scarcely credible that Robert thought of himself as choosing a 'constructed' saint as his patron, but Robert could not have known any other version of Anianus than that presented in the hagiographic texts or in his clerical advisers' rendering of those texts.[72]

In making the 'fathers' of the diocese present for a contemporary audience, the hagiographers expressed the wish that their works serve a real purpose in the spiritual lives of that audience. The key word employed by them in the prologues to their works was 'imitation'. The living Christians who heard and read these examples – those who, as Adrevald suggested, saw the presence of the saints through the mirror of these texts – were supposed to imitate the *virtus* which those stories illustrated. Lucifer claimed that he composed his work so that it would be imitated by the 'ignorant'.[73] The author of the *Vita s. Lifardi* was less imperious, saying, 'If I myself am unable to imitate [Lifardus], at least I make accessible in writing what ought to be imitated by others.'[74] In the eleventh century Letaldus echoed many of these standard Carolingian phrases in the conclusion of the prologue to his *Vita s.*

---

[70] Needham 1972.

[71] Helgaud of Fleury, *Epitoma vitae Rotberti regis pii*, c. 22, p. 106.

[72] An interesting critique of similar tendencies in the historiography of a later period has been offered by Clark 1983.

[73] 'Idcirco justo libramine mercedis unius retributionem diu multumque pensantes, ut et nos participes simus eorum, qui praedictorum auctores sunt, maluimus sancti ac beatissimi Evurtii episcopi, qualiter in rebus humanis conversatus est, honorabili stylo vitam pandere, et ad notitiam ignorantium pro imitatione edicere.' Lucifer of Orléans, *Vita s. Evurtii II*, prologue, p. 52.   [74] *Vita s. Lifardi*, c. 1, p. 154.

Juliani, 'When the peace of the church was thus restored, various men shone forth throughout the world, who, marvellous for the light of their virtues and noteworthy for the lustre of their faith, would appear worthy of imitation for the meek of heart who wished to follow in the footsteps of Christ.'[75] Moreover the praise of such *virtus* itself was enough to win the patronage of the saints, a patronage which aided in the forgiveness of sins.[76]

Individuals shaped and interpreted the experience of their own lives through the examples and images provided in the lives of the saints. Aimo told the story of a monk named Drogo who left Fleury to live as a hermit. Drogo was assailed by demons during his long fasts and vigils. One night when these visions were particularly disturbing he called on the protection of Benedict, the patron of his monastery. When flames suddenly burst out around him, he remembered a story from the life of Benedict. According to Gregory the Great the saint had been simply unable, through miraculous intervention, to see imaginary flames which devils had employed in an effort to trick the saint's monks. Strengthened by this example Drogo concluded that these flames were also a demonic illusion:

Then the soldier of Christ having recourse to a well-known protection armed himself on the forehead with the sign of the cross and threw himself completely against the phantom fire, clearly mindful, we may conjecture, of the works of his lord and master Benedict who, helped by the gift of divine grace, called his disciples into his presence and declared that the burning flames had been imaginary.[77]

Stories from the lives of the diocese's 'fathers' could also be used by the community at large to interpret its contemporary circumstances. When, during the reconstruction of the early eleventh century, a treasure was discovered in the excavations for the cathedral of Sainte-Croix, people noted the similarity to the story of Evurtius' original construction of the cathedral related in the *Vitae s. Evurtii*.[78]

---

[75] Letaldus of Micy, *Vita s. Juliani*, c. 7, col. 786A.
[76] 'Hanc itaque certitudinem spei et nos habentes, carissimi, veneremur martyrum certamina, collaudemus confessorum pietatis opera, ut qui peccando aeternae claritatis amisimus palatia, ad eadem redeamus, patrocinantibus sanctorum meritis, peccaminum condonati venia.' *Vita s. Laeti*, prologue, p. 72.
[77] *Miracula s. Benedicti*, II.4, p. 102. The story he remembered is Gregory the Great, *Dialogues*, II.10, II, 173.
[78] Rodulfus Glaber, *Historiarum libri quinque*, II.5.9, pp. 66–7.

While scripture and monastic rules were the primary guide as to
how to live a good life, the hagiographers claimed that their lives of
the saints presented examples of how to put such divine wisdom
into practice. Vitalis of Fleury expressed the relationship of
scripture to his hagiographic composition:

For in sacred scriptures we find the rule for living by the law (*norma iure
vivendi*); but in the examples of preceding fathers we find models of good
behaviour (*forma bene operandi*) . . . Whence the life of Blessed Paul shines
full of examples, which shows to us true simplicity tempered by the
keenness of prudence and demonstrates humility's path to the celestial
joys.[79]

The saints lived out the message contained in the Bible; imitating
their example meant following the true path laid out in scripture.
According to Aimo of Fleury contemporary individuals – those
like his hero, Abbo, who would come to be known as saints – could
also provide such *exempla*.[80]

Just as hagiography embodied sacred wisdom, so too the saintly
lives it recounted could surpass worldly learning. Bertholdus of
Micy noted that the Greeks had 'falsely' composed the acts of their
great philosophers and kings to keep alive their memory. If pagans
took the example of such people so seriously, Christians ought
more to imitate the true example of their saints, whose lives
contained the 'highest philosophy'.[81] Bertholdus' anonymous
successor drew a comparison between scripture and the works of
the ancient philosophers, showing how the sacred books reached
the truths sought in various fields of philosophy: 'In the spirit of
these little ones, omnipotent wisdom destined, in our place and era,
Maximinus, one not swollen with wordly wisdom, but conspi-

[79] Vitalis of Fleury, *Vita s. Pauli Aureliani*, c. 1, p. 112.
[80] Aimo of Fleury, *Vita s. Abbonis*, dedicatory epistle, p. 37. On the relationship of the
exempla told in the lives of the saints to the miracles told in the bible see Van Uytfanghe
1981.
[81] 'Quippe cum Gentillium studia maximum sibi favorem contraxerint, modo prosaico
scribentes, modo metrico opere ludentes in describendis actibus vel moribus atque
exercitiis liberalium artium tam magnorum Regum quam Philosophorum, quos
mendax Graecia maxima laude consuevit efferre: ipsi partim ingenia sua commendantes,
partimque temporalis commodi lucra ab eis quibus placere gestiebant captantes,
memoriam sui multorum notitiam miserunt. Nam si quaerimus eos quos Domino
placere confidimus fragilitatis nostrae interventores habere, non pigeat habere eorum
memoriam nos saepius ad mentem reducere, omnipotentem quoque Deum in eorum
fide, moribus, doctrina et actibus collaudemus, cujus exercitiis edocti nobis exercitia
summae Philosophiae imitanda dedere.' Bertholdus of Micy, *Vita s. Maximini I*, c. 1, p.
592.

cuous in the clearness of virtue, worthy in deed and name.' His audience could attain truer wisdom by becoming a disciple of the saint than by following Pythagoras or Plato.[82] Rodulfus Tortarius likewise condemned classical learning in favour of studying sacred learning, and, in particular, the lives of the saints. In the preface to the *Passio s. Mauri* he reviewed a wide spectrum of Greek and Latin literature, pointedly parading his grasp of classical tradition in order to condemn it. As he remarked, 'It is ridiculous to believe the false words of the Greeks / It is ridiculous to lose time in these trifles.'[83] Letaldus of Micy emphasized the didactic value of hagiography without attacking other literature. In the *Vita s. Eusicii* he metaphorically compared Christ to the sun and the saints to the sun's rays.[84] Just as the rays bring light to the world, so the saints teach and enlighten the church. In a parallel passage in the *Vita s. Martini Vertavensis*, he considered how various types of saints preached the message of Christ: the patriarchs and prophets looked to the future, the apostles taught what they knew directly, the martyrs spoke through their blood, and the confessors continued to express *virtus* equivalent to that of the martyrs, although in different circumstances.[85]

These hagiographic works could reach a large audience with this message of saintly *virtus* because they provided the *lectiones*, or liturgical readings, used on the feasts of the saints. Their primary audience was monks and canons, particularly those whose communities fell under the patronage of the saint described in the life. The stories of the life of the saint presented that audience with images which the monks and canons came to know, venerate, and imitate. The lives of the 'fathers' of the diocese had a natural liturgical importance, since the celebration of their feasts was required throughout the diocese. Texts about the translation and invention of relics were also read on the appropriate feastdays. Aimo of Fleury mentioned a now-lost account of the translation of Paul Aurelian 'appreciated many times, and, just as we learned it by hearing it from our predecessors, so too we must hand it on as worthy [to our successors]'.[86] Such liturgical use meant that hagiographic texts were heard as much, or perhaps even more,

---

[82] *Vita s. Maximini II*, cc. 1–3, pp. 581–2.
[83] Rodulfus Tortarius, *Passio s. Mauri*, prologue, in *Rodulfi Tortarii Carmina*, p. 349.
[84] Letaldus of Micy, *Vita s. Eusicii*, prologue edited in Head 1989.
[85] Letaldus of Micy, *Vita s. Martini Vertavensis*, c. 1, p. 805.
[86] *Miracula s. Benedicti*, III.11, p. 155.

than they were read. M. T. Clanchy has remarked, 'The medieval recipient prepared himself to listen to an utterance rather than to scrutinize a document visually as a modern literate would.'[87] The repetition of such hagiographic texts also meant that they became, as Aimo implied, familiar.

On a feastday two types of texts were read which related directly to the saint: prayers, said most particularly at mass, which invoked intercession of the saint directly, and *lectiones*, which were stories concerning the life and miracles of the saint heard during the night and morning offices, as well as in the refectory. Feasts did not all receive equal liturgical attention. The night office contained either three- or twelve-part *lectiones*. Specific hymns, vestments, or other additions could be specially required on important feasts.[88]

Such commemorations reveal the relative importance of feasts in given communities. By the middle of the thirteenth century Fleury celebrated a large number of feasts specific to its own history and relics – such as that of St Paul Aurelian – as well as to the saints of the Orléanais. Although it is dangerous to extrapolate such usages to an earlier period, this customary provides a picture of the commemoration of the saints at Fleury at the very end of the period under consideration here. The *proprium sanctorum* contained three feasts of St Benedict, four of the Virgin Mary (to whom the abbey was formally dedicated), eleven of saints associated with Fleury, and six of saints associated with the diocese of Orléans.[89] Anselme

---

[87] Clanchy 1979, p. 214.

[88] While the general form of the monastic liturgy and the commemoration of the saints within that liturgy is well known, it is not easy to reconstruct the particulars of practice for the houses of the Orléanais. Liturgical books survive only from Fleury and Micy, and most date to the thirteenth century and later. There were several major waves of liturgical reform during the period we are studying, particularly in the ninth and the twelfth centuries, so that it is by no means certain that such manuscripts reflect earlier usages. The sketch of the liturgy of the saints which follows uses material from different houses and several periods to reconstruct the general lines along which the monks and canons of the Orléanais venerated their 'fathers' in their liturgy.

[89] The details may be found in a thirteenth-century customary, the *Consuetudines Floriacenses*. The feasts of St Benedict: *transitus* (21 March); *adventus* (11 July); *illatio* (4 December). The feasts of the Virgin: the Purification (2 February); Annunciation (25 March); Assumption (15 August); and Nativity (8 September). The feasts particular to Fleury: Scholastica (the sister of Benedict, 10 February); Oswald (a monk of Fleury who later became archbishop of York, 28 February); Paul Aurelian (combined with the feast of Gregory the Great, 12 March); Mummolus (an early abbot of Fleury, 8 August); Tenestina (a virgin from the Maine whose relics may have been brought to Fleury, 24 August); Aigulphus, Frongentius, and Mansuetus (the combined feast of the monk who translated the relics of Benedict, a Breton saint brought to Fleury in the tenth century, and the abbot of a monastery in Toul which had close ties to Fleury, 3 September); Denis

Davril has divided the feasts at Fleury into nine grades of celebration.[90] The feasts of the highest rank included all three feasts of Benedict, the feast of the dedication of the abbey's church, as well as such feasts of the universal church as the Assumption (given particular attention at Fleury as a Marian feast), Christmas, and Easter; those of the second rank included the Purification of Mary, the octave of the *translatio* of Benedict, Maurus the martyr, and the *translatio* of Paul Aurelian; while those of the third rank included the Annunciation, the Conception of Mary, and St Scholastica, sister of St Benedict. Thus eleven of the twenty-six most solemn liturgical events of the year at Fleury were connected to the dual patrons of the abbey and to other saints whose relics it possessed. The remaining seven celebrations of saints associated with the abbey were all twelve-lesson feasts. All of the feasts of the diocese also received twelve readings and relatively extensive instructions for the liturgy.[91]

The extant breviaries and missals from Fleury and Micy contain numerous examples of prayers addressed directly to saints during the mass. Most date, however, like the Fleury customary, to the thirteenth century.[92] These prayers were primarily hymns of praise and requests for intercession.[93] On the feast of St Maximinus, for example, the monks of Micy prayed that their sins not interfere with the function of God's mercy and their saint's patronage: 'O eternally omnipotent God, on this festival day grant the more powerful benefits of your kindness to your devout people who are praying to you, and grant through your accustomed piety

and his companions, Rusticus, Eleutherius, and Sebastian (saints of whom some relics had been donated to Fleury by the abbey of Saint-Denis in the ninth century, 11 October); the *translatio* of Paul of Léon (10 October); Abbo (on the feast of Bricius, 13 November); Maurus the martyr (21 November); and the dedication of the church of the Virgin (30 December). The feasts particular to the diocese of Orléans: Lifardus (3 June); the *translatio* of Anianus (14 June); Avitus, Gundulfus, and Posennus (including two other obscure local saints on the same feast as Avitus, 17 June); Evurtius (7 September); the exaltation of the cross (14 September); Anianus (17 November); and Maximinus (15 December). These include all the feasts of Bishop Walter's list.

90 Davril 1974, 24–5.
91 The only exceptions were those of St Lifardus and the *translatio* of St Anianus, which were simple three-lesson feasts.
92 Avranches, BM 41 (late twelfth-century sacramentary from Fleury, see Leroquais 1924, I, 89); Trier, Seminarbibliothek 187 (thirteenth-century missal from Fleury); Orléans, BM 125 (thirteenth-century breviary from Fleury, see Leroquais 1934, III, 292–5); Orléans, BM 121 (early thirteenth-century missal from Micy, see Leroquais 1924, II, 93); Orléans, BM 721 (early thirteenth-century missal from Micy, see Leroquais 1924, II, 92).
93 On the development of prayers to St Benedict during the middle ages, see Grégoire 1965.

to the patron blessed Maximinus your confessor that which, dragged down by the weight of sins, it would not be possible to obtain.'[94] Their prayers at the *sanctus* of the mass showed the shared duties taken by Christ and the patron saint in bringing intercessory aid: 'Displaying the salvation-bringing host and the great munificence of your majesty, O Lord, we ask in our most humble prayers that you will cause us to come to the tranquillity of heavenly happiness through the support of blessed Maximinus your confessor, who always complied with your advice.'[95] These prayers emphasized both the presence of the relics of the patron in the community's church and the sins which had caused the gathered community to seek the help of the saint. They tended to be formulaic and contained little distinctive detail about the character of the saint in question. Nevertheless these prayers were an essential part of the request for a patron's intercession which marked the monastic liturgy.

Lectiones, on the other hand, were taken from hagiographic texts directly or with minor adaptation. Monastic librarians and scribes faced a major task in locating and preserving hagiographic texts, both those which concerned local saints and those of the universal church, in order to fulfil the needs of a community's liturgical calendar. The monastic calendar changed as the cult of a patron saint developed. Micy provides an excellent case in point. The feast of Maximinus (15 December) – and presumably those of his disciples Avitus (17 June) and Carileffus (1 July) – had been celebrated since the ninth century. The invention of the relics of Maximinus and his disciples in the early 1020s caused the addition of a feast marking that *inventio* (27 May) as well as a feast of Theodemir (19 November), the presumed second abbot of Micy. The abbey's scriptorium kept pace. When a version of the Wandelbertian martyrology was copied at Micy, the scribe added verses to the basic text for the celebration of these five feasts.[96] A

[94] Orléans, BM 121, fo. 119; Orléans, BM 721, fo. 89v.
[95] Orléans, BM 121, fo. 119; Orléans, BM 721, fo. 89v.
[96] Paris, BN lat. 7521, fos. 13–29. The base text may be found in *MGH, Poetae aevi Carolini*, II, 578–602. The additions read as follows. The *translatio* of Maximinus (fo. 18v): 'Corpore Miciaco Maximini atque duorum / Cuiuc qui patris clari maniere clientes.' Lifardus (fo. 18v): 'Aureliana suum plebes redolitque Lifardum.' Avitus (fo. 19): 'Hic scandit gaudens Avitus sydera celi / Magnificus meritis abbas qui Miciacensis.' Theodemir (fo. 27): 'Miciacasque bonum celebrat nunc Theodericum.' The *inventio* of Maximinus (fo. 21): 'Miciaco sentiet inventio reliquarum / Insignis meriti Maximini

deluxe copy of the relevant hagiographic texts, including a beautiful miniature of St Maximinus, was also produced in the abbey scriptorium about this time.[97]

Two extant twelfth-century calendars from the house show how the calendar developed over the course of the following century. Each included the celebration of the specific feasts of Micy and those of the local 'fathers' recommended by Bishop Walter for the entire diocese.[98] These calendars also added the celebration of the feasts of Euspicius (20 July), a portion of whose relics had been returned to the abbey in 1029; of Julian of Le Mans (27 January) and Martin of Vertou (24 October), both saints about whom Letaldus of Micy had written; and of Viator (5 August) and Laetus (5 November), saints who had come into local prominence since the time of Bishop Walter.[99] By the twelfth century the abbey also celebrated the feasts of other saints associated with Micy such as Lifardus, Launomaurus, and Leonard.[100] Thus the tree which was the legacy of Maximinus continued to grow and to be celebrated throughout the life of the abbey.

The development of elaborate liturgical calendars made it essential for monasteries to possess a number of hagiographic texts, usually collected into manuscripts known as legendaries which exclusively contained hagiographic material suitable for *lectiones*.[101] The marginalia in an eleventh-century copy of the

atque duorum / Cuius qui patris clari maniere clientes.' The *transitus* of Maximinus (fo. 28): 'Ac invisu famis populos per tempora servans / Insuper extinguis Hydra modiciticione [*sic*] / Hic vivens per agis spectacula denique clara / Sed multo maiora facis nec presule Christi / Aureliana ferax prebent cui sura hieum.'

[97] Vatican, Reg. lat. 621, fos. 34–54 (the miniature is on fo. 34). See Head 1984, pp. 235–6.
[98] Both calendars did omit the feast of the *inventio* of Maximinus' relics. This feast did continue to be celebrated at the abbey, however, for a thirteenth-century breviary from Micy contains prayers for the feast: Orléans, BM 121, fos. 161–2. See also Leroquais 1924, II, 93.
[99] Paris, Bibliothèque d'Arsenal 371, fos. 87–92 (see Martin 1885–94, I, 234–5), and Vatican, Reg. lat. 1263, fos. 65–74 (see Delisle 1876, pp. 489–90). The feast of Laetus is contained in the latter. The former curiously listed the feast of Avitus on 19 December, rather than 17 June.
[100] Launomaurus (19 January): Vatican, Reg. lat. 1263, fo. 55v, and Paris, Bibliothèque d'Arsenal 371, fo. 87. Leonard of Corbion (15 October): Vatican, Reg. Lat. 1263, fo. 73. Leonard of Noblat (6 November): Paris, Bibliothèque d'Arsenal 371, fo. 92. The feast of Lifardus (3 June) was celebrated throughout the diocese: Vatican, Reg. Lat. 1263, fo. 69v, and Paris, Bibliothèque d'Arsenal 371, fo. 81v. The difference between the calendars over which Leonard's feast was celebrated probably reflects the confusion over the identity of the Leonard associated with Micy.
[101] On the nature of these manuscripts, see Philippart 1977 and 1981.

martyrology of Usuard made and used at Fleury (Orléans BM 322) indicate how such hagiographic resources were used to provide *lectiones*. A monastic scribe noted, for part of the liturgical year, what texts should be used on given feastdays and where those texts might be found. From these marginalia Elisabeth Pellegrin has identified the texts and in some cases the very manuscripts which provided the liturgical readings.[102] On the 4 December feast of the burial of St Benedict's relics, for instance, the monks heard readings from Theodoric's *Illatio s. Benedicti* during the office, while in the refectory they heard selections from a sermon in praise of the saint composed by Aimo.[103] During the octave they heard, again in the refectory, readings *in libro miraculorum*, that is from a manuscript containing a variety of texts concerning the saint. These included a sermon by Odo of Cluny, himself a former abbot of Fleury, as well as a story taken from Aimo's so-called *libelli*.[104] In the thirteenth century the monks heard readings from Gregory the Great's life of St Benedict on the feast of his death, from Adrevald's *Historia translationis s. Benedicti* on that of his translation, and from the sermon of Odo of Cluny on that of his burial. They also heard such texts as the *Vita s. Pauli Aureliani*, the *Vita s. Aigulphi*, the *Miracula s. Abbonis*, and the locally composed lives of Evurtius, Anianus, and Maximinus on the relevant feastdays.[105] The liturgy did not provide the only means of celebration. On the various feasts of their patron the monks were treated in the refectory with such

[102] Pellegrin 1963.
[103] The marginal note reads, 'Translationem require in epistulis Pauli glosatis et in ystoria romana, In crastinum lege ad prandium sermonem Aymoini in libro floriac. abbatum et romana priuil.' Orléans, BM 322, p. 248. Pellegrin has identified the manuscript of the glossed Pauline epistles as a combination of Orléans, BM 82, and Bern, Burgerbibliothek 196. The extant fragments do not, however, contain a *translatio* text. Pellegrin (1963, pp. 24–6) has identified this *translatio* as the *Illatio s. Benedicti* of Theodoric for three reasons: the *Historia translationis s. Benedicti* of Adrevald was primarily associated with the 11 July feast; the *Illatio* explains the origin of the 4 December feast; and a twelfth-century lectionary from Fleury (Paris, BN lat. 12606) contains the *Illatio* among readings for the month of December. The text of Adrevald does, however, contain readings directly relating to the origin of the 4 December feast and would be more likely referred to as a *translatio*.
[104] Pellegrin (1963, pp. 26–8) has identified the manuscript as a combination of Orléans, BM 337, and parts of Orléans, BM 323, as well as texts represented in a later copy (Vatican, Reg. lat. 591). Marginal notes from these manuscripts correspond to and expand upon those in the martyrology.
[105] *Consuetudines Floriacenses*, pp. 155, 157, 169, 189–90, 217–18, 234, 252, 254, and 264. Pellegrin (1963, p. 14) has identified Vatican, Reg. lat. 585, fos. 13–24v, as the copy of the *Vita s. Maximini II* in use at Fleury in the eleventh century.

delights as a cake made from fruit, a malt cake, three measures of fish, and a *pitantia* of good wine.[106]

The liturgical needs of a community could often change as when a community gained new relics, became a priory of a large community, or simply enlarged its calendar. Such changes generated a need for new texts. In the eleventh century the monks of Fleury sent a manuscript to their priory at Perrecy which contained the miracle collections of Adrevald and Aimo, as well as announcements of the deaths of Abbots Abbo and Gauzlin.[107] Around the year 1100 a legendary (Vatican, Reg. lat. 528) was assembled – probably at the abbey of Saint-Denis – to meet that abbey's new needs in celebrating the feasts of saints from the Orléanais.[108] An extant manuscript was dismembered and then bound together with two new *libelli*, which contained texts about Maximinus of Micy and Benedict of Nursia. A scribe then added a table of contents to the first folio of the codex, noting the date of the feasts on which each text would be read. *Lectio*-markings were also added to the new *libelli*.

106 *Consuetudines Floriacenses*, pp. 158, 191, 193, 265. The celebratory meal was more elaborate for the two feasts particular to the cult of Benedict's relics at Fleury than to the more universal commemoration of his death.
107 The manuscript is Dijon, BM 1118. See *CGMBPF*, v, 279–81; Lejay 1896; Vidier 1965, pp. 29–30 n. 10.
108 On Vatican, Reg. lat. 528 see *Catal. Vat.*, pp. 354–6. The sections are fos. 1–41 (eleventh century); fos. 42–184 (late ninth or tenth century); fos. 185–92 (tenth century); and fos. 193–232 (late ninth or tenth centuries). The second and the fourth sections are in the same hand and constitute the original codex. The first section contains the anonymous *Vita s. Maximini II*, Letaldus of Micy's *Miracula s. Maximini*, and Odo of Cluny's *Sermo de s. Benedicto*. The third section contains Adrevald of Fleury's *Historia translationis s. Benedicti*. The fourth section (fos. 193–209) contained the life of Benedict from the *Dialogues* of Gregory the Great. The table of contents (late eleventh or twelfth centuries) is found on fo. 1. The approximate date of assembly is provided by this hand. According to the table of contents, the selection from Gregory the Great's *Dialogues* was read on the traditional 21 March feast of Benedict's death, while Adrevald of Fleury's *Historia translationis s. Benedicti* was to be read on the 10 July feast of the *translatio* and Odo of Cluny's *Sermo* on the 4 December feast of the *illatio*. These seem to have been the same readings as were in use at Fleury at this time. Apparently the March feast had already been celebrated at the abbey where the manuscript was assembled, while the other two feasts were added to the calendar along with the celebration of the feast of Maximinus of Micy. As part of the table of contents, the scribe included a list of thirteen disciples of St Maximinus, based on Letaldus' *Miracula s. Maximini*.
  There are marginal notes in a thirteenth-century hand on fos. 1v and 2 which read 'hic est liber beati Dionysii', suggesting that the manuscript was probably assembled at Saint-Denis in Paris. Since many of the feasts noted in the table of contents were not celebrated at either Fleury or Micy the original codex certainly did not come from the Orléanais, although the added *libelli* may have been obtained from the region, since they have palaeographic similarities to work done at the scriptoria of Fleury and Micy. On the assembling of legendaries, see Dolbeau 1981a.

In producing legendaries scribes could significantly alter the content of a text. In many eleventh-century copies of the *Vita s. Aniani I*, for instance, a passage taken from Gregory of Tours was substituted for part of the original description of Anianus' defence of the city of Orléans.[109] So, too, the choice of which excerpts were to be read on a feastday affected the reception of a hagiographic text. The *Sermo de inventione s. Maximini et eius discipulorum*, for example, was read at the abbey of Micy on the feast which commemorated the reburial of those relics during the reconstruction of the church under Abbot Albert in the late 1020s, an event described in some detail at the end of the *Sermo*. The sole medieval manuscript of the text, which comes from Micy itself, indicates that this historical narrative was not read during the liturgy. Rather the *lectiones* consisted of a description of Maximinus tutoring his disciples in the monastic life, a section which contained the metaphorical comparison of Maximinus and his disciples to the root and spreading branches of a tree.[110] The monks of Micy thus heard a description of the spiritual achievements of the saint rather than of the event which the feastday commemorated. Similarly the monks of Saint-Denis chose to hear the description of the miracles worked by Maximinus during his life, rather than the story of the foundation of Micy, on the feast of that saint.[111]

In addition to such common legendaries, a monastic scriptorium would sometimes produce special volumes containing texts about that community's own patron. The best example from the Orléanais is an illuminated codex (Archives du Loiret H 20) which

---

[109] On the relationship of the two texts, see above chapter 1 n. 4. Renaud (1978a, n. 14) identified twenty-three medieval manuscripts of *BHL* 473. Although she was aware of the substitution in question (see n. 22), she did not record how many scribes made it. Mlle. Renaud has kindly provided me with her unpublished list. Of these, I have identified six which use the substitute passage from Gregory of Tours: Paris, BN lat. 5278, fos. 373v–6; Paris, BN lat. 5308, fos. 268–70; Vatican, Reg. lat. 496, fos. 173–80; Vienna, Nationalbibliothek 420, fos. 110–15; Troyes, BM 1171, fos. 210–13v; Trier, Stadtbibliothek 1151, fos. 49–52. Of these, at least the first three are probably from the middle Loire valley. Cuissard (1886, pp. 201–2) mistook the text of Paris, BN lat. 5278, as the original text of *BHL* 473 and so erroneously concluded that Gregory of Tours had followed that source almost verbatim.

[110] Vatican, Reg. lat. 621, fos. 40–2. On the manuscript, see Head 1984, pp. 235–6.

[111] The *lectio*-markings for the copy of the *Vita s. Maximini II* found in Vatican, Reg. lat. 528, are on fos. 9–12v. They correspond approximately to cc. 24–33, pp. 587–9. There are no *lectio*-markings in the copy of Letaldus' *Miracula s. Maximini* in this manuscript, suggesting that the monks did not hear readings from that work. Presumably the choices of liturgical readings would have differed at Micy itself.

was executed at the Fleury scriptorium beginning in the late tenth century. It contained Gregory the Great's life of St Benedict, Adrevald's *Historia translationis s. Benedicti*, sermons of Odo of Cluny and Aimo of Fleury, as well as the miracle collections of Adrevald and Aimo.[112] The manuscript included a full-page miniature of the saint. Such a manuscript would have played a role in the cult of the patron's relics, as it contained basic readings for the three feasts of the saint. This manuscript was kept in the reliquary of the saint by the seventeenth century and may have been closely associated with the shrine itself at an earlier date. Similarly a copy of Abbo of Fleury's life of King Edmund belonged to the keeper of that saint's shrine at Bury St Edmunds.[113]

Prayers and *lectiones* were not the only readings which a monastic community heard during the course of a patron's feast. Sermons also appear to have been preached as part of the mass. One of the goals of the Carolingian reform had been to incorporate sermons as a regular part of the liturgy in both monastic communities and parishes.[114] Before the advent of the mendicants, however, preaching was not an enterprise in which the preacher was responsible for the composition, or at least the redaction, of the sermon. Usually sermons were based directly on patristic models. Most manuscript collections of sermons, called *homiliaria*, primarily contain material for Sunday services culled from such writers as Augustine and Caesarius of Arles. The few sermons on saints in these collections (most did not include a separate *proprium sanctorum*) also betray the overbearing hand of tradition.[115] Odo of Cluny's sermon on St Benedict, for example, became a ritual text, repeated at Fleury and elsewhere on the December feast of Benedict's burial.[116]

In the eleventh century members of the religious communities of the Orléanais produced sermons for use on the feasts of their patrons which were based on patristic and Carolingian texts. Aimo of Fleury, for example, began his *Sermo in festivitatibus s. patris Benedicti* with a long comparison of Benedict to the prophet Elijah, supported with numerous quotations from scripture and Gregory

---

[112] Vidier 1965, pp. 137–8; Grémont 1963–4, p. 238; Van der Straeten 1982, pp. 80–1.
[113] British Library, Cotton MS Tiberius B ii, bears the inscription *Liber feretrariorum*. See Wormald 1974, pp. 94–5.
[114] McKitterick 1977, pp. 80–114; Gatch 1977, pp. 27–39; Wallace-Hadrill 1983, pp. 280–2.
[115] On Carolingian *homiliaria* from nearby Auxerre, see Barré 1962.
[116] Pellegrin 1963, p. 26.

the Great's life of the saint. This introduced a *florilegium* of passages from both prose and verse works about St Benedict by such authors as Gregory, Paul the Deacon, and Smaragdus.[117] This work was later lavishly praised by Andrew: '[Aimo] also composed a *sermo* in praise of father Benedict, which sparkled with the beautiful inclusion of verses. Collecting the declarations of preceding fathers, he produced a most precious pearl of signs [*signa*, that is miracles], so that this man should be regarded as equal in virtue to the attesting patriarchs.'[118] Two anonymous authors composed sermons in honour of Benedict and of Anianus.[119] Both were based on the same sermon of Caesarius of Arles, whose works had long provided the basis for many Sunday sermons collected in *homiliaria*. That sermon of Caesarius was available in the library of Fleury.[120] The author of the Benedict text, probably a monk of that monastery, added substantial sections of original material about his subject to quotations from Caesarius' work. The author

---

[117] *PL*, CXXXIX, cols. 851D–70C. Introductory comparison of Benedict and Elijah: cols. 851D–8A; from Gregory the Great's *Dialogues*: cols. 858A–9A; from Gauzbert of Fleury's verse *vita*: cols. 859A–C; from Odo of Glanfeuil's *Miracula*: cols. 859C–D; from Mark of Monte Cassino's verses to Benedict: cols. 859D–61B; from Paul the Deacon's *Historia Langobardorum*: cols. 861B–4A; from a hymn by Iambicus Archilochius: cols. 864A–5A; references to Paul the Deacon and Odo of Cluny: col. 865A; from Smaragdus' verse commentary on Benedict's rule: cols. 865B–6D; from Aldhelm of Malmesbury's *De laude sanctorum*: cols. 866D–8A; concluding section on the love of Benedict's pupils or foster-sons (*alumni*), the monks of Fleury, for their patron: cols. 868A–70C.

[118] Andrew of Fleury, *Vita Gauzlini*, c. 2, pp. 32–4.

[119] The sermon about St Benedict was read in the monastic refectory at Fleury on the night before the feast of the saint's translation, see Pellegrin 1963, p. 27.

[120] The *Sermo 'Ad illuminandum' s. Benedicti* (also known as the *Sermo in translatione s. Benedicti*) survives in three manuscripts: Dijon, BM 1118 (eleventh century, Perrecy, a priory of Fleury), fos. 127–32v; Paris, BN lat. 2627 (eleventh century, Moissac), fos. 89–91v; and Vatican, Reg. lat. 591 (twelfth century, Fleury?), fos. 79–81v. On these manuscripts, see Pellegrin 1963, p. 27 n. 4.

The *Sermo 'Ad illuminandum' s. Aniani*, also known as the *Sermo in festivitate s. Aniani*, survives in one manuscript: Vatican, Reg. lat. 585 (eleventh century), fo. 57v. The two texts cannot be dated with certainty, but the Benedict text must date at least to the first half of the eleventh century on the evidence of the manuscripts. Since the Anianus text is so similar in form, I would date it to the same period.

The source text was Caesarius of Arles, sermon 214, pp. 853–6. While this sermon was absent from most manuscript collections of Caesarius' works, significantly it was included in a copy produced at Fleury. Morin used Orléans, BM 131 (seventh century, Fleury), p. 344, as the primary source for his edition of sermon 214. There are only two other known manuscripts. Sermon 215, a sermon in honour of St Felix, was thought to be the work of Faustus of Rietz. This work has been assumed to be the source for the sermon on St Anianus, but sermon 214 contains all the material used in both the Benedict and Anianus texts, and, unlike sermon 215, was available in a manuscript at Fleury. Thus it would seem to be the most likely source of both eleventh-century works.

of the Anianus text simply altered sections of Caesarius' work by changing the name of the saint, as well as an original conclusion.[121] Both Aimo's work and the anonymous sermon on Benedict were read in the Fleury refectory in conjunction with the December feast of the saint's burial.[122]

The elaborate process of reading and hearing texts which was required on the feastdays of universal, local, and patron saints points out one way in which monasteries functioned as communities of interpretation. Monks and canons listened to stories about the saints and even about their saint. From these texts they learned an ideal of *virtus* which they should imitate; just as the saints had encapsulated the life of Christ in their lives, so, too, the members of religious communities were supposed to imitate the lives of the saints in their own. They also learned of the ongoing *patrocinium* which their 'father' provided their community.

The laity were to a large degree excluded from this communal process of interpretation. The hagiography from the Orléanais was composed — like most extant western hagiography prior to the twelfth century — in Latin, a learned language whose use was primarily confined to the clergy.[123] Moreover, the liturgical uses of hagiography discussed so far pertained to the canonical hours of the monastic *opus Dei*. The stories about the 'fathers' of the diocese, and the ideals of sanctity which they contained, thus circulated first and foremost among the monks, canons, and priests of the diocese. There is abundant evidence that the laity attended monastic liturgies. In the ninth century the monks of Fleury worried whether they would have enough food to serve the 'crowd of many people which usually came to the monastery' on the feast of St Benedict.[124] In the eleventh century the feast of St Maximinus

---

[121] These eleventh-century authors sometimes inserted their own concerns and language into the source texts from which they borrowed. One, for example, modernized the patristic text by substituting the phrase *poterunt intercedere* for Caesarius' *poterunt commendare* in a description of how the saints plead the cases of those who pray to them.

[122] Pellegrin 1963, pp. 24–7. Pellegrin noted that she was unable to locate the 'liber floriac abbatum et romana priuil' which contained Aimo's sermon. That manuscript apparently contained the lost work of Aimo on the abbots of Fleury which Andrew of Fleury mentioned several times (*Miracula s. Benedicti*, IV.prologue, p. 173, V.6, p. 202, VI.13, p. 237, and VII.13, p. 270).

[123] For a review of the evidence of Latin as a clerical language, see Grundmann 1958; Clanchy 1979, pp. 154–64 and 177–91; Stock 1983, pp. 19–30. While no medieval vernacular versions of any hagiographic works from the Orléanais survive, one of the earliest manuscripts of a vernacular saint's romance (Orléans, BM 347), the *Chanson de Ste Foi* was held in the library at Fleury. On this text, see Grémont 1969.

[124] *Miracula s. Benedicti*, I.22, pp. 51–2.

was described as an event 'attended by all men, and most particularly by the brothers [of Micy] and the whole people of the Orléanais'.[125] These examples could be multiplied. Lay attendance was not confined to the feastdays of the saints. The *custodes* of the cathedral of Sainte-Croix were charged with opening the doors of the church so that people could enter and attend matins.[126] Most importantly, the purpose of Bishop Walter's legislation on the celebration of feastdays was to require liturgical commemoration of the diocese's 'fathers' in parish churches.

The laity who attended these liturgical events, either at the monasteries or their parish churches, would not have directly understood most prayers, *lectiones*, or sermons in Latin. The Carolingian reform programme did not simply inculcate preaching, however, but began to institute preaching in the vernacular language on the parish level.[127] Theodulf of Orléans had stressed his priests' duty to undertake the catechetical teaching of their flocks. Bishop Walter required that a martyrology and a *homiliarium* be kept in parish churches.[128] The priests ordinarily provided renderings of Latin texts in the vernacular to their lay audiences in a part of the liturgy known as the *Prone*. Presumably these talks were based on hagiographic *lectiones* on the feastdays of the 'fathers'. Thus the devout laity of the diocese had some contact – albeit through intermediaries – with the hagiographic traditions of the region. Their primary contact with the 'fathers', however, was not based on hearing hagiographic traditions, but on their experience of the *patrocinium* of the saints as pilgrims to their relic shrines or as servants of the saints on the lands of their monasteries.

The institution of relic cults was treated by the authors of the *vitae* of the saints in highly stereotyped passages on the burial and posthumous miracles of the saint which concluded their works. These passages served a dual purpose: they connected a saint to a specific tomb, and they linked the living and the posthumous personalities of that saint. First, the saints foresaw, frequently with the aid of a divinely inspired vision, their impending deaths. Some arranged for the continued function of their office. Evurtius left his

[125] *Miraculum s. Maximini*, pp. 244–5.
[126] Rodulfus Glaber, *Historiarum libri quinque*, II.5.8, pp. 64–7.
[127] McKitterick 1977, pp. 84–7; Gatch 1977, pp. 37–9. The first requirement for preaching in the vernacular is usually assumed to have been at the Council of Tours in 813 (*capitula* 4 and 17 in *MGH, Concilia*, II.1, p. 288).
[128] Walter of Orléans, *Capitularia Walterii*, c. 7, p. 189.

office as bishop to make way for his successor, while Maximinus put the affairs of Micy in order.[129] Others looked to their own burial. Avitus promised relics to the citizens of Châteaudun, and Viator went so far as to prepare his own tomb.[130]

According to the hagiographers the burial of a saint was a major liturgical event, attended by prominent churchmen. Maximinus was interred by Eusebius, his friend and bishop of Orléans; Viator by Trijetius, his first abbot.[131] Sometimes, as in the case of Maximinus and Avitus, the saint was buried in a church, while for others, such as Anianus and Evurtius, churches were later constructed over their tombs. The construction of these churches was financed by those seeking the patronage of the saints. Among those on Bishop Walter's list, the churches for Avitus, Anianus, and Evurtius (the three patrons of canonical foundations) were all built by lay patrons, while those for Benedict, Maximinus, and Lifardus (the patrons of monasteries) were built by clerical patrons.[132] These buildings were described in terms closer to reliquaries than to actual edifices.[133] The authors all claimed that many people were cured of illnesses at the shrines thereafter. The lists of cures were *topoi* which contained little detail about the cures, although they stressed lameness, blindness, and leprosy. The author of the *Vita s. Aniani II* noted, 'Light was returned to the blind there, and hoped for solace to the depressed, demons were exorcized, oaths were very frequently made, and corresponding gifts were

129 *Vita s. Evurtii I*, cc. 14–15, pp. 318–19. *Vita s. Maximini II*, c. 33, p. 589; compare Bertholdus of Micy, *Vita s. Maximini I*, c. 22, pp. 596–7.
130 *Vita s. Aviti I*, c. 12, p. 62; *Vita s. Viatoris*, c. 9, p. 102.
131 Bertholdus of Micy, *Vita s. Maximini I*, c. 22, pp. 596–7; *Vita s. Viatoris*, c. 10, pp. 102–3.
132 On Evurtius: *Vita s. Evurtii II*, c. 20, p. 58; *Acta translationis s. Evurtii*, cc. 4–9, pp. 59–60. On Avitus: *Vita s. Aviti I*, c. 13, pp. 62–3; *Vita s. Aviti III*, in Paris, BN lat. 3789, fo. 113. On the relics of the cross: *Vita s. Evurtii I*, cc. 9–10, pp. 315–17; Lucifer of Orléans, *Vita s. Evurtii II*, cc. 8–13, pp. 55–6. On Lifardus: *Vita s. Lifardi*, c. 13, p. 157. On Benedict: Adrevald of Fleury, *Historia translationis s. Benedicti*, cc. 4–7, pp. 4–8. On Maximinus: Bertholdus of Micy, *Vita s. Maximini I*, c. 25, p. 597.
133 'Postea vero cressente devotione fidelium, multorum curriculis annorum labentibus ad orientalem plagam civitatis Aurelianensium, extructo templo mirifico, argento et auro gemmisque fulgentibus exornato, concurrente nobilium conventu cum choris psallentium, crucibus, candelabris ac vario lumine radientium lampadarum sanctum corpus illius translatum est in triumpho, operante clementia Christi virtutum fulget congeries.' *Vita s. Aniani II*, c. 9, p. 33. Compare Bertholdus' generic description of reliquaries: 'Sanctorum praeconia virorum Ecclesiae Fidelium per orbem diffusae summa laude concelebrant, quorum piam memoriam nunc sepulcra auri argentique metallis, pretiosorum quoque ordinibus lapidum ac marmorum crustis redimita testantur'. Bertholdus of Micy, *Vita s. Maximini I*, c. 1, p. 592.

presented to the petitioners through the work of our Lord Jesus Christ, who glorifies his saints with crowns of laurel.'[134] Not only did the saints continue to exercise the *virtus* given them by Christ at their shrines, but they did so by bringing living petitioners into their service and forming personal relationships with them, just as they had with other holy people during their own lives.

Nevertheless the *patrocinium* of the saints was not the main focus of these works. Subsequently collections of miracle stories added flesh to the skeletal *topoi* found in their lists of posthumous miracles. The authors of those collections painted a portrait of how the saints continued to exhibit the same *virtus* after their deaths which had been attested in their *vitae*. It is in those collections that the personal relationships formed between living Christians – both clerical and lay – and the 'fathers' of the diocese were most fully described.

[134] *Vita s. Aniani II*, c. 9, p. 33.

Chapter 4

THE POSTHUMOUS PATRONAGE OF THE SAINTS

SAINTLY PATRONAGE AND THE COLLECTION OF MIRACLE STORIES

As the authors of the lives of the 'fathers' of the Orléanais stressed, the *virtus* which those saints had exhibited during their lifetimes continued to be efficacious posthumously at the shrines containing their relics. Bertholdus of Micy wrote, 'The exercise of spiritual powers, in which the saints once exerted themselves either bodily or spiritually . . . even today does not cease to show forth around their remains.'[1] While a living holy person had numerous ways in which to exercise *virtus*, such as asceticism and teaching the monastic life, the posthumous exercise of that *virtus* was virtually synonymous with miracles. Odo of Cluny echoed Bertholdus in the mid-tenth century when he preached to the monks of Fleury, 'The Holy Spirit adorns [St Benedict] spiritually both with the signs of miracles and with the exercise of powers in order that he, through whom [the Holy Spirit] has placed the multitude of the higher order under a rule, might now appear worthy in the world.'[2]

The monks of Fleury took the presence of Benedict in their house seriously and literally. Odo's biographer related how one had been confronted by St Benedict himself in front of the abbey's gates. The saint had ordered him, 'Go and tell the brothers that, since they give me no peace, I am going to leave these buildings.' The purpose of the saint's journey was to bring Odo, a renowned

---

[1] Bertholdus of Micy, *Vita s. Maximini I*, c. 1, p. 592.

[2] Odo of Cluny, *Sermo de s. Benedicto*, col. 722. The word *informaret* in the printed edition has been corrected to *innormaret* according to Vatican, Reg. lat. 528, fo. 41. Odo's words were repeated in the prayers for the feast of Benedict's *illatio* in two thirteenth-century breviaries: Paris, BN lat. 1020, fo. 181v (a breviary for the winter months copied for the diocese of Orléans *c.* 1230; Leroquais 1934, III, 462–3), and in Orléans, BM 125, fo. 264v (Fleury; Leroquais 1934, III, 292–5). Both these texts use *innormaret*. Other readings for the feast differed in the two manuscripts and the liturgical traditions represented by the two seem to be independent.

reformer, to the house. The monks of Fleury reacted to this pronouncement, not with the tears and prayers of repentance which the Cluniac hagiographer thought their best recourse, but by mounting on horseback and riding off in an attempt to force the saint to return.[3] Such a reaction should hardly be surprising in light of the traditions about the saint which had been collected by Adrevald only half a century earlier. In a similar vision, St Benedict had once promised the community that, if they vowed to live the monastic life properly according to his rule, 'Your patron will in his grace deny you nothing good.' His fellows responded enthusiastically and prayerfully to the offer of their 'most faithful father'. Later that day, the troops of Count Odo of Orléans, who had been oppressing the community, were defeated and the count himself perished.[4] When the monks of Fleury mounted their horses, they sought to bring back this 'father' who attacked his enemies and cured his friends.[5] Nor were the monks the only ones devoted to this patron. Continuing his praise of Benedict's miraculous *virtus*, Odo of Cluny noted,

[Because of these signs, a multitude] turns out on [Benedict's] days, both on this feast [of his burial] and on many others dedicated to him, many times through the year; some devoutly, others for pleasure, from all over they come to his most holy tomb. Not only countryfolk, but even people from the city, a mingling of noblemen and distinguished clerics, as well as of some puffed-up sorts, they stream together rejoicing and devoutly seek [the saint's] patronage (*patrocinium*) in common.[6]

Collections of miracle stories provide the primary evidence for the posthumous *patrocinium* of the 'fathers' of the Orléanais.[7] These

[3] John of Salerno, *Vita s. Odonis*, III.8, cols. 80D–1A.
[4] *Miracula s. Benedicti*, I.20–1, pp. 47–51 (the quotation is on p. 49).
[5] *Miracula s. Benedicti*, I.21, p. 50.
[6] Odo of Cluny, *Sermo de s. Benedicto*, col. 722B.
[7] The vast bulk of this evidence comes from the abbey of Fleury, so that this portrait may sometimes seem to be more a picture of the relationship between St Benedict and his servants than a general description of the 'fathers'. The miracle collections composed by Adrevald, Aimo, Andrew, Rodulfus Tortarius, and Hugh at Fleury contain the descriptions of over 150 miracles, while those from all the other houses in the diocese only include about one third that number.
It should be noted that not all the miracles described at Fleury are attributed primarily or solely to St Benedict. The Fleury collections have been studied by several scholars for the light they shed on early medieval society and the idea of the miraculous, see Leclercq 1975; Ward 1981 and 1982, pp. 42–56; Rollason 1985. The 'fathers' were not the only saints who performed miracles. Several miracles collected in the *Miracula s. Benedicti* (II.19, III.11, VI.7, VIII.20–1, VIII.23, VIII.27, VIII.37, IX.10), particularly in the work of

were works of historiography. They were one of the means by which medieval writers – in this period primarily monks and canons – recorded the actions of human society and its interaction with the sacred.[8] Since these authors wished to discuss the ways in which the 'fathers' of their communities exercised patronage, it should not be surprising that they often discussed the social context of that patronage, thus providing much information about what might be termed secular history. The writers themselves would have made no such firm distinction between events inside and outside a monastery's walls.[9] They cast their nets widely in order to narrate the story of the patronage provided by their 'fathers'.

The form in which these authors told their histories of saintly patronage did not remain constant. In the third quarter of the ninth century Adrevald of Fleury composed the first such collection in the Orléanais. That work provided a model for the first two collections of the Capetian period, those of Letaldus of Micy and Aimo of Fleury. The latter explicitly noted that he wrote in Adrevald's tradition. All three authors welded together the stories of their patron saint and their community into a single narrative.[10] Their primary focus was on the miracles through which the saint protected his lands and servants, not on cures performed at his shrine. In the middle third of the eleventh century new concerns can be sensed. While Andrew of Fleury shared his predecessors'

Rodulfus Tortarius, were attributed to such other saints as Maurus the martyr whose relics were also enshrined at Fleury. The author of the *Miracula s. Euspicii* collected four miracles attributed to the power of the uncle of Micy's patron, some of whose relics were enshrined on a side altar in the monastic church. Abbo of Fleury and Gregory of Nicopolis were both thought to have performed miracles after their deaths, although those attributed to Abbo were largely confined to the priory of La Réole where he had been murdered.

[8] On the connections between miracle collections and historiography see primarily Sigal 1980, as well as Bautier 1970, p. 837, and Labande 1970, pp. 752–3. Most discussions on the relationships between hagiography and historiography focus, as do most discussion of hagiography as a genre, on *vitae*, see, for example, Günter 1949; Genicot 1965; and Gaiffier 1970.

[9] Andrew of Fleury's work, for example, is one of the major sources for such varied events as the burning of the heretics of Orléans in 1022 and the infamous militia organized in 1038 by Archbishop Aimo of Bourges to enforce the oaths of the Peace of God. On Andrew as a historical source, see Head 1987a, pp. 513–18. Many modern historians, however, have drawn too firm a divide between historiography and hagiography. Vidier (1965, p. 206), for instance, remarked, 'For [Andrew] the miracles were less his purpose than the pretext he had taken for writing history.' More recently Duby (1980, p. 185) moderated that judgement only slightly, 'Although a hagiographer, [Andrew] did not refuse a historian's role.' Such remarks threaten to obscure the fact that Andrew saw the two roles as virtually identical.   [10] *Miracula s. Benedicti*, II.prologue, p. 92.

focus on Benedict's protection of their community, he organized his work geographically, around Fleury's many dependencies, rather than fashioning a continuous narrative.[11] The anonymous author of the *Miracula s. Aniani*, on the other hand, used the historiographical form pioneered by Adrevald, but emphasized miracles, particularly cures, performed at Anianus' shrine. The later miracle collections, composed from the last quarter of the eleventh century through the twelfth century, were simply loose collections of stories with little or no narrative theme which consisted primarily of miracles performed at the shrines of the saints. Rodulfus Tortarius even chose to ignore the works of his predecessors in the prologue to his work.[12]

No matter what the overall form of the work, however, each individual miracle story told a drama of sacred power in action. They provide examples of how the 'fathers' were perceived and their actions were explained by a medieval audience, or, perhaps more accurately, of how the actions of the saints were used to explain other events, such as injuries, cures, and court judgements. The stories were written by clerical authors and most directly reflect their mentality. Many concerned the laity and their dealings with the saints and their communities of monks and canons. The collections also provide precious evidence concerning the interaction of clergy and laity and thus serve as an excellent mirror of what is generally called popular religion. Taken together they detail a logic of saintly patronage which was developed in monastic circles, but which, as we shall see, the laity, at least in part, accepted as an accurate description of the powers of the saints. The social function of the cult of the saints was grounded in this logic of patronage.

THE WORK OF ADREVALD OF FLEURY

A vivid picture of St Benedict's patronage emerged in the work of Adrevald, the earliest of the collections. Benedict's shrine was located in the church of the Virgin Mary at Fleury. Large numbers of lay pilgrims came throughout the year, but most particularly on the feasts of the saint.[13] They came at times from great distances

---

[11] Andrew stated that he wrote in the tradition of both Adrevald and Aimo, see *Miracula s. Benedicti*, IV.prologue, p. 173. On Andrew's style, see Vidier 1965, pp. 199–207 and Head 1987a, pp. 514–15.   [12] *Miracula s. Benedicti*, VIII.1, pp. 277–8.

[13] *Miracula s. Benedicti*, I.22, p. 51, and I.23 (incorrectly numbered 33 in the Certain edition), p. 53.

and their numbers included all levels of society from peasants to the high nobility.[14] Pilgrims had the custom of leaving tokens for the saint, mostly of gilded bronze, tied to the bellropes of the church. Women, however, were prevented by what Adrevald variously termed *antiqua auctoritas* and *religio monastica* from going past the exterior gates of the monastery.[15] When new relics of martyrs were received from the abbey of Saint-Denis, a tent was set up outside the main gate of the monastery to allow the multitudes of pilgrims from the region, including many women, access to these novelties under the watchful eye of the monks.[16] The monks provided food for pilgrims on the feasts of the saint and maintained separate hospices for the poor and the nobility.[17] They also took an avid interest in what happened to the pilgrims, witnessing several cures, questioning the validity of another, and talking, sometimes at length, to their lay visitors.[18] Those pilgrims could cause a considerable spectacle. One man 'possessed by a particularly cruel demon' was chained to a column in the church, foaming at the mouth and screaming, for three days.[19] Adrevald was not, however, primarily interested in such stories of miraculous cures

[14] Various pilgrims were described as being from the 'upper parts of the Loire' (*Miracula s. Benedicti*, 1.31, p. 68); the viscount of Tonnerre (1.32, p. 69); and a *pauper* (1.23, p. 54). Adrevald suggested that German, the native language of the monk Christian, was common among the pilgrims (1.26, p. 59).

[15] Adrevald described the presence of laymen in the church of the Virgin at Fleury. The only woman whom he mentioned as having been cured by the saint (*Miracula s. Benedicti*, 1.36, p. 79) positioned herself in the *fores* of a church in Orléans where the relics were housed after the destruction of the monastery by the Normans. She was apparently barred from entering the church, but there was no monastic enclosure to keep her from approaching its doors. Evidence from Micy suggests that such prohibitions were not universally enforced in the monastic houses of the region. Bertholdus (*Vita s. Maximini I*, c. 25, p. 597), who wrote shortly after the return of the body of Maximinus to Micy in the early ninth century, said that a number of laypeople of all classes and ages and both sexes joined the assembled clerics and the community of Micy in the celebration. Several decades later the anonymous author of the *Vita s. Maximini II* (c. 37, p. 591) emphasized that the same event had particularly attracted the infirm and women. It is impossible to determine, however, whether such remarks were simply *topoi* or reflect the actual presence of women within the cloister walls at Micy in the ninth century.

[16] *Miracula s. Benedicti*, 1.28, pp. 63–5.

[17] The foundation of both a *hospitale nobilium* and a *hospitale pauperum* by Louis the Pious was recalled in a bull of Pope John VIII in 878 (*Recueil des chartes de Saint-Benoît*, no. 29, 1, 80–3).
This bull was later confirmed by Charles the Simple (no. 34, 1, 92–5, reedited in *Recueil des actes de Charles le Simple*, no. 34, p. 74). On the provision of food and the function of the hospice for the poor, see *Miracula s. Benedicti*, 1.23, p. 54, and 1.24, p. 56. On monastic *hospitia*, see Lesne 1910–45, VI, 102–9.

[19] *Miracula s. Benedicti*, 1.31, pp. 68–9.

and exorcisms – he included only six such stories, none of which concerned a monk of Fleury.[20]

Physical contact with the saint's relics played a small role in Adrevald's description of the cult of Benedict. Many of the miracles which the monk related, both cures and more particularly chastisements, occurred far from Fleury. While pilgrims to the church of the Virgin stood in the presence of the saint, none of those who were cured actually touched the tomb. At the time when Benedict's relics were located in the city of Orléans, removed from Fleury out of fear of the Normans, the saint still punished a man who took a false oath in the market of the village attached to the monastery.[21] Adrevald related four stories in which Benedict appeared to members of the community and to laypeople who had attacked the monastery. Hercambaldus, who had one of these visions, described Benedict as having appeared *in specie corporea*.[22] For Adrevald the relics – that is the physical matter which had once formed the saint's living body – were the focus of Benedict's presence at Fleury. They did not completely constitute the saint's posthumous existence, however, for he appeared elsewhere in this world in this 'body-like manner'. Presumably the saint had still another form in the court of heaven.

To abstract a general picture of the cult of Benedict is to suggest that Adrevald's work was simply a hodgepodge of stories, when it was a carefully organized argument concerning the patronage which St Benedict offered to his community. Both because of the rival claims of Monte Cassino and the threats provided by local bishops and counts, Adrevald wished to demonstrate that Benedict himself was present at the monastery and that he provided strong protection for his servants. Since Benedict had not come from the region, Adrevald's first priority was to show that Fleury was the saint's chosen home. In the first third of his work he described the life of Benedict, the later abandonment of Benedict's abbey at Monte Cassino, the foundation of Fleury, and the translation of

---

[20] This range of interest sets Adrevald apart from the authors of most Carolingian miracle collections, whose work tended to be short, to focus on curing miracles, and to contain little of the historiographic detail in which Adrevald's work abounded. On such collections, see in particular Rouche 1981. For examples, see the *Miracula s. Richarii* (BHL 7230) or the *Miracula s. Germani* (BHL 3462). The ninth-century miracle collection closest in form to Adrevald's work was the *Historia translationis corporis s. Mauri abbatis in Fossatense monasterium* (BHL 5775) of Odo of Glanfeuil, an author who seems to have been strongly influenced by Adrevald of Fleury.

[21] *Miracula s. Benedicti*, 1.35, pp. 77–8.   [22] *Miracula s. Benedicti*, 1.21, p. 50.

Benedict's relics there. Adrevald borrowed his account of the translation of Benedict's relics from Paul the Deacon, who was from Italy and a partisan of Monte Cassino. Thus he emphasized that Fleury's claim to possess the relics was widely accepted. Adrevald argued that the seat of both monastic and secular authority had moved from Italy to the land of the Franks.

Adrevald had first developed his argument that Fleury was Benedict's chosen home in the *Historia translationis s. Benedicti*. In that earlier text, miracles marked each major episode in the translation of Benedict's relics to Fleury, confirming that the translation was in accord with divine providence and the personal will of the saint. Abbot Mummolus of Fleury was inspired by a 'divine oracle' to set the search for the body of Benedict in motion. His emissary, Aigulphus, joined a group of monks from Le Mans who were seeking the relics of Scholastica as the result of a similar vision.[23] When the party arrived at Monte Cassino an old man appeared to tell them where the relics of both saints were located.[24] Although the pope was warned in a dream that the relics were being taken out of his country, he was unable to stop the Frankish monks. Adrevald used language from Exodus to describe how shadows hid the monks from the pope's eyes, thus making this journey parallel to the flight of the Israelites from Egypt.[25] When the monks arrived in the *pagus Aurelianensis*, the sick among the crowds which greeted them were cured.[26] Later at Fleury the bones of Benedict and Scholastica, contained in a single coffin, were separated by divine will in response to the prayers of the people.[27] Mummolus first decided to bury Benedict in the church of St Peter, but a great storm and accompanying flash of light from the church of the Virgin convinced him that God wished that church to house the relics.[28]

In the miracle collection the transition of monastic authority

[23] Adrevald of Fleury, *Historia translationis s. Benedicti*, c. 3, p. 4 and c. 4, p. 5.
[24] Adrevald of Fleury, *Historia translationis s. Benedicti*, c. 6, pp. 5–7.
[25] 'Nam Omnipotentis potentia tenebrarum densitate ita eos occuluit, ut sibi quidem nil obesset, persecutoribus vero eorum omnem facultatem se inveniendi auferret, sicque famuli Dei, malorum timore sublato ocius redirent.' Adrevald of Fleury, *Historia translationis s. Benedicti*, c. 8, pp. 8–9.
[26] Adrevald of Fleury, *Historia translationis s. Benedicti*, cc. 9–11, pp. 9–10. These were not miracle stories, but simple notations of the towns in which they occurred and what diseases were cured.
[27] Adrevald of Fleury, *Historia translationis s. Benedicti*, cc. 12–13, pp. 11–12.
[28] Adrevald of Fleury, *Historia translationis s. Benedicti*, c. 15, pp. 13–14.

from Monte Cassino in Italy to Fleury in Gaul culminated in the attempt by the newly restored abbey of Monte Cassino to regain the relics of Benedict around the middle of the eighth century.[29] Carloman – who had served, along with his brother Pippin, as governor of the palace for Childeric III – decided (*c.* 746) to become a monk and settled at Monte Cassino. After Pippin had usurped the throne with the blessing of Pope Stephen in 751, Carloman and the brothers of Monte Cassino decided to secure the return of the precious relics of their founder. He went to Rome and obtained a letter of support from Pope Zachary. He then left for France to petition his brother for help in obtaining the treasure. Faced with both familial and papal claims on his allegiance, Pippin dispatched Archbishop Remigius of Rouen to Fleury.

On the arrival of the delegation at Fleury, Abbot Medo unwillingly agreed to the request. His speech reveals much about the relationship of the community to their patron, at least as envisaged in the ninth century:

The most holy father permitted himself to be brought here by his own will, and by a sacred vision he invited his servants for the purpose of carrying him off. We, though unworthy, received the most holy members of the great father: we received the pious remains; we have devoutly preserved [them] until now. And if, by means of our intervening sins, it is pleasing to him to leave Gaul and to seek again his native country, I acknowledge that it appears to be possible for him, nor is it proper that our wish in any way interfere.[30]

After these brave words he ordered the church locked and several servants to sleep in front of the doors. The monks retired to the church of St Peter to pray for divine help in retaining the relics, a gift which God had given 'by grace alone', not as the result of their merits.[31] The monks were in the powerless position of serfs; all authority resided in their lord, the saint. When the archbishop's delegation gained entrance to the church to exhume the relics, the tomb emitted a flash of light which blinded the party. In the ensuing confusion the archbishop was reduced to humble prayer and Abbot Medo led the *violatores* from the church. A terrified Remigius later warned Pippin against removing the relics and the monks of Monte Cassino went home satisfied with the gift of a few

---

[29] *Miracula s. Benedicti*, I.15–17, pp. 37–42.
[30] *Miracula s. Benedicti*, I.16, p. 40.   [31] *Miracula s. Benedicti*, I.17, pp. 40–1.

minor relics of Benedict.[32] The *pignus* of the saint remained in place at Fleury. The original meaning of *pignus* was a pledge and the word came to signify relics only through usages such as this.

This episode, taken together with the *Historia translationis s. Benedicti*, certified Benedict's choice of Fleury as his home. He had pledged his patronage to the monks of that community through the symbol of his body. Those monks had become, in Adrevald's word, the saint's *familia*.[33] Geary has pointed out that one of the purposes of translation accounts in general, and of the accounts of relic thefts (among which he numbers Adrevald's work) in particular, was to prove that it was the will of the saint that his or her relics be moved to a new home:

The historical significance of the *translationes* is drastically altered if the relics are recognized as living persons. The theft of such relics then becomes a ritual kidnapping and the *translatio* becomes the story of how an important powerful individual leaves his home, wanders through many dangers, and finally is welcomed into a position of honor and authority in a new community.[34]

The story of a saint's patronage, however, only began with such a welcome.

Seen from the perspective of later records of the saint's patronage, rather than of the translation itself, the relics look less like living persons. Certainly Benedict continued to live after the death of his physical body and his relics were intimately related to that continued existence. At the same time, the saint did not exist only through his relics. He was free to wander his territory and the world at large, aiding his servants and rebuking his enemies. The remainder of Adrevald's work chronicled those very actions. If there was a simple equation between the relics of a saint and that saint's posthumous existence, then the monks of Fleury at the time of Odo of Cluny need not have worried that Benedict had left them, since his relics were still safely enshrined in their church.

---

[32] Remigius was later regarded as a saint in Normandy and is recorded in a tenth-century work, the *Vita s. Remigii* (*BHL* 7174). The author of that work made Remigius the brother of Carloman and Pippin. Other than the elaboration of these obviously ahistorical details concerning the archbishops's family and youth, the author depended directly on the work of Adrevald. I am grateful to Felice Lifshitz for informing me of this text.

[33] See particularly his description of the monks praying together in church for the safety of Benedict's relics, *Miracula s. Benedicti*, I.17, p. 41.   [34] Geary 1978, p. 154.

Geary was correct to emphasize the personal, as opposed to material or magical, nature of relics. For Adrevald, however, those relics were not the equivalent of the living saint, they were rather the personal pledges of an ongoing relationship between Benedict and the saint's servants.

In the three stories following the repulse of Remigius, Adrevald discussed the mutual recognition of the roles of patron and servant by Benedict and his monks. He began by triumphantly relating how Charlemagne came into sole possession of royal power and subjugated Italy.[35] The monk shrewdly noted, however, that, because of the 'suspect faith' of the Franks, Charlemagne had to recruit a number of men from the *nobile genus* to serve as intermediate authorities. Raho, the man chosen as count of the Orléanais, was quickly 'shown to be most cruel in his greed'. Seeing that most of the region's resources were subject to his control, with the exception of the community of St Benedict, he plotted to kill its abbot, Radulfus. Benedict shortly proved the efficacy of his patronage as the 'founder' (*conditor*) of Fleury. The count summoned the abbot for a meeting at his palace. Meanwhile he retired to luxuriate in a bath. Radulfus stopped by the priory of Saint-Gondon where he met a dwarf 'who served the count with jests'. That man informed him of the count's intention and the abbot immediately returned to Fleury. He need not have worried. Raho got up from his bath and lay down on a couch, placing his head in the lap of his concubine. While napping there, an old man dressed as a monk and accompanied by a young attendant appeared to him. The figure demanded, 'O count, what have I done to merit your wish to kill my abbot?' When Raho denied any such intention, the figure raised his *baculus*, or staff of office, and struck the count saying, 'I swear by your head that punishment will most certainly come to you for such a senseless act.' The count then awoke and recounted this vision in terror. He quickly fell into a depression and died the following night.

Immediately following this punishment of comital arrogance was a story which emphasized the secular rights of the monastic community.[36] Fleury possessed a royal grant to maintain four

---

[35] *Miracula s. Benedicti*, 1.18, pp. 42–6.
[36] *Miracula s. Benedicti*, 1.19, pp. 46–7. On the importance and interpretation of this story, see Ganshof 1959, pp. 485–90, and Rollason 1985, p. 78.

boats on the Loire exempt from duties.[37] An agent of Count Raho confiscated one of these boats and brought it to Orléans to subject its cargo to a taxation for the *fisc* 'in contempt of royal authority'. There was a special harbour set aside for boats awaiting such taxation. On a Sunday afternoon the boat from Fleury came loose from its moorings and returned upstream to the abbey with no one aboard to pilot it. Adrevald observed, 'People from the city ran from all sides to see this unbelievable miracle. Amazed they raised their voices with rejoicing and adulation.'

In Adrevald's view the secular oppression of the religious communities of the region continued in the reign of Louis the Pious: 'The church of Orléans with the nearby houses of the saints, which were considered to be subject to the rule of clerics and monks of the Lord, was afflicted by not a little hardship.'[38] After Count Matfrid rebelled against Louis in 830, a noble named Odo was substituted in his place and soon decided to gain control of the rich properties of Fleury and Saint-Aignan. The monks of Fleury sent a delegation to him, who 'bearing relics of the saints and in all ways bearing themselves humbly in prayer [begged] him not to incur such a sin and not to transfer the property (*res*) set aside for the sacral order to impious use'. The petition fell on deaf ears. In 833 Matfrid and his ally Count Lambert again revolted in support of Louis' son, Lothar.[39] Odo organized an expedition against the rebels and pressed, among many others, Abbot Boso into service. He proposed to march into Burgundy along the northern bank of the Loire and to support his troops in part by plundering Fleury's lands. Boso decided to transfer the abbey's serfs and such movable goods as livestock to the southern shore.

Three days after the abbot departed on the expedition Hercambaldus, who was charged with arranging the transfer, fell asleep in the early morning hours, exhausted by his labours. An elderly man carrying an abbatial staff and followed by a young attendant appeared to him, as to Raho. This spectral abbot mocked the

---

[37] Adrevald places these events during the reign of Charlemagne. An extant charter of Louis the Pious (*Recueil des chartes de Saint-Benoît*, no. 8, 1, 23, and no. 15, 1, 33–6) granting these rights confirmed a series of earlier royal acts, including one of Charlemagne. There is no reason to doubt the authenticity of either the extant charter or its predecessors. The monastery of Micy possessed a similar right ('Chartes de Micy', no. 1, pp. 13–17).

[38] *Miracula s. Benedicti*, 1.20–1, pp. 47–51 (the quotation is on p. 47).

[39] For a summary treatment of these rebellions, see McKitterick 1983, pp. 170–2, and the works cited there.

monks for their lack of trust and then offered to make a pact with them:

It is remarkable that our brothers find fault with me for ignoring them, as if I have no care for their problems and, weighed down by laziness, I sleep instead of relieving them . . . If you will take care to obey the precepts of the almighty and will without hesitation take an oath to follow the commands of the Rule which has been handed down by God through me to you, then all your adversities will turn to prosperity, your enemies will become friends, and your patron (*fautor*) in his grace will deny you nothing good . . . Have faith in the Lord and in him you will be comforted.[40]

The attendant then identified the speaker as Benedict. Hercambaldus immediately got up and extended his arms 'as if he might be able to grasp the vestiges of the one whom he had seen'. He set off for the monastery and told the monks of the pact which their patron had offered. They immediately prayed to God in acceptance.

That evening an exhausted messenger arrived and told the community of a battle in which Odo, in addition to many others, had died. The monks were saddened by news of the death of so many 'Christian people', even though some were their enemies who merited punishment. Calling to mind Christ's injunction to love one's enemies (Matthew 5:44), they prayed together for the dead 'so that, if they did not merit absolution from eternal punishment, they might at least be touched lightly by softer penalties than strict justice required'.[41] Those who had earned punishment wrought through Benedict's protective patronage and divine justice were thus reincorporated, at least partially, into the Christian family. Not only did the saint's patronage have power, but so did the prayers of his monastic *familia*.

These episodes signalled the formation of a pact between the monks of Fleury and their patron St Benedict, a pact implicitly sworn over the pledge of the saint's relics (*pignora*). The recognition of this relationship by the laity, which Adrevald recognized as *opinio vulgus*, remained essential. In the next pair of stories Adrevald told how Benedict's reputation spread. He turned his attention to the 4 December feast of the burial of the saint's relics 'when a crowd of many people always flowed to the monastery on

---

[40] *Miracula s. Benedicti*, i.20, p. 49.   [41] *Miracula s. Benedicti*, i.21, p. 51.

account of the memory of such a father'.[42] It was the custom of the monks to provide a feast for the pilgrims, albeit one in accord with monastic dietary restrictions. One year the community was particularly anxious as to whether they would have enough food to satisfy the multitude. The night before the feast one monk had a dream-vision of an area of the Loire river which he recognized. A venerable-looking monk gestured to that stretch of the river with his abbatial staff. After the completion of the office of matins the monk told the community of his dream. A number of them went to the indicated spot on the river and caught an abundance of fish, which Adrevald described as a 'booty' provided by the 'beloved knight of Christ for his fellow knights'.[43]

The number of pilgrims grew, even apart from the festal celebrations of the saint's honour. 'Popular opinion began to spread through the world that the excellent grace of Christ was present for those mortals who laboured under some bodily disability. From every region they began to seek the door of Benedict, the confessor of Christ, and his monastery, since they were accustomed to find there a hoped-for remedy.'[44] One in particular came who, having lost the use of his legs, was forced to travel on his knees, using a crude form of bench for support. He prayed for a cure through the intercession of Benedict at his shrine in the church of the Virgin and then retired to the hospice maintained for the poor. The next day he got up and was able to walk upright, but the monks suspected a hoax. While the community was gathered in chapter, Abbot Adalgaud called the anonymous pilgrim before them. As he stood there, another figure, using an abbatial staff as a crutch, suddenly appeared. The monks recognized Benedict, described here as their *patronus*, and gave thanks to God for the miracles by singing hymns.

Together the stories provided proof that Benedict had taken pilgrims to his shrine under the protection of his patronage. The *baculus* which the saint had wielded in wrath against his noble opponents was used in these appearances to sustain this new group of servants. These laypeople were also linked to the saint by an implicit oath taken over the saint's *pignora*. Adrevald next

---

[42] *Miracula s. Benedicti*, 1.22, p. 51.   [43] *Miracula s. Benedicti*, 1.22, p. 53.

[44] *Miracula s. Benedicti*, 1.23, p. 53 (note the chapter is incorrectly numbered 33 in the Certain edition).

described two court cases from the abbacy of Boso (833–45) in which Fleury clashed with another monastery over the possession of some serfs.[45] The first was to be heard by the local *vicarius* (a deputy of the count) and Boso sent monks to visit him with a gift of two silver bowls. The other abbey, however, had already provided the judge with a – presumably larger – gift. Thus 'corrupted' he spurned the gift of Fleury, swearing by his sword that the serfs would no longer belong to St Benedict. Shortly thereafter he was thrown from his horse and died. The *advocatus* of Fleury was then able to secure a hearing before a different judge and 'lawful judgement' prevailed.

The second dispute pitted Fleury against Saint-Denis. It was first held before local judges assembled by both sides and witnessed by royal legates, including Bishop Jonas of Orléans and Count Donatus of Melun. 'But as they were unable to reach judgement in that court (*placitum*), due to the fact that these judges of the Salic law were not able to settle properly a matter of ecclesiastical property which was contained under Roman law, the case (*placitum*) was moved to Orléans under *missi dominici*.' It is unclear exactly what the term 'Roman law', of which relatively little would have been current in the late ninth century, means here.[46] Nevertheless it is significant that a question of competence could cause a change of venue. The distinction between Roman and Salic laws also indicates a growing recognition of the differences both between the laws pertaining to ecclesiastical and civic matters and those between laws based on written tradition and on custom. Even after the move, no judgement could be reached and it was suggested that judicial combat be used to decide the case. One of the doctors of law present – a man from the Gâtinais with a 'bestial name' who must be Servatus Lupus – had been 'corrupted' and suggested that 'it was not right that witnesses should make judgement in an ecclesiastical matter by means of war and that it was much better for the *advocati* [to arrange] among themselves that the serfs be divided.'[47] Viscount Genesius favoured this course of action over the objections of Fleury. This time St Benedict merely struck the 'corrupt' doctor mute. Brought by his friends to Fleury, he made peace with the saint and afterwards praised his powers, but Benedict never regained the lost serfs.

---

[45] *Miracula s. Benedicti*, 1.24–5, pp. 55–7. Also see Rollason 1985, p. 82, and Nelson 1986, pp. 45 and 63.   [46] Riché 1965, p. 20.   [47] *Miracula s. Benedicti*, 1.25, p. 57.

The law was not, in these cases, an idealized code which was impersonally applied. Judges were sometimes ignorant of the relevant laws and the law often failed to produce a judgement. First judicial combat, and finally simple compromise, had to be suggested in its place. Gifts, which were implied to be corrupt bribes when given by the enemies of St Benedict, were exchanged freely. Such means of reaching compromise were common in the Carolingian world. As Janet Nelson has suggested, the evidence of miracle collections can help to illuminate the record of diplomatic sources: 'The judicial records, by their very nature, stress adversarial procedure: winners and losers. Agreements, mediations and arbitrations must have resolved very many ninth-century disputes, but either they were unrecorded, or the records have been lost, partly because churches, as disputants, were more interested in victory than in compromise.'[48] Just such a judicial record can be found in a contemporary *placitum* which survives in the Fleury cartulary.[49] It recorded a judgement favourable to Fleury in a dispute with a vassal named Gysleharius over the rights to several *villulae*. Bishop Jonas and Count Hugh, the *missi dominici* who heard the case, ruled on the basis of written evidence that the rights had been given to Fleury by Pippin.

This diplomatic record in turn sheds light on the miracle collection. St Benedict appeared in the *placitum* only as the patron of Fleury. The scribes of the royal chancery did not mention the saint's protective power.[50] When written documentation was available, chastisement by the saint was irrelevant. Adrevald, as a monk of Fleury, chose to record a disputed judgement neglected by the royal chancery because, in citing the power of St Benedict, he was able to claim a limited victory in these cases. What mattered to Adrevald was not written law, but the personal power of his patron. In his miracle collection he could gather together traditions concerning the property of the abbey which would not otherwise find their way into its archives. The diplomatic records of an application of Roman law and the narrative records of a search for

---

[48] Nelson 1986, p. 63.
[49] *Recueil des chartes de Saint-Benoît*, no. 19, I, 43–6. The diploma is dated 24 August 835 and mentioned Boso as abbot.
[50] Even the formulaic phrase 'the place where St Benedict is buried' was not used for Fleury, although it appeared in many other Carolingian charters.

consensus by appeal to the sacred coexisted easily in the Carolingian world.[51]

Adrevald now turned his attention back to the shrine of Benedict. He focused on a monk named Christian who had been chosen by lot to be the guardian (*custos*) of the sanctuary, a post which Adrevald compared to that of guardian of the temple under Mosaic custom.[52] The monk worked as an *agent provocateur* for his patron, going to the sanctuary and pretending disaffection with the saint in order to incite similar calumnies from onlookers, which the monk would then roundly condemn. One night, while Christian was sleeping, some thieves entered the church and stole some of the bronze ex-votos left by pilgrims there. Discovering the theft, Christian immediately turned to the person most responsible for allowing it to happen:

Since he with utmost simplicity had faith that St Benedict would hear, he spoke in the language of a pilgrim feigning rusticity (for he was a German by birth), 'O St Benedict, you lazy-bones, why are you sleeping? Why do you so negligently provide for your home that you would allow thieves to take away secretly the gift which I gave to you in honour? I'm certain that I couldn't care if someone stole your breeches, since you let them take my amulets. Believe me, if your amulets aren't given back to me, I won't light even one candle to you.'

Then he struck the saint's tomb with a staff (*baculus*). Both by his use of the staff and by reprimanding the saint for being asleep, Christian neatly reversed the symbolism inherent in earlier stories and effectively coerced the saint to act in the manner of a patron.[53] Shortly thereafter the thieves were apprehended during a second robbery and then revealed the hiding place of the pilgrim offerings, which were returned to their place of honour in the church.

There was no simple demarcation of monastic from lay and learned from popular cultures. A monk talked to lay pilgrims near the site of Benedict's body. Some of the laity acted as the saint's enemies, others devoutly brought gifts to him. The monk sometimes acted in the manner of the laity (*vulgari mortalium more*)

---

[51] On the coexistence, at later periods, of 'rational' law with 'irrational' or miraculous ideas, see the perceptive comments of Cheyette 1970, Brown 1975, and White 1978.

[52] *Miracula s. Benedicti*, 1.26, pp. 58–60. Adrevald used the verb *sortior* to describe the choice of Christian as *custos*, a word which strongly suggests an element of chance, although Adrevald went on to emphasize the holiness of Christian's character.

[53] For similar examples, see Geary 1979a.

and was able to mime the speech of a peasant pilgrim, presumably in his native German. Moreover this monk assumed that such pilgrims would expect, just as he expected, St Benedict to meet the obligations which he had to his servants. Christian did not strike his patron's tomb as the *custos* of the church, but in the place of all the anonymous pilgrims who had made themselves Benedict's servants by providing him with gifts. If Benedict would not live up to his end of the bargain, then those pilgrims would stop giving gifts and lighting candles. While this story was told by a monastic chronicler and concerned a monk, it indicates that the monks of Fleury in the ninth century thought that their lay neighbours recognized and acted according to the logic of patronage which governed the relationships between the saint and his servants, lay as well as monastic.

Adrevald's collection was an exposition of this logic of saintly patronage. A web of personal relationships centred on the saint and the pledge of power found in his relics. Through careful presentation of his material Adrevald had shown that the saint was obliged to care for his servants, first his monks, then his pilgrims, and finally the serfs attached to his lands. They in turn were obliged to serve him, by such means as obeying his rule, donating land to his monastery, or bringing ex-voto offerings to his shrine. Benedict jealously protected the belongings which he received in this manner. The relics were the physical focus of the saint's power, but that power did not emanate by way of sympathetic magic. Rather Benedict himself personally exercised that power, as the vision stories dramatically demonstrated. The monks had an idea of what Benedict in his posthumous existence actually looked like. He was an elderly man, but a figure of strength and authority. He carried a symbol of that authority, his *baculus*, and was accompanied by at least one attendant. Each miracle story was a drama in which this *patronus* exercised his power. The miracles depended on the network of personal relationships which the saint had developed with the living. Since the saint was himself a servant of Christ, divine power emanated through a chain of personal ties. Christ used his power through the intercession of his servant Benedict in favour of the servants of the saint. These personal relationships, a contract for mutual service based on oath taking and gift giving, were similar to the social ties of military and agricultural service which bound secular society together. The saint served as an effective foil to the Carolingian nobility. This was the *patrocinium* which Bishop Walter, writing only a few years after Adrevald, invoked and celebrated. Like the monk of Fleury, the bishop assumed that the laypeople of his diocese understood that saintly *patrocinium*.

SAINTLY PATRONAGE IN THE ELEVENTH AND TWELFTH CENTURIES

This image of the posthumous personality and patronage of the 'fathers' of the diocese was revived by numerous authors, such as Aimo of Fleury and Letaldus of Micy, in the Capetian period. What follows is a general picture of the patronage provided by the 'fathers' of the Orléanais in the eleventh and twelfth centuries.[54] While that patronage was in many respects similar to that described by Adrevald, it had subtly changed to fit new social circumstances. For Adrevald, writing within the Carolingian imperial order, the high nobility provided the most important enemies of his patron Benedict and royal agents were the prime dispensers of justice. His eleventh-century successors, Aimo and Andrew, described knights as Benedict's most contentious lay foes and a judicial system under the control of the local nobility.[55] The 'dislocation of the *pagus*' can be clearly traced in the miracle collections of Neustria.[56]

The 'fathers' of the Orléanais possessed the property of the foundation dedicated to them; they were named in its charters; they gave and received its gifts. Thus they were fully involved as active participants in the contemporary economy of gift exchange. Miracles were performed not by material objects, that is by the relics of the saints, but by people, that is the 'fathers' themselves – or, as the medieval authors insisted, by God working through the

---

[54] Sigal (1985) has provided a statistical study of those miracle collections composed in the eleventh and twelfth centuries in the region between the Loire and the Seine. His work provides a wealth of useful comparative material for the following description. Other useful comparative material may be found in Gonthier and Lebas 1974, Hermann-Mascard 1975, Finucane 1977, and Ward 1982. Some particularly salient comparisons will be provided in the notes. The following description is primarily intended to treat the function and development of the cult of local 'fathers' in the Orléanais itself, but is written in the belief that the posthumous cult of the saints is best studied within such a local framework.

[55] For a full account of the change in the sources, see Rollason 1985, pp. 81–5. A similar focus can be seen in the collections from other communities. The Fulk who, according to Letaldus, tried to take the *villa* of Bezillis from Micy (*Miracula s. Maximini*, c. 30, p. 606) was described as a *miles*, while the Gilbert who ravaged the lands of Saint-Aignan (*Miracula s. Aniani*, c. 13, p. 269) was likely of the same station given the description of his actions. [56] Lemarignier 1951, particularly pp. 401–2.

intercession of the saints. At the same time the cult of the saints had a strongly material character. Relics provided the focus for the veneration of a saint. The relationship between these physical remains and the personal being, or soul, of a saint had been more completely worked out by the late tenth century than it had been in the time of Adrevald. Saints were, or could be, present at their interred bodies in a way that differed from ordinary dead Christians. Abbo of Fleury described the relationship thus, 'Of [Edmund], as of all other saints who now reign with Christ, it is certain that, although his spirit is in celestial glory, his presence (*presentia*) is not either day or night far from visiting his body, in union with which it merited those things through which it now experiences the joy of blessed immortality.'[57] If the living body had once been a saint's means of expressing *virtus* and meriting salvation, posthumously the saint's relics continued to express that *virtus* in miracles performed through the saint's intercessory presence. In a contemporary text, Letaldus used that same term in noting that at Micy 'the grace of God . . . demonstrates [Maximinus'] presence (*presentia*) through a most frequent abundance of miracles'.[58]

While this *presentia* of the saints was particularly focused on their relics, it was by no means limited to their tombs. The full sense of this term was expressed in a long speech which a monk of Fleury placed in the mouth of St Benedict himself.[59] The saint was addressing the abbot of Monte Cassino, telling him in no uncertain terms that his relics had been removed from their original tomb to Fleury with the saint's approval. Nevertheless Monte Cassino, as the saint's original community, shared in the patronage which he also provided for his adopted home of Fleury: 'As both places were consigned to my custody . . . there remains for both one single glory, one oversight, one custody, one defence.' While Benedict might intercede for the monks of Monte Cassino in a manner indistinguishable from that provided for the monks of Fleury, he was not present at the Italian community in the same way. He concluded his talk, 'You must be content that my presence (*presentia*) is always here spiritually (*spiritualiter*).' Such a purely spiritual presence would seem to differ from the materially grounded presence that Benedict had at Fleury, or, for that matter,

---

[57] Abbo of Fleury, *Vita s. Edmundi*, c. 16, p. 86.
[58] Letaldus of Micy, *Miracula s. Maximini*, c. 28, p. 605.
[59] *Miracula s. Benedicti*, VII.15, pp. 273–4.

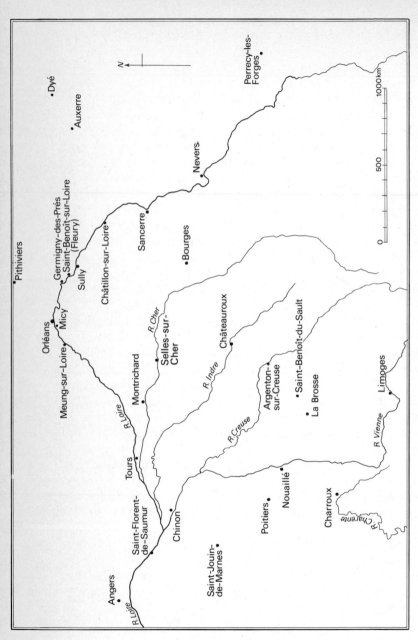

Map 2 Places associated with the collections of miracle stories

Source: based on D. W. Rollason, 'The miracles of St Benedict: a window on early medieval France', in Henry Mayr-

Maximinus had at Micy. The physical pledge provided by the *pignora* of the saint had real, if not exclusive, value in making that saint become present in this material world and thus carry out both miracles in that realm and intercession in the realm of 'celestial glory'.

The personal pledges which the 'fathers' had provided were therefore carefully enshrined by the communities protected by the patronage of those same 'fathers'. Relics of a patron thus became the most prized possession of a community. The monks and canons of the Orléanais had gone to great lengths to defend their relics during the invasions of the Normans. Sometimes they also had to defend them against one another. Theodoric of Fleury composed the *Illatio s. Benedicti* (BHL 1122), a mythical account of the struggles against the Normans.[60] One manuscript of the work preserves an interesting variant.[61] The monks of Fleury brought the relics of Benedict to the church of Saint-Aignan for safekeeping. The monks of that community responded by attempting to keep the relics for themselves and thus make Fleury 'destitute of its own patron'. Those monks (described as *litigantes*) pointed out that Fleury had been founded from Saint-Aignan. Since the monks of Fleury had been forced to leave their monastery because of their sins, those of Saint-Aignan reasoned that the relics constituted a gift of God to their community. The monks of Fleury responded that the many miracles and visions granted by Benedict to their community, despite their sins, showed that he wished his body to remain there. The miraculous return of Benedict's relics to Fleury proved their claim. While the passage was suppressed, it indicates

---

60 The text was composed 1010–18. On the circumstances of composition, see Poncelet 1908, pp. 20–5, and Vidier 1965, pp. 170–80. According to Theodoric, the monks knew of the approach of the Norman raiding parties and so sent the relics of their patron by boat to Orléans where they were placed in the church of Saint-Aignan. The Normans burnt the church of the Virgin at Fleury and killed sixty of the community's monks, but they were later destroyed by Count Gislolfus, who fought aided by a vision of Benedict. When it came time to return, the monks placed the relics in the same boat, although the river was frozen. Miraculously the boat managed the trip to Fleury on 4 December and the relics were reburied at the saint's home. That date was later celebrated as the feast of the *illatio* or burial. Theodoric's text is curious. He evidently conflated the stories told by Adrevald and Adelarius, but he also included an explanation for the origin of the December feast which was clearly in conflict with that given by Adrevald (*Historia translationis s. Benedicti*, p. 14).

61 Paris, BN lat. 17641, fos. 4v–6v. The base text of this passage is Theodoric of Fleury, *Illatio s. Benedicti*, c. 8, pp. 353–4. Some of the variants are printed in *Catal. Paris.*, III, 422–3. Vidier (1965, pp. 177–9) discusses all the additions. In his opinion this manuscript provides the primitive version of the text.

that a tension existed between the two communities during the eleventh century, perhaps created by jealousy of the senior community for the success of its junior.

Later in the eleventh century Monte Cassino challenged Fleury's claim to possess the true relics of Benedict. In 1066 Abbot Desiderius began to rebuild the main church of that foundation. During the construction, probably in 1068, a tomb was discovered under the floor of the old sanctuary. It was identified as that of Benedict. Desiderius ordered it to be covered up and then altered his construction plans. He also claimed that miracles occurred at the rediscovered tomb and implied that these events proved Fleury's claim to the relics false.[62] Around this time – and quite possibly in response to these events – an author from Fleury composed a brief collection of miracle stories.[63] He began by noting that in 1056 – on the 21 March feast of Benedict's death – a column of light had appeared over the monastery of Fleury, making it appear that the buildings were on fire. Many people were attracted from the city of Orléans by the spectacle, 'some not lacking in nobility and priests endowed with honour'. The members of the community were 'exhilarated in their hearts and bodies' by this sign of God's love for their patron. More important was a report given by Abbot Gervinus of Saint-Riquier at a gathering which included the abbots of Fleury, Saint-Denis, and Saint-Medard. Gervinus had gone to Italy on business with the papal court and stopped at Monte Cassino. He related that Abbot Richer had led the community in a

---

[62] Meyvaert 1955; Davril 1979a. On the miracles at the rediscovered tomb, see Desiderius of Monte Cassino, *Dialogi de miraculis s. Benedicti*, II.14–15 and 17–18, pp. 443–6.

[63] *Miracula s. Benedicti*, VII.14–17, pp. 271–6. Unfortunately the only known manuscript of this collection (Vatican, Reg. lat. 592) is incomplete, breaking off in the middle of a story. The collection is generally considered to be an anonymous appendix added to the work of Andrew. Despite the arguments of Vidier (1965, pp. 202–3), Andrew completed the first three books of his collection in 1043. At some later point he added a fourth book (Book VII of the Certain edition). Vidier reasonably claims (p. 204) that the stories in question here formed an even later addition to that book, for they appeared in a different hand in Vatican, Reg. lat. 592, and were not included in Rodulfus Tortarius' verse synopsis of Andrew's work. Vidier also claims that the author of this appendix was not Andrew. Bautier (1969, p. 90 n. 5) is in agreement. I do not think that it is easy to discount Andrew's authorship of this appendix. Vidier's main argument is that the author showed a preoccupation with the presence of the relics of Benedict at Fleury which was not evident in Andrew's work. The changed circumstances of mid-century could easily account for such a change in Andrew's attitude. Moreover the final story in the extant portion of the appendix (VII.17, pp. 275–6) concerns a fire at the monastery in 1026, which Andrew discussed in detail in his *Vita Gauzlini* (c. 67, p. 136). While these chapters certainly form an addition to the original text, the identity of their author must remain an open question.

three-day fast, designed to seek guidance in recouping the lost relics of their patron.[64] On the final day Benedict appeared to the abbot, and, in the speech discussed above, warned him not to violate the saint's tomb, for he had gone to Fleury willingly. Benedict's message for the monks of Monte Cassino, carefully worked out by a monk of rival Fleury, was a mixed one. They could enjoy the saint's patronage, defence, and intercession, but they could not aspire to recouping his relics.

Much later an author compiled a synopsis of the *Historia translationis s. Benedicti* and the *Illatio s. Benedicti* in French.[65] He worked probably toward the end of the thirteenth century and in a style which marks him as a Burgundian. It was the only example, however, of a vernacular version of any of the hagiography from the Orléanais composed before the early modern period. The work was an attempt to make the story of Benedict's choice of Fleury as his home, so important in these monastic disputes, available in the vernacular, presumably to a lay audience.

SANCTUARIES, FEASTS, AND PILGRIMAGE

The churches of the monastic communities of the Orléanais served as homes to the relics of the 'fathers'. In them the monks and canons enacted the most important rituals of the cults of these patrons and pilgrims sought to be in the presence of a saint. Those churches also served as the setting for the daily round of the *opus dei*, or monastic office. They were not static environments. Frequent additions and alterations were made in their fabric to accommodate changes in ritual and style. Other changes were necessitated by destruction wrought by violence or by fire.

The best evidence, both textual and architectural, for the appearance and function of such a church comes from Fleury, whose Romanesque structure is still largely extant.[66] According to

---

[64] Since Richer (1038–58) was still abbot, the event must be placed between 1056 and 1058.

[65] Vidier 1965, pp. 220–6, provides both an edition and discussion of this text.

[66] The most comprehensive description of the church at Fleury remains the works of Chenesseau (1931a and 1936). Laporte (*DHGE*, xvii, 441–76) provides an updated summary. Bautier (1969) has traced the changes in the structure in the early Capetian period (988–1032) by comparing architectural and textual evidence. Berland (1982) has studied the Romanesque altar, while he (1979b), Grémont (1963–4), and Verdier (1977) have each separately studied the sculpted capitals. These studies have been superseded, to one degree or another, by Vergnolle's (1985) analysis of the eleventh-century sculpture in which she also considers many other aspects of the architectural history of Fleury.

Adrevald, the relics of Benedict had been housed in the central sanctuary of the church of the Virgin Mary from the time of Abbot Mummolus, but there are few extant descriptions of either the reliquary or the church itself during the Carolingian period.[67] The church had to be reconstructed after the destruction of the monastery by the Normans in 865, a task which seems to have been largely completed within a single decade. Odo of Cluny (abbot of Fleury, *c.* 930–43) constructed the first subterranean crypt in which to place the relics. At that time they were preserved in a lead reliquary decorated with gems. At the time of the reception of the relics of St Paul Aurelian, Abbot Wulfadus (948–63) moved the relics of Benedict from the crypt to the upper church. There the reliquaries (*loculi*) of the two saints were placed in a single repository (*scrinium*) covered with gold.[68] At the turn of the century masses were celebrated by some ordained members of the community in the crypt and Aimo knew of two miracles which had occurred during such masses.[69] By that time, and probably much earlier, a tower had been constructed at the western end of the church. The monks used to gather there to recite psalms as part of the office and also for the performance of such liturgical dramas as the *Quem quaeritis?* at Easter. Aimo numbered among the miracles of Benedict an incident in which the monks were kept dry during their office despite a storm which raged outside the open edifice.[70] Abbot Abbo (988–1004) commissioned the monk Gauzfredus, who served as *custos* of the relics, to fashion a new reliquary for Benedict encrusted with plaques of gold and various gems and decorated with scenes from the life of the saint.[71]

One of Abbo's explicit concerns in commissioning the new reliquary was that the relics be kept safe from fire (*ad repellendam ignis*). The threat of fire posed significant problems for monastic communities. True relics were believed to be immune from fire.

[67] Bautier 1969, p. 78.
[68] *Miracula s. Benedicti*, VII.16, p. 275. The description of the *scrinium* is found in a passage from Aimo, *Miracula s. Benedicti*, III.11, p. 155. Bautier (1969, p. 91) reasonably suggests that some form of crypt probably dated back to the reconstruction of the church in the late ninth century. On the layout of this crypt, see Vidier 1965, pp. 189–90 and 232–3; Bautier 1969, pp. 90–3; Berland 1983–4, pp. 15–16.
[69] Aimo of Fleury, *Libelli miraculorum s. Benedicti*, cc. 2–3, pp. 227–8.
[70] Aimo of Fleury, *Libelli miraculorum s. Benedicti*, c. 1, p. 227. See also Vidier 1965, pp. 229–32; Bautier 1969, pp. 93–6. Heitz (1963, pp. 189–209) discusses the *Quem quaeritis?* and the importance of Fleury in the development of this liturgical drama.
[71] Aimo of Fleury, *Vita s. Abbonis*, c. 15, p. 51. Gauzfredus was directly appointed to this office, not chosen by lot as the monk Christian had been in the ninth century.

Occasionally relics of dubious authenticity were tested through an ordeal by fire and in some cases relics were used to fight fires. Fires at monasteries were generally interpreted as a sign of divine punishment and their containment credited to a saint's patronage. In 974 several of Fleury's buildings, including the church of St Peter, burned to the ground. The flames suddenly subsided when they reached the church of the Virgin.[72] In interpreting this event Aimo wrote,

[It was] as if the Lord said to his servants, not in words, but in actions, 'Although to you I seem to be angry for the sins you have committed, nevertheless having been softened by the prayers of my faithful ones, whom I have chosen to be guardians in this place, I leave some homes for you to live in.'

The church of the Virgin successfully weathered two fires which started in neighbouring buildings in 1002 and again in 1005, both times on the eve of the feast of Benedict's translation.[73] In 1026 it was so badly damaged by fire that Abbot Gauzlin began major restorations which were interrupted by his death.[74] Toward the end of his life he waited impatiently for the arrival of an artist summoned from Byzantium to oversee the construction of a mosaic floor.[75] Abbot William (1067–80) began the construction of an essentially new church, replacing the older structure by sections as had been done at Micy in the 1020s.[76] Only the chevet and the entrance tower, begun by Gauzlin, were finished during the eleventh century.[77] During his abbacy the saint's body was placed in a new bronze reliquary. The wooden box which served as the inner portion of the older reliquary was broken up and its pieces were associated with miraculous cures.[78] According to Rodulfus Tortarius, who was a member of the community during much of this construction, Benedict continued to look after this new home. On Easter Monday of 1095, a fire started in a barn in the neighbouring town.[79] The monks rushed to the church. The younger ones began to take down the silken draperies hung for the

---

[72] *Miracula s. Benedicti*, II.9, pp. 110–12.
[73] *Miracula s. Benedicti*, III.2, pp. 128–30, and III.19, pp. 166–9.
[74] Bautier (1969, pp. 96–112) discusses this fire and Gauzlin's building programme from the evidence provided by Andrew of Fleury (*Vita Gauzlini*, c. 57, pp. 104–8).
[75] Andrew of Fleury, *Vita Gauzlini*, c. 67, p. 137.
[76] *Miracula s. Benedicti*, VIII.25, pp. 318–19.
[77] For a discussion of the tower, see Vergnolle 1985, pp. 24–199.
[78] *Miracula s. Benedicti*, VIII.42, p. 347.   [79] *Miracula s. Benedicti*, VIII.27, pp. 321–4.

feast, the older ones carried the relics out of the church, while the more infirm and the oblate children chanted prayers under the direction of the abbot. The monastery was spared 'by the merits of [the Virgin] and of father Benedict', but the wooden church of Saint-Denis and much of the town were destroyed. Shortly thereafter the saint also healed the injuries of a workman who fell while toiling on the new walls.[80] Letaldus had similarly claimed that a monk of Micy had had his life saved after a fall. The monk had been placing a new cross on the roof of that community's church.[81]

The church of the Virgin constructed in the late eleventh century contained sculpted capitals in the apse and the nave which depicted various sacred and natural subjects. Nine of them portrayed vignettes from the life of Benedict found in Gregory the Great's *Dialogues*.[82] None represented stories from the collections of posthumous miracles.[83] Only one of the stories concerned a cure effected by the saint. The others involved such varied examples of his *virtus* as the avoidance of diabolic temptation, the liberation of a prisoner, and the chastisement of two recalcitrant oblates. The artists, of whom there were at least two, focused on the gestures involved in the miracles. In four scenes Benedict raised his hand in a blessing, causing the miracle to occur, while in two, divine hands carried out a similar gesture.[84] In another, Totila, the king of the Goths, demonstrated his deference to the saint by kneeling at his

---

[80] *Miracula s. Benedicti*, VIII.30, pp. 327–8.

[81] Letaldus of Micy, *Miracula s. Maximini*, c. 33, p. 607. See also Finucane 1977, p. 110, and Sigal 1985, p. 267 n. 6.

[82] Ten different scenes are depicted, as one column contains two scenes. Of these nine, seven capitals are still in place, while two from the transept have fallen and are now preserved in the museum of the abbey of Fleury. On the iconography of these capitals, see Grémont 1963–4, pp. 235–52; Verdier 1977; Berland 1979b; Vergnolle 1985, pp. 226–30 and 248–54. Verdier provides textual identifications of the subjects.

[83] Two have been commonly identified as such. The first is a fallen capital from the transept. Verdier (1977, pp. 135–6) suggested that it depicted a man who hanged himself in a story told by Rodulfus Tortarius (*Miracula s. Benedicti*, VIII.44, pp. 349–51). Vergnolle (1985, p. 228, particularly n. 632) points out that the identification is mistaken, and that the man is not hanging from a gibbet, but simply carrying a stylized object. A second capital has been interpreted as depicting men engaged in judicial combat. Grémont (1963–4, p. 250) identifies it with a story told by Rodulfus Tortarius (*Miracula s. Benedicti*, VIII.11, pp. 288–90), while Verdier (1977, pp. 132–3) suggests that it portrays a story told by Adrevald (*Miracula s. Benedicti*, I.25, pp. 56–7). Berland (1979b, pp. 16–18), however, claims that it does not concern judicial combat at all, but represents a touring group of *jongleurs*.

[84] Vergnolle 1985, figures 229 (both Christ and Benedict), 252, 254, 256, and 257.

feet, although Gregory had more simply recorded that the king asked for the saint's blessing.[85] Benedict always appeared in monastic garb, but with a relatively youthful face, not the aged abbot of the visions. His staff, or *baculus*, was depicted three times.[86] The artist responsible for part of this cycle was named Hugh, almost certainly the writer of hagiography and historiography in the early twelfth century.[87] The figure of this monk is to be found on three separate capitals, in the presence of Christ, the Virgin Mary, and Benedict.[88] He was accompanied in one case by two knights and in another by a group of monks. In all three Hugh and his companions were depicted in gestures of subservience, bringing gifts to their sacred patrons. While these representations show how monastic artists of the eleventh and early twelfth centuries pictured the saint and the stories about him, the actual impact of these sculptures on people visiting the church, either monastic or lay, would have been small, given their location high on the walls of the church.

Two other pieces of sculpture had more obvious value as propaganda. A relief above the north door, dated by Philippe Verdier to the late twelfth century, contained four scenes from Adrevald's *Historia translationis s. Benedicti*.[89] It put all who entered on notice that the relics within were truly those of St Benedict. The second was a bas-relief of a human head on the exterior wall of the same transept. It was alleged to be the Norman chieftain Rainald. According to Aimo, the monks of Fleury had made an effigy in marble after St Benedict had caused his death. In Aimo's time it was visible on the wall of the church.[90] That structure was destroyed in 1026 and it is unlikely that such a sculpture would have survived. The extant mask is a copy, probably executed in the twelfth century in an attempt to be faithful to the story told by Aimo.[91] As in the early eleventh century, this tortured depiction of a victim of Benedict's chastisement would have been an effective symbol of his patronage.

During the long period of construction at Fleury the relics were kept in the nave. After the dedication of the two main altars on 20

[85] Vergnolle 1985, figure 258. Cf. Gregory the Great, *Dialogues*, II.15, p. 182.
[86] Vergnolle 1985, figures 256, 258, and 264.   [87] Vergnolle 1985, pp. 254–7.
[88] Vergnolle 1985, figures 250, 263, and 264.
[89] Grémont 1963–4, p. 250; Verdier 1977, pp. 140–52.
[90] *Miracula s. Benedicti*, II.2, p. 98.   [91] Verdier 1977, pp. 133–5.

March 1108, they were placed in the new crypt, which was located behind that altar.[92] In 1207 the reliquary was removed and elevated on a pillar in the sanctuary behind the main altar, but it is uncertain how long it remained there.[93] In the other churches of the region the relics of the 'fathers' were also kept within the main sanctuary. At Micy and at Meung, for example, they were buried in the ground under the main altar. The monks of the former community referred to that part of the church as a *crypta* even though it was not recessed.[94] The new churches built at Saint-Aignan, Saint-Euverte, and Saint-Avit after the devastating fire of the early eleventh century were all provided with subterranean crypts.[95]

These churches served as the primary theatres in which the drama of the cult of the saints was played out. The veneration of the 'fathers' included much pomp and ritual. Occasions such as inventions – the formal ritual of enshrining the saints – and translations – the formal ritual of moving their relics – became major public displays of the 'father' and his power. The communities attempted to assemble as many ecclesiastical dignitaries as possible to witness the celebration of their patronage, although the number varied with the importance of the foundation. In the early 1020s Abbot Albert of Micy gathered Odolric, his own bishop, and Arnulf, archbishop of Tours, for the invention of the relics of St Maximinus. It was a celebration of family as well as communal power, for Odolric was related to Albert by marriage, while Arnulf was the abbot's son.[96] Later in that decade Robert the Pious looked on as the new church of Saint-Aignan, whose construction he had largely financed, was rededicated and the relics of Anianus brought out from their tomb. Robert assembled the ecclesiastical magnates of his immediate lands: the archbishops of Sens and Tours; the bishops of Orléans, Chartres, Meaux,

---

[92] The central altar was still dedicated to the Virgin Mary, while that in the apse, which stood above the crypt, was dedicated to Benedict. *Chronique de Saint-Pierre-le-Vif*, pp. 150–3. See also Berland 1975a, p. 387, and 1982, particularly pp. 12–19.

[93] This elevation is reported in two indulgences (*Recueil des chartes de Saint-Benoît*, nos. 248–9, II, 186–9) promulgated for the participants after the ritual. It is also mentioned at the end of a compilation in Old French of episodes from the *Historia translationis s. Benedicti* and the *Illatio s. Benedicti* (edited in Vidier 1965, p. 226). See also Verdier 1977, p. 144.

[94] *Sermo de inventione s. Maximini* (c. 3), p. 252; *Translatio s. Lifardi*, cc. 4–5, p. 158. See also J. Hubert 1951.

[95] Rousseau 1975a, particularly pp. 463–4; Lenormant 1862; Jouvellier 1975, p. 452.

[96] *Sermo de inventione s. Maximini* (c. 7), p. 253. On these relationships, see figure 1.

Beauvais, and Senlis; Abbot Odilo of Cluny; and Gauzlin, who was both abbot of Fleury and archbishop of Bourges.[97] A single commmunity would be able to muster varying numbers of dignitaries on different occasions. When the monks of Fleury consecrated the two main altars of their new church in 1108, and at the same time returned the relics of Benedict to the crypt, only two bishops, those of Orléans and Auxerre, were present, although lustre was added by the presence of Louis VI who would shortly ascend the throne.[98] In 1207, however, the monks gathered the archbishops of Sens and Bourges, as well as the bishops of Orléans, Paris, Nevers, and Auxerre at the elevation of the relics of Benedict.[99]

The fullest description of such a liturgy is found in the *Translatio s. Lifardi*, a lively eyewitness narrative of the rededication of the monastic church of Meung in 1105. That rededication was unusual because it was not due to reconstruction, but to the fact that the church had been polluted by the spilling of blood in a revolt against the bishop two years earlier.[100] The word *translatio* was used to describe the ritual because the relics of the patron had to be removed from the church, apparently because of the pollution, before they could be returned and reinterred. This event, which was to a large degree a celebration of the reimposition of control over Meung by its lord the bishop of Orléans, was attended by King Philip I, Archbishop Ralph of Tours, Bishops Guato of Paris and John of Orléans, and Abbot Christian of Micy.

The text was composed by one of the clerical participants, who made it clear that he belonged to this exalted company, although he also remained anonymous.[101] The author carefully avoided any mention of the revolt of the citizenry of Meung against the bishop which had caused the deaths which had polluted the church. In fact, he did not offer any explanation of the reason behind this ritual. The process took two days. On the first, the clerics said mass and removed the relics from their place of burial. During the ceremony the abbot of Micy and the author lay down directly on the earth of the tomb, while the author shed tears because of his unworthiness. He saw himself in direct contact with the world of the saints. When

[97] Helgaud of Fleury, *Epitoma vitae regis Rotberti pii*, c. 22, pp. 106–15.
[98] Clarius, *Chronicon S. Petri Vivi Senonensis*, p. 150.
[99] *Recueil des chartes de Saint-Benoît*, nos. 248–9, II, 186–9.
[100] Suger of Saint-Denis, *Vie de Louis VI, le Gros*, c. 6, p. 28.
[101] *Translatio s. Lifardi*, c. 1, p. 157.

the priests withdrew the bones from the tomb, the author felt a sense of awe at seeing the actual bones of the saint. At this point the author contemplated stealing part of the relics, only to chastise himself again for the paradoxical impiety of such a 'pious theft'. During the mass a young boy was cured of blindness, and the bishop of Orléans, amidst his own tears and those of the congregation, led the boy to the main altar to be near the relics. The relics were then brought overnight to the nearby parish church of Saint-Pierre, where St Lifardus was described as the guest of St Peter. The next day the prelates first rededicated the altar of the church of St Lifardus and then brought the relics back from Saint-Pierre. Crucial to this service were sermons given by the bishops to the gathered laity, instructing them with 'proclamations of truth' and instituting that day as a feast. Some form of indulgence was also provided for those present.[102] The author ended by instructing the canons of Meung to be happy in the dual feasts of their saint, since they could celebrate both the corporeal and spiritual benefits he brought them.[103]

The feasts of the 'fathers' were also occasions for ritual displays, although less elaborate ones. Aimo recalled Odo of Cluny in stating, 'When the festival day of the translation of the glorious father recurred each succeeding year, there came to see his celebration – as a certain wise man said in his praise – not only countryfolk, but even cityfolk and persons of the clergy.'[104] On that day the reliquary, which still stood in the sanctuary, was surrounded by candles and the walls hung with silken banners. The canons of Saint-Aignan, 'as was usual according to the custom of ancient piety', kept candles burning throughout the night before the tomb of their patron. Once, when the lamps inexplicably went out, the *custos* claimed to have seen Anianus himself relight them.[105] Numerous people from the city of Orléans came to the abbey of Micy for the morning office on the feast of Maximinus. A monk described the scene, '[As] the holy *Te Deum Laudamus* was being finished with the rough harmony of people singing psalms and rejoicing together and of the well-rung bells fittingly alternating . . . the end of vigils approached in the rising dawn.'[106]

---

[102] 'Quatenus in die anniversaria semper conveniant pro festivitate geminata geminatam exultationem habituri, et poenitentiarum relaxationem et peccatorum remissionem percepturi.' *Translatio s. Lifardi*, c. 8, p. 159.
[103] *Translatio s. Lifardi*, c. 10, p. 159.   [104] *Miracula s. Benedicti*, III.2, p. 128.
[105] *Miracula s. Aniani*, c. 14, pp. 269–70.   [106] *Miraculum s. Maximini*, pp. 246–7.

On the feast of Anianus, the crowd which filled the church of Saint-Aignan was of such size that a mother was separated from her mute daughter.[107] The saints were perceived as particularly likely to use their intercessory power to perform miracles on these feasts or at other times of sacred importance. Of the eight cures recorded in the *Miracula s. Aniani*, for instance, three occurred on feastdays of the saint, two on Sundays, one on Easter, and one during the dedication of the church.[108]

Lay pilgrims came to visit the shrines of the saints throughout the year. They came to Fleury from widely scattered locations. Hugh noted the cures of eight pilgrims over the course of two months in 1114.[109] A girl from Châteauneuf-sur-Loire, afflicted with deformities of both body and speech, was brought the few kilometres to Fleury on Ascension Sunday. A poor man from the Auvergne assisted his lame sister on the long journey. She recovered at the shrine, but half-way home she became lame again and had to return for a second miracle. A blind farmer from the Berry had first gone with his son to the shrine of St Martin in Tours. Returning from this unsuccessful trip he happened to hear, in Montrichard, of Benedict's reputation and turned his steps to Fleury. An Italian youth, lame for twelve years, had wandered from shrine to shrine on his crutches before he was told in a vision to go to Fleury. The others included a poor woman from neighbouring Sully who had been mute for seven years, a mute woman from Gien who had suffered for three years, a boy from the Berry mute from birth, and a Burgundian man possessed by a demon. Pilgrims even went to Fleury's priories seeking the patronage of St Benedict. The lord of Sémur-en-Brionnois, experiencing a head ailment which caused memory loss, went to nearby Perrecy-les-Forges after visits to other saints – including St Peter at Cluny and St Philibert at Tournus – proved fruitless.[110] The other shrines of the Orléanais did not have so widespread a reputation.

When lay pilgrims arrived at a church, they were only able to stand in the presence of the 'fathers', not come into direct contact with them. Not a single miracle story from the region describes a layperson as being present in the crypt of a church or as touching a

107 *Miracula s. Aniani*, c. 16, pp. 270–1.
108 *Miracula s. Aniani*, cc. 7, 9, 10–13, 15–18.
109 *Miracula s. Benedicti*, IX.2–4 and IX.6–9, pp. 361–6.
110 *Miracula s. Benedicti*, VIII.42, pp. 346–7.

reliquary.[111] Canon law actually prohibited the laity from handling the *res sacra*.[112] There was no trace of incubation, the practice of sleeping on a reliquary.[113] Pilgrims did, however, regularly sleep in the churches.[114] Some homeless people even lived in their outer porches out of necessity.[115] Robert-Henri Bautier has suggested that at Fleury lay pilgrims were unable to go beyond the monastic choir.[116] They would lay down or sleep before the main altar in the centre of the church for vigils which could last many hours.[117] Sometimes they lay instead before a silver crucifix kept elsewhere in the church.[118] Abbot Gauzlin encouraged them to pray at the altar of St Andrew, which housed relics of Christ's burial shroud.[119] By the eleventh century women were allowed into the monastic church, although it was closed to all laypeople during certain hours of the divine office.[120] Large numbers of laity attended the office of matins on feastdays and

---

[111] The only layperson recorded to have touched a reliquary was a man named Mark whose paralysed arm was blessed with a hand-held reliquary containing some minor relics of Benedict. The blessing occurred at the church of Vitry-aux-Loges, not at Fleury (*Miracula s. Benedicti*, VIII.26, pp. 320–1). Also, one of the *pauperes* housed in the monastic hospice was recorded to have served the mass of a monk in the crypt (Aimo of Fleury, *Libelli miraculorum s. Benedicti*, c. 2, pp. 227–8), but such a permanent guest of the community was virtually a member of the house.

[112] Herrmann-Mascard 1975, pp. 201–3. Sigal (1985, pp. 35–40) has concluded that, during the eleventh and twelfth centuries, pilgrims had relatively little direct contact with relics other than by incubation. In many churches, however, they were allowed freer access to the tombs of the saints than in the Orléanais.

[113] Incubation had been one of the chief means of contact with relics in antiquity and was revived through much of Francia during the eleventh and twelfth centuries. See in particular Sigal 1985, pp. 135–44, and Foreville and Keir 1987, pp. cv–cvii. The only case of incubation from the Orléanais concerned a man who slept under the reliquary of St Maurus the martyr when it had been taken outside the church of Fleury to the suburbs of the city of Orléans (*Miracula s. Benedicti*, II.19, p. 125).

[114] The author of the *Miracula s. Aniani* (c. 14, p. 270) stated that pilgrims were not allowed to sleep in the church of Saint-Aignan in those rare cases when the lights inside the church were extinguished, but his language indicates that this was an exceptional circumstance. Among the stories which describe pilgrims sleeping during a vigil kept in the church are *Miracula s. Benedicti*, III.14, pp. 160–1; VIII.28–9, pp. 324–6; IX.2, p. 361; IX.7, pp. 364–5; IX.11, pp. 369–70.

[115] *Miracula s. Aniani* c. 10, p. 267. According to Letaldus (*Miracula s. Maximini*, c. 44, p. 610) a poor man lived with his wife and six children under an overhanging rock near Micy. [116] Bautier 1969, p. 106.

[117] *Miracula s. Benedicti*, VIII.31, p. 329, and IX.3–4, p. 362.

[118] *Miracula s. Benedicti*, VIII.28, p. 325; IX.7, pp. 364–5; IX.11, p. 370.

[119] *Miracula s. Benedicti*, VII.6, p. 257; Andrew of Fleury, *Vita Gauzlini*, c. 20, pp. 60–2.

[120] The earliest mention of a woman in the monastic church at Fleury concerned Adela, who was both mute and paralysed. She was cured on the July feast of Benedict's translation in 1005 (*Miracula s. Benedicti*, III.17, p. 164). On the closing of the church, see *Miracula s. Benedicti*, IX.1, p. 360.

pilgrims spending the night in the church generally attended vigils.[121]

Customs were similar elsewhere. At Saint-Aignan a woman left her cured infant on the altar for a period of thanksgiving.[122] A pilgrim at Micy, seeking a cure from paralysis, lay down within the monastic choir during the celebration of the feast of St Maximinus.[123] The four recorded recipients of miracles at Pithiviers prostrated themselves before the altar, one of them naked, either seeking or giving thanks for a miracle.[124] The crucifix served as a focus of devotions at Meung, particularly during Lent.[125] Matins drew crowds of laity on holy days and the canons of Meung allowed pilgrims to approach their patron's tomb more closely on the Sunday after Easter.[126] On occasion the monks and canons directed the pilgrims as to how and where to make their obeisances to their saintly patron.[127] The canons of Sainte-Croix even sent one man suffering from fevers across the river to Micy to seek his cure.[128]

More direct contact with the relics was limited to the monks, or perhaps more precisely to the abbots. Abbot Andrew of Micy (1171–82) touched the relics of Euspicius against his tumour and was cured, while Abbot Veranus of Fleury (1080–6) successfully suppressed a fever which had defied his medical knowledge by drinking water which had been used to wash the relics.[129] Still the presence of relics – and, more importantly, of the *presentia* and *patrocinium* of the 'fathers' which they represented – mattered more than physical contact. Some communities did not even know the exact location of their relics. When the monks of Micy reconstructed their church in 1021 they had to search for the casket of their patron, even expressing fear that the corpse had been stolen, although they did not doubt the efficacy of the saint's miraculous power for the community.[130] A century later, the newly installed

121 See, for example, *Miracula s. Benedicti*, IX.10–11, pp. 367–71.
122 *Miracula s. Aniani*, c. 17, p. 272.   123 *Miraculum s. Maximini*, p. 244.
124 *Miracula ss. Georgii et Laeti*, cc. 1–4, pp. 78–9.
125 *Miracula s. Lifardi*, cc. 10 and 12, p. 162.
126 *Miraculum s. Maximini*, p. 244; *Miracula s. Lifardi*, c. 17, p. 163.
127 Letaldus of Micy, *Miracula s. Maximini*, c. 34, p. 607.
128 Letaldus of Micy, *Miracula s. Maximini*, c. 54, p. 612.
129 *Miracula s. Euspicii*, c. 2, p. 315; *Miracula s. Benedicti*, VIII.25, pp. 318–19. On the similar use of water which had touched relics, see Finucane 1977, pp. 63, 90, and 94. Laypeople sometimes drank wine in which a minor reliquary had been submerged, see, for example, *Miracula s. Euspicii*, c. 3, p. 315.
130 *Sermo de inventione s. Maximini*, c. 2, p. 252.

Victorine canons of Saint-Euverte were unsure of the exact location of Evurtius' tomb. They suggested that their predecessors had ignored the relics of their patron out of fear that they would attract pilgrims and thus bring attention to their own unreformed lives.[131]

Petitioners did not expect miracles to happen immediately. One man spent eight sleepless days shaking with fever in the church of Micy.[132] A mother, convinced that Benedict would cure her deaf-mute son, remained at Fleury for two years.[133] Not infrequently pilgrims would visit several shrines before they were cured or before their cure became complete.[134] Visitors, particularly those suffering from demonic possession, sometimes disturbed monastic quiet and the liturgy.[135] Some miracles occurred simply and silently, perhaps not even recognized until the recipient awoke from a slumber. On the other hand, a female serf who lived on lands belonging to St Benedict near Troyes was amazed when, during the reading of the gospel at mass one Sunday, her badly deformed spine began to snap back into place. A lame man was inspired during the reading of another gospel passage (Luke 6:36) to try walking and found his legs healed. The ringing of a bell told a canon of Saint-Aignan that he was cured from deafness, while panic caused a mute girl to yell and discover that she was cured.[136] Many cures were accompanied by visions of the saint or of other preternatural beings.[137] If the miracle occurred during a liturgy, all those in the church were quickly gathered round. Even if it did not, the monastic community might be summoned. Once the monks of Fleury ran from the chapter-room, attracted by the exultant screams of a man released from demonic possession.[138] On their arrival the clerics sometimes held an investigation to determine the authenticity of the miracle.[139] They usually turned

[131] *Inventio s. Evurtii*, pp. 59–60.

[132] Letaldus of Micy, *Miracula s. Maximini*, c. 52, p. 612.

[133] *Miracula s. Benedicti*, IX.10, p. 367.

[134] Head 1984, pp. 222–4 and the bibliography cited there.

[135] Letaldus of Micy, *Miracula s. Maximini*, c. 35, p. 608; *Miracula s. Benedicti*, VIII.31, pp. 328–9; *Miracula s. Aniani*, c. 15, p. 270.

[136] *Miracula s. Benedicti*, VIII.13, p. 293, and IX.9, p. 366; *Miracula s. Aniani*, c. 9, p. 266, and c. 16, p. 271.

[137] Such visions occurred at every shrine for which there are records, except Pithiviers. See, for example, *Miraculum s. Maximini*, p. 246; *Miracula s. Benedicti*, IX.10, pp. 367–8; *Miracula s. Aniani*, cc. 11 and 12, pp. 268–9; *Miracula s. Lifardi*, c. 14, pp. 162–3.

[138] *Miracula s. Benedicti*, VIII.29, p. 326.

[139] *Miracula s. Aniani*, c. 16, p. 271; *Miraculum s. Maximini*, p. 249.

such an occasion into a ritual celebration of their 'father's' patronage, ringing bells and singing hymns, most commonly the *Te Deum*, or, at Saint-Aignan, the *Gloria*.[140]

The brief records of most curing miracles focused on the events surrounding the cure itself and do not provide a full picture of the overall experience of a lay pilgrim. A monk of Micy did, however, compose a more detailed description of a pilgrim named Henry who had been cured of lameness at his house during the 1060s.[141] Henry possessed considerable wealth, if not noble rank. One night he was told in a dream that God had decreed that he would be cured through the services of St Maximinus. He quickly rounded up his retainers and told them to make ready for a journey, but was unsure where to go. One of his servants told him of the shrine of St Maximinus of Trier and so the group set off for that city.[142] After sleeping for many nights at that saint's tomb, he again had a vision in his sleep which told him that he had come to the wrong saint and would have to search for his cure in Gaul. While travelling westward he met a man who told him that there was a shrine in Chinon for the relics of one of St Martin's disciples. The informant, however, was uncertain whether the saint was named Maximinus or Maximus.[143] After making the difficult journey to Chinon, Henry began to have doubts once he found out that the saint was indeed named Maximus. The vision returned to him in his sleep and this time upbraided him for his mistakes, 'Why do you consider that which [God] offers to you kindly as some form of a jest?' This time Henry was provided with more exact instructions: to retrace his steps to Orléans and look for the tomb of Maximinus there.

Coming to the abbey of Micy on 5 December he was welcomed by the monks, who assured him that he would be cured on the upcoming feastday of the saint (15 December). At first he sat in front of fires in the monastic calefactory where 'he renewed with their heat the strength which the cold of winter had drawn away, for it was in the month of December'. He was introduced to the community in the chapter-room the next day and then spent his

---

140 *Miraculum s. Maximini*, p. 249; *Miracula s. Benedicti*, VIII.29, p. 326; IX.7, p. 365; IX.8, p. 366; *Miracula s. Lifardi*, c. 17, p. 163; *Miracula s. Aniani*, c. 9, p. 266; c. 10, p. 268; c. 12, p. 269.
141 For an edition, translation, and more complete discussion of this text, see Head 1984.
142 On St Maximinus of Trier, see *VSBP*, V, 565–6, and *BS*, VII, 33–4.
143 On St Maximus of Chinon, see *VSBP*, VIII, 369–70, and *BS*, IX, 39–40.

time in prayer while living in Micy's guesthouse. On the vigil of Maximinus' feast he spent the day in fasting and then lay 'as a supplicant' in the monastic choir through the night. During matins a large crowd of laypeople from the city gathered in the monastic church. While the monks were chanting the office, Henry audibly cried out for forgiveness and asked those brothers who looked his way to join in his prayers. His presence must have added a strange and dramatic element to the familiar ritual for both the local clergy and laity. As the end of the service neared, and nothing had happened, Henry decided to leave the sanctuary stealthily with the rest of the crowd. He encountered a white-haired man, supporting himself with a staff (*baculus*), who addressed him, 'Where are you going, fool? . . . Resist being foolish. The time comes. You will soon have respite.' Then the old man struck Henry on the face. Although the blow was light, Henry fell down as if dead. When he recovered, he found that he was no longer lame and that the bandages which had covered his leg had been scattered through the church.

A crowd of laypeople gathered around Henry and their murmuring attracted the abbot and those monks who were gathered around the altar with incense. They waited until the rest of the community had finished the office and then summoned those brothers as well. The laypeople shouted in celebration, while the monks sang the *Te Deum* and rang the church bells. Meanwhile Henry explained what had happened to whoever would listen and said, 'In whatever land I will live, I vow myself to be a servant [of Maximinus], I will be so now and forever.' Then 'as if he had Maximinus before his eyes, he quickly prostrated himself in order to hold the saint's feet'. The experience had been a debilitating one, Henry's face was 'wet with exertion' and his breath laboured. After his miraculous cure and vow of service, Henry lived at Micy for some time. Even after he left, he continued 'to preach with a glorious cry the sublime power of that faithful protector [Maximinus] to people far removed from our home [Micy]'. These incidents indicate that – while the monks of Micy welcomed the laity in their guesthouse and on feastdays and even allowed Henry a remarkable degree of latitude for his conduct in the monastic choir – they still held themselves apart from the outside world. They sought to preserve the integrity of the monastic office and celebrated the miracle with Latin hymns, as opposed to the more free-form celebrations of the gathered laity. The monastic cloister of Micy was a world separate from that of the city of Orléans, but the cult of Maximinus provided one of the means of real contact between the two.

The language which the monk of Micy used to interpret and narrate Henry's experience provides a glimpse into the psychology of the experience of the miraculous. The author described Henry's journey as a movement from uncertainty to certitude. Henry's servants at first identified St Maximinus 'confidently'. After his lack of success in Trier, he labelled their efforts 'worthless' and 'vain'. When the servants reported to him about the saint of Chinon, they 'did not know for certain whether he was called Maximinus or Maximus'. After Henry 'was made certain of the name', the third vision called him 'unwise' and 'worthless'. When he finally arrived at Micy he did so 'with certainty'. This confidence was reinforced by the words of the monk. On the feastday of Maximinus, however, doubt again assailed the pilgrim: 'since he had many times been in error, perhaps he was still in doubt'. He thought 'that the divine vision was mistaken'; he 'was overcome by a debilitating feeling'; he considered 'fleeing in fear'. When he was about to give in to this doubt, he met the saint, was reassured, and then cured. As he turned to the crowd, his first words in making his vow of servitude ('believe for certain') underlined the final certitude of his belief in the powers of Maximinus' patronage. For this monastic author, steadfastness of belief was essential. Without it a 'father' would not come to the aid of his servants, clerical or lay. The language of the narrative directly reflects a monastic mentality. Henry, however, showed by his actions – even if they were affected by the instructions of the monks – that he understood the logic of patronage. He sought his cure through rendering homage and service to his patron, not through some form of sympathetic magic effected by contact with the relics.

People desired contact with the 'fathers' even after their own death. At Fleury many monks and laypeople sought the privilege of being buried near its great patron. A number of anonymous tombs, dating from the tenth century on, have been uncovered, all positioned to provide proximity to the patron's relics. Jean Marie Berland has identified them as the tombs of local lay magnates.[144] Philip I, who according to Orderic Vitalis held the monastery of

[144] Berland 1979a.

Fleury and its patron in the highest esteem, was buried on 2 August
1108 'between the choir and the altar'. He was one the few
Capetian kings not buried at Saint-Denis.[145] Many of the abbots of
Fleury were also interred in the church.[146] Finally, some favoured
members of the community were allowed burial there. Andrew
recorded how one holy monk had a vision of heaven shortly before
his death. He then told his fellows that he wished to be buried on
the 'exterior of the crypt of the Holy Cross'. He posthumously
upbraided them when his wishes were not carried out.[147]

THE MIRACULOUS PROTECTION OF MONASTIC PROPERTY AND SERVANTS

As Pierre-André Sigal has noted, the power of the saints was
perceived to be strong not simply at the shrine of their relics, but
also in those areas which they possessed, that is the properties of
their foundations.[148] Aimo stated, 'As the blessed Pope Gregory
said, the holy martyrs show forth miracles just as frequently at
those places which are dedicated to their memory, as in those
where their sacred bodies are kept.'[149] In fact, the great majority of
the miracles recorded in the collections of the Orléanais did not
occur at the shrine of the saint. Most of these distant miracles
involved the protection of properties and rights through the
chastisement of those enemies of the monastic community who
sought to infringe them.[150]

If a community required the saint's power at some point distant
from the shrine, the relics could be brought from the church.
When the troops of a local knight tried to take possession of a field
belonging to Micy, the monks went to defend their property
armed with the relics of Maximinus.[151] In the time of Hugh Capet
they similarly brought the relics when they approached the armed

[145] Berland 1982, pp. 24–5.
[146] According to Andrew of Fleury (*Vita Gauzlini*, c. 75, p. 146) Gauzlin was buried 'to the right of the altar of the mother of God'. The tomb of Veranus (1080–6), one of the abbots responsible for the church's construction, was discovered in the nineteenth century, see Berland 1982, p. 11.
[147] *Miracula s. Benedicti*, VII.13, pp. 270–1.   [148] Sigal 1985, pp. 60–4.
[149] *Miracula s. Benedicti*, III.4, p. 132. The reference is to Gregory the Great, *Dialogues*, II.38, II, 246–8.
[150] For comparative material, see Gaiffier 1932; Hermann-Mascard 1975, pp. 217–34; Platelle 1978–9; Sigal 1976a and 1985, pp. 276–82.
[151] Letaldus of Micy, *Miracula s. Maximini*, c. 30, p. 606.

retainers of Hugh's prefect Salomon.[152] A short time earlier Bishop Arnulf (970–1003) dispatched some armed men to keep the servants of Fleury from harvesting grapes in a disputed vineyard located in the suburbs of Orléans.[153] In response the monks went in procession bearing the relics of the martyrs Maurus and Frogentius to enforce Benedict's claim to the property. The episcopal troops, like those of the knight and prefect, were dispersed by this ritual display of sacred power.

This procession – or delation to use the technical term – had an unexpected side-effect. Many people from the region came out to see the 'pomp of the passers-by'. One of them suffered from a debilitating fever which had deprived him of control over his limbs. He spent a night sleeping under the reliquary, apparently believing it to be that of St Benedict, and awoke cured. He went on to build a small hut over the site of his cure and similarly afflicted people continued to sleep there in search of cures. This hut provided in a sense an extension of the shrine of Benedict whose existence was due to a layman, an excellent example of the lay adaptation of clerical religion.

Relic processions served as a means of combating epidemics as well. The brothers of Fleury decided, 'along with the people of that same area', to take the relics of Maurus on a procession to the parish church of the town outside the monastic walls.[154] The express purpose was to 'placate father Benedict with prayers'. Rodulfus Tortarius' description provides a vivid picture of how such a penitential procession appeared. The whole assemblage – 'the sacred order as well as the people, along with the poor and women' – went barefoot, singing litanies. They had tears in their eyes and their lamenting increased as they neared the church. On arrival they celebrated mass, and suddenly the humid south wind replaced the dry wind from the north. The rains which followed brought relief from both drought and fever.[155]

About the same time Gallebertus, the monk charged with acquiring building stone for the construction of Fleury's new church, found himself running low on funds. He went on a

---

[152] Letaldus of Micy, *Miracula s. Maximini*, c. 46, p. 610.
[153] *Miracula s. Benedicti*, II.19, pp. 123–5.
[154] *Miracula s. Benedicti*, VIII.20, pp. 304–6.
[155] Benedict had earlier (*Miracula s. Benedicti*, III.19, pp. 166–9) demonstrated his command over the elements by sending a wind to protect the church of the Virgin from fire.

fundraising tour of the surrounding countryside, taking some relics of the saints as well as some preachers with him. From Rodulfus Tortarius' summary, it seems that Gallebertus knew how to work a crowd:

He entered the church [at Vitry-aux-Loges near Châteauneuf] and reminded the people with a hortatory sermon to flee the uncertainty of the present life and to seek the stability of the future life with the passion of an inflamed heart. He also entreated with flattering persuasion on other topics, after which the whole sermon built to its climax, as he enjoined them to provide some help, even if it was to give just a little money, for his work.[156]

In this particular case the impact of the monk's appeal was heightened when a man in the crowd successfully asked for Benedict's aid in curing his paralysed arm.

The relics of saintly patrons were not brought forth from a monastic church only to protect the interests of that saint's community. The last decades of the tenth century witnessed the beginnings of a movement known by some medieval writers, and modern historians following them, as the Peace of God. Bishops, first in the Aquitaine and later in Francia itself, held a series of regional synods at which they undertook the defence of the property of the unarmed – that is of the clergy and of the poor elements of society – against the power of the armed – that is of nobles and knights.[157] The relics of the patrons of local monasteries were commonly brought to these councils and, in some cases, the male population of a region was required to swear an oath over such relics that they would maintain the peace.[158] While no Peace councils were held in the Orléanais, and there is no record of the major relics of its 'fathers' having been brought to such councils, the monks of the region were certainly aware of the movement and of the role of relics and saintly patronage in it.

---

[156] *Miracula s. Benedicti*, VIII.26, pp. 319–21. Rodulfus called the preachers *seminiverbii*, a rare word used to describe St Paul as a preacher in Acts 17:18. Such tours of relics to elicit donations, particularly for monastic building projects, were common in the late eleventh and twelfth centuries. See Héliot and Chastang 1964–5; Hermann-Mascard 1975, pp. 296–305; Sigal 1976b; Ward 1982, pp. 150–8; Koziol 1987.

[157] For a review of literature of the Peace of God, see Paxton 1987.

[158] Töpfer 1957, pp. 40–54 and 103–10; Cowdrey 1970b, pp. 44–53; Sargent 1985, pp. 220–8.

In the *Delatio corporis s. Juniani*, Letaldus of Micy recorded how the monks of Nouaillé brought the relics of their patron to the Council of Charroux in 989.[159] He composed the work at the request of his former abbot, Constantine, who had become abbot of Nouaillé.[160] In it he briefly described the role played by relics:

It pleased bishops, abbots, and other religious men that a council be held at which the taking of booty would be prohibited and the property of the saints, which had been unjustly stolen, would be restored. Other evils which fouled the fair countenance of the holy church of God were also struck down by the sharp points of anathemas. I think that this council was held at the monastery of Charroux and that a great crowd of many people gathered there from the Poitou, the Limousin, and neighbouring regions. Many bodies of saints were also brought there. The cause of religion was strengthened by their presence, and the impudence of evil people was beaten back. That council – convoked, as it was thought, by divine will – was adorned through the presence of these saints by frequent miracles.[161]

The council brought a variety of potent elements – the traditional patronage of the saints, the popular enthusiasm represented by the *multorum concursus populorum*, and the episcopal prerogative of excommunication by anathema – together and forged from them a powerful weapon.

Although the word *pax* occurred in neither the canons promulgated by the council nor in Letaldus' description, the monk of Micy correctly implied that the purpose of the council was to curb violence, specifically that directed against the church. Letaldus saw that that bishops, monks, and laity, not to mention the saints, all had a hand in defeating the 'impudence of evil people'. Not all the monks of the Orléanais were so approving. Andrew of Fleury cast the efforts of Archbishop Aimo of Bourges to enforce Peace oaths in a decidedly negative light. The monk suggested that the levy or militia which Aimo collected in order to force the nobility of the Berry into submitting to such oaths broke the very *fidelitas* crucial to the oaths themselves: 'They forgot that God is the strength and rampart of his people, and ascribed the

---

[159] Töpfer 1957, p. 59; Bonnaud-Delamare 1961, pp. 419–26; Hoffmann 1964; pp. 25–8. Töpfer's defence of the traditional date of 989 for the council seems to withstand the arguments of Bonnaud-Delamare.   [160] Head 1990.
[161] Letaldus of Micy, *Delatio corporis s. Juniani*, c. 2, p. 434.

power of God to their own apostate power.' Thus Aimo and his allies merited the overwhelming defeat which they suffered at the hands of Odo of Déols in a pitched battle on the banks of the Cher river.[162] Despite Andrew's disapproval of what he took to be a misappropriation of sacral power, the public display and use of relics of the 'fathers' at Charroux, Bourges, and other centres of the Peace increased lay awareness of the power and patronage of the saints. Letaldus recorded how peasants erected makeshift shrines at places where the relics of Junianus had stopped on their way to Charroux, shrines which were apparently still the focal point of lay devotions some years after the event.[163]

In some cases it was on the initiative of laypeople that relics were brought forth from their resting places. In 956 Count Lambert of Chalon-sur-Saône deputized a nobleman named Bernard to be the leader of his troops on an expedition against a raiding party from the Auvergne. Lambert and Bernard went to Perrecy-les-Forges, a priory of Fleury, and donated property in exchange for the right to bring some of the community's relics, presumably of St Benedict, on the expedition.[164] At the same time they turned over other properties to the priory which had belonged to retainers of Lambert who had died in a recent battle. The purpose was to secure the prayers of the monks for the salvation of the men's souls. These nobles sought two different forms of sacred power from the monastic community in exchange for land. Such use of relics was not limited to the nobility. In 994 an epidemic of ergotism attacked the Limousin.[165] The local inhabitants 'took council in common' and asked the prior of Saint-Benoît-du-Sault, another dependency

---

[162] *Miracula s. Benedicti*, v.2–4, pp. 192–8; Head 1987a, particularly pp. 515–19.

[163] Letaldus of Micy, *Delatio corporis s. Juniani*, c. 3, pp. 434–5. Similar shrines were erected in celebration of the *delatio* of relics of St Bercharius (*De diversis casibus Dervensis coenobii et miraculis s. Bercharii*, c. 28, pp. 859–60).

[164] *Recueil des chartes de Saint-Benoît*, no. 51, I, 127–30. On Perrecy, see Berland 1985, who does not discuss this act in any detail. According to Aimo (*Miracula s. Benedicti*, III.15, pp. 161–2) the priory had received relics of Benedict when it was acquired by Fleury in 876, but it also possessed an impressive collection of its own. The act does not specify which saint's relics were to be used. While this act was unusual in form, even containing the purported words of a conversation between Lambert and Bernard, it was contained in the cartulary of Perrecy and there is no reason to doubt its authenticity.

[165] Ergotism, known in the middle ages as *ignis sacer* and later as St Anthony's fire, is a febrile disease caused by a rot which grows on improperly stored grain, most particularly rye. The rot is chemically similar to several hallucinogenic substances and the fevers frequently cause visions and hysteria. For a fuller treatment of ergotism, see Chaumartin 1946.

of Fleury, to loan them the relics of Benedict enshrined there.[166] They brought these in a procession to the shrine of a local saint, St Martial, in the city of Limoges and the disease soon ended. When, in the late eleventh century, the inhabitants of Sancerre suffered from a vaguely described 'pestilence', they requested that the monks of Fleury bring the body of Maurus the martyr to their town.[167] There the reliquary was immersed in many vats of wine to produce a *confectio medicinalis*, of which the inhabitants strove to drink as much as possible.

The number of these incidents should not give the impression that the monks and canons of the Orléanais or other regions removed the relics of their patrons from their crypts on the slightest of whims. Gallebertus used a hand-held reliquary which contained only some minor relics of his patron. The reliquaries of Benedict at Perrecy and Saint-Benoît-du-Sault were probably similar. The monks of Fleury used the relics of Maurus the martyr in processions, apparently thinking it unnecessary to risk the displacement of their greatest treasure. In any case, the clerics became skilled in the use of relics to create an environment in which there was a heightened chance of achieving their goals, whether that be to settle a dispute, to raise funds, to end an epidemic, or to enforce the Peace of God.

According to authors from the Orléanais, the 'fathers' frequently protected their properties against hostile nobles through visionary appearances in which they punished those enemies with illness, accident, or death. Adrevald had presented a picture of the saint who stood behind the relics: the elderly abbot, Benedict, accompanied by an attendant, who attacked those who opposed him with his staff of office. The image continued to have force in the eleventh century.[168] According to Letaldus a soldier of Robert the Pious, who was illegally pasturing his horse on lands of Micy, blasphemed against its patron.[169] That night Maximinus appeared

---

[166] *Miracula s. Benedicti*, IV.I, pp. 174–7. Ademar of Chabbanes (*Chronicon*, III.35, p. 158) described the *delationes* as having occurred in conjunction with a Peace council, an association significantly ignored by Andrew. For a comparison of the accounts, see Head 1987a, pp. 525–6.   [167] *Miracula s. Benedicti*, VIII.21, pp. 306–10.

[168] This image was not confined to authors from the Orléanais. See, for example, Odo of Glanfeuil, *Historia translationis corporis s. Maurus abbatis in Fossatense monasterium*, c. 6, pp. 169–70, and Bernard of Angers, *Liber miraculorum s. Fidis*, I.13, p. 46, and I.25, pp. 64–5. Both authors were from the Anjou; the former wrote shortly after Adrevald, the latter shortly after Aimo.

[169] Letaldus of Micy, *Miracula s. Maximini*, c. 48, p. 611. See also cc. 19–20, p. 603.

to him in his sleep and struck him with a *baculus*. The soldier awoke, cried out that he had been given a blow by the saint, and breathed his last. Aimo told how Rainald had led a group of Normans up the Loire, intending to loot the property of Fleury.[170] One night he dreamed of two monks, one an old man, the other a child. The elder demanded why the Norman wished to disturb the place where his bones rested, threatened the leader's head with a *baculus*, and predicted his impending death. Rainald awoke and told his entourage of the vision. When he died shortly thereafter, his leaderless band fled back to Rouen, after cremating his body. The monks of Fleury placed a marble carving of his face on the wall of their church to warn future intruders of the power of their patron.[171]

Even when the saint did not make an appearance, his personal patronage was implicitly understood to extend to his properties. When one knight came to a village which 'pertained by law to the monastery of St Benedict', he entered the house of a widow to take grain for his horses.[172] She warned him, 'If you hold me in contempt by taking the poverty of my widowhood, at least pay reverence to most holy Benedict. The country in which I dwell is under his law.' The knight, taking the grain, responded, 'I fear St Benedict as much as I do you.' Not far away he was thrown from his horse and severely injured. Aimo concluded, 'He told of his punishment and preached the example to others, lest they make a habit of condemning the saints.' Some nobles respected the protective powers of the saints. When Count Odo II of Blois withdrew from his defeat at Pontlevoy in 1016 his troops crossed lands belonging to Fleury.[173] Odo was careful to instruct his men not to pillage 'out of reverence for the friend of God'. Monastic communities saw a need to guard the fruits of their properties against the depredations of the groups of armed men – be they Norman raiders, a local knight, or a soldier of the presumptive heir to the throne. Not even animals were exempt. Rodulfus Tortarius recorded how dogs, pigs, and birds who violated the sanctuary of the church at Germigny-des-Prés were punished.[174]

Sometimes the monks and their lay allies themselves took an active hand in aiding the protection of monastic property provided

[170] *Miracula s. Benedicti*, II.2, p. 97. See also II.7, p. 108.
[171] The same image still had force for Andrew (*Miracula s. Benedicti*, VII.8, p. 265).
[172] *Miracula s. Benedicti*, II.14, pp. 116–17.   [173] *Miracula s. Benedicti*, VI.12, pp. 236–7.
[174] *Miracula s. Benedicti*, VIII.2–3, and VIII.5, pp. 278–82.

by the patron saint. Aimo told of battles waged to protect the lands of Fleury's priory of Saint-Benoît-du-Sault in the late tenth century, while Andrew recounted a similar defence of another priory at Châtillon-sur-Loire a half-century later.[175] The troops allied to Fleury fought under the banner of St Benedict, used his name as a battle cry, and once even went forth fortified by bread which had been blessed in the presence of his relics.[176] In Andrew's words the saint provided protection 'like a rampart'. In some cases the lands of Fleury and its possessions were defended by nobles friendly to the community, such as Geilo, lord of Sully. At other times the abbey, or more properly its priory, was served simply by a levy of men from a neighbouring *castrum*, such as those from Argenton-sur-Creuse who defended Saint-Benoît-du-Sault during the wars between Gerald, viscount of Limoges, and William IV, count of Poitiers. The right to use the banner of the saint belonged to the lay advocate of Saint-Benoît-du-Sault, while its provost initiated the use of the saint's name as a battle-cry.[177] These lay *defensores ecclesiarum*, unlike those criticized by Abbo, fulfilled their duties.

The monks of Fleury's priories did not themselves engage in combat, although Andrew approvingly recounted stories he had heard during a journey in Spain of monks who had fought against the Muslims.[178] Carl Erdmann has seen in these and similar military actions the origin of the idea of 'holy war', although he points out that actual force of arms was not frequently ascribed to saints.[179] Such patronage of the saints in battle was not found in the diocese of Orléans itself. The custom of using relics and other symbols of saintly patronage in battle seems to have originated in the Aquitaine around the year 1000 and slowly spread northward.[180]

A similar *patrocinium* served when monks became involved in court cases.[181] Aimo described a man named Walter who falsely claimed ownership of some land used by Fleury. When he found

[175] *Miracula s. Benedicti*, II.15–16, pp. 117–21; III.4–6, pp. 132–46; V.15, pp. 212–13. See Rollason 1985, pp. 82–7.
[176] *Miracula s. Benedicti*, II.15, p. 118; III.5, p. 139; V.15, pp. 212–13; III.7, p. 148.
[177] *Miracula s. Benedicti*, II.15, p. 118, and III.5, p. 139.
[178] *Miracula s. Benedicti*, IV.9–11, pp. 185–91.   [179] Erdmann 1935, pp. 40–5.
[180] Rollason 1985, pp. 85–6. On the varied military uses made of the relics and banner of St Lambert during later periods in the diocese of Liège, see Gaier 1966.
[181] While cases of the chastisement of enemies were common in the miracle collections from other communities, the only descriptions of actual court cases come from the collections composed at Fleury.

himself riding near the disputed property in a party which included
Abbot Abbo, Walter decided to press his claim. He offered to
undertake judicial combat to prove the truth of his words, but was
then thrown from his horse and died. Aimo concluded, 'Thus he
fought alone the combat which he had proposed and, through the
will of God, a judgement on the merits of his beloved confessor
Benedict was made manifest.'[182] Andrew later told four stories
about how Benedict's patronage caused the monks of Fleury to
win such contests. When Geoffrey, the viscount of Bourges, laid
claim to a wood which belonged to a priory of Fleury, Châtillon-
sur-Loire, he challenged a champion of the monks to a judicial
duel.[183] Geoffrey was struck blind. His sight returned to his right
eye when he agreed that he had given false testimony. The canons
of the cathedral of Bourges resorted to an ordeal by fire to uphold
their false testimony in a case involving the same priory.[184] The
hand of their advocate at first appeared to be free from harm, but
then miraculously festered, showing the truth of the claim of the
Fleury monks. When the niece of a cleric who had donated a
church *in precaria* to Fleury disputed the inheritance, she became
paralysed.[185] A serf named Stabilis moved to a village in
Burgundy where he pretended to be a freeman.[186] His fortunes
improved to the point that he was able to purchase the material
necessities of the military class – including a horse, weapons, and
hounds – and to marry a woman of free status. Then a monk of
Fleury discovered him and brought him before the count of
Troyes. Stabilis feigned ignorance even of his patron Benedict's
name and played an almost clever trick. While holding an *obolus*, a
coin which symbolized his servile duties to the saint, hidden from
view, he stated that he owed nothing more to St Benedict. The
coin miraculously grew in size, unmasking his treachery.

Virtually all court cases recorded in these hagiographic works
involved some form of the ordeal or judicial duel.[187] This was not

---

[182] *Miracula s. Benedicti*, III.10, pp. 153–4.   [183] *Miracula s. Benedicti*, V.7, pp. 203–5.
[184] *Miracula s. Benedicti*, V.13, p. 211.
[185] *Miracula s. Benedicti*, V.17 (numberless in the Certain edition), pp. 215–16.
[186] *Miracula s. Benedicti*, VI.2, pp. 218–221.
[187] A judicial duel was used to adjudicate a dispute between Fleury and Bishop Isembard
(1033–63) over possession of a serf (*Miracula s. Benedicti*, VIII.11, pp. 287–9), while in the
time of Bishop Manassas another duel solved a dispute between the canons of Meung
and a local knight (*Miracula s. Lifardi*, cc. 18–21, p. 164). It is uncertain whether Manassas
of Garland (1147–85) or Manassas of Seignelay (1207–21) figured in the latter story. On
these procedures, see particularly Colman 1974; Morris 1975; Brown 1975; Asad 1983;
Bartlett 1986.

the case in other regions. In the twelfth century the monks of Marchiennes, for example, recorded legal disputes in which the relics of St Rictrude or oaths taken over those relics were ritually manipulated to bring the case to a satisfactory conclusion.[188] In all the cases at Fleury and Marchiennes, however, the monks sought to remove the judicial case from the realm of written law by means of an appeal to the miraculous. Such an appeal lay, as Peter Brown has rightly pointed out, at the very heart of the ordeal.[189] Some have argued this search for the miraculous was an example of the basic irrationality of early medieval culture used out of fear.[190] Others have countered that they provided a means of seeking consensus in the absence of clear proof. As Brown concludes, 'What we have found in the ordeal is not a body of men acting on specific beliefs about the supernatural; we have found instead specific beliefs held in such a way as to enable a body of men to act.'[191]

Neither the psychological nor the functionalist analysis seems to fit these cases. The monks of Fleury were not seeking an acceptable consensus, still less were they quaking in fear of their lord, either Benedict or Christ. They claimed to have sought with certitude the reimposition of a supernatural order which had been violated. The lands and serfs in question belonged to Benedict. There was no possibility, at the very least no admitted possibility, that his patronage would fail to protect them. The ordeals did not serve so much as a means of protecting Benedict's property as they provided a venue in which the saint acted to protect them on his own. The saint's other acts of chastisement were similar in many ways to ordeals. In them God acted through the saint to set right what was wrong, to reimpose order on a disordered society.

THE VARIETY OF SAINTLY INTERCESSION

Chastisements, in their various guises, were not the only sorts of miracles which were recorded far from a saint's shrine. A man riding to a market on a deserted road called on St Benedict's assistance when he thought himself pursued by demons.[192] When Abbot Amalricus of Micy saw a blind man in danger of drowning and was unable to go to his aid, he invoked the aid of St

---

[188] Platelle 1978–9.   [189] Brown 1975, particularly pp. 135–7.
[190] Notably Rousset 1948 and Radding 1978.
[191] Colman 1974, pp. 575–80; Brown 1975, pp. 138–40 (the quotation is on p. 140).
[192] *Miracula s. Benedicti*, VIII.45, pp. 351–2.

Maximinus.[193] A mother prayed to Benedict to save her son, a convicted thief, from hanging.[194] Prisoners prayed for their release.[195] A number of boatmen – a profession vital to the economic well being of Micy and Fleury – prayed to the patrons of both houses for rescue.[196] When a tunnel collapsed on workmen in a field owned by Micy, the monk who had been supervising their labour invoked the name of Maximinus.[197] Miracles saved people injured while working on the fabric of the churches which housed the relics of the 'fathers'.[198] Cures from chronic illness were also obtained through invocation. A woman from a town near Fleury who was unable to move heard of the many miracles performed at the tomb itself, and prayed for Benedict's intercession until he appeared in a dream and cured her.[199]

Frequently the recipients of such miracles came to pray at the tomb of the saint at a later time. Victims who survived the punishments of the saint came to beg forgiveness. Some released prisoners had to seek sanctuary in the church before those who had held them in bondage accepted the miraculous release.[200] One was even transported mirculously to the church of Fleury from his cell.[201] The woman cured by Benedict immediately went, during the night, to her local church and then, the next day, to Fleury in order to praise the saint.[202] Service had to be rendered to the patron either to mend a broken relationship or in return for the services the saint had rendered.

The descriptions of the miraculous powers of the saints did not remain static through the Capetian period. Earlier writers, such as

---

[193] Letaldus of Micy, *Miracula s. Maximini*, c. 43, p. 610.

[194] *Miracula s. Benedicti*, VIII.44, pp. 349–51.

[195] *Miracula s. Benedicti*, VI.6, pp. 226–7, and IX.1, pp. 359–61; *Miracula s. Aniani*, c. 11, p. 268; *Miracula ss. Georgii et Laeti*, c. 1, p. 78; *Miracula s. Lifardi*, cc. 3–6 and 14–17, pp. 160–3. See Sigal 1985, pp. 268–71. The cases from the Orléanais confirm Sigal's general conclusions that the release of prisoners was frequently accompanied by an appearance of the saint, but almost never by any contact with the relics. Many of the cases from this region also occurred, like other forms of miracles, on the feastday of the saint.

[196] Letaldus of Micy, *Miracula s. Maximini*, c. 29, p. 606; c. 31, pp. 606–7; c. 32, p. 607; c. 43, p. 610; *Miracula s. Benedicti*, I.19, pp. 46–7; II.18, pp. 122–3; III.9, pp. 151–3.

[197] Letaldus of Micy, *Miracula s. Maximini*, c. 42, pp. 609–10.

[198] Letaldus of Micy, *Miracula s. Maximini*, c. 33, p. 607; *Miracula s. Benedicti*, II. 11, pp. 113–14.

[199] *Miracula s. Benedicti*, IX.5, p. 363. Sigal (1985, p. 64) notes that most cures which occurred at a distance from a shrine during this period concerned people who were unable to travel because of the severity of their illness.

[200] *Miracula s. Aniani*, c. 11, p. 268; *Miracula ss. Georgii et Laeti*, c. 1, p. 78; *Miracula s. Lifardi*, cc. 14–17, pp. 162–3.

[201] *Miracula s. Benedicti*, IX.1, pp. 360–1.

[202] *Miracula s. Benedicti*, IX.5, p. 363.

Aimo and Letaldus, emphasized miracles which occurred away from the shrines of the saints, most particularly miracles of chastisement. Slowly authors changed their focus to curing miracles, most of which occurred at the shrine itself. Hugh of Fleury, writing in the early twelfth century, included only cures and a single case of a prisoner released from confinement. This latter type of miracle did not occur in any work before that of Andrew.[203] By the late eleventh century the saints appeared to cure their servants rather than to punish their enemies. One such recipient was a female paralytic who lived in the porch of the church of Saint-Samson supported solely by alms.[204] She had tried following the advice of doctors, but they had failed to cure her. One night, a *vir venerabilis* appeared to her in a dream and told her to go to the church of Saint-Aignan. The woman awoke and dismissed the vision as a dream. When the man appeared to her a second time, she decided she was unable to make the relatively short journey because of her infirmity. Only when he appeared a third night in a row did the woman go to Saint-Aignan. There, during the Easter vigil service, Anianus appeared to her in the garb of a bishop and struck her diseased limbs with his *virga*. She found herself cured and went up to the altar to announce the miracle. The same saint cured a man possessed by a demon with a similar blow, while the lame pilgrim Henry was cured by a blow from the *baculus* of Maximinus.[205] The purpose of the blows delivered by the saints had changed from those which had killed Count Radulphus and the Norman leader Rainald.

THE COMPOSITION AND USE OF MIRACLE COLLECTIONS

The purpose for which miracle stories were collected also seems to have undergone change. Adrevald of Fleury's collection survives in more than twenty medieval manuscripts.[206] The diffusion indicates that this Carolingian work became widely popular in Neustria. None of the collections from the Capetian period, however, survives in more than three medieval manuscripts.[207]

---

[203] *Miracula s. Benedicti*, VII.8, pp. 264–5.   [204] *Miracula s. Aniani*, c. 10, p. 267.

[205] *Miracula s. Aniani*, c. 15, p. 270; *Miraculum s. Maximini*, p. 246.

[206] Vidier 1965, pp. 151–2 (to which should be added Rouen, BM 635 (A 365)).

[207] Letaldus' *Miracula s. Maximini* survives in a single complete copy, Vatican, Reg. lat. 528 (eleventh century, copied either at or for Saint-Denis; *Catal. Vat.*, pp. 354–5), fos. 14v–35. There is also a partial copy (Paris, BN 5366, fos. 23v–7v) executed at Micy in the fifteenth century, probably from an eleventh-century exemplar. This manuscript also

Most versions seem to have been copied by, and usually for, the community where the miracles had occurred. In the eleventh century the Fleury scriptorium, for example, produced two manuscripts which contained selections of hagiographic works about St Benedict including the collections of miracles composed by Adrevald and Aimo. One (Archives du Loiret, H 20), which was beautifully executed and illuminated, was apparently kept in close proximity to the reliquary, while the other (Dijon BM 1118) was sent to the priory of Perrecy.[208]

It is uncertain when and where, or even if, these works were read aloud. While the liturgical use of other genres of hagiography was common and remains well documented, there is only scattered evidence for such use of posthumous miracle stories as *lectiones*. Most of the known manuscripts of the miracle collections lacked *lectio*-markings. In a Saint-Denis manuscript which contains both the *Vita s. Maximini II* and Letaldus' *Miracula s. Maximini* only the former was divided into readings, suggesting that the latter was not used liturgically on the saint's feast.[209] The only posthumous miracle stories which were certainly used for liturgical purposes were the *libelli* composed by Aimo.[210] The evidence suggests, however, that the miracle collections of the eleventh century were

contains (fos. 27v–9) the only known medieval copy of the *Miracula s. Euspicii*. On this manuscript, see Poncelet 1905, pp. 103–4. Aimo's collection survives in three copies from the eleventh and twelfth centuries (of which at least two are from the Fleury scriptorium) and two more from the fifteenth century. On these, see Vidier 1965, pp. 181–2. Andrew's collection survives in only a single complete copy. This is contained in Vatican, Reg. lat. 592, in which the only other work is Andrew's *Vita Gauzlini*. This volume, executed in the Fleury scriptorium in the eleventh century, bears marks on the verso side of the first folio ('Andreas composuit hunc libellum' and 'Bernardus scripsit') which suggest that it was copied under Andrew's direction. On this manuscript, see Vidier 1965, pp. 197 and 201, and *Catal. Vat.*, p. 385. Extracts from Andrew's works are also found following Aimo's collection in four manuscripts, see Vidier 1965, pp. 197–8. The *Miracula s. Aniani* survives in two manuscripts, see Renaud 1976, pp. 245–9. There are no complete extant manuscripts of the collections of either Rodulfus Tortarius or Hugh of Fleury, although extracts from both works do survive, see Vidier 1965, pp. 209–10 and 213. The *Miraculum s. Maximini* survives in a single incomplete manuscript, probably an author's autograph (see Head 1984, pp. 234–5). There are no surviving copies of the *Miracula ss. Georgii et Laeti*. The edition, which is incomplete, was made from a now-lost manuscript from Pithiviers. I have been unable to locate any medieval copies of the *Miracula s. Lifardi*. Mabillon made his edition from an early modern copy of Vion Herouval.

[208] On the former, see Vidier 1965, pp. 137–8, and Van der Straeten 1982, pp. 80–1.

[209] Vatican, Reg. lat. 528, fos. 2–35.

[210] Pellegrin 1963, pp. 26–7. This brief collection may have been specifically intended for liturgical use. All four stories in the text concern aspects of the veneration of the saint's relics in the churches of Fleury or its priories.

largely intended to serve an audience within the communities dedicated to the 'fathers' whose powers they celebrated.

Writers such as Aimo and Letaldus did not write to prove the sanctity of men such as Benedict and Maximinus, for their sanctity was fully accepted. They rather wrote to aid their own community in celebrating their patron's honour. The authors of these collections emphasized their desire to preserve traditions for future generations. Aimo, for example, said that Abbot Gauzlin had ordered him to write down 'some of the miracles of our common patron most holy Benedict for the memory of posterity'.[211] The importance of such an aid to communal memory was underlined by his later complaint that so little record remained of the miracles which Benedict had worked in the time of Odo of Cluny, a lack due 'partly to antiquity and partly to the negligence of writers'.[212]

In this emphasis on memory, collections of posthumous miracle stories made in the early Capetian period had strong similarities to cartularies which monastic communities began to collect around the same time. Charters often served simply to confirm memory.[213] Letaldus of Micy highlighted this purpose in the opening of a charter which he copied, and may well have composed:

Every time a record of a grant and donation is justly and legally set down in writing for future memory, it serves as a conveyance for memory, in order that, if death is the inevitable end for living men, this mode of setting down might be in this fleshly world a testimony of the handing-over and be preserved as a written testament.[214]

In their descriptions of those miracles which involved the properties of the saints, most particularly chastisements, writers such as Letaldus, Aimo, and Rodulfus Tortarius carefully included a number of precise details. These could include the location and

---

[211] *Miracula s. Benedicti*, II.prologue, p. 90. In introducing his collection of the miracles of Abbo (*Miracula s. Abbonis*, c. 1, p. 57), he similarly stated that he wrote for the 'notice of posterity'. See also parallel passages from other writers collected by Sigal 1980, pp. 244–6.

[212] *Miracula s. Benedicti*, II.4, p. 101. See the similar complaints of the twelfth-century canon from Meung-sur-Loire, *Miracula s. Lifardi*, c. 2, p. 160.

[213] Constable 1983, p. 23.

[214] 'Quotiens largitionis et donationis ordo juste et legaliter diffinitus fuerit ad memoriam futurorum scripto, id convenit memore deportasse; ut si inevitabili mortis casu presentium hominum, carnea claustra deserentium defuerit testimonium diffinitionis modus per succedentia labentium annorum curricula scripturae testamento servetur.' 'Chartes de Micy', no. 11, p. 62.

name of the property, how it had come to belong to their community, as well as the name, lineage, and social rank of the person who disputed the community's ownership or attempted to steal its fruits.

This sort of information is what one would expect to find in a diplomatic source. In the one case where Andrew says such a record was available in the archives of Fleury he did not bother to include such a precise record.[215] These details were in some sense irrelevant to the description of the miraculous powers of the saints. The authors of miracle collections rarely approached such precision in recording miraculous cures. None of the disputes over property catalogued in the miracle collections from the Orléanais, however, was also recorded in an extant diplomatic source. The authors do not seem to have used such written records as sources for miracle stories with any frequency. Those who emphasized the miraculous protection of monastic property in their collections may well have sought to gather together oral traditions concerning their community's properties and rights which were not adequately attested in written records. Miracle collections may in part have been used as an adjunct to, or substitute for, collecting charters.

The anonymous author of the *Miracula s. Lifardi* said that he began his collection only after he was unable to locate diplomatic records concerning the properties of his monastery in the episcopal archives. He concluded, 'Since we are unable to restore stolen property, let us try to restore, in as much as it will prove possible, the praises of God in his saint.'[216] In his work he included the details of several chastisements and court cases, showing, for example, that the canons of Meung, and not the precentor of the local parish church, possessed a property called 'Alnetus'.[217] The search of this canon calls to mind that described by the monk of the abbey of Saint-Père of Chartres who collected together the charters of his community around the year 1080. The community's archives had been partially destroyed by fire and Paul sought to provide a record for the future.[218] His explanation of why his predecessors had neglected to provide sufficient records was strikingly and poignantly similar to that provided by the canon of

[215] *Miracula s. Benedicti*, VI.9, pp. 230–1.
[216] *Miracula s. Lifardi*, c. 2, p. 160.   [217] *Miracula s. Lifardi*, c. 7, p. 161.
[218] *Cartulaire de Saint-Père de Chartres*, I.1, I, 3–4. See also Stock 1983, pp. 76–7.

Meung.[219] Like the hagiographers of the Orléanais, Paul included much general background on the history of his community in his cartulary, including the story of the 1022 trial of heretics at Orléans in which one of the donors of property to his monastery had participated.[220] The parallel breaks down, of course, in that Paul found written records of the property of his community, while the canon of Meung did not. The community of Meung, however, possessed in the relics of their saintly founder and 'father' a sort of treasure which the community of Saint-Père lacked. In collecting together the miracles of that 'father', the anonymous canon, like his predecessors Letaldus and Aimo, found an alternative manner of proving the power and wealth of his community.

Authors such as Hugh of Fleury became increasingly concerned to record the miraculous cures performed at the shrines of the 'fathers'. They gradually changed their focus from the preservation of communal memories to the celebration of present events. While that change did not occur simultaneously in all communities – the canon of Meung was still concerned with the properties of his community in the twelfth century – the hagiographers of the Orléanais began altering the style of their collections around the year 1100. Quite possibly they did so partially in response to the new practice of holding inquests into the miraculous powers of recently deceased holy people as part of the evolving process of canonization. Certainly Aimo's collection of miracles performed by his martyred friend and leader Abbo was far different in character than his collection of the posthumous miracles of his patron and 'father' Benedict.

THE LOGIC OF SAINTLY PATRONAGE

What did not change was that at the heart of all of the experiences of the miraculous which they described in their collections – whether it be the cure of Henry, the punishment of Geoffrey of Bourges, or the judgement of Stabilis – lay personal relationships

---

[219] 'Utrum autem vetustate abolitae sunt [cartae], aut hostium igne crematae, aut nunquam scriptae, scribarum penuria, minime scio.' *Cartulaire de Saint-Père de Chartres*, I.7, I, 48. 'De hoc sancto antecessores nostri quamvis pauca admodum sive scriptorum inopia, seu bellorum inquietudine, aliisve aliquibus de causis scripta, nobis tamen quanta fecerit ex amplissima praediorum largitione manifestissime docent.' *Miracula s. Lifardi*, c. 2, p. 160.

[220] *Cartulaire de Saint-Père de Chartres*, VI.3, I, 108–15. See also Stock 1983, pp. 107–15.

which relied on an explicit or implicit contract between the 'father' and his servants. The monks and canons who had vowed to serve their patrons had become the legal equivalent of serfs.[221] Many of the inhabitants of the property of a monastery were also part of the *familia* of that community's patron. They were supposed to refrain from work on their patron's feasts. Local priests had the responsibility of announcing the coming feast to their congregations, but, at least occasionally, a parish priest, angered by the revenues taken by the monastery, would see that a feast went uncelebrated.[222] Some miracle stories told how violators of this custom were punished.[223] Two different peasants who insisted on working their fields on the feast of Benedict had their ploughs break in two.[224] A woman who lived in a village belonging to Fleury, but not herself a member of the *familia* of the saint, thought herself exempt from the prohibition and worked on the feast of his translation.[225] She was injured later in the day and the bleeding did not stop until she went to the village church, where her fellows were celebrating the feast, and vowed her service to the saint.

A story from Micy provides the general structure of these relationships.[226] Teduine, an inhabitant of a village neighbouring Micy, was asked by his lord to dig ditches, forgetting that it was the feast of St Maximinus. Teduine's hands became paralysed and he ran off to the house of his lord, who suddenly realized that it was the feastday of a saint. The lord then directed his serf to the church of Micy. Teduine arrived during mass and his cries led the monks at first to think him possessed. After mass they learned of his predicament and sent him to have a meal, after which one of the brothers interviewed him at length about the cause of his malady. Hearing the story the monk led Teduine to the altar of the church and told him to implore the aid of the saint. Unable to do proper obeisance because of his paralysis, Teduine promised to become a

---

[221] Blecker 1966.

[222] Rodulfus Tortarius (*Miracula s. Benedicti*, VIII.12, p. 291) described how a parish priest announced an upcoming feast. Earlier, Andrew (*Miracula s. Benedicti*, VI.10, pp. 232–3) had discussed a priest who failed to do so and was punished by the saint.

[223] In a study of fourteenth-century England, Harvey (1972) has shown that, in that period, peasants guarded their right not to work on feastdays against landlords who attempted to force them to work.

[224] *Miracula s. Benedicti*, V.12, pp. 210–11, VIII.12, pp. 291–2.

[225] *Miracula s. Benedicti*, VIII.32, pp. 329–30. Also see two other instances told by Andrew (*Miracula s. Benedicti*, VI.10, pp. 232–3).

[226] Letaldus of Micy, *Miracula s. Maximini*, cc. 34–5, pp. 607–8. See also *Miracula s. Benedicti*, VI.10, p. 233; VIII.12, p. 292; and VIII.32, p. 330.

servant of Maximinus should the saint cure him.[227] Motion returned to his limbs and he returned yearly to lay a payment on the altar. Teduine and the other inhabitants of monastic territory were bound to the service of their saints just as they were to their overlords. When they did not render proper service to their patron, they were forced to pay a fine or an alternate form of service.

This same logic of patronage and servitude governed the actions of other lay supplicants. Some explicitly entered the service of the saints in order that those patrons would protect them, thus returning the service rendered. Bonded service may seem a radical step to take, even as a means of seeking refuge from a crippling disease. The noble parents of a young lame woman named Adelaide vowed her servitude to Benedict if she was cured.[228] Aimo commented that her children were still useful servants of the abbey years after her cure. Other supplicants donated gifts to the saint in place of service. Andrew told how his community acquired two of its most important properties from people who vowed to part with them in exchange for a cure.[229] The hagiographers employed the language and gestures of social contracts. Rodulfus Tortarius, for example, termed the gold which was given to Fleury by the parents of a young knight killed in battle against the abbey a *vadimonium*. Such a payment was a pledge of good faith designed to lessen the posthumous punishment for his sins and to win the prayers of the saint and his monks.[230]

As they were founded upon an exchange of gifts, these relationships between saintly 'fathers' and their servants were reciprocal. The living Christians bound to the saint were required to perform certain services. Aimo described one calamity which occurred at Fleury as possible because Benedict had withdrawn 'the right hand of his protection' due to the sins of the monks.[231] Rodulfus Tortarius openly ridiculed Abbot Veranus of Fleury for seeking the help of 'doctors (so he thought) of medicine' for relief from recurrent fevers. The abbot was cured only when he remembered the existence close at hand of more powerful

---

227 Letaldus of Micy, *Miracula s. Maximini*, c. 35, p. 608.
228 *Miracula s. Benedicti*, III.20, pp. 169–70.
229 *Miracula s. Benedicti*, III.4, pp. 132–3, and v.5, pp. 199–200.
230 *Miracula s. Benedicti*, VIII.35, pp. 334–6. The service which a young man vowed to St Laetus after the saint released him from prison was called a *capitis censum*, see *Miracula ss. Georgii et Laeti*, c. 1, p. 79.   231 *Miracula s. Benedicti*, III.19, pp. 166–7.

medicines, and had himself carried into the church to drink water which had touched the relics.[232] Henry's vision had told him that he would be cured through the merits of Maximinus of Micy, and prayer at the shrines of Maximinus of Trier and Maximus of Chinon brought him no relief.[233]

If much was expected of both the monks and the *familia* of the saints, those saints were expected to uphold their end of the bargain as well. A formula copied at Fleury around the year 1100 promised that the serfs who belonged to Benedict would be provided *securitas*.[234] When the 'fathers' failed, they were seen by their servants to be quite literally sleeping on the job. Adrevald had described the monk Christian who berated his patron when amulets were stolen from the shrine and accused him of sleeping. Likewise, when Benedict had appeared to Hercambaldus in the ninth century, he had asked whether his monks thought him asleep. That image, like that of Benedict carrying the *baculus*, had a long life. Over 150 years later an elderly woman who lived on Fleury's lands and was maltreated by a local nobleman rushed into the church, threw back the altar cloths, and began beating on it with her fists.[235] Her words echoed those of the Carolingian monk, 'Benedict old man, you lazy person, you sloth, what are you doing? Why do you sleep? Why do you submit your servants to such improprieties?'

Monastic communities had more formal ways of coercing a saint to perform his or her duties as a patron. Ritualized curses could be aimed at those who attempted to harm the monks themselves or their property.[236] These curses were attempts to bring down miraculous punishments similar to the ones described in the miracle collections. Rodulfus Tortarius recorded how two members of the castellan family from Châtillon-sur-Loing tried to

[232] *Miracula s. Benedicti*, VIII.25, pp. 318–19.
[233] *Miraculum s. Maximini*, pp. 238–42.
[234] 'In Dei nomine ille abbas monasterii sanctae Mariae, sancti Petri et sancti Benedicti Floriacensis. Notum sit omnibus fidelibus sancte Dei aecclesiae quia postulavit nos quidam homo sancti Benedicti, servus, nomine ille, vel femina similiter sancti Benedicti, ancilla, nomine illa, ut ei et infantibus ejus scriptum securitatis faceremus, hoc est quod eam et infantes ejus nulli unquam homini daremus aut commutaremus, sed eos semper in nostro in dominicatu teneremus. Nos autem eorum petitioni consentientes hoc ea fecimus ratione ut annis singulis debitum nobis servitutem reddant, hoc est IIII denarios singuli de suo capite receptum quoque nobis faciant sicut servi sancti Benedicti tempore oportuno.' Transcribed by Prou (1893, p. 218 n. 1) from Vatican, Reg. lat. 479, fo. 61.
[235] *Miracula s. Benedicti*, VIII.6, pp. 282–3.
[236] Little 1975a and 1979; Reynolds 1987, pp. 418–19.

take control of nearby La-Cour-Marigny, which belonged to Fleury. The monks pronounced a curse, which Rodulfus vaguely described as an *anathema*, against the members of the clan who each in turn died a horrible death at the hands of St Benedict.[237]

The probable form of such a curse can be learned from one contained in a later collection of prayers from Fleury:

Lord Jesus, redeemer of the world, we come before the holy altar and before your most holy body and blood, and we turn to you because of our sins for which we are justly held culpable before you. We come to you, Lord Jesus, and we who are prostrate cry out, since the unjust and the proud confident of their power over us invade, rob, and devastate the lands of Holy Mary, of St Peter, and of St Benedict. For these reasons Lord impose justice on them by your power and make them recognize their wrongdoing and free us in your mercy.

A marginal note in the vernacular shows that this curse was once employed against Beatrice, countess of Chalon-sur-Saône. In 1204 she is known to have been involved in a legal dispute with Fleury over certain properties belonging to the priory of Perrecy. The monks saw no contradiction in the use of both miraculous and judicial weapons against their enemies.[238] Such curses were used by monastic communities in the Loire valley throughout our period, although they began to decline in fashion in the later middle ages.[239]

---

[237] *Miracula s. Benedicti*, VIII.15–16, pp. 296–300. On the confusing terminology of excommunication, anathema, and malediction, see Reynolds 1987, particularly pp. 406 and 417.

[238] The *Clamor in malefactoribus* is contained in Orléans, BM 123, pp. 339–40: 'Ante sanctum altare et sanctissimum corpus et sanguinem tuum, Domine Iesu, redemptor mundi, accedimus et de peccatis nostris pro quibus iuste affligimur culpabiles contra te nos reddidimus. Ad te, Domine Iesu, venimus, ad te prostrati clamamus quia iniqui et superbi suisque viribus confisi super nos insurgunt terras sanctae Mariae, sancti Petri, sanctique Benedicti invadunt depraedantur et vastant. Propterea Domine, sicut suis iustifica eos in uirtute tua et fac eis reconoscere prout tibi placet sua malefacta et libera nos in misericordia tua. Amen.' A colophon has been added in a later hand just before the Amen: 'qui cum patre et spiritu sancto uiuis et regnas dominus per omnia saecula saeculorum'. A marginal note, which is in a later hand and not completely legible, reads 'Beatrix la contesse de . . . Hugo de Dignone. Richardus de Digone.' In 1204 Beatrice of Chalon-sur-Saône came to an agreement with the abbot of Fleury to quit certain claims against the priory of Perrecy and to make donations to St Benedict in recompense for the injuries which she had committed against the community. See *Recueil des chartes de Saint-Benoît*, no. 292, II, 179–81.

[239] In 1204 Innocent III sent a letter (PL, CCXVII, 107D–108C) to the prior of La Charité-sur-Loire approving the use of such a prayer against *malefactores*. Apparently the prior had worried that this already somewhat antique usage might be canonically improper. I am grateful to Lester Little for this reference.

Occasionally communities even cursed their own patrons in times of distress in an attempt to force them to exercise their patronal powers. The monks of Micy apparently raised such a *clamor* against Maximinus when their simoniacal abbot was unduly oppressing them.[240] Other communities went so far as to use a ritual of humiliation, in which the relics of the saint were taken from their shrine, put in full view of the community, and criticized in prayer and ritual curses.[241] These monks simply formalized the complaints about the saint's laziness made by the *custos* Christian and the elderly female serf at the church of Fleury. As Geary has pointed out, such chastisements of the saints, whether informally by individuals or formally by communities, were a symbolic and ideological inversion of the chastisement of enemies by the saints according to the logic of patronage.[242]

As the *clamor* from Fleury makes clear, a strong link was seen between sin and the disasters which a monastic community suffered. The enemies of a community also sinned in their lack of regard for its 'father', hence they earned the chastisements inflicted on them by the saints. Similarly disease, as it afflicted both clerics and laity, was usually seen as a sign of moral failure. In order to recover from their varied punishments, the clerics and laity of the Orléanais had to do penance for their sins and thus place themselves once again in right relationship with their 'fathers' and their God. As the monk of Micy remarked about the pilgrim Henry, 'he came to penance more through necessity than through desire'.[243] Pointing to scriptural authority, Hugh of Fleury drew an explicit connection between sin and disease. For him the monastic life was the best remedy and means of salvation, but a pilgrimage conducted in a suitably penitential manner could produce the sort of curing miracles which he recorded.[244] Such varied rituals as the use of the *clamor* by the monks of Fleury, their barefoot procession with their lay neighbours carrying the relics of St Maurus to the church of Saint-Denis, or the prostration of numerous pilgrims before the altars and tombs of the saints were all expressions of penitence designed to call upon the 'fathers' for miraculous

---

[240] Letaldus of Micy, *Miracula s. Maximini*, c. 20, p. 603.
[241] Geary 1979b, but see also the modifications made by Martimont 1978, pp. 224–7, and Reynolds 1987, p. 420. There is no recorded use of a formal humiliation in the Orléanais.   [242] Geary 1979a.
[243] *Miraculum s. Maximini*, p. 238.
[244] *Miracula s. Benedicti*, IX.prologue, pp. 357–9.

assistance. A correct relationship between the living and their saintly 'fathers' was essential to their well-being in both this world and the next.

When one died in a state of sin, eternal damnation could be the result. Therefore the people of the Orléanais particularly called upon the aid of their 'fathers' in avoiding hell and reaching heaven. To be part of the *familia* of such a 'father' was a great boon after death. The monastic servants of those patrons themselves aided in the process of salvation through prayers said on behalf of the deceased servants of their patron. This process of intercessory prayer was one of the most important functions of monastic communities from at least as early as the Carolingian period. Evidence for it can be found in a wide variety of literary and liturgical sources, including necrologies and prayers for the dead. Unfortunately, little detailed evidence remains extant from the Orléanais itself concerning this aspect of monastic life. Certainly the monks of Fleury, Micy, and Meung were involved in memorializing those deceased laypeople who had, through their donations or service, become part of the monastic *familia* and themselves servants of the saintly 'fathers'.[245]

Clamores, on the other hand, served to remove the enemies of a monastery from the *familia* of their patron. To curse an enemy was to sever all bonds between that enemy and the monks themselves, as well as to deny the efficacy of that person's claims on the protective power of the saintly 'father'. Such curses stopped short of outright excommunication, which marked a complete break between an individual and the entire community of the church. Whereas, for example, excommunication would prohibit burial in any consecrated ground, a monastic curse could only prohibit burial in the cemeteries controlled by the monks themselves. In the early eleventh century excommunication became one of the chief weapons used by bishops involved in the Peace of God in their struggles against lay usurpation of ecclesiastical property. Excommunication, however, was an episcopal prerogative and not directly available to a monastic community. Indeed the monastic communities of the Orléanais were often on bad terms with their own bishops. One of the most interesting formulae of excommunication – which came to be contained in the *Pontificale Romano-*

---

[245] The most comprehensive treatment of monastic prayers for the dead is McLaughin 1985. Unfortunately it remains unpublished.

Germanicum – had one of its earliest usages in a letter of Pope Leo VII on behalf of the monks of Fleury. At the request of Odo of Cluny, then abbot of Fleury, the pope threatened a group of bishops with excommunication if they attempted to usurp properties of St Benedict. While the letter is of suspect authenticity, it was certainly of medieval origin and thus demonstrates that the connection between theft of the property of a 'father' and excommunication was made in the mind of the monks of Fleury, if not in the mind of the pope himself.[246] Monastic communities could, like their divine and saintly overlords, relent from anger. The use of intercessory prayer on behalf of a defeated enemy occurred as early as the ninth century, when the monks of Fleury prayed that the torments of the recently deceased Count Odo of Orléans be diminished.[247]

The importance of membership in the *familia* of a saintly 'father' can be seen in the story of the castellan Herbert of Sully. According to Aimo, he donated certain incomes from a church to Fleury in *beneficium*, a gift which would have gained him such membership and the protective patronage of St Benedict. Later, however, Herbert attempted to deny the gift.[248] The monks tried both prayer and a court action in order to resolve the situation. They even summoned the local populace to join in their prayers by ringing the bells of the church, thereby symbolically gathering the entire *familia* of Benedict. Herbert remained obdurate. One night while sleeping he heard a voice repeating the words of John 11:10, 'He who walks in the night offends, since the light is not in him.' He then saw St Benedict approach. The saint then struck Herbert between the shoulder blades with his *baculus*. The castellan's shouts attracted his fellow knights. Shortly before dying he asked them to bring him to the tomb of the saint. They brought his body to the monastery and, after some initial reluctance, the monks agreed to bury him in the churchyard, a symbolic acceptance of his deathbed repentance. Posthumously Herbert was reincorporated into the *familia* of the saint and presumably awarded once again the benefits of Benedict's patronage and intercession. In similar fashion, Abbot

---

[246] *Recueil des chartes de Saint-Benoît*, no. 45, I, 114–19; Little 1979, pp. 52–3; Reynolds 1987, pp. 415–16. On the development of the rituals of excommunication, see Reynolds 1987, pp. 407–15. On the canon law of excommunication, see Vodola 1986, particularly pp. 12–20 on the Carolingian period and pp. 24–7 on the effects of the bull *Quoniam multos* (1078).

[247] *Miracula s. Benedicti*, I.21, p. 51.   [248] *Miracula s. Benedicti*, II.7, pp. 107–9.

Abbo once allowed a lay property-owner named Walter – who had died as a result of a miraculous punishment while wrongfully disputing Fleury's claim to a piece of property – to be buried in the cemetery at Fleury since Walter had shown the abbot personal respect on a journey they once had taken together.[249]

The intercession of the saint was deemed capable of preventing death as well as damnation. Letaldus told how a canon from Saint-Martin of Tours named Vivianus came for a visit to Micy.[250] He was expelled from the community, however, after his behaviour repeatedly disturbed the monastic routine, particularly by making excessive noise. Returning to Tours he had the temerity to cross the Loire at a treacherous point. His boat was wrecked and he floated for many hours holding on to a plank before he was rescued by a fisherman. Brought back to Micy, he was assumed to be dead and the monks regretted having turned him away. At midnight, however, he revived and told them how St Maximinus had brought him back from the river Arvernus and the very grasp of the devil. He repented of his sins, asked the *indulgentia* of the monks, and began to lead a good and humble life. Letaldus' description of the geography of the afterlife was borrowed almost completely from Virgil. Such a classicizing touch certainly appealed to that author, who also imitated Virgil in his poetry, but it also betrays the fact that the fate of an ordinary, that is non-saintly, soul between the time of death and the final judgement had yet to be determined with any theological rigour.

Not all people who offended a saint were as lucky as Vivianus. A knight named Arnustus was stricken and died after he had broken a pact with the monks of Fleury. Aimo's description indicates that the monks may have invoked some form of ritual *clamor* in their prayers for help to their patron. The knight's friends prayed in vain to the Lord and Benedict to save Arnustus from death, but there is no record of the disposition of his body.[251] Apparently the goodwill of the monks was seen as being essential to the intercession of the saint and the dispensation of divine forgiveness. Sometimes the living could find solace denied to the dead in monastic cemeteries. According to generally accepted custom, cemeteries were considered to be a place of sanctuary for criminals.

---

[249] *Miracula s. Benedicti*, III.10, p. 154.
[250] Letaldus of Micy, *Miracula s. Maximini*, c. 32, p. 607.
[251] *Miracula s. Benedicti*, II.5, p. 105.

A murderer sought out one which had been donated to St Benedict on at least one occasion.[252]

Belief in the intercessory powers of the 'fathers' and their monastic servants undergirded the complex system of memorial prayers, as well as of monastic profession *ad succurrendum*, which developed from the Carolingian period on, most spectacularly in houses associated with Cluny. Although no memorial books or necrologies survive from this period in our region, the monks of the Orléanais certainly were involved in praying for the dead. The exact relationship between such intercessory prayer and the cult of the saints has yet to be fully explored. As John van Engen remarks, however, 'The veneration of relics . . . and Benedictine prayer [for the dead] were surely two different religious phenomena. Yet monks often served as guardians of relics and thus appeared as the primary coworkers of the saints interceding in the divine court.'[253] As a property-owner put it when he became a monk of Fleury, 'Believing the promises [of eternal life] . . . [I] hope to give service to the commands of father Benedict and to Jesus Christ his lord.'[254]

The language of charters leaves little doubt that one major purpose of donating property to a monastic foundation and its patron was to secure the prayers of the monks for the safety of the donor's soul. A charter from Perrecy dated 889, that is after it had become a priory of Fleury, opened,

If any of the faithful wish to give from their goods to the places of the saints of the holy church of God, they may without doubt be confident that it will be returned to them in eternal beatitude. Therefore, I, Vulfardus, fearing the day of the final call, lest I be found burdened with a mass of sins and without the fruit of good works, and since I have heard in the Gospel 'Whoever gives up father and mother . . . will possess eternal life (Mt. 19:29)', therefore I give [the following properties to Fleury] for the safety of my soul.[255]

Similar sentiments were repeated time and time again. Even though the language of charters was based on standard formulae, it reflects the fact that the donations of properties to monastic and canonical communities was grounded firmly in the logic of saintly patronage. The donor entered into a gift-giving relationship with

---

[252] *Miracula s. Benedicti*, VIII.17, pp. 300–2.   [253] Van Engen 1986, p. 296.
[254] *Recueil des chartes de Saint-Benoît*, no. 73, I, 190–2.
[255] *Recueil des chartes de Saint-Benoît*, no. 31, I, 85–8.

the patron of the community and that relationship would posthumously serve to benefit the donor.

The relationships formed in these charters were based on the same logic of patronage which we have found in the collections of miracle stories. The patronage of the saints, most particularly those who were resident through their relics in a place like Fleury, was a powerful inducement for donations. Bernard Töpfer has stressed the importance of the cult of relics in attracting the lay support which helped to finance the church building of the early eleventh century. He has gone so far as to claim that 'relics were . . . the chief instrument of churchly propaganda'.[256] On one level, the logic of patronage simply made good business sense. Relics attracted pilgrims, pilgrims provided donations, donations allowed the construction of grander churches and reliquaries, these grander structures attracted even more pilgrims than before. While there were many important Romanesque churches which did not house important relics, Töpfer is correct in suggesting that the logic of saintly patronage was not limited to the monasteries and associated clerics, but exercised a profound attraction to the laity of western Christendom. Laypeople did accept that they could be cured of their illnesses, spiritual as well as physical, through the intercession of the saints. It was a good thing to be a friend of Benedict, or of Maximinus, or of Anianus, all of whom were themselves intimate friends of Christ. Nor was it by any means unusual that gifts be exchanged between the living and the dead. Moreover ecclesiastical institutions naturally became the arbiters of such exchanges.[257]

The process by which information about the powers of the saintly 'fathers' was disseminated to the laity remains unclear. Certainly the miracle collections themselves, which were composed in Latin and received only a limited distribution, did not aid in this process. Some of the stories which they contain, however, provide some illumination. At least one monk of Fleury went to parish churches with relics of his patron to preach about that saint's powers and thus obtain resources for the reconstruction of the church at his monastery.[258] Some laypeople were impressed by seeing the relics of the saint brought forth on liturgical processions.[259] Those who had suffered punishments from the saints

---

[256] Töpfer 1956 (the quotation is on p. 438).
[258] *Miracula s. Benedicti*, VIII.26, pp. 319–21.
[257] Oexle 1983 and Geary 1986a.
[259] *Miracula s. Benedicti*, II.19, p. 125.

or who had been cured by them often proved to be effective promoters of a cult. A knight who had been thrown from his horse after illegally obtaining fodder on the lands of Benedict 'offered this example to others'. A man who had been chastised by Anianus in a vision 'kept the memory always before his eyes' and his words 'deterred many and recalled them from evil'. The pilgrim Henry, after he had been cured by Maximinus, 'sought, through the aid and merits of our most faithful father Maximinus, to help the unfortunate and to preach with a glorious cry the sublime power of that faithful protector to people far removed from our home'.[260] While the laity certainly seem to have accepted the logic of saintly patronage, their appreciation of the powers of the saints may well have differed in its particulars from clerics who lived in the monastic communities under the patronage of the 'fathers'.

The basic piety of intercessory prayer and the theology of the forgiveness of sins were to undergo important refinement during the twelfth century. A more interiorized form of penitence was promoted as the surest route to the heavenly kingdom, although it did not win universal assent. There are no parallels from the Orléanais to the ghost stories concerning personal penitence and purgatory which Sharon Farmer has found at Marmoutier. She has identified in these stories a piety characteristic of the later twelfth century which informed new interpretations of the role of intercession. As she concludes, 'The monastic ghost stories . . . indicate that the participants in, and advocates of, monastic suffrages for the dead were themselves aware that men had, or needed, personal motivations for joining in those rituals.'[261] The chastisement stories told by Letaldus, Aimo, and even by Rodulfus Tortarius writing in the early twelfth century, were emblematic of an earlier piety. They offered motivation to both clergy and laity by threat of external force. The 'personal motivation' offered to laypeople by the appearances of 'fathers' such as Benedict and Maximinus swinging their abbatial staffs as weapons differed greatly from the meeker monastic ghosts with their stories of posthumous torment found in the stories from Marmoutier. One story from the Touraine, however, did in part concern a 'father' of the Orléanais. According to its author Evurtius once appeared along with St Martin and two other bishops to a canon of the

---

[260] *Miracula s. Benedicti*, II.14, p. 117; *Miracula s. Aniani*, c. 13, p. 269; *Miraculum s. Maximini*, p. 238. [261] Farmer 1985, the quotation is on p. 237.

church of Saint-Martin.[262] In the course of Martin's advice to the canon concerning penitence, he identified Evurtius, saying that each day 'during the present age' God freed a soul from the 'place of penance' on account of that saint's merit.

The miracle collections from the Orléanais reveal much about eleventh- and early twelfth-century society. Both the social and the natural worlds simmered with the constant threat of disaster. The military order was almost nonchalant about the use of violence to obtain its goals. Written title to property often had little meaning in the face of a drawn sword. The truly poor, such as the woman living in the portico of Saint-Samson or the family squatting near Micy, had virtually no protection against the ravages of the physical world. Letaldus even described the monks of Micy cowering in their church during a particularly severe storm.[263] Dimly understood illnesses of a stunning variety afflicted people of every class and could alter the fortunes even of such evidently wealthy people as Henry and Adelaide suddenly and forever. Communication was fraught with problems caused by differences of language and the difficulties of traversing even moderate distances. At the same time people of all classes made surprisingly long and obviously arduous journeys. Even a move to Burgundy was insufficient to hide the serf Stabilis from a chance observation by the vigilant eyes of one of his former masters.

These stories demonstrate that the idea of patronage was not a legal fiction, but an extension of deeply held assumptions about the nature both of the saints themselves and of social relationships more generally. Carolingian and early Capetian society was a network of personal allegiances based on complex and overlapping ties of service defined by such factors as family, vows, and the possession of property. As historians such as Marc Bloch and Georges Duby have stressed, gift giving provided the very foundations of these

---

[262] The text *Pretiosi confessoris* (*BHL* 5661) was written sometime after 1141; see *lectio* 3, p. 19. While it probably originated in the Touraine, it is included in at least two late medieval manuscript collections from the Orléanais of material dealing with St Evurtius: (1) Paris, BN lat. 910 A (fourteenth century; Saint-Euverte de Vilhermerico; *Catal. Paris.*, I, 18) which also contained the *Vita s. Evurtii II* on fos. 26–36; (2) Vatican, Reg. lat. 623 (fifteenth century; *Catal. Vat.*, p. 391, and Renaud 1976, pp. 247–8) which also contained a collection of Evurtius material on fos. 99v–103v. Martin was a very popular saint and many hagiographers sought to associate less well-known subjects with him. The author of the *Miracula s. Aniani* (c. 4, pp. 260–1), for example, included an historically impossible story about Martin (d. 397) praying at the tomb of Anianus (d. c. 455).   [263] Letaldus of Micy, *Miracula s. Maximini*, c. 37, p. 608.

social relationships. In that world the idea of faithfulness or fidelity was crucially important. One had to trust one's lord – be that Jesus Christ, St Benedict, the king of the Franks, or the knight who controlled a nearby castle – for protection. When such trust was called into question, society itself was in danger of failing. Rodulfus Tortarius told of a serf named Robert who was given by Abbot Hugh of Fleury to Tescelin of Pithiviers.[264] Robert preferred the patronage and protection of Benedict as an overlord to that provided by a human castellan, for he 'had faith (*fiducia*) in father Benedict, who was his lord by law'. With the miraculous support of the saint, the serf successfully maintained that he could not be removed from Benedict's *familia* and was eventually returned to the lands of Fleury. For the logic of patronage to function such *fiducia* was essential.

The saints were perceived by monastic authors to act according to, and to be constrained by, the duties of personal allegiance in much the same way as was any ordinary living person. The specific language and actions of patronage discussed here were not present in all of the stories. Nevertheless I would suggest that this logic of patronage – that is the submission of a person to the power of a saint and the request that the power be used to protect and intercede for the petitioner – governed the full array of relationships between the 'fathers' and their servants, including pilgrimage and the donation of property to monastic communities. Pilgrims brought their gifts and their prayers to leave at the tombs, and through their gestures in the churches they made obeisance to the saints. They sought the patronage of the saints as forcefully, if less formally, as did those people who vowed their service to the saints.

The miraculous did not depend on physical contact with the relics. Miracles were not some sort of 'sympathetic magic' or 'thaumaturgy', but resulted from the personal patronage of the 'fathers'. They often involved contact with a saint through the invocation of the saint's name, the veneration of the saint's relics, or even a vision of the saint. Such contact was, however, subordinate to the duties of patronage which required a saint to act on behalf of a servant. Saintly patronage was based on the powerful bond of exchanged gifts. The saint provided relics to servants as a pledge of the saint's own personal power. In return the petitioner offered some form of gift which could be prayers, ex-voto offerings, the

---

[264] *Miracula s. Benedicti*, VIII.11, p. 287–8.

donation of property, or personal service. The clerics and laity of the Orléanais became the servants of the saints in a variety of ways: monks and canons by means of their religious vows; serfs, such as Teduine, by their legal position; the ill seeking cures, like Adelaide and Henry, by their vows of service; ordinary pilgrims by their ex-voto offerings and prayers. In all these cases the *patrocinium* provided by a saint was clear: the servant gave gifts and honour to the 'father', the 'father' brought divine *virtus* to the aid of the servant.

Chapter 5

SAINTLY PATRONAGE AND EPISCOPAL AUTHORITY AT THE ABBEY OF MICY

As the stories of miraculous cures, chastisements, and court cases indicate, the beliefs of the clerics and laity of the Orléanais rendered the patronage provided by the 'fathers' of the diocese very powerful indeed. While this sense of the miraculous was crucial to that patronage, the 'fathers' did not exercise their power solely in those events deemed to be miracles. As the patrons of abbeys and collegiate churches, the 'fathers' also wielded an ongoing lordship over communities of monks and canons. They were important figures in the structures of ecclesiastical authority within the region. The power of the patron saints can be seen in the history of the abbey of Micy, which had a proud legacy from the 'fathers' of the Merovingian age. According to tradition it had been founded in the sixth century by Clovis as a gift to two holy men from Verdun, Maximinus and his elderly uncle, Euspicius. The former became not only the first abbot of the new monastery, but a renowned teacher of the contemplative life as well. Sacked and abandoned during the wars of the eighth century, Micy was refounded by Bishop Theodulf of Orléans (*c.* 790–818). From that time it remained firmly under episcopal control, a power that often worked, in the eyes of the monks, to their detriment. Although the monastery had originally been dedicated to St Stephen, the monks primarily venerated the memory of their first abbot, Maximinus. While they named both saints as patrons in their charters, it was to Maximinus that the members of the community regularly turned for support in their struggles against the inimical effects of episcopal authority.

The early history of the community remains obscure. The only account of the abbey prior to the refoundation is that contained in the various lives of Maximinus, themselves composed in the ninth century. All charters which allegedly predate the refoundation have been shown to be forgeries based on these Carolingian works.[1] In addition to inventing diplomatic sources, the authors of those lives adapted traditions about Maximinus from the extant lives of his disciples, St Avitus and St Carileffus. Their works served in turn as sources for eleventh-century authors from the Orléanais who claimed other saints, most importantly St Viator and St Laetus, as disciples of Maximinus. Meanwhile hagiographers from neighbouring regions – including the authors of the lives of St Leobinus of Chartres, St Leonard of Noblat, and St Launomaurus of Blois – also borrowed from and contributed to the traditions about Maximinus' tenure at Micy. Thus a tangled web of hagiographic tradition formed which was centred on Micy's first abbot. It is not surprising that Micy has acquired a reputation for being 'one of the most famous workshops for forgeries of the Middle Ages'.[2]

The documented history of the abbey begins with Theodulf of Orléans, one of that remarkable group of intellectuals recruited by Charlemagne to develop and enforce ecclesiastical reform. By 796 Theodulf had received the bishopric of Orléans as well as the abbacies of Fleury and of Saint-Aignan from the emperor. The bishop later asked the noted monastic reformer Benedict of Aniane to send a delegation of monks 'of regular discipline' who would repopulate the buildings of Micy then standing empty and ruined across the river from his episcopal city.[3] In order to celebrate the refoundation Theodulf, an accomplished poet, composed verses in the conceit of a letter to Benedict.[4] The bishop believed that an abbey had existed there for some time and that Maximinus had been its abbot. In a line redolent of Prudentius he attributed the abandonment of the abbey to the work of 'barbarians'. A monk of Micy would later note more precisely that the sack occurred in 749

---

[1] Havet 1885, pp. 224–33; Poncelet 1905, pp. 6–10; 'Chartes de Micy', pp. vi–vii.

[2] Jacques Dubois in *VSBP*, XI, 297. The Bollandist Albert Poncelet established (1905) a stemma of the many texts associated with the abbey of Micy. Unfortunately virtually all the published work on the history and hagiography of Micy (the best known being Vergnaud-Romagnesi 1842, Cochard 1877, and Jarossay 1902) predated this article and is therefore of little value for the history of the abbey prior to the twelfth century. Poncelet himself (pp. 1–14) points out some of the problems and errors of Jarossay. Although some alterations to his conclusions have been suggested before, notably by Goffart (1966, pp. 339–48), and still others will be offered here, the work remains the basis for research on the history of Micy.

[3] Ardo, *Vita s. Benedicti Anianensis*, c. 24, p. 209. It is impossible to date the refoundation precisely, but Ardo included it before the death of Charlemagne (814) in his narrative, thus providing a firm *terminus ad quem*.   [4] *MGH, Poetae aevi Carolini*, I, 520–2.

during the war between Pippin II and King Waifarius of the
Aquitaine.[5] Theodulf found a number of tombs at the abbey and
mistakenly believed that of Maximinus to be among them. Even
granting poetic licence, he had high hopes for the new abbey. He
suggested that, through the reform of Micy, Benedict of Aniane
could follow in the tradition of the patron of Fleury: 'What
Benedict was as director in Italian lands, so you; Benedict will be in
our lands.'[6]

Although Theodulf himself may have served for a time as abbot
of the newly refounded community, a man named Druectesindus
held that office by 815.[7] In 826 Bishop Jonas, who succeeded to the
see after Theodulf's spectacular fall from favour, obtained imperial
approval for a grant of limited exemptions for Micy, including the
right to elect its own abbot. These exemptions do not seem to have
had much practical effect. The right of free election, for example,
was exercised only sporadically over the following centuries. In the
words of the imperial act, Micy was 'under the command of its
bishop' and its monks were required 'to stand firm under the law
and power of its diocese'.[8]

At the time of Micy's refoundation there were already several
hagiographic traditions concerning its foundation and patron saint
circulating among the monastic communities of the middle Loire
valley. According to the *Vita s. Aviti I*, St Avitus had been a monk
of Micy under the tutelage of Abbot Maximinus.[9] After Maximinus' death the monks of the abbey, with the approval of the bishop
(*pontifice iubente*), attempted to elect Avitus as their abbot. He
refused to return from his hermitage, although he later founded his
own monastic community near Châteaudun. The author later
suggested that the citizens of Orléans had used Avitus' connection
to Micy as the grounds for their request for the return of Avitus'
relics from Châteaudun.[10] The author did not, however, mention

[5] Letaldus of Micy, *Miracula s. Maximini*, c. 12, p. 601.
[6] *MGH, Poetae aevi Carolini*, I, 521.
[7] 'Chartes de Micy', no. 3, pp. 13–17. This diploma of Louis the Pious dated 8 January 815 is the earliest genuine charter extant from Micy. On its authenticity see *Regesten des Kaiserreichs*, no. 568; 'Chartes de Micy', pp. lxxxi–lxxxii.
[8] *Cartulaire de Sainte-Croix*, no. 38, pp. 75–8.
[9] There is no mention of Micy in the Merovingian sources about St Avitus. Poncelet (1905, pp. 15–16) demonstrates that the reference to Avitus' abbacy of Micy found in some editions of Gregory of Tours' *Historia Francorum*, III.6, is a later interpolation.
[10] *Vita s. Aviti I*, cc. 3 and 11, pp. 57–8 and 61.

the foundation of Micy. His successor embellished the account by stating that Micy had been founded by Bishop Eusebius of Orléans.[11] The author of the *Vita s. Aviti III* repeated this passage almost verbatim.[12] In all three versions the bishop clearly exercised the final right to choose Micy's abbot.[13] In the first decades of the ninth century a monk from the Maine used these traditions to form the basis for the story of his patron, St Carileffus, whom he identified as St Avitus' companion on his journey. Micy and its abbot retained an important place in his narrative as the original monastic home and teacher of his hero. That author did, however, make several factual errors concerning the monastery in the Orléanais.[14] The author of the *Vita s. Lifardi*, another early ninth-century work, also knew of Micy. While he avoided any mention of St Maximinus, he described how Lifardus had a vision of the soul of Micy's newly deceased abbot, Theodemir, entering heaven and had later reported the vision to Theodemir's nephew and successor, who was named Maximinus.[15] Through these texts Micy was already gaining a reputation as having been a cradle of saints during the Merovingian age.

The writing of hagiography at Micy began with the composition of the *Vita s. Maximini I* by a monk named Bertholdus.[16] The monk dedicated his work to Bishop Jonas (818–43) in a poem

---

[11] 'Est autem cominus Aurelianam urbem Miciacense monasterium quod est iuris matris ecclesiae Sanctae Crucis, a praedicta urbe dispescens fere tribus milibus; ubi tunc beatus Maximinus ab Eusebio Aurelianensis ecclesiae pontifice constitutus coenobiali praeerat ordini.' This portion of the *Vita s. Aviti II* is printed by Poncelet 1905, p. 20. See also Paris, BN lat. 12606, fo. 54v, and Vatican, Reg. lat. 585, fo. 28v.

[12] This section of the only extant manuscript of the *Vita s. Aviti III* (Paris, BN lat. 3789, fo. 105v) was altered by a later scribe. An ultraviolet reading of the manuscript, however, confirms Poncelet's suggestion (1905, p. 20) that the original text was virtually identical to that of the *Vita s. Aviti II*.

[13] The extant manuscripts of all three versions date to the eleventh century or later. Of the eleven medieval manuscripts I have located of the *Vita s. Aviti I*, ten are German or Austrian in origin, while the three extant manuscripts of the later versions (Paris, BN lat. 12606; Vatican, Reg. lat. 585; Paris, BN lat. 3789) are all from the Orléanais. The provenance of these manuscripts suggests that the closely related later versions became the standard texts of the life in the Orléanais, while the *Vita s. Aviti I* was widely circulated in eastern Frankish lands.

[14] *Vita s. Carileffi I*, c. 3, p. 72. As Goffart points out (1966, p. 343), the author placed Micy on the north bank of the Loire and made Maximinus the bishop of Orléans.

[15] *Vita s. Lifardi*, c. 11, p. 156. While it was composed in the ninth century, this text is more difficult to date and may not predate the work of Bertholdus.

[16] Bertholdus was identified as a monk of Micy by Letaldus (*Miracula s. Maximini*, prologue, p. 598).

which used standard *topoi* to excuse the author's poor style and to praise the bishop's literary attainments. Bertholdus undertook his work in the latter part of Jonas' episcopate, after the bishop had relinquished the abbacy of Micy to Heric (*c.* 828–42).[17] Playing on his subject's name he noted that 'Divine providence provides for us a shepherd, namely the most blessed Maximinus, who was given to us just as is written down here and who strove in the lasting record of his name to adorn his own life with an abundance of the highest (*maxima*) spiritual virtues.'[18]

Bertholdus deftly altered the story of the foundation of Micy found in the later versions of the life of Avitus. According to him (and works from Micy are the sole sources for these events) the citizens of Verdun revolted against the rule of Clovis, who immediately invested the city. As defeat appeared imminent the inhabitants asked Euspicius, a local priest noted for his wisdom, to plead their case. He successfully persuaded Clovis to show mercy. Impressed by the demeanour of this priest, the king offered him the vacant see of the town. After Euspicius refused, Clovis asked the priest to accompany him to Orléans, which he did with Maximinus, his nephew. There Clovis built a new monastery for the two men and Bertholdus carefully specified certain properties (*municipia*) which were added to the grant. Euspicius allowed his nephew to become the first abbot. Shortly after the foundation and the elevation of Maximinus to the priesthood by Bishop Eusebius, Euspicius died and was buried in the church of Saint-Aignan.

In this new foundation legend Clovis became the founder of Micy, while Bishop Eusebius served simply as a friend and adviser to Maximinus. Indeed the bishop undertook to console the abbot after his uncle's death by bringing him to the 'basilica of Mary' where he was healed from his grief by blessings and prayer.[19] From that time on the virtues of Maximinus' life drew followers from the secular world to study in his 'gymnasium of spiritual philosophy'.[20] In a passage which served to introduce his account of the lives of Avitus and Carileffus, Bertholdus played on the theme, introduced in his prologue, of how the life lived by a saint and the text which recounted that life should serve as an example for imitation by others. To show such imitation at work he

---

[17] Bertholdus of Micy, *Vita s. Maximini I*, c. 25, p. 597.
[18] Bertholdus of Micy, *Vita s. Maximini I*, c. 2, p. 592.
[19] Bertholdus of Micy, *Vita s. Maximini I*, c. 12, p. 594.
[20] Bertholdus of Micy, *Vita s. Maximini I*, c. 13, p. 594.

summarized the earlier *Vita s. Aviti III* and *Vita s. Carileffi I*.[21]
Drawing mostly on the latter he described how Avitus and
Carileffus had come from the Aquitaine, resided for a while at
Micy, and eventually left for the Perche. Thus the monk of Micy
expertly turned the extant traditions about his abbey into a part of
his own story.

A series of miracle stories completed Bertholdus' portrait. In one
which used a common hagiographic *topos* Maximinus slew a
dragon who inhabited a cave above the Loire.[22] Soon afterward he
died and was buried, according to his stated wishes, in that grotto.
His relics did not remain there long. A servant of a nobleman
named Agilus ran away and sought sanctuary at the tomb. Agilus
tried to enter and carry the man off, but he was struck down with
excruciating pain. Carried out by his other servants, he repented
and vowed to build a basilica to house the tomb of the saint.[23] The
exact location of this church is unclear, and even its existence is
historically dubious. By the eleventh century, however, a church
had been built to commemorate the spot.[24] In the seventh century
Bishop Sigobert constructed a new church in the city to house
Maximinus' relics.[25] Thus at the time of the refoundation of the
abbey, the relics of both Euspicius and Maximinus were enshrined
within the city walls. Abbot Heric requested the return of
Maximinus' relics from Bishop Jonas. His body, along with the

[21] Poncelet 1905, pp. 51–2. Goffart (1966, pp. 347–8) has shown that Bertholdus used the
Vita s. Carileffi I, and not the *Vita s. Carileffi II* as thought by Poncelet. That the story of
the hermits' departure from Micy was borrowed from the *Vita s. Avitti III*, rather than
the intermediary source from the Maine, can be seen by comparing *Vita s. Maximini I* (c.
16, p. 595) with *Vita s. Aviti III* (*lectio* 4, in Paris, BN Lat. 3789, fo. 107v). The author of
the *Vita s. Carileffi I* used this story in a different context.

[22] On this *topos*, see A. Thomas 1889, pp. 75–7.

[23] Neither Bertholdus (*Vita s. Maximini I*, c. 23, p. 597) nor, following him, the author of
the *Vita s. Maximini II* (c. 35, p. 590), said anything further about Agilus. In the early
eleventh century the author of the *Sermo de inventione s. Maximini*; Vatican, Reg. Lat.
621, fo. 40v) included Agilus in his list of the saints of the abbey. This tradition was
elaborated in the *Vita s. Agili*, a work to which Poncelet (1905, p. 83) assigns a 'relatively
recent' date. Comte de Pibrac (1861) recounts the growth and popularity of the legend of
this nobleman-turned-saint (called variously Agile, Ay, and Y) during the modern
period.

[24] The extant church contains fabric from the early Romanesque period, see Banchereau
1931c. This, or its predecessor, may well be the 'capella quae dicitur sancti Maximini
secus Ligerim sita' mentioned in a charter of 973 ('Chartes de Micy', no. 11, p. 64).

[25] Bertholdus of Micy, *Vita s. Maximini I*, c. 24, p. 597. Its existence as an episcopal
possession is attested by a coin of this period, see Lesne 1910–45, I, 271 n. 3. This church
was located close to that of Saint-Aignan. In the fourteenth century it became a
possession of the chapter of Sainte-Croix; *Cartulaire de Sainte-Croix*, pp. xl and 541. The
'cella Sancti Maximini' or 'capella Sancti Maximini iuxta muros' which appears

bodies of one Theodemir (identified by Bertholdus as a monk of Micy cured by one of Maximinus' miracles) and two unnamed companions, were translated to a newly prepared shrine in the main church at Micy. Jonas was also, according to a later tradition, responsible for completing the reconstruction of the sanctuary and crypt.[26]

Whether Bertholdus based his foundation narrative on traditions current among his community or simply invented it out of expediency is impossible to determine. By grounding the community's original foundation in the authority of Clovis and by ignoring the refoundation of the abbey by Theodulf, Bertholdus attempted to separate Micy from the power of the bishops of Orléans. His anonymous successor dedicated the second version of the life of Maximinus to Charles the Bald rather than to his contemporary bishop.[27] Over a century later Letaldus recalled that Bishop Jonas had undertaken the translation of Maximinus' remains to Micy only on the instigation of Louis the Pious.[28] These signs hint that the struggle between the abbey and its bishop, which was to dominate the concerns of Micy around the year 1000, had already begun in the generation following its refoundation.

Micy remained under episcopal control in the ninth century. Charles the Bald ascended the throne in 840, and before the death of Jonas of Orléans in 843 he confirmed the possessions of the bishopric, including the *monasterium* of St Maximinus.[29] The abbey remained listed among the episcopal possessions in all later confirmations.[30] Nevertheless the community – itself the beneficiary of the efforts of Benedict of Aniane – began to exert some

alongside the monastery of Micy in several lists of episcopal possessions dating from the ninth and tenth centuries is probably not this church, but a small church, later known as Saint-Mesmin de l'Aleu, which served as a lodging place or refuge for the monks inside the city. This second church probably dates to the ninth century, see *Cartulaire de Sainte-Croix*, pp. xxxix–xl; Gaillard and Debal 1987, pp. 12 and 34.

26 Letaldus of Micy, *Miracula s. Maximini*, c. 14, p. 601.
27 *Vita s. Maximini II*, dedicatory poem, pp. 580–1.
28 Letaldus of Micy, *Miracula s. Maximini*, c. 15, p. 602.
29 *Recueil des actes de Charles le Chauve*, no. 25, 1, 63. Also printed in *Cartulaire de Sainte-Croix*, no. 33, p. 64.
30 *Cartulaire de Sainte-Croix*, no. 19, p. 38 (Leo VII, 938); no. 376, p. 520 (Lothar, 956); no. 63, p. 126 (Hugh Capet, 975); no. 39, p. 79 (Hugh Capet, 990); no. 40, p. 86 (Robert the Pious, 991); no. 23, p. 51 (Eugenius III, 1151); no. 175, p. 263 (Honorius III, 1218); no. 387, pp. 537–8 (list of episcopal revenues, 1321). A confusing passage in the diploma of Lothar has sometimes been interpreted as attributing numerous possessions outside the Orléanais to Micy (see *Cartulaire de Sainte-Croix*, pp. xliv–xlvi), but this seems unlikely given the wording of the passage.

influence in the monastic reform movement. At the command of
Louis the Pious, Abbot Heric and a number of monks were sent to
reform the abbey of Curbion (Moutiers-Saint-Lomer) near Blois.
In 843 Heric still served as abbot of that house and traditions about
his rule there were known to Letaldus.[31] There were many signs of
intellectual vigour in the community during this period. Letaldus
recorded the names of five 'noble and zealous fathers who shone
forth in that place': Bertholdus, Abbots Dructesindus and Peter,
and two otherwise unknown figures, Haymo and Stenegaudus.[32]
The eleven extant manuscripts from the early ninth century
marked with the *ex-libris* of Micy bear eloquent testimony to an
ambitious programme of book acquisition and production. The
list features several works of Jerome, patristic biblical commentaries, Josephus' *History of the Jewish Wars* with a set of fine line
drawings, and Gregory of Tours' *History of the Franks*. Abbot
Peter was responsible for much of this activity.[33]

---

[31] The reform of Curbion was recorded in a diploma of Charles the Bald issued after the
Council of Germigny and dated 14 October 843 (*Recueil des actes de Charles le Chauve*, no.
27, I, 67–71). On the history of the abbey, see Godet 1891. Letaldus recorded a miracle
worked at that abbey in the time of Heric. As to his source for the story he noted, 'Quod
ego veridica seniorum relatione cognoscens nequaquam silentio passus sum abscondi:
proculdubio credens, quia etsi sunt rari nunc miracula facientes, multi tamen in sancta
sunt Ecclesia, qui vitae merito operatoribus miraculorum dispares non sunt.' *Miracula s.
Maximini*, c. 16, p. 602.

[32] Letaldus of Micy, *Miracula s. Maximini*, prologue, p. 598.

[33] The evidence concerning Micy's medieval library is summarized in Traube 1902, pp. xii–
xx, and Poncelet 1904.

    A note in an eighth-century copy of Jerome's commentary on Jeremiah shows that it
was corrected (*relectus*) by Abbot Peter, who replaced four or five folios of corrupted
text: Paris, BN lat. 1820 (Lauer *et al.* 1939–66, II, 187). Delisle (1868–81, II, 408–9)
concludes that fos. 9–13 had been replaced by Peter, while Marie-Madeleine Lemarignier
('Chartes de Micy', pp. xcvi–xcvii n. 1) thinks that fo. 221 was his addition as well. Rand
(1929, I, 87–8) notes that the original manuscript was copied by the same scribe from the
Tours scriptorium responsible for Paris, BN lat. 1572. The *ex-libris* of three other
manuscripts state that they were copied at the abbot's order and that he placed them as an
offering on the main altar, which was dedicated to St Stephen and St Maximinus, on the
feast of Holy Thursday. These three manuscripts are: Paris, BN lat. 1862, fos. 1–82,
which contains Jerome's commentary on Psalms, Alcuin's *Quaestiones super Genesim*, and
some fragments of patristic works (Lauer *et al.* 1939–66, II, pp. 201–2); Vatican, Reg. lat.
95, which contains Hilary of Poitiers' commentary on Psalms (Wilmart 1937–45, I, 208–
9); Leiden, University Library, Codex Vossiani Latini Quarto 110, which contains
Jerome's translation of Eusebius' *Historia Ecclesiastica* (Meyier 1975, pp. 244–6). The full
ex-libris of the Paris manuscript reads (fo. 82v), 'Hic liber Sancti Maximini monasterii
quem Petrus Abbas scribere iussit et dies caenae domini cum salutari hostias super
sanctam altare Sancti Stephani primi in Christo martyris domino et sancto Maximino
habendum obtulit sub huius modi voto ut quisquis eum de isto loco non redditurus
abstulerit cum Iuda proditore, Anna et Caiphas, atque Pilato dampnatiomem accidit.'
The others bear similar inscriptions, although that of the Leiden manuscript adds that the

During the reign of Charles the Bald an anonymous author, certainly a monk of Micy, retold the community's hagiographic traditions in the *Vita s. Maximini II* (*BHL* 5814–16). While this author did not describe his sources, he for the most part expanded upon the extant narrative of Bertholdus.[34] There was only one significant difference between the two works. In describing the translation of Maximinus' body from Orléans to Micy the anonymous author mentioned only the bodies of the two nameless companions, omitting that of Theodemir. This difference, while minor, suggests that the later text was written well after the translation. It is unclear why a new and substantially similar life should have been composed no more than a generation after the work of Bertholdus. The distribution of extant manuscripts suggests, however, that the new work replaced that of Bertholdus as the standard life of the saint in the Orléanais. The next document known to have been composed at Micy was a charter dated 973. Intellectual life, however, had certainly not ground to a halt over the course of the intervening century. There are seven extant manuscripts dating from the later ninth or tenth centuries which

scribe was a monk named Helias (for partial printings see Poncelet 1904, pp. 82–3 and the catalogues mentioned above). Delisle (1868–81, II, 409) suggests that Paris, BN lat. 1866, a collection of works by Jerome (Lauer *et al.* 1939–66, II, pp. 206–7), should also be assigned to the abbacy of Peter because of the similarity of its book curse (fo. 207) to those above. The original opening of this manuscript is to be found in Paris, BN lat. 1790, fos. 40–4 (Lauer *et al.* 1939–66, II, p. 176). Traube and Poncelet, not realizing that only those folios came from Micy, both mistakenly assigned this manuscript to the eleventh century.

There are six other manuscripts of the early ninth century which are known to have come from Micy: Paris, BN lat. 15679, which contains scriptural commentaries by Jerome, Bede, and Isidore of Seville; Paris, BN, nouvelle acquisition latine 1572, which contains Augustine's commentary on Genesis; Vatican, Reg. lat. 1953, which contains Isidore of Seville's *Etymologia*; Leiden, Codex Vossiani Latini Quarto 17, fos. 3–72, which contains a collection of Gregory the Great's letters (Meyier 1975, pp. 49–51); Leiden, Codex Vossiani Latini Quarto 87, which contains Solinus' grammar (Meyier 1975, pp. 204–6); and Leiden, Public Library 21, which contains Gregory of Tours' *Historia Francorum* and Ambrose's translation of Josephus' *De bello Judaico*.

34 There were certain minor changes such as the omission of one entire story and a minor change in the order of another: Bertholdus of Micy, *Vita s. Maximini I*, cc. 16–17 and 18. The latter was used in *Vita s. Maximini II*, c. 21. Some details were slightly altered or expanded. After the death of Euspicius, for instance, Maximinus sought consolation through solitary contemplation and largely ignored the blandishments of Bishop Eusebius. Bertholdus' sparse description of Clovis' siege of Verdun was expanded. The anonymous author was also less concerned than Bertholdus with how a saint's life could serve as an example of monastic virtue.

bear the marks of the abbey's library. These include works of
Priscian and Prudentius, as well as Josephus' *Antiquities*.[35]

In the 970s Letaldus, who was to become the community's most
accomplished and prolific author, began his literary career.[36] He
entered the community of Micy as a youth (*infantulus*) during the
abbacy of Anno (*c.* 960–70).[37] He was probably a nephew or other
relation of an abbot of Micy named Letaldus who had served in the
940s. Our author described that abbot as a *vir nobilis*, a phrase
which certainly indicates a family of high standing even though it
was not used with precision in this period.[38] By 973 the monk had
risen to the post of *cancellarius* in the community of Micy and later
events show that he had much higher ambitions.[39] Sometime in

---

[35] The evidence is summarized in Traube 1902, pp. xii–xx, and Poncelet 1904. The seven
manuscripts of the later ninth and tenth centuries are: Avranches, BM 32, fos. 137–267,
Origen's commentary on the epistle to the Romans (*CGMBPF*, x, 18); Bern,
Bibliotheca Bongarsiana 50, Josephus' *Antiquitates* (Hagen 1874, pp. 74–5, and, on the
illuminations, Homburger 1962, pp. 91–3 and plates 33–5); Bern, Bibliotheca
Bongarsiana 283, Gregory the Great's *Regula Pastoralis* (Hagen 1874, p. 307); Bern,
Bibliotheca Bongarsiana 312, Isidore of Seville's *Sententiae* (Hagen 1874, p. 323); Bern
Bibliotheca Bongarsiana 344, Jerome's commentary on the Pauline epistles (Hagen 1874,
p. 335); Bern, Bibliotheca Bongarsiana 394, Prudentius' *Carmina* followed by some
selections of Alcuin's poetry (Hagen 1874, pp. 362–3); Bern, Bibliotheca Bongarsiana
432, a grammatical collection including Priscian (Hagen 1874, p. 378). Bern, Bibliotheca
Bongarsiana 394 does not bear a Micy *ex-libris*, but Traube 1902 assigned it to the abbey
on the grounds of palaeographical similarities. Cf. Poncelet (1904 p. 84) who suggests
that three of these Bern manuscripts (Bibliotheca Bongarsiana 312, 344, and 432) date
from the earlier part of the ninth century.
[36] *HLF*, vi, 528–37; Hauréau 1843–52, ii, 1–10; Manitius 1911–31, ii, 426–32. These
accounts of Letaldus' career are unreliable and do not recognize the full canon of his
works as enumerated here. The brief notice by John Howe in *DMA* vii, 552, is more
complete. In a study of one of Letaldus' poems, Bonnes (1943, pp. 29–33) provided a
biographical sketch which improved on these earlier accounts, but which is still
incomplete on certain crucial particulars. The most recent study of his poetry
(Ziolkowski 1984), while excellent in terms of literary analysis, repeats many of the
errors of these accounts. Letaldus' reputation has remained mixed among historians.
Leclercq (1957, p. 152) cited Letaldus as a prominent example of 'critical judgement'
among monastic authors, but Erdmann (1935, p. 81 n. 81) dismissed him as an
'insignificant' hagiographer.
[37] Letaldus of Micy, *Miracula s. Maximini*, c. 34, p. 607. Ledru's claim (1906, pp. 326–8) that
he was born near Micy is based on a misreading of this passage. Letaldus composed the
work approximately thirty years after his profession, see c. 33, p. 607.
[38] Letaldus of Micy, *Miracula s. Maximini*, cc. 21–2, pp. 603–4. Martindale 1977, pp. 20–36,
particularly pp. 32–5. Martindale comments about Francia in the later tenth century (p.
32), 'It will probably come as no surprise to discover that the upper ranks of the
"nobility" can be fairly easily identified, but that it is extremely difficult to discover what
its lower limits were.'
[39] 'Chartes de Micy', no. 11, p. 67. There is no reason to accept Werner's suggestion (1960,
pp. 81–2 n. 45) that Letaldus was actually schooled at Fleury. Letaldus' works

the following decade Letaldus composed his first work, the *Miracula s. Maximini*.[40] Beginning with the life of the patron saint and the foundation of the abbey, the hagiographer described the history of his community down to his own age, concluding with contemporary miracles worked through Maximinus' patronage. He noted that 'the place which the man of God [Maximinus] constructed, namely Micy, has sometimes flourished and other times suffered most abjectly, only to attempt to rise up again'. God and the divine servant Maximinus exhibited their patronage both generally, through a providential guidance of the community, and more directly, through miracles. Letaldus recounted both for the consolation of the *vacillantes et trepidi* among his audience.[41]

Letaldus based his account of the early history of his abbey on various Carolingian lives from the region.[42] He conflated the stories of Micy's foundation from the extant lives of Maximinus.[43] In his hands the story of Maximinus' disciples was again transformed. Avitus was alleged, against the explicit statement of his source, to have accepted the abbacy of Micy.[44] Letaldus added five names to the list of Maximinus' disciples, including two saints, Lifardus and Viator, whose relics were venerated elsewhere in the Orléanais.[45] He also claimed that Bishop Sigobert (*c.* 670–81) had donated the church in which he buried the body of Maximinus to

demonstrate that he was intimately acquainted with the manuscripts possessed by his own community and could easily have received his education there. Several historical works which Letaldus (*Vita s. Juliani*, cc. 3–4, cols. 783–4) cited, such as Gregory of Tours' *Historia Francorum* and Jerome's translation of Eusebius' *Historia Ecclesiastica*, were to be found in Micy's library.

[40] The earliest known manuscript (Vatican, Reg. lat. 528, fo. 14v, an eleventh-century copy from either Micy or Fleury) provided Letaldus' name. Arnauldet, who suggests (1903) that the work is a modern invention, ignored this and other medieval manuscripts. On the date of the work, see above, chapter 2, n. 1.

[41] Letaldus of Micy, *Miracula s. Maximini*, prologue, p. 598.

[42] Poncelet 1905, pp. 45–7 and 52–3. Letaldus also employed Adrevald of Fleury's *Miracula s. Benedicti*, see Werner 1960, pp. 81–2 n. 45.

[43] Poncelet (1905, pp. 52–3) suggests that he knew Bertholdus only by name and was unfamiliar with his work (*BHL* 5817), but rather relied solely on the anonymous life (*BHL* 5814) as his source. In the case of the only substantive disagreement between the two lives, which concerns the translation of Maximinus' relics in the ninth century, Letaldus (c. 15, p. 602) agreed with the anonymous life in stating that three bodies, not four, were translated to Micy.

[44] Letaldus of Micy, *Miracula s. Maximini*, c. 6, p. 600. Letaldus (c. 4, p. 599) restored the story of Avitus' first eremitic journey to the Perche in accordance with the *Vita s. Aviti III*.   [45] Letaldus of Micy, *Miracula s. Maximini*, prologue and c. 4, pp. 598–9.

the abbey of Micy.[46] In describing the return of the saint's relics from that church to Micy, he attributed the translation more to the will of Louis the Pious than to the generosity of Bishop Jonas.[47] Thus Letaldus attempted to extricate, in so far as he could, the cult of Maximinus from the control of the bishops of Orléans.

For Letaldus the history of Micy from this translation to his own lifetime – a period for which his work is the only source – was a saga of the problems which plagued a foundation controlled by an unsympathetic and at times malevolent bishop.[48] In the late ninth century a 'noble cleric' named Frederick duped the drunken Bishop Trohannus (*c.* 900) into granting him the vacant abbacy of Micy.[49] 'Frederick obtained the name of abbot in the gift of the drunkard, but shunned the office in all ways.' This nominal abbot maltreated the few remaining monks and dissipated the monastic property. After the monks demanded the aid of their patron saint through the ritual curse known as a *clamor*, Maximinus appeared to both the bishop and the abbot while they lay sleeping and punished them with death.[50]

The community's lot improved somewhat under the abbacy of Letaldus who was elected by the monks *c.* 940 from their own number with the approval of Bishop Theodoric I.[51] This abbot

---

[46] Letaldus of Micy, *Miracula s. Maximini*, c. 11, p. 601. That this church existed, under episcopal control, in the eighth century is proven by a coin of that vintage, see Lesne 1910–45, I, 271 n. 3.

[47] Letaldus of Micy, *Miracula s. Maximini*, c. 10, p. 600, and c. 15, p. 602. Letaldus identified the two bodies translated with that of Maximinus as belonging to the saint's successors as abbot. He obtained their names, Theodemir and Maximinus II (the saint's own nephew), from the *Vita s. Lifardi*, c. 11, p. 156.

[48] For parallel cases, see Lesne 1910–45, II.2, 132–43 and 212–16.

[49] Letaldus of Micy, *Miracula s. Maximini*, cc. 19–20, p. 603. Frederick's brother was named Ermentheus. It is unlikely that this Ermentheus was, as Boussard (1970, p. 177) suggests, the same man who served as bishop of Orléans from 956 to 974.

[50] Apparently the monks did not employ the more elaborate ritual of humiliating their patron's relics. Letaldus (*Miracula s. Maximini*, c. 20, p. 603) simply says, 'Cuius clamoribus famuli excitati clamoris causas inquirunt'. Compare the almost contemporary reactions of the monks of a community in Reims, who used the *clamor* to complain to their patron about similar despoliations (Adso of Montierender, *Translatio s. Basoli*, c. 12, p. 141). On the *clamor* more generally, see Geary 1979a.

[51] Letaldus of Micy, *Miracula s. Maximini*, cc. 21–2, pp. 603–4. The abbot Letaldus was elected by his fellows and confirmed by Bishop Theodoric I. Theodoric's predecessor Anselm received a confirmation of episcopal property in 938 from Pope Leo VII (*Cartulaire de Sainte-Croix*, no. 19, pp. 37–43). His successor, Ermentheus, received a confirmation of episcopal property in 956 from King Lothar (*Cartulaire de Sainte-Croix*, no. 376, pp. 519–21).

would seem to have been a relative, likely an uncle, of the author. His term proved to be only a brief respite for the community. The next bishop, Ermentheus (pre-956–70), returned to the practice of exploiting his control of the abbacy of Micy for his own gain. He first gave the office to his provost, Benedict, who built a country house on the abbey's riverside property and deprived the monks of their fishing rights. He took the revenues of lands which had been given to Micy 'by kings and by certain of the faithful for the salvation of their souls' and used them to support the soldiers of the episcopal guard. Ignoring the pleas of the monks, he fed them 'bread, meagre vegetables, and wine only rarely'.[52]

Later Ermentheus threw Benedict out and sold the abbacy of Micy three times. The first two recipients were refugees from Brittany, a region which was racked by civil war and invasion during this period.[53] Another Benedict, the count-bishop of Quimper, paid 30 *livres*.[54] His successor, Jacob, the former abbot of a Breton monastery, was charged twice that price on Benedict's death.[55] The next abbot of Micy was Anno, the abbot of the Norman community of Jumièges and relative by marriage of the powerful noble family of Bellême. Anno's brothers bought him the abbacy of Micy for the devalued price of only 20 *livres*.[56] Although a simoniac, Anno proved to be a great leader in Letaldus' judgement. Under his guidance the rule of St Benedict was followed with renewed vigour and the life of the monks improved. More importantly, Anno actively fought the bishop on the community's behalf.[57] Letaldus recorded Maximinus' approval by noting the comparative frequency of his miracles during Anno's abbacy.[58]

Anno died on the feast of the Epiphany in 970. Bishop

---

[52] Letaldus of Micy, *Miracula s. Maximini*, cc. 22–3, p. 604.

[53] Devailly 1980, pp. 49–50.

[54] Letaldus of Micy, *Miracula s. Maximini*, c. 24, p. 604; *GC*, XIV, 874; *Cartulaire de Quimper*, p. 4; Latouche 1910, pp. 70–1.

[55] Letaldus of Micy, *Miracula s. Maximini*, c. 27, p. 605. On the death of Bishop Conan of Pol-de-Léon, Count Alain Barbetorte appointed Jacob his successor. Jacob's successor was Mabbo (*GC*, XIV, 974), who later brought the relics of St Paul Aurelian to Fleury.

[56] Letaldus of Micy, *Miracula s. Maximini*, c. 28, pp. 605–6. A charter from Jumièges (*Chartes de Jumièges*, no. 15, I, 51–3) described Abbot Albert of Micy as both the nephew of Abbot Anno and the son of Hildeburgis of Bellême. For Albert's wider family relations, see figure 1. On Anno's abbacy at Jumièges, see Loth 1882, I, 135–6.

[57] Letaldus of Micy, *Miracula s. Maximini*, cc. 28 and 38, pp. 605 and 609.

[58] Letaldus of Micy, *Miracula s. Maximini*, c. 28, p. 605. Cf. a similar statement concerning the time of Abbot Heric, c. 16, p. 602.

Ermentheus of Orléans, Abbot Richard of Fleury, and 'various nobles' attended the funeral. The abbot was buried in the confines of the church next to a noble named Suthard who had been an important benefactor of Micy. The monks soon elected one of their number to replace the *decanus* who had died only nine days before Anno. They would have to wait over a year until a new abbot was appointed. Bishop Ermentheus became sick at this time and retired to Micy, where he took the monastic habit. He was replaced by his nephew, Arnulf.[59] When Ermentheus attempted to impose a monk of Fleury named Hermenaldus as the new abbot, the monks successfully appealed to Arnulf to block the appointment. In his stead Amalricus, the *decanus* of Fleury, was named abbot of Micy. The entire process of replacing Anno had taken a year and eight days. Ermentheus died a little over a year later.[60] Letaldus recorded only three miracle stories for the decade or two between Amalricus' election and the composition of his work.[61]

In discussing his sources Letaldus prided himself on their accuracy: 'Where . . . there is some question as to whether an event happened or not, all men will be silent with me.'[62] He even supplemented his written sources with reference to archaeological evidence.[63] He also emphasized the reliability of his oral sources.[64] Behind these claims, however, Letaldus cleverly hid an argument concerning the abbey of Micy. He claimed that Bishop Arnulf had favoured Micy by returning some properties which had been taken

---

[59] Letaldus of Micy, *Miracula s. Maximini*, cc. 38–40, p. 609. These events are usually assigned to either 971 or 972. In 973, however, Arnulf signed a charter ('Chartes de Micy', no. 11, p. 67) which was dated as being in the third year of his episcopate. Therefore the death of Anno, the retirement of Ermentheus, and the succession of Arnulf occurred in 970. Arnulf died in 1003. On him, see Certain 1853; *DHGE*, IV, 616–17. Many scholars (see, for example, *HLF*, VI, 521, and *GC*, VIII, 1428–30) have distinguished two bishops named Arnulf whose terms were separated by the episcopacy of Manassas. This Manassas allegedly subscribed the acts of the synod of Sens held in 980 (*Chronique de Saint-Pierre-le-Vif*, pp. 252–4). The only copy of that act, however, was marred by scribal error and the Manassas in question was bishop of Troyes.

[60] Letaldus of Micy, *Miracula s. Maximini*, cc. 4, p. 609.

[61] Letaldus of Micy, *Miracula s. Maximini*, cc. 42–4, pp. 609–10. Letaldus was reminded of the remaining stories in his collection (cc. 45–55, pp. 610–13) by his fellows after he had completed his first draft. They date to earlier periods, mostly the abbacy of Anno. The final chapters in the work (cc. 56–7, p. 613) were added by another monk of Micy after 1041. Letaldus composed his work sometime in the decade after 982.

[62] Letaldus of Micy, *Miracula s. Maximini*, prologue, p. 598. See also c. 28, p. 605.

[63] Letaldus of Micy, *Miracula s. Maximini*, prologue and c. 13, pp. 598 and 601. Letaldus used as sources the *ex-libris* of the manuscripts copied for Abbot Peter and an inscription in the church of Germigny-des-Près.

[64] Letaldus of Micy, *Miracula s. Maximini*, cc. 16 and 33, pp. 602 and 607.

from it and by exempting its properties from certain forms of episcopal control. Furthermore Arnulf had, still according to Letaldus, obtained a papal decree which enumerated those privileges and added that no bishop would appoint an abbot from outside the community without the consent of the brothers. This decree had allegedly been copied from the Roman original (described as being on papyrus) and placed in the archives at Micy.[65] No copy survives of this decree, but the immunities claimed by Letaldus were certainly never granted. If such a text were ever placed in the abbey's archives, it was a forgery.[66] Ironically the abbey had, in 973, received an important concession from Arnulf, the exemption of the altars in five churches from all episcopal rights.[67] This grant meant that the community had essentially free control over the revenues from certain churches located on its lands. Letaldus' reference to a non-existent privilege, however, was designed to win a much wider exemption for his house.

Several extant documents were also fabricated at the abbey around this time: a diploma of Charles the Bald granting certain properties;[68] the purported foundation grant of Clovis;[69] and a diploma of Louis the Pious and Lothar I confirming spurious donations of Merovingian kings.[70] The first successfully duped Hugh Capet, who confirmed it in 987, the latter two were probably composed during the 990s.[71] It is tempting to see Letaldus' hand, as the sometime *cancellarius* of Micy, in these forgeries. These documents represent a programmatic campaign to obtain rights and exemptions for Micy through the use of forged evidence. At a time when written records were slowly replacing a

---

[65] Letaldus of Micy, *Miracula s. Maximini*, c. 41, p. 609. Papyrus was the usual medium used by the papal chancery during the early middle ages, see Poole 1915, pp. 197–8. Letaldus added that detail to lend verisimilitude to his account. Eadmer of Canterbury used a reference to papyrus in a similar manner, see Clanchy 1979, p. 119.

[66] 'Chartes de Micy', pp. cix–cxxxi.

[67] 'Chartes de Micy', no. 11, pp. 62–7. The right is referred to by the term *altare*, which is the earliest use of this term to distinguish episcopal rights over altars and the masses said on them from rights to the church in which the altar stood. For a thorough discussion of this distinction, its novelty, and its importance, see Lemarignier 1937, pp. 84–90.

[68] *Recueil des actes de Charles le Chauve*, no. 478, II, 589–93; 'Chartes de Micy', no. 8, pp. lxxxiv–xcvii *bis* and 49–54.

[69] *GC*, VIII, *instrumenta* 479; *MGH, Diplomata*, I, 120–1; 'Chartes de Micy', pp. lxx–lxxix, and no. 2, pp. 6–12; Havet 1885, pp. 224–33.

[70] *RHF*, VI, 554; *Regesten des Kaiserreichs*, no. 955; 'Chartes de Micy', pp. x–xi, particularly n. 3, lxxxiv–xcv, and no. 6, pp. 27–42.

[71] Lot 1891, p. 405; 'Chartes de Micy', no. 12, pp. lxxxiv–xcvii *bis* and 68–71.

reliance on human memory, the monks of Micy under the lead of
Letaldus – who himself made a strict distinction between written
and oral sources – felt compelled to produce a written tradition to
shore up long-held convictions concerning their independence
from the bishops of Orléans.[72]

Despite these efforts the three men who served as abbot from 970
until 1014 were all outsiders, monks from important monasteries
of the middle Loire valley. Amalricus had been *decanus* at Fleury
before he became abbot in 971.[73] Bishop Arnulf appointed
Constantine I, another monk of Fleury and friend of the influential
Gerbert of Reims, as Amalricus' successor.[74] Constantine may
well have been a failed rival to Oylbold and Abbo in the
controversial abbatial elections at Fleury. He was later moved from
Micy to the abbacy of Nouaillé in the Haut-Poitou (*c.* 994). Robert
of Blois, the abbot of Saint-Florent-de-Saumur, was installed in his
stead at Micy.[75] These changes were engineered by Arnulf,
probably with the connivance of Gerbert. Robert of Blois
campaigned during his abbacy to protect the interests of his other
abbey of Saumur and of his relatives, the counts of Blois. Their
primary enemy was Fulk Nerra, the count of the Angevins, who
was vigorously expanding his power in the middle Loire valley. In
particular, Fulk sought control over Saumur as a means of
threatening the city of Tours.[76] Robert's installation at Micy and
that of Constantine at Nouaillé were part of a larger strategy
pursued by the counts of Blois and their allies to shore up the
independent power of monastic communities on the borders of
Fulk's territories. Those events also destroyed any illusion of
exemption from episcopal control which might have been
harboured at Micy. In 994 Abbo of Fleury was moved to mention

---

[72] For a detailed discussion of the development of written records in English monasteries of
this period, see Clanchy 1979, pp. 79–80 and 116–20, and Keynes 1980, pp. 19–27. On the
vexed question of forgery and intentionality, see Constable 1983, particularly pp. 20–3.

[73] Letaldus of Micy, *Miracula s. Maximini*, c. 40, p. 609; *GC*, VIII, 1530.

[74] Andrew of Fleury, *Vita Gauzlini*, c. 2, p. 38. On the friendship between Constantine and
Gerbert of Reims, see Gerbert's *Opera mathematica*, pp. 6–8 and 23–35, and *Epistolae*, no.
86, p. 114; no. 142, pp. 168–9; no. 191, pp. 229–30. This Constantine has frequently been
confused with another Constantine who was *decanus* of Micy in 1004 and became abbot
after the death of Robert of Blois in 1011. The distinction between these two men named
Constantine was first recognized by Warren (1909) and later confirmed by Bautier and
Labory (1965, pp. 23–4).

[75] Cf. Lot 1903, p. 115; Guillot 1972, II, 61; Bachrach 1978, p. 132. The earliest charter to
record Robert of Blois as abbot of Micy is a donation of Robert the Pious, dated 14
April, 1001 ('Chartes de Micy', pp. 75–8).   [76] Bachrach 1978.

the plight of Letaldus as a fellow victim of the machinations of Arnulf which were done 'unmindful of injury to priestly dignity and without any legality'.[77] After Robert's replacement of Constantine I as abbot of Micy, Letaldus composed brief hagiographic works for Constantine's new abbey at Nouaillé and for Robert's home at Saumur.[78] In the *Delatio corporis s. Juniani* (*BHL* 4565) he described how the monks of the abbey of Nouaillé in 989 brought the relics of their patron to the Council of Charroux and how those relics had worked miracles on the route.[79] It is surely not coincidental that the abbey of Nouaillé began a major building programme under Constantine's leadership after this advertisement of the potency of Junianus' patronage.[80] Letaldus' primary composition for Saumur was a heroic poem, the *Versus de eversione monasterii Glomnensis*, which described the flight of the monks from their original home at Mont Glonna when it was sacked by the Normans in the ninth century.[81] The story of the courage of Saumur's monks may have been intended to strengthen them in the face of recent Angevin advances. Letaldus also composed a liturgical poem in honour of Saumur's patron saint.[82]

In the following years Letaldus composed texts for two monastic houses which shared anti-Angevin sentiments with Robert of Blois: the *Vita et miracula s. Martini Vertavensis* (*BHL* 5667–8), written for the monks of Saint-Jouin-sur-Marne in the Poitou most probably between 994 and 1004, and the *Vita et miracula s.*

---

[77] Abbo of Fleury, *Apologeticus*, col. 469A. On Abbo's enmity for Bishop Arnulf, see Certain 1853; Cousin 1954, pp. 113–41; Lemarignier 1957, pp. 384–5.

[78] On the use of hagiography and forged charters by the community of Saumur to win exemptions during this period, see Hamon 1971 and 1972; Ziezulewicz 1985.

[79] Letaldus is mentioned as author in the dedication. On the council, see particularly Töpfer 1957, p. 59; Bonnaud-Delamare 1961, pp. 419–26; Hoffman 1964, pp. 25–8. Töpfer's defence of the traditional date of 989 for the council withstands the arguments of Bonnaud-Delamare.   [80] Crozet 1939; Vergnolle 1985, p. 140 n. 425.

[81] Lot (1907, pp. 41–57) first demonstrated that the poem was not by a contemporary, but dated from the late tenth or eleventh centuries. Bonnes (1943, pp. 32–3) suggested Letaldus as author on the grounds of stylistic similarity to the *Versus de quodam piscatore*. Letaldus' affiliation with Saumur through Abbot Robert of Blois, unknown to Bonnes, strengthens the argument for Letaldus' authorship. Cf. Lutz's (1970, p. 99 n. 13) dismissal of Letaldus' authorship.

[82] Letaldus' authorship of this brief poem is indicated both by its stylistic similarity to his known poetic works, the *De eversione* and the *De quodam piscatore*, and, more importantly, by the fact that the sole known exemplar is found on the endpaper of a manuscript from Micy (Paris, BN lat. 1866, fo. 207v). Du Méril (1843, p. 259 n. 3) included a faulty edition of it, provided on the basis of a letter from Dom Lobineau, in a note to his edition of the *De eversione*.

Eusicii (*BHL* 2754 and 2756), written for the monks of Selles–sur–Cher in the Berry most probably between 1002 and 1004.[83] Both communities were, like Robert's community of Saumur, forced to protect their properties against threats posed by Fulk Nerra's territorial expansionism. As Letaldus had done earlier at Micy, he gathered together traditions held about the patron saints of these communities in order to defend them against claims made by an outside authority, although in this case the presumed predator was a secular, rather than an ecclesiastical, magnate.

The monks of Vertou, located near Nantes, had abandoned their abbey after its destruction by the Normans in 843 and moved to Saint–Jouin with the relics of Martin, their first abbot.[84] A text apparently dating from that era had described the life of the saint and posthumous miracles worked at both Vertou and Saint–Jouin. The only copy of that cherished record, however, had been destroyed by a fire in the nearby city of Thouars. Rainald, the provost of Saint–Jouin, engaged Letaldus to compose a prose version of an inferior verse life which still survived (the *vita*) and to reconstruct the lost Carolingian text from the memories of the older monks still alive at Saint–Jouin (the *miracula*). Using these oral witnesses Letaldus recorded many episodes from the life of the saint, the early history of the community, and miracles which had occurred over a century earlier.[85]

The purpose of the text becomes clear in light of the contemporary situation of the community of Saint–Jouin. The monastery was located within the Mauges, a region controlled by the viscounts of Thouars.[86] They were members of the *Aimeri* clan

---

[83] Krusch (*MGH, SRM*, IV, 771–2) first ascribed the *Vita et miracula s. Martini Vertavensis* to Letaldus. See also Poncelet 1904, p. 78. Many historians are unaware of the text's authorship, see, for example, Poulin 1975, p. 179. On the attribution of the *Vita et miracula s. Eusicii* to Letaldus, see Head 1989.

[84] Martin of Vertou (*VSBP*, x, 810–11) was a sixth-century deacon of the church of Nantes who was sent by Bishop Felix to evangelize a district south of the Loire. On the successful completion of his mission, he went on pilgrimage to Rome, returning to lead an eremitic life at Vertou. He was eventually buried in a church dedicated to John the Baptist, which later served as the basis for a monastic community. Martin came to be considered, along with St Jovinus, as one of the dual patrons of Saint–Jouin. In a charter of 916 that monastery was described as 'sub patrocinio Beati Martini et Sancti Jovini', while in another charter of c. 990 it was described as 'congregacio Sancti Martini vel Sancti Jovini' (*Cartulaire de Saint-Jouin de Marnes*, pp. 14–15).

[85] Letaldus of Micy, *Miracula s. Martini Vertavensis*, prologue, in *MGH, SRM*, III, 567–8. On Letaldus' use of source material, see also above, chapter 2, pp. 81–9.

[86] Painter 1956; Garaud 1929, 1959–60, pp. 364–77, and 1964, pp. 6 (n. 14), 12–13, 39–43, and 71–2.

which claimed roots among the *vassi dominici* of Charles the Bald.[87] The community also relied on the patronage of the *Rainaldi*, a noble family of Poitevin origin which held property in Anjou.[88] Men named Aimery and Savary (the primary names among the *Aimeri*), as well as Rainald and Hervaeus (the primary names among the *Rainaldi*) regularly appeared in the charters of Saint-Jouin as donors, monks, and witnesses.[89] Members of the latter family also figured prominently in Letaldus' work. One member had been the abbot who brought the monks of Vertou and the relics of Martin to Saint-Jouin in 843, thus effectively refounding the community.[90] Another was the duke who repented of his despoliation of St Martin's property.[91] A third was the provost of the abbey who commissioned Letaldus' composition.[92] A fourth, Rainald the Thuringian, was praised as the witness of various contemporary miracles performed by Martin.[93]

In the time of Letaldus, Fulk Nerra was extending Angevin influence southward and attempting to take control of monastic property in areas such as the Mauges on the borders of the Poitou.[94] The monks of Saint-Jouin thus lived in a precarious balance between their traditional lords and this new threat. Robert of Blois and the abbey of Saint-Florent were similarly threatened by the expansion of Fulk Nerra's power in another direction. On first becoming abbot, Robert wished to weaken the eastward thrust of Angevin power toward Saumur. Later, however, he also began to sow discord on Fulk's southern frontiers, in part by allying himself with both the *Aimeri* and the *Rainaldi*. In 987 Rainald the Thuringian took an oath to protect the property of Saumur against the depredations of Fulk Nerra in spite of his status as the count's subject.[95] In 994 the viscount's son and heir, Bishop

---

[87] Beech 1974. Also note, however, Bouchard's (1981, p. 508 n. 25) criticism.

[88] Hogan 1981.

[89] These names appear in virtually every charter preserved from the tenth and eleventh centuries, see *Cartulaire de Saint-Jouin de Marnes*, pp. 2–27.

[90] Letaldus of Micy, *Miracula s. Martini Vertavensis*, c. 9, in *MGH, SRM*, III, 573–4; Hogan 1981, p. 40.

[91] Letaldus of Micy, *Miracula s. Martini Vertavensis*, c. 18, in *MGH, SRM*, III, 575; Hogan 1981, p. 39.

[92] Letaldus of Micy, *Miracula s. Martini Vertavensis*, prologue, in *MGH, SRM*, III, 567. This Rainald was not considered by Hogan (1981) but was, I would submit, a member.

[93] Letaldus of Micy, *Miracula s. Martini Vertavensis*, c. 1, in *MGH, SRM*, III, 569; Hogan 1981, pp. 36–7.

[94] Halphen 1906, pp. 17–28; Guillot 1972, I, 39–43; Bachrach 1976, pp. 111–21.

[95] Bachrach 1978, pp. 126–9; Guillot 1972, I, 206–8; Hogan, 1981, pp. 36–7, particularly n. 7. Cf. Halphen 1906, p. 98 n. 1; Bouchard 1981, p. 516 n. 18.

Rainald of Angers, adjudicated a court case in favour of Robert of Blois against Angevin interests. About that time Robert also courted the support of Aimery III, the viscount of Thouars, who had recently had the title of count of Nantes taken away by Fulk Nerra. Aimery donated property directly to Saint-Florent as a sign of his new allegiance.[96] By the time he became abbot of Micy, Robert of Blois had thus already forged alliances with the two noble families who exerted the most influence over the community of Saint-Jouin. It would seem that Robert of Blois had Letaldus compose the *Vita et miracula s. Martini Vertavensis* – including as it did both the praise of the *Rainaldi* clan and the implicit warning to Fulk Nerra described above – as a service for the monks of Saint-Jouin and their noble patrons. The composition probably took place between the flowering of the alliances between Robert and both the *Aimeri* and the *Rainaldi* in 994 – which approximately corresponded with his election to the abbacy of Micy – and Letaldus' revolt against Robert's authority in 1004.

Letaldus most particularly directed one story in his work against Fulk. It concerned the attempts of King Dagobert to tax the monastery of Vertou.[97] The monks did not complain about a deduction from their resources to aid the royal fisc similar to that made at other monasteries, but a nobleman named Centulfus prodded the king into taking more, plotting to pilfer some of the monastery's goods for his own. The patrons of Vertou – Martin and John the Baptist – appeared to Centulfus in a dream. After they verbally chastised him, the nobleman died a painful death. While the story was included among the original Carolingian traditions which Letaldus collected as oral tradition, he retold it using much language specific to the early eleventh century. Bernard Bachrach has noted how this language particularly applied to Fulk Nerra and could have been interpreted as a warning to Fulk not to take property from Saint-Jouin.[98] The warning and the family alliances from which the text had sprung were both unsuccessful. A few years later Fulk Nerra had the monks of Saint-Jouin establish two churches at his castle of Vihiers.[99] The monastery was eventually

---

[96] Garaud 1964, p. 40; Bachrach 1978, pp. 129–30.

[97] Letaldus of Micy, *Miracula s. Martini Vertavensis*, c. 7 in *MGH, SRM*, III, 571–2.

[98] Bernard Bachrach has kindly shared his research on this topic with me. It will appear under the title 'Fulk Nerra's exploitation of the *facultates monachorum* ca. 1000'.

[99] *Cartulaire de Saint-Jouin de Marnes*, pp. 19–20. Grandmaison dates the act to *c.* 1016, but Guillot (1972, II, 58–9) states that it can be dated no more precisely than 1006–39.

stripped of its liberties by the Angevins, only to have them returned much later by the same family.[100] The allegiances formed by Robert of Blois had more influence on his own community of Saint-Florent. The *Aimeri* would continue to exercise some influence at Saumur while that monastery remained in the hands of the Blèsois. In 1013 Count Odo II of Blois engineered the election of Gerald of Thouars – a monk of Saint-Florent and relative of the viscounts – as abbot of Saumur in order to counteract Angevin influence in the Poitou. Unfortunately Gerald despoiled the fisc of his monastery and had to be deposed by Odo in 1020.[101] Shortly thereafter Saint-Florent fell, like Saint-Jouin, under the control of the Angevins.

In a similar fashion Fulk Nerra's campaigns in the Berry against the house of Blois, much closer to the seat of Robert of Blois' family power, threatened the independence of the abbey of Selles-sur-Cher.[102] That abbey was under the protection of Geoffrey of Bonzy, the lord of Saint-Aignan and a vassal of the count of Blois.[103] In composing the *Vita et miracula s. Eusicii* Letaldus worked with scantier source material than he had used at Saint-Jouin. He recorded only that Odulfus, presumably the abbot, had requested that he undertake the project. While this work was simpler than the *Vita et miracula s. Martini Vertavensis*, he again included useful precedents. In particular he noted how Clovis had exempted Selles from duties to the local nobility.[104] In one of the posthumous miracle stories Letaldus also recorded how St Eusicius had chastised a force of Fulk Nerra when the soldiers plundered the property of the abbey of Selles during the course of a raid probably launched from nearby Graçay.[105] As at Saint-Jouin, however, the struggles of the monastic community, the support of Robert and his master the count of Blois, and the literary efforts of Letaldus all went for naught. Geoffrey of Bonzy died languishing in Fulk Nerra's jail, and control of the town, and possibly the monastery, of Selles passed to Evrard of Le Four, lord of Issoudon.[106]

---

[100] *Cartulaire de Saint-Jouin de Marnes*, pp. 20–1.   [101] Ziezulewicz 1988, pp. 293–4.
[102] Halphen 1906, 13–51; Guillot 1972, I, 20–43; Devailly 1973b, pp. 123–35 and 161–8.
[103] Paris, BN lat. 12742, pp. 490–1; printed in Pierre de Sainte-Catherine 1892, cols. 29–30; incorrectly reported in *GC*, II, 183. The town of Saint-Aignan in the Berry held the name of Bishop Anianus of Orléans, but was not connected to the monastery of Saint-Aignan in that city.   [104] Letaldus of Micy, *Vita s. Eusicii*, p. 376.
[105] Letaldus of Micy, *Miracula s. Eusicii*, c. 6, p. 465.
[106] *Gesta Ambaziensium dominorum*, p. 80. The testament of Evrard is paraphrased in Thaumas de la Thaumassière 1689, I, 366.

Both these works included, like the *Miracula s. Maximini*, a defence of monastic immunities as an implicit theme. Such a defence of foundations which shared common interests with Robert of Blois, a foreigner whose leadership had been forced on the community of Micy by its bishop, must have seemed ironic to Letaldus.[107] In late 1004 he instigated an attempt to unseat Robert. In the recent past the abbot had lost two of his strongest allies, through the death of Bishop Arnulf and King Robert the Pious' repudiation of his marriage to Bertha of Burgundy, the abbot's relative.[108] The abbot was moreover resident not at Micy, but at far-off Saumur. The community accused their absent abbot of misconduct and tried to convince Arnulf's successor, Fulk, to depose him. Abbo of Fleury, who as a long-time adversary of Arnulf and partisan of Robert the Pious might have been presumed to endorse these efforts, instead immediately wrote to the monks of Micy condemning them.[109] He compared their actions to those of Frederick, a schoolmaster of Marmoutier who only a few years previously had led a revolt of that community against its abbot and who was then undertaking a penitential pilgrimage to Jerusalem.[110] Both rebellions were like a plague (*pestis*) and bordered on heresy.[111] Abbo singled out Letaldus – whom he called the *conspirationis caput* – for special blame and accused him of desiring to become abbot in Robert's place.[112] The abbot of Fleury was determined to uphold the independent power of abbots against internal and external conspiracies. Letaldus may well have deemed Micy's abbacy, once held by his relative, to have

---

[107] The *Liber niger* of Saint-Florent contains one example (Halphen 1906, pp. 352–4; Bachrach 1978, p. 133) of how Robert of Blois despoiled the property of Micy by bringing one of its serfs to Saumur without compensation.

[108] *GC*, VIII, 1430; Guillot 1972, I, 24–6.

[109] Abbo of Fleury, *Epistolae*, no. 11, cols. 436D–8B. See also Cousin 1954, pp. 169–71; Mostert 1987, pp. 62–3. This letter was written between December 1003 (the death of Bishop Arnulf) and December 1004 (the death of Abbo). It provides the only evidence for the incident. The letter was addressed to Constantine, the dean of the community. Cousin, Mostert, and most other analysts mistakenly identify this dean with Constantine of Fleury, who had served as abbot of Micy prior to the abbacy of Robert of Blois and was at this time abbot of Nouaillé.

[110] Abbo had interceded in that quarrel as well. See *Epistolae*, nos. 8 and 9, cols. 429A–33A; Cousin 1954, pp. 162–7; Mostert 1987, pp. 61–2.

[111] Abbo of Fleury, *Epistolae*, no. 11, col. 437B.

[112] Abbo of Fleury, *Epistolae*, no. 11, col. 438A. As Ledru (1906, p. 326) has shown, the traditional assumption that Letaldus was exiled to the abbey of Saint-Pierre-de-la-Couture in the Maine as a result of the rebellion at Micy is unfounded.

been an office rightfully his which had been usurped by outsiders. In any case, the attempt to unseat Robert was unsuccessful.[113]

Sometime thereafter Letaldus composed a piece of hagiographic propaganda, the *Vita s. Juliani* (*BHL* 4544), not for another ally of Robert of Blois, but for Bishop Avesgaud of Le Mans. That man was a member of the family of Bellême and thus a relative by marriage of Micy's former abbot Anno and an ally of Fulk Nerra.[114] With Fulk's support Avesgaud was engaged in a struggle against the counts of Le Mans.[115] As later events indicate Letaldus desired to enlist Avesgaud's powerful family once again in the support of his community of Micy. Having failed in a direct assault on Robert of Blois' authority, Letaldus set about using the vehicle of hagiography to construct for his own, or rather for his community's, purposes the same sort of family alliances that he had sought to build for Robert's sake at Saint-Jouin and Selles. The hagiographer's task was to rewrite a Carolingian life of Julian (*BHL* 4546), the first bishop of Le Mans. Ironically, according to Goffart, this source had been composed in the early ninth century by the so-called 'Le Mans forger', who made a pastiche of local traditions and hagiographic sources in order to support the claim of the bishop of Le Mans over the monastery of Saint-Calais.[116] By the early eleventh century those claims – which had constituted an attack on the principle of monastic immunity – were no longer of importance to the bishop and the Carolingian text had become outdated.

Letaldus himself realized that much of the work consisted of thinly veiled borrowings from other hagiographic works, sources

[113] Cf. Bachrach (1978, pp. 132–3 n. 5 and p. 134 n. 3) who suggests that Robert was forced out of Micy and the community's dean, Constantine, consecrated abbot in his place.

[114] Ledru (1906, pp. 326–8) incorrectly attempted to distinguish Letaldus the author of the *Vita s. Juliani* from Letaldus the author of the *Vita s. Maximini*. The two works are obviously by the same hand and Bonnes (1943, p. 24) correctly rejected Ledru's argument as 'hypercritical'. According to Latouche (1910, pp. 134–5) Avesgaud became bishop of Le Mans sometime between October 997 and 1004. There is no further indication of the date of Letaldus' text. According to the *Actus pontificum Cenomannis* (c. 30, p. 357; see also Boussard 1951, pp. 45–7, 1962, pp. 312–13, and 1970, pp. 181–3) Avesgaud was the son of Ivo and Godehildis of Bellême. He also had a sister named Hildeburgis who was, according to a charter of Jumièges (*Chartes de Jumièges*, no. 15, pp. 51–6), the sister-in-law of Abbot Anno of Micy. On these connections of Abbot Anno to the family of Bellême, see figure 1.

[115] *Actus pontificum Cenomannis*, cc. 29–30, pp. 351–62; Latouche 1910, pp. 14–26; Oury 1978b, Bachrach 1985, pp. 25–7. The struggle began under Avesgaud's predecessor, his uncle Sigifridus, and continued under his successor, his nephew Gervasius.

[116] Goffart 1966, pp. 50–5.

which he accurately identified.[117] Letaldus claimed to see past his corrupt source to an authentic antique tradition. He indeed omitted much of this borrowed material, although he otherwise followed the order, and sometimes the words, of his source. Letaldus, however, retained two stories borrowed from the *Virtutes s. Fursaei* which helped to confirm the bishop's independence from the local count.[118] While these stories did not directly concern monastic immunity, they were historical precedents which could serve to protect an ecclesiastical institution against an outside power, making this work similar in thrust to Letaldus' earlier works for Micy, Saint-Jouin, and Selles. His retention of the stories borrowed from the *Virtutes s. Fursaei* ran counter to his stated, and otherwise practised, standards of verification. By including these stories Letaldus aided a family which had itself formerly supported the monks of Micy in a struggle against allies of the counts of Blois, and intentionally used source material, whose falsity he recognized, in a manner which can only be called forgery.

These indirect efforts to unseat Robert, like most of Letaldus' earlier efforts, were unsuccessful in the short term. Robert died peacefully while resident at Micy in 1011, his power there and the properties of his beloved Saumur intact. A monk of Saumur noted that he 'defended this sheepfold [Micy] from treacherous wolves with the care of a shepherd'.[119] Avesgaud and his family, on the other hand, successfully held off all efforts of the counts of Le Mans to control the bishopric for over half a century. Not all of Letaldus' writing was prompted by concern for monastic rights and the cult of the saints. He composed a charming mock epic poem, the *Versus de quodam piscatore*. This story of the miraculous deliverance of a fisherman who has been eaten by a whale bears many of the stylistic marks and spiritual concerns of Letaldus' other works.[120]

The date of Letaldus' death is unknown, although he was mentioned in a note of the death of Constantine I, then abbot of Nouaillé, in 1014, indicating that he outlived Robert of Blois.[121] He may well be, as Bautier and Gillette Labory have suggested, the Letaldus whom Robert the Pious made *decanus* of Saint-Aignan in

[117] Letaldus of Micy, *Vita s. Juliani*, c. 2, col. 783A.
[118] Letaldus of Micy, *Vita s. Juliani*, cc. 15–20, cols. 787A–90A.
[119] *Historia s. Florentii Salmurensis*, pp. 263–4.
[120] For a fuller treatment, see Ziolkowski 1984.
[121] *La Chronique de Saint-Maixent* for 1014, p. 108.

the 1020s.[122] That foundation was very important to Robert, who oversaw its reconstruction during this time. Over the following years, its *decani* were to serve as officials in the Capetian royal government.[123] If this identification is correct, then Letaldus was finally rewarded for his partisanship.

Letaldus was a writer of great erudition and stylistic grace who put his talents at the service of his own community, of his friends and potential allies, and of his abbot and the allies of that unwanted interloper, all in order to defend monastic, or more generally ecclesiastical, rights and immunities. Lacking the power and stature of the office of abbot, Letaldus carried out his campaign against the secular and episcopal domination of monasteries in a more clandestine fashion, through the composition of hagiography. Although he frequently emphasized the accuracy of his source material, he tailored that source material, even to the point of forgery, in order to suit the interests of the communities for which he wrote. In this, in his apparent indifference to simony, and in his willingness to question abbatial authority, he differed significantly from his contemporary Abbo of Fleury. It is not surprising that Abbo, who in 994 sympathized with Letaldus' plight, shook his head in disappointment in 1004:

Finally to you, my one time friend Letaldus, let my words now be directed, whose singular wisdom my own inability admires and seeks to extol with the greatest praises. Of what interest is it to you to gnaw away at the life of a miserable man, a little man whose vices mark him out, since it is written that the wise man should not seek vengeance? . . . I beg and implore you, dearest friend, to recall your own weakness, open your heart to compassion, censure your brothers, 'reprove, entreat, rebuke in all patience and doctrine' (2 Tim. 4:2) . . . For you are the head of the conspiracy; you take for your own the office of your lord abbot, Robert, a thing which is criminal.[124]

It is striking how consistently Letaldus failed in what would seem to have been his goals. Outsiders – Constantine I and Robert of Blois – were made abbots of Micy in the years following the composition of the *Miracula s. Maximini*. Both the abbeys of Saint-Jouin-de-Marnes and Selles-sur-Cher came under the domination of Fulk Nerra and his allies. Robert of Blois controlled Micy until his death. Forgery, the manipulation of historic precedent, and

---

[122] Bautier and Labory 1965, p. 24 n. 3.
[123] Griffiths 1988.   [124] Abbo of Fleury, *Epistolae*, no. 11, col. 438.

even the much-publicized patronage of a saint were insufficient by
themselves to free religious communities from the control of
outside powers, secular or ecclesiastical. Letaldus' career and works
serve as excellent reminders of the often harsh social and economic
realities which, in addition to the motivations of pious interest and
liturgical necessity, shaped the composition of medieval
hagiography.

Robert of Blois' successor as abbot was Constantine II, who, as
former *decanus* of the abbey, was the first monk of the community
to be raised to its abbacy in many years.[125] Little is known of
Constantine's term. His successor was Albert, the nephew of the
former abbot Anno. The new abbot was related, through his
mother, to the lords of Bellême and, through his wife, to the lords
of Châteaudun.[126] His relatives, who thus included some of the
most powerful ecclesiastics of the middle Loire valley, did much to
enrich Micy during his tenure. Albert's son, Archbishop Arnulf of
Tours, donated properties on the occasion of various important
ritual celebrations.[127] The archbishop also used his influence to
cause Bishop Odolric of Orléans to give the monks half the
revenues of a local church 'for both the salvation of my soul and the

[125] Constantine II was listed as *decanus* in the letter of Abbo of Fleury (*Epistolae*, no. 11, col. 437) and as abbot in a donation of June 1015 ('Chartes de Micy', no. 15, pp. 79–82).

[126] Albert was first mentioned as abbot in a charter of 1022–3 ('Chartes de Micy', no. 18, pp. 87–90, and Newman 1937a, no. 58, pp. 75–6) and last in a charter of 1044 ('Chartes de Micy', no. 27, pp. 142–7). He was described as the son of a man named Albert and of Hildeburgis of Bellême in a charter dated 1030/1 (*Chartes de Jumièges*, no. 15, pp. 51–6). According to another charter which antedated 1047 (*Actus pontificum Cenomannis*, pp. 370–1), Bishop Gervasius of Le Mans was the nephew of Bishop Avesgaud of Le Mans and the son of Hildesburgis of Bellême and Haymo of Château-sur-Loir. Hildeburgis was apparently married twice. The dates of the charters suggests that Albert was her first husband. Abbot Albert was thus the nephew of both Abbot Anno of Micy (brother of the elder Albert) and of Bishop Avesgaud (brother of Hildeburgis), as well as the half-brother of Bishop Gervasius. He married a daughter of Hugh of Châteaudun and thus became the brother-in-law of Archbishop Hugh of Tours (*GC*, XIV, 56; Bry 1620, pp. 137–8; Boussard 1951, p. 46 n. 4.) Albert was not an only child ('Chartes de Micy', no. 25, p. 132), the names of Albert's sibling and wife are unknown. Albert's son Arnulf succeeded his maternal uncle as archbishop of Tours (*Chartes de Jumièges*, no. 9, p. 24; 'Chartes de Micy', no. 22, pp. 111–15; cf. Bautier (1975a, p. 87) who describes Albert and Arnulf as brothers).
  Albert's marriage also provided him with a distant connection to Bishop Odolric of Orléans. Albert's sister-in-law, Milesend, had a son named Geoffrey of Châteaudun (also lord of Mortagne). This nephew of Albert in turn married Heloise, the sister of Bishop Odolric of Orléans. Note that Boussard (1970, pp. 189–90, particularly n. 145) is incorrect in distinguishing two abbots of Micy named Albert during this period. A second Albert (*GC*, VIII, 1533) served as abbot during the twelfth century. For a family tree detailing the relations of Albert, see figure 1.

[127] *Sermo de inventione s. Maximini*, p. 253; *Translatio s. Euspicii*, p. 314.

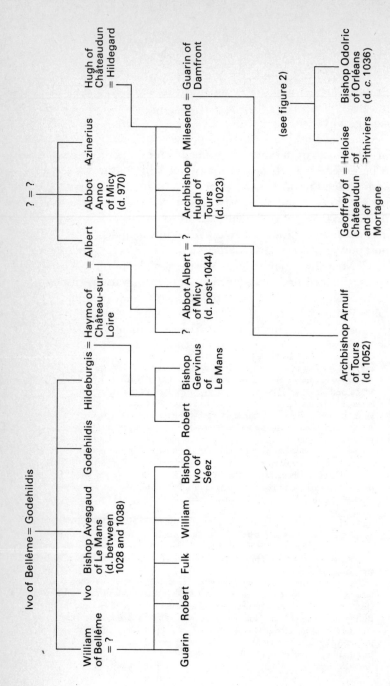

Figure 1 The relations of Abbot Albert of Micy

salvation of the soul of [Arnulf's father]'.[128] Albert later received the abbacy of Saint-Julien of Tours from his son.[129] The abbot's nephew, Hervaeus, donated the church of Ferté-Avrain. This archdeacon of Sainte-Croix had founded that church to house 'most holy relics of the tomb of our Lord Jesus Christ', which he had brought back from the Holy Land.[130] Bishop Avesgaud of Le Mans, the abbot's uncle, released his rights of *synodalia* and *circadae* in a church located in his diocese which had been given to the monks of Micy by a knight from the Maine.[131] Albert also apparently had allegiances to the royal family. Shortly after the trial of heretics at Orléans in 1022, Robert the Pious donated two mills to Micy 'through the intercession of the Queen [Constance] and her cleric Tetduin'.[132] When Letaldus three years later donated another mill to his old community, he did so 'by the order and intercession of my lord king, Robert, who is lord and abbot of this monastery [Saint-Aignan]'.[133]

Albert continued the campaign to win recognition of the abbey's possessions and rights. In particular he wrote to Pope John XIX (1024–31) seeking papal confirmation of Micy's properties. The abbot carefully outlined the foundation of his abbey, stressing the role of Clovis and the patronage provided by Euspicius and Maximinus. Then he cited the contemporary support of Queen Constance and asked that the pope provide his seal for two 'tomes'. The first named the properties donated by the queen, while the other contained 'the confirmation of the substance of our community'.[134] Such papal approval, while less sweeping in scope

---

128 The act was dated 29 October 1027. 'Chartes de Micy', no. 22, pp. 111–15.
129 *GC*, XIV, 59. Despite the bitter reaction of the monks of that abbey to Albert's appointment, there is no evidence to suggest that he utilized this second benefice to enrich the abbey of Micy.
130 The act was not dated. 'Chartes de Micy', no. 25, pp. 128–33.
131 The act was dated 1036. 'Chartes de Micy', no. 26, pp. cxviii–cxxiii and 134–41; Lemarignier 1937, pp. 85–8.
132 Stein 1895; 'Chartes de Micy', no. 18, pp. 87–90; Newman 1937a, no. 58, pp. 75–6. This Tetduin is probably the Teduin who witnessed, as archdeacon, the donation made by Odolric in 1027.
133 'Chartes de Micy', no. 20, pp. 105–8. Despite Griffiths' suspicion (1988, p. 461), the donation appears to be authentic.
134 Abbo of Fleury, *Epistolae*, no. 13, cols. 439–40. While this letter was composed by Albert of Micy some years after the death of Abbo of Fleury, it was fortuitously preserved in the collection of Abbo's letters. It is contained in the earliest known manuscript of that collection copied at Fleury in the mid-eleventh century (British Library, Additional Manuscript 10972, fo. 23). On the date, see *GC*, VIII, 1531. Cf. Mabillon 1703–39, IV, 203–4, and Jarossay 1902, pp. 486–7.

than the rights of exemption claimed in earlier forgeries, would have provided important support for the abbey. There is, however, no record of a favourable reply. A use of similar tactics can be seen in a manuscript of the *Vita s. Aviti III* copied in the scriptorium of Micy during the eleventh century. Although the text itself clearly stated that the saint never accepted the abbacy of Micy, the scribe named Avitus *abbas Miciacensis* in the title. More importantly the original text, which stated that Micy was founded by Bishop Eusebius, was altered by a contemporary hand to state that the monastery had been founded by Clovis.[135]

Albert's most significant accomplishment was the rebuilding of the abbey church. Two major liturgical rituals marked this rebuilding programme: the invention of the relics of Maximinus and his disciples, which had been enshrined in the church since the ninth century, and the translation to Micy of some relics of Euspicius, who was enshrined in the church of Saint-Aignan. The church which commemorated Maximinus' victory over the dragon may also have been built about this time.[136]

In the *Sermo de inventione s. Maximini* an anonymous monk of the abbey described the invention of the putative coffins of the community's three earliest abbots. He introduced this account with a long discussion of the lives of Maximinus and his disciples which was excerpted from earlier hagiography. The concluding section provides a fascinating glimpse into how a monastic community related to the relics of their patron.[137] The old church at Micy had a main altar dedicated to St Stephen at its centre and a

---

[135] The title (Paris, BN lat. 3789, fo. 105v) reads: 'Vita sancti ac beatissimi Aviti confessoris atque abbatis Miciacensis monasterii.' The explanation of the foundation of Micy (fo. 106v) reads: 'Est Miciacensis monasterii locus ab Aureliani urbe tribus distans milibus. Cuius in loci coenobio tunc beatissimus Maximinus a Chlodoveo primo rege Francorum christianissimo constitutus, coenobiali praeerat ordini. Illuc famulus Domini Avitus perniciter veniens ab abbate comam capitis in morem clericorum sibi secari poposcit. Quo peracto monasticae professionis iugum devote suscepit.' The words 'a Chlodoveo primo rege Francorum christianissimo' were written over an erasure. Poncelet (1905, p. 21) suggests that the original text was 'ab Eusebio Aurelianensis ecclesiae pontifice'. An ultraviolet reading of the text confirms this suggestion. Both the original hand and that of the correction are of the eleventh century, but the manuscript is difficult to date more precisely on palaeographic grounds.

[136] Banchereau 1931c. The church stands near the traditional spot of the grotto where the contest took place. Most of the fabric dates from the eleventh century. There is no evidence of earlier construction, although the *Vita s. Maximini* claim that Agilus first built a church at that site.

[137] This is the only section of the work which has been edited, see *Sermo de inventione s. Maximini*, pp. 252–3.

secondary altar in the apse, whose dedication is unknown but might well have been to St Maximinus.[138] The monk described how his fellows rebuilt this church by pulling it down in sections and putting up the new one over it. He referred to a central area of the church – 'which is covered by a vault of lead-coloured bricks and in which is located the principal altar of the blessed protomartyr' – as a *crypta*, although none of it was subterranean.[139] When the time came to renovate this section, in which the monks assumed their patron to be buried, they began to tremble 'lest in some way the sacred bones had been removed from the place of Micy'. Although Letaldus had collected numerous traditions concerning the miracles of the patron in the preceding generation, and the community saw his operation as being intimately connected with their own welfare, they had apparently not had direct contact with the relics themselves within living memory.

Four monks were charged with the actual search for Maximinus' relics: the prior, the procurator, the guardian of the sanctuary, and the chief builder. Under the main altar they uncovered three caskets. The monks immediately informed Abbot Albert of their discovery and the community was gathered together around the excavations in order to chant hymns of praise and thanksgiving.[140] In the heat of the moment the monks frankly expected a miracle. In fulfilment of their hopes, a tremendous noise erupted when the first efforts were made to open the middle casket, 'as if the Lord spoke in a great voice through his confessor'. When they finally managed to open the casket, they found not only a corpse, but a lead tablet with uncial lettering identifying the body as that of Maximinus and the

---

138 A similar configuration was followed in contemporary churches, such as that of Fleury. It would seem that Micy had been originally dedicated to St Stephen and the patronage of St Maximinus was added at some point after his death. While the ninth-century sources agree that the church was dedicated to Stephen, thus suggesting that he had been the original patron, all the charters of that period refer to Micy as being solely dedicated to Maximinus. In the eleventh century, however, reference to Stephen's patronage was revived and all charters of that period referred to the monastery under a double dedication to both Maximinus and Stephen. The vintage of this church is unclear. When Theodulf refounded the abbey, he suggested that he merely repaired extant buildings. There is no reference to the construction or reconstruction of a church at Micy in the intervening period.

139 J. Hubert (1951) discusses the uses of the word *crypta* in this and other texts, suggesting that it first referred to the use of a liturgical space to enshrine relics and only later came to have a specifically subterranean connotation.

140 Albert is not mentioned by name, but the author did describe (*Sermo de inventione s. Maximini*, p. 253) the abbot as the father of Archbishop Arnulf of Tours.

other two caskets as those of Theodemir and Maximinus II, the nephew of the first abbot. In one of them, however, the monks to their surprise found two corpses.[141] The community quickly announced the uncovering of the relics and the accompanying miracle to the bishop of Orléans and placed the caskets on an altar in the already-completed apse of the church to await the completion of the entire structure. On 25 July a solemn celebration was held to place the relics in a new resting place, once again under the main altar, presided over by Bishop Odolric, who was related by marriage to Albert, and Archbishop Arnulf of Tours, the abbot's own son.[142]

The author of the account of this invention also composed the *Vita et translatio s. Euspicii* in which he introduced a brief description of the translation of Euspicius' relics with an account of the saint's life. Euspicius' relics had been conserved at the church of Saint-Aignan since at least the ninth century.[143] During the dedication of the reconstructed church there in 1029, they were solemnly placed in a new altar.[144] Abbot Albert was in attendance at the ceremony and petitioned King Robert the Pious, who had supported the rebuilding effort, to return some of the abbot's relics to Micy.[145] The anonymous author noted how important the voice of Tedelin, the *decanus* of Saint-Aignan (1029–36), was in persuading the king, although the presence of Albert's son, Archbishop Arnulf, probably also helped the cause of Micy.[146] On the following day two monks – the guardian of the sanctuary and

---

[141] Bertholdus stated (*Vita s. Maximini I*, c. 25, p. 597) that Maximinus was buried at Micy in the ninth century with Theodemir, a man whom Maximinus had cured, and two other *socii*. According to Bertholdus' anonymous successor (*Vita s. Maximini II*, c. 37, p. 591.), Maximinus was buried with two anonymous *discipuli*. Letaldus (*Miracula s. Maximini*, c. 14, p. 602) had agreed with the anonymous life and identified the *discipuli* as Maximinus' successors Theodemir and Maximinus II in accordance with the *Vita s. Lifardi* (c. 11, p. 156). The tablet discovered by the monks agreed with the narrative of Letaldus. The monks were clearly surprised to find the fourth corpse, which the description of Bertholdus would have led them to expect. Their reaction provides the best evidence that Bertholdus' life of Maximinus had been eclipsed by the anonymous life as the basic source for the traditions about Maximinus at Micy during the Capetian period.
[142] There may have been another participant. In the sole known manuscript of this work (Vatican, Reg. lat. 621, fo. 45r and 45v) a phrase has been erased before both occurrences of the name of Bishop Odolric.
[143] Bertholdus of Micy, *Vita s. Maximini I*, c. 11, p. 594; *Vita s. Maximini II*, c. 18, p. 585.
[144] Helgaud of Fleury, *Epitoma vitae regis Rotberti pii*, c. 22, p. 110.
[145] *Translatio s. Euspicii*, p. 314.   [146] On Tedelin, see Griffiths 1988, p. 461.

the builder who had both earlier helped to discover Maximinus'
relics – brought an urn containing Euspicius' arm to their
church.[147] The author simply stated that they were received 'with
praise and honour' and did not specify where the relics were placed
in the recently completed abbey church.

During his tenure as abbot, Albert thus orchestrated ritual
displays of the community's saintly patronage. Faced with the near
certainty of episcopal control of his abbey, he also attempted to
enrich and improve Micy by means of his alliances with important
ecclesiastical and secular leaders, including the bishops of Orléans
themselves. He was remarkably successful in appealing to the
various factions in the turbulent power struggles of the west
Franks. In 1024, for example, Fulbert of Chartres, a supporter of
Bishop Odolric, expressed his intention of passing Christmas at
Micy when Robert the Pious called him, against his will, to attend
a council in Orléans.[148] In 1022 and again in 1025, however,
Robert himself caused significant donations of property to be
made to Micy.[149] Albert thus wooed royal support while keeping
his house a safe haven for those who opposed the royal will.
Although certainly married, and quite possibly a simoniac like his
uncle, Albert provided the same strong leadership which Letaldus
had earlier praised in the person of Anno. Nevertheless the abbey
remained under episcopal control.[150] Albert's abbacy marked the
end of important hagiographic composition at Micy.

From the time of its refoundation under Theodulf, the abbey of
Micy lay under the dominion of the bishops of Orléans who
frequently exploited its resources. The ancient Merovingian
community of Micy had been surrounded by the aura of sanctity
emanating from its first abbot, Maximinus, and those traditions
remained of crucial importance. In a striking simile one of its
hagiographers compared that saint and his numerous disciples to a

---

[147] Their names were Laterius (Leterius) and Odo. See *Sermo de inventione s. Maximini*, p.
252, and *Translatio s. Euspicii*, p. 314. These references suggest that a specific group of
monks – including the procurator, the guardian of the sanctuary, and the chief builder,
as well as the abbot and prior – were charged with the preservation of the cult of relics
at Micy.   [148] Fulbert of Chartres, *Letters*, no. 94, pp. 170–3.

[149] Stein 1895; 'Chartes de Micy', nos. 18 and 20, pp. 87–90 and 105–8; Newman 1937a, no.
58, pp. 75–6.

[150] *Cartulaire de Sainte-Croix*, nos. 23 (Eugenius III, 10 February 1151), 175 (Honorius III,
17 November 1218), and 387 (revenues of the dean of Orléans, 15 March 1321), pp. 51,
263–4, and 537–8.

single root which sprouted many trees.[151] From the Carolingian to the early Capetian period, the monks of Micy assiduously took advantage of two patronage networks: the first, that of the holy dead oriented to the kingdom of God, and the second, that of powerful living patrons oriented to the royal court. While these patrons never effectively exempted the abbey from episcopal control, they did allow it to flourish to a far greater degree than other episcopally controlled houses in the Orléanais. By the twelfth century the canons of Saint-Euverte had forgotten the location of the relics of Evurtius, while those of Meung-sur-Loire desperately searched for traditions about Lifardus. Unlike the monks of Micy, they had largely forfeited the powerful patronage of their 'fathers'.

---

[151] 'Testis adest Perticus Auito atque Karileppho magnis duobus illuminata luminibus. Silua etiam quae Longinqua dicitur, quam diuinis sanctus Leonardus exercitiis coluit, suique ospitio corporis celebrem reddidit. Hoc quoque testando manifestat Secalonia, egregium Viatorem seruans in Viatoria, Beatum quoque Dulchardum necminus ex praecellentissimi patris Maximini clientela Biturigensis possidet parrochia, nec prorsus silet Belsica illustrata in sancto uiro nomine Leto, quem nunc corpore sanctum Piueris dicitur retinere. Illustrem quoque uirum Agilum post uiri dei Maximini obitum causa sanitatis illi redditae nouimus ad habitum sanctitatis conuersum. Nulli uero sit ambiguum floruisse ex eius regulari ordine beatum Leobinum Carnotensium episcopum, sanctum quoque Constantinum, nichilominus sanctissimum Launoraurum et beatum Lifardum. Ut enim multi arboris yami ex una radice prodeunt sic isti et alii multi quorum nomina sunt cognita deo soli ex eius sancta disciplina pullulando ipsi et sequaces eorum in uirtutum culmen euasserent. Sicquidem ante patrem Maximinum eiusque auunculum Euspicium regularem disciplinam in hac prouincia aliquis patrum tenuisse nimine legendo inuenitur.' Vatican, Reg. lat. 621, fos. 40v–41. Part of this text is printed by Poncelet (1905, p. 78 n. 1) from a Bollandist notebook (itself copied from Vatican, Reg. lat. 621). The image of the root and trees may be borrowed from Theodulf of Orléans, *MGH, Poetae latinae*, I, 521. This author added four new saints to the litany of Maximinus' disciples provided by Letaldus: Laetus, a hermit from the Perche; Leobinus, the bishop of Chartres; Constantine, a hermit from the Maine; and Agilus, the nobleman who chased his escaped servant into the grotto of Maximinus. The monks of Micy continued to draw on the hagiographic traditions current in the middle Loire valley to enrich the history of their own abbey. A later scribe added yet another seven saints (Phrambaldus, Urbicius, Senardus, Amator, Pavacius, Rigomarus, and a second Leonard) to the list of disciples appended to the original dedicatory poem of the *Vita s. Maximini II* (see *AASSOSB*, I, 581). The only known copy comes from a manuscript of the fifteenth century, but the addition probably dates to the eleventh century, see Poncelet 1905, pp. 79–81. These verses were inscribed in a bronze cross erected in the grotto of St Maximinus by the diocese of Orléans on 13 June 1858, see Mantellier 1858. The list was further amplified by local antiquarians in the nineteenth century. Cochard (1877), for instance, lists twenty-eight saints as disciples of Maximinus. Poncelet (1905, pp. 78–98) investigated the connections of no less than forty saints to Maximinus and Micy.

Chapter 6

SAINTS, ABBOTS, AND ECCLESIASTICAL POLITICS AT FLEURY AND PITHIVIERS

SOCIAL CHANGE AND THE DEFENCE OF ECCLESIASTICAL PROPERTY

During the first decades of Capetian rule local magnates, both secular and ecclesiastical, sought to exert dominion over the inhabitants, institutions, and lands of their territories. The properties of monastic communities provided particularly tempting prizes. Such communities of the unarmed had to find ways of defending themselves and their possessions against attempts to assert external control, interference which was often backed by armed force. As Lemarignier has noted, 'Vassalage and feudovassalic practices always carried within them the ferment of anarchy and a menace of disorder for society. Against them the leaders, whom we would call the public powers, were forced to seek some cure, with means differing according to the times.'[1]

Under these circumstances the abbots and monks of Fleury supplemented the traditional protection provided by their 'father' Benedict by developing new ideas of saintly, or more accurately sacred, patronage. They appealed to law and the public powers as a supplement to – although certainly not a substitute for – the personal power exerted by their patron. Writers from the community in large part developed these ideas in a novel form of hagiographic literature, that is the lives of contemporary figures.[2] The bishops of Orléans, for their part, resisted the new rights which the community of Fleury won in this fashion, rights which anticipated the celebrated immunities of Cluny. The bishops, too, appealed to a tradition of law and to the patronage provided by

[1] Lemarignier 1957, p. 373.
[2] The richness of the interrelated hagiographic, historiographic, and biographical works produced at Fleury during this period has been emphasized by many scholars, most importantly Bautier 1975b. I would also particularly like to thank Frederick Paxton of Connecticut College for sharing with me an unpublished paper which is most provocative in its assessment of this same corpus.

certain 'fathers' of the diocese. On occasion, they even resorted to the use of armed force.

The struggles between the community of Fleury and their opponents, both ecclesiastical ones such as the bishops of Orléans and secular ones such as castellans whose properties neighboured those of Fleury, were in many ways typical of the problems which engulfed Francia in the first half-century of Capetian rule. Saintly patronage played a significant role in these struggles, as we have already seen in the case of the abbey of Micy. As Frankish society was changing, however, so too did the concept of the patronage exerted by the saintly 'fathers' of the realm. The Franks increasingly looked to contemporaries as heroic examples of holiness and as agents of divine providence. The role played by traditional 'fathers', while still important, was diminished. By the end of the twelfth century, as we have seen, chastisement miracles were less common and the ancient saints of Francia began to perform cures at their shrines almost to the exclusion of other miracles. Monastic communities looked ever more to law, both royal and canon, and to the courts which enforced that law for defence of their properties. The process of monastic reform, as found in Cluniac houses and elsewhere, came to serve as a firmer guarantee of exemptions than had the presence of a saintly 'father'. The monastery of Fleury, which we shall now examine, played, particularly under its celebrated abbots Abbo and Gauzlin, a leading role in these developments.

THE PRIVILEGES AND EXEMPTIONS OF FLEURY

The abbey of Fleury had greater resources than did any other monastic community of the Orléanais: more elaborate traditional rights, a more famous patron saint, greater library holdings, and a larger cadre of educated monks. From at least the time of Louis the Pious it had been protected by royal authority against the power of local courts, both secular and ecclesiastical. The community had the right to elect its own abbot in accordance with the rule of St Benedict and its properties lay under royal *defensio*.[3] Thus Fleury was an independent, or 'royal', monastery, not under episcopal control as were such abbeys as Micy and Meung-sur-Loire or such

---

[3] *Recueil des chartes de Saint-Benoît*, no. 14, I, 31–3. This act made reference to similar acts of Pippin and Charlemagne which are now lost (no. 4, I, 22, and no. 7, I, 23).

chapters of canons as Saint-Euverte and Saint-Avit. That protection had palpable effect. When Bishop Jonas came to the abbey, for
example, he did so as a royal *missus* investigating legal claims which
were eventually adjudicated in the monks' favour.[4] While
Adrevald had recorded many invasions of Fleury's property by
secular lords during the ninth century, attacks which were repelled
through the patronage of St Benedict, he never mentioned the
bishops of Orléans as opponents of the community. He also
described how royal defence sometimes had to be supplemented by
saintly patronage in order to protect the community of Fleury in
the courts of the Carolingian *pagus*. It is worth remembering that
one of these cases had to be moved from a *placitum* held before local
judges near Fleury to the city of Orléans because the local judges
were competent only in Salic and not Roman law.[5]

Fleury continued under royal protection as one of the last
vestiges of Carolingian influence in the Loire valley during the
middle years of the tenth century.[6] In 967 and again in 974 Lothar
confirmed the privileges originally granted by Louis the Pious,
both times at the request of Abbot Richard. These charters
elaborated the defences which guarded the abbey against non-
royal authorities.[7] In this period, however, royal protection did
not always function. At one point the monks unsuccessfully
petitioned both Lothar and Hugh Capet, then *dux Francorum*, to
obtain justice against Herbert of Sully. In the absence of royal
justice they turned instead to the miraculous *patrocinium* afforded
by their 'father' Benedict.[8] The privileges, moreover, did not
exempt the abbey from royally sanctioned interference. The
community elected Amalbert as Richard's successor, but the
election had to be approved by Lothar, his son Louis V, and the
local count.[9] The new abbot obtained yet another confirmation of
royally granted immunities when Louis was crowned co-ruler on 8
June 979.[10] The show of royal concern for Fleury was not unique.
Louis confirmed the possessions and privileges of the see of Orléans

[4] *Recueil des chartes de Saint-Benoît*, no. 19, I, 43–6; *Miracula s. Benedicti*, I.25, pp. 56–7.
[5] *Miracula s. Benedicti*, I.24–5, pp. 55–7. [6] Newman 1937b, p. 70.
[7] *Recueil des chartes de Saint-Benoît*, no. 55, I, 136–8, and no. 60, I, 147–8. For newer editions,
see *Recueil des actes de Lothaire et de Louis V*, no. 27, pp. 66–8, and no. 34, pp. 83–6. The
right of free election of the abbot is mentioned only in the second.
[8] *Miracula s. Benedicti*, II.7, pp. 107–9; Lot 1891, p. 81 n. 3.
[9] *Miracula s. Benedicti*, II.17, p. 120.
[10] *Recueil des chartes de Saint-Benoît*, no. 64, I, 167–70. For a newer edition, see *Recueil des
actes de Lothaire et de Louis V*, no. 70, pp. 173–6.

for Bishop Arnulf on almost the very same day.[11] Both bishop and abbot seem to have particularly wished to guarantee that their rights would continue under the next royal administration. Amalbert died in April 985.[12] He was succeeded by Oylbold, whose election was also approved by Lothar.[13]

By this time, Abbo, destined to become Fleury's greatest leader, had already become the master of the abbey's school. He was from a relatively humble family.[14] His parents evidently had him become a monk and attend that same school in order to gain advancement. From Fleury he travelled over northern France in search of an education which was to make him the scholarly rival of his contemporary Gerbert of Reims.[15] Shortly after Oylbold's election, a request came from the English abbey of Ramsey that the monks of Fleury provide that house with a schoolmaster.[16] Abbo himself accepted the charge and left for a two-year sojourn in those rather isolated environs, quite probably out of disappointment at not receiving the abbacy of Fleury.[17]

About this same time Bishop Arnulf of Orléans began to oppose the privileges of Fleury. He was a man of high birth whose uncle had previously held the bishopric.[18] He disputed the right of the monks of Fleury to harvest grapes in some fields located near the city of Orléans. According to Aimo, '[Arnulf] never unconditionally loved the abbots of Fleury, mostly because, as they only gave honour to the command of the king, they never adhered to the command of his own will, subjection to which he loved beyond moderation.' In response the monks brought a reliquary to the harvest in order to protect themselves against episcopal troops. Again according to Aimo, some laypeople along the route described the procession as 'Benedict going to the suburbs of

[11] *Cartulaire de Sainte-Croix*, no. 64, pp. 125–9. For a newer edition, see *Recueil des actes de Lothaire et de Louis V*, no. 69, pp. 169–73.

[12] Mostert 1986, p. 202.   [13] *Miracula s. Benedicti*, II.18, p. 121.

[14] Aimo of Fleury, *Vita s. Abbonis*, c. 1, p. 38.

[15] Aimo of Fleury, *Vita s. Abbonis*, c. 3, p. 39.

[16] The school of Fleury had earlier served a number of English monks, including Oswald the founder of Ramsey, and the abbey had thus become one of the fountainheads of the tenth-century monastic reform in England. On the connections of Fleury to England, see Cousin 1954, pp. 60–7; Grémont and Donnat 1966, pp. 769–77 (particularly pp. 770–2 nn. 143, 144, and 157 on Oswald); Vezin 1977; John 1983, pp. 303–15; Berland 1984b; Hallinger 1984, pp. 351–9.   [17] Mostert 1986, pp. 203–4.

[18] Rodulfus Glaber, *Historiarum libri quinque*, II.5.9, pp. 66–9; Letaldus of Micy, *Miracula s. Maximini*, c. 40, p. 609; Boussard 1970, pp. 177–8; Martindale 1977, p. 35. Note that Boussard incorrectly distinguishes two bishops of Orléans named Arnulf in the late tenth century.

Orléans in order to carry out the defence of his vines.' For the moment, this recourse to traditional saintly patronage served the monks of Fleury. It was a contest of personal wills between bishop and saint which the former could not hope to win. Arnulf withdrew his claim.[19]

Carolingian power was crumbling. Archbishop Adalbero of Reims and others were plotting against the royal family. Gerbert, then the archbishop's adviser, remarked, 'Lothar is king of Francia only in name.'[20] The king died suddenly on 2 March 986. The succession of Louis V was not disputed, but his reign was short-lived. He died in a hunting accident the following May. Within weeks Hugh Capet was elected by his fellow magnates as Louis' successor, over the claim of Louis' uncle, Charles of Lotharingia. On 3 July 987 Hugh was anointed by Adalbero at Noyon and in December his son Robert was elected co-ruler at Orléans.[21] Within the year Abbot Oylbold obtained a confirmation of Fleury's traditional privileges from the new king. Hugh chose to repeat verbatim much of the language from the acts of Lothar and Louis V.[22] His solicitude for Fleury was not surprising as his father, Hugh the Great, had helped to sponsor the reform carried out there by Odo of Cluny.[23] The new monarch moreover wished to secure the allegiance of that important community. Within the year, however, Oylbold was dead. Hugh then confirmed the election of Abbo, whom Oylbold had earlier recalled from his putative exile in England. According to Aimo, however, 'some of the brothers perversely resisted the election'.[24] About the same time, Constan-

---

[19] *Miracula s. Benedicti*, II.19, pp. 123–5. Note that Aimo included this story in the first book of his collection prior to the death of King Lothar. The relics which the monks brought with them were actually those of Maurus the martyr and Frongentius.

[20] Gerbert of Reims, *Epistolae*, no. 48, p. 77.

[21] For a guide to the thorny problems surrounding the dynastic change, see, among others, McKitterick 1983, pp. 324–34; Lewis 1981, pp. 14–21; Sassier 1987, pp. 177–98.

[22] *Recueil des chartes de Saint-Benoît*, no. 69, I, 181–2.

[23] *Recueil des chartes de Saint-Benoît*, no. 44, I, 110–14.

[24] *Miracula s. Benedicti*, III.1, p. 127; Aimo of Fleury, *Vita s. Abbonis*, c. 7, p. 41. Oylbold's letter requesting Abbo's return has been edited by Mostert 1986, pp. 206–8. Mostert (p. 206) concludes that Abbo returned before Oylbold's death. The date of Abbo's election can be fixed in 988, for he had served as abbot for sixteen years at his death in December 1004 (Aimo, *Vita s. Abbonis*, c. 16, p. 51). Around this time Gerbert of Reims criticized an abbot of Fleury (*Epistolae*, no. 69, pp. 99–100; nos. 86–8, pp. 114–16; no. 95, pp. 124–6; and no. 142, pp. 168–9). Gerbert never used a proper name, but referred to the abbot as an 'intruder' (*pervasor*). The identification of this abbot has been controversial. Julien Havet, the original editor of Gerbert's correspondence, thought that Oylbold was the *pervasor* and so dated the letters in question to 986–7. Lot (1891, pp. 188–9, particularly n.

tine, who had replaced Abbo as schoolmaster, was consecrated abbot of Micy by Bishop Arnulf. Constantine was a long-time friend of Gerbert of Reims, himself no friend of Abbo, and it is tempting to see in this move a second defection from Fleury by an unsuccessful candidate for the abbacy, similar in motivation to Abbo's own journey to England.[25]

THE WORK OF ABBO OF FLEURY

Abbo came to the governance of an abbey in difficult straits. The community was apparently rent by factionalism. The brothers lived under the authority of their third king and their second – or possibly even third – abbot in three years. Royal control over supposed vassals, both lay and ecclesiastical, had seriously eroded over the previous half-century.[26] The bishop of Orléans was plotting to gain some control over the most important monastery in his diocese.[27] Viscounts, castellans, and other *milites* – such as Herbert of Sully, Ademar of Limoges, and Bernard of Uzon – cast covetous eyes on the rich properties of Fleury and its priories.[28] Lemarignier has seen the appearance of a new 'seigneurie banale' in

4) rejected this identification on the grounds that the upright man described by Aimo could not have been deemed a *pervasor* by contemporaries. Most scholars since (see, for example, Cousin 1954, pp. 91–2, and Mostert 1986, pp. 202–3) have followed Lot's lead. If they are correct, the letters must be redated to 988, for Oylbold was still alive in 987. Since Aimo twice (in the passages cited above) described Abbo as the immediate successor of Oylbold, Lot and his followers suggest that the hagiographer was covering up a scandalous episode in his community's history. For a resumé of the debate, see the discussion by Weigle (Gerbert of Reims, *Epistolae*, pp. 99–100 n. 4). Weigle himself keeps neutral, but his persistence in dating the letters to 986–7 suggests that he is in agreement with Havet. I would be inclined to identify Oylbold, whose election had been supported and confirmed by Lothar, as the abbot deemed a *pervasor* by Gerbert, who was a supporter of the Capetians.

25 Andrew of Fleury, *Vita Gauzlini*, c. 2, p. 38. It is impossible to date this move with any precision, but it must have occurred *c.* 990. On the friendship of Constantine and Gerbert, see Gerbert of Reims, *Opera mathematica*, pp. 6–8 and 23–35, and *Epistolae*, no. 86, p. 114, no. 142, pp. 168–9, and no. 191, pp. 229–30. This last letter includes an attack on Abbo. If Oylbold was indeed the *pervasor* described by Gerbert (see previous note), the minority of the monks of Fleury who opposed the election of Abbo according to Aimo's account (*Vita s. Abbonis*, c. 7, p. 41) might then be identified as the partisans of Constantine, rather than of the anonymous *pervasor*.

26 Lemarignier 1955, particularly pp. 141–3 and 156.

27 For specific examples, see *Miracula s. Benedicti*, II.19, pp. 123–4, and *Recueil des chartes de Saint-Benoît*, no. 70, I, 182–5.

28 On the attacks of these castellans, all dating to the decades around the year 1000, see *Miracula s. Benedicti*, II.7, pp. 107–9; III.5–6, pp. 135–43; III.16, pp. 163–4. These examples could be multiplied.

these attempts by local authorities to extend their judicial rights over monastic property.[29] The very laymen (*advocati*) who had been charged with protecting the property rights of the monastery in the judicial system of the old Carolingian *pagus* were now often conspiring against the community. The land of the western Franks was suffering from a crisis of *fidelitas*.[30] Although Hugh Capet had indeed renewed the traditional Carolingian privileges of the abbey of Fleury, Abbo recognized such a guarantee of royal defence would no longer suffice in and of itself. It was necessary to redefine what royal support of monastic rights entailed and in the process to reformulate the very definitions of the offices of king, bishop, and abbot. A skilled scholar with an unusually rich library at his disposal, Abbo took up this formidable task in a series of works composed over the next sixteen years. In the process he would almost single-handedly give impetus to the movement for monastic exemption which would lead to the development of Cluny's unique liberties.[31]

Abbo began this enterprise in his sole work of hagiography, the *Vita s. Edmundi*, which concerned the death of King Edmund of East Anglia at the hands of the invading Danish chieftain Hinguar.[32] He chose to claim sanctity for Edmund by portraying him as a martyr who embraced death by giving up his arms and refusing to submit to the demands of the victorious barbarians – even though earlier traditions did not preclude the possibility that Edmund had died in battle.[33] Although the work was undertaken at the request of English monks and Abbo had gathered his material while in England, Marco Mostert has argued that he did not actually compose it until after his return to Fleury in 987.[34] Abbo's

---

[29] Lemarignier 1977, pp. 361–2.
[30] I am grateful to Thomas Bisson of Harvard University, who proposed this phrase as a useful understanding of the problems of the early Capetian period in a paper soon to be published.
[31] A number of scholars have provided a much fuller reading of Abbo's programme. See Lemarignier 1950, pp. 303–7, 1957, pp. 384–6, and 1977, pp. 359–70, on the problem of exemption; Constable 1964, pp. 80–1, 84, 147, and 165, on that of ecclesiastical revenue; Batany 1975 and Duby 1980, pp. 87–92, on Abbo's contribution to the idea of threefold division of society; Mostert 1987 on his 'political theology'.
[32] On this work, see particularly Cousin 1954, pp. 69–72; Folz 1978, pp. 227–30; Gransden 1985, pp. 3–9; Mostert 1987, pp. 40–5; Ridyard 1988, pp. 211–14.
[33] Whitelock 1970, pp. 217–18; Folz 1987, pp. 226–8; Gransden 1985, p. 2.
[34] Mostert 1987, p. 45. The work was dedicated to Archbishop Dunstan of Canterbury, who died on 19 May 988, and thus it may still predate Abbo's election to the office of abbot.

chief purposes were to prove the king's sanctity and to discuss the origin of the shrine of his relics, which was to become the important abbey of Bury St Edmunds.[35] Thus this work fits the definition proposed here of 'local hagiography', but within an English context. Edmund was a saint of a type very different from the 'fathers' of the Orléanais and there is no indication that his feast was ever celebrated at Abbo's home. In the midst of the local concerns of his text, however, Abbo laid the groundwork for his future discussion of kingship.

The choice to portray Edmund as a martyr allowed Abbo to focus almost exclusively on the circumstances of the Danish invasion, the king's death and dismemberment, the miraculous rejoining of his head to his body, and the subsequent internment of the relics. Whereas a bishop such as Anianus or an abbot such as Maximinus imitated Christ during the course of their lives through their teaching, their asceticism, and most importantly through their miracles, martyrs imitated Christ most clearly and poignantly in their own deaths.[36] The king need not have performed miracles or otherwise exhibited unusual holiness during his life. Edmund had been, according to Abbo, a model king: 'He tempered the cunning of the shrewd serpent with the gentleness of the simple dove.'[37] He was famed both for being a humble man who exhibited liberality to the poor and for being a skilled warrior whose abilities forced the Danes to use strategic ruses.[38] There was no suggestion, however, that he would have been considered a saint in the absence of a heroic death. In Abbo's words, 'from his boyhood he grasped the ladder of virtue which divine piety knew beforehand he would complete in martyrdom'.[39]

---

[35] For a discussion of these later developments, see Whitelock 1970; Gransden 1975; Ridyard 1988, pp. 211–33.

[36] An extraordinary example of how the paradigm of Christ could be used to portray the lives of the saints, in particular that of a martyr, comes from a twelfth-century manuscript of the *Vita s. Edmundi*, probably from Bury St Edmunds and now in the Pierpont Morgan Library (Morgan 736). It contains thirty-two full-page miniatures illustrating the passion of the saint. The paintings appear to be based on a series of scenes of Christ's passion. Wormald (1952–3, pp. 251 and 260–1) provides pictures of a strikingly similar pair of flagellation scenes, one of Edmund from Morgan 736 and the other of Christ from the St Alban's Psalter (see the plates between pp. 252–3).

[37] Abbo of Fleury, *Vita s. Edmundi*, c. 4, p. 71. The phrase, a common *topos*, is an adaptation of Jesus' advice to his disciples in Matthew 10:16: 'Be therefore wise as serpents and simple as doves.'   [38] Abbo of Fleury, *Vita s. Edmundi*, c. 4, p. 71; c. 6, p. 73.

[39] Abbo of Fleury, *Vita s. Edmundi*, c. 3, p. 70.

To be sure, Edmund was an unusual, and particularly Anglo-Saxon, form of martyr. He had been killed by pagans, as had the martyrs of Christian antiquity, but not for professing faith in Christ. A number of murdered Anglo-Saxon royal and episcopal figures were venerated as saints in pre-Conquest England.[40] They had died, frequently at the hands of fellow Christians, for reasons other than holding the Christian faith. A century later Archbishop Lanfranc of Canterbury was thus reported by Eadmer to question the sanctity of his predecessor Ælfheah:

This man they not only number among the saints, but even among the martyrs, although they do not deny that he was killed, not for professing the name of Christ, but because he refused to buy himself off with money. For – to use the words of the English themselves – when his foes, the pagan enemies of God, had captured him, out of respect for his dignity they gave him the possibility of buying himself off, and demanded in return an immense sum of money from him. But since he could only have obtained this by despoiling his own men and possibly reducing some of them to a wretched state of beggary, he preferred to lose his life, rather than to keep it on such conditions.

This description almost exactly fits the case of Edmund. In response Anselm, then abbot of Bec and later Lanfranc's successor, replied that Ælfheah was a saint in that he had gone beyond simple confession of faith to meet the responsibilities of his episcopal office and thus his duties to Christ. According to Eadmer, Anselm thus convinced Lanfranc that he should not hinder the veneration of Ælfheah's relics.[41]

Abbo seemed almost to foreshadow Anselm's reasoning by implying that Edmund's death was a martyrdom because in it he fulfilled his royal office and thus proved his faith in Christ. That office had been conferred by a combination of both birth and election. The first was a necessary precondition, but a king had to have the consent of his subjects to rule: 'Born to kingly ancestors . . .

---

[40] Rollason 1985. On a different group of saints who were considered martyrs although they were neither persecuted nor killed by pagans, the Cordoban martyrs, see Wolf 1988, particularly pp. 86–104.

[41] Eadmer of Canterbury, *Vita s. Anselmi*, I.30, pp. 50–4. Guibert of Nogent (*De pignoribus sanctorum*, I.I, cols. 614D–15A) later approvingly cited Lanfranc's scepticism with no notice of Anselm's defence of Ælfheah's sanctity. The Normans have sometimes been seen as generally opposed to Anglo-Saxon saints. For a useful corrective to this view, see Ridyard 1988.

[Edmund] was, by the unanimous favour of all his fellow provincials, not so much elected in succession of birth as forced to rule over them with the authority of the sceptre.'[42] Abbo detailed the duties of kingship in two speeches placed in Edmund's mouth, the first to a bishop who advised capitulation to the Danes, the second to the Danes themselves. As he reminded his episcopal adviser, the kingly office was a sacred one conferred by holy unction (*sanctificatus chrismatis perunctione*) no less than three times: baptism, confirmation, and the royal election. The king himself – as king and not as saintly martyr – thus formed a connection between heaven and earth. Edmund acknowledged that he had been unable to protect the lives and properties of his *fideles*, and so now had no wish to outlive them: 'It is proper for me to die for my fatherland.' Later, addressing Hinguar's messenger, he claimed to be 'unarmed according to the teachings of Christ'. Thus the king became in his last moments monk-like, but that transformation did not diminish his royal virtues, it only served to enhance his saintly ones. Edmund resolutely refused, however, the 'serf-like' (*servilis*) path of compliance in the Danish violence and theft by which he would have become 'something less than a king' (*rex diminutus*). Having failed to protect his subjects' liberty by force of arms, he must now suffer the consequences of being their sacred protector, 'For it is more proper to defend liberty without ceasing, if not by arms, then at least by speech.' Thus he must die – in Abbo's words 'become a standard-bearer in the camp of the eternal king' – in order to uphold the honour of his office and his sacred duties. Edmund's martyrdom thus became a defence of the office of kingship and speech about liberty – that is a kind of law – over force of arms. He died being faithful to his office.[43]

Abbo in a sense anticipated the famous words which the aging Bishop Adalbero of Laon was to address to Robert the Pious some forty years later, 'Although first among Franks, you are a serf (*servus*) in the order of kings.'[44] It was just such servile status that Edmund had shunned. Abbo well recognized the crisis of fidelity which racked the early Capetian realm. He was to remark, as he stood at his priory of La Réole in Gascony, 'I am more powerful

---

[42] Abbo of Fleury, *Vita s. Edmundi*, c. 3, p. 70. The word used by Abbo for 'fellow provincials' is *comprovinciales*, a word frequently used by a metropolitan bishop of his suffragans.   [43] Abbo of Fleury, *Vita s. Edmundi*, cc. 8–9, pp. 74–8.
[44] Adalbero of Laon, *Poème au roi Robert*, line 390, p. 30.

than our lord the king of the Franks in these lands where no one fears his rule.'[45] In a society in which secular lords and even bishops brought out their troops to invade the properties of unarmed subjects, the abbot keenly wished that his monarch would keep faith with his sacred office and those *fideles* whom he had been elected to protect, most particularly the unarmed monks of Fleury. Abbo had witnessed first-hand the growing power of those armed men known generically as *milites*. Their increased power and pretensions had led to widespread feuding and fostered a society in which violence was seemingly endemic. The buying and selling of both churches and ecclesiastical offices, which was promoted by both the lay and ecclesiastical nobility, led to the alienation of church properties and rights. Those who stood 'unarmed according to the teachings of Christ' – either by choice, as Edmund, or by canonical requirement, as the monks of Fleury – had to place trust in rule by law, or at the very least by royal command, over rule by force of arms. Saintly patronage, like the Carolingian royal privileges, would not by itself suffice.

In the years following his election, Abbo came into frequent, open, and bitter conflict with his bishop, Arnulf. The first occasion was the trial of another Arnulf, the archbishop of Reims, for treason, which was held at the church of Saint-Basle-de-Verzy in June 991. Speaking for the prosecution, Arnulf of Orléans argued that such an episcopal council did indeed have the authority to depose a bishop in a matter of treason. A number of abbots and schoolmasters, Abbo prominent among them, stood up to claim that only the pope could perform such an action. Like Arnulf they cited canonical and patristic texts which they had brought with them to the proceedings. The defence of Arnulf of Reims was ultimately unsuccessful. He was deposed and replaced by Gerbert, an act which caused a serious rift between Pope John XV and Hugh Capet.[46] Although he had opposed the royal cause at Saint-Basle, Abbo was able, in a court case some two years later, to secure Hugh Capet's defence of specific properties belonging to Fleury which were located near the castle of Yèvre. The castellan, yet another man named Arnulf who was a nephew of the bishop of Orléans,

---

[45] Aimo of Fleury, *Vita s. Abbonis*, c. 20, p. 54.

[46] Gerbert of Reims, *Acta concilii Remenensis*, pp. 666–71; Richer, *Histoire de France*, IV.66–8, pp. 254–7. See also Lot 1903, pp. 31–81; Cousin 1954, pp. 113–18; Mostert 1987, pp. 46–8.

seized power as the lay vicar of Fleury's possessions and enacted certain *malae consuetudines*.[47] He thus attempted to institute a form of lay lordship, or 'seigneurie banale'. Hugh reversed the castellan's actions, although he required Fleury to provide Arnulf a small amount of wine each year in recompense. In this manner the royal defence of monastic property became less theoretical.[48] So, too, did episcopal pressure. About this same time, armed retainers of Bishop Arnulf prevented Abbo from journeying to Tours in order to celebrate the feast of St Martin. They insulted the abbot and almost wounded some members of his suite.[49]

Before Lent 994 an episcopal council was held at the abbey of Saint-Denis on the subject of tithes and the conflicting episcopal and monastic claims to such revenues. When it became known that the bishops were discussing the possible usurpation of monastic revenues, the local populace, who were indirectly dependent on such revenues, rioted and chased the gathered prelates to the walls of Paris. Thoroughly angered, the bishops found a convenient scapegoat in Abbo, whom they had regarded as a troublemaker since Saint-Basle.[50] In response to their accusations, Abbo composed his *Apology to Kings Hugh and Robert*. In that work he vigorously defended monastic rights against episcopal and secular interference by citing patristic and conciliar sources. Abbo was spectacularly successful; he succeeded in reversing royal opinion and placed Gerbert and Arnulf on the defensive.[51] The degree of Abbo's success can be gauged from the bitterness of Arnulf's written response.[52]

The following years were busy ones for Abbo. In the autumn of 994 he journeyed to Rome on behalf of Hugh Capet in order to seek reconciliation on the matter of the archbishopric of Reims. Two years later, after the deaths of both Hugh Capet and Pope John XV, Abbo again set off for Rome, this time as a representative of Robert the Pious to Gregory V. He sought not only an end to

[47] On the usages of the word *consuetudines* during this period, see Lemarignier 1951.
[48] *Recueil des chartes de Saint-Benoît*, no. 70, I, 182–5; Lemarignier (1977, pp. 363–4) has stressed the novelty of Hugh's action.
[49] Aimo of Fleury, *Vita s. Abbonis*, c. 8, p. 42.
[50] Aimo of Fleury, *Vita s. Abbonis*, c. 9, pp. 43–4; Gerbert of Reims, *Epistolae*, no. 209, p. 251. See also Pfister 1885, p. 315; Lot 1903, p. 88 n. 1; Lemarignier 1950, pp. 307–8; Cousin 1954, pp. 132–4; Constable 1964, pp. 79–80; Mostert 1987, pp. 48–9.
[51] Gerbert of Reims, *Epistolae*, no. 190, pp. 227–9.
[52] The only manuscript of Arnulf's *De cartiligene* is incomplete. For the extant text, see Lauer 1898, pp. 493–4. On Gerbert's attitude toward the ideas of Abbo, see Lot 1903, pp. 149–57.

the controversy over the bishopric of Reims, but also to secure a dispensation so that Robert could marry Bertha, the widow of Count Odo I of Blois.[53] Successful in the former case and not the latter, Abbo also scored a spectacular coup on behalf of the community of Fleury by successfully urging the pope to grant a sweeping set of privileges to the monastery. In the charter, which was not issued until the following year, Gregory V declared that the abbot of Fleury was 'first among the abbots of Gaul' and could be judged only by a provincial council or by the papal court.[54] Thus the possessions of the monastery were guarded against the interference of any local ecclesiastical power or court. The almost extravagant language of the act was borrowed in part from a bull – attributed to Gregory IV – which had been earlier forged by Abbo, or at least under his direction.[55] As a result of the charter Fleury gained, in theory at least, virtually complete independence from its bishop. The community now had its rights defended against bishops and castellans by both papal and royal authority. It would be another year or two before Odilo – the man dubbed 'king' of Cluny by Adalbero of Laon – secured a somewhat more extensive guarantee of the rights of his community.[56]

Over these same years Abbo gathered together a *Collection of Canons* – that is patristic and conciliar passages – which concerned royal, episcopal, and abbatial power, as well as a letter to an unidentified 'G' which contained similar material specifically related to episcopal–monastic relations.[57] Taken together with his *Apology*, these works formed an impressive attempt 'to defend liberty . . . by speech' – to use Abbo's own phrase from the *Vita s. Edmundi* – that is an attempt to define an appeal to law. According to extant accounts Abbo read from similar collections of passages at the Councils of Saint-Basle and Saint-Denis, as well as in his

[53] Aimo of Fleury, *Vita s. Abbonis*, c. 11, pp. 47–8; Mostert 1987, p. 55; Moehs 1972, pp. 44–52 and 55–7.
[54] *Recueil des chartes de Saint-Benoît*, no. 71, I, 187; Jaffé–Wattenbach, no. 3872. For a new edition, see *Papsturkunden 896–1046*, II, 655–7. On this work, see particularly Lot 1903, p. 275; Lemarignier 1950, pp. 303–5, 1962, pp. 56–7, and 1977, p. 367; Mostert 1987, pp. 57–9. Those scholars have defended the bull against all earlier suspicions as to its authenticity.
[55] *Recueil des chartes de Saint-Benoît*, no. 18, I, 39–43; Mostert 1987, pp. 57–8.
[56] On the relationship of Abbo's work to Cluny's rights, see Lemarignier 1950, pp. 301–15, and Cowdrey 1970a, pp. 19–36.
[57] Abbo of Fleury, *Collectio canonum*, cols. 473–4, and *Epistolae*, no. 14, cols. 440–60. On the date of these works, see respectively Mostert 1987, pp. 52–3, and Lemarignier 1962, p. 56. As Constable (1964, p. 81 n. 2) emphasizes, the identity of 'G' remains uncertain.

conversations with Gregory V. Around the year 1000 such collection and citation of passages culled from the works of the 'fathers' and the acts of ancient kings and popes essentially constituted canon law.

For Abbo the monastic *ordo* was at the summit of the social hierarchy, above the clerical and the lay *ordines*. Monks and clerics should ideally work with one another, complementary as Mary to Martha, for the good of the whole church. Monks must ideally live 'by the alms of good men and the labour of their own hands'.[58] In fact, however, monks were subject to attack from both the other orders, whose members attempted to wrest these very alms from monastic control. Bishops and priests engaged in the heretical practice of simony.[59] Because of this heresy clerics gave church property 'to *milites* as gifts or dispersed it as benefices' and thus 'ecclesiastical oblations do more good for the horses and dogs of laymen than they do for pilgrims, orphans, and widows, or even for the restoration of churches'.[60] The laity themselves were also directly at fault. 'Those who are these days called defenders of churches defend for themselves that which by law (*ius*) belongs to the church against the authority of laws (*leges*) and canons. Thus inflicting violence on clerics and monks, they rob the property of churches and monasteries for their own use and profit.' They thus deprive the monks of that which has been given 'by the alms of good men'.[61] Abbo seems to have grasped how the familial relationships of those clerics still in the world could influence their dispersal of church property. One of the proofs of the moral superiority of monks and nuns was their virginity; hence he strongly urged episcopal and even clerical celibacy in anticipation of later reform movements.[62]

Abbo often compared his opponents to heretics of the ancient church.[63] In his eyes lay attempts to control church property and

---

[58] Abbo of Fleury, *Apologeticus*, cols. 463A–5A. See also Batany 1975, pp. 15–16, and Duby 1980, pp. 89–90. [59] Abbo of Fleury, *Apologeticus*, cols. 466C–8B.

[60] Abbo of Fleury, *Epistolae*, no. 14, cols. 440D–1A. See also *Collectio canonum*, c. 13, cols. 483C–4A; Constable 1964, p. 81; Lemarignier 1977, pp. 365–9; Mostert 1987, pp. 95–6.

[61] Abbo of Fleury, *Collectio canonum*, c. 2, cols. 476D–7A. The repetition of the phrase from the *Apologeticus* (col. 464D) is significant.

[62] Abbo of Fleury, *Vita s. Edmundi*, c. 17, pp. 86–7; *Apologeticus*, cols. 463B–C; *Epistolae*, no. 14, cols. 452A–B, 455A–B, and 454C; *Collectio canonum*, c. 32, cols. 491D–2D, and c. 40, col. 496B.

[63] See, for example, Abbo of Fleury, *Apologeticus*, cols. 462D–3A and 467B; *Epitome de XCI Romanorum pontificum vitis*, cc. 36–8, cols. 541C–2B; *Collectio canonum*, c. 3, col. 477C.

episcopal attempts to restrict monastic rights were heretical, as being contrary to the good order of the church. The monks of Fleury were greatly concerned about such heresy. The tenth-century customs of the community specified that the *armarius* – an office once held by Abbo – was responsible for the 'refutation of heretics'.[64] Later monks of Fleury combed a copy of the *Registrum* of Gregory the Great in the library at Fleury for references to heretics from the early church.[65] Their concern in this offensive against perceived heresy was not so much with doctrine as with the defence of monastic property and rights.

Charges of moral misconduct bordering on heresy and the reforms recommended for its amelioration were not abstractions to Abbo. The words he used in the *Collection of Canons* could easily have been applied directly to the actions of Arnulf of Orléans and his nephew Arnulf of Yèvre against the monks of Fleury. It was to condemn such enemies that Abbo brought together his collections of authoritative passages and read out from them at church councils. He wished to show that the *gravis contumelia* inflicted on him when his bishop prevented him from journeying to Tours and the *malae consuetudines* enacted by the lay vicar of Yèvre were against *auctoritas legum et canonum*.[66] In that phrase Abbo would seem to distinguish secular from ecclesiastical law. Indeed Abbo quoted many capitularies of the Carolingian monarchs, as well as some Roman law, in addition to standard ecclesiastical citations. Thus he was able to demonstrate that an enemy of monastic rights was not just a 'thief of property', but a 'perverter of laws' as well.[67] Through assiduous scholarship Abbo had filled an important gap in Fleury's defences.[68]

---

[64] *Consuetudines Floriacenses*, p. 17.

[65] Mostert 1987, pp. 72–3, particularly nn. 31 and 39. The interest in Jews might be explained by the almost contemporary charges against the Jewish community of Orléans (Rodulphus Glaber, *Historiarum libri quinque*, III.7.25, pp. 136–7) concerning their responsibility for the burning of the Holy Sepulchre.

[66] The quoted phrases come from Aimo of Fleury, *Vita s. Abbonis*, c. 8, p. 42; *Recueil des chartes de Saint-Benoît*, no. 70, I, 183–4; Abbo of Fleury, *Collectio canonum*, c. 2, col. 476D.

[67] 'Quis rerum extortor legumque contortor funiculos ecclesiasticae haereditatis miscendo confundere praesumat'. Abbo of Fleury, *Apologeticus*, col. 461D. See also Mostert 1987, p. 116.

[68] As Aimo later remarked (*Vita s. Abbonis*, c. 7, p. 42) of another, now lost, work, that his learned abbot had 'extracted passages from the authority of many fathers ... in order that he have in hand defences against the bishop of the church of Orléans, who had required certain things from him unjustly'. On the question of this lost dossier, see Lemarignier 1950, p. 303, and Mostert 1987, pp. 58, 65, and 70–1.

If a defence of monastic property by law was to work, if bishops
like Arnulf of Orléans and castellans like Arnulf of Yèvre were to
be prevented from repeating their past misconduct, there had to be
a functioning legal system, or, perhaps more accurately, systems.
Thus Abbo was also at pains in his canonical works to define the
royal office according to the ideal adumbrated in the *Vita s.
Edmundi.*[69] The abbot addressed both his *Apology* and his
Collection of Canons to his sovereigns. He described the *Collection*
as being specifically 'for the defence of the monastic order',[70]
Royal authority was a necessary complement to papal authority in
defending the church.[71]

The qualifications which Abbo outlined for kingship have great
interest. Royal blood was a necessary qualification.[72] It was
election, however, which conferred sacred authority upon the king
and required his *fideles* to obey his commands. Abbo also discussed
the importance of unction to this process in the *Vita s. Edmundi*.
Thus a king was like a bishop or abbot, chosen by his fellows and by
God both to rule and to serve. Abbo's ideal king Edmund had even
been celibate. Thus bishops and the lay *primores* of the kingdom
had to show faith in and fidelity to their sovereign.[73] Monastic
authorities had to obey the king: 'If it is canonical, we follow it; if it
is truly not canonical, we suffer it in as much as we are able to
without sin.'[74] In return for this obedience, the king was expected
to enforce the laws, even, as was true in the case of Edmund, to the
point of death. Thus the king of the Franks might be called upon –
as he was in the case of Yèvre – to discipline those very bishops and
lay defenders of the church who constituted the royal retinue.
Abbo had made an important distinction between office and office-
holder. In doing so he had made the holder of the royal office an
executor of divine will, not unlike a bishop, or abbot. By outlining
such a system of rule by *fidelitas* rather than by force of arms, Abbo

---

69 For a far more detailed, and perhaps overly systematic, analysis of this question, see
   Mostert 1987, pp. 135–56.
70 Abbo of Fleury, *Apologeticus*, cols. 461B and 470D; *Collectio canonum*, preface, cols.
   473A–4A.
71 Abbo of Fleury, *Apologeticus*, cols. 467C–D; Aimo of Fleury (quoting a lost letter of
   Abbo), *Vita s. Abbonis*, c. 10, p. 45.
72 Abbo of Fleury, *Vita s. Edmundi*, c. 3, p. 70; *Apologeticus*, col. 470D; *Collectio canonum*, c.
   3, col. 477C. Abbo used the same quotation from Horace ('atauis regibus aeditus' = *Odes*
   1.1.1) to describe both Edmund of East Anglia and Robert the Pious.
73 Abbo of Fleury, *Vita s. Edmundi*, c. 3, p. 70; *Collectio canonum*, c. 4, cols. 478A–9A.
74 Abbo of Fleury, *Collectio canonum*, c. 42, col. 497B. Note that this is said equally of
   obedience to imperial (or here royal) and episcopal authority.

attempted to give added weight to the royal and papal guarantees of Fleury's independence which he and his predecessors had so carefully gathered.

Abbo's efforts in this direction did not mean that he and his fellow monks had turned away from the traditional patronage offered by their 'father' Benedict. His student Aimo composed a miracle collection shortly after the abbot's death.[75] According to Aimo, the abbot once attributed to the power of Benedict the death of a laymen who lied in the midst of a property dispute with Fleury. He was quite willing to accept that the saint might intervene in the manner of an ordeal when someone tried to alienate property which, after all, belonged to that patron.[76] Aimo also made it clear that the monks of Saint-Benoît-du-Sault, a priory of Fleury located in the Limousin, had to rely on the power of armed men fighting under the miraculous protection of Benedict, rather than on recourse to the voice of law, in order to protect their lands.[77]

The varied defences provided by king, pope, and patron saint could not always protect monks against attacks. Abbo died at Fleury's priory of La Réole from wounds suffered in an armed scuffle between the local Gascon monks and the abbot's party of Franks who had come to enforce monastic discipline. Shortly thereafter Abbo's student and friend Aimo composed the *Vita et miracula s. Abbonis* which portrayed the abbot's death as a martyrdom. The community of Fleury came to celebrate a feast in the abbot's honour (13 November), although he was buried at La Réole and the posthumous miracles associated with him occurred there.[78] Abbo's sanctity was attested by later writers at Fleury and elsewhere.[79] The idea that an important abbot of a community, other than its 'father' or patron, could enjoy a reputation for sanctity was no novelty in the Orléanais. Fleury celebrated a feast for Abbot Mummolus and a reliquary of the Merovingian period has been discovered with his name etched in the top.[80] Letaldus

[75] *Miracula s. Benedicti*, III.19, p. 166.
[76] *Miracula s. Benedicti*, III.10, pp. 153–4.   [77] *Miracula s. Benedicti*, III.5, pp. 135–42.
[78] Paris, nouvelle acquisition latine, 7299, fo. 8v; Orléans, BM 322, fo. 8; Orléans, BM 123, fo. F; Trier, Seminarbibliothek 187, fo. 7; Orléans, BM 125, fo. 243.
[79] *Miracula s. Benedicti*, v.6, p. 202, and VII.13, p. 270; Rodulfus Glaber, *Historiarum libri quinque*, III.3.11, pp. 112–13; Ademar of Chabannes, *Chronicon*, III.39, p. 161.
[80] Orléans, BM 129, fo. 241v. The reliquary has been published in Berland 1980b, pp. 69–70. On the discovery of the reliquary in 1642, see p. 61. Cf. Cousin 1954, pp. 172–3, particularly n. 2.

noted that the body of Abbot Anno of Micy was found to be incorrupt – a traditional sign of sanctity also noted by Abbo of Edmund – when it was removed from its coffin twelve years after his death.[81] What was novel was that Aimo chose to compose a life of his murdered abbot.

Aimo was aware that his hero did not fit traditional models of sanctity:

If however someone therefore should believe that it detracts from him that [Abbo] hardly performed any miraculous sign in his life, let him read the lives of the most excellent teachers, Augustine and Jerome, and he will find the things to be praised in them not prodigies of temporal signs, which the wicked can often perform, but purity of life, eloquence of sound doctrine, and constancy in faith.[82]

Abbo's life had been a dutiful and holy practice of the monastic rule, but was hardly marked by exceptional events. Aimo was able to tell only two stories which might even be construed as miraculous. A monk suffering from leprosy came to the abbot in the belief that the learned man might cure him. Abbo washed his limbs in blessed water and told the monk that only his faith in God would provide a cure.[83] Aimo also tentatively implied that Abbo's companions in a boat crossing to England were saved from a storm by his presence and prayers.[84]

In place of miracle stories, Aimo made the first two-thirds of his work into a virtual *florilegium* of passages culled from Abbo's writings, particularly from the *Apology* and his letters. These include key passages on the canonical justification of papal jurisdiction over bishops and on the sin of simony.[85] The reader would also learn of Abbo's defence of monastic rights at Saint-Basle, Saint-Denis, at the papal and royal courts, and in other disputes. Indeed it does not seem that Aimo intended the bulk of this life for public use as a *lectio*, for it was the posthumous miracle stories which were used in the liturgy on Abbo's feast.[86] Thus Aimo charted how Abbo over the course of his career as an author defined the duties of the abbatial, as well as the royal and episcopal, offices in the protection of monastic property. He noted that one canonical dossier compiled by Abbo was no longer able to be

---

[81] Letaldus of Micy, *Miracula s. Maximini*, c. 39, p. 609.
[82] Aimo of Fleury, *Vita s. Abbonis*, preface, p. 38.
[83] Aimo of Fleury, *Vita s. Abbonis*, c. 14, pp. 50–1.
[84] Aimo of Fleury, *Vita s. Abbonis*, c. 4, p. 40.
[85] Aimo of Fleury, *Vita s. Abbonis*, cc. 8–9, pp. 42–4, and c. 10, pp. 45–7.
[86] *Consuetudines Floriacenses*, p. 252.

found in the library at Fleury.[87] In this light, Aimo's own compilation of extracts from Abbo's works seems virtually a practical necessity.

In order to portray Abbo as a martyr, and thus as a saint, Aimo used the model of Abbo's own *Vita s. Edmundi*. The hagiographer even described the abbot as a man who 'combined the simplicity of a dove with the cunning of a serpent', a *topos* earlier used by Abbo to describe Edmund.[88] Abbo's death, like that of Edmund, became a fulfilment of the duties of his office as expounded over the earlier course both of Aimo's work and of Abbo's own life. The narration of Abbo's fateful trip to La Réole occupied the final third of Aimo's work. The hagiographer himself was one of three monks, and apparently a number of servants as well, who accompanied the abbot. He described the journey in extraordinary detail, describing each stage of the trip south, including a stop at the *villa* called 'Ad Francos' which belonged to the author's parents.[89] The journey was into a foreign country. Aimo, himself a native of the Aquitaine, consistently identified his party as Franks in distinction to the 'barbarous' Gascons.

The purpose of the visit was to reestablish monastic discipline. The rule was indeed laxly observed at La Réole: there was a group of women who lived outside the monastic enclosure who appear to have been the wives or concubines of some of the monks.[90] On the second day after the party arrived, Abbo chastised a member of the community for leaving the monastery without his abbatial permission. That monk left the building and began loudly to stir up resentment among his fellows, who surrounded some of the Franks. When one of the visitors struck a Gascon with a staff, a riot broke out. Abbo, who was engaged in correcting some *computus* tables within the monastic enclosure, came out and tried to seek the safety of the guesthouse up the hill. One of the Gascons struck him with a lance. He was brought to the guesthouse and then sent Aimo back into the fray to calm the situation. By the time the Gascons

---

[87] Aimo of Fleury, *Vita s. Abbonis*, c. 7, p. 42.

[88] 'Inerat ei columbina simplicitas serpentinae copulata astutiae, ut et per mansuetudinem leniret benivolos'. Aimo of Fleury, *Vita s. Abbonis*, c. 2, p. 39. Compare 'Siquidem ita columbinae simplicitatis mansuetudine temperauit serpentinae calliditatis astutiam'. Abbo of Fleury, *Vita s. Edmundi*, c. 4, p. 71. The language is adapted from Matthew 10:16, see above, n. 36.   [89] Aimo of Fleury, *Vita s. Abbonis*, c. 18, p. 53.

[90] Aimo latinized the Gascon name of the place as *Regula*. The irony was perhaps intentional, as Ademar of Chabannes (*Chronicon*, III.39, p. 161) later used the more elaborate *Regulatense*.

had dispersed, however, Abbo had died. The terrified Franks were left in possession of the monastery by the monks. There they buried their dead, tended their wounded, and set off some days later for home under the protection of the local viscount.[91]

The blow from which Abbo died was a random one struck in the heat of combat. His assailant was a Christian monk. Aimo claimed martyrdom for him, however, by following the same logic which Abbo had used concerning Edmund. The Gascons were engaged in what Aimo perceived to be a conspiracy against abbatial authority. Abbo died because he had exercised that authority. Moments before his death he had been peacefully engaged in the sort of activity which had characterized his career as scholar and reformer. Earlier in the journey he had encouraged William V (c. 993–c. 1030), duke of the Aquitaine, to protect the possessions of the monastery of Salx against its lay *advocati* and defended an abbot against attacks by his own monks.[92] Aimo was aware that this claim of martyrdom could have been controversial: '[Abbo] did not convert men from the cult of idols, but he laboured to free men from servitude to vice, a task which is greater.'[93] The hagiographer backed up his claim of sanctity – as Abbo had in the case of Edmund – by including posthumous miracles, four of which occurred in the week between Abbo's burial and the departure of his companions for Fleury.[94] The title of martyr was generally accepted, for Rodulfus Glaber applied it to Abbo some years later.[95]

Aimo in effect made Abbo himself an example of Abbo's own ideal formulation of the office of abbot. He also composed a work now lost on the abbots of Fleury which may well have been an extended development of this ideal as found in the history of his community.[96] He certainly elaborated on the office of king in his *History of the Franks*, the first work to describe fully the story of the holy oil with which Clovis was anointed. Thus he laid a claim to the traditional importance of unction for the rulership of the Franks.[97] He emphasized the elective nature of Hugh Capet's accession in accord with Abbo's *Collection of Canons* and

[91] Aimo of Fleury, *Vita s. Abbonis*, c. 20, pp. 54–6.
[92] Aimo of Fleury, *Vita s. Abbonis*, cc. 17–18, p. 52–3.
[93] Aimo of Fleury, *Vita s. Abbonis*, preface, p. 37.
[94] Aimo of Fleury, *Miracula s. Abbonis*, cc. 1–4, pp. 57–8.
[95] Rodulphus Glaber, *Historiarum libri quinque*, III.3.11, pp. 112–13.
[96] *Miracula s. Benedicti*, v.6, p. 202.
[97] Aimo of Fleury, *Historiae francorum*, 1.16, cols. 654–5; Lemarignier 1955, pp. 10–11.

description of Edmund.[98] Aimo also was the first monk of Fleury in over a century to collect together the stories of miracles which exhibited the *patrocinium* of the community's 'father'. Over the first years of the eleventh century, this monk composed an ambitious cycle of works which detailed the various forms of patronage – personal and legal, sacred and secular – which could protect his community.

The years 1003–4, like those of 985–8, marked the end of a generation in the struggles for power in the Orléanais. Abbo's sudden death came only a year after the deaths of his long-time opponents Bishop Arnulf and Gerbert of Reims, who had since become pope. Three powerful men passed from the scene. Moreover, Robert the Pious repudiated, for a time, his canonically unacceptable marriage to Bertha of Burgundy and thus ended his rapprochement with the counts of Blois at almost the same time.[99] Letaldus of Micy, for one, appreciated the significance of these changes. He chose early 1004 to lead the monks of Micy to the newly installed Bishop Fulk in order to seek the expulsion of Abbot Robert of Blois. Ironically it was Abbo – the man who had once supported Letaldus against the attacks of Bishop Arnulf which were done 'without any legality' – who now condemned his efforts as being 'against the authority of canons'.[100] Once again Abbo's language in concrete situations echoed that of his more theoretical works. The principles of law, both those of secular society and the canons of the church, had become, largely through Abbo's own efforts, crucial to the exercise of ecclesiastical authority within the Orléanais.

THE LEGACY OF ABBO AND ARNULF

Two new antagonists now came on the scene, Bishop Fulk of Orléans and Abbot Gauzlin of Fleury. Fulk's exact origins remain obscure, although he appears to have been an intimate of Bishop Arnulf.[101] According to Andrew of Fleury, Gauzlin came 'from

---

[98] *Miracula s. Benedicti*, III.1, p. 127.

[99] Guillot 1972, I, 25–6. Cf. Pfister 1885, pp. 60–1 n. 3.

[100] Abbo of Fleury, *Apologeticus*, col. 469A, and *Epistolae*, no. 11, col. 437D.

[101] Boussard (1970, p. 178) suggests that Fulk came from the region of Beauvais. In 994, however, Gerbert of Reims (*Epistolae*, no. 190, p. 228) referred to one Fulcho as 'filius vester' in a letter to Arnulf of Orléans. While no one has suggested that this figure was the future bishop, the identification seems a likely one. The phrase could certainly have been used metaphorically.

one of the most noble lineages of Gaul' and assumed the abbacy without incident.[102] The two soon continued the conflict of Arnulf and Abbo. Fulk arrived at the monastery of Fleury on the celebration of a feast of St Benedict on 11 July, probably in 1008. He intentionally violated the privileges which Abbo had obtained from Gregory V by not first asking permission of Gauzlin. The bishop was testing the durability of those papal protections. When he entered the town which bordered the monastery, the townspeople drove him away both with blows and with invocations of the name of St Benedict. Fulk immediately appealed to his archbishop, Leothericus of Sens, a 'defender of clerics in all matters'. The archbishop convoked a council at which the monks of Fleury produced and read out a copy of Gregory's privilege. Fulk's party thereupon threatened to throw the offending document into the fire.[103] In this world, law could be as fragile as the papyrus or parchment on which it was copied.

Bishop Fulbert of Chartres – taking up the role of Gerbert of Reims in opposition to Fleury's claim of monastic rights – then wrote to Fulk and Gauzlin. He reversed the claim of the monks, by praising Fulk's resolve in upholding episcopal authority. In a manner similar to Abbo, albeit with a different purpose, Fulbert wished to elaborate a theory of law. As he wrote to Fulk, there were too few 'defenders of law' in contemporary society. The king, who ought to be the 'fountainhead of justice', was weakened by treachery. Thus the bishop ought not to worry excessively about matters pertaining to secular law, but attempt only to force the abbot of Fleury to abide by the appropriate canons (*subiectio canonica*). A few months later, Fulbert rebuked Gauzlin in similar terms, 'I cannot find a law or any manner of reasoning that might release you from the yoke of this obedience [to your bishop].'[104]

Fulbert and Fulk thus rejected as illegal the very sort of papal protection of monastic rights which had been elaborated by Abbo.

---

[102] Andrew of Fleury, *Vita Gauzlini*, c. 1, p. 33. Ademar of Chabannes (*Chronicon*, III.39, p. 161), on the other hand, described Gauzlin as the bastard son of Hugh Capet and suggested that Robert the Pious confirmed this illegitimate half-brother as abbot of Fleury over the objections of the community. There is, however, every reason to suspect Ademar as a hostile source, since Gauzlin, as archbishop of Bourges, had placed the diocese of Limoges under interdict.

[103] Andrew of Fleury, *Vita Gauzlini*, c. 18, pp. 50–3. Abbo (*Collectio canonum*, c. 15, cols. 485D–6B) had discussed the rights of an abbot to refuse his bishop entrance into the monastic enclosure. [104] Fulbert of Chartres, *Letters*, nos. 7 and 8, pp. 16–21.

Pope John XVIII, however, heard of the matter through a papal legate who had happened to attend Leothericus' council. The pope addressed separate letters to King Robert, Leothericus, Fulk, and Gauzlin supporting the cause of Fleury and expressing outrage that so little regard had been shown to papal privileges. The litigants were summoned to Rome; both Fulk and Leothericus were threatened with excommunication.[105] Such an appeal to the papal court over a local episcopal council was exactly what Abbo had envisioned. The martyred abbot and canonist emerged triumphant. The episode, however, turned Fulbert into an enemy of the community and its abbot. Shortly thereafter he opposed the appointment of Gauzlin as archbishop of Bourges.[106]

Fulk died sometime before 1013 and was succeeded by a monk from the Senonais named Theodoric.[107] Odolric, the son of the castellan of Pithiviers and nephew of Bishop Roger of Beauvais, forcibly opposed the election of the new bishop. The struggle for control of the see bitterly divided the Orléanais for some years. Ensuing events were to demonstrate that monks were not the only ones who could manipulate the patronage of the 'fathers' and the sanctity of contemporaries for their advantage. Indeed, the castellans of Pithiviers – a family who would control the see of Orléans for three generations – exhibited a canny understanding of how to use the cult of the saints to augment their prestige.

PITHIVIERS

We must, therefore, turn our attention from the abbey of Fleury to the town of Pithiviers, located 42 kilometres north-east of Orléans. It first appeared (under the name *Pedeverius*) as a *villa* in the list of episcopal possessions confirmed by Charles the Bald.[108] The earliest known members of the family were a couple named Rainard and Heloise. Odolric was their only son, although they also had a daughter named Heloise and Rainard had apparently

---

[105] Andrew of Fleury, *Vita Gauzlini*, c. 18, pp. 52–9.
[106] Fulbert of Chartres, *Letters*, no. 26, pp. 48–51.
[107] Newman 1937a, no. 53, p. 69 n. 4; *GC*, VIII, 1430–3.
[108] *Recueil des actes de Charles le Chauve*, no. 25, I, 64, and *Cartulaire de Sainte-Croix*, no. 33, p. 65. The *villa* also appeared (under the name *Petverius*) in the reconfirmation of those possessions in bulls of Leo VII (9 January 938; *Cartulaire de Sainte-Croix*, no. 19, p. 39) and Benedict VII (974–80; no. 20, p. 45).

had another son, Isembard, by a previous marriage.[109] Rainard remains an obscure figure who predeceased his wife.[110] He certainly possessed territory in the Beauce, between Orléans and Châteaudun.[111] Heloise was the sister of Bishop Roger of Beauvais, one-time chancellor of Hugh Capet.[112] On her husband's death she took control of the castle and added a strong tower.[113]

This woman, later remembered under the curious title 'duchess of Orléans' (*ducissa Aurelianensis*), oversaw her family's rise to ecclesiastical prominence.[114] She founded, 'for the salvation of the soul of her husband', a college of canons dedicated to St George.

[109] The author of the *Vita s. Gregorii Nicopolitani* (c. 7, p. 463) described Odolric as the only son of Heloise and Rainard. See also *Garin le Loheren*, lines 808–9, p. 134. Odolric, however, had a half-brother named Isembard and a sister named Heloise. Bur (1977, p. 212) has suggested, not without reason, that Isembard was Rainard's son by a previous marriage. On Isembard, see *GC*, VIII, *instrumenta* 491; Devaux 1886, pp. 119–23. Isembard sired two sons, Hugh Bardoul and (despite Bur's uncertainty) Isembard. The younger Heloise – who married Geoffrey, the viscount of Châteaudun and of Mortagne – would almost certainly have been named after her mother. On her, see *Cartulaire de Saint-Père de Chartres*, I, 400; Devaux 1886, pp. 116–17 n. 2; Lot 1889, p. 275. The younger Heloise had one son, Hugh of Mortagne. Andrew of Fleury later referred (*Miracula s. Benedicti*, VI.18, p. 244) to Hugh as Odolric's nephew. See the family tree in figure 2.

[110] The sole mention of Rainard is in the *Vita s. Gregorii Nicopolitani*, c. 7, p. 463: 'Erat autem in eodem oppido quaedam nobilis matrona, Ailuisa nomine bonae memoriae, quae et ipsa genitrix unigenitum suum, nomine Odolricum, illius videlicet oppidi haeredem, que et ipse postea Aurelianensis Ecclesiae factus est Episcopus, Patre suo Rainardo iam defuncto atque ante fores Romanae Ecclesiae sepulto; amicabiliter educabat.'

[111] According to the *Vita s. Gregorii Nicopolitani* (c. 7, p. 463) Heloise had received in dowry (*dotalitia lege*) from Rainard an allod called *Usselus*. According to a charter of 1024 (*GC*, VIII, *instrumenta* 491), Odolric and his half-brother Isembard possessed a church near Châteaudun where a serf named Hilduin was described as *casatus noster*, whose rights must have been inherited from their father. According to a charter of 1028 (*GC*, VIII, *instrumenta* 296), Odolric also possessed *in vicaria* a church in the Orléanais from his father. Rainard did not appear by name in either of these charters. See, also, Devaux 1885, p. 252.

[112] Devaux 1885, p. 253; Lot 1889, p. 275; Boussard 1970, p. 179 n. 82; Bur 1977, p. 212. The relationship is proven by a reference to Roger as the uncle of Odolric in a charter of 1028 (Newman 1937a, no. 72, p. 90). Heloise and Roger were not, as Devaux claims, the children of Count Odo I of Blois. Lot suggests that their family came from the region of Chartres.

[113] Devaux 1885, pp. 254–6; Lot 1889, pp. 275–6; Chenesseau 1931d, p. 428. Heloise's construction of the tower is reported by *Garin le Loheran* (lines 802–4, p. 134). According to Orderic Vitalis (*The Ecclesiastical History*, VIII.24, IV, 290) the architect was a man named Lanfred 'who was then famous above all other architects in France for his skill' and who later designed the famed castle of Ivry.

[114] Devaux 1886, p. 319 n. 1; Lot 1889, p. 279. She was also recorded in the *Garin le Loheran* (lines 802–9 and 2368–72, pp. 134 and 171) as the eldest daughter of Hervil of Metz, the sister of Garin of Lotharingia, and the wife of one Hernaïs of Orléans.

Their son brought Rainard's body to Rome for burial near the basilica of St Peter, presumably to be close to the graves of the martyrs.[115] For the lords of Pithiviers, as for many castellan families during this period, the new church was a means of increasing familial power, not dissimilar to the stone fortifications whose construction Heloise also undertook.[116] She obtained the relics of a saint named Laetus as a second patron for her canons. This saint's cult had first emerged during the ninth century.[117] His body was enshrined at that time in a village bearing his name, Saint-Lyé-la-Forêt, just to the north of Orléans. Bishop Ermentheus (pre-956–70), Arnulf's uncle, had caused the relics to be translated to Pithiviers, presumably at Rainard and Heloise's request.[118] The parish church of Pithiviers also contained significant relics, those of St Salomon, the martyr-king of Brittany, which probably had been translated there in the mid-tenth century.[119]

Some decades later, during Odolric's episcopacy and presumably at his request, a canon of Pithiviers composed the *Vita s. Laeti*.[120] The purpose of the text was to identify Laetus as a 'father' of the Orléanais, similar in stature to such patrons as Maximinus. The work was divided into two parts: the first nine chapters, which concerned the saint's life, were a reworking of the *Vita s. Viatoris*,

---

115 *Vita s. Gregorii Nicopolitani*, c. 7, p. 463; *Miracula ss. Georgii et Laeti*, c. 4, p. 79. The former text is corrupt, substituting the name of St Gregory for that of George. On the architecture of the church, see Chenesseau 1931d.

116 Lemarignier 1959, pp. 23–8.

117 He was mentioned in the martyrology of Usuard (*Le Martyrologe d'Usuard*, p. 336).

118 *Vita s. Laeti*, c. 10, p. 76. See also *commentarius praevius*, p. 67 n. 4, on the date of the translation. Elsewhere Poncelet (1905, p. 65) claims that the church of Saint-Lyé-la-Forêt came under the patronage of the college of canons in Pithiviers by the twelfth century. Cf. *Patron* 1870–1, I, 443.

119 *Vita s. Gregorii Nicopolitani*, c. 10, p. 464. There is no independent verification of either the veneration of these relics or the saint's liturgical commemoration in the diocese of Orléans. Salomon was a ninth-century king of Brittany who retired to the monastery of St Maxentius and was assassinated by rebellious barons in 874. On his career, see Lobineau 1725, pp. 193–204; *VSBP*, VI, 425–6; *BS*, XI, 590–1; *AASS*, June VI, pp. 248–59; Smith 1982. He was well known as a heroic character in several *chansons de geste* of the twelfth century (Borderie 1892). Since he seems to have ascended to the throne through murder, his reputation for sanctity must have been based on his later life and, in particular, on the manner of his death. No independent hagiographic account, however, of his life survives. His relics were originally kept at the abbey where he died and it is known that they left the monastery during the tenth century, but there is no account of the translation other than this source from the Orléanais. On the cult of these relics, see *VSBP* VI, 426; *BS*, XI, 591. The best general treatment of the translation of Breton saints to the middle Loire valley during the civil wars of the tenth century remains that of Plaine (1899).

120 *Vita s. Laeti*, c. 10, p. 77; *AASS*, Nov. III, *commentarius praevius*, p. 68 n. 4.

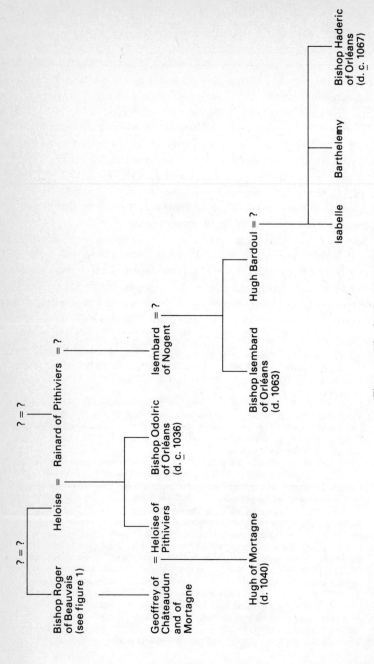

Figure 2 The family of Pithiviers

while the lengthy final chapter detailed the translation of the relics in the tenth century and a miracle later witnessed by Odolric himself.[121] The author simply intended his life to provide a plausible background to the narrative which he considered important, that is the construction of the church in Pithiviers, the translation of the relics, and a miracle observed by his bishop. By borrowing from the *Vita s. Viatoris*, the author made Laetus a man who had studied the monastic life under Maximinus at Micy and later accompanied Avitus into his eremitic exile. When Avitus was made abbot of Micy, Laetus fled further into the forest. There he constructed a hut which served as his dwelling until his death. The borrowing was so servile that the author from Pithiviers even gave *Viatoria*, the name of Viator's hermitage, as the original name for *Laogium*, the dwelling-place of Laetus. Through this adaptation, Laetus, like Viator before him, became identified as one of the eremitic saints who had been a disciple of Maximinus of Micy. Thus his stature as a 'father' of the diocese was assured.

The connection between Laetus and the abbey of Micy, which was unknown even to Letaldus in the late tenth century, may well have been provided for the first time by the author of the *Vita s. Laeti*. In the 1020s the monks of Micy became aware of the link, quite possibly through Bishop Odolric himself.[122] The traditions of that abbey simply provided convenient source material for clothing otherwise obscure saints with an aura of antiquity and authority. For their part, the monks of Micy were more than willing to adopt such newly identified 'fathers' as their own. During those same years Bishop Odolric took an active role in the promotion of the cult of Laetus. He was, for example, the source of a story of a deaf-mute who had 'frequented the dwelling of the blessed confessor [Laetus]' and was cured by the saint's help. When another boy was cured of paralysis in the same sanctuary on the feast of All Saints, the bishop gathered a crowd together to celebrate the event.[123]

In the first decades of the eleventh century, before Odolric was raised to the episcopacy, Heloise of Pithiviers was able to add a

---

121 Poncelet 1905, pp. 65–71; *AASS*, Nov. III, pp. 67–8. The only details which are changed are the name of the saint, the place to which Laetus and Avitus go to lead the eremitic life (*Laogium*, that is Saint-Lyé, for *Tremulus-vicus*, and the date of the death of the saint (5 November for 5 August).

122 *Sermo de inventione s. Maximini*, in Vatican, Reg. lat. 621, fo. 39v.

123 *Vita s. Laeti*, c. 10, pp. 77–8.

third saint – this time a living holy man – to her family's patrons. The man was Gregory, allegedly an Armenian bishop, who settled near Pithiviers as a hermit.[124] The acquisition of relics of traditional 'fathers' such as those of Laetus through a translation was not uncommon in eleventh-century Francia. The arrival of a holy man from a far-off land, however, must have seemed truly fortuitous. Although the *Vita s. Gregorii Nicopolitani* was not composed until the 1040s, well after Odolric's death, it nevertheless reveals much about the religious life of the region during his lifetime. According to the author, probably a canon of the church of St George, Gregory had been 'archbishop of the city of Nicopolis of the Armenians'.[125] The would-be saint was attracted to a religious life early, memorizing the scriptures as a boy. This *athleta Christi* demonstrated his spiritual martyrdom through fasts and bodily mortification. Recalling the gestures of the 'fathers' of the Orléanais, among them Laetus, this foreigner had become a servant of God by means of long prayer vigils in which he 'prostrated himself before the face of God with his whole body, laying on the pavement'.[126] He progressed quickly through the ranks of the clergy, becoming an exemplary archbishop, but then he decided to leave his diocese as he feared that he might fall victim to pride.

Therefore Gregory set off one night on a long journey which took him across the Alps. At length he arrived in Pithiviers, where he requested lodging from the priest charged with the care of the churches of the town. That night Gregory had a vision which told

---

[124] *Vita s. Gregorii Nicopolitani*, c. 1, p. 462, and c. 6, p. 463.

[125] *Vita s. Gregorii Nicopolitani*, c. 1, p. 462. Despite these claims, the actual origins of Gregory remain obscure. The story of his abandonment of his episcopal duties for the eremitic life is somewhat unusual. The city of Nicopolis (Le Quien 1840, I, 427–30) in Armenia Minor was founded by the Roman general Pompey after his victory over Mithridates. It grew to be an important Christian see praised by Basil of Caesarea, but it was destroyed by an earthquake in 499. The damage was irreparable and Nicopolis never regained its former stature. There are, in fact, no certain records of any bishops after the earthquake. The Latin life from Pithiviers is the only extant record of Gregory; his name does not occur in any Armenian source. Nevertheless it remains possible that Gregory had been the bishop of that see. It is also quite possible that he was an Armenian monk who was something of an imposter and falsely claimed to be the bishop of an historically important see which would have been known in the west. A third possibility, more remote, is that Gregory was in fact from a different city named Nicopolis, located in the ancient province of Thrace (*DACL*, XIV, cols. 2003–6). That city was an archbishopric until the region fell into the hands of the Bulgarians around 640, only to be restored by the Byzantine emperor Basil II in the late tenth century. The only recent commentator on the text (*VSBP*, III, 353) seems to confuse these two cities.

[126] *Vita s. Gregorii Nicopolitani*, c. 2, p. 462.

him to take up residence in a church dedicated to St Martin of Vertou which was located outside the town. His arrival occurred after the death of Rainard and before the consecration of Odolric, most likely in the first decade of the eleventh century.[127] Gregory asked Heloise, who by this time controlled the fortified town, for permission to use its church as a hermitage. She offered him instead the use of the newly constructed church of St George and St Laetus. He declined, however, citing the dictates of the vision. Heloise then gave her permission and persuaded an unnamed bishop – probably Fulk – to provide permission for the hermit to live there (*habitandi licentia*). Thus Gregory became connected not to a lineage of saints, as were Avitus and Viator when they arrived at Micy, but to the house of Pithiviers.

Gregory lived in the small church of St Martin for seven years. He was very particular about his fasting; indeed his diet was described in extraordinary detail. Four days a week Gregory ate nothing at all. On Wednesdays and Fridays he ate one meal prepared by his own hand. It was always the same, consisting of lentils which had been sprouted in water, three 'ounces' (*unciae*) of barley-bread boiled into a mash, and the roots of wild herbs. On Sundays and certain feasts he partook of a common meal, but never of meat or offal. On these occasions he invited parish and monastic priests, 'and even some lay monks', to his table where they were provided 'not only bodily food, but spiritual food as well'. Thus Gregory became a significant teacher of the religious life. These meals also became the centre of a more widely spread personal cult, for his asceticism had earned him a reputation for holiness among the local populace: 'On those days [Sundays and feasts] cityfolk and wealthy countryfolk – just about anyone who was able – sought him out in recognition of his sanctity.' Gregory preached to these uninvited guests and then blessed them, after which 'they returned home joyful'. Yet a third group – the poor – was also present and remained after the hermit's blessing, for this holy man distributed alms, probably food. At one time, while en route home, one of the peasants was afflicted by a demon whom Gregory later exorcized. This was the sole miracle explicitly attributed to Gregory during his lifetime, but the author implied that others had taken place.[128] In terms of his personal asceticism, his spiritual teaching, and his

---

127 *Vita s. Gregorii Nicopolitani*, c. 7, p. 463.
128 *Vita s. Gregorii Nicopolitani*, c. 8, p. 463.

ability to inspire crowds of laypeople, Gregory appears to have been a very early example of the eremitic revival in the west which would later include such figures as Robert of Arbrissel and Stephen of Muret.[129]

By the time of Gregory's death, he was apparently already perceived, and thus later remembered, according to the model of sanctity associated with the ancient hermits of the diocese, such as Laetus. The year of Gregory's death is uncertain, although it probably occurred in the second decade of the eleventh century; the traditional day was 16 March, which later served as his feastday.[130] The author asserted that a great crowd – 'not only from nearby, but also from far-flung regions, as many devoted laypeople as clergy' – gathered for his funeral. At first he was buried next to the altar of the church of St Martin of Vertou. Further indication of Gregory's sanctity came posthumously. He continued to gather the local populace to his side, for his body soon gained the reputation for working miracles: 'Whatever diseased person came to him, that person left that place made healthy and sound from whatever disease had afflicted him.'[131] Heloise recognized the potential of this growing cult, which seems to have had little clerical supervision. She had the saint's body translated to the church of St Salomon within the walls of Pithiviers. There miracles continued to occur, two of which the author specified: a peasant was cured of blindness after prostrating himself in prayer before the saint's tomb, while the paralysed hand of a woman was cured when she made it touch, on the suggestion of a priest, the reliquary itself.[132]

Gregory of Nicopolis was a different sort of saint from Edmund of East Anglia and Abbo of Fleury. He had a widespread reputation for miracle-working and asceticism during his lifetime. Much of the description of his life was in fact similar to the lives of those 'fathers' of the Orléanais who had themselves been hermits. Although there is no extant record of his feast having been

---

[129] Leyser 1984, particularly pp. 18–28 and 69–77; Chenu 1954.
[130] On the basis of an alternate version of the text, which dated Gregory's death specifically to a Sunday, the Bollandists (*AASS*, March II, p. 464 n. a) have suggested either 1004 or 1010, when 16 March fell on that day of the week. The passage, however, is not only of a late date, but also sounds too much like a *topos* to be given much credence.
[131] *Vita s. Gregorii Nicopolitani*, c. 9, p. 464.
[132] *Vita s. Gregorii Nicopolitani*, c. 10, p. 464.

commemorated in the diocese, the mere existence of the *Vita s. Gregorii* suggests that it was celebrated at least at Pithiviers. Certainly the shrine dedicated to him attracted pilgrims and miracles were perceived to occur there. The part played by the local laity, especially the *rustici*, in establishing both Gregory's reputation for sanctity during his life and his posthumous cult is striking. They came as uninvited guests to his Sunday repasts to receive his blessing and his alms. They came again to his funeral and later sought out his aid through his relics at both the churches of St Martin and of St Salomon. While the clergy of the region also recognized Gregory's holiness both before and after his death, there was an element of popular canonization at work in his cult. In addition to direct knowledge of recent events, the author of his life relied on stories told by people who had been present at the saint's Sunday gatherings and by his own 'relatives and friends' who had frequented his shrine. The clergy and laity who had once heard the hermit preach continued to seek out his aid and to interpret his actions long after his death.

The presence of the miracle-working relics of Laetus and Gregory brought prestige to Pithiviers and Heloise's family. The members of her clan, however, had pretensions to much greater power than the lordship of such a fortified town. When Bishop Fulk died and Theodoric, an outsider to the diocese, was imposed on the see by Leothericus of Sens and Robert the Pious, Odolric tried to seize ecclesiastical authority within the diocese and, in so doing, defy royal power. According to an author sympathetic to Theodoric, Odolric actually entered the cathedral of Orléans during the consecration ceremony bearing arms.[133] In addition, Fulbert of Chartres, who was present at the consecration as a fellow suffragan of the archbishop of Sens, refused to lay his hands on the new bishop. From his testimony it seems that Odolric was not the only one to bring weapons into Sainte-Croix that day, but that an armed mêlée between factions supporting two rival candidates had taken place.

In a letter to Theodoric, Fulbert later cited a number of reasons for his refusal, among them the fact that the candidate had been

---

[133] *Vita s. Theodorici II*, c. 2, p. 197. This author described Odolric as *quidam clericus*, while the author of the *Vita s. Gregorii Nicopolitani* (c. 6, p. 463) described Odolric as the son of Heloise of Pithiviers and the 'heir to the town' (*oppidi haeredis*).

charged with homicide. Most important, however, was the fact that his election had been carried out by 'intimidation'. Fulbert suggested that in canonical terms no true election had taken place.

> When for these reasons we did not dare to place our hands on you . . . since we would not be transgressors of the law, O sacrilegious impiety! In the very heart of holy mother church we were nearly killed by your partisans and, indeed, we were so glad to have escaped alive that our loss during the plundering which followed seems insignificant.

Like Abbo before him, but in a different cause, he gathered together the testimony of the past in his favour. In particular he cited canons of the Councils of Nicaea, Antioch, and (erroneously) Riez. He went on to criticize Theodoric for saying mass in a church which had been 'violated but not reconciled'.[134]

Opposition to Theodoric continued. Fulbert wrote to Leothericus, criticizing him for having violated canon law by consecrating Theodoric, and later Gauzlin of Fleury as archbishop of Bourges, without Fulbert's consent.[135] Odolric physically attacked the bishop, knocking him from his horse and threatening him with a sword. This opposition to Theodoric was so bitter and prolonged that he eventually agreed to have Odolric designated as his successor.[136] Later Fulbert ordained Odolric to the priesthood in preparation for his consecration. He then had to defend his actions to Leothericus, although he did little to conceal his dislike for his metropolitan. The bishop of Chartres was, in any event, the man seen as most responsible for Odolric's success in gaining the see of Orléans.[137] Odolric's consecration almost certainly preceded Theodoric's death and it would seem that the rivals had worked out some form of condominium by the early 1020s.

Their conflict, however, came to a head during the trial of canons of Sainte-Croix on charges of heresy in 1022. As Bautier has pointed out in an important reinterpretation of that episode, the disputed episcopal election pitted two of the most powerful factions in the realm against one another: on one side, the royal

---

[134] Fulbert of Chartres, *Letters*, no. 22, pp. 38–45.
[135] Fulbert of Chartres, *Letters*, no. 26, pp. 48–50.
[136] *Vita s. Theodorici* II, c. 3, p. 197.
[137] Fulbert of Chartres, *Letters*, nos. 42–3, pp. 74–7. Behrends interprets Fulbert's statement about the laying on of hands in the second letter as a reference to his ordination of Odolric as priest. I rather think that it refers to his earlier refusal to consecrate Theodoric as bishop.

party, on the other, the partisans of Odo II of Blois, represented in this matter by Fulbert of Chartres.[138] Robert the Pious' earlier renunciation of his marriage to Odo's widowed step-mother, Bertha of Burgundy, and subsequent marriage to Constance of Arles had caused a long-simmering rift with the house of Blois. That dispute emboldened Odolric, a powerful local castellan who could count on Odo's support, to dispute the king's traditional right to control appointments to the see of Orléans.[139] When charges of heresy involving clerics formerly of the royal entourage came to light Odolric seized upon them as an ideal means of discrediting his rival and the royal party.

The heretical canons of Sainte-Croix represented a religious movement of great enthusiasm and rigour. They kept to a vegetarian diet and discussed their teachings among themselves and conventicles of possible converts, both clerical and lay.[140] Such behaviour by itself, however, was hardly unorthodox or uncommon. The followers of Gregory of Nicopolis had met for vegetarian meals and spiritual discourse in a manner which sounds, on one level, much like the conventicles in which Arefast participated. Bautier has dismissed the 'popular', that is lay, associations of the these heretics and, by describing the origins of the case in factional disputes, has also diminished its specifically religious dimensions.[141] On the other hand, Stock has reasserted the influence which these heretics had on lay piety.[142] Gregory's enthusiastic audiences, in which clergy and laity mingled, bear eloquent testimony to the fact that there was a great deal of ferment in the religious life of the Orléanais at this time. Those in attendance at Gregory's hermitage and those who sought counsel from the canons of Sainte-Croix both fit Stock's definition of 'textual communities', that is groups who shared in common an authoritative interpretation, or interpreter, of a text.[143] In the

---

[138] Bautier 1975a. Bautier provides a thorough discussion of the various sources concerning this episode.

[139] Odolric was the nephew of Bishop Roger of Beauvais (Newman 1937a, no. 72, pp. 90-2) and thus allied to the Blèsois cause. Bautier (1975a, pp. 77-8) overstates the likelihood that Odolric was a direct relative of Odo II.   [140] Bautier 1975a, pp. 69-77.

[141] Bautier 1975a, pp. 76-7 and 88. Moore, who has been convinced by this argument, claims (1987, p. 16), 'If its intellectual background is similar to that of the Monforte group . . . the origin of the affair nevertheless lies in the world of the court and political power, and not in that even of learned, let alone popular heresy.'

[142] Stock 1983, p. 115.   [143] Stock 1983, pp. 90-2.

former case the group's hermeneutic was considered orthodox, in the latter heterodox, although much of their behaviour might have seemed similar to less-tutored participants.

The canons also rejected much of the accepted written tradition of Christianity and instead trusted in direct illumination by the Holy Spirit. Gauzlin of Fleury attended the trial as archbishop of Bourges and brought with him several of the 'more learned' of the community of Fleury. These learned monks produced 'the testimony of divine books' against the heretics, who had been 'educated from childhood in holy religion, and instructed in divine as well as secular letters'.[144] Although imbued in written culture, the canons rejected such 'things written on the membranes of animals' in favour of 'the law written in the interior of a man by the Holy Spirit'.[145] The entire process brought intellectuals into bad repute. Gauzlin of Fleury – who was among the bishops presiding at the trial, but also a member of the royal party under attack – felt compelled to make a declaration of orthodoxy modelled on one made earlier by Gerbert.[146]

In any case, the accused canons refused to abjure their beliefs under questioning by the assembled bishops and were burned on 28 December, the feast of the Holy Innocents. According to Ademar of Chabannes, Robert the Pious had much loved one of the heretics for the 'sanctity which the king had believed to be in him'. Sanctity was not simply in the eye of the beholder; it required proof and its celebration required the careful supervision of ecclesiastical authorities. The proof that the canons completely lacked sanctity came when they were executed by being burned on a pyre. Again according to Ademar, 'Without delay they were so completely reduced into ash that no trace of their bones could be discovered.'[147] Just as the canons were not saints, but heretics, so too their bones were not relics, for they had not survived the fire but were burned to nothingness. Only a few years earlier Abbot Gauzlin had explicitly employed an ordeal by fire to test the authenticity of relics of Christ's burial shroud which he wished to purchase while in Rome.[148] This technique was widely used in western Christendom at this time and had sprung in part from the

---

[144] *Miracula s. Benedicti*, VI.20, p. 247.
[145] *Cartulaire de Sainte-Père de Chartres*, VI.3, p. 114.
[146] Andrew of Fleury, *Vita Gauzlini*, c. 56, pp. 98–103.
[147] Ademar of Chabannes, *Chronicon*, III.59, p. 185.
[148] Andrew of Fleury, *Vita Gauzlini*, c. 20, p. 60.

tradition that relics survived church fires.[149] Ademar, at least in part, viewed the execution of the heretics as such an ordeal in reverse.

A curious coda to these events was provided by Andrew of Fleury.[150] He had probably accompanied Gauzlin to the trial as one of the *sapientiores* of the monastic community. One night shortly after the trial, a monk of Fleury had a vision of devils who entered the cloister through openings provided by the monastic latrines. Benedict himself then appeared and attacked the demons with his abbatial staff, driving them through the northern door of the monastery. This episode puts much of Andrew's demonology, particularly his fear of demonic pollution, into sharp focus. These heretics were explicitly servants of the devil. After their execution their familiar demons sought other victims and tried to invade Fleury through an appropriate break in its supernatural defences. The saintly patron immediately routed their forces. Andrew believed that the monastery was surrounded by demons, as was dramatized by another story concerning a sinful cellarer who was almost carried off by demons one night when outside the monastic enclosure.[151] For Andrew the monastery was not simply an island of holiness in a secular world, but an oasis in the midst of demonic pollution. This story demonstrates the sheer novelty which the heretical canons of Sainte-Croix held for Andrew. These canons differed radically from the heretics confronted only a few decades before by Abbo. Those figures had been simoniacs or bishops, like Arnulf, who improperly hungered for control over monastic rights and properties. His invocation of the term *haeretici* had implied what a great threat such men posed to Abbo's concept of church order. The canons, however, represented a basically different conception of Christianity, one opposed to saintly patronage, to the power of intercessory prayer, and to the holy texts on which the beliefs and power of the community of Fleury were based. Such deviance could only, in Andrew's mind, be due to demonic inspiration.

The judgement and execution of the canons led to Odolric's final triumph. Theodoric left Orléans to bring a complaint to the

---

[149] The only comprehensive modern treatment of the testing of relics by the ordeal by fire is that of Hermann-Mascard (1975, pp. 134–6) which is marred by the misinterpretation of several important passages.
[150] *Miracula s. Benedicti*, VI.20, pp. 246–8.
[151] *Miracula s. Benedicti*, VI.8, pp. 229–30.

papal court, but he died unexpectedly on 27 January in Tonnerre while visiting his cousin, the local count.[152] Odolric consolidated his hold on the see of Orléans over the course of the following years. This castellan-turned-bishop also possessed two important sets of land-holdings: the castle of Pithiviers and surrounding lands, inherited from his father, and the lordship of Nogent-le-Roi near Chartres, inherited from his mother's family. As lord of Pithiviers, the bishop came into conflict with the monks of Fleury over the castle of Yèvre.[153]

The 1030s witnessed the end of this second generation of ecclesiastical conflict in the Orléanais. Fulbert of Chartres, Gauzlin of Fleury, Robert the Pious, Leothericus of Sens, and Odolric of Pithiviers all died within the space of a few years.[154] The factional rivalry of the previous decades had been intense, but erratic. Leothericus of Sens had banded with Fulbert against Gauzlin in his court case with Bishop Fulk, but with Gauzlin and Robert the Pious in support of Theodoric. Abbot Albert of Micy had conducted cordial, and profitable, relations with both sides.

BIOGRAPHY AT FLEURY

Over the next decade two monks of Fleury, Helgaud and Andrew, attempted to elaborate the function of the royal and abbatial offices by composing lives of two of the main protagonists in these struggles: Robert the Pious and Abbot Gauzlin. Historians have argued over whether the *Epitoma vitae regis Rotberti pii* and the *Vita Gauzlini* were biography or hagiography.[155] The question seems

---

[152] *Chronique de Saint-Pierre-le-Vif*, p. 114; *Vita s. Theodorici I*, c. 5, p. 196; *Vita s. Theodorici II*, cc. 4–5, pp. 197–8. Bautier (1975a, pp. 78–9) has convincingly argued that these sources are correct in placing Theodoric's death in January 1023. Most earlier historians, such as Newman (1937a, no. 53, p. 69 n. 4) and Behrends (Fulbert of Chartres, *Letters*, p. lxxviii), placed Theodoric's death in January 1021. Others (for example *GC*, VIII, 1433) accepted the fact that Theodoric and Odolric shared the episcopal power, but placed Theodoric's death in January 1022.

[153] Andrew of Fleury, *Vita Gauzlini*, cc. 41–3, pp. 76–81; *Miracula s. Benedicti*, VI.19, pp. 245–6.

[154] Fulbert on 10 April 1028 (Fulbert of Chartres, *Letters*, p. xxi); Gauzlin on 8 March 1030 (Andrew of Fleury, *Vita Gauzlini*, c. 78, pp. 150 and 151 n. 1); Robert on 20 July 1031 (Helgaud of Fleury, *Epitoma vitae regis Rotberti pii*, c. 29, p. 134); Leothericus in 1032 (*Chronique de Saint-Pierre-le-Vif*, p. 116); Odolric most probably in early 1036 (the last charter to bear Odolric's name is dated November 1035; *Recueil des chartes de Saint-Benoît*, no. 74, I, 194).

[155] See, for example, Bautier and Labory, 1965, pp. 21, 35, and 36; Rosenthal 1971, p. 9; Bautier 1975b, p. 28; Lomastro 1975, p. 522; Lauranson-Rosaz 1987, p. 443.

misplaced. Neither Helgaud nor Andrew compared their protagonists to the traditional 'fathers' of the diocese. The monks did
indeed suggest that Robert and Gauzlin had been raised to heaven
and thus were saints in the restricted sense of the term.[156] There is
no evidence, however, that a feastday was ever celebrated in
honour of either king or abbot. More importantly there is no
evidence that either man was venerated at his tomb or performed
posthumous miracles. Thus it seems doubtful that Helgaud's work
was used either as a liturgical reading for a commemoration of
Robert at Saint-Aignan or as a reading in the refectory at Fleury as
has been suggested.[157]

Helgaud and Andrew modelled their works on the earlier lives
of a king and of an abbot composed by Abbo and Aimo.[158] Like
their predecessors, the new generation at Fleury were interested in
detailing the offices which their subjects held rather than in fully
presenting their lives. Helgaud, for example, was only interested in
certain aspects of kingship, saying that he would leave the military
life and achievements of Robert 'to the historians'.[159] These four
works from Fleury together constitute a distinctive literary
tradition very different in character from the traditional hagiography of the Orléanais. At base all four authors were more
interested in the sacred character of the offices which their subjects
held than in the sanctity of the men themselves. The relationship of
office to office-holder had become, largely owing to Abbo, a
problem which the community took very seriously indeed.

The character of these works demonstrates that it is necessary to
distinguish various degrees of sanctity when discussing hagiography. In the Orléanais prior to the thirteenth century, the local
'fathers', those great heroes of the distant past who served as
patrons of monastic communities and whose relics were the focus
of significant local shrines, most certainly held pride of place.
Secondly there were those people like Edmund, Abbo, and
Gregory of Nicopolis who had been raised to heaven on their death
and who also continued to have a special presence – *presentia* is the
term used by Abbo about Edmund – at their tombs.[160] That

[156] Helgaud of Fleury, *Epitoma vitae regis Rotberti pii*, c. 30, pp. 136–41; Andrew of Fleury,
Vita Gauzlini, cc. 74–5, pp. 144–7.
[157] Bautier and Labory 1965, p. 35; Carozzi 1981, p. 427.
[158] Helgaud also used Odo of Cluny's influential *Vita s. Geraldi* as a literary model for the
composition of life of a layman, as Carozzi (1980) has suggested.
[159] Helgaud of Fleury, *Epitoma vitae regis Rotberti pii*, c. 30, p. 138.
[160] Abbo of Fleury, *Vita s. Edmundi*, c. 16, p. 68.

presence was confirmed by posthumous miracles. Although the tombs of all three men became the goal of pilgrims, Gregory was the only one buried in the Orléanais itself. A canon of Pithiviers composed the *Vita s. Gregorii Nicopolitani* only after Gregory's relics had survived the burning of the church of St Salomon in 1044.[161] That event served as an implicit ordeal by fire – of the sort which the bodies of the heretical canons had failed – which guaranteed that the bones were indeed relics and that the hermit had a posthumous presence in them. Thirdly there were men like Robert and Gauzlin who had been raised to heaven, but who had no posthumous presence in this world. In this light it is not surprising that there was little of the miraculous, and no suggestion at all of posthumous miracles, in these works. Andrew discussed at length how Fleury's patrons, Benedict and the Virgin Mary, used supernatural power to protect the community, but he did not attribute any such power to his abbot.[162] Helgaud attributed to Robert the ability to cure certain diseases in a manner that later became associated with the 'royal touch', but that tradition of curing had more to do with the sacred quality of the office than the personal holiness of the office-holder.[163]

The lives of Robert and Gauzlin demonstrate the continued development of the ideas of saintly patronage and of sacred offices in the community of Fleury.[164] At the beginning of his work Helgaud placed King Robert in the context of sacred rulership:

The dignity of the celestial empire . . . has elected in the secular world powerful princes who rule with the sceptres of that world. Just as the holy church, which is our mother, obtains for itself bishops, abbots, and other ministers of the sacred order for ruling the people of God, so in this world

---

[161] *Vita s. Gregorii Nicopolitani*, c. 11, p. 464.
[162] Andrew of Fleury, *Vita Gauzlini*, cc. 24–5, pp. 64–71.
[163] Helgaud of Fleury, *Epitoma vitae regis Rotberti pii*, c. 27, pp. 126–9; Bloch 1924, pp. 36–41.
[164] Both have, unlike any of the works of hagiography about the traditional 'fathers' of the Orléanais, received modern critical editions. Partly as a result of these editions, they have become the most carefully studied eleventh-century texts from the region and I will not attempt a full discussion of these works here. On the *Epitoma vitae regis Rotberti pii*, see Rosenthal 1971; Lomastro 1975; Duby 1980, pp. 181–5; Carozzi 1980 and 1981. On the *Vita Gauzlini*, see Lomastro 1975. Also, for both works, see the fine introductions provided by Robert-Henri Bautier and Gillette Labory (respectively 1965 and 1969) who have together edited both texts.

it elects emperors, kings, and princes for punishing malefactors and for reprimanding the audacity of evil-doers.[165]

This was Abbo's idea of kingship, particularly as, only a few lines later, Robert was described as *filius Hugonis regis*.[166] Robert's was a sacred office, similar to that of bishops and abbots. He obtained it both by royal birth and by election. The monk left the matter of unction moot at this point, but later said that Robert particularly loved Orléans as the city in which he had been baptized and later anointed king, two of the three blessings mentioned by Abbo in the *Vita s. Edmundi*. Helgaud also later gave Robert the title 'king by holy blessing' (*sanctae benedictionis rex*).[167] Secondly, Helgaud placed Robert in the context of saintly patronage. He appended his work to a copy of the *Testamentum Leodebodi*, the foundation charter of Fleury. In that document an abbot of Saint-Aignan had cared for the properties of a saint. So, too, in this work it was to be shown how Robert, as a 'most dutiful king' (*piissimus rex*), cared for the properties of the saints and, in particular, 'enriched, loved, and honoured [St Anianus] in as much as he was able'. The relationship between the seventh-century foundation charter and the eleventh-century life was crucial for the monastic hagiographer. Not only did it make the offices of abbot and king parallel in function, but it also made them similar in the way abbots and kings served the saintly 'fathers' of the region. Such dutiful service brought the king into close contact with the saints and – in word which Helgaud added in his own hand to the first version of his work – made the king's life 'something to be imitated by present and future generations'.[168]

Robert had been connected to the 'fathers' of the Orléanais since childhood. The future king was born in that city. When in his youth he fell deathly ill, his mother had him brought to the cathedral of Sainte-Croix – 'the oldest church in Orléans which St Evurtius founded according to the wish of God' – and there he was

---

[165] Helgaud of Fleury, *Epitoma vitae regis Rotberti pii*, c. 1, p. 56. In the lines that follow Helgaud described Robert simply as 'precipuus pater' in the first draft, but added 'scilicet R[otbertus] Francorum rex gloriosus' in the margin at a later time.

[166] Helgaud later added in his own hand, called 'C' by the editors, more information on Robert's parentage, which made him *origine natus nobilissima*.

[167] Helgaud of Fleury, *Epitoma vitae regis Rotberti pii*, c. 15, p. 86; c. 22, p. 110.

[168] Helgaud of Fleury, *Epitoma vitae regis Rotberti pii*, c. 1, p. 58. The addition was made in hand 'C'.

blessed. When the boy soon recovered his father Hugh donated a large silver vase 'which remains even in our times in that holy house of God'. When he grew up, Robert commemorated his deliverance by restoring an important set of lands to the cathedral chapter which Bishop Fulk had given away. The king also, presumably at different times, gave magnificent gifts to both the rival claimants of the see of Orléans, Theodoric and Odolric. Helgaud followed this narrative with the record of several other gifts made by Robert to important monastic houses and their patron saints including 'our father Benedict'.[169]

The intimate relationship between king and patron saints also appeared clearly in Helgaud's detailed description of the rebuilding of the church of Saint-Aignan.[170] Anianus was Robert's 'particular advocate before God'. A saint could play the role of *advocatus* for a layman in the divine court, just as a layman played that role for monastic communities in the royal court. According to Helgaud, the king spoke eloquently to his entourage of the virtues and powers of this 'father'. The church which housed his relics had been destroyed in the fire which had devastated Orléans in the late tenth century. The chapter of canons attached to it had long been controlled by Robert's family and he was probably its lay abbot. Therefore he financed the construction of a large and elaborate new church. For its consecration in 1029 he gathered together eight bishops of Neustria and other notable clerics such as Odilo of Cluny. The episode was so important to Helgaud that he drew up a first draft of his text, presumably to have certain factual details corroborated.[171] It remained so important to the canons of Saint-Aignan that they later copied it, along with a parallel incident from the life of Louis IX, under the title 'Mirabilia gesta regis Roberti de sancto Aniano'.[172]

Helgaud also described how Robert made a long journey south of the Loire in search of saintly patronage.[173] The trip sounds very much like a pilgrimage to the major relic cults of the Aquitaine: 'Travelling during one Lent, he went to those saints with whom he was united in the service of God. He prayed to them, honoured

---

[169] Helgaud of Fleury, *Epitoma vitae regis Rotberti pii*, c. 15, pp. 84–91.
[170] Helgaud of Fleury, *Epitoma vitae regis Rotberti pii*, c. 22, pp. 106–15.
[171] Vatican, Reg. lat. 585, fo. 58. On this draft, see Auvray 1887; Bautier and Labory 1965, pp. 37–42.
[172] Vatican, Reg. lat. 623, fos. 142–4. On this manuscript, see Renaud 1976, pp. 248–9.
[173] Helgaud of Fleury, *Epitoma vitae regis Rotberti pii*, c. 27, pp. 124–9.

them, made their ears ring with humble and wholesome prayers in order that he would be able to be found worthy with them and all the saints in the praise of God.' In short, Robert was worried about his death and the question of his salvation. He went outside the effective limits of his kingdom to areas where Abbo had once joked he had virtually no power in order to seek out the patron saints of that territory. From Helgaud's list of saints an itinerary can be worked out.[174] Christian Lauranson-Rosaz has inferred that this journey took slightly more than one year and most probably occurred either in 1019/20 or 1020/1. As he points out, this royal progress would seem to have been an ambitious attempt to extend royal authority, or at least to lay the foundations for such an extension, to the south.[175] As part of his strategy he chose the most powerful allies he could win with some ease in the region, the saints. Robert the Pious recognized the power of the traditional 'fathers' of the Aquitaine and cannily attempted to win their advocacy not just in the celestial court, but in the courts of local princes. Robert saw saintly patronage not just as a religious duty, but as a potential means of governance.

Robert's dutiful performance of religious acts which was so lovingly recorded by Helgaud has often perplexed historians. A recognition of the importance both of saintly patronage and of Abbo's theory of kingship in the intellectual milieu of Fleury, as well as in the world of the west Franks more generally, makes this piety more comprehensible. Helgaud wished quite simply to show how Robert served as the agent of divine providence and saintly patronage through the proper exercise of his office. Thus Robert's *pietas* was above all his sense of duty. For his own part, Robert seems to have grasped intuitively the important place held by the saintly 'fathers' in the fractious society he was attempting to govern. He tried to use their patronage as one way of inculcating the *fidelitas* which he, like Abbo before him, recognized as lacking in his kingdom. Service to saintly 'fathers' was part of the very fibre of west Frankish social and religious life.

Just as Helgaud presented Robert as the exemplary king, so his

---

[174] St Stephen at the cathedral of Bourges; St Maiolus of Cluny at the abbey of Souvigny; St Julian at the abbey of Brioude; St Giles at the abbey of Saint-Gilles-du-Gard; St Saturninus at the abbey of Saint-Saturnin in Toulouse; St Vincent at the abbey of Castres; St Antoninus at the abbey of Saint-Antonin near the Garonne; St Faith at the abbey of Conques; and St Gerald at the abbey founded by the saint in Aurillac.

[175] Lauranson-Rosaz 1987, pp. 442–53.

contemporary Andrew wished to portray Gauzlin as the model abbot. The primary theme of his work was how the abbot protected the property of his community against the depredations of both laymen and clerics, as well as enriched its properties by soliciting gifts. The editors suggest that Andrew began this work around 1042, at the same time as he was composing the first three books of his collection of the posthumous miracles of St Benedict.[176] In one case the monk reused a story almost verbatim from the miracle collection.[177] Several other incidents, persons, and places are common to both works. Thus Andrew composed the life of Gauzlin, in a manner once again reminiscent of Aimo's life of Abbo, as part of a larger project which included the celebration of the miraculous patronage provided by Fleury's 'father'. The first book of the *Vita Gauzlini* was essentially a collection of *exempla*, that is stories or even summaries of documents, which served to illustrate the author's argument about the office of abbot. Andrew's narrative was dry, using the language of legal transactions. A typical summary reads, 'William, count of Avranches, gave some land in the *villa* of Beuvron for the construction of a church and some more for the making of a mill in order to redeem his sins.'[178] At one point he noted that the record of a certain gift to the monastery could be found 'in our archives'.[179] He also included the complete texts of various documents, including letters from the papal chancery and some texts composed by Gauzlin himself. Indeed, as the editors have noted, in the absence of an extant cartulary, this work provides the best record of Fleury's property during this period.[180] Gauzlin defended the abbey's holdings against members of the high nobility who attempted to seize whole properties – as in the case of the 'despicable' Odo II of Blois – castellans and knights who plundered goods from priories – as in the case of Hildebert of Limoges – and bishops who defied Fleury's papal and royal privileges – as in the case of Fulk of Orléans.[181] Gauzlin also enriched his abbey by soliciting gifts from the same social groups in the persons of Fulk Nerra, the family of Bellême, and Odolric of

[176] Bautier and Labory 1969, p. 13.
[177] Andrew of Fleury, *Vita Gauzlini*, c. 25, pp. 66–71 = *Miracula s. Benedicti*, IV.5–6, pp. 179–82.   [178] Andrew of Fleury, *Vita Gauzlini*, c. 30, p. 72.
[179] Andrew of Fleury, *Vita Gauzlini*, c. 8, p. 42.
[180] Bautier and Labory 1969, p. 13.
[181] Andrew of Fleury, *Vita Gauzlini*, c. 10, pp. 42–5; c. 18, pp. 50–9; c. 25, pp. 66–71.

Pithiviers.[182] A picture emerges of an efficient administrator, wise in the ways of both the secular and ecclesiastical worlds.

In Gauzlin's conflict with Bishop Fulk, the recently elected abbot relied upon the legal defences which his predecessor Abbo had obtained for Fleury from the papal court. Gauzlin, however, was also willing to seize the initiative. He paid 400 *sous* for rights over the church in the *castrum* of Yèvre, doubtless wishing to gain some control over this castellanry which had caused so many problems for the properties of Fleury in previous generations.[183] Sometime later, however, the castellan of nearby Pithiviers became bishop. Odolric rebuilt the castle of Yèvre and reinstituted the same *malae consuetudines* which Arnulf had previously enacted over lands belonging to Fleury. Gauzlin now went so far as to make a direct cash payment to the bishop of $9\frac{1}{2}$ gold *livres* for the rights to the castle, which he proceeded to destroy. Along with uprooting the castle of Yèvre itself, Gauzlin renounced the same legal rights which had caused troubles for the lands of his abbey since the time of Abbo. He also paid 195 silver *livres* to the king for a royal confirmation and obtained an anathema against Odolric from 'all the bishops of Gaul'. As penance Odolric gave the monks of Fleury rights to the small abbey of Saint-Gualt which he himself had founded at Yèvre.[184] Over the coming decades the abbey of Fleury was to use the newly acquired town of Yèvre as the basis for the creation of a 'seigneurie ecclésiastique', that is an enclave of monastic properties and privileges. An incipient bastion of castellan power had thus been successfully seized by monks.[185]

The first book ended with the trial of the heretical canons of Sainte-Croix, an event of epochal proportions for contemporaries in the Orléanais. In the second book, Andrew, turning to the years 1026–9, provided full and colourful descriptions of events which he had witnessed. He began with the fire of 30 July 1026 which ruined much of the monastery. In this adversity Gauzlin showed his true genius. He stood almost literally in the same ashes of this seeming disaster and addressed his monks, rallying their spirits. He had the relics of Benedict taken out of the crypt where they had been protected, paraded round the nearby lands of the monastery, and then returned to the cloister and the severely damaged church of

---

[182] Andrew of Fleury, *Vita Gauzlini*, c. 15, pp. 46–9; c. 28, p. 70–1; c. 42, pp. 78–81.
[183] Andrew of Fleury, *Vita Gauzlini*, c. 6, p. 40.
[184] Andrew of Fleury, *Vita Gauzlini*, cc. 41–3, pp. 76–81; *Miracula s. Benedicti*, VI.19, pp. 245–6.   [185] Lemarignier 1965, pp. 628–30.

the Virgin. This ceremonial procession served as a symbolic beginning of the renewal of Benedict's house. Gauzlin himself, according to Andrew, pointed out the biblical parallel of the people of Israel wandering in the desert before coming to the promised land. Andrew added a classical comparison to the Trojans under Aeneas seeking the promise of Rome.[186] In the following years Gauzlin undertook an energetic programme of building. In particular, the walls of several new buildings were decorated with cycles of frescoes – pictures of the Apocalypse and of the life of Peter in the church dedicated to that saint, scenes from Aesop's fables in the monastic refectory. While these pictures have vanished, Andrew described them in detail and his work provides an important source for the history of painting and its function in the early eleventh century.

For Andrew his abbot had been above all else a good shepherd, a *pastor* – a word which he applied to Gauzlin no less than ten times – who guarded and enriched the flock which had been entrusted to him.[187] In that role Gauzlin served Christ and the patrons of Fleury – the Virgin Mary, St Peter, and 'father' Benedict. The abbot understood his role in terms of service. In a speech placed in his mouth by Andrew, Gauzlin said,

I do not think of myself as being frustrated in this hope [of salvation], rather, by the offer of my pure devotion, since I have made the submission required by our condition and . . . I have declared the singular trust of my hope in the unblemished mother of my Lord, in my unique advocate (*advocatus*) before the Lord, St Benedict, and in the keeper of the celestial gate [St Peter].[188]

A faithful executor of his office, Gauzlin, like Robert, still made use of the advocacy offered by the 'fathers' of his house and region. The legacy of Abbo had strengthened, not replaced, the legacy of Benedict.

The works of Helgaud and Andrew demonstrate that a generation after the death of Abbo the monks of Fleury continued to place their faith in the ability of their saintly patron, their elected abbot, and their anointed king to carry out the commands of divine providence and thus protect their rights and properties. These lives are best understood as portraits of Abbo's idealized king

[186] Andrew of Fleury, *Vita Gauzlini*, c. 58, pp. 108–15.
[187] Andrew of Fleury, *Vita Gauzlini*, pp. 34, 44, 84, 106, 110, 134, 142, 146, and 148.
[188] Andrew of Fleury, *Vita Gauzlini*, c. 72, p. 142.

and abbot in action. They also demonstrate the continued vitality of intellectual life at Fleury. Andrew included a long description of the literary attainments of his fellows in the community.[189] The ability of these monks – not only Helgaud and Andrew, but also Aimo, Isembard, Constantine, Vitalis, Gerald, and others – to articulate and make public the historical and legal claims of the community was crucial to the contemporary success of the monks of Fleury in protecting, and even augmenting, their rights and properties.

It is not surprising to find that, during this very period, the monks of Cluny themselves, as well as monks from important dependencies, were also choosing to articulate their reform ideology in the lives of contemporary figures. In particular they composed a number of related texts concerning Abbot Maiolus, a near contemporary of Abbo. These served as part of a campaign to win the abbot's canonization and several of them served a known liturgical function.[190] Dominique Iogna-Pratt has unravelled the interrelationships of this hagiographic dossier and analysed its major themes. The literature about Maiolus exhibited a greater interest in such traditional themes of monastic spirituality as humility, virginity, and the communal life than it did in institutional problems such as election and the protection of property. These 'spiritual' themes, however, were central to the Cluniac method of reform and thus to Cluny's control of dependent houses. Around the year 1000, the monks of Cluny found themselves between the Carolingian tradition of reform – of which presumably Fleury continued to be an example – and the inchoate beginnings of Gregorian ideology.[191]

Not all contemporary saints were reforming abbots. No less than six members of the Ottonian clan, who served as the royal and later imperial family of Saxony, had gained some reputation for sanctity by the year 1000.[192] All but one of these saints was female. While Cluniac influence can be found in the cult of Empress Adelaide, the literature concerning the others represents a general acceptance in Saxony of the Ottonians which was a sacred clan (*beata stirps*) celebrated by authors as diverse as Hrotsvit of

---

[189] Andrew of Fleury, *Vita Gauzlini*, c. 2, pp. 32–9.
[190] Iogna-Pratt 1988, pp. 19–20, 26–7, 65, and 147–8.
[191] Iogna-Pratt 1988, pp. 320–96, particularly 344, 350–1, and 394–6.
[192] Queen Mathilda (+968), Hathumoda, abbess of Gandersheim (+874), Duchess Oda (+912), Queen Edith (+946), Bishop Bruno of Cologne (+965), and Empress Adelaide (+999).

Gandersheim and Thietmar of Merseburg. According to Patrick Corbet, who has studied the ensemble in remarkable detail, these lives represented a concerted attempt on the part of the clergy to inculcate ascetic and other Christian ideals in the lives of the nobility. The fact that it was the female and clerical (hence virginal) members of the dynasty who were its exemplars of sanctity demonstrates that it was the clan itself, rather than the secular offices occupied by its male members, which was sacred.[193] These works exemplified the older traditions of dynastic rulership and sacral kingship which were far less oriented toward law than was the theory of elective kingship expounded by Abbo.

Like Ottonian Saxony, Anglo-Saxon England had possessed a strong tradition of royal sanctity, encompassing both male and female members of the West-Saxon and East-Anglian families. The lives of these saints were discussed by authors from the time of Bede down to the first generations of the conquering Normans, who sometimes objected to the political implications of these native cults. Susan Ridyard has skilfully shown how these cults were created and nurtured by various religious communities and institutions to enhance their prestige. Ecclesiastics used the distinctly Christian concept of sanctity as a means of exerting influence over secular rulers and rulership, as well as a means of recognizing the centrality of royal power in England. As she concludes, 'The church in promoting or sanctioning the cults of the royal saints not only acknowledged and reinforced the social dominance of kings and royal dynasties. It also gave voice to its own interpretation of kingship and society.'[194] Abbo of Fleury had written about Edmund, one of these Anglo-Saxon saints. Ridyard has noted, however, that his work differed substantially from the native hagiographic tradition of royal saints: 'it has little theoretical content and concerns itself not at all with the relationship of royal birth to the attainment of sanctity; its subject is located instead within the distinct hagiological tradition of the martyred innocent'.[195] Even in England where the hagiographic traditions of Fleury were known, the local traditions of royal hagiography developed in another direction.

---

[193] Corbet 1986, particularly pp. 65–72. See also pp. 79, 94–6 (notes), 105, 227, and 240–1, for some comparisons to the work of Helgaud.

[194] Ridyard 1988, particularly pp. 234–52 (the quotation is on p. 250).

[195] Ridyard 1988, p. 235. On Abbo's work more generally, see pp. 62–9, 93–5, and 211–14. Ridyard's interpretation of this work differs somewhat from that presented here.

These hagiographic traditions differed from the four lives of contemporaries composed at Fleury in several crucial ways. First, they were more concerned with the posthumous cult than were those from Fleury. Secondly, the authors of these works all presented the offices of abbot and king as defined more in terms of person – which could mean spiritual attainment, birth, or charismatic power – than in terms of law. Most importantly, none of these other bodies of hagiography were built on the work of as brilliant a legal theorist as Abbo. None of them attained the concise continuity exhibited by the works from Fleury, which were, after all, composed by four members of the same monastic house over a period of less than fifty years.

At Fleury the literary tradition of Abbo and his followers – a tradition for which hagiography provided the vital core – continued to 'flourish' (the pun on the name of Fleury was Andrew's own) down to the early twelfth century in the works of Rodulfus Tortarius and Hugh. The patronage provided by 'father' Benedict always remained the focus of these claims. The lives of contemporary figures, however, added an important dimension: the appeal, not to the personal power of a saint, but to the power of law and of sacred offices, such as king and abbot, instituted by God, but conferred through the agreement (*electio*) of one's fellows. Those ideas were in many ways elaborated in the historiographic and political works of Hugh of Fleury, which were to become crucial texts in the Gregorian reform. In the eleventh century the hagiographers of Fleury called not only for service to a saintly 'father', but also for fidelity both to an emergent system of laws and to the rulers, entrusted through election and anointing, with the execution of those laws. Bishops might enter through their gates uninvited and lay lords might enact *malae consuetudines* on their lands, but the monks of Fleury trusted that joint appeals to the miraculous powers of Benedict and to the defences found in the privileges granted them by crown and papacy would confound their enemies.

CONCLUSION

The patronage of the saints was part of the very fibre of Frankish society. The Franks had adopted the belief in this miraculous power, and the relics which served as its focus, from the conquered Gallo-Roman population as part of the process of their conversion to Christianity. Until the twelfth century many, indeed most, of the important saintly patrons within the Frankish realms were the martyrs, bishops, and abbots of Gallo-Roman society. Ironically the Gallo-Romans themselves, as we know from the works of Gregory of Tours, had seen these saints and their relics as one of their most powerful defences against the Germanic invaders. When that bishop retold the story of how Bishop Anianus had turned away the attacking Huns from Orléans, it must have had particular resonance for an audience themselves embattled by the Franks. In an extraordinary process of cultural synthesis, the Franks made such patrons as Anianus their own. The cult of the saints had been and continued to be an eminently local phenomenon. Anianus was above all a patron for the Orléanais, its Gallo-Roman population, the Franks who conquered and settled it, and the Christian descendants of mixed race who were the progeny of the invasions.

A story told by Hariulf in the early twelfth century demonstrates how those descendants clung to the patronage provided by their local saints. When the members of the First Crusade took ship to go to the Holy Land, they included 'men of diverse nations, namely Franks, Burgundians, Aquitanians, Gascons, Spaniards, Italians, Sicilians, Calabrians, and other nations as well'. While at sea, a severe storm broke out. Threatened with drowning, the clerics and monks on board began to chant psalms and canticles.

Behold [what we did] was not pleasing to God, and so, thinking that a general invocation of the saints might be able to save us from this danger, each one of us invoked those saints whom we knew as particular (*peculiares*) to our own locales and we sought, through the suffrages made to them, to evade grave danger. And so all gave praise, and those from the

Conclusion

Ile de France began to invoke Denis, those from Poitiers Hilary, those from Tours Martin, those from Orléans Anianus, those from Limoges Martial, those from Toulouse Saturninus, those from Auxerre Germanus, those from Reims Remigius, those from the Vermandois Quintinus, and those from other cities knew and called upon the names of other notable saints.

The eventual outcome was, not surprisingly, that St Richarius, the patron of Hariulf's own monastery, quelled the storm.[1] Other than Richarius himself, the list of saints invoked by the crusading clerics reads like a roll call of early bishops who had become the saintly patrons of prominent Gallo-Roman *civitates*.

   The study of the Orléanais we have undertaken here provides one picture of the overall development of this 'pious local patronage' – to invoke once again the phrase of Bishop Walter with which we began this study – from its Merovingian roots to the time of Hariulf. The tombs of the great Christian heroes originally lay in cemeteries located outside the walls of Gallo-Roman *civitates*. Gradually the faithful constructed churches over these tombs, turning them into symbols of patronage and shrines for pilgrimage. Gregory of Tours knew of two shrines near the city of Orléans, those of Anianus and of Avitus. Both were apparently under the control of the Gallo-Romans.[2] According to later traditions, however, the Franks became actively involved in this process of honouring the holy dead from an early date. In Carolingian *vitae*, for example, it was Clovis himself who provided Euspicius and Maximinus, members of the Gallo-Roman aristocracy of Vienne, with the properties needed to found the abbey of Micy. As monastic communities came to be associated with shrine churches, Frankish donations became increasingly more important for the upkeep of the cults of the saints. In the seventh century it was a Frankish queen who supported the reform of the house of Saint-Aignan.[3] The Franks also brought the beloved trappings of their new religion, both monasticism and the cult of the saints, into the further reaches of the countryside. Abbot Leodebodus of Saint-Aignan founded the monastery of Fleury, which was originally dedicated to the Virgin and to Peter, but which soon acquired a

[1] Hariulf, *Libellus de miraculis s. Richarii factis post eius relationem*, c. 3, p. 569.
[2] The recently deceased Bishop Namatius had been buried in the church of Anianus, while Gregory himself had received the Frankish King Guntram in a house located near the shrine of Avitus. See Gregory of Tours, *Historia Francorum*, IX.18, p. 432; VIII.2, pp. 371–2.   [3] *Vita s. Balthildis*, c. 9, p. 493.

distinctive saintly patron of its own. The names of the saints – Avitus, Anianus, Evurtius, Benedictus – had a pure Latin ring. Those of their servants – Balthildis, Leodebodus, Mummolus, Aigulphus – came to be ever more exclusively Germanic.

What was true of the Orléanais was also true of other regions dominated by the Franks. The tombs of Albinus at Angers, Germanus at Auxerre, Benignus at Dijon, Maximinus at Trier, and numerous others first became suburban shrines, quite often in the Gallo-Roman period itself, and later important monasteries which were eventually incorporated within the expanding circuit of city walls. The shrine of Martin, patron of Gregory of Tours' own episcopal seat, was already a virtual city-within-a-city by Gregory's own lifetime.[4] Meanwhile, rural shrines and their attached monastic communities – that of Denis near Paris and that of Richarius at Centula in the Ponthieu, as well as that of Benedict at Fleury – steadily gained in wealth and prestige through the gifts of the Frankish nobility. In this manner each of these saints developed his – and sometimes, as in the case of Faith at Conques or Geneviève at Paris, her – own network of patronage. The more Romanized regions south of the Loire and those less Romanized reaches beyond the Rhine each followed its own, unique pattern of development, somewhat different from that of Neustria. The cults of Faith herself, of Martial at Limoges, of the relics of the holy cross obtained by Radegund for Poitiers, and of the relics of Liborius which were translated from Le Mans to the new see of Paderborn in 836 all point to the fact that saintly patrons were to be found, native or imported, in those very regions as well.

It was to provide a history for these patrons and their communities that authors, most of them monks, undertook the projects of hagiographic composition which mark the Carolingian period in Neustria. These works served the dual purposes of piety and institutional prestige. During this process of consolidation and regularization – of Carolingian reform if you will – the cults of many Gallo-Roman saints whose tombs had not been graced by shrines and monastic communities, and who had thus not attained the status of saintly patrons, slipped from view. Developments within the Orléanais were paralleled in regions as different as the Maine, where the so-called Le Mans forger staked out episcopal claims to authority under the guise of saintly lives, and Reims,

---

[4] Van Dam (1985, pp. 230–55) provides a fine portrait of this shrine and monastery.

where Hincmar considered the *Vita s. Remigii* as the crowning achievement of his career.[5] Joseph-Claude Poulin has also charted the richness, as well as the difference of focus, in contemporary hagiography coming from the Aquitaine.[6] Not all Frankish regions were as ravaged by the brutal invasions and civil wars of the tenth century as were the valleys of the Loire and the Seine. Many regional hagiographic traditions remained quite lively, in contrast to the moribund Orléanais, during this period.

During the first century of Capetian rule the clerics of the Orléanais once again celebrated the miraculous patronage of their local 'fathers'. The dominant hagiographic genre of this period was not the life of the patron saint, although some new patrons were created along traditional lines, but collections of the stories of posthumous miracles attributed to those patrons. While the composition of such collections was on the wane in the Orléanais by 1100, this vogue continued unabated through the twelfth century, most particularly in the region bounded by the Loire and the Rhine. The diocese of Liège, for example, experienced a hagiographic renaissance similar to that of the Orléanais during the eleventh century, although it was far from the heartland of Capetian power. In that milieu lives of the saints, in particular the distinctive literary genre of verse lives, were as important as miracle collections.[7] It may have taken a travelling scholar from Angers named Bernard to begin, around the second decade of the eleventh century, the collection of miracle stories associated with the prominent shrine of St Faith deep in the Aquitaine. Thereafter, however, the collection of the posthumous miracle stories of local saints' patronage – most significantly at such important stops on the pilgrimage routes to Compostela as Limoges, Mende, Saint-Guilhem-le-Désert, and Saint-Gilles-du-Gard – became almost as common south of the Loire as in the north.[8]

In the lands of the eastern Franks, now Ottonian Saxony, the renewal of monastic houses often went hand-in-hand with the invocation of saintly patronage. Some time between 973 and 983, just before Letaldus of Micy composed his *Miracula s. Maximini* and began the second productive age of hagiographic composition in the Orléanais, Hrotsvit of Gandersheim undertook the task of recording the traditions which concerned the foundation of her

[5] Goffart 1966, *passim*; Wallace-Hadrill 1983, pp. 301–2.
[6] Poulin 1975.   [7] Gaiffier 1967.   [8] Sigal 1976a.

community in the *Primordia coenobii Gandeshemensis*. Like Letaldus, one of Hrotsvit's overriding purposes was to show that the bishop of her diocese had little in the way of traditional rights over her monastery.[9] In 978 Archbishop Egbert began the reform of the monastery of St Eucharius in the city of Trier. The centrepiece of his project was the ritual invention, the following year, of the newly discovered relics of St Celsus. It occurred in the monastery's church before a large gathering of clerics and laity. As the monk Theodoric later recalled, 'After the text from the holy gospel had been read, the bishop of the city spoke to the people in an admonitory manner . . . describing the discovery of the saint's relics. He exhorted them that they should not forget to visit blessed Celsus frequently.'[10] Once again monks and bishops with Germanic names enshrined the relics of a saint presumed to come from the antiquity of late Roman Christianity.

The evolution of the cults of saintly patrons demonstrates yet one more way in which the institutions of the Carolingian empire were renewed and reworked in the period around the year 1000. Just as the old Carolingian aristocracy for a while foundered under the brunt of the tenth-century invasions, only to reemerge – albeit with many partners from families of more recent origin – in the eleventh century, so too the ancient saintly 'fathers' of Neustria tenaciously clung to their power. The monastic *familia* of those saints invoked by the crusaders accompanied by Hariulf – Denis and Richarius, Martin and Martial – were all powerful communities, once linked to the Carolingian aristocracy, now to the emergent Capetian dynasty. In the Orléanais, Anianus and Benedict had weathered the 'dislocation of the *pagus*' described by Lemarignier and others. Other ancient patrons and their communities – like Lifardus and Evurtius – had a more difficult time, but they still survived in the new age, more dependent on the episcopacy or the new reforming orders. The old saintly aristocracy, like their secular counterparts, were joined by *novi homines*, saints like Laetus at Pithiviers or Celsus at Trier whose cults were newly celebrated.

The revival of the cult of the saints in the eleventh and twelfth centuries was not limited to the lands of the Franks. Paolo Golinelli has shown that Italian cities also celebrated the civic patronage

[9] Head 1987b.
[10] Theodoric of Saint-Eucharius, *Historia inventionis s. Celsi*, c. 22, p. 406.

provided by their early bishops during the early eleventh century.[11] By the latter part of that century Norman bishops newly arrived in England desired to organize, and thus control, the cults of native Anglo-Saxon saints, which sometimes served as the focus of troublesome native sentiment.[12] Over the following century the collection of attestations of miraculous cures became the norm at the shrines of such various saints as the ancient Anglo-Saxon nun Frideswide, the more recent Anglo-Saxon hermit Godric of Finchale, and two victims of murder, William of Norwich and Thomas Becket.[13]

At the heart of the cult of saints lay the concept of saintly patronage. According to its logic, the saints would protect, both in this world and in the kingdom of God, those people who chose to become their servants. The bond between those servants – be they the members of monastic communities, the peasants who worked their lands, noble benefactors of those communities, or pilgrims who came to their shrines – and their saintly patrons was a highly personal one grounded in a vital belief in the miraculous power of the saints. While the relationships between saintly patrons and their servants mirrored in many ways the relationships between lords and vassals in secular society, a merely functionalist explanation of the cult of the saints fails to take the importance of this belief into account. The saints were not fictions created by monastic hagiographers to serve a useful end, but lively presences who owned property, appeared in visions, cured the sick, and dispensed justice. Hagiography provided the prism through which relics were viewed and interpreted, but a literary genre could not invent the presence of saintly patrons.

To see the belief in the miraculous powers of relics as some form of pagan survival is to mistake the reality of Christianity in the late-antique and medieval worlds. Educated Gallo-Romans such as Sulpicius Severus and Gregory of Tours – not to mention such products of a more pristinely Roman education as Augustine and Ambrose – believed in the miraculous power of the saints as exhibited in their relics. The Franks came to understand the patronage exerted by the saints in terms of their own social system, that is in terms of gift giving and charismatic personal power in the Merovingian period and in terms of incipient vassalage by the Carolingian age. In whatever terms it was conceived, however, the

[11] Golinelli 1980, pp. 65–94.   [12] Ridyard 1988.   [13] Finucane 1977, pp. 100–29.

miraculous patronage of the saints, like the miraculous powers invoked in the ordeal which apparently had more purely Germanic roots, was seen by contemporaries as functioning in an authentically Christian manner.[14] Those medieval clerics, such as Bernard of Angers and Guibert of Nogent, who criticized certain relic cults as inauthentic, certainly accepted the power inherent in true saints and their relics. At one point Bernard admitted to having compared the statue-reliquaries of such saints as Gerald at Aurillac and Faith at Conques to classical images of the pagan gods, but he later came to a firm, even impassioned, belief in the patronage of St Faith.[15]

The bulk of evidence for saintly patronage, both in the Orléanais and elsewhere in the old Carolingian lands, comes from the collections of posthumous miracle stories compiled in the eleventh and twelfth centuries.[16] The authors of these collections, however, developed ideas already present in the less numerous collections of the ninth and tenth centuries. By the year 1000 the *ordo* of monks, celibate and withdrawn from the world for prayer and contemplation, was generally recognized to occupy a position closer to the celestial realm than that of other humans. The monks, and to some extent other celibate clergy such as regular canons, served as intercessors between the court of heaven and the other, more worldy, *ordines* of human society, however the map of that society might be drawn. The prayers offered by monks were central to this intercessory venture, as the necrologies compiled by monastic communities from the ninth century on attest. In the words of the researchers who have done the most to exploit this material, the prayers of the monks created a 'community of common interest' (*Gemeinschaft*) with the laity, not only the dead for whom they prayed but their living descendants as well.[17]

Saintly patronage served a similar intercessory function.[18] The vital cults of traditional saintly patrons were, in the eleventh and

---

[14] See Bartlett's (1986, pp. 34–42 and 153–66) powerful arguments against interpretation of the ordeal in terms either of functionalism or of pagan survivals.

[15] Bernard of Angers, *Liber miraculorum s. Fidis*, I.13–15, pp. 46–51.

[16] Sigal (1985) provides the most comprehensive survey of this material, although he focuses almost exclusively on the west Frankish lands and the Aquitaine, that is on the territory of modern France and Belgium.

[17] For the general argument, see Wollasch and Schmid 1967.

[18] Van Engen 1986, p. 296, would seem to make too great a distinction when he writes, 'The veneration of relics, the other primary means of intercession in that age, and Benedictine prayer were surely two different religious phenomena.'

twelfth centuries, largely associated with those abbeys whose roots reached back to the Carolingian age and further. To be sure, in the Orléanais for example, the canonical communities of Saint-Aignan and Meung-sur-Loire publicized the miraculous powers of their patrons. Both had been founded, however, as communities of monks and both miracle collections were associated with a reform of the community. The unreformed canons of Saint-Euverte ignored the relics of their 'father'; the new generation of regular canons, bringing reform from Saint-Victor, took pains to rediscover his relics and celebrate his patronage. Such communities were, like the monks of Fleury and Micy, involved in praying for the deceased laity.[19] The saintly patrons validated and reinforced the prayers of their monks and canons. They did not just aid their servants during their lifetimes by, for example, curing physical illnesses which resulted from sins. The servants of the saints could be buried in their churchyards, while enemies were excluded. Saintly patrons could even, as the canon who drowned after leaving Micy discovered, serve as guides through the underworld.[20]

The laity who came to relic shrines as pilgrims or who otherwise sought the intercession of a saintly 'father' brought with them important gifts and services. If miracle collections were, in a sense, a form of monastic propaganda, advertising the powers of a given patron, then there was a lay audience for that rhetoric.[21] As has been emphasized in this study, the interaction between monastic communities and the laity in the cult of the saints was complex and remains difficult to study with any precision. Nevertheless, it existed. The laity who became servants of a 'father' – the peasants who worked the saint's lands, the landholders who made donations to a community, the pilgrims who came to a shrine, and those who entered into voluntary servitude because of a cure or other miracle – formed, with the monks or canons who also served that saint, a 'community of common interest'. Their interests were not simply of this world, but were oriented to the court of heaven in which the 'fathers' lived as servants of God and in which they could provide unmatched patronage. The figure of St Faith, depicted on the early twelfth-century tympanum at Conques, whispering into the ear of

---

[19] According to Jean-Loup Lemaître, in an unpublished paper, an early modern necrology from Saint-Aignan bears strong traces of a medieval original.

[20] Letaldus of Micy, *Miracula s. Maximini*, c. 32, p. 607.

[21] For one discussion of the propagandistic values of miracle stories, see Töpfer 1956.

Christ on behalf of her servants at the last judgement encapsulates this form of patronage.[22]

Another crucial aspect of saintly patronage was the protection of monastic property, a goal which could not be served as directly by intercessory prayer. Violence was endemic in eleventh-century Francia and its neighbouring regions. The lands of monastic communities were frequently exploited by bishops or plundered by castellans.[23] Thus the wide variety of protective miracles, discussed here as chastisements, also had important value as propaganda. Nor was the protection offered by saints limited to the telling of stories, but involved powerful actions steeped in symbol and ritual. In the Orléanais the monks of Fleury took out their relics to face the armed servants of their bishop in a dispute over property, while the monks of Micy similarly used the relics of their 'father' against the retainers of a castellan.[24] Elsewhere the monks of Conques brought the relics of St Faith to protect their rights in a 'place alienated from St Faith by a lawless intruder'.[25] The standard of St Lambert was used in battle near Liège.[26] In the Touraine, monks used their powers of intercessory prayer to reconcile feuding nobles, while in Flanders the monks of Lobbes used the relics of their patron to similar ends.[27] Monks and canons, like those at Saint-Martin in Tours, humiliated the relics of their patrons when the expected protection of their property was not forthcoming.[28] These examples could all be multiplied many times over.

A general survey of miracle collections from Francia suggests that, as in the Orléanais, over the course of the eleventh and twelfth centuries saints exercised their miraculous patronage progressively less to protect the property of their communities, in what might be termed chastisement miracles, and more to cure or otherwise materially to aid pilgrims who came to their shrine. Such a development does not mean that the economic well being of monastic communities was any less at stake. As Francia became more stable over the course of the twelfth century, the income

---

22 On this image, see Bonne 1984, pp. 243–51. It is reproduced as figure 6 at the beginning of Bonne's work.

23 It was not, of course, the nature of lay violence against the church that was novel, but its frequency. In the ninth century Bishop Jonas of Orléans (*De institutione laicali*, 1.10, col. 138) had already described the *milites* as men whose hands were stained with blood.

24 *Miracula s. Benedicti*, 11.19, pp. 123–4; Letaldus of Micy, *Miracula s. Maximini*, c. 30, p. 606.

25 Bernard of Angers, *Liber miraculorum s. Fidis*, 11.4, p. 100.   26 Gaier 1966.

27 White 1986; Koziol 1987.   28 Geary 1979b, particularly pp. 29–33.

from these shrines, encouraged by the 'propaganda' provided by hagiographic literature, did much to enrich such traditional centres of monasticism as Fleury, Saint-Denis, and Saint-Philibert. At some monasteries – for example, to the north at Marchiennes and to the south at Mende – chastisement miracles continued to dominate collections, presumably in areas where the violent plundering of castellans continued to present significant threats to monastic property and well being.[29]

The cults of traditional saintly patrons were organized and controlled by the clergy, particularly monks and regular canons. The laity to varying degrees accepted this ideal of saintly patronage, participated in the official cults, and even, as Guibert of Nogent and others noted, sometimes organized unofficial cults of their own.[30] In as much as the laity did accept this ideal, it provided the monks with power to solicit donations and to protect the property which they already owned. By the eleventh century, however, monks were also searching for other means of self-protection. The royal and papal privileges forged by Letaldus and numerous others on the basis of saintly patronage provided one possible avenue. Abbo of Fleury's more programmatic development of law as a basis for real privileges had greater impact. Armed with such privileges – real or forged – monks frequented law courts armed with weapons other than the relics or miraculous powers of their patron. They did so not only to protect their own rights and properties, but even, as in the case of the abbey of Noyers, to solve the feuds of their lay neighbours.[31] The justice provided by the miraculous powers of a saintly 'father' mirrored the logic of the ordeal. In the eleventh and twelfth centuries monks began to trust legal processes based less on appeal to the immanent power of God.

The monks of Cluny eagerly followed Abbo of Fleury's lead in gathering papal privileges which exempted them from the power of the local bishop. As a house of relatively recent foundation, however, Cluny did not have the same access to the patronage of traditional 'fathers' as did such older centres as Fleury, Saint-Denis, or Saint-Philibert. While Cluny possessed many relics and

[29] See, for example, the various collections of *Miracula s. Rictrudi* (BHL 7249–51) and the *Miracula s. Privati* (BHL 6935) as studied by Platelle 1978–9 and Sigal 1976a, particularly p. 50 n. 3, and p. 55.
[30] On shrines organized by the laity, see, for example, Letaldus of Micy, *Delatio corporis s. Juniani*, c. 3, pp. 434–5; *Miracula s. Benedicti*, II.19, p. 125; *De diversis casibus Dervensis coenobii et miraculis s. Bercharii*, c. 28, pp. 859–60; Guibert of Nogent, *De pignoribus sanctorum*, I.2, col. 621. [31] White 1986.

attracted pilgrims, the tombs of its patron Peter lay elsewhere and its monks relied particularly on the power of their own intercessory prayer for their prestige. Peter was, after all, the gatekeeper of the kingdom of heaven, so that, in the absence of a shrine dedicated to him, his monastic servants could still beseech his aid. As Rodulfus Glaber, one of the fervent publicists of the Cluniac movement, recorded a hermit as saying, 'in the Roman world [Cluny] exceeds all in the number of souls it liberates from demonic control'.[32] The monks of Cluny forged their liturgical prayers into a kind of spiritual weapon for combat which was as effective as the miraculous powers of the saints in countering aggression based in lay society.[33] Still other houses of recent foundation, such as La Trinité at Vendôme, followed Cluny's lead in using papal privileges, an appeal to law, and the currency of prayer in the absence of significant relics.[34] Over the course of the eleventh and twelfth centuries monastic houses thus became less dependent on traditional saintly patronage in defending against bishops and laymen.

The bishops themselves had to protect other forms of ecclesiastical property against lay predators. The cathedrals of Francia, however, lacked significant relics of traditional patrons. In the Merovingian period bishops were not buried in their episcopal churches, but in suburban cemeteries. Most cathedrals came to be dedicated to the Virgin Mary, the protomartyr Stephen, or, as in Orléans, the holy cross. Thus the relics of Anianus, Denis, Germanus, and the other episcopal 'fathers' of the region did not lie under the control of bishops. Fulbert of Chartres represented one response to the problems facing the episcopate. Like Abbo of Fleury, he assiduously developed a tradition of canon law, but one favourable to episcopal rather than monastic claims. He also celebrated the miraculous powers of the Virgin and attempted to develop a cult focused on her veil, which was allegedly possessed by his cathedral.

Further south the bishops of the Aquitaine began to gather together in synods which issued legislation threatening with excommunication those who plundered church property or otherwise violated the peace. These synods gave impetus to the

---

[32] Rodulfus Glaber, *Quinque libri historiarum*, v.1.13, pp. 234–5.
[33] Rosenwein 1971.   [34] Johnson 1981, particularly pp. 69–102.

movement which became known as the Peace of God. In many cases oaths were required of the lay populace that they would renounce violence against the church and fellow Christians and thus observe peace. It was a novel and bold response to endemic violence, very different from traditional monastic responses to social upheaval. To be sure, monks participated in these synods, bringing with them the relics of their patrons whose presence was a standard mark of Peace councils.[35] The Peace of God differed, however, in its logic from the appeal to the miraculous protective powers called upon by monks through the relics of their saintly 'fathers'. Whereas the servants, both clerical and lay, of a saintly patron were linked through that saint to divine providence in a kind of hierarchical order, the people who administered and accepted Peace oaths, again both clerical and lay, were making divine providence present in the world through their own communal action. The saints whose relics were gathered at such a council served more simply as witnesses, rather than as the direct conduits of divine power.[36]   These new ideas of how divine power could be made manifest in human society – the legal tradition advocated by Abbo and Fulbert, the reliance on monastic prayer found at Cluny and its followers, the communal oaths and threats of excommunication employed in the Peace of God – all indicate that the winds of change were blowing through Francia and its neighbouring regions in the eleventh century. Over the course of the twelfth century interest in composing literary monuments dedicated to traditional 'fathers' waned, earlier in the Orléanais than elsewhere in Francia. After the twelfth century, the only texts composed about a 'father' of the Orléanais were several versions of the *Vita s. Dulchardi*, which proposed a new 'father' for veneration in much the same manner as the *Vita s. Laeti*.[37] The waning of literary activity, however, did not mean that the cult of these saints perished. Quite the contrary, liturgical evidence shows that these saints – be they Anianus and Benedict in the Orléanais, Denis and Geneviève in Paris, or still other saints in other regions – continued to be venerated.

New saintly patrons, however, emerged. Contemporary men

---

[35] Töpfer 1957, pp. 40–54 and 103–10; Cowdrey 1970b, pp. 44–53; Sargent 1985, pp. 220–8.   [36] For a fuller version of this argument, see Head 1987a.

[37] Poncelet 1905, pp. 73–6. The texts are difficult to date. Dulchardus was commonly included in liturgical calendars by the sixteenth century.

Conclusion

and women, many of them associated with reformed monastic orders, were recognized as potential saints during their lifetimes. Frequently the relics of such figures became, like those of the wandering hermit Gregory of Nicopolis, the focus of veneration. In the neighbouring diocese of Chartres, for example, the cults of Adiutor and Bernard, both monks of the abbey of Tiron, and of Gilduinus, a bishop of Dol who died at the abbey of Saint-Père, became popular. After Gregory, however, no saints emerged in the Orléanais itself.[38] The problems associated with this newer concept of sanctity led to the development of papally controlled canonization procedures. It was the shrines of newly canonized saints such as Thomas Becket and Francis of Assisi which now captured the religious imagination of western Europe. Miraculous relics and statues associated with Mary or crucifixes, images of the saviour himself, also gained in popularity as the focus of shrines and pilgrimages. Such statues of the Virgin would be found in the Orléanais in the suburb called *Avenum*, where it later attracted the attention of Jeanne d'Arc, and at the town of Cléry.[39]

Chartres and Canterbury, Jerusalem and Assisi, even Rome and Compostela – shrines of the apostles and martyrs, oldest of all Christian saints – these were to be the dominant shrines of the later middle ages. Traditional monasteries such as Saint-Denis and, to a lesser degree, Fleury would continue to have great importance as they were linked to the Capetian royal family, not as pilgrimage shrines. Sanctity became something expressed in terms of the affective contemplation of the Cistercians, the fervour for the apostolic life of the mendicants, or the intensely physical devotion to the Eucharist of women in the cities of late medieval Italy. The Franks, however, did not abandon the relics of their more traditional 'fathers'. In the thirteenth century, for example, Louis IX provided new reliquaries and churches for a number of such saints, Anianus among them.[40] The 'pious local patronage' of Bishop Walter's 'fathers', and of their counterparts in the dioceses of the Franks and of the old Carolingian empire more generally, slowly receded from a position of central importance in the religious life of western Europe. Those saints and their patronage –

[38] Some figures who came from the region, but lived elsewhere, were recognized as saints, such as Odo of Tournai whose cult was centred in his episcopal see of Cambrai.
[39] Vincent of Beauvais, *Bibliotheca mundi*, VII.83, IV, 251; Jarry 1899.
[40] Carolus-Barré 1965, particularly pp. 1093–4.

explored here in terms of a single exemplary region – had been at the very centre of one important phase in the development of the practice of Christianity and the life of the society which that religion moulded.

BIBLIOGRAPHY AND REFERENCES

PRIMARY SOURCES

Abbo of Fleury, *Apologeticus. PL*, cxxxix, 461–72.

Collectio canonum. PL, cxxxix, 473–508.

Epistolae. PL, cxxxix, 419–61.

Epitome de XCI Romanorum pontificum vitis. PL, cxxxix, 535–70.

Quaestiones Grammaticales, ed. Anita Guerreau-Jalabert. Paris, 1982.

Vita s. Edmundi (BHL 2392), ed. Michael Winterbottom. In *Three Lives of English Saints*. Toronto, 1972, pp. 67–87.

Acta translationis s. Evurtii (BHL 2801). *AASS*, Sept. iii, pp. 59–60.

Actus pontificum Cenomannis in urbe degentium, ed. Gustave Busson and Ambroise Ledru. Archives historiques du Maine, 2. Le Mans, 1901.

Adalbero of Laon, *Poème au roi Robert*, ed. and trans. Claude Carozzi. Les classiques de l'histoire de France au moyen âge, 32. Paris, 1979.

Ademar of Chabannes, *Chronicon*, ed. Jules Chavanon. Collection des textes pour servir à l'étude et à l'enseignement de l'histoire, 20. Paris, 1897.

Adrevald of Fleury, *Historia translationis s. Benedicti (BHL* 1117). In Certain 1858, pp. 1–14.

De corpore et sanguine Christi contra ineptias Iohannis Scoti. PL, cxxiv, 947–54.

Miracula s. Benedicti (BHL 1123). In Certain 1858, pp. 15–83.

Vita s. Aigulphi (BHL 194). *AASSOSB*, ii, 656–65.

Adso of Montierender, *Translatio et miracula s. Basoli (BHL* 1034). *AASSOSB*, iv.2, 137–42.

Aimo of Fleury, *Fert animus linguam. PL*, cxxxix, 797–802.

Historiae francorum libri quatuor. PL, cxxxix, 627–851.

In annuis terrenorum. PL, cxxxix, 851–70.

Libelli miraculorum s. Benedicti (BHL 1136–9). In Vidier 1965, pp. 227–8.

Miracula s. Benedicti (BHL 1125). In Certain 1858, pp. 90–172.

Sermo in festivitatibus s. patris Benedicti. PL, cxxxix, 851–70.

Vita et miracula s. Abbonis (BHL 3). *AASSOSB*, vi.1, 37–58.

Anastasius Bibliothecarius, *Liber Pontificalis. MGH, Gesta Pontificum Romanorum*, i.

Andrew of Fleury, *Miracula s. Benedicti (BHL* 1126). In Certain 1858, pp. 173–248.

Vie de Gauzlin, abbé de Fleury. Vita Gauzlini abbatis Floriacensis monasterii, ed. and trans. Robert-Henri Bautier and Gillette Labory. Sources d'histoire médiévale publiées par l'Institut de Recherches et d'Histoire des Textes, 2. Paris, 1969.

Bibliography and references

Annales de Saint-Bertin, ed. Felix Grat, Jeanne Vielliard, and Suzanne Clémenet. Paris, 1964.

Annales Floriacenses. In Vidier 1965, pp. 217–20.

Annales Laureshamenses. MGH, SS, I, 22–39.

Ardo, *Vita s. Benedicti Anianensis (BHL* 1096). *MGH, SS,* xv.1, 200–20.

Arnulf of Orléans, *De cartiligene*. In Lauer 1898, pp. 493–4.

Bernard of Angers, *Liber miraculorum s. Fidis (BHL* 1942), ed. A. Bouillet. Collection des textes pour servir à l'étude et à l'enseignement de l'histoire, 21. Paris, 1897.

Bertarius of Verdun, *Gesta pontificum s. Virdunensis ecclesiae. PL,* cxxxii, 502–28.

Bertholdus of Micy, *Vita s. Maximini I (BHL* 5817). *AASSOSB,* I, 591–7.

Caesarius of Arles, *Sermones*, ed. Germain Morin. Corpus Christianorum series latina, 103–4. Turnhout, 1953.

Cartulaire de l'abbaye de Saint-Père de Chartres, ed. B. Guérard. 2 vols. Collection des cartulaires de France, 1 and 2. Paris, 1840.

Cartulaire de l'église de Quimper, ed. Paul Peyron. Quimper, 1909.

Cartulaire de Notre-Dame de Chartres, eds. Eugène Lépinois and Lucien Merlet. 2 vols. Chartres, 1862.

Cartulaire de Sainte-Croix d'Orléans (814–1300), ed. Joseph Thillier and Eugène Jarry. Mémoires de la Société archéologique et historique de l'Orléanais, 30. Paris, 1906.

Cartulaire de Saint-Jouin de Marnes, ed. Charles Grandmaison. *Mémoires de la Société de statistique du département des Deux-Sèvres,* 17, part 2. Niort, 1854.

Cartulaire des abbayes de Saint-Pierre de La Couture et de Saint-Pierre de Solesmes, ed. les Bénédictins de Solesmes. Le Mans, 1881.

Cartulaire du chapitre de Saint-Avit-d'Orléans, ed. Gaston Vignat. Collection des cartulaires du Loiret, 2. Orléans, 1886.

Les Chartes de l'abbaye de Jumièges (v. 825 à 1204), ed. Jules Vernier. 2 vols. Paris, 1916.

('Chartes de Micy'.) 'Etudes sur les anciennes chartes de l'abbaye Saint-Mesmin de Micy et essai de reconstitution des cartulaires', ed. Marie-Madeleine Lemarignier. Thèse de l'Ecole des Chartes. Typescript. Paris, 1937.

Chronicon Dolensis coenobii. In Léopold Delisle, ed., *Recueil des historiens des Gaules et de la France,* 13 vols. (Paris, 1738–86), xi, 387–8.

Chronique de l'Abbaye de Saint-Bénigne de Dijon, ed. E. Bougard and Joseph Garnier. Analecta Divionensia, 9. Dijon, 1875.

La Chronique de Saint-Maixent, 751–1140, ed. and trans. Jean Verdon. Les classiques de l'histoire de France au moyen âge, 33. Paris, 1979.

Chronique de Saint-Pierre-le-Vif de Sens, dite de Clarius, ed. and trans. Robert-Henri Bautier and Monique Gilles. Sources d'histoire médiévale publiées par l'Institut de Recherche et d'Histoire des Textes, 3. Paris, 1979.

Conseutudines Floriacenses saeculi tertii decimi, ed. Anselme Davril. Corpus Consuetudinum Monasticarum, 12. Siegburg, 1976.

De diversis casibus Dervensis coenobii et miraculis s. Bercharii (BHL 1179). *AASSOSB,* ii, 844–61.

De translatione reliquiarum s. Aigulfi in castrum Pruviense (BHL 195). *AASS,* Sept. 1, pp. 755–6.

Desiderius of Monte Cassino, *Dialogi de miraculis s. Benedicti (BHL* 1141). *AASSOSB*, IV.2, 425–61.

Eadmer of Canterbury, *Vita s. Anselmi (BHL* 526), ed. and trans. R. W. Southern. Nelson's Medieval Texts. London, 1962. Repr. Oxford Medieval Texts. Oxford, 1972.

Ermoldus Nigellus, *Poème sur Louis le Pieux et épîtres au roi Pépin*, ed. and trans. Edmond Faral. Les classiques de l'histoire de France au moyen âge, 14. Paris, 1932.

Exercitiunculae de gestis s. Saviniani (BHL 7436). *AASSOSB*, VI.1, 259–66.

Flodoard, *Les Annales de Flodoard*, ed. Philippe Lauer. Collection des textes pour servir à l'étude et à l'enseignement de l'histoire, 39. Paris, 1905.

Fredegar, *Chronicon*. *MGH, SRM*, II, 18–193.
   The Fourth Book of the Chronicle of Fredegar with its Continuations, trans. and ed. J. M. Wallace-Hadrill. Nelson's Medieval Texts. London, 1960.

Fulbert of Chartres, *The Letters of Fulbert of Chartres*, ed. and trans. Frederick Behrends. Oxford Medieval Texts. Oxford, 1976.

Garin le Loheren. According to Manuscript A (Bibliothèque de l'Arsenal 2983), ed. Josephine Vallerie. Ann Arbor, Mich., 1947.

Gerbert of Reims, *Acta concilii Remensis*. In *MGH, SS*, III, 658–86.
   Epistolae. In *Die Briefsammlung Gerberts von Reims*, ed. Fritz Weigle. *MGH, Die Briefe der deutschen Kaiserzeit*, II. Berlin, 1966.
   Opera mathematica, 972–1003, ed. Nikolai Bubnov. Berlin, 1899.

Gesta Ambaziensium dominorum. In *Chroniques des comtes d'Anjou et des seigneurs d'Amboise*, ed. Louis Halphen and René Poupardin, pp. 74–132. Collection des textes pour servir à l'étude et à l'enseignement de l'histoire, 48. Paris, 1913.

Gregory of Tours, *Historia Francorum*. *MGH, SRM*, I, 1–450.
   Libri octo miraculorum VIII. Liber in gloria confessorum. *MGH, SRM*, I, 744–820.

Gregory the Great. *Dialogues*, ed. Adalbert de Vogüé. 3 vols. Sources chrétiennes, 251, 260, and 265. Paris, 1978–80.

Guibert of Nogent, *De pignoribus sanctorum*. *PL*, CLVI, 607–80.
   Autobiographie, ed. and trans. Edmond-René Labande. Les classiques de l'histoire de France au moyen âge, 34. Paris, 1981.

Le Guide du pèlerin de Saint-Jacques de Compostelle, ed. and trans. Jeanne Vielliard. 5th edition. Mâcon, 1978.

Hariulf, *Libellus de miraculis s. Richarii factis post eius relationem (BHL* 7235). *AASSOSB*, V, 567–73.

Heiric of Auxerre, *Miracula s. Germani (BHL* 3462). *AASS*, July VII, pp. 255–83.

Helgaud of Fleury, *Vie de Robert le Pieux. Epitoma vitae regis Rotberti pii*, ed. and trans. Robert-Henri Bautier and Gillette Labory. Sources d'histoire médiévale publiées par l'Institut de Recherches et d'Histoire des Textes, 1. Paris, 1965.

Herimanus, *Liber de restauratione monasterii Sancti-Martini Toracensis*. *MGH, SS*, XIV, 270–81.

Hieronymian Martyrology. *AASS*, Nov. II, part 1.

Hilary of Arles, *Vie de Saint Honorat (BHL* 3975), ed. and trans. Marie-Denise Valentin. Sources chrétiennes, 235. Paris, 1977.

Bibliography and references

Historia s. Florentii Salmurensis. In *Les Chroniques d'Anjou,* ed. Paul Marchegay and Emile Mabille. 2 vols. (Paris, 1869), II, 207–328.

Historia translationis reliquiarum s. Juniani abbatis e Mariacensi monasterio in Nobiliacense apud Pictones (BHL 4564). *AASSOSB,* IV.1, 432–3.

Hugh of Fleury, *Historia ecclesiastica. MGH, SS,* IX, 349–53.

 Liber de regia potestate et sacerdotali dignitate. MGH, Libelli de lite imperatorum et pontificum saeculi XI et XII conscripti, II, 465–94.

 Liber modernorum regum. PL, CLXIII, 875–940.

 Miracula s. Benedicti (BHL 1135). In Certain 1858, pp. 357–71.

 Vita et miracula s. Sacerdotis (BHL 7456–9). *PL,* CLXIII, 769–1004.

Jerome, *Sancti Eusebii Hieronymi Epistulae,* ed. Isidore Hilberg. Corpus Scriptorum Ecclesiasticorum Latinorum, 54–5. Vienna, 1910.

John of Ripoll, *Letter to Abbot Oliba.* In Andrew of Fleury, *Vita Gauzlini,* pp. 180–3.

John of Salerno, *Vita s. Odonis* (BHL 6292–7). *PL,* CXXXIII, 43–86.

Jonas of Orléans, *De imaginis sanctorum. PL,* CVI, 305–88.

 De institutione laicali libri tres. PL, CVI, 121–280.

 De institutione regia ad Pippinum regem. PL, CVI, 280–306.

 Vita et translatio s. Huberti (BHL 3994–5). *AASS,* Nov. I, pp. 806–18.

Letaldus of Micy, *Delatio corporis s. Juniani ad synodem Karoffensem* (BHL 4565). *AASSOSB,* IV.1, 434–5.

 Miracula s. Maximini (BHL 5820). *AASSOSB,* I, 598–613.

 Versus de eversione monasterii Glomnensis. MGH, Poetae latini aevi Carolini, II, 146–9.

 Versus de quodam piscatore quem ballena absorbuit. In Pascal 1987.

 Vita et miracula s. Eusicii (BHL 2754 and 2756). *Nova bibliotheca mss.,* II, 372–6 and 463–6.

 Vita et miracula s. Martini Vertavensis (BHL 5667–8). *AASS,* Oct. X, pp. 805–17. Prologue and selections in *MGH, SRM,* III, 567–75.

 Vita s. Juliani (BHL 4544). *PL,* CXXXVII, 781–96.

Liber historiae Francorum. MGH, SRM, II, 238–328.

Lucifer of Orléans, *Vita s. Evurtii II* (BHL 2799). *AASS,* Sept, III, pp. 52–8.

Lupus of Ferrières, *Correspondance,* ed. and trans. Léon Levillain. 2 vols. Les classiques de l'histoire de France au moyen âge, 10 and 11. Paris, 1927–35.

 Vita s. Maximini Treverensis (BHL 5824). *MGH, SRM,* III, 74–82.

 Vita s. Wigberti (BHL 8879). *AASSOSB,* III.1 673–82.

Miracula s. Aigulfi (BHL 196). *AASSOSB,* II, 667–72.

Miracula s. Aniani (BHL 476 b and d). In Renaud 1976, pp. 256–74.

Miracula s. Carileffi (BHL 1572). *AASSOSB,* I, 650–4.

Miracula s. Euspicii (BHL 2759). *AASSOSB,* VI.1, 314–15.

Miracula s. Lifardi (BHL 4933). *AASSOSB,* I, 159–64.

Miracula ss. Georgii et Laeti (BHL 3398 d). *AASS,* Nov. III, pp. 78–9.

Miraculum s. Maximini (BHL 5821 b). In Head 1984, pp. 238–51.

Odo of Cluny, *Sermo de s. Benedicto. PL,* CXXXIII, 721–9.

 Vita s. Geraldi Auriliacensis comitis (BHL 3411). *PL,* CXXXIII, 639–704.

Odo of Glanfeuil, *Historia translationis corporis s. Mauri abbatis in Fossatense monasterium* (BHL 5775–6). *AASSOSB,* IV.2, 167–83.

Odorannus of Sens, *Chronique*. In *Opera omnia*, ed. and trans. Robert-Henri Bautier and Monique Gilles (Sources d'histoire médiévale publiées par l'Institut de Recherches et d'Histoire des Textes, 4. Paris, 1972), pp. 84–113.

Orderic Vitalis, *The Ecclesiastical History of Orderic Vitalis*, ed. and trans. Marjorie Chibnall. 6 vols. Oxford Medieval Texts. Oxford, 1969–80.

Ouenus of Rouen, *Vita s. Eligii* (BHL 2474). *PL*, cxxxvii, 479–594.

Papsturkunden 896–1046, ed. Harald Zimmermann. 2 vols. Vienna, 1984–5.

Passio et translatio s. Baudelii (BHL 1045 b and c). In Renaud 1978b, pp. 160–6.

Passio s. Baudelii (Nimausi) (BHL 1043). *AASS*, May v, pp. 195–6.

Passio s. Clementis (BHL 1848). In Mombrizio 1479?, i, 193–5.

Passio s. Dionysii (BHL 2171). *MGH*, *AA*, iv, 101–5.

Paul the Deacon, *Historia Langobardorum*. *MGH*, *Scriptores rerum Langobardicarum*, i.

Peter the Deacon, *Divinae pietatis*. *Analecta Bollandiana*, 1 (1882), 79–84.

    Historica relatio de corpore s. Benedicti Casini (BHL 1142). *AASS*, March iii, pp. 288–97.

Peter the Venerable, *The Letters of Peter the Venerable*, ed. Giles Constable. 2 vols. Cambridge, Mass., 1967.

Pretiosi confessoris (BHL 5661). *Catal. Paris*, i, 19–21.

Recueil des actes de Charles II le Chauve, roi de France, ed. Georges Tessier. 3 vols. Paris, 1943–55.

Recueil des actes de Charles III le Simple, roi de France (893–923), ed. Philippe Lauer. Paris, 1949.

Recueil des actes d'Eudes, roi de France (888–898), ed. Robert Henri Bautier. Paris, 1968.

Recueil des actes de Lothaire et de Louis V rois de France (954–987), ed. Louis Halphen. Paris, 1908.

Recueil des actes de Louis IV, roi de France (936–954), ed. Philippe Lauer. Paris, 1914.

Recueil des chartes de l'abbaye de Saint-Benoît-sur-Loire, ed. Maurice Prou and Alexandre Vidier. 2 vols. Documents publiés par la Société historique et archéologique du Gâtinais, 5. Paris, 1900–32.

Regino of Prüm, *Chronicon*. *MGH*, *SS*, ii, 537–612.

Relatio qualiter corpus sanctae Scholasticae virginis, sororis sancti Benedicti, Cenomannis advenerit et a Berario eiusdem urbis episcopo susceptum et conditum sit (BHL 7525). In Goffart 1967, pp. 134–41.

Richer, *Histoire de France*, ed. and trans. Robert Latouche. 2 vols. Les classiques de l'histoire de France au moyen âge, 12 and 17. Paris, 1967 and 1964.

Rodulfus Glaber, *Historiarum libri quinque*, ed. J. France. Oxford Medieval Texts. Oxford, 1989.

Rodulfus Tortarius, *Miracula s. Benedicti* (BHL 1129). In Certain 1858, pp. 277–356.

    Rodulfi Tortarii Carmina, ed. M. G. Ogle and D. M. Schullian. Papers and Monographs of the American Academy in Rome, 8. Rome, 1933.

Roger of Saint-Euverte, *Inventio s. Evurtii* (BHL 2802). *AASS*, Sept. iii, p. 61.

Sermo de inventione s. Maximini et eius discipulorum Theodemiri et alterius Maximini (BHL 5821). *AASSOSB*, vi.1, 252–3.

Sidonius Apollinaris, *Epistolae et Carmina*. *MGH*, *AA*, viii.

Bibliography and references

Sigebert of Gembloux, *De scriptoribus ecclesiasticis*. PL, CLX, 547–92.

Stephen of Liège, *Vita s. Lamberti* (BHL 4683). *MGH, SRM*, VI, 385–92.

Suger of Saint-Denis, *Vie de Louis VI le Gros*, ed. and trans. Henri Waquet. Les classiques de l'histoire de France au moyen âge, 11. Paris, 1929.

Theodoric of Fleury, *Consuetudines Floriacenses antiquiores*, ed. Anselme Davril and Lin Donnat. Corpus Consuetudinum Monasticarum, 7, part 3. Sieburg, 1984.

  Illatio s. Benedicti (BHL 1122). *AASSOSB*, IV.2, 350–5.

  Passio ss. Tryphoni et Respicii (BHL 8340). Prologue in Mai 1839–44, IV, 291–3.

  Vita s. Firmani (BHL 3001). Excerpts in Poncelet 1899b, pp. 22–9.

  Vita s. Martini papae (BHL 5596). Prologue in Mai 1839–44, IV, 293–5. Text in *Hist. SS.*, XI, 421–40.

Theodoric of Saint-Eucharius, *Historia inventionis s. Celsi* (BHL 1720). *AASS*, Feb. III, pp. 402–6.

Theodulf of Orléans, *Carmina*. *MGH, Poetae latini aevi Carolini*, I, 437–581.

  Libri Carolini sive Caroli Magni Capitulare de Imaginibus. *MGH, Concilia*, II.3.

Translatio s. Benedicti (BHL 1116). In Weber 1952, pp. 141–2.

Translatio s. Euspicii (BHL 2758). *AASSOSB*, VI.1, 313–14.

Translatio s. Lifardi (BHL 4932). *AASSOSB*, I, 157–9.

Usuard, *Le Martyrologe d'Usuard, texte et commentaire*, ed. Jacques Dubois. Subsidia hagiographica, 40. Brussels, 1965.

La Vie et les miracles de saint Viâtre, dont le corps est dans l'église de Trembelvif en Sologne, diocèse d'Orléans. Orléans, 1736.

Vincent of Beauvais, *Bibliotheca mundi, seu Speculi maioris Vincentii Burgundi praesulis Bellovacensis Ordinis Praedicatorum, theologi ac doctoris eximii*. 4 vols. Douai, 1624.

Virtutes s. Fursaei (BHL 3213). *MGH, SRM*, IV, 440–9.

Vita Hludovici imperatoris. *MGH, SS*, II, 604–28.

Vita s. Balthildis reginae (BHL 905). *MGH, SRM*, II, 477–508.

Vita s. Genovefae (BHL 3335). *MGH, SRM*, III, 215–38.

Vita s. Gertrudi (BHL 3490). *AASSOSB*, II, 463–8.

Vita s. Montanae (BHL 6008). *Nova bibliotheca mss.*, II, 593–6.

Vita s. Adonis (BHL 82). *AASSOSB*, IV.2, 262–5.

Vita s. Agili (BHL 147). *AASS*, Aug. VI, pp. 566–8.

Vita s. Aldrici (BHL 263). *AASSOSB*, IV.1, 539–46.

Vita s. Almiri (BHL 305). *AASS*, Sept. III, pp. 803–6.

Vita s. Aniani I (BHL 473). *MGH, SRM*, III, 108–17.

Vita s. Aniani II (BHL 474). In Theiner 1832, pp. 27–33.

Vita s. Aniani III (BHL 476). In Theiner 1832, pp. 34–6.

Vita s. Aviti I (BHL 879). *Catal. Brux.*, I, 57–63.

Vita s. Aviti IV (BHL 882). *AASS*, June III, pp. 351–9.

Vita s. Carileffi I (BHL 1568). *Hist. SS*, VII, 71–82.

Vita s. Carileffi II (BHL 1569–70). *AASSOSB*, I, 642–50.

Vita s. Constantiani (BHL 1931). *Nova bibliotheca mss.*, II, 515–17.

Vita s. Eucherii (BHL 2660). *AASS*, Feb. III, pp. 217–19.

Vita s. Evurtii I (BHL 2800). *Catal. Paris.*, II, 312–19.

Vita s. Gregorii Nicopolitani (BHL 3669). *AASS*, March II, pp. 462–4.

Vita s. Huberti I (BHL 3993). *AASS*, Nov. I, pp. 798–805.

Vita s. Juliani (BHL 4545). In *Actus pontificum Cenomannis in urbe degentium*, pp. 10–27.

Vita s. Laeti (BHL 4672). *AASS*, Nov. III, pp. 72–8.

Vita s. Launomauri (BHL 4733). *AASSOSB*, I, 335–8.

Vita s. Leobini (BHL 4847). *AASSOSB*, I, 123–8.

Vita s. Lifardi (BHL 4931). *AASSOSB*, I, 154–7.

Vita s. Lupi Senonensis (BHL 5082–3). *MGH, SRM*, IV, 179–87.

Vita s. Maximini II (BHL 5814–16). *AASSOSB*, I, 580–91.

Vita s. Rigomari (BHL 7256). *AASS*, Aug. IV, pp. 786–8.

Vita s. Theodorici I (BHL 8052). *AASSOSB*, VI.1, 194–6.

Vita s. Theodorici II (BHL 8053). *AASSOSB*, VI.1, 197–8.

Vita s. Viatoris (BHL 8551). In Poncelet 1905, pp. 98–103.

Vitalis of Fleury, *Vita s. Pauli Aureliani* (BHL 6586). *AASS*, May II, pp. 111–20.

Walter of Orléans, *Capitularia Walterii*. *MGH, Capitula episcoporum*, I, 185–93.

Wormonoc of Landévennec, *Vita s. Pauli Aureliani* (BHL 6585), ed. Bede Plaine. *Analecta Bollandiana*, I (1882), 209–58.

SECONDARY WORKS

Arnauldet, M. P., 1903. 'Notice sur la plus ancienne bibliothèque de France et les livres historiques de l'abbaye de Saint Mesmin de Micy au VIe siècle', *Bulletin de la Société nationale des Antiquaires de France*, 270–7.

Asad, Talal, 1983. 'Notes on body pain and truth in medieval Christian ritual', *Economy and Society*, 12, 287–327.

Aubert, Marcel, 1930. 'Ferrières-en-Gâtinais', *Congrès archéologique de France*, 93, 219–32.

Auvray, Lucien, 1887. 'Une source de la "Vita Roberti regis"', *Mélanges d'archéologie et d'histoire publiés par l'Ecole française de Rome*, 7, 458–71.

Babonaux, Yves, 1983. 'De l'Orléanais au terroir d'Orléans', in Debal 1983, pp. 7–45.

Bachrach, Bernard, 1976. 'A study in feudal politics: relations between Fulk Nerra and William the Great, 995–1030', *Viator*, 7, 111–21.

1978. 'Robert de Blois, Abbot of Saint-Florent de Saumur and Saint-Mesmin de Micy (985–1011). A study in small power politics', *Revue Bénédictine*, 88, 123–46.

1985. 'Geoffrey Greymantle, Count of the Angevins, 960–987: a study in French politics', *Studies in Medieval and Renaissance History*, 7, 3–67.

Banchereau, Jules, 1931a. 'Eglise Saint-Aignan', *Congrès archéologique de France*, 93, 52–70.

1931b. 'Saint-Avit', *Congrès archéologique de France*, 93, 70–7.

1931c. 'La Chapelle Saint-Mesmin', *Congrès archéologique de France*, 93, 271–8.

Bar, Francis, 1937. *Les Epîtres latines de Raoul le Tourtier (1065?–1114?). Etude des sources*. Paris

1975. 'Raoul le Tourtier, moine de Fleury et poète latin à la fin du XIe siècle', in Louis 1975, pp. 1–8.

Bibliography and references

Barbier, Paul, 1898. *Histoire de Saint-Euverte; le saint, l'abbaye, l'église, le pensionnat.* Orléans.

Barralis, Victor, 1603. *Chronologia sanctorum et aliorum virorum illustrium ac abbatum sacrae insulae Lerinensis.* Lyon.

Barré, Henri, 1962. *Les Homéliaires carolingiens de l'école d'Auxerre. Authenticité – inventaire – tableaux comparatifs – initia.* Studi e testi, 225. Rome.

Bartlett, Robert, 1986. *Trial by Fire and Water. The Medieval Judicial Ordeal.* Oxford.

Batany, Jean, 1975. 'Abbon de Fleury et les théories des structures sociales vers l'an mil', in Louis 1975, pp. 9–18.

Bauchy, Jacques-Henri, 1983. 'Aspects de la renaissance carolingienne en Orléanais', in Oury 1983a, pp. 54–60.

Bauerreiss, Romuald, 1950. 'Wer ist der Verfasser des ältesten Translationsberichtes der Benediktinus-reliquien?', *Studien und Mitteilungen zur Geschichte des Benediktinerordens*, 62, 8–12.

Bautier, Robert-Henri, 1964. 'L'*Epitoma vitae regis Rotberti Pii*, du moine Helgaud', *Académie des Inscriptions et Belles-Lettres. Comptes rendus des séances de l'année 1963*, pp. 361–71. Paris.

1969. 'Le Monastère et les églises de Fleury-sur-Loire sous les abbatiats d'Abbon, de Gauzlin et d'Arnaud (988–1032)', *Mémoires de la Société nationale des Antiquaires de France*, 9th series, 4, 71–156.

1970. 'L'Historiographie en France aux Xe et XIe siècles (France du Nord et de l'Est)', in *La storiografia altomedievale*, II, 793–850. Settimane di studio del Centro italiano di studi sull'alto Medio Evo, 17. Spoleto.

1975a. 'L'Hérésie d'Orléans et le mouvement intellectuel au début du XIe siècle. Documents et hypothèses', in *Enseignement et vie intellectuelle*, pp. 63–88. Actes du 95e Congrès national des sociétés savantes, Reims, 1970. Section de philologie et d'histoire jusqu'à 1610, Tome I. Paris.

1975b. 'La Place de l'abbaye de Fleury-sur-Loire dans l'historiographie française du IXe au XIIe siècle', in Louis 1975, pp. 25–34.

Bautier, Robert-Henri, and Gillette Labory, 1965. 'Introduction', to Helgaud of Fleury, *Vie de Robert le Pieux*, pp. 2–53.

1969. 'Introduction', to Andrew of Fleury, *Vie de Gauzlin, abbé de Fleury*, pp. 7–30.

Bédier, Joseph, 1929. *Les Légendes épiques. Recherches sur la formation des chansons de geste.* 3rd edition. 4 vols. Paris.

Beech, George, 1974. 'The origins of the family of the Viscounts of Thouars', in *Etudes de civilisation médiévale (IXe–XIIe siècles). Mélanges offerts à Edmond-René Labande*, pp. 25–31. Poitiers.

Beeson, C. H., 1930. *Servatus Lupus as Scribe and Text Critic.* Cambridge, Mass.

Belton, Louis, 1893. 'Les Reliques de Saint Calais', *Loir et Cher historique*, 6, 139–41.

Berland, Jean-Marie, 1975a. 'La Crypte romane de Saint-Benoît-sur-Loire', in Louis 1975, pp. 387–402.

1975b. 'Présentation des vestiges anciens et objects d'art préromans conservés dans l'abbaye', in Louis 1975, pp. 403–12.

1978a. 'A propos de Saint-Aignan d'Orléans: une expression d'Helgaud de

Fleury dans sa "Vita Roberti"', *Bulletin de la Société archéologique et historique de l'Orléanais*, 49, 171–3.

1978b. 'Les Origines de l'église d'Orléans (IVe–VIIe siécles)', *Bulletin de la Société archéologique et historique de l'Orléanais*, 49, 19–78.

1978c. 'Saint-Pierre-aux-Boeufs, une église orléanaise fantôme', *Bulletin de la Société archéologique et historique de l'Orléanais*, 49, 79–82.

1979a. 'La Nécropole "ad sanctum" de Saint-Benoît-sur-Loire', *Studia Monastica*, 21, 303–12.

1979b. 'Les Chapiteaux historiés du triforium de l'église abbatiale de Saint-Benoît-sur-Loire', *Cahiers de Saint-Michel de Cuxa*, 11, 1–48.

1979c. 'Présence du corps de saint Benoît a Fleury-sur-Loire du Haut Moyen Age à nos jours', *Studia Monastica*, 21, 279–302.

1980a. 'Saint-Benoît-sur-Loire: l'abbaye et le village', *Bulletin de la Société historique, archéologique et artistique du Giennois*, 28, 1–47.

ed., 1980b. *Val de Loire Roman.* 3rd edition. Pierre-qui-Vire.

1981. 'La Presence bénédictine dans le diocèse d'Orléans', *Bulletin de la Société historique, archéologique et artistique du Giennois*, 29, 3–56.

1982. 'L'Autel roman, dédié à Saint Benoît en 1108 à Saint-Benoît-sur-Loire, et son environnement', *Cahiers de Saint-Michel de Cuxa*, 14, 5–61.

1983–4. 'Un moine aquitain de l'an mil: Aimoin de Fleury', *Revue historique de Bordeaux et du département de la Gironde*, 30, 5–32.

1984a. 'Les Prieurés normands de l'abbaye de Fleury aux XIe et XIIIe siècles', in *Questions d'histoire et de dialectologie Normande*, pp. 107–24. Actes du 105e Congrès national des sociétés savantes, Caen, 1980. Section de philologie et d'histoire jusqu'à 1610, Tome II. Paris.

1984b. 'L'Influence de l'abbaye de Fleury-sur-Loire en Bretagne et dans les îles britanniques du Xe au XIIe siècle', in *Questions d'histoire de Bretagne*, pp. 275–99. Actes du 107e Congrès national des sociétés savantes, Brest, 1982. Section de philologie et d'histoire jusqu'à 1610, Tome II. Paris.

1985. 'La Place du monastère de Perrecy et de ses églises parmi les prieurés de Fleury', in *L'Encadrement religieux des fidèles au Moyen-Age et jusqu'au Concile de Trente. La paroisse – le clergé – la pastorale – la dévotion*, pp. 621–43. Actes du 109e Congrès national des sociétés savantes, Dijon, 1984. Section d'histoire médiévale et de philologie, Tome I. Paris.

Bernois, Charles, 1918. *Histoire de l'abbaye royale de Saint-Euverte d'Orléans.* Orléans.

Bernoulli, Carl, 1900. *Die Heiligen der Merowinger.* Tübingen.

Biémont, René, 1837. *La Collégiale de Saint-Aignan à Orléans.* Orléans.

Bimbenet, Jean-Eugène, 1861. *Episcopats de St. Euverte et de St. Aignan, ou l'église d'Orléans aux IVe et Ve siècles.* Orléans.

1884–8. *Histoire de la ville d'Orléans.* 5 vols. Orléans.

Bischoff, Bernhard, 1984. 'Briefe des neunten Jahrhunderts', in *idem*, ed., *Anecdota Novissima. Texte des vierten bis sechzehnten Jahrhunderts*, pp. 123–38. Quellen und Untersuchungen zur lateinischen Philologie des Mittelalters, 7. Stuttgart.

Blanchet, Adrien, and Adolphe Dieudonné, 1912–36. *Manuel de numismatique française.* 4 vols. Paris.

Bibliography and references

Blecker, Michael, 1966. 'The civil rights of the monk in Roman and canon law. The monk as *servus*', *American Benedictine Review*, 17, 185–98.

Bloch, Marc, 1924. *Les Rois thaumaturges. Etude sur le caractère surnaturel attribué à la puissance royale particulièrement en France et en Angleterre*. Publications de la Faculté des lettres de l'Université de Strasbourg, 19. Strasbourg.

Boesch Gajano, Sofia, ed., 1976. *Agiografia altomedioevale*. Bologna.

Boesch Gajano, Sofia, and Lucia Sebastiani, eds., 1984. *Culto dei santi, istituzioni e classi sociali in età preindustriale*. Collana di studi storici, 1. Aquila.

Bonnaud-Delamere, Roger, 1961. 'les Institutions de paix en Aquitaine au XIe siècle', *Recueils de la Société Jean Bodin pour l'histoire comparative des institutions*, 14, 415–87.

Bonne, Jean-Claude, 1984. *L'Art roman de face et de profil. Le tympan de Conques*. Paris.

Bonnes, Jean-Paul, 1943. 'Un lettré du Xe siècle. Introduction au poème de Letald', *Revue Mabillon*, 33, 23–47.

Borderie, Arthur de la, 1892. 'Salomon roi de Bretagne dans les chansons de geste', *Revue de Bretagne, de Vendée et d'Anjou*, 7, 395–408.

Bosl, Karl, 1965. 'Adelsheilige, Idealtypus und Wirklichkeit. Gesellschaft und Kultur im merowingerzeitlichen Bayern des 7.–8. Jahrhunderts', in Clemens Bauer, ed., *Speculum historiale. Geschichte im Spiegel von Geschichtschreibung und Geschichtsdeutung. Festschrift für J. Spörl*, pp. 167–87. Munich.

Bouchard, Constance, 1981. 'The origins of the French nobility, a reassessment', *American Historical Review*. 86, 501–32.

Boussard, Jacques, 1951. 'La Seigneurie de Bellême aux Xe et XIe siècles', in Perrin 1951, pp. 43–54.

1962. 'L'Origine des familles seigneuriales dans la région de la Loire moyenne', *Cahiers de civilisation médiévale*, 5, 303–22.

1970. 'Les Evêques en Neustrie avant la réforme grégorienne (950–1050 environ)', *Journal des Savants*, 161–94.

Broderick, John, 1966. 'A census of the saints (993–1955)', *American Ecclesiastical Review*, 135, 87–115.

Brooke, Rosalind, and Christopher Brooke, 1984. *Popular Religion in the Middle Ages. Western Europe 1000–1300*. London.

Brown, Peter, 1971. 'The rise and function of the holy man in late antiquity', *Journal of Roman Studies*, 61, 80–101.

1975. 'Society and the supernatural. A medieval change'; *Daedalus*, 104, 133–51.

1981. *The Cult of the Saints. Its Rise and Function in Latin Christianity*. Chicago.

1982. 'Relics and social status in the age of Gregory of Tours', in *idem, Society and the Holy in Late Antiquity*, pp. 222–50. Chicago.

Brühl, Carlrichard, 1968. *Fodrum, Gistum, Servitium Regis*. Cologne.

Bry, Gilles, 1620. *Histoire des pays et comté du Perche et duché d'Alençon*. Paris.

Bullough, Donald, 1983. 'Alcuin and the kingdom of heaven. Liturgy, theology, and the Carolingian age,' in Uta-Renate Blumenthal, ed., *Carolingian Essays*, pp. 1–70. Washington, D.C.

Bur, Michel, 1977. *La Formation du comté de Champagne v.950–v.1150*. Nancy.

Callahan, Daniel, 1976. 'The sermons of Adémar of Chabannes and the cult of St.

Martial of Limoges', *Revue Bénédictine*, 86, 251–95.

Canard, Marius, 1965. 'La Destruction de l'église de la résurrection par le Caliphe Hakim et l'histoire de la descente du feu sacré', *Byzantion*, 35, 16–43.

Carey, Frederick, 1923. 'De scriptura Floriacensi', *Harvard Studies in Classical Philology*, 34, 193–5.

Carolus-Barré, Louis, 1965. 'Saint Louis et la translation des corps saints', in *Etudes d'histoire du droit canonique dediées à Gabriel Le Bras*, pp. 1088–112. Paris.

Carozzi, Claude, 1978a. 'La Tripartition sociale et l'idée de paix au XIe siècle', in *La Guerre et la paix*, pp. 9–22. Actes du 101e congrès national des sociétés savantes, Lille, 1976. Section de philologie et histoire jusqu'à 1610, Tome I. Paris.

1978b. 'Les Fondements de la tripartition sociale chez Adalberon de Laon', *Annales. Economies, sociétés, civilisations*, 33, 683–702.

1980. 'La Vie de Robert par Helgaud de Fleury, historiographie et hagiographie', *Annales de Bretagne et des Pays de l'Ouest*, 87, 219–36.

1981. 'Le Roi et la liturgie chez Helgaud de Fleury', in Patlagean and Riché 1981, pp. 417–32.

Caspar, Erich, 1909. *Petrus Diaconus und die Monte Cassineser Fälschungen. Ein Beitrag zur Geschichte des Italienischen Geisteslebens im Mittelalter*. Berlin.

Certain, Eugène de, 1853. 'Arnoul, évêque d'Orléans', *Bibliothèque d'Ecole des Chartes*, 14, 425–63.

ed., 1858. *Les Miracles de Saint Benoît écrits par Adrevald Aimoin, André, Raoul Tortaire et Hugues de Sainte Marie moines de Fleury*. Paris.

Chabaneau, Camille, 1882. 'Sur quelques manuscrits provençaux perdus ou égarés', *Revue des langues romanes*, 21, 209–17.

Chapman, J., 1903. 'A propos des martyrologes. La recension gallicane du martyrologe de Saint Jérôme. Les fêtes de Saint Benoît aux VII–IXe siècles', *Revue Bénédictine*, 20, 281–313.

Charles, Jacques, 1976. 'Quelques réflexions sur les origines de l'abbaye de Micy-lez-Orléans', *Bulletin de la Société archéologique et historique de l'Orléanais*, 47, 395–401.

Chaumartin, Henry, 1946. *Le Feu Saint-Antoine et le mal des ardents*. Paris.

Chédeville, André, 1973. *Chartres et ses campagnes (XIe–XIIIe siècles)*. Paris.

Chenesseau, Georges, 1921. *Sainte-Croix d'Orléans; histoire d'une cathédrale gothique rééedifiée par les Bourbons, 1599–1829*. 3 vols. Paris.

1925. *Monographie de la cathédrale d'Orléans*. Orléans.

1931a. *L'Abbaye de Fleury à Saint-Benoît-sur-Loire. Son histoire, ses institutions, ses édifices*. Paris.

1931b. 'Cathédrale Sainte-Croix', *Congrès archéologique de France*, 93, 11–51.

1931c. 'Eglise Saint-Euverte', *Congrès archéologique de France*, 93, 78–111.

1931d. 'Pithiviers', *Congrès archéologique de France*, 93, 419–36.

1936. *Les Reliques de Saint Benoît et le mobilier liturgique à l'église de Saint-Benoît-sur-Loire*. Orléans.

1938. 'Les Fouilles de la cathédrale d'Orléans (septembre-décembre 1937)', *Bulletin monumental*, 97, 73–94.

Chenesseau, Georges, and Jules de la Martinière, 1939. 'A propos des origines chrétiennes d'Orléans', *Revue d'histoire d'église de France*, 25, 193–211.

Chenu, Marie-Dominique, 1954. 'Moines, clercs, laics. Au carrefour de la vie évangélique', *Revue d'histoire ecclésiastique*, 51, 59–89.

Chevalier, Ulysse, 1903–7. *Répertoire des sources historiques du Moyen Age. Bio-bibliographique*. 2nd edition. 2 vols. Paris.

Cheyette, Fredric, 1970. 'Suum cuique tribuere', *French Historical Studies*, 6, pp. 287–99.

Christian, William, 1981. *Local Religion in Sixteenth-Century Spain*. Princeton.

Clanchy, M. T., 1979. *From Memory to Written Record. England, 1066–1307*. Cambridge.

Clark, Stuart, 1983. 'French historians and early modern popular culture', *Past and Present*, 100, 62–99.

Classen, Peter, 1974. *Burgundio von Pisa. Richter – Gesandter – Übersetzer*. Heidelberg.

Clercq, Charles de, 1936–58. *La Législation religieuses franque. Etude sur les actes des conciles et les capitulaires, les statuts diocésains et les règles monastiques*. 2 vols. Louvain and Antwerp.

Cochard, Theophile, 1877. 'Micy, son histoire, son influence sociale au VIe siècle', *Lectures et Mémoire de l'Académie de Sainte-Croix d'Orléans*, 3, 76–224.

1879. *Les Saints de l'église d'Orléans*. Orléans.

Collins, Fletcher, 1980. 'The home of the Fleury playbook', *Comparative Drama*, 14, 312–20.

Colman, Rebecca, 1974. 'Reason and unreason in early medieval law', *Journal of Interdisciplinary History*, 4, 571–91.

Comte de Pibrac (Anatole du Faur), 1861. 'Le Tombeau de Saint Ay', *Mémoires de la Société d'agriculture, sciences, belles-lettres et arts d'Orléans*, 6, 5–27.

Constable, Giles, 1964. *Monastic Tithes from their Origins to the Twelfth Century*. Cambridge Studies in Medieval Life and Thought, new series, 10. Cambridge.

1982. 'Renewal and reform in religious life. Concepts and realities', in Robert Benson and Giles Constable, eds., *Renaissance and Renewal in the Twelfth Century*, pp. 37–67. Cambridge, Mass.

1983. 'Forgery and plagiarism in the middle ages', *Archiv für Diplomatik*, 29, 1–41.

Corbet, Patrick, 1986. *Les Saints ottoniens. Sainteté dynastique, sainteté royale et sainteté féminine autour de l'an Mil*. Beihefte der Francia, 15. Sigmaringen.

Cottineau, Laurent, 1939–70. *Répertoire topo-bibliographique des abbayes et prieurés*. 3 vols. Mâcon.

Couderc, Camille, 1893. 'Note sur une compilation inédite de Hugues de Sainte-Marie et sa vie de saint Sacerdos évêque de Limoges', *Bibliothèque d'Ecole des Chartes*, 54, 468–74.

Courcelle, Pierre, 1953. 'L'Enfant et les sorts bibliques', *Vigiliae Christianae*, 7, 146–250.

Cousin, Patrice, 1954. *Abbon de Fleury-sur-Loire. Un savant, un pasteur, un martyr à la fin du Xe siècle*. Paris.

Cowdrey, H. E. J., 1970a. *The Cluniacs and the Gregorian Reform*. Oxford.

1970b. 'The peace and the truce of God in the eleventh century', *Past and Present*, 46, 42–67.

Cracco, Giorgio, 1969. 'Spunti storici e storiografici in Elgaldo di Fleury (a proposito di una recente edizione)', *Rivista Storica Italiana*, 8, 118–32.

1981. 'Un problema sempre aperto: l'origine dell'eresia medievale', *Cultura e scuola*, 79, 102–12.

Crapanzano, Vincent, 1973. *The Hamadsha. A Study in Moroccan Ethnopsychiatry*. Berkeley.

Crozet, René, 1939. 'Nouaillé', *Bulletin monumentale*, 101, 256–97.

Cuissard, Charles, 1875. *L'Ecole de Fleury à la fin du Xe siècle et son influence*. Orléans.

1880. *Catena Floriacensis de existentia corporis sancti Benedicti in Galliis*. Paris.

1885. *L'Inventaire des manuscrits de la Bibliothèque d'Orléans (Fonds de Fleury)*. Orléans.

1886. 'Les Premiers Evêques d'Orléans, examen des difficultés en présentant leurs actes', *Mémoires de la Société archéologique et historique d'Orléanais*, 21, 1–299.

1889. *Les Manuscrits de la bibliothèque publique d'Orléans*. Catalogue général des manuscrits des bibliothèques publiques de France, 12. Paris.

1900. *Les Chanoines et dignitaires de la cathédrale d'Orléans d'après les nécrologes manuscrits de Sainte-Croix*. Orléans.

Davies, Wendy, and Paul Fouracre, eds., 1986. *The Settlement of Disputes in Early Medieval Europe*. Cambridge.

Davril, Anselme, 1974. 'La Vie à l'abbaye de Fleury-Saint-Benoît au XIIIe siècle', *Bulletin de la Société archéologique et historique d'Orléanais*, 45, 5–29.

1975. 'Un moine de Fleury aux environs de l'an mil, Thierry, dit d'Amorbach', in Louis 1975, pp. 97–104.

1979a. 'La Tradition cassinienne', *Studia Monastica*, 21, 377–408.

1979b. 'Le Culte de Saint-Abbon au moyen âge', in *Actes du colloque du millénaire de la fondation du prieuré de La Réole*, pp. 143–58. Bordeaux.

Debal, Jacques, 1974. 'De Cenabum à Orléans', *Bulletin de la Société archéologique et historique de l'Orléanais*, 45 (supplement), 1–24.

et al., eds. 1983. *Histoire d'Orléans et de son terroir. Tome I: Des origines à la fin du XVIe siècle*. Roanne/Le Coteau.

Delahaye, Paul, 1905. *Notre Dame des Miracles. Son histoire – son culte – ses merveilles*. Paris.

Delaruelle, Etienne, 1951. 'En relisant de "De institutione regia" de Jonas d'Orléans', in Perrin 1951, pp. 185–92.

1975a. *Le Pieté populaire au moyen âge*. Turin.

1975b. 'Le Problème du clocher au haut moyen âge et la religion populaire', in Louis 1975, pp. 125–31.

Delehaye, Hippolyte, 1930. 'Loca Sanctorum', *Analecta Bollandiana*, 48, 5–64.

Delisle, Léopold, 1868–81. *Le Cabinet des manuscrits de la Bibliothèque Nationale*. 3 vols. Paris.

1876. 'Notice sur vingt manuscrits du Vatican', *Bibliothèque d'Ecole des Chartes*, 37, 470–527.

1879. 'Les Bibles de Théodulphe', *Bibliothèque d'Ecole des Chartes*, 40, 6–47.

Delooz, Pierre, 1962. 'Pour une étude sociologique de la sainteté canonisée dans l'église catholique', *Archives de sociologie des religions*, 13, 17–43.

1969. *Sociologie et canonisation*. Collections scientifiques de la faculté de Droit de l'Université de Liège, 30. La Haye.

Deperis, P., 1898. 'Memoriale intorno a S. Mauro, patrono di Parenzo', *Atti e Memorie della Società Istriana di Archeologia e Storia Patria*, 14, 1–37.

Dereine, Charles, 1948. 'Odon de Tournai et la crise du cénobitisme au XIe siècle', *Revue du Moyen Age latin*, 4, 137–54.

Dermenghem, Emile, 1954. *Le Culte des saints dans l'Islam maghrébin*. Paris.

Deshusses, Jacques, and Jacques Hourlier, 1979. 'Saint Benoît dans les livres liturgiques', *Studia Monastica*, 21, 143–204.

Deug-Su, I., 1983. *L'opera agiografica di Alcuino*. Biblioteca degli 'Studi Medievali', 13. Spoleto.

Devailly, Guy, 1966. 'La Vie religieuse dans les pays de la Loire au IXe siècle', *Bulletin philologique et historique*, 2, 639–49.

1973a. 'La Pastorale en Gaule au IXe siècle', *Revue d'histoire de l'église de France*, 59, 23–54.

1973b. *Le Berry du Xe au milieu du XIIe siècle*. Paris.

1980. 'L'Eglise médiévale', in Guy-Marie Oury, ed., *Histoire religieuse de Bretagne*, pp. 41–93. Paris.

1984. 'Les Grandes Familles et l'épiscopat dans l'ouest de la France et les pays de la Loire', *Cahiers de civilisation médiévale*, 27, 49–55.

Devaux, Jules, 1885. 'Essai sur les premiers seigneurs de Pithiviers, 1–2', *Annales du Gâtinais*, 3, 186–78 and 250–65.

1886. 'Essai sur les premiers seigneurs de Pithiviers, 3–4', *Annales du Gâtinais*, 4, 94–129 and 290–321.

D'Haenens, Albert, 1969. 'Les Invasions normandes dans l'empire franc au IXe siècle', in *I Normanni e la loro espansione in Europa nell'alto medioevo*, pp. 233–98. Settimane di studio del Centro italiano di studi sull'alto medioevo, 16. Spoleto.

Dolbeau, François, 1976. 'Sur la genèse et la diffusion du Liber de Notabiliis', *Revue d'histoire des textes*, 6, 143–95.

1979. 'Anciens possesseurs des manuscrits hagiographiques conservés à la Bibliothèque Nationale de Paris', *Revue d'histoire des textes*, 9, 184–238.

1981a. 'Notes sur l'organisation interne des légendiers latins', in Patlagean and Riché 1981, pp. 11–31.

1981b. 'Un vol de reliques dans le diocèse de Reims au milieu du XIe siècle', *Revue Bénédictine*, 91, 172–84.

Donnat, Lin, 1975a. 'L'Abbaye de Ferrières-en-Gâtinais', in Louis 1975, pp. 522–4.

1975b. 'Recherches sur l'influence de Fleury au Xe siècle', in Louis 1975, pp. 165–75.

Dubois, Jacques, 1978. *Les Martyrologes du Moyen Age latin*. Typologie des sources du Moyen Age occidental, A-VI.A.1. Turnhout. 1978.

Dubois, Jacques, and Geneviève Renaud, 1981. 'Influence des Vies de saints sur le développement des institutions', in Patlagean and Riché 1981, pp. 491–513.

Duby, Georges, 1968. 'Les Laïcs et la paix de Dieu', in *I laici nella 'societas christiana' dei secoli XI e XII*, pp. 448–61. Miscellanea del Centro di studi medioevali, 5. Milan.

1971. *La Société aux XIe et XIIe siècles dans la région mâconnaise.* Paris.

1980. *The Three Orders. Feudal Society Imagined*, trans. Arthur Goldhammer. Chicago.

Duchateau, Eugène, 1888. *Histoire du diocèse d'Orléans, depuis son origine jusqu'à nos jours.* Orléans.

Du Chesne, André, ed., 1619. *Historiae Normannorum Scriptores antiqui.* Paris.

1631. *Histoire généalogique des maisons de Broyes et de Châteauvillain.* Paris.

Duchesne, Louis, 1894–1915. *Fastes épiscopaux de l'ancienne Gaule.* 3 vols. Paris.

Duine, F., 1922. *Catalogue des sources hagiographiques pour l'histoire de Bretagne jusqu'à la fin du XIIe siècle.* Paris.

Dumas, Auguste, 1940. 'La Notion de la propriété ecclésiastique du IXe au XIe siècle', *Revue d'histoire d'église de France*, 26, 14–34.

Du Méril, Edélestrand, 1843. *Poésies populaires latines antérieures au XIIe siècle.* Paris.

Dümmler, Ernst, 1894. *Uber Leben und Schriften des Mönches Theodoric (von Amorbach).* Philosophische und historische Abhandlungen der Königlichen Akademie der Wissenschaften zu Berlin. Berlin.

Dupré, Louis, 1854. 'Tremblevif en Sologne', *Bulletin de la Société archéologique et historique de l'Orléanais*, 2, 190–2.

Erdmann, Carl, 1935. *Die Entstehung des Kreuzzugsgedankens.* Forschungen zur Kirchen- und Geistesgeschichte, 6. Stuttgart.

Evans-Pritchard, E. E., 1937. *Witchcraft, Oracles and Magic Among the Azande.* Oxford.

1965. *Theories of Primitive Religion.* Oxford.

Ewig, Eugen, 1960a. 'Der Petrus- und Apostel-Kult im spätrömischen und fränkischen Gallien', *Zeitschrift für Kirchengeschichte*, 71, 215–51.

1960b. 'Die Kathedralpatrozinien im römischen und im fränkischen Gallien', *Historisches Jahrbuch*, 79, 1–60.

Farmer, Sharon, 1985. 'Personal perceptions, collective behavior: twelfth-century suffrages for the dead', in Richard Trexler, ed., *Persons in Groups. Social Behavior as Identity Formation in Medieval and Renaissance Europe*, pp. 231–9. Binghamton, N.Y.

Fichtenau, Heinrich, 1952. 'Zum Reliquienwesen im früheren Mittelalter', *Mitteilungen des Instituts für österreichische Geschichtsforschung*, 60, 60–89.

Finucane, Ronald, 1977. *Miracles and Pilgrims. Popular Beliefs in Medieval England.* Totowa, N.J.

Folz, Robert, 1978. 'Naissance et manifestations d'un culte royal: Saint Edmond, roi d'est-anglie', in Karl Hauk and Hubert Mordek, eds., *Geschichtsschreibung und geistiges Leben im Mittelalter. Festschrift für Heinz Löwe zum 65. Geburtstag*, pp. 226–46. Cologne.

Fontaine, Jacques, 1979. 'Bible et hagiographie dans le royaume franc mérovingien (600–750)', *Analecta Bollandiana*, 97, 387–96.

Foreville, Raymonde, and Gillian Keir, eds., 1987. *The Book of St Gilbert.* Oxford Medieval Texts. Oxford.

Fossier, Robert, 1971. 'Les Mouvements populaires en occident au XIe siècle', *Académie des Inscriptions et Belles-Lettres. Comptes rendus des séances de l'année 1971*, pp. 257–69. Paris.

Fouracre, Paul, 1979. 'The Work of Audoenus of Rouen and Eligius of Noyon in extending episcopal influence from the town to the country in seventh-century Neustria', *Studies in Church History*, 16, 77–91.

Freeman, Ann, 1957. 'Theodulf of Orléans and the *Libri Carolini*', *Speculum*, 32, 663–705.

Frolow, Anatole, 1961. *La Relique de la vraie croix. Recherches sur le développement d'un culte.* Paris.

Gaier, Claude, 1966. 'Le Rôle militaire des reliques et de l'étendard de saint Lambert dans la principauté de Liège', *Le Moyen Age*, 72, 235–49.

Gaiffier, Baudouin de, 1932. 'Les Revindications de biens dans quelques documents hagiographiques du XIe siècle', *Analecta Bollandiana*, 50, 123–38.

    1962. 'Hagiographie salernitaine. La translation de S. Matthieu', *Analecta Bollandiana*, 80, 87–90.

    1966. 'Miracles bibliques et Vies de saints', *Nouvelle revue théologique*, 88, 376–85.

    1967. 'L'Hagiographie dans le marquisat de Flandre et le duché de Basse-Lotharingie au XIe siècle', in *idem., Etudes critiques d'hagiographie et d'iconologie*, pp. 415–507. Subsidia hagiographica, 43. Brussels.

    1968. 'Mentalité de l'hagiographie médiéval d'après quelques travaux récents', *Analecta Bollandiana*, 86, 391–9.

    1970. 'Hagiographie et historiographie. Quelques aspects du problème', in *La storiografia altomedievale*, II, 139–66. Settimane di studio del Centro italiano di studi sull'alto Medio Evo, 17. Spoleto.

Gaillard, Louis, and Jacques Debal, 1987. *Les Lieux de culte à Orléans de l'antiquité au XXe siècle.* Orléans.

Galli, Déodat, 1954. *Saint Benoît en France.* Fleury-sur-Loire.

Gams, Pius Bonifacius, ed., 1873. *Series episcoporum ecclesiae catholicae.* Regensburg.

Ganshof, François, 1959. 'A propos du tonlieu à l'époque carolingienne', in *La città nell'alto medioevo*, pp. 485–508. Settimane di studio del Centro italiano di studi sull'alto medioevo, 6. Spoleto.

Garand, M. C., 1983. 'Un manuscrit d'auteur de Raoul Glaber? Observations codicologique et paléographique sur le ms. Paris, BN, latin 10912', *Scriptorium*, 37, 5–28.

Garaud, Marcel, 1929. 'Les Vicomtes du Poitou (Xe–XIIe siècle)', *Revue d'histoire du droit français et étranger*, 36–68.

    1959–60. 'Observations sur les vicissitudes de la propriété ecclésiastique dans le diocèse de Poitiers du IXe au XIIIe siècle', *Bulletin de la Société des antiquaires de l'Ouest*, 4th series, 5, 357–77.

    1964. *Les Châtelains de Poitou et l'avènement du régime féodal, XIe et XIIe siècles.* Mémoires de la Société des antiquaires de l'Ouest, 4th series, 8. Poitiers.

Gariépy, R. J., 1968. 'Lupus, Carolingian scribe and text critic', *Mediaeval Studies*, 30, 90–105.

Garsoïan, Nina, 1967. *The Paulician Heresy. A Study of the Origin and Development of Paulicianism in Armenia and the Eastern Provinces of the Byzantine Empire.* Publications in Near and Middle East Studies, Columbia University, Series A, 4. The Hague.

Bibliography and references

Gatch, Milton, 1977. *Preaching and Theology in Anglo-Saxon England: Aelfric and Wulfstan*. Toronto.

Geary, Patrick, 1978. *Furta Sacra: Thefts of Relics in the Central Middle Ages*. Princeton.

1979a. 'La Coercition des saints dans la pratique religieuse médiévale', in Pierre Boglioni, ed., *La Culture populaire au Moyen Age. Etudes présentés au Quatrième colloque de l'Institut d'études médiévales de l'Université de Montréal, 2–3 avril, 1977*, pp. 145–61. Montreal.

1979b. 'L'Humiliation des saints', *Annales. Economies, sociétés, civilisations*, 34, 27–42.

1979c. 'The ninth-century relic trade. A response to popular piety?', in James Obelkevich, ed., *Religion and the People, 800–1700*, pp. 8–19. Chapel Hill, N.C.

1986a. 'Echanges et relations entre les vivants et les morts dans la société du haut moyen âge', *Droit et cultures*, 12, 3–17.

1986b. 'Vivre en conflit dans une France sans état: typologie des mécanismes de règlement des conflits (1050–1200)', *Annales. Economies, sociétés, civilisations*, 41, 1107–33.

Geertz, Clifford, 1983. 'Local knowledge: fact and law in comparative perspective', in *idem*, *Local Knowledge. Further Essays in Interpretive Anthropology*, pp. 167–70. New York.

Gellner, Ernest, 1969. *Saints of the Atlas*. Chicago.

1981. 'Saints and their descendants', in *idem*, *Muslim Society*, pp. 207–13. Cambridge Studies in Social Anthropology, 32. Cambridge.

Genicot, Léopold, 1962. 'La Noblesse au Moyen Age dans l'ancienne "Francie"', *Annales. Economies, sociétés, civilisations*, 17, 1–22.

1965. 'Sur l'intérêt des textes hagiographiques', *Académie royale de Belgique. Bulletin de la classe des lettres et des sciences morales et politiques*, 5th series, 51, 65–75.

Giradot (Baron de), 1880. 'Conservation des églises et des reliquaires de l'ancienne abbaye de Ferrières', *Revue des sociétés savantes des départements*, 7th series, 2, 243–7.

Godefroy, Jean, 1937. 'L'Histoire du prieuré Saint-Ayoul de Provins et le récit des miracles du saint', *Revue Mabillon*, 27, 94–107.

1938. 'L'Histoire du prieuré Saint-Ayoul de Provins et le récit des miracles du saint (suite)', *Revue Mabillon*, 28, 29–48, 84–98, and 112–17.

Godet, Henri, 1891. 'L'Abbaye et le prieuré de Moutiers-en-Perche (ancien Corbion)', *Bulletin de la Société historique de l'Orne*, 10, 20–7.

Goffart, Walter, 1966. *The Le Mans Forgeries. A Chapter from the History of Church Property in the Ninth Century*. Harvard Historical Studies, 76. Cambridge, Mass.

1967. 'Le Mans, St Scholastica, and the literary tradition of the translation of St. Benedict', *Revue Bénédictine*, 77, 107–41.

Golinelli, Paolo, 1980. *Culto dei santi e vita cittadina a Reggio Emilia (secoli IX–XII)*. Modena.

1984. 'Istituzioni cittadine e culti episcopali in area matildica avanti il sorgere dei Comuni', in Boesch Gajano and Sebastiani 1984, pp. 141–97.

Gonthier, Dominique, and Claire Lebas, 1974. 'Analyse socio-économique de quelques recueils de miracles dans la Normandie du XIe au XIIIe siècles', *Annales de Normandie*, 24, 3–36.

Goodich, Michael, 1975. 'The politics of canonization in the thirteenth century: lay and mendicant saints', *Church History*, 44, 294–307.

1976. 'A profile of thirteenth-century sainthood', *Comparative Studies in Society and History*, 18, 429–37.

1982. *Vita perfecta: The Ideal of Sainthood in the Thirteenth Century*. Monographien zur Geschichte des Mittelalters, 25. Stuttgart.

Goody, Jack, 1977. *The Domestication of the Savage Mind*. Cambridge.

Gransden, Antonia, 1975. *Historical Writing in England c. 550 to c. 1307*. London.

1985. 'The legends and traditions concerning the origins of the abbey of Bury St. Edmunds', *English Historical Review*, 100, 1–24.

Graus, Frantisek, 1965. *Volk, Herrscher und Heiliger im Reich der Merowinger. Studien zur Hagiographie der Merowingerzeit*. Prague.

1974. 'Sozialgeschichtliche Aspekte der Hagiographie der Merowinger- und Karolingerzeit', in Arno Borst, ed., *Mönchtum, Episkopat und Adel zur Gründungszeit des Klosters Reichenau*, pp. 131–76. Vorträge und Forschungen, 20. Sigmaringen.

1977. 'Der Heilige als Schlachtenhelfer. Zur Nationalisierung einer Wundererzählung der mittelalterlichen Chronisten', in *Festschrift für Helmut Beumann zum 65. Geburtstag*, pp. 330–48. Sigmaringen.

Grégoire, Réginald, 1965. 'Prières liturgiques médiévales en l'honneur de Saint Benoît, de Sainte Scolastique et de Saint Maur', *Studia Anselmiana*, 54, 1–85.

Grellet-Balguerie, Charles, 1882. *Authenticité et date précise de la translation du corps de Saint Benoît en France*. Orléans.

Grémont, Denis, 1963–4. 'Les Miracles de Saint Benoît et leur iconographie dans la basilique de Saint-Benoît', *Bulletin de la Société archéologique et historique de l'Orléanais*, 45, 235–52.

1969. 'Le Culte de sainte Foi et de sainte Marie-Madeleine à Conques au XIe s. d'après le ms. de la Chanson de sainte Foi', *Revue de Rouergue*, 23, 165–75.

1975. 'Le Culte de la Madeleine à Fleury', in Louis 1975, pp. 203–26.

Grémont, Denis, and Lin Donnat, 1966. 'Fleury, Le Mont Saint-Michel et l'Angleterre à la fin du Xe et au début du XIe siècle, à propos du manuscrit d'Orléans no. 127 (105)', in *Millénaire monastique du Mont Saint-Michel*, I, 751–93. 3 vols. Paris.

Grémont, Denis, and Jacques Hourlier, 1979. 'La Plus Ancienne Bibliothèque de Fleury', *Studia Monastica*, 21, 253–64.

Griffiths, Quentin, 1988. 'Les Gens du roi de la collégiale Saint-Aignan d'Orléans et le gouvernement capétien', *Revue Mabillon*, 61, 447–70.

Grundmann, Herbert, 1958. 'Litteratus-illitteratus. Der Wandel einer Bildungsnorm vom Altertum zum Mittelalter', *Archiv für Kulturgeschichte*, 40, 1–65.

Guenée, Bernard, 1975–6. 'Temps de l'histoire et temps de la mémoire au Moyen Age', *Annuaire-Bulletin de la Société de l'Histoire de France*, 25–35.

Guerreau-Jalabert, Anita, ed., 1982. *Abbo Floriacensis. Quaestiones grammaticales*. Paris.

Guillot, Olivier, 1972. *Le Comte d'Anjou et son entourage au XIe siècle*. 2 vols. Paris.

Günter, Heinrich, 1949. 'Hagiographie und Wissenschaft', *Historisches Jahrbuch*, 62–9, 43–88.

Guth, Klaus, 1970. *Guibert von Nogent und die hochmittelalterliche Kritik an der Reliquienverehrung*. Studien und Mitteilungen zur Geschichte des Benediktiner-Ordens und seiner Zweige, 21. Ottobeuren.

Guyon, Symphorien, 1647–50. *Histoire de l'église et diocèse, ville et université d'Orléans*. 4 vols. Orléans.

Hagen, Herman, 1874. *Catalogus codicum Bernensium (Bibliotheca Bongarsiana)*. Bern.

Hajdu, Robert, 1977. 'Family and feudal ties in Poitou, 1100–1300', *Journal of Interdisciplinary History*, 8, 117–39.

Hallinger, Kassius, ed., 1984. *Consuetudinum saeculi X/XI/XII monumenta introductiones*. Corpus Consuetudinum monasticarum, 7.1. Siegburg.

Halphen, Louis, 1906. *Le Comté d'Anjou au XIe siècle*. Paris.

Hamon, Maurice, 1971. 'La Vie de Saint Florent et les origines de l'abbaye du Mont-Glonne', *Bibliothèque d'Ecole des Chartes*, 129, 215–38.

    1979. 'Un aspect de la reconstruction monastique dans l'Ouest: les relations entre Saint-Florent de Saumur et les abbayes de la Loire moyenne (950–1026 environ)', *Bulletin philologique et historique du Comité des travaux historiques et scientifiques, année 1972*, 87–94.

Häring, Nikolaus, 1973. 'Hilary of Orléans and his letter collection', *Studi medievali*, 3rd series, 14, 1069–122.

Harmening, Dieter, 1979. *Superstitio. Uberlieferungs- und theoriegeschichtliche Untersuchungen zur kirchlich-theologischen Aberglaubensliteratur des Mittelalters*. Berlin.

Harvey, Barbara, 1972. 'Work and *Festa ferienda* in medieval England', *Journal of Ecclesiastical History*, 23, 284–308.

Hauréau, Barthélemy, 1843–52. *Histoire littéraire du Maine*. 4 vols. Le Mans.

    1849. 'Versus Lethaldi monachi de quodam piscatore quem ballena absorbuit (X s.)', *Bulletin du comité historique des monuments écrits de l'histoire de France*, 1, 178–83.

Havet, Julien, 1885. 'Questions mérovingiennes. II. Les découvertes de Jérôme Vignier', *Bibliothèque d'Ecole des Chartes*, 46, 205–71.

Head, Thomas, 1984. '"I vow myself to be your servant": an eleventh-century pilgrim, his chronicler and his saint', *Historical Reflections / Refléxions Historiques*, 11, 215–51.

    1987a. 'Andrew of Fleury and the Peace League of Bourges', *Historical Reflections / Réflexions Historiques*, 14, 513–29. Revised version to appear in *idem* and Richard Landes, eds., *'Without Peace No One May See God': Essays on the Peace of God* (Ithaca, N.Y., forthcoming).

    1987b. 'Hrotsvit and the historical traditions of monastic communities', in K. Wilson 1987, pp. 143–64.

    1989. 'Letaldus of Micy and the hagiographic traditions of Selles-sur-Cher', *Analecta Bollandiana*, 107, 393–414.

Heinzelmann, Martin, 1977. 'Sanctitas und "Tugendadel". Zur Konzeptionen von "Heiligkeit" im 5. und 10. Jahrhundert', *Francia*, 5, 741–52.

Bibliography and references

Heitz, Carol, 1963. *Recherches sur les rapports entre architecture et liturgie à l'époque carolingienne*. Paris.

Héliot, Pierre, and M.-L. Chastang, 1964. 'Quêtes et voyages de reliques au profit des églises françaises du moyen âge', *Revue d'histoire ecclésiastique*, 59, 789–822.

1965. 'Quêtes et voyages de reliques au profit des églises françaises du moyen âge (suite)', *Revue d'histoire ecclésiastique*, 60, 5–32.

Herrmann-Mascard, Nicole, 1975. *Les Reliques des saints. Formation coutumière d'un droit*. Société d'histoire du droit, Collection d'histoire institutionnelle et sociale, 6. Paris.

Hertling, Ludwig, 1933. 'Der mittelalterliche Heiligentypus nach den Tugendkatalogen', *Zeitschrift für Askese und Mystik*, 8, 260–8.

Hoffmann, Hartmut, 1964. *Gottesfriede und Treuga Dei*. Schriften der Monumenta Germaniae Historica, 20. Stuttgart.

1967. 'Die älteren Abtslisten von Monte Cassino', *Quellen und Forschungen aus italienischen Archiven und Bibliotheken*, 47, 224–354.

Hogan, Robert, 1981. 'The *Rainaldi* of Angers: "new men" or descendants of Carolingian *Nobiles*?', *Medieval Prosopography*, 2, 35–62.

Homburger, Otto, 1962. *Die Illustrierten Handschriften der Bürgerbibliothek Bern. Die vorkarolingischen und karolingischen Handschriften*. Bern.

Hourlier, Jacques, 1979a. 'La Lettre de Zacharie', *Studia Monastica*, 21, 247–52.

1979b. 'La Translation d'après les sources narratives', *Studia Monastica*, 21, 213–46.

1979c. 'La Translation de sainte Scholastique à Juvigny', *Studia Monastica*, 21, 335–48.

1979d. 'La Translation de sainte Scholastique au Mans', *Studia Monastica*, 21, 313–34.

1979e. 'Le Témoignage de Paul Diacre', *Studia Monastica*, 21, 205–12.

Hourlier, Jacques, and Jean Deshusses, 1979. 'Saint Benoît dans les livres liturgiques', *Studia Monastica*, 21, 143–204.

Howe, John, 1986. 'Saints and society through the centuries', *Catholic Historical Review*, 52, 425–36.

Hubert, Jean, 1951. '"Cryptae inferiores" et "cryptae superiores" dans l'architecture religieuse de l'époque carolingienne', in Perrin 1951, pp. 351–7.

1959. 'Évolution de la topographie et de l'aspect des villes de Gaule du Ve au Xe siècle', in *La città nell'alto medioevo*, pp. 529–58. Settimane di studio del Centro italiano di studi sull'alto medioevo, 6. Spoleto.

1968. 'La Place faite aux laïcs dans les églises monastiques et dans les cathédrales aux XIe et XIIe siècles', in *I laici nella 'societas christiana' dei secoli XI e XII*, pp. 470–87. Miscellanea del Centro di studi medioevali, 5. Milan.

Hubert, M.-J., 1934. 'Note sur l'histoire de l'abbaye de Ferrières', *Annales de la Société historique et archéologique du Gâtinais*, 42, 95–114.

Hubert, Robert, 1661. *Antiquitez historiques de l'église royale Saint-Aignan d'Orléans*. Orléans.

Huyghebaert, Nicolas, 1968. 'Les Femmes laïques dans la vie religieuse des XIe et XIIe siècles dans la province ecclésiastique de Reims', in *I laici nella 'Societas*

Bibliography and references

Christiana' dei secoli XI e XII, pp. 364–6. Miscellanea del Centro di studi medioevali, 5. Milan.

Iogna-Pratt, Dominique, 1988. *Agni Immaculati. Recherches sur les sources hagiographiques relatives à Saint Maieul de Cluny, 954–994*. Paris.

Jarossay, Eugène, 1901. *Ferrières-en-Gâtinais, ordre de Saint-Benoît (508–1790). Son influence religieuse, sociale et littéraire*. Orléans.

  1902. *Histoire de l'abbaye de Micy-Saint-Mesmin-lez-Orléans (502–1790). Son influence religieuse et sociale*. Orléans.

Jarry, Louis, 1899. *Histoire de Cléry et de l'église collégiale et chapelle royale de Notre-Dame de Cléry*. Orléans.

John, Eric, 1983. 'The world of Abbot Aelfric', in Patrick Wormald, ed., *Ideal and Reality in Frankish and Anglo-Saxon Society*, pp. 300–16. Oxford.

Johnson, Penelope, 1981. *Prayer, Patronage, and Power: The Abbey of La Trinité, Vendôme. 1032–1187*. New York.

Jouvellier, Pierre, 1975. 'La Crypte de l'église Saint-Avit d'Orléans', in Louis 1975, pp. 450–3.

Kee, Howard, 1983. *Miracle in the Early Christian World. A Study in Sociohistorical Method*. New Haven.

Kehr, Paul, 1907–57. *Italia pontificia, sive Repertorium privilegiorum et litterarum a Romanis pontificibus ante annum MCLXXXXVIII*. 10 vols. Berlin.

Keynes, Simon, 1980. *The Diplomas of King Aethelred 'The Unready' (978–1016). A Study in their Use as Historical Evidence*. Cambridge Studies in Medieval Life and Thought, 3rd series, 13. Cambridge.

Kiekhefer, Richard, 1984. *Unquiet Souls. Fourteenth-Century Saints and their Religious Milieu*. Chicago.

Koziol, Geoffrey, 1987. 'Monks, feuds, and the making of peace in eleventh-century Flanders', *Historical Reflections / Réflexions Historiques*, 14, 531–49.

Labande, Edmond-René, 1966. '"Ad limina": le pèlerin médiéval au terme de sa démarche', in Pierre Gallais and Yves-Jean Riou, eds., *Mélanges offerts à René Crozet* I, 283–91. 2 vols. Poitiers.

  1970. 'L'Historiographie de la France de l'Ouest aux Xe et XIe siècles', in *La storiografia altomedievale*, pp. 751–91. Settimane di studio del Centro italiano di studi sull'alto Medio Evo, 17. Spoleto.

Labbe, Philippe, and Gabriel Cossaert, 1728–33. *Sacrosancta concilia ad regiam editionem exacta . . . ab initiis aerae Christianae ad annum MDCCXXVII*. 21 vols. Venice.

Lacroix, Benoît, 1971. *L'Historien au moyen âge*. Conférence Albert-le-Grand 1966. Paris.

Lagomarsini, Girolamo (Golmario Marsigliano), 1726. *Vita di s. Fermano abate dell'ordine di s. Benedetto descritta da Golmario Marsigliano e dedicata al Reverendissimo padre Don Leandro Porzia, abate de s. Paolo*. Treviso.

Lambert, Malcolm, 1977. *Medieval Heresy. Popular Movements from Bogomil to Hus*. London.

Landes, Richard, 1987. 'The dynamics of heresy and reform in Limoges: a study of popular participation in the "Peace of God" (994–1033)', *Historical Reflections / Réflexions Historiques*, 14, 467–511.

Laporte, Jacques, 1979. 'Vues sur l'histoire de l'abbaye de Fleury aux VIIe et VIIIe siècles', *Studia Monastica*, 21, 109–42.

Larnage, H. de, 1895. 'Mézières-en-Sologne, ses relations avec l'abbaye de Micy, les souvenirs de St. Avit, la paroisse et le château', *Lectures et Mémoires de l'Académie de Sainte-Croix d'Orléans*, 6, 101–39.

Latouche, Robert, 1910. *Histoire du comté du Maine pendant le Xe et le XIe siècle*. Paris.

　　1968. 'Le Maine sous les carolingiens', *La Province du Maine*, 70, 265–76.

　　1970. 'Coup d'oeil sur le Maine féodal, sous les comtes héréditaires, 900–1100', *La Province du Maine*, 72, 1–14.

Lauer, Philippe, 1898. 'Le Manuscrit des *Annales de Flodoard* Reg. lat. 633 du Vatican', *Mélanges d'archéologie et d'histoire de l'Ecole française de Rome*, 18, 491–523.

　　1900. *Le Règne de Louis IV d'Outre-Mer*. Paris.

Lauer, Philippe, *et al.*, eds., 1939–66. *Catalogue général des manuscrits latins de la Bibliothèque nationale de Paris*. 5 vols. Paris.

Lauranson-Rosaz, Christian, 1987. *L'Auvergne et ses marges (Velay, Gévaudan) du VIIIe au XIe siècle. La fin du monde antique?*. Le Puy-en-Velay.

Leccisotti, Tommaso, 1951. 'Il sepolcro di s. Benedetto. La testimonianza storica', *Miscellanea Cassinense*, 27, 120–50.

Leclercq, Jean, 1957. *Initiation aux auteurs monastiques du moyen âge. L'Amour des lettres et le désir de Dieu*. Paris.

　　1959. 'Anciennes prières monastiques', *Studia monastica*, 1, 379–92.

　　1963. 'La Rencontre des moines de Moissac avec Dieu', *Annales du Midi*, 85, 405–17.

　　1964. 'Les Méditations d'un moine de Moissac au XIe siècle', *Revue d'ascéticisme et de mysticisme*, 40, 197–210.

　　1975. 'Violence et dévotion à Saint-Benoît-sur-Loire au moyen âge', in Louis 1975, pp. 247–56.

Le Cointe, Charles, 1665–83. *Annales ecclesiastici Francorum*. 8 vols. Paris.

Ledru, Ambroise, 1904. 'Saint Julien, évêque du Mans, part IV', *La Province du Maine*, 12, 113–21.

　　1906. 'Origines de Lethald, moine de Micy (fin du Xe siècle)', *La Province du Maine*, 16, 326–8.

Lefranc, Abel, 1896. 'Le Traité des reliques de Guibert de Nogent et les commencements de la critique historique au Moyen Age', in Ernest Lavisse, ed., *Etudes d'histoire du Moyen Age dédiées à Gabriel Monod*, pp. 285–306. Paris.

LeGoff, Jacques, 1967. 'Culture cléricale et traditions folkloriques dans la civilisation mérovingienne', in L. Bergeron, ed., *Niveaux de culture et groupes sociaux*, pp. 21–32. Paris.

　　1970. 'Culture ecclésiastique et culture folklorique au Moyen Age: Saint Marcel de Paris et le dragon', in Luigi de Rosa, ed., *Ricerche storiche ed economiche in memoria de Corrado Barbagallo*, II, 53–90. 2 vols. Naples.

　　1985. 'Mentalities: a history of ambiguities', in Jacques LeGoff and Pierre Nora, eds., *Constructing the Past: Essays in Historical Methodology*, trans. Colin Lucas, pp. 166–80. Cambridge.

Bibliography and references

LeGoff, Jacques, and J.-P. Valery Patin, 1975. 'A propos de la typologie des miracles dans le *Liber de miraculis de Pierre le Vénérable*', in *Pierre Abélard. Pierre le Vénérable. Les courants philosophiques, littéraires, et artistiques en Occident au milieu du XIIe siècle*, pp. 181–90. Paris.

Lejay, Paul, 1896. 'Catalogues de la bibliothèque de Perrecy (XIe s.)', *Revue des bibliothèques*, 6, 225–34.

Le Maire, François, 1648. *Histoire et antiquitez de la ville et duché d'Orléans. Ensemble le tome ecclésiastique, contenant la fondation et nombres des églises, histoires des évesques . . . .* 2nd edition. Orléans.

Le Maître, Philippe, 1982. 'Image du Christ, image de l'empereur. L'exemple du culte du Saint Sauveur sous Louis le Pieux', *Revue d'histoire d'église de France*, 68, 201–12.

Lemarignier, Jean-François, 1937. *Etude sur les privilèges d'exemption et de juridiction ecclésiastique des abbayes normandes depuis les origines jusqu'en 1140*. Archives de la France monastique, 44. Paris.

1950. 'L'Exemption monastique et les origines de la réforme grégorienne', in *A Cluny. Congrès scientifique. Fêtes et cérémonies liturgiques en l'honneur des saints abbés Odon et Odilon 9–11 juillet 1949*, pp. 288–340. Dijon.

1951. 'La Dislocation du "pagus" et le problème des "consuetudines" (X–XI siècles)', in Perrin 1951, pp. 401–10.

1955. 'Les Fidèles du roi de France (936–987)', in *Recueil de travaux offert à M. Clovis Brunel*, II, 138–62. 2 vols. Mémoires et documents publiés par la société de l'Ecole des Chartes, 12. Paris.

1957. 'Structures monastiques et structures politiques dans la France', in *Il Monachesimo nell'alto Medioevo*, pp. 357–400. Settimane di studi di Centro italiano di studi sull'alto medioevo, 4. Spoleto.

1959. 'Aspects politiques des fondations de collégiales dans le royaume de France au XIe siècle', in *La Vita comune del clero nei secoli XI e XII*, I, 19–49. 2 vols, Miscellanea del Centro di studi medioevali, 3. Milan.

1962. 'Les Institutions ecclésiastiques en France de la fin du Xe au milieu du XIIe siècle', in Lot and Fawtier 1962, pp. 3–139.

1965. *Le Gouvernement royal aux premiers temps capétiens (987–1108)*. Paris.

1968. 'Aux origines de l'état français. Royauté et entourage royal aux premiers temps capétiens (987–1108)', in *L'Europe aux IXe–XIe siècles. Aux origines des Etats nationaux*, pp. 43–55. Warsaw.

1977. 'Le Monachisme et l'encadrement religieux des campagnes du royaume de France situées au nord de la Loire, de la fin du X à la fin du XIe siècle', in *Le istituzioni ecclesiastiche della "Societas Christiana" dei secoli XI–XII. Diocesi, pievi e parrocchie*, pp. 357–95. Miscellanea del Centro di studi medioevali, 8. Milan.

Lenormant, Charles, 1862. 'Mémoire sur le tombeau de Saint Euverte', *Mémoires de la Société archéologique et historique d'Orléanais*, 5, 1–25.

Le Quien, Michael, 1840. *Oriens Christianus, in quatuor patriarchatus digestus; quo exhibentur ecclesiae, patriarchae, caeterique praesules totius orientis*. 3 vols. Paris.

Leroquais, Victor, 1924. *Les Sacramentaires et les missels manuscrits des bibliothèques publiques de France*. 4 vols. Paris.

1934. *Les Bréviaires manuscrits des bibliothèques publiques de France*. 6 vols. Paris.

1943. *Les Psautiers latins manuscrits des bibliothèques publiques de France.* 3 vols. Paris.

Lesne, Emile, 1910–45. *Histoire de la propriété ecclésiastique en France.* 6 vols. Mémoires et travaux publiés par des professeurs de la faculté Catholique de Lille. Lille and Paris.

Lettinck, Nico, 1981. 'Pour une édition critique de l'Historia Ecclesiastica de Hugues de Fleury', *Revue Bénédictine*, 91, 386–97.

Lewis, Andrew, 1981. *Royal Succession in Capetian France: Studies on Familial Order and the State.* Harvard Historical Studies, 100. Cambridge, Mass.

Leyser, Henrietta, 1984. *Hermits and the New Monasticism. A Study of Religious Communities in Western Europe, 1000–1150.* London.

Little, Lester, 1975a. 'Formules monastiques de malédiction aux IXe et Xe siècles', *Revue Mabillon*, 58, 377–99.

1975b. 'Intellectual training and attitudes toward reform, 1075–1150', in *Pierre Abélard. Pierre le Vénérable. Les courants philosophiques, littéraires et artistiques en Occident au milieu du XIIe siècle*, pp. 235–54. Paris.

1979. 'La Morphologie des malédictions monastiques', *Annales. Economies, sociétés, civilisations*, 34, 43–60.

Lobineau, Gui-Alexis, 1725. *Vies des saints de Bretagne.* Rennes.

Lomastro, Francesca, 1975. 'Umiltà e buone opere nella spiritualità dell' XI secolo (dalla *Vita Roberti* di Elgaldo e dalla *Vita Gauzlini*, di Andrea di Fleury)', *Studia Patavina*, 22, 521–41.

Longère, Paul, 1982. 'La Prédication sur Saint Benoît de Xe au XIIIe siècle', in *Sous le règle de Saint Benoît. Structures monastiques et sociétés en France du Moyen Age à l'époque moderne. Abbaye bénédictine Sainte-Marie de Paris, 23–25 octobre, 1980*, pp. 433–60. Geneva.

1983. *La Prédication médiévale.* Paris.

Loos, Milan, 1974. *Dualist Heresy in the Middle Ages.* Prague.

Lot, Ferdinand, 1889. 'Helois de Peviers, soeur de *Garin le Lorrain*', *Romania*, 28, 274–9.

1891. *Les Derniers Carolingiens: Lothaire, Louis V, Charles de Lorraine (954–991).* Bibliothèque de l'Ecole des Hautes Etudes, 87. Paris.

1903. *Etudes sur le règne de Hugues Capet et la fin du Xe siècle.* Bibliothèque de l'Ecole des Hautes Etudes, 147. Paris.

1907. *Mélanges d'histoire bretonne (VIe–XIe siècle).* Paris.

1915. 'La Loire, l'Aquitaine et la Seine de 862 à 866. Robert le Fort', *Bibliothèque d'Ecole des Chartes*, 76, 473–510.

Lot, Ferdinand, and Robert Fawtier, 1962. *Histoire des institutions françaises au moyen âge. Tome III: Institutions ecclésiastiques.* Paris.

Loth, Julien, 1882. *Histoire de l'abbaye royale de Saint-Pierre de Jumièges.* 3 vols. Rouen.

Louis, René, ed., 1975. *Etudes ligériennes d'histoire et d'archéologie médiévales. (Mémoires et exposés présentés à la Semaine d'études médiévales de Saint-Benoît-sur-Loire du 3 au 10 juillet 1969).* Auxerre.

Lowe, Elias Avery, 1934–66. *Codices latini antiquiores. A Palaeographical Guide to Latin Manuscripts prior to the Ninth Century.* 11 volumes. Oxford.

Loyen, André, 1969. 'Le Rôle de saint Aignan dans la délivrance d'Orléans', in

Bibliography and references

Académie des Inscriptions et Belles-Lettres. Comptes rendus des séances de l'année 1969, pp. 64–74. Paris.

Luchet (Le Marquis de), 1766. Histoire de l'Orléanais depuis l'an 703 de la fondation de Rome jusqu'à nos jours. Paris.

Lutz, Cora, 1970. 'Letaldus, a wit of the tenth century', Viator, 1, 97–106.

Mabillon, Jean, 1703–39. Annales ordinis Sancti Benedicti. 2nd edition. 6 vols. Paris.

McCulloh, John, 1983. 'Historical martyrologies in the Benedictine cultural tradition', in W. Lourdaux and D. Verhelst, eds., Benedictine Culture, 750–1050, pp. 114–31. Louvain.

MacKinney, Loren, 1930. 'The people and public opinion in the eleventh-century peace movement', Speculum, 5, 181–206.

McKitterick, Rosamond, 1977. The Frankish Church and the Carolingian Reforms, 789–895. London.

 1979. 'Town and monastery in the Carolingian period', Studies in Church History, 16, 93–102.

 1983. The Frankish Kingdoms under the Carolingians, 751–987. London.

McLaughlin, Megan Molly, 1985. 'Consorting with saints: prayers for the dead in early medieval French society'. Unpublished doctoral dissertation. Stanford University.

Mai, Angelo, ed., 1839–44. Spicilegium romanum. 10 vols. Rome.

Manitius, Max, 1911–31. Geschichte der lateinischen Literatur des Mittelalters. 3 vols. Handbuch der Altertumswissenschaft, IX, 2. Munich.

Manning, Eugène, 1962. 'La Signification de militare – militia – miles dans la Règle de Saint Benoît', Revue Bénédictine, 72, 135–8.

Manselli, Raoul, 1974. 'La religione popolare nel medio evo: prime considerazioni metodologiche', Nuova rivista storica, 58, 29–43.

 1975. La Religion populaire au moyen âge. Problèmes de méthode et d'histoire. Montreal.

Mansi, Johannes, 1903–24. Sacrorum conciliorum nova et amplissima collectio, 55 vols. Reprint. Paris.

Mantellier, P., 1858. 'Rapport à la Société archéologique de l'Orléanais, sur la fête célébrée le 13 juin 1858', Bulletin de la Société archéologique et historique de l'Orléanais, 2, 454–83.

Martimort, Aimé-Georges, 1978. La documentation liturgique de Dom Edmond Martène. Etude codicologique. Studi e testi, 279. Vatican City.

Martin, Henry, 1885–94. Catalogue des manuscrits de la bibliothèque de l'Arsenal. 9 vols. Paris.

Martindale, Jane, 1977. 'The French aristocracy in the early middle ages: a reappraisal', Past and Present, 75, 5–45.

Martinière, Jules de la, 1939. 'Les Origines chrétiennes d'Orléans', Revue d'histoire d'église de France, 25, 5–32.

Mayr-Harting, Henry, 1975. 'Functions of a twelfth-century recluse', History, 60, 337–52.

 1985. 'Functions of a twelfth-century shrine: the miracles of St Frideswide', in Mayr-Harting and Moore 1985, pp. 193–206.

Mayr-Harting, Henry, and R. I. Moore, eds., 1985. Studies in Medieval History Presented to R.H.C. Davis. London.

Ménard, Leon, 1750–8. *Histoire civile, ecclésiastique et littéraire de la ville de Nîmes.* 7 vols. Paris.

Meyier, Karl de, 1975. *Codices Vossiani latini. Pars II, Codices in quarto.* Leiden.

Meyvaert, Paul, 1955. 'Peter the Deacon and the tomb of St. Benedict. The Cassinese Tradition', *Revue Bénédictine,* 65, 3–70.

1959. 'L'Invention des reliques Cassiniennes de St. Benoît en 1484', *Revue Bénédictine,* 69, 287–336.

Michalowski, Roman, 1984. 'Il culto dei santifondatori nei monasteri tedeschi dei secoli XI e XII. Proposte di ricerca', in Boesch Gajano and Sebastiani 1984, pp. 105–40.

Mikoletsky, Leo, 1949. 'Sinn und Art der Heiligung im frühen Mittelalter', *Mitteilungen des Instituts für österreichische Geschichtsforschung,* 57, 83–122.

Mireux, Marie-Danielle, 1977. 'Guibert de Nogent et la critique du culte des reliques', in *La Piété populaire au Moyen Age,* pp. 293–302. Actes du 99e Congrès national des sociétés savantes, Besançon, 1974. Section de philologie et d'histoire jusqu'à 1610, Tome I. Paris.

Moehs, Teta, 1972. *Gregorius V, 996–999. A Biographical Study.* Päpste und Papsttum, 2. Stuttgart.

Molinier, Auguste, 1901–6. *Les Sources de l'histoire de France des origines aux guerres d'Italie (1494).* 6 vols. Paris.

Mombrizio, Bonino, ed., 1479? *Sanctuarium, seu Vitae sanctorum,* 2 vols. Milan.

Moore, R. I., 1977. *The Origins of European Dissent.* London.

1980. 'Family, community and cult on the eve of the Gregorian reform', *Transactions of the Royal Historical Society,* 5th series, 30, 49–69.

1987. *The Formation of a Persecuting Society. Power and Deviance in Western Europe, 950–1250.* London.

Morin, Gustave, 1902. 'La Translation de s. Benoît et la chronicle de Léng', *Revue Bénédictine,* 19, 337–57.

Morris, Colin, 1972. 'A critique of popular religion: Guibert of Nogent on *The Relics of the Saints*', *Studies in Church History,* 8, 55–60.

1975. '*Judicium Dei*: the social and political significance of the ordeal in the eleventh century', *Studies in Church History,* 12, 95–111.

Mostert, Marco, 1986. 'Le Séjour d'Abbon de Fleury à Ramsey', *Bibliothèque de l'Ecole des Chartes,* 144, 199–208.

1987. *The Political Theology of Abbo of Fleury. A Study of the Ideas About Society and Law of the Tenth-Century Monastic Reform Movement.* Middeleeuwse Studies en Bronnen, 2. Hilversum.

Muller, François, 1987. 'Les Formes du pouvoir en Orléanais (814–923)', *Bulletin de la Société archéologique et historique de l'Orléanais,* new series, 10, 7–26.

Munding, Emmanuel, 1930. *Palimpsesttexte aus der Codex Latinus Monacensis 6333 (Freising. 133, Clm 308).* Texte und Arbeiten, 15–18. Beuron.

Murray, Alexander, 1978. *Reason and Society in the Middle Ages.* Oxford.

Musy, Jean, 1975. 'Mouvements populaires et hérésies au XIe siècle en France', *Revue historique,* 513, 33–76.

Needham, Rodney, 1972. *Belief, Language, and Experience.* Chicago.

Nelson, Janet, 1972. 'Society, theodicy and the origins of heresy: towards a reassessment of the medieval evidence', *Studies in Church History,* 9, 65–77.

1977. 'On the limits of the Carolingian renaissance', *Studies in Church History*, 14, 51–67.

1979. 'Charles the Bald and the church in town and countryside', *Studies in Church History*, 16, 103–18.

1986. 'Dispute settlement in Carolingian west Francia', in Davies and Fouracre 1986, pp. 45–64.

Newman, William, 1937a. *Catalogue des actes de Robert II roi de France*. Paris.

1937b. *Le Domaine royal sous les premiers capétiens (987–1180)*, Paris.

Nichols, Stephen, 1983. *Romanesque Signs. Early Medieval Narrative and Iconography*. New Haven.

Niermeyer, J. F., 1976. *Mediae Latinitatis lexicon minus*. Leiden.

Oexle, Otto, 1983. 'Die Gegenwart der Toten', in Herman Braet and Werner Verbeke, eds., *Death in the Middle Ages*, pp. 19–77. Mediaevalia Lovaniensia, 1.9. Louvain.

Oheix, André, 1900. 'Note sur la translation des reliques de saint Paul Aurélian à Fleury', *Bulletin de la Société archéologique de Nantes*, 41, 216–21.

Oury, Guy-Marie, 1970–5. 'L'Erémitisme dans l'ancien diocèse de Tours au XIIe siècle', *Revue Mabillon*, 58, 43–92.

1977. 'Divers aspects du monachisme carolingien dans le Maine: une lecture des vies de saint Calais', *La Province du Maine*, 79, 2–15.

1978a. 'L'Eglise du Mans sous les carolingiens', in *idem, Histoire religieuse du Maine*, pp. 37–48. Chambray-lès-Tours.

1978b. 'Moines, comtes et laïcs au temps des comtes héréditaires', in *idem, Histoire religieuse du Maine*, pp. 49–58. Chambray-lès-Tours.

ed., 1983a. *Histoire religieuse d'Orléanais*. Chambray-lès-Tours.

1983b. 'L'Enseignement de quelques biographies chartraines de l'époque carolingienne', in Oury 1983a, pp. 73–81.

1983c. 'Moines, évêques et chanoines du Xe au XIIIe siècle', in Oury 1983a, pp. 85–100.

Painter, Sidney, 1956. 'Castellans on the plain of Poitou in the eleventh and twelfth centuries', *Speculum*, 31, 243–57.

Pascal, Paul, 1987. 'The poem of Letaldus. A new edition', in K. Wilson 1987, pp. 211–28.

Patlagean, Evelyne, 1968. 'Ancienne hagiographie byzantine et histoire sociale', *Annales. Economies, sociétés, civilisations*, 23, 106–26.

Patlagean, Evelyne, and Pierre Riché, eds., 1981. *Hagiographie, cultures et sociétés. IVe–XIIe siècles. Actes du Colloque organisé à Nanterre et à Paris (2–5 mai 1979)*. Paris.

Patron, Jean-Baptiste, 1870–1. *Recherches historiques sur l'Orléanais, ou essai sur l'histoire de l'Orléans proprement dit depuis l'époque celtique jusqu'au nos jours*. 2 vols. Orléans.

Paxton, Frederick, 1987. 'The Peace of God in modern historiography: perspectives and trends'. *Historical Reflections / Réflexions Historiques*, 14, 385–404.

Pellegrin, Elisabeth, 1963. 'Notes sur quelques recueils de vies de saints utilisés pour la liturgie à Fleury-sur-Loire au XIe siècle', *Bulletin d'information de l'Institut de recherches et d'histoire des textes*, 12, 7–30.

1982. 'Une prologue et un argument inédits à l'*Historia translationis Sancti Benedicti*', *Analecta Bollandiana*, 100, 365–72.

Pelletier, Victor, 1855. *Les Evêques de l'église d'Orléans depuis les origines jusqu'à nos jours*. Orléans.

Penco, Gregory, 1968. 'Le figure bibliche del *Vir Dei* nell'agiographia monastica', *Benedictina*, 15, 1–13.

Pergot, Auguste, 1865. *Vie de Saint Sacerdos, évêque de Limoges et patron de l'ancien diocèse de Sarlat*. Perigaux.

Perrin, Charles-Edmond, ed., 1951. *Mélanges d'histoire du moyen âge dédiés à la mémoire de Louis Halphen*. Paris.

Pesante, Giovanne, 1891. *S. Mauro protettore della città e diocesi di Parenzo*. Parenzo.

Petersen, Joan, 1983. 'Dead or alive? The holy man as healer in east and west in the late sixth century', *Journal of Medieval History*, 9, 91–8.

Pfister, Christian, 1885. *Etudes sur le règne de Robert le Pieux (996–1031)*. Bibliothèque de l'Ecole des Hautes Etudes, 64. Paris.

Philippart, Guy, 1977. *Les Légendiers latins et autres manuscrits hagiographiques*. Typologie des sources du Moyen Age occidental, A-VI.D.9. Turnhout.

1981. 'L'Edition médiévale des légendiers latins dans le cadre d'une hagiographie générale', in Hans Bekker-Nielson *et al.*, eds., *Hagiography and Medieval Literature. A Symposium*, pp. 127–58. Odense.

Plaine, Bede, 1899. 'Les Invasions des Normands en Armorique et la translation générale des Saints bretons', *Bulletin de la Societé archéologique du Finistère*, 26, 209–38 and 310–35.

Platelle, Henri, 1978–9. 'Crime et châtiment à Marchiennes. Etude sur la conception et le fonctionnement de la justice d'après les Miracles de sainte Rictrude (XIIe s.)', *Sacris Erudiri*, 24, 156–202.

Plongeron, Bernard, ed., 1975. *La Religion populaire dans l'occident chrétien. Approches historiques*. Paris.

Pohlkamp, Wilhelm, 1977. 'Hagiographische Texte als Zeugnisse einer "histoire de la sainteté". Bericht über ein Buch zum Heiligkeitsideal im karolingischen Aquitanien', *Frühmittelalterliche Studien*, 11, 229–40.

Poncelet, Albert, 1899a. 'Saints d'Istrie et de Dalmatie', *Analecta Bollandiana*, 18, 370–84.

1899b. 'La Vie de S. Firmanus, abbé au diocèse de Fermo par Thierry d'Amorbach', *Analecta Bollandiana*, 18, 22–33.

1904. 'La Bibliothèque de l'abbaye de Micy au IXe et au Xe siècle, *Analecta Bollandiana*, 23, 76–84.

1905. 'Les Saints de Micy', *Analecta Bollandiana*, 24, 5–104.

1908. 'La Vie et les oeuvres de Thierry de Fleury', *Analecta Bollandiana*, 27, 5–27.

Poole, Reginald, 1915. *Lectures on the History of the Papal Chancery*. Cambridge.

Poulin, Joseph-Claude, 1975. *L'Idéal de sainteté dans l'Aquitaine carolingienne d'après les sources hagiographiques (750–950)*. Quebec City.

1977. 'Hagiographie et politique. La première vie de Saint Samson de Dol', *Francia*, 5, 1–19.

Prinz, Friedrich, 1965. *Frühes Mönchtum in Frankreich. Kultur und Gesellschaft in*

Gallien, den Rheinlanden und Bayern am Beispiel der monastischen Entwicklung (4. bis 8. Jahrhundert). Munich.

1967. 'Heiligenkult und Adelherrschaft im Spiegel merowingischer Hagiographie', *Historische Zeitschrift*, 204, 528–44.

1973. 'Gesellschaftsgeschichtliche Aspekte frühmittelalterlicher Hagiographie', *Zeitschrift für Literatur, Wissenschaft und Linguistik*, 3, part 2, 17–36.

Prou, Maurice, 1893. 'Les Serfs de Saint-Benoît-sur-Loire', *Bulletin de la Société nationale des antiquaires de France*, 6th series, 4, 216–20.

Quentin, Henri, 1903. 'Le Martyrologe Hiéronymien et les fêtes de saint Benoît', *Revue Bénédictine*, 20, 351–424.

Radding, Charles, 1978. 'Evolution of medieval mentalities: a cognitive–structural approach', *American Historical Review*, 83, 577–97.

1985. *A World Made by Men. Cognition and Society, 400–1200.* Chapel Hill.

Rand, Edward, 1929. *A Survey of the Manuscripts of Tours.* 2 vols. Cambridge, Massachusetts.

Reinhardt, Hans, 1933. 'Etude sur les églises-porches carolingiennes et leur survivance dans l'art roman', *Bulletin monumentale*, 92, 331–65.

1937. 'Etude sur les églises-porches carolingiennes et leur survivance dans l'art roman (suite)', *Bulletin monumentale*, 96, 425–65.

Renaud, Geneviève, 1976. 'Les Miracles de Saint Aignan d'Orléans. XIe siècle', *Analecta Bollandiana*, 94, 245–74.

1978a. 'Saint Aignan et sa legende, les "vies" et les "miracles"', *Bulletin de la Société archéologique et historique de l'Orléanais*, 49, 83–109.

1978b. 'Une passion de saint Baudele, sous-diacre à Orléans et martyr à Nîmes (XIe s.)', *Analecta Bollandiana*, 96, 154–66.

Reviron, Jean, 1930. *Les Idées politico-religieuses d'un évêque du IXe siècle. Jonas d'Orléans et son 'De institutione regia'.* Paris.

Reynolds, Roger, 1987. 'Rites of Separation and Reconciliation in the Early Middle Ages,' in *Segni e riti nella chiesa altomedievale occidentale*, I, 405–33. 2 vols. Settimane di studio del Centro italiano di studi sull'alto medioevo, 33. Spoleto.

Riché, Pierre, 1965. *Enseignement du droit en Gaule du VIe au XIe siècle.* Milan.

1969. 'Conséquences des invasions normandes sur la culture monastique dans l'occident franc', in *I Normanni e la loro espansione in Europa nell'alto medioevo*, pp. 705–21. Settimane di studio del Centro italiano di studi sull'alto medioevo, 16. Spoleto.

1976a. 'Le Mythe des terreurs de l'An Mille', in *Les terreurs de l'an 2000*, pp. 21–30. Paris.

1976b. 'La "Renaissance" intellectuelle du Xe siècle en Occident', *Cahiers d'histoire*, 21, 27–42.

Riché, Pierre, and Guy Lobrichon, eds., 1984. *Le Moyen Age et la Bible. Bible de tous les temps*, 4. Paris.

Ridyard, Susan, 1988. *The Royal Saints of Anglo-Saxon England. A Study of West Saxon and East Anglian Cults.* Cambridge Studies in Medieval Life and Thought, 4th series, 9. Cambridge.

Rocher, Jacques-Napolean-Michel, 1865. *Histoire de l'abbaye royale de Saint-*

Benoît-sur-Loire. Orléans.

1867. *Notice sur la paroisse de Saint-Hilaire-Saint-Mesmin*. Orléans.

Roisin, Simone, 1947. *L'Hagiographie cistercienne dans le diocèse de Liège au XIIIe siècle*. Recueil de travaux d'histoire et de philologie, 3rd series, 27. Louvain.

Rollason, D. W., 1985. 'The miracles of St Benedict: a window on early medieval France', in Mayr-Harting and Moore 1985, pp. 73–90.

Rosenthal, Joel, 1971. 'Edward the Confessor and Robert the Pious: 11th century kingship and biography', *Mediaeval Studies*, 33, 7–20.

Rosenwein, Barbara, 1971. 'Feudal war and monastic peace: Cluniac liturgy as ritual agression', *Viator*, 2, 129–57.

1982. *Rhinoceros Bound. Cluny in the Tenth Century*. Philadelphia.

Rothkrug, Lionel, 1980. *Religious Practices and Collective Perceptions: Hidden Homologies in the Renaissance and Reformation*. Published as *Historical Reflections / Réflexions Historiques*, 7, part 1.

Rouche, Michel, 1981. 'Miracles, maladies et psychologie de la foi à l'époque carolingienne en Francie', in Patlagean and Riché 1981, pp. 319–36.

Rouse, Richard, 1979. 'Florilegia and Latin classical authors in twelfth- and thirteenth-century Orléans', *Viator*, 10, 131–60.

Rousseau, Pierre, 1975a. 'La Crypte de Saint-Aignan d'Orléans', in Louis 1975, pp. 454–73.

1975b. 'L'Eglise Saint-Pierre de Ferrières-en-Gâtinais', in Louis 1975, pp. 525–30.

Rousset, Paul, 1948. 'La Croyance en la justice immanente à l'époque féodale', *Le Moyen Age*, 54, 225–48.

Russell, Jeffrey, 1965. *Dissent and Reform in the Early Middle Ages*. Los Angeles.

Sackur, Ernst, 1892–4. *Die Cluniacenser in ihrer kirchlichen und allgemeingeschichtlichen Wirksamkeit bis zur Mitte des elften Jahrhunderts*. 2 vols. Halle.

Sainte-Catherine, Pierre de, 1889–97. *Loir et Cher historique*, 2 (1889), pp. 6–7, 21–4, 81–2, 98–100, 118–20; 3 (1890), pp. 11–16, 39–41, 97–100, 143–4, 150–2, 186–91; 4 (1891), pp. 29–32, 81–8, 138–41; 5 (1892), pp. 22–32, 120–7, 255–6, 312–19, 347–52; 7 (1894), pp. 25–30, 50–64, 91–4, 124–8, 138–59, 185–91, 213–23, 247–56, 284–8, 335–42, 374–7; 8 (1895), pp. 19–32, 53–64, 92–6, 121–7, 141–58, 178–91, 215–23, 278–86, 300–20, 339–52; 9 (1896), pp. 157–60, 182–92, 218–24, 245–56, 279–88, 375–82; 10 (1897), pp. 25–9, 53–64, 87–96, 106–19, 156–60, 161–84. (Transcription of Blois, Archives de Loir-et-Cher, 30.H.32, in quarto.)

Salmon, Pierre, 1959. *L'Office divin. Histoire de la formation du bréviaire*. Lex orandi, 27. Paris.

Saltet, Louis, 1925. 'Une discussion sur Saint Martial entre un Lombard et un Limousin en 1029', *Bulletin de littérature ecclésiastique*, 26, 163–86 and 279–302.

1926. 'Une prétendue lettre de Jean XIX sur Saint Martial fabriqué par Adémar de Chabannes', *Bulletin de littérature ecclésiastique*, 27, 117–39 and 145–60.

Sargent, Steven, 1985. 'Religious responses to social violence in eleventh-century Aquitaine', *Historical Reflections / Réflexions Historiques*, 12, 219–40.

Sassier, Yves, 1987. *Hugues Capet. Naissance d'une dynastie*. Paris.

Saussaye, Charles de la, 1615. *Annales ecclesiae Aurelianensis, saeculis et libris*

Bibliography and references

sexdecim, addito tractatu accuratissimo de veritate translationis corporis s. Benedicti ex Italia in Gallias ad monasterium Floriacense. Paris.

Saussaye, Louis de la, 1856. 'Chronique de l'église de Tremblevif en Sologne', *Mémoires de la Société des sciences et des lettres de la ville de Blois*, 5, 359–98.

Schlegel, G., 1947. 'Medieval prayers to Saint Benedict', *Ephemerides liturgicae*, 61, 253–5.

Schmitt, Jean-Claude, 1976. '"Religion populaire" et culture folklorique', *Annales. Economies, sociétés, civilisations*, 31, 941–53.

1979. *Le Saint lévrier. Guinefort, guérisseur d'enfants depuis le XIIIe siècle.* Paris.

1984. 'La Fabrique des saints', *Annales. Economies, sociétés, civilisations*, 39, 286–300.

Schreiner, Klaus, 1966a. '*Discrimen veri et falsi*. Ansätze und Formen der Kritik in der Heiligen- und Reliquienverehrung der Mittelalters', *Archiv für Kulturgeschichte*, 48, 1–53.

1966b. 'Zum Wahrheitsverständnis im Heiligen- und Reliquienwesen des Mittelalters', *Saeculum*, 17, 131–69.

Sejourné, Edmond, 1905. *Les Reliques de Saint Aignan évêque d'Orléans. Histoire et authenticité d'après les documents originaux et inédits.* Orléans.

Sigal, Pierre-André, 1969. 'Maladie, pèlerinage et guérison au XIIe siècle: les miracles de Saint Gibrien à Reims', *Annales. Economies, sociétés, civilisations*, 24, 1522–39.

1971. 'Comment on concevait et on traitait la paralysie en Occident dans le Haut Moyen Age (Ve-XIIe siècles)', *Revue d'histoire des sciences*, 24, 193–211.

1972–3. 'Le Culte des reliques en Gévaudan aux XIe et XIIe siècles', *Bulletin de la Société des lettres, sciences et arts de la Lozère*, 19–20, 103–15.

1976a. 'Un aspect du culte des saints: le châtiment divin aux XIe et XIIe siècles d'après la littérature hagiographique du Midi du France', in M.-H. Vicaire, ed., *La Religion populaire en Languedoc du XIIIe à la moitié du XIVe siècle*, pp. 49–59. Cahiers de Fanjeaux, 11. Toulouse.

1976b. 'Les Voyages des reliques aux XIe–XIIe siècles', in *Voyage, quête, pèlerinage dans la littérature et la civilisation médiévales*, pp. 75–104. Senefiance, 2. Paris.

1980. 'Histoire et hagiographie: les *Miracula* aux XIe et XIIe siècles', *Annales de Bretagne et des Pays de l'ouest*, 87, 237–57.

1982. 'Miracle in vita et miracle posthume aux XIe et XIIe siècles', in Jean de Vigurie, ed., *Histoire des miracles*, pp. 41–9. Publications du Centre de recherches d'histoire religieuse et d'histoire des idées, 6. Angers.

1985. *L'Homme et le miracle dans la France médiévale (XIe-XIIe siècle).* Paris.

Silvestre, Hubert, 1960. 'Le Problème des faux au Moyen Age. (A propos d'un livre récent de M. Saxer)', *Moyen Age*, 66, 351–70.

Smith, Julia, 1982. 'The "archbishopric" of Dol and the ecclesiastical politics of ninth century Brittany', *Studies in Church History*, 18, 59–70.

1985. 'Celtic asceticism and Carolingian authority in early medieval Brittany', *Studies in Church History*, 22, 53–63.

Sorokin, Pitirim, 1950. *Altruistic Love. A Study of American 'Good Neighbors' and Christian Saints.* Boston.

Sot, Michel, 1978. 'Historiographie épiscopale et modèle familial en occident au

IXe siècle', *Annales. Economies, sociétés, civilisations*, 33, 433–49.

1981. 'Arguments hagiographiques et historiographiques dans les "Gesta episcoporum"', in Patlagean and Riché 1981, pp. 95–104.

Stancliffe, C. E., 1979. 'From town to country: the christianisation of the Touraine, 370–600', *Studies in Church History*, 16, 43–59.

Stein, Henri, 1895. 'Un diplôme du roi Robert', *Annales de la Société historique et archéologique du Gâtinais*, 13, 108–9.

1907. *Bibliographie générale des cartulaires français ou relatifs à l'histoire de France.* Manuels de bibliographie historique, 4. Paris.

Stock, Brian, 1983. *The Implications of Literacy. Written Language and Models of Interpretation in the Eleventh and Twelfth Centuries.* Princeton.

Tambiah, Stanley, 1976. *World Conqueror and World Renouncer. A Study of Buddhism and Polity in Thailand against a Historical Background.* Cambridge Studies in Social Anthropology, 15. Cambridge.

1984. *The Buddhist Saints of the Forest and the Cult of Amulets. A Study in Charisma, Hagiography, Sectarianism, and Millennial Buddhism.* Cambridge Studies in Social Antropology, 49. Cambridge.

Thaumas de la Thaumassière, Gaspard, 1689. *Histoire de Berry.* 2 vols. Bourges.

Theiner, Augustin, 1832. *Saint Aignan, ou Le siège d'Orléans, par Attila. Notice historique suivie de la Vie du saint, tirée des manuscrits de la bibliothèque du Roi.* Paris.

Thomas, Alexandre, 1889. *Saint Pol-Aurélian et ses premiers successeurs.* Quimper.

Thomas, Keith, 1971. *Religion and the Decline of Magic.* London.

Töpfer, Bernard, 1956. 'Reliquienkult und Pilgerbewegung zur Zeit der Klosterreform im burgundisch-aquitanischen Gebiet', in H. Kretzschmar, ed., *Vom Mittelalter zur Neuzeit. Zum 65. Geburtstag von Heinrich Sprömberg*, pp. 420–39. Berlin.

1957. *Volk und Kirche zur Zeit der beginnenden Gottesfriedensbewegung in Frankreich.* Neue Beiträge zur Geschichtswissenschaft, 1. Berlin.

Tourquat, E. de, 1853. 'Histoire de l'église et du chapitre de Saint-Avit-d'Orléans', *Mémoires de la Société archéologique et historique de l'Orléanais*, 2, 323–44.

1857a. 'Note sur la restauration de l'église de Saint-Euverte d'Orléans', *Bulletin de la Société archéologique et historique de l'Orléanais*, 2, 312–17

1857b. 'Rapporte sur la crypte de l'église Saint-Aignam, à l'occasion des travaux de Déblai opérés en 1857', *Bulletin de la Société archéologique et historique de l'Orléanais*, 2, 369–80.

Traube, Ludwig, 1902. *Hieronymi Chronicorum codicis Floriacensis fragmenta Leidensia Parisina Vaticana phototypice edita.* Lyon.

Trier, Jost, 1924. *Der heilige Jodocus. Sein Leben und seine Verehrung.* Germanistische Abhandlungen, 56. Breslau.

Vallery-Radot, Jean, 1931a. 'Eglise Saint-Lifard et la tour Manassès de Garlande', *Congrès archéologique de France*, 93, 279–301.

1931b. 'Yèvre-le-Chatel', *Congrès archéologique de France*, 93, 401–18.

Van Dam, Raymond, 1985. *Leadership and Community in Late Antique Gaul.* Berkeley.

Bibliography and references

Van der Essen, Léon, 1907. *Etude critique et littéraire sur les Vitae des saints mérovingiens de l'ancienne Belgique.* Louvain.

Van der Straeten, Joseph, 1982. *Les Manuscrits hagiographiques d'Orléans, Tours et Angers, avec plusieurs texts inédits.* Subsidia hagiographica, 64. Brussels.

Van der Vyver, André, 1929. 'Les Etapes du développement philosophique du haut moyen âge', *Revue Belge de philologie et d'histoire*, 8, 425–52.

   1935. 'Les Oeuvres inédites d'Abbon de Fleury', *Revue Bénédictine*, 47, 123–69.

Van Engen, John, 1986. 'The "Crisis of Cenobitism" reconsidered: Benedictine monasticism in the years 1050–1150', *Speculum*, 61, 269–304.

Van Luyn, P., 1971. 'Les Milites dans la France du XIe siècle: examen des sources narratives', *Le Moyen Age*, 77, 5–51.

Van Uytfanghe, Marc, 1976. 'La Bible dans les Vies de saints mérovingiennes', *Revue d'histoire d'église de la France*, 62, 103–12.

   1977. 'Les Avatars contemporains de l'"hagiologie". A propos d'un ouvrage récent sur Saint Séverin du Norique', *Francia*, 5, 639–71.

   1981. 'La Controverse biblique et patristique autour du miracle, et ses répercussions sur l'hagiographie dans l'Antiquité tardive et le haut Moyen Age latin', in Patlagean and Riché 1981, pp. 205–33.

   1984. 'Modèles bibliques dans l'hagiographie', in Riché and Lobrichon 1984, pp. 449–88.

Vauchez, André, 1974. '"Beata Stirps": Sainteté et lignage en occident aux XIIIe et XIV siècles', in Georges Duby and Jacques LeGoff, eds., *Famille et parenté dans l'occident médiéval*, pp. 261–71. Collection de l'Ecole française de Rome, 30. Rome.

   1981. *La Sainteté en occident aux derniers siècles du Moyen Age d'après les procès de canonisation et les documents hagiographiques.* Bibliothèque des Ecoles françaises d'Athènes et de Rome, 241. Rome.

Verdier, Philippe, 1977. 'La Vie et les miracles de Saint Benoît dans les sculptures de Saint-Benoît-sur-Loire', *Mélanges de l'Ecole française de Rome*, 89, 119–53.

Vergnaud-Romagnesi, Charles-François, 1842. *Mémoire sur l'ancienne abbaye de St.-Mesmin de Mici, près Orléans.* Orléans.

Vergnolle, Eliane, 1985. *Saint-Benoît-sur-Loire et la sculpture du XIe siècle.* Paris.

Vermeesch, Albert, 1966. *Essai sur les origines et la signification de la commune dans le nord de la France (XIe et XIIe siècles).* Studies Presented to the International Commission for the History of Representative and Parliamentary Institutions, 30. Heule.

Vezin, Jean, 1977. 'Leofnoth. Un scribe anglais à Saint-Benoît-sur-Loire', *Codices manuscripti*, 4, 109–20.

Vicaire, Marie-Humbert, 1963. *L'Imitation des apôtres: moines, chanoines et mendiants, IVe–XIIIe siècles.* Tradition et spiritualité, 2. Paris.

Vidier, Alexandre, 1906. 'Ermitages orléanais au XIIe siècle. Le Gué de l'Orme et Chappes', *Le Moyen Age*, 19, 57–96 and 134–56.

   1907. 'Notices sur des actes d'affranchissement et de précaire concernant Saint-Aignan d'Orléans (IXe–Xe siècles)', *Le Moyen Age*, 20, 289–317.

   1965. *L'Historiographie à Saint-Benoît-sur-Loire et les Miracles de Saint Benoît.* Posthumously edited and annotated by the monks of Saint-Benoît de Fleury (Denis Grémont). Paris.

Bibliography and references

Vielliard-Troïekouroff, May, 1976. *Les Monuments religieux de la Gaule d'après les oeuvres de Grégoire de Tours*. Paris.

Villette, Guy, 1983. 'La Christianisation des Carnutes', in Oury 1983a, pp. 15–51.

Vodola, Elisabeth, 1986. *Excommunication in the Middle Ages*. Berkeley.

Wallace-Hadrill, J. M., 1981. 'History in the mind of Archbishop Hincmar', in R. H. C. Davis and J. M. Wallace-Hadrill, eds., *The Writing of History in the Middle Ages. Essays Presented to Richard William Southern*, pp. 43–70. Oxford.

1983. *The Frankish Church*. Oxford.

Ward, Benedicta, 1981. 'The miracles of St. Benedict', in E. Rozanne Elder, ed., *Benedictus. Studies in Honor of St. Benedict of Nursia*, pp. 1–14. Cistercian Studies Series, 27. Kalamazoo.

1982. *Miracles and the Medieval Mind*. Philadelphia.

Warren, Francis, 1909. 'Constantine of Fleury (985–1014)', *Transactions of the Connecticut Academy of Arts and Sciences*, 15, pp. 286–92.

Weber, Robert, 1952. 'Un nouveau manuscrit du plus ancien récit de la translation des reliques de St. Benoît', *Revue Bénédictine*, 62, 140–2.

Weinstein, Donald, and Rudolph Bell, 1982. *Saints and Society. The Two Worlds of Western Christendom, 1000–1700*. Chicago.

Werner, Karl Ferdinand, 1960. 'Die literarischen Vorbilder des Aimoin von Fleury und die Entstehung seiner *Gesta Francorum*', in H. R. Jauss and D. Schaller, eds., *Medium Aevum Vivum: Festschrift für Walther Bulst*, pp. 69–103. Heidelberg.

1977. 'Liens de parenté et noms de personne. Un problème historique et méthodologique', in Georges Duby and Jacques LeGoff, eds., *Famille et parenté dans l'occident médiéval*, pp. 13–18 and 25–34. Collection de l'Ecole française de Rome, 30. Rome.

1979. 'Kingdom and principality in twelfth-century France', in Timothy Reuter, ed., *The Medieval Nobility. Studies on the Ruling Classes of France and Germany from the Sixth to the Twelfth Centuries*, pp. 243–90. Amsterdam.

1980. 'L'Acquisition par la maison de Blois des comtés de Chartres et de Châteaudun', in P. Basten, ed., *Mélanges de numismatique, d'archéologie et d'histoire offerts à Jean Lafaurie*, pp. 265–72. Paris.

White, Stephen, 1978. '"Pactum . . . Legem Vincit et Amor Judicium". The settlement of disputes by compromise in eleventh-century western France', *American Journal of Legal History*, 22, 281–308.

1986. 'Feuding and peace-making in the Touraine around the year 1100', *Traditio*, 42, 195–263.

Whitelock, Dorothy, 1970. 'Fact and fiction in the legend of St. Edmund', *Proceedings of the Suffolk Institute of Archaeology*, 31, 217–33.

Wilmart, André, 1936. 'Le Poème heroique de Letald sur Within le pêcheur', *Studi medievali*, 2nd series, 9, 188–203.

1937–45. *Bibliotheca apostolica Vaticana. Codices reginenses latini*. 2 vols. Vatican City.

Wilson, Katherina, ed., 1987. *Hrotsvit of Gandersheim. Rara avis in Saxonia?*. Ann Arbor, Mich.

Wilson, Stephen, ed., 1983. *Saints and their Cults. Studies in Religious Sociology, Folklore and History*. Cambridge.

Wollasch, Joachim, and Karl Schmid, 1967. 'Die Gemeinschaft der Lebenden und Verstorbenen in Zeugnissen des Mittelalters', *Frühmittelalterliche Studien*, 1, 365–405.

Wolf, Kenneth, 1988. *Christian Martyrs in Muslim Spain*. Cambridge Iberian and Latin American Studies. Cambridge.

Wood, I. N., 1979. 'Early Merovingian devotion in town and country', *Studies in Church History*, 16, 61–76.

Wormald, Francis, 1952–3. 'The illustrated manuscripts of the lives of the saints', *Bulletin of the John Rylands Library*, 25, 248–66.

    1974. 'The monastic library', in Ursula McCracken, L. Randall, and R. Randall, eds., *Gatherings in Honor of Dorothy T. Miner*, pp. 93–109. Baltimore.

Wühr, Wilhelm, 1948. 'Die Wiedergeburt Montecassinos unter seinem ersten Reformabt Richer von Niederaltarich (d. 1055)', *Studi Gregoriani*, 3, 369–450.

Ziezulewicz, William, 1985. 'Etude d'un faux monastique à une periode de réforme: une charte de Charles le Chauve pour Saint-Florent-de-Saumur (8 juin 848)', *Cahiers de civilisation médiéval*, 28, 201–11.

    1988. 'Abbatial elections at Saint-Florent-de-Saumur (ca. 950–1118)', *Church History*, 57, 289–97.

Ziolkowski, Jan, 1984. 'Folklore and learned legend in Letaldus' whale poem', *Viator*, 15, 107–18.

Zoepf, Ludwig, 1908. *Das Heiligen-Leben im 10. Jahrhundert*. Leipzig.

INDEX

Abbo, St, abbot of Fleury, 71, 158, 179–80, 238–55, 291; death of, 127, 253–4; election of, 74, 239–40; feast of, 126, 251–2; and Letaldus of Micy, 217–18, 223, 226; miracles performed by, 73, 252; relics and shrine of, 73, 99n, 271
  work about: *see under* Aimo, monk of Fleury
  works of: *Apologeticus*, 246–50, 252; *Collectio canonum*, 247–50, 254; *Epistolae*, 68, 217–18, 223, 226, 252; *Vita s. Edmundi*, 58, 59n, 78–9, 129, 153, 241–50, 255, 273, 280
Adalbero, archbishop of Reims, 239
Adalbero, bishop of Laon, 244, 247
Adelaide, noblewomen, 189
Adelaide, St, empress, 279
Adelarius, monk of Fleury, work of: *Miracula s. Benedicti*, 53
Ademar, viscount of Limoges, 240
Ademar of Chabannes, 256n, 268–9
Adrevald, monk of Fleury, 32, 39, 115; also known as Adalbert, 40n; manuscripts of the works of, 127, 129, 183; use by, of the works of earlier hagiographers, 39–40, 47, 103
  works of: *Historia translationis s. Benedicti*, 39, 126–7, 141, 143, 161; *Miracula s. Benedicti*, 12, 27, 39–40, 46, 52, 73–4, 136–52, 177, 190; *Vita s. Aigulphi*, 41, 126
Ælfheah, St, archbishop of Canterbury, 243
Aetius, 21
Agilus, St, 207, 234n
Agius, bishop of Orléans, 47
Aigulphus, St, monk of Fleury and abbot of Lèrins, 39–40, 116, 141; feast of, 99n, 126; relics and shrine of, 99n
  work about: *see under* Adrevald, monk of Fleury

Aimery III, viscount of Thouars, 221
Aimo, archbishop of Bourges, 175–6
Aimo, monk of Ferrières, 69
Aimo, monk of Fleury, 70–1, 74, 79, 183; home of, 253; manuscripts of the works of, 126–7, 129, 184n; praised by Andrew of Fleury, 130; use by, of works of earlier hagiographers, 76, 121, 129–30, 137, 164, 172
  works of: *Historia translationis s. Benedicti*, 59n; *Historiae francorum*, 254; *Libelli miraculorum s. Benedicti*, 126, 158, 184; *Miracula s. Benedicti*, 17–18, 55–6, 59n, 70, 74, 76–7, 172, 178–80, 185, 189; *Sermo in festivitatibus s. patris Benedicti*, 126, 129–30; *Vita et miracula s. Abbonis*, 59n, 71, 73, 78–80, 120, 126, 251–5
Albert, abbot of Micy, 62, 66, 162, 214n, 227–33; abbot of Saint-Julien of Tours, 229
Aldagaud, abbot of Fleury, 147
Aldric, bishop of Le Mans, 49
al-Hakim, caliph of Jerusalem, 61
Amalbert, abbot of Fleury, 74, 237–8
Amalricus, abbot of Micy, 181–2, 215–17
Amator, St, 234n
Anastasius the Librarian, 90
Andaine, abbey, 42
Andrew, abbot of Micy, 97, 167
Andrew, monk of Fleury, 71; manuscripts of the works of, 184n; use by, of works of earlier hagiographers, 70–1
  works of: *Miracula s. Benedicti*, 59n, 70–1, 74–7, 137–8, 175–80, 186, 269; *Vita Gauzlini*, 59n, 78, 130, 146n, 255–7, 270–2, 275–9
Angers, bishop of, *see* Rainald
Anianus, St, bishop of Orléans, 104, 117–18; burial of, 37; consecration of, by St Evurtius, 35, 106–7, 114; feasts of, 1, 31–2, 98n; Orléans saved

Index

Edmund, St, king of East Anglia (*cont.*)
241–4
work about: *see under* Abbo, St, abbot
of Fleury
Egbert, archbishop of Trier, 286
Einhard, 47
Elisiardus, count, 55
Erdmann, Carl, 179
ergotism, 176–7
Ermentheus, bishop of Orléans, 63,
214–15, 259
Ermoldus Nigellus, 26
Eugenius III, pope, 52
Eusebius, bishop of Orléans, 133, 206
Eusicius, St, founder of Selles-sur-Cher,
85–6, 104, 121, 122
work about: *see under* Letaldus, monk
of Micy
Euspicius, St, monk of Micy, 104; feast
of, 9, 99n, 125; and foundation of
Micy, 109, 202; patronage of, 97,
229; relics and shrine of, 9;
translation of, to Micy, 62, 230,
232–3
works about: *Miracula s. Euspicii*, 59n,
97; *Vita et translatio s. Euspicii*, 59n,
66–7, 232
Evrard of Le Four, lord of Issoudon, 222
Evurtius, St, bishop of Orléans, 104;
burial of, 36; consecration by, of
Anianus, 35, 106–7, 114;
consecration of, 35–6, 105, 116;
construction by, of the cathedral of
Sainte-Croix, 105–7, 119; feast of, 1,
31–2, 98n; lack of miracles
performed by, 112; relics and shrine
of, 7, 25–6, 31, 133
works about: *Acta translationis s. Evurtii*,
51–2; *Inventio s. Evurtii*, 59n, 95–6;
Pretiosi confessoris, 198–9; *Vita s.
Evurtii I*, 35–6, 67, 105–6, 111; *see
also under* Lucifer of Orléans
excommunication, 190–5
ex-voto offerings, 139, 150–1

Faith, St, 73, 284–5, 290
Farmer, Sharon, 198
Felix, hermit from Brittany, 75
Ferrières, abbey, 8, 26, 68–9; abbot of, *see*
Servatus Lupus
fire, miraculous protection from, 119,
158–60
Firmanus, St, abbot, 89, 91n, 104
work about: *see under* Theodoric, monk
of Fleury

Fleury (Saint-Benoît-sur-Loire), abbey,
6–7, 23–4, 52–6, 135–201 *passim*,
235–57, 270–81; abbots of, *see* Abbo,
Aldagaud, Amalbert, Boso, Gauzlin,
Medo, Mummolus, Oylbold,
Radulfus, Ragnerius, Richard,
Theodulf of Orléans, Veranus,
William, Wulfadus; burials at,
171–2, 194–6, *see also under* Philip I;
church of St Dionysius at, 72, 192;
church of St Peter at, 141–2, 159;
church of the Virgin Mary at, 32,
138, 141–2, 157–62, 163, 166, 171–2,
190, 277–8; dedication to the Virgin
Mary and St Peter, 22–3; destruction
of, by Normans, 52, 158; dispute
with abbey of Saint-Denis, 30, 45,
148; fires at, 158–9; foundation of,
22–3, 115, 283; hospice of, 139, 147;
immunities of, 30, 145, 236–8,
240–1, 246–51, 255–7; library of, 41;
liturgy at, 122–3, 125–7, 131, 146,
156, 188, 256; monks of, *see*
Adelarius, Adrevald, Aimo, Andrew,
Christian, Drogo, Gallebertus,
Gauzfredus, Giraldus, Helgaud,
Hercambaldus, Hermenaldus, Hugh,
Isembard, Rodulfus Tortarius,
Theodoric, Vitalis; pilgrimage to, 55,
131, 138–40, 146–7, 150–1, 165–9;
priories of, see Charité-sur-Loire,
Châtillon-sur-Loire, La Réole,
Perrecy-les-Forges, Saint-Benoît-du-
Sault; property of, 72, 144–7,
172–201 *passim*, 236–40, 246–7, 249,
255–7, 275–8, *see also* La-Cour-
Marigny, Yèvre; reform of, by Odo
of Cluny, 54–5; relics and shrines at,
see under Benedict of Nursia, St,
burial shroud, Dionysius, St,
Frogentius, St, Maurus of Brittany,
St, Paul Aurelian, St, Rusticus and
Eleutherius, Ss; royal protection of,
55, 65, 236–8; school of, 59;
translation of relics to, *see under*
Benedict of Nursia, St, Dionysius,
St, Paul Aurelian, St; *Vetus Floriacus*,
22, 41
Flosculus, St, bishop of Orléans, 31–2
forgery, 33–4, 38–9, 51–2, 86–9, 216–17,
247
Francis of Assisi, St, 4, 100, 294
Frederick, schoolmaster of Marmoutier,
223
Frideswide, St, hermit, 287

334

Index

Frogentius, St, relics of, 173
Fulbert, bishop of Chartres, 233, 256–7, 265–70; death of, 270
Fulk, bishop of Orléans, 255–7, 274, 276–7
Fulk Nerra, count of the Angevins, 217–26 *passim*, 276
Fursaeus, St, abbot, 87–9
    work about: *Virtutes s. Fursaei*, 87–9, 225

Gaiffier, Baudouin de, 19
Gallebertus, monk of Fleury, 173–4, 177
Gauzfredus, monk of Fleury, 158
Gauzlin, abbot of Fleury, 163, 166, 185, 255–7, 274–9; attendance of, at the Council of Orléans, 71, 266–9, 277; construction at Fleury undertaken by, 62, 159; death of, 127, 270
    work about: *see under* Andrew, monk of Fleury
Geary, Patrick, 5, 45–6, 143–4, 192
Geilo, lord of Sully, 179
Genesius, viscount, 148
Geoffrey, viscount of Bourges, 180
Geoffrey of Bonzy, lord of Saint-Aignan, 222
Geoffrey of Châteaudun, 227n
Gerald, St, count of Aurillac, 117
Gerald, viscount of Limoges, 179
Gerald of Thouars, abbot of Saint-Florent, 222
Gerard, St, monk of Saint-Aubin, 117
Gerbert, archbishop of Reims, 217, 238, 239–40, 245–6, 255
Germigny-des-Près, abbey, 178
Gertrude of Nivelles, St, 69
Gervasius, bishop of Le Mans, 227n
Gervinus, abbot of Saint-Riquier, 75
Gien, 165
Giraldus, monk of Fleury
    work of: *Historia translationis s. Benedicti*, 59n
Gloria, hymn, 169
Godric of Finchale, St, hermit, 287
Goffart, Walter, 86, 224
Golinelli, Paolo, 286–7
Goths, king of, *see* Totila
Gregory, bishop of Tours, 21, 87, 128, 209, 283, 287; description by, of St Avitus, 8, 21–2
Gregory, St, archbishop of Nicopolis, 294
    work about: *Vita s. Gregorii Nicopolitani*, 59n, 78–9, 262–5, 272
Gregory I (the Great), pope

works of: *Dialogues*, 39, 41, 103, 119, 126, 129–30, 160, 172; *Registrum*, 249
Gregory IV, pope, 247
Gregory V, pope, 246–7
Guato, bishop of Paris, 163
Guibert of Nogent, 17, 94–5, 288
Gysleharius, 149

hagiography: and art, 160–1; composition of, 32–45, 58–60, 69–94, 105–10, 135–8, 205–8, 211–25, 230–3, 241–4, 251–5, 270–2; and laity, 74–9, 131–2; and liturgy, 69–70, 98–9, 121–32, 270–1; purpose of, 14–18, 66, 102–5, 183–7, 219–22, 288–90
Hariulf, 282–3
Heccard, count, 52
Helgaud, monk of Fleury, 71–2, 118; builder of church of Saint-Denis, 72
    work of: *Epitoma vitae regis Rotberti pii*, 59n, 71, 78, 79–80, 118, 270–4
Heloise of Pithiviers, 258–62
Henry, lay pilgrim, 13–14, 72, 78, 169–71, 190, 192, 198
Herbert, lord of Sully, 194–5
Hercambaldus, monk of Fleury, 12–14, 74, 140, 145–6, 190
heresy, 61–2, 71, 229, 249; trial for, at Orléans in 1022, 266–9, 277
Heric, abbot of Micy, 206–9
Hermenaldus, monk of Fleury, 215
Hervaeus, archdeacon of Sainte-Croix, 229
Hilary of Orléans, 95
Hildebert, viscount of Limoges, 276
Hildeburgis of Bellême, 214n, 228
Hilduin, abbot of Saint-Denis, 46
Hinguar, chieftain of the Danes, 241, 244
Holy Sepulchre, church of, 61
Hrotsvit of Gandersheim, 279–80, 285–6
Hubert, St, bishop of Tongres-Liège, 42–3, 104
Hugh, abbot of Fleury, 192, 200
Hugh, archbishop of Tours, 227n
Hugh, count, 149
Hugh Capet, king, 6, 63, 74, 114, 237, 239, 241, 245–6, 254
Hugh (Hugh de Sainte-Marie), monk of Fleury, 71, 74–5, 161; as sculptor, 71, 160–1
    works of: *Historia ecclesiastica*, 92–3; *Liber de regia potestate et sacerdotali dignitate*, 71; *Miracula s. Benedicti*, 18, 59n, 73, 74–5, 183, 192; *Vita et miracula s. Sacerdotis*, 36n, 59n, 91–3

335

Index

Hugh the Abbot, duke of the Franks, 48, 53, 55
Hugh the Great, duke of the Franks, 55, 57, 63, 239
Huns, 20–1, 35, 282

imitation, of Christ, 113–14, 133–4, 242; of saints, 103, 118–20
immunity, 30–1, 64–5, 100, 145, 204, 215–17, 235–8, 240–1, 245–57
incubation, 166
Iogna-Pratt, Dominique, 279
Isembard, bishop of Orléans, 72
Isembard, monk of Fleury
  work of: *Vita, translatio et miracula s. Judoci*, 59n

Jacob, abbot of Micy, 214
Jeanne d'Arc, St, 98n, 100, 294
Jews, 61–2
John, bishop of Orléans, 163
John XV, pope, 245, 246
John XVIII, pope, 257
John XIX, pope, 229
John of Salerno, monk of Cluny
  work of: *Vita s. Odonis*, 54, 135–6
Jonas, bishop of Orléans, 6, 25, 30, 42–5, 47; approval by, of exemptions for Micy, 204; death of, 208; relics of Maximinus returned to Micy by, 207, 213; as royal legate, 148–9, 237
  works of: *De institutione laicali*, 45; *De institutione regia*, 45; *Vita et translatio s. Huberti*, 42–3, 49
Josephus, 209, 211
Judocus, St, abbot, 104
  work about: *see under* Isembard, monk of Fleury
Julian, St, bishop of Le Mans, 86–9, 104, 224–5; feast of, 99n, 105, 125
  works about: *see under* Letaldus, monk of Micy, and 'Le Mans forger'
Jumièges, abbey, 214
Junianus, St, abbot of Mairé, 218
  work about: *see under* Letaldus, monk of Micy

Karlamagnussaga, 36

La-Cour-Marigny, castle, 191
Lacroix, Benoît, 81
Laetus, St, monk of Micy, 70, 97, 104, 110, 203, 234n; feast of, 32, 125; relics and shrine of, 17, 32, 63, 259;

translation to Pithiviers, 259
  works about: *Miracula ss. Georgii et Laeti*, 59n, 72; *Vita s. Laeti*, 59n, 66, 109, 259–61, 293; *see also under* Viator, St
Lambert, count of Chalon-sur-Sâone, 176
Lambert, count of Orléans, 145
Lanfranc, archbishop of Canterbury, 243
Laon, bishop of, *see* Adalbero
La Réole, priory of Fleury, 73, 244, 251, 253–4
Lateran Council, fourth, 4, 73, 95
Launomaurus of Blois, St, abbot of Curbion, 203; feast of, 125
Lauranson-Rosaz, Christian, 275
law, 149, 180–1, 245–56; Roman, 148, 150, 237, 249; Salic, 148, 237
LeGoff, Jacques, 14
Le Mans, 49, 86–9, 114, 141; bishops of, *see* Aldric; Avesgaud; Gervasius; Julian, St
'Le Mans forger', 86–9, 284
Lemarignier, Jean-François, 64–5, 235, 240, 286
Leo VII, pope, 194
Leo of Meung, 63
Leobinus, St, bishop of Chartres, 203, 234n
Leodebodus, abbot of Saint-Aignan, 22, 116, 283
  work of: *Testamentum Leodebodi*, 80–1, 273
Leonard of Noblat, St, hermit, 203, 234n; feast of, 125
Leonard of Vandoeuvre, St, hermit, 234n; feast of, 125
Leothericus, archbishop of Sens, 256–7, 265; death of, 270
Lèrins, abbey, 116
Letaldus, abbot of Micy, 213–14
Letaldus, monk of Micy, 6, 71, 81–9, 183, 211–27, 255; *cancellarius* of Micy, 185, 211, 216; possibly dean of Saint-Aignan, 225, 229
  works of: *Delatio corporis s. Juniani*, 59n, 175–6, 218; *Miracula s. Maximini*, 58, 59n, 70, 72, 73, 74, 81–2, 104, 127, 137, 153, 184, 207n, 212–16; *Versus de eversione monasterii Glomnensis*, 218; *Versus de quodam piscatore*, 225; *Vita et miracula s. Eusicii*, 59n, 85–6, 121, 222; *Vita et miracula s. Martini Vertavensis*, 10, 59n, 82–5, 104, 121, 218–22; *Vita s. Juliani*, 59n, 86–9, 93, 224–5

Index

libraries, monastic, *see under* Fleury, Micy
Liège, 42, 285; bishop of, *see* Walcaudus
Lifardus, St, abbot of Meung-sur-Loire,
   25, 104, 110, 234; feasts of, 1, 31–2,
   98n, 125, 163; relics and shrine of, 7,
   25–6, 31, 100; translation of, in 1105,
   11, 163–4
   works about: *Miracula s. Lifardi*, 59n,
      96–7, 186; *Translatio s. Lifardi*, 11,
      59n, 65n, 163–4; *Vita s. Lifardi*, 38,
      110, 118, 205
Lifshitz, Felice, 143n
Limoges, viscount of, *see* Ademar;
   Hildebert
Little, Lester, 191n
liturgy, 98–9, 121–3, 126–7, 166–7; for
   burial of saints, 133–4; calendars for,
   125–7; for *inventiones* of saints,
   162–4, 232, 274; *lectiones* for, 16,
   69–70, 84, 88, 121–7, 131–2, 184–5,
   270–1; and manuscripts, 121–31; in
   parishes, 188; *see also* prayers;
   sermons; and *also under* Fleury and
   Micy
Lothar, king, 145, 237–8, 239
Louis V, king, 63, 237, 239
Louis VI, king, 163
Louis the Pious, king, 29–30, 47, 145,
   208–9, 213, 237; episcopal
   appointments by, 6, 25; forged
   diploma of, 216
Lucifer of Orléans, work of: *Vita s.
   Evurtii II*, 34–5, 105–6

Mabbo, bishop of Pol-de-Lèon, 56, 214n
McKitterick, Rosamond, 49
Maine, duke of, *see* Rainald
Mainz, Council of, 2
Maiolus, St, abbot of Cluny, 279
Manasses of Garland, bishop of Orléans,
   96
Manasses of Seignelay, bishop of Orléans,
   97
manuscripts, 121–31, 183–5; at shrine,
   128–9, 184
   Avranches: BM 41, 123n, 211n
   Bern: Bibliotheca Bongarsiana 50,
      211n; Bibliotheca Bongarsiana 283,
      211n; Bibliotheca Bongarsiana 312,
      211n; Bibliotheca Bongarsiana 344,
      211n; Bibliotheca Bongarsiana 394,
      211n; Bibliotheca Bongarsiana 432,
      211n; Burgerbibliothek 196, 126n
   Bordeaux: BM 11, 93n

Dijon: BM 1118, 40n, 127n, 130n, 184
Leiden: Public Library 21, 87n, 210n;
   University Library, Codex Vossiani
   Latini Quarto 17, 210n; Codex
   Vossiani Latini Quarto 87, 209n;
   Codex Vossiani Latini Quarto 110,
   87n, 209n
Le Mans: BM 217, 67n
London: British Library, Cotton MS
   Tiberius B ii, 129n
Orléans: Archives du Loiret H 20, 184;
   BM 82, 126n; BM 121, 123–5nn;
   BM 123, 33n, 98n, 99n, 191n; BM
   125, 55n, 99n, 123n; BM 129, 98n,
   99nn; BM 131, 130n; BM 322, 33n,
   98n, 99n, 126; BM 323, 126n; BM
   337, 126n; BM 721, 123n
Paris: Bibliothèque d'Arsenal 371, 9n,
   33n, 98n, 99nn, 125nn; BN lat. 1020,
   98n; BN lat. 1572, 209n; BN lat.
   1790, 210n; BN lat. 1820, 209n; BN
   lat. 1862, 209n; BN lat. 1866, 210n;
   BN lat. 2627, 130n; BN lat. 3789,
   34n, 113n, 205nn, 207n, 230n; BN
   lat. 5278, 128n; BN lat. 5308, 128n;
   BN lat. 5366, 183n; BN lat. 5575,
   92n; BN lat. 7299, 33n, 98n; BN lat.
   7521, 33n, 98n, 99n, 124–5n, BN lat.
   12606, 34n, 86n, 113n, 126n, 205nn;
   Bn lat. 15679, 210n; BN 17641,
   155n; BN nouvelle acquisition latine
   1572, 210n; BN nouvelle acquisition
   latine 7299, 99n
Trier: Seminarbibliothek 187, 33n, 98n,
   99nn, 123n; Stadtbibliothek 1151,
   128n
Troyes: BM 1171, 128n
Vatican: Reg. lat. 95, 209n; Reg. lat.
   318, 86n; Reg. lat. 479, 190n; Reg.
   lat. 496, 128n; Reg. lat. 528, 127,
   128n, 183n, 184n; Reg. lat. 566, 80;
   Reg. lat. 585, 34n 80, 126n, 113n,
   205nn; Reg. lat. 591, 130n; Reg. lat.
   592, 156n, 184n; Reg. lat. 621, 9n,
   67nn, 78, 115n, 125n, 128n, 207n;
   Reg. lat. 1263, 33n, 98n, 99nn,
   125nn; Reg. lat. 1953, 210n
Vienna: Nationalbibliothek 420, 128n
Marchiennes, abbey, 181
Marmoutier, abbey, 198
Martin, St, bishop of Tours, 117, 198–9,
   feast of, 246; shrine of, 21, 165, 284
Martin I, St, pope, 90–1, 104; works about:
   see under Theodoric, monk of Fleury

337

Index

Martin of Vertou, St, hermit, 82–5, 104,
121, 218–22; church dedicated to,
near Pithiviers, 263–4; feast of, 99n,
105, 125
work about: *see under* Letaldus, monk
of Micy
martydrom, 116–17, 242–4, 251–3
martyrology: of Adon, 32n; of Florus of
Lyon, 24, 38n; of Jerome, 23–4,
31–2; of Usuard, 31–2, 125–6; of
Wandelbert, 32n, 124–5
Matfrid, count of Orléans, 30n, 145
Maurus of Brittany, St, martyr, 8, 68, 69,
97, 116; feast of, 99n, 123; relics of,
173, 177, 192
works about: *Passio s. Mauri*, 59n, 68,
116; *see also under* Rodulfus Tortarius
Maurus of Istria, St, martyr, 68
Maximinus, St, abbot of Micy, 104, 115;
feasts of, 1, 31–2, 98n, 99n, 123–5,
128, 131–2, 169–70, 188–9; image of,
124–5; invention of, 62, 66, 162,
230–3; patronage of, at Micy, 133,
202, 214, 229; prayers to, 123–4;
relics and shrines of, 7, 24, 26, 31;
translation to Micy, 207–8;
translation to Orléans, 24, 207
works about: *Miraculum s. Maximini*,
59n, 78, *see also* Henry, lay pilgrim;
*Sermo de inventione s. Maximini et eius
discipulorum Theodemiri et alterius
Maximini*, 59n, 66, 128, 230–1; *Vita
s. Maximini II*, 34n, 66–7, 109, 127,
184, 207n, 208, 210, 212, 234n; *see
also under* Avitus, St; Bertholdus,
monk of Micy, St; Carileffus, St;
Laetus, St; Letaldus, monk of Micy;
Viator, St
Maximinus, St, archbishop of Trier, 13,
85, 104, 169, 171
work about: *see under* Servatus Lupus
Maximinus II, St, abbot of Micy, 232
Maximus, St, abbot of Chinon, 13, 169,
171
Medo, abbot of Fleury, 52, 142
memory, 74–5, 83–4, 185–7, 217
Meung-sur-Loire, abbey, later chapter of
canons, 7, 25, 54, 62–3, 96–7, 100,
110, 186–7, 234; abbot of, *see*
Lifardus, St; church of, 11, 163–4;
possession of bishops of Orléans, 29,
65, 96–7; relics and shrines at, *see
under* Lifardus, St
Micy (Saint-Mesmin-de-Micy), abbey, 7,

24, 30, 115–16, 202–34, 261; abbots
of, *see* Albert, Amalricus, Andrew,
Anno, Benedict of Quimper,
Christian, Constantine I, Constantine
II, Dructesindus, Heric, Jacob,
Letaldus, Maximinus, St, Maximinus
II, St, Peter, Robert of Blois,
Theodemir, St; church of St Stephen
at, 66–7, 162, 167; immunities of,
204; library of, 87, 209–11; liturgy
at, 123–25, monks of *see* Avitus, St,
Bertholdus, Carileffus, St, Laetus, St,
Letaldus, Viator, St; patronage of,
see under Maximinus, St, Stephen, St;
pilgrimage to, 13, 132, 167, 168–71;
possession of bishops of Orléans, 29,
54, 65, 204, 213–18; property of,
152n, 172, 177, see also under Robert
II; refoundation of, 25, 37, 202–4;
sack of, in 749, 203–4
miracles: and asceticism, 111; and battle,
53, 109, 176–7, 179; and candles,
164; chastisements, 12, 21–2, 77, 140,
144–6, 150–1, 172–4, 177–83,
187–90, 194–5; and court cases,
147–9, 180–1; cures 12–13, 111–13,
131, 139–40, 165–72, 176–7, 182–3,
187–90, 252, 261; and drowning,
181–2; as evidence of sanctity, 10,
102–3, 112, 252, 264–5, 272;
exorcisms, 139–40, 168; and
feastdays, 165, 169–70; and fire, 119,
158–60; and fundraising, 174, 197–8;
and natural phenomena, 39, 75, 141,
142, 158, 252; and the Peace of God,
175–6; performed in imitation of
Christ, 112–13; release of prisoners,
182, 183; resurrections, 113, 195; and
workmen, 182
Monitor, St, bishop of Orléans, 31–2
Montana, St, abbess, 8; translation to
Ferrières, 69
work about: *Vita s. Montanae*, 59n, 69
Monte Cassino, abbey, 23–4, 75, 90,
140–1, 153; abbot of, *see* Desiderius;
attempts to regain relics of Benedict,
11, 23, 142, 156–7; monk of, *see* Paul
the Deacon; original tomb of
Benedict, 7
Moore, R. I., 62
Mostert, Marco, 241
Mummolus, St, abbot of Fleury, 39, 116,
141; feast of, 99n, 251; relics and
shrine of, 99n, 251

Index

Namatius, bishop of Orléans, 21
Needham, Rodney, 118
Nelson, Janet, 149
Nicaea, Council of, 266
Nicopolis, 262
Nogent-le-Roi, castle, 270
Normans, raids by, 47–8, 50–4, 161, 178
Nouaillé, abbey, 217–18

Odilo, St, abbot of Cluny, 163, 247, 274
Odo, count of Orléans, 12, 27, 136,
 145–6, 194
Odo, king, 53–4
Odo, lord of Déols, 176
Odo, St, abbot of Cluny, 54–7, 74,
 135–6, 158, 164, 194, 239
 works of: *Sermo de s. Benedicto*, 55–6,
 126, 129, 135; *Vita s. Geraldi*, 117
Odo I, count of Blois, 247
Odo II, count of Blois, 178, 222, 267, 276
Odolric of Pithiviers, bishop of Orléans,
 66, 162, 227, 232, 257–61, 265–70,
 274, 276–7; death of, 270
Odulfus, abbot of Selles-sur-Cher, 222
oral traditions, use of, 37, 41, 73–7, 79,
 82–6, 93–5, 146, 197–8, 215, 219
ordeal, judicial, 180–1
Orderic Vitalis, 171–2
Orléans, 6, 25–7, 63–4; bishops of, *see*
 Agius, Anianus, Arnulf, Diclopetus,
 Ermentheus, Eusebius, Evurtius,
 Flosculus, Isembard, John, Jonas,
 Manasses of Garland, Manasses of
 Seignelay, Monitor, Namatius,
 Odolric of Pithiviers, Prosper?,
 Rainerius, Sigobert, Theodulf,
 Trohannus, Walter; cathedral of, *see*
 Sainte-Croix, *and under* Stephen, St;
 churches of, *see* Saint-Laurent;
 Council of, in 1022, 71, 266–9, 277;
 counts of, *see* Lambert, Matfrid,
 Odo, Raho; destroyed by fire, 60–1;
 destroyed by Normans, 47, 50–1;
 religious foundations of, *see* Saint-
 Aignan, Saint-Avit, Saint-Euverte,
 Saint-Pierre-le-Puellier; religious
 foundations of, in surrounding
 diocese, *see* Fleury, Micy, Meung-
 sur-Loire, *see also under* Pithiviers
Oylbold, abbot of Fleury, 217, 238–9

Paris, bishop of, *see* Dionysius, St; Guato
parish churches, 132
Pastor, St, 31

patronage: provided by saints, 1–2, 10–14,
 135–8, 152–7, 187–201, 172–81,
 282–91; provided by nobility, 21,
 199–200; *see also under* Benedict of
 Nursia, St; Maximinus, St; miracles
Paul, monk of Saint-Père of Chartres,
 186–7
Paul Aurelian, St, bishop, 8, 68, 120–1;
 feasts of, 99n, 105, 122–3, 126;
 translation to Fleury, 56, 158, 214n
 works about: *see under* Vitalis, monk of
 Fleury; Wormonoc of Landévennec
Paul the Deacon, monk of Monte
 Cassino, work of: *Historia
 Langobardorum*, 24, 39, 41, 130
Pavacius, St, hermit, 234n
Paxton, Frederick, 235n
Peace of God, 174–6, 193, 292–3
Perrecy-les-Forgers, priory of Fleury, 75,
 76, 127, 165, 176, 177, 184, 191, 196
Peter, abbot of Micy, 209–10n, 215n
Peter of Poitiers, 18
Peter the Venerable, abbot of Cluny, 18
Philip I, king, 63, 64, 163; buried at
 Fleury, 171–2
Phrambaldus, St, hermit, 234n
pilgrimage, 55, 13, 131–2, 138–40, 146–7,
 150–1, 164–72, 265; monastic life as,
 192
Pippin II, mayor of the Austrasian palace,
 204
Pippin III, king, 141, 143n
Pithiviers, 257–70; canons of, 65, 72,
 78–9, 258; lords of, 63, 227n, 257–8,
 and *see* Rainard; Tescelin; parish
 church of, 259
placitum, 30, 45, 148–9, 237
Plato, 121
Poissey, abbey, 108
Poitiers, count of, *see* William IV;
 William V
Poncelet, Albert, 6
Pontificale Romano-Germanicum, 194
Pontlevoy, battle of, 178
Porec (Porenzo), 68
Poulin, Joseph-Claude, 285
prayers: for dead, 194–9, 288–9; to patron
 saints, 123–4
Priscian, 211
Prosper, St, bishop of Orléans?, 31–2
Prudentius, 203, 211
Pythagoras, 121

Quimper, bishop of, *see* Benedict

Index

Tryphon and Respicius, Ss, 89, 104
  works about: *see under* Theodoric,
    monk of Fleury

Urbicius, St, 110, 234n
Ursinus, St, 49–50
Uzon, lord of, *see* Bernard

Van Engen, John, 196
Veranus, abbot of Fleury, 167, 189–90
Verdier, Phillipe, 161
Verdun, 109, 202, 206
vernacular languages, 76–7, 131–2, 150–1,
  157
Viator, St, 70, 104, 110, 133, 203, 234n;
  feast of, 125; relics and shrine of, 63
  works about: *Vita s. Viatoris*, 59n,
    65–6, 109, 259–61; *see also under*
    Laetus, St
Victorine canons, 95–6, 100, 167–8
Vidier, Alexandre, 6
Vihiers, castle of, 221–2
Vincent of Beauvais, 98n
Virgil, 115n, 195
Virgin Mary, feasts of, 1, 122–3
visions: of God, 106; of messengers, 169;
  of saints, 12, 13, 144, 145–6, 147,
    153, 157, 170, 177–8, 183, 194–5, 269
Vitalis, monk of Fleury, 120; praised by
  Andrew of Fleury, 68
  work of: *Vita s. Pauli Aureliani*, 59n,
    68–9, 104

Vivianus, canon of Saint-Martin-de-
  Tours, 195

Waifarius, king of Aquitaine, 204
Walcaudus, bishop of Liège, 42
Walter, bishop of Orléans, 48; statutes of,
  1–19 *passim*, 25–6, 32–3, 48–50, 102,
    107, 132–4, 283
Wigbert of Hessia, St, abbot, 104
  work about, *see under* Servatus Lupus
William, abbot of Fleury, 159
William, count of Avranches, 276
William IV, duke of Aquitaine and count
  of Poitiers, 179
William V, duke of Aquitaine and count
  of Poitiers, 254
William of Norwich, St, martyr, 287
wine, 127, 177
witnesses, 41, 74–7, 139
women, entry of, into monastic churches,
  139, 166
Wormonoc of Landévennec, work of:
  Vita s. Pauli Aureliani, 68
written sources, use of, 34–8, 41–4, 76–7,
  79–95, 205–8, 211–22, 247–9, 252–3
Wulfadus, abbot of Fleury, 56, 158

Yèvre: castle, 249–50, 270, 277; lord of,
  see Arnulf

Zachary, pope, 23, 142